CONCISE
EARTH
HISTORY

EARTHHISTORY

Editor:
Anders Røhr, J.W. Cappelens Forlag, Oslo

Production management:
Bo Gramfors, Maps International, Stockholm
Siv Eklund and
Mats Halling, GLA Kartor, Stockholm

Historical consultant:
Prof. Knut Mykland

Historical timetable:
Lars Ove Larsson, Stockholm

World Today Text:
Tor Åhman

English translation:
Jim Manis and
Randy Morse, Reidmore Books, Edmonton

Drawings in upper margin:
Ellen Bakke, Oslo

Technical production:
Boksenteret A/S, Oslo

EARTHHISTORY ISBN 1-877731-15-3
Library of Congress Catalog Card Number 90-085870

Published in the United States of America by
EARTHBOOKS, INCORPORATED
7000 N. Broadway #103
Denver, Colorado 80221

President:
Steven W. Schmidt

EARTHHISTORY© 1991
EARTHBOOKS, INCORPORATED

Cover Design:
Randy Nelsen

Copyright© 1991
J.W. Cappelens Forlag A/S, Oslo
GLA Kartor AB, Stockholm
Maps International AB, Stockholm

Printed in Italy

Our lives are borrowed from history.

Events, decisions, accidents, incidents and sheer coincidence shape history as well as our daily lives.

History is formed by people, through their interactions with one another and nature. Through genius and blind ambition; lust for power and quest for grace; wisdom and folly; love and hate, previous generations have presented with us a stage to act our lives upon. It is now up to us – each of us – to decide what parts we will play.

How will we be remembered? As the final arbiters of planetary peace, or torch bearers passing on the age-old flames of death and destruction?

Will ours be looked back upon as the era of irreversible environmental degradation, or as the time when ecological madness on a global scale was finally brought to a halt?

Will future generations remember the last years of the 20th century as a pivotal – and positive – period for humankind?

Only time – and future historians – can tell. One thing, for now, is certain: moving ahead is always made easier by knowing what has gone before. This modest book will provide you with basic background. As for *future history*, it is yours for the making.

Bo Gramfors

Contents

6 Prehistoric Times

7 The Earliest Humans

8 Europe and the Mid-East in the Early Bronze Age

9 Celtic Culture. La Tène

10 Indus Valley Culture. The Birth of Egypt

11 Mesopotamia

12 The Treasures of Ur

13 The Persian Empire

14 The Egypt of the Pharaohs

15 Ancient Israel

16 Phoenicians and Greeks

17 Greece under Pericles

18 The Olympic Games

19 The Acropolis of Athens

20 Magna Graecia (Greater Greece)

21 The Empire of Alexander the Great

22 The Roman Empire to ca. 300 BC

23 The Punic Wars

24 The Roman Empire to 44 BC

25 Caesar Conquers Gaul

26 Palestine in the Time of Christ

27 Imperial Rome

28 The Roman Empire to 117 AD

29 Britain in the Roman Age

30 Earliest Times in China

31 The Chinese Empire

32 China under the Sui and the T´Ang

33 China under the Han Dynasty

34 Genghis Khan

35 China under the Ming and Ch´In

36 The Great Religions

37 The Arab World-Power

38 India under the Maurya Dynasty and the Harsha

39 Indochina and the Khmer Kingdom

40 The Rule of the Mongols

41 The Spread of Islam and Christianity

42 The Byzantine Empire

43 The Germanic Migrations

44 The Empire of Charles the Great (Charlemagne)

45 South-Eastern Europe

46 Viking Expeditions

47 The German Empire in the 900s

48 The Age of the Great Crusades

49 Universities in the Middle Ages

50 Frederick II´s Roman Empire

51 Russia around 1000 AD

52 England and France 1154-1328

53 The German Empire 1024-1250

54 Industry and Trade in Europe

55 The Black Death

56 The Hundred Years´ War between England and France

57 The Hansa Traders. Italy during the Renaissance

58 Martin Luther and the Reformation

59 The Roman Catholic Church

60 Discovering the World

61 Columbus and Vasco da Gama

62 The Colonizing of North and South America

63 Aztec and Mayan Culture

64 India from the 1300s to the 1600s

65 Africa in the 1500s

66 The Netherlands and the Great Fire of London in 1666

67 England in the Time of Elizabeth I

68 Spanish World-Power 1580

69 The Thirty Years´War. Sweden´s Expansion

70 The Peace of Westphalia 1648

71 The Russia of Peter the Great. The Ottoman Empire

72 Europe 1721

73 The Three Divisions of Poland. Catherine the Great

74 The Musical Life of the 1700s. The Seven Years´War

75 Frederick the Great of Prussia

76 Population Density 1800

77 Transportation and Commerce around 1800

78 Revolution in Europe

79 The French Revolution

80 Napoleon 1796-1800

81 Napoleon in Spain and Portugal

82 Napoleonic France 1801-14

83 Russia 1762-1812

84 The Congress of Vienna in 1815

85 The Battle of Waterloo in 1815

86 The Uniting of Germany 1865-71

87 The Uniting of Italy 1859-61

88 Greece Gains Independence

89 The Crimean War 1853-56

90 The Railways

91 Population Density and Transportation

92 The United States of America

93 The American Civil War

94 Spanish America

95 Latin America

96 Africa in the 1800s

97 The Boer War

98 The British Empire

99 The Colonizing of India

100 South-Eastern Europe 1878

101 The Congress of Berlin

102 Japanese Expansion 1868-1939

103 The Balkan Wars. The Shot Fired in Sarajevo

104 The First World War 1914-18

105 The Eastern and Western Fronts

106 Civil War in Russia 1918-21

107 The Inter-War Period

108 The Near East 1917-26. Germany 1918-39

109 Fascism in Europe

110 The Second World War 1939-41

111 The Second World War in the Far East

112 The Second World War 1942-45

113 The Second World War 1942-45

114 The End of Nazi Germany 1945

115 The UN and Economic Alliances after WW2

116 Military Alliances after WW2

117 The Soviet Union and Communist China

118 Israel. The Middle East

119 The Middle East. The Korean War 1950-53

120 Rich and Poor Nations

121 The Cuban Missile Crisis

122 The Liberation of Africa

123 The Congo Crisis 1960-65

124 French Indochina

125 North and South Vietnam 1955-76

126 Indonesia 1942-76

127 India 1939-89. Bangladesh 1947-84

128 The World Today

133 Map Index

163 Index, Subject and Name

173 Historical Timeline

Reconstruction of a dwelling from ca. 20 000 BC.

Mammoth carved in horn. Probably a 15 000-year old handle.

The «Venus» of Willendorf. From Early Palaeolithic times.

Left: The Black Ox. Detail from a 15 000 year old (est.) cave painting from Lascaux in France (map nr. 7, p. 9). The Lascaux cave contains the largest and best preserved man-made images from prehistoric times.

1. THE EARLIEST HUMANS

The Earliest Humans

We don't know anything for certain about mankind's earliest roots – not yet. We can't even say with complete accuracy where these origins are to be found. Nor can we say exactly when the first tools were produced, or when language evolved. These remain among the many unsolved riddles of our common human heritage.

Yet, in spite of the fact that some fundamental questions remain unanswered, year by year we add a bit more to our knowledge of mankind's age, origins and evolution. In Asia, and especially in Africa, many discoveries have been made, in the past as well as in more recent times, that help to shed some light on the haziest chapters in mankind's biological prehistory.

Certain areas of southern and eastern Africa have proved to be especially productive hunting grounds for geological and paleontological «man-hunters». New dating methods have made it possible to date skeletal remains with far greater accuracy than ever before.

While only a few years ago researchers might have had to guess at a number to indicate the absolute age of their finds, they can now order their material sequentially millions

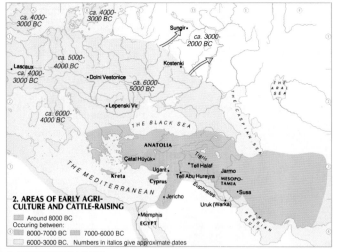

2. AREAS OF EARLY AGRI-CULTURE AND CATTLE-RAISING

Around 8000 BC
Occuring between:
8000-7000 BC   7000-6000 BC
6000-3000 BC.   Numbers in italics give approximate dates

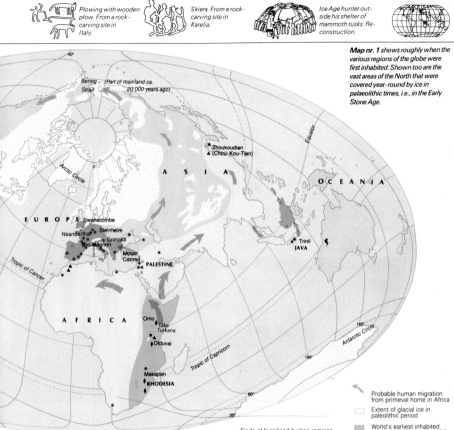

Plowing with wooden plow. From a rock-carving site in Italy.

Skiers. From a rock-carving site in Karelia.

Ice Age hunter outside his shelter of mammoth tusks. Reconstruction.

Map nr. 1 shows roughly when the various regions of the globe were first inhabited. Shown too are the vast areas of the North that were covered year-round by ice in palaeolithic times, i.e., in the Early Stone Age.

Bering Strait – (Part of mainland ca. 20 000 years ago)

Zhoukoudian (Chou-Kou-Tien)

A S I A

O C E A N I A

Arctic Circle

E U R O P E   Swanscombe
Steinhelm
Neanderthal   Grimaldi
Cro-Magnon   Mount Carmel
PALESTINE

Trinil
JAVA

Tropic of Cancer

A F R I C A   Omo   Lake Turkana
Olduvai
Makapan
RHODESIA

Tropic of Capricorn

Antarctic Circle

Probable human migration from primeval home in Africa

Extent of glacial ice in paleolithic period

World's earliest inhabited areas. 3.5-1.5 mill. years BC

Inhabited areas 1.5 mill. - 500.000 years ago

Areas inhabited 500.000-100.000 years ago

First inhabited 100.000-10.000 years ago

Finds of fossilized human remains
♦ Australopithecus
■ Homo habilis
▲ Pithecantropus
● Neanderthal Man
○ Homo sapiens sapiens Cro-Magnon

of years back in time.

We are steadily gaining new insight into the time when man was a naked creature with no knowledge of tools, competing ruthlessly with the other animals.

And yet, even the oldest and most primitive skeletal remains come from the species known as *Homo Erectus* – «upright-walking man».

It now seems most likely that Africa was the area on Earth where creatures like us first evolved. It is at any rate here that the fossil remains are most numerous, oldest and best documented.

Anders Hagen, *Cappelens verdenshistorie*, v.1

The drawing at the left gives an overview of a number of domestic animals, with approximate dates of domestication. Beneath the dates the areas in which they were first domesticated are also given.

	SHEEP approx. 8500 BC Iraq
	DOG approx. 8400 BC Idaho, USA
	GOAT approx. 7500 BC Iran
	PIG approx. 7000 BC Turkey
	OX/COW approx. 6500 BC Anatolia
	LLAMA approx. 3500 BC Peru
	DONKEY approx. 3000 BC Egypt
	CAMEL approx. 3000 BC Southern part of Soviet Union
	DROMEDARY approx. 3000 Saudi Arabia
	HORSE approx. 3000 BC Ukraine
	CHICKEN approx. 2000 BC Pakistan
	CAT approx. 1600 BC Egypt
	GOOSE approx. 1500 BC Germany
	ALPACA approx. 1500 BC Peru

Below: A cromlech, or circular arrangement of monoliths, at Keswick in Cumberland, Great Britain from the megalithic period (approx. 3000 BC). Several theories have been offered to explain the purpose of these stone monuments. Yet, the only thing we can say with some certainty is that they must have been connected to religious practices.

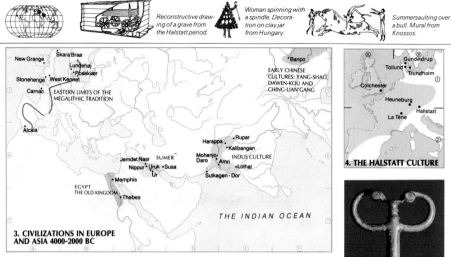

Reconstructive drawing of a grave from the Halstatt period.

Woman spinning with a spindle. Decoration on clay jar from Hungary.

Summersaulting over a bull. Mural from Knossos.

EARLY CHINESE CULTURES: YANG-SHAO, DAWEN-KOU AND CHING-LIAN'GANG

3. CIVILIZATIONS IN EUROPE AND ASIA 4000-2000 BC

THE INDIAN OCEAN

EASTERN LIMITS OF THE MEGALITHIC TRADITION

SUMER

EGYPT THE OLD KINGDOM

INDUS CULTURE

4. THE HALSTATT CULTURE

Right: *Bronze dagger (6th century BC) from Halstatt, a small town in the Austrian Alps, which in the Early Iron Age was an important centre of industry and trade in Central Europe. Finds there have given the name to a group of related cultures in Central and Western Europe (map nr. 4).*

on the other hand, there lived only nomads and loosely assembled tribes, whose stages of development varied, but with a significant exchange of cultural products along what we now take to be the most likely trading routes of the time (map nr. 5).

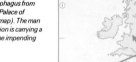

Above: *A funeral procession placing sacrificial animals and containers of wine or blood before a priest. From a sarcophagus from Hagia Triada in the Palace of Knossos (see right map). The man leading the procession is carrying a ship, symbolizing the impending cosmic journey.*

Civilization moves westward

From about the year 1500 BC we can trace established, orderly societies in the east, with towns and organized trade. In most of Europe,

5. EUROPE AND THE MIDDLE EAST 1500-1000 BC

- Areas with organized trade, government, towns and villages
- Sparse agricultural settlement
- Nomads
- Trade routes
- → Major trade routes in Europe

EARLY BRONZE AGE

BALTIC BRONZE AGE

LAUSITZER CULTURE

URN FIELD CULTURES

THE CASPIAN SEA

THE BLACK SEA

URARTU

THE MEDITERRANEAN

EGYPT

To the cities of the Indus Valley

Log house from
La Tène period. Re-
constructive draw-
ing.

Celtic warrior on
horseback. Relief
from 4th century BC.

Grave monument from
Monolithic period.
Cornwall, S. Eng-
land.

**7. CAVES FROM PRE-HISTO-
RIC TIMES IN SOUTHERN
FRANCE AND SPAIN**

**6. CELTIC EXPANSION
TO 200 BC - LA TÈNE**

Before 400 BC

400-200 BC

Celtic civilization

The Celts first settled in the central
areas of Europe, but sometime
between 400 and 200 BC they
began migrating both west and east
(map nr. 6). In La Tène by Lake
Neuchâtel in Switzerland large
numbers of iron weapons and tools
from this period have been found.

Above: Detail from a grave
complex, West Kennet in southern
England (map nr. 3). From the
so-called Megalithic Period, a name
taken from Greek: megas large, and
lithos stone. We can only marvel that
people 5 000 years ago, without the
benefit of machinery, managed to
transport and erect these heavy,
roughly hewn stones.

Right: The fortress town of
Biskupin on an island in western
Poland (map nr. 6). Ca. 30 000 oak
timbers have been driven into the
ground, to protect the town from
the marsh, as well as against
enemies. A causeway of oak leads
to the mainland. The houses, all built
of pine and oak timbers, are
thatched with sod. By the main gate
is a small market square. At the
height of its development, i.e.,
around 550–400 BC, Biskupin
must have had at least 1500
inhabitants (Drawing by Lars
Tangedal)

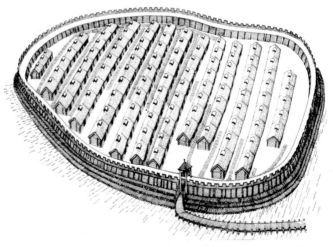

Dancing girl from Mohenjo-Daro.

Axes from the Indus culture.

Hittite warrior from the 14th century BC.

8. MESOPOTAMIA AND THE INDUS REGION

▨ Kingdom of Sargon I 2330 BC
▨ Indus cultures
— Trade routes

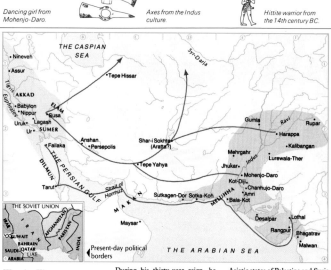

The Indus Valley Civilization

Along the Indus River in present-day Pakistan a unique and highly advanced civilization existed from about 2500–1800 BC (map nr. 8). In the early 1920s extensive excavations were carried out at the sites of two ancient cities, Harappa and Mohenjo-Daro (illust. p. 11). Both here, and at other sites excavated later, archaeologists have uncovered ruins of highly sophisticated cities. Harappa and Mohenjo-Daro are thought to have had around 40 000 inhabitants each.

Below: *Soldiers from Kush (Nubia), the area between the 2nd and 3rd cataracts (map nr. 10). Wood carving from the Second Kingdom in Egypt (ca. 2000 BC). The total size of the artifact is 193 × 73 cm, with forty soldiers marching four abreast. It is now in the Cairo Museum.*

Warrior King Thutmos III

Because of his many campaigns of conquest, Thutmos, who became Pharaoh in Egypt in 1468 BC, has been called the Napoleon of Antiquity.

During his thirty-year reign, he undertook a total of seventeen campaigns of conquest in Asia. The eighth of these took his troops all the way to the Euphrates.
Under Thutmos's predecessor, Queen Hatshepsut, whose reign had been quite peaceful, the small

Asiatic states of Palestine and Syria had formed a coalition, led by the new Hurrittic kingdom of Mitanni. It was this coalition, and the Hittite Empire further to the north, that Thutmos III wanted to bring into line. His soldiers won many battles, and much booty – in the form of slaves, cattle and precious metals – was brought home to Egypt.
However, when Thutmos died at about the age of 55 in 1438 BC, the Mitanni Empire had yet to be subdued.

The map below shows areas attacked by Thutmos III's legions, and counter-attacks by the Hittite and Mitanni empires.

9. THUTMOS III's CAMPAIGNS

Sumerian chariot from Ur. Ca. 2500 BC.

Mesopotamian warrior with tunic and battle axe.

Hammurabi standing before the sun-god Shamash.

Left: The excavation of Mohenjo-Daro in the Indus Valley soon revealed that all the houses had been built of very costly fired ceramic brick. Seen here is the same standardized brick (7 × 14 × 28 cm), used in one of the city's wells.

Right: Statue from Uruk in Sumer is from ca. 3000 BC, thought to represent one of the very first Mesopotamian rulers. The figure, eighteen cm high, is worked in alabaster. The eyes are mother-of-pearl and lapis lazuli, inlaid in asphalt.

lished Mesopotamia's first high civilization about 3000 BC, with Uruk as its cultural and administrative centre. The entire area corresponds approximately to present-day Iraq.

It was not, however, until around 1800 BC that the great law-giver, king Hammurabi, unified most of

the area in one kingdom with Babylon as its capital (map nr. 10). Babylon was one of the youngest cities in Mesopotamia, but it became in Hammurabi's time the cultural hub of the entire Near East, a position the city maintained long after it had lost its independence.

The Land Between the Rivers

Mesopotamia is originally a Greek name and means «the land between the rivers», in this case, between the Euphrates and the Tigris. Settlements some 12 000 years old have been discovered in this area, and in the south, the Sumerians estab-

Below: Statue of the Egyptian feudal lord Ka-aper, who governed one of the country's in all 42 fiefs or noms. Found in Sakkara, it is one of the most famous artifacts from the Old Kingdom (2665–2155 BC). Now in the Cairo Museum.

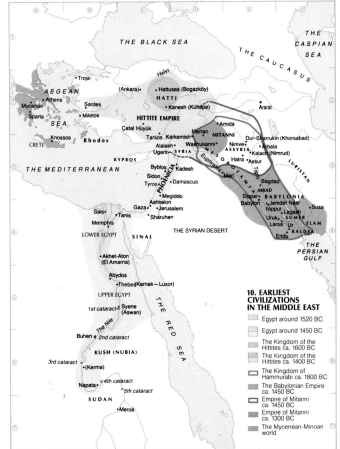

THE BLACK SEA

THE CASPIAN SEA

THE CAUCASUS

• Troja   Halys

AEGEAN   (Ankara)• • Hattusas (Bogazköy)
Mycenae   HATTI
Athens   Sardes   • Kanesh (Kültepe)   • Ararat
Sparta • Miletos   HITTITE EMPIRE
      SEA   Çatal Hüyük   • Amida
Knossos Rhodos   Tarsos Karkemish• Harran MITANNI Dur-Sharrukin (Khorsabad)
CRETE   Alalakh• Washukanni• Ninive• •Arbela
         Ugarit• •SYRIA ASSYRIA •Kalach (Nimrud)
KYPROS   Hatra• •Assur
                  Byblos• Kadesh
THE MEDITERRANEAN Sidon• •Damascus   Mari• Bagdad•
                  Tyros•   AKKAD
                      •Megiddo   Sippar• BABYLONIA
              Gaza• Ashkelon Babylon• •Jemdet Nasr •Susa
          Sais• •Jerusalem   Nippur• Lagash ELAM
       •Tanis •Sharuhen   Uruk• •SUMER
     Memphis   Larsa• •Ur •KALDEA
LOWER EGYPT SINAI   THE SYRIAN DESERT   Eridu•

• Akhet-Aton (El Amarna)   THE PERSIAN GULF

Abydos•

•Thebes Karnak – Luxor

UPPER EGYPT

1st cataract• •Syene (Aswan)

Buhen • 2nd cataract

         KUSH (NUBIA)

3rd cataract •(Kerma)

Napata• 4th cataract
              5th cataract

SUDAN

• Meroë

10. EARLIEST CIVILIZATIONS IN THE MIDDLE EAST

- Egypt around 1520 BC
- Egypt around 1450 BC
- The Kingdom of the Hittites ca. 1600 BC
- The Kingdom of the Hittites ca. 1400 BC
- The Kingdom of Hammurabi ca. 1800 BC
- The Babylonian Empire ca. 1450 BC
- Empire of Mitanni ca. 1450 BC
- Empire of Mitanni ca. 1300 BC
- The Mycenean-Minoan world

Tiled dwelling from Ur. Attempted reconstruction.

Temple tower (the Ziggurat) in Ur. 22nd century BC.

Helmet hammered out of 15 carat gold. From Ur in Sumeria.

11. THE KINGDOM OF SARGON I IN THE 24TH CENTURY BC

Map labels: THE BLACK SEA · THE CASPIAN SEA · Halys · Hattusas · Kanesh · Taurus · Diyarbakir · Tigris · Ebla · Niniveh · Urbillum (Erbil) · Cyprus · Assur · Lullubi (Sulaimanya) · Ecbatana · THE MEDITERRANEAN · Mari · Euphrates · Kermanshah · Amanus · Tuttul (Hit) · Opis · ELAM · Babylon · Kish · Susa · Memfis · Umma · Lagash · SUMER · Uruk · Larsa · Ur · Anshan · Persepolis · Shar-i Sokhta (Aratta?) · EGYPT · Thinis · Nagada · Thebes · Hie
ankonpolis · THE RED SEA · THE PERSIAN GULF · Dilmun (Bahrain) · GULF OF OMAN · Strait of Hormuz · MAKRAN (OMAN)

Above: In 2382 BC Sargon I came to power in the city of Kish in Akkad, Mesopotamia. The map shows the boundaries of the kingdom he established during the fifty-six years of his reign.

Left: Warrior from the 8th century BC, i.e., at the time when the Assyrian empire had reached its peak (map nr. 12). The Assyrians, armed with coats of mail, spears and shields, were fearsome warriors.

The Treasures of Ur

The first archaeological studies in Ur in Chaldea were undertaken by J.E. Taylor in 1854. But it wasn't until the end of the 1920s that the famous Treasures of Ur were uncovered during excavations lead by the British archaeologist Sir Leonard Woolley. Several royal tombs were found that had not been looted in ancient times, brimming with jewelry of gold, silver and precious stones, together with weapons and golden vessels. Today the nearly 5 000 year old treasures from Ur are one of the major attractions at the British Museum in London.

12. THE NEAR EAST AROUND 600 BC
- ☐ The Kingdom of the Medes
- ▨ Cilicia
- ☐ Lydian Empire
- ▨ The New Babylonian Empire
- — The Assyrian Empire ca. 700 BC

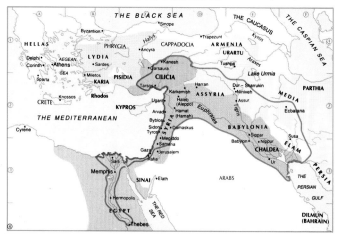

Map labels: THE BLACK SEA · THE CAUCASUS · THE CASPIAN SEA · Byzantion · Sinope · Trapezunt · Kyros · HELLAS · PHRYGIA · Halys · CAPPADOCIA · ARMENIA · URARTU · Delphi · Ancyra · Araxes · Corinth · LYDIA · Kanesh · Tushpa · Athens · Sardes · Garsaura · Lake Urmia · AEGEAN SEA · Sparta · Miletos · PISIDIA · CILICIA · Tarsos · Dur-Sharrukin · PARTHIA · KARIA · Rhodos · Karkemish · Niniveh · MEDIA · Knossos · KYPROS · Harran · ASSYRIA · Ecbatana · CRETE · Ugarit · Haleb (Aleppo) · Assur · THE MEDITERRANEAN · Arvad · Hamat (Hamah) · Euphrates · Tigris · Byblos · BABYLONIA · Cyrene · Sidon · Damaskus · Tyros · Megiddo · Sippar · Susa · ELAM · Samaria · Babylon · Nippur · Gaza · Jerusalem · CHALDEA · PERSIA · Sais · Rafia · Ur · Memphis · SINAI · Elath · ARABS · THE PERSIAN GULF · Hermopolis · THE RED SEA · EGYPT · DILMUN (BAHRAIN) · Thebes

Darius I on lion hunt. Relief from 5th or 6th century BC.

Median princes walking up the stairs to Persepolis.

Scythian warrior on horseback. Statuette from 5th century BC.

Left: *Detail from one of the artifacts from Ur, a billy goat, produced in gold leaf, lapis lazuli and mother-of-pearl.*

Right: *A gilded wagon with a four-horse team carries a Persian king or satrap. Miniature from about 500–200 BC, belonging to the so-called Oxus Treasure. Now in the British Museum, London.*

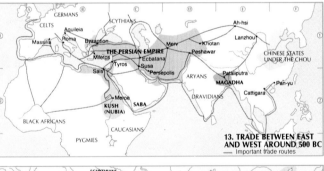

The Persian Empire
559–479 BC

In 559–529 BC Cyrus II of the Achaemenid, becomes king of the Persians, conquers the Median Empire, defeats the Lydian king Croesus, and annexes Lydia and the Greek city-states on the coast of Asia Minor in 546. He conquers Babylon and allows the Jews to return to Palestine. Cyrus II falls against the Scythians in 529.

529–522 King Kambyses II rules the empire and conquers Egypt in 525. He also carries out campaigns in Libya and Nubia.

522–479 Darius I founds Susa and Persepolis and organizes the empire into twenty administrative districts, with standing armies at the Kings disposal. Darius attacks Egypt in 518, advances toward the Indus in 513, crosses the Bosporus in 512 and makes dependencies of Thrace and Macedonia, but is stopped by the Scythians. A rebellion in the Greek city-states in Asia Minor is put down in 500–494. A punitive mission against Greece ends in the destruction of Eretria, but the Persians suffer defeat at the hands of the Athenians under Miltiades at Marathon in 490. In 485 Xerxes I comes into power in the Persian Empire and he puts down revolts in Babylonia and Egypt. Under his campaign against the Greeks 480–479 he defeats the spartans under Leonidas at Termopylene and Athens is burnt down. But the Persian fleet is crushed by Themistokles at the battle of Salamis and the Persian army is routed while withdrawing, following the battle at Plataiai in 479 BC.

13. TRADE BETWEEN EAST AND WEST AROUND 500 BC
— Important trade routes

14. THE PERSIAN EMPIRE AROUND 500 BC
→ Campaigns against Greece 490 BC
⇒ Xerxes' attacks Greece 480 BC
— The royal highway

Dead man's heart is weighed against the feather of truth. Egyptian papyrus.

Egyptian woman playing a harp. Detail from a grave painting.

Egyptian woman grinding corn with a hand-mill.

15. THE EGYPT OF THE PHARAOHS

- Arable land
- Desert and steppes
- ▲ Pyramids
- ◇ Quarries and mines
- ▪▪▪ Southernmost border 2665-2155 BC (The Old Kingdom)
- ▪▪▪ Southernmost border 2061-1650 BC (Middle Kingdom)
- — Caravan routes

Left: One of Egypt's best known Pharaohs is Tutankhamen, (1346–1337 BC). His fame does not rest so much with his political deeds as with the sensation created by the opening of his tomb in the 1920s. Among the many treasures was the king's throne, carved in wood, covered with gold and silver and inlaid with gems, faience and glass. In the detail of the back of the throne shown here, Tutankhamen himself is seen in all his splendour.

Below: A detail from an Egyptian tomb painting from the period of the New Kingdom – Woman with duckling.

THE MEDITERRANEAN

Joppe
Jerusalem
Ashkelon
Gaza
Present-day coastline
(Alexandria)
(Rosetta)
GOSEN
Pelusion
(Naucratis) Sais Busiris
Tanis
(Naucratis)
Bubastis
Wadi Tumulat
LOWER EGYPT
Giza • Heliopolis
Abusir ▲
Sakkara ▲
Dashur ▲ Memphis (Cairo) ▲
Klysma (Suez)
Eziongeber
Lake Moeris
Faiyum Oasis ▲ Afroditopolis
Herakleopolis
Copper and iron
Gemstones
◇ Alabaster
◇ Malachite
Wadi Maghara
◇ Quarry
SINAI
Hermopolis • Beni Hassan
Myos Hormos
• Akhet-Aton (El Amarna)
◇ Alabaster
Assiut • ◇ Alabaster
◇ Porphyry
UPPER EGYPT
◇ Granite and gold
• Chemmis (Panopolis)
Abydos • Nagada
Koptos • Gold
Valley of the Kings
Deir el Bahri ◇ Thebes (Luxor – Karnak)
THE GREAT OASIS (KHARGA OASIS)
• Esna ◇ Gold
Gold
Hierakonpolis • Edfu ◇ Gold
Sandstone ◇ • Silsile Emeralds
Ombos •
◇ Gemstones
Syene (Aswan) • ◇ Lead
1st cataract • Elephantine
◇ Gold and copper
Talmis •
THE RED SEA
Diorite ◇
to Punt
Aniba •
◇ Gold
Abu Simbel •
Buhen • Wadi el-Allaki
Abka • 2nd cataract
Semna • Kumma
KUSH (NUBIA)
◇ Gold

Egypt 3050–1438 BC

About 3050 BC begins a period of national consolidation. The two centres of power, Lower Egypt in the Nile delta and Upper Egypt in the south, are united under one ruler.

The Old Kingdom

Around 2630 BC the royal architect Imhotep builds a stair-step pyramid, the Stairway to Heaven, at Sakkara. Power is centred around the Pharaoh and his residence in Memphis, the country's only capital city.

2575–2550 Under king Cheops kingship develops into absolute monarchy. Construction of the great pyramid of Cheops is begun.
2540–2515 In king Chephren's day the Sphinx is carved out of sandstone.
2480–2154 A new dynasty, the «Sons of Ra», has come to power. Majestic temples are built in honour of the sun god, Ra. Art and culture blossom. With time highly placed civil servants become royal princes, with large, hereditary estates. Rivalries develop, leading to internal squabbling. Finally, royal power is weakened and the

An unconventional form of coitus. Drawing from an Egyptian papyrus.

Cross section of Cheops pyramid with the king's chamber in the centre.

Egyptian Ibis from the 3rd century BC.

16. THE PYRAMIDS AT GIZA
Smaller tombs around the pyramids are not marked

Right: The pyramids at Giza. In the foreground queens' pyramids in front of the pyramid of Mycerinus, followed by the pyramid of Chephren, and furthest back, the grandest of them all, the great pyramid of Cheops. Together they cover an area of about 200 acres, and the distance in a straight line from the nearest corner of the pyramid of Mycerinus to the farthest corner of Cheops is approximately 1.2 km. We can get some idea of the size by observing the two riders. The Cheops pyramid was 230 m at the base.

country falls into a state of chaos. 2154–2000 All against one, and one against all. The royal princes exploit the peasants mercilessly. The tombs of the kings are plundered. The country is divided into small fiefdoms.

The Middle Kingdom
Ca. 2000–1970 BC Amenemhet I unites the kingdom once again. A great fortification, «the Walls of the Kings», is built across the Isthmus of Suez. Under Amenemhet and Sesostris III, Egypt experiences a golden age of literature, science, art and architecture.
Ca. 1860 The «Land of Gold», Nubia, is conquered to the Second Cataract. The End of the fiefdoms.
1650–1544 BC The age of the Hyksos. Asiatic peoples migrate into the Kingdom and occupy large areas of land. A Semitic dynasty takes power in the Delta, while the southern parts remain in the hands of the Egyptians.

The New Kingdom
Ca. 1540 BC the Asiatic invaders are driven out of Egypt, the Nubians are defeated, and Egypt is reunited. Thebes again becomes the country's capital, and Amon-Ra the chief deity.
1468–1438 BC Under Thutmos

III Egyptian conquest was carried to the Euphrates, including the northern Sudan, Phoenicia and Syria (map nr. 10, p. 11).

Israel ca. 1030–931 BC
Approx. 1030–1015 BC Israel's first king, Saul, battles the Philistines who are invading the country. He is successful at first, but falls in

17. ISRAEL UNDER DAVID AND SOLOMON (CA. 1005-925 BC)
▨ The Kingdom of Israel

battle in 1015.
Ca. 1015–972 David succeeds Saul as king. He defeats the Philistines, conquers Jerusalem, which becomes his governmental seat, and builds a tabernacle to house the «Ark of the Covenant», for the stone tablets with the Ten Commandments written by God.
Ca. 972–931 Under king Solomon the kingdom has its period of greatest achievement, blossoming both intellectually and materially.
931 The kingdom is divided after

Solomon's death. The rebel leader Jeroboam becomes king of Israel, the area inhabited by the northern tribes, while Solomon's son, Rehoboam becomes king of the southern tribes in Judah.

18. ISRAEL AND JUDAH CA. 860 BC
▨ The Kingdom of Israel
▨ The Kingdom of Judah
— Assyria's southern border 721 BC

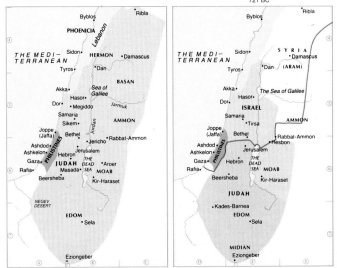

ANCIENT ISRAEL 15

Female athlete from Sparta. Contemporary bronze statuette.

Reconstructive drawing of a bourgeois home in Athens.

Phoenician ships, loaded with logs. Relief from the 8th century BC.

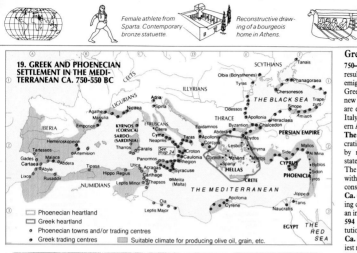

19. GREEK AND PHOENICIAN SETTLEMENT IN THE MEDITERRANEAN CA. 750-550 BC

SCYTHIANS
Tanais
Olbia (Borysthenes)
Phanagoraea
Tyras
CELTS
ILLYRIANS
Adria
LIGURIANS
Agathe
Nicaea
Spina
Odessos
THE BLACK SEA
Trapezunt
Sinope
Amisos
THRACE
Apollonia
Heraclea
Massilia
Emporion
ETRUSCANS
Caere
Epidamnos
Byzantion
Chalcedon
Abydos
PERSIAN EMPIRE
IBERIA
KYRNOS (CORSICA)
Neapolis
Taras
Apollonia
Abdera
Smyrna
Mallos
Hemeroskopeion
SARDO (SARDINIA)
Cyme
Corcyra
Lesbos
Side
Al Mina
Tartessos
Tharros
Caralis
See map 24
Croton
Corinth
Athens
Miletos
Byblos
Gades
Malaca
Abdera
Panormos
Caulonia
Sparta
Sidon
Cartaea
Abyle
Tipasa
Utica
Acragas
Rhegion
HELLAS
CYPRUS
Tyros
Lixos
Hippo Regius
Carthage
Syracuse
PHOENICIA
Rusaddir
Leptis Minor
Thapsos
Melita (Malta)
CRETE
NUMIDIANS
THE MEDITERRANEAN
Joppe
Oia
Apollonia
Tanis
Leptis Major
Cyrene
Naucratis

☐ Phoenician heartland
☐ Greek heartland
● Phoenician towns and/or trading centres
● Greek trading centres
▨ Suitable climate for producing olive oil, grain, etc.

EGYPT
THE RED SEA

750–650 Overpopulation and the resulting food shortage leads to emigration from mainland Greece. Greek men are forced to seek out new land. Agricultural settlements are established in Sicily, southern Italy, southern France and northern Africa (map nr. 19).

The 6th Century BC Aristocratic constitutions are overturned by revolutions in several Greek states, where tyrants seize power. The Age of Tyrants is interspersed with periods that see democratic constitutions evolve.

Ca. 600 The first method of striking coins is invented. This leads to an increase in trading activities.

594 Solon proposes a new constitution for Athens.

Ca. 570 Sparta is one of the mightiest military powers of the age.

552–527 The tyrant Peisistratos lays the groundwork for an Athenian age of greatness.

546–449 The cities in Asia Minor submit to Persian rule, and Persia attempts to conquer Greece itself (see p. 13). The Persian Wars begin with rebellions in the Greek cities in Asia Minor in 500, and the Persians are not stopped before they have reached Marathon (490) and Salamis (480). These victories make Athens a great-power, and Sparta's bitter rival.

Above: A votive shield from Greece (6th century BC) depicts an offering to the gods, as gifts and various trappings are carried in a procession to the alter. A young boy is ready with the offer while the alter is sprinkled with consecrated wine.

The Phoenicians

were known for their prowess as seafarers and traders. The heart of this activity, the Phoenician homeland, was present-day Lebanon (map nr. 19). Tyros and Sidon became the major trading centres in the ancient world.

The Phoenicians traded throughout the Mediterranean. In the period 750–550 there was also extensive emigration to new settlements in this area. Carthage and Utica in present-day Tunisia were among the first to be established.

20. CENTRAL GREECE IN ANTIQUITY

▨ Dorians
▨ Ionians
▨ Aeolians
☐ Arcadians
▨ Northwestern Greeks
— Important road

Hypata
Gulf of Maliakos
Cerinthos
AEGEAN SEA
Aperantia
Heraclaea
Termopylebe
Stratos
AITOLIA
Elatea
Opos
EASTERN LOCRIS
Cyme
Myonia
PHOCIS
THERMOS
Parnassos
Orchomenos
CHALKIS
Pleuron
WESTERN LOCRIS
DELPHI
Chaironia
Copais
BOEOTIA
Eretria
Oiniadai
Calydon
Naupaktos
Askra
THEBES
Cape Araxos
Patras
GULF OF CORINTH
Leuctra
Thespia
Plataiai
Tanagra
Afidnai
Rhamnos
ACHAIA
Aegium
Aigeira
Sikyon
Elevsis
ATTICA
Hyrmine
Dyme
Leontium
MEGARIS
MEGARA
ATHEN
Marathon
ELIS
Aigina
Salamis
Pireus
Brauron
Elis
Psophis
Cleitor
Stymphalos
CORINTH
Nemea
Phaleron
Hymettos
PELOPONNESE
Mycenae
Aigina
AIGINA
SARONIC
Thorikos
Helena
Letrini
ARCADIA
ARGOS
Epidauros
Hieron
Cape Sounion (Colonna)
CHIOS
OLYMPIA
Mantineia
Lerna
Tiryns
Calaurea
GULF
Alfeios
Macistus
Dipaia
Asine
Troizen
THE IONIAN SEA
Pyrgos
Phigalia
Tegea
MEGALOPOLIS
Thyreia
Hermione
Hydrea
MESSENIA
Euotas
Prasiai
Pityussa
Messene
Thuna
Farai
SPARTA
LACONIA
Pylos
Pharis

Loom with counter-weights from classical Greece.

The Acropolis of Athens, built in the 5th century BC.

Pericles, Athens' leader during her period of greatness in the 5th cent. BC.

21. THE PELOPONNESIAN WAR 431-404 BC

- Athens, The Delian League and its allies
- Sparta and her allies
- Neutral states
- → Main campaigns by Athens and the Delian League
- → Main campaigns by Sparta and her allies
- ★ Important battle sites with dates

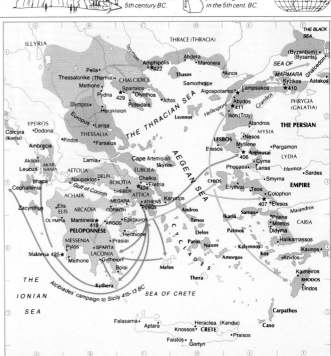

The Delian League

In 478 BC a maritime confederation was formed between Athens and other Greek city-states, primarily a defense league against the Persian Empire, under the military leadership of Athens. The League's headquarters was in Athens as well, but the war chest was maintained in the Temple of Apollo on the island of Delos.

The allied states were to provide either warships or money. Since most parties preferred the latter option, the League's fighting fleet and the Athenian navy soon became one and the same force.

During the Peloponnesian War (see below) it became a major objective for Sparta to crush the Delian League, and with Sparta's victory in 404 BC the League was dissolved.

The Peloponnesian War

The reign of the great statesman and strategist Pericles (ca. 500–429 BC), Athens' age of greatness. Not only did the city become a centre of international trade, but the Athenians were also busy building up an empire in the Mediterranean. This was the reason Sparta went to war with Athens in 431.

It is called the Peloponnesian War, and did not end until an alliance of Spartans and Persians crushed the main body of the Athenian navy at Aegospotami in 405. Only eight vessels, under the strategist Conon, managed to make their way to Cyprus. One year later Athens had to capitulate.

Right: The Greek dramatist Sophocles (496–406 BC) was influenced by myth and legend, but his topics and his characters made the plays contemporary dramas that had important things to say about the politics of his day. F. ex. in his «Oedipus Rex», which is not only Sophocles' masterpiece, but that of ancient drama on the whole. Here a modern production of the play at the Herodes Atticus Theatre at the Acropolis (map nr. 23, p. 19).

Discus thrower. Greek marble statue from ca. 450 BC.

Greek distance runners.

Olympic sprinter ca. 500 BC.

Gymnasium (210.5 m long)
(Practice area for wrestlers and boxers.)

East Hall

Roman bath

Covered entrance for athletes and judges

Palaestra (Sports arena, surrounded by baths, recital halls. etc.)

Prytanaeum 1) ca. 160 BC

Herodes Atticus 1) Exedra (ca. 160 AD)

Treasuries (for votive gifts)

Heraion
Temple of Hera Alter Metroum 2)
Philippaeum Alter to Zeus
Pelopium 3) Hall of echoes STADIUM length: 1 Olympic stadium = 192 m)

Theocoleum (Priests' residence)

ALTIS (festival grounds)

Temple to Zeus (456 BC)

Roman hot springs

Workshop of Phidias (sculptor) from the middle of the 5th century

Paeonius' statue of Nike (421)

Nero's Palace

Leonidaeum (Built as a guest house by Leonidas, it later became the governor's residence)

Agora (square)

Bouleuterium (Council chambers)

Hippodrome →

South Hall

0 20 40 60 80 100 metres

1) On the Altar of Hestia in the Prytanaeum the Olympic flame burned during the Games. In one of the great halls in the building a banquet was held for the victors.

2) The Metroum was dedicated to the mother-goddess Rhea (magna mater), who gave birth to all of the chief gods of Olympus: Zeus, Hades, Poseidon, Hera, Demeter, and Hestia.

3) The Greek hero of legend, Pelops, is considered the originator of the Olympic Games. The Pelopium, a shrine, consisting of a raised open area, is dedicated to him.

Above: The ruins of the Pronaia temple in Delphi, which, like the temple of Apollo, was destroyed during the great earthquake in 373 BC. Three years later, however, it was rebuilt. It was at the cult centre of Delphi that the sibyl Pythia delivered the judgments of the Oracle.

Below left: Greek sprinters as depicted on a victory vase from around 470 BC. Right: Charioteer from Delphi. Bronze statue from around 470 BC. Both in Olympia and at the Pythian Games in Delphi, the chariot races were a highpoint of the games.

The Olympic Games

The first athletic contests in Greece probably took place in Olympia in 776 BC, or even earlier.

They were held in the summer every four years, and lasted five days. On the first day participants made offerings, prayed to the gods and took the Olympic oath. The following day there were chariot races in the Hippodrome, then the pentathlon in the stadium, with competition in the discus, long jump, javelin, sprints and wrestling. The third day was the day of the full moon. This day began with religious rituals in the morning, and sprints, boxing and wrestling for juniors in the afternoon.

On the fourth day there were two races, one of one stadium length, and one covering two lengths (1 stadium length = 92 m), and a distance run of twenty-seven stadium lengths (c. 5 kms). In the afternoon contestants competed in boxing, wrestling and **pankration**, no-holds-barred combat. The final event of the games was a race, twice the length of the stadium, in full armour.

The fifth day was the awards ceremony.

22. OLYMPIA

Buildings from Classical period (5th century BC)

Constructed in the Hellenic period

From the time of Imperial Rome

The earliest known Olympic games were held in 776 BC, the last in 394 AD

It was during an excavation in Olympia that French archaeologist and pedagogue, Baron Pierre de Coubertin (1863–1937), first had the idea of reviving the Games. The first modern games were held in Greece in the summer of 1896. The first Winter Games took place in Chamonix in 1924.

Grecian temple in the Dorian style. Ca. 450 BC.

Ionian column and capital arch from the Acropolis 430s BC.

Greek amphitheatre from around 350 BC.

Above: *The world around 500 BC, according to the Greek philosopher and scientist Hekataios. Libya (Africa) has been run together with Asia, thus becoming about the same size as Europe. Hekataios produced also a «Description of the World», containing hundreds of place names.*

Left: *One of the colonnades in the Parthenon of the Acropolis.*

23. THE ACROPOLIS OF ATHENS

▨ Buildings from Classical period (5th century BC)

▨ Constructed in the Hellenic period

▨ From the time of Imperial Rome

The Acropolis of Athens

Construction of the Acropolis in Athens in the classical period was begun under Pericles in 447 BC, and the first building completed was the Parthenon according to drawings by the architects Iktinos and Kalikrates. The temple, erected in honour of the goddess Athena, the city's guardian deity, was built in the Dorian style and dedicated in

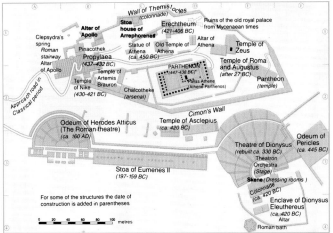

Wall of Themistocles (colonnade)

Alter of Apollo

Stoa house of Arrephorenes

Erechtheum (421-406 BC)

Ruins of the old royal palace from Mycenaean times

Clepsydra's spring

Roman stairway

Altar of Apollo

Pinacothek

Propylaea (437-432 BC)

Temple of Nike (430-421 BC)

Temple of Brauron

Statue of Athena

Old Temple of Athena (ca. 450 BC)

Altar of Athena

PARTHENON (447-438 BC)

Pallas Athene (Athene Parthenos)

Chalcotheke (arsenal)

Temple of Zeus

Temple of Roma and Augustus (after 27 BC)

Pantheon (temple)

Approach road in Classical period

Odeum of Herodes Atticus (The Roman theatre) (ca. 160 AD)

Cimon's Wall

Temple of Asclepius (ca. 420 BC)

Theatre of Dionysus (rebuilt ca. 330 BC)

Theatron

Orchestra (Stage)

Skene (Dressing rooms)

Odeum of Pericles (ca. 445 BC)

Stoa of Eumenes II (197-159 BC)

For some of the structures the date of construction is added in parentheses.

Colonnade (ca. 420 BC)

Enclave of Dionysius Eleuthereus (ca. 420 BC)

Altar

Roman bath

0 20 40 60 80 100 metres

438 BC. A short time later (437–432 BC) the pompous complex of arched entryways, the Propylaea, was built in both the Dorian and Ionic styles. Pericles' Odium, which served as a concert hall, was

Left: *During performances at the Dionysian and other Greek theatres, music was an important element. Seen here is an actor with a tambourine, made of a round wooden frame with hide stretched across one side. Bits of metal sound when the instrument is struck or shaken.*

added around 445 BC. It was situated close to the Theatre of Dionysus, rebuilt around 330 BC.

From 421 to 406 a temple – Erechtheum – was built north of the Parthenon, and dedicated to Athena, Erechtheus and Poseidon. Construction was begun in order to occupy workers in a period of great unemployment. Pericles commissioned the sculptor Peidias to decorate the Parthenon and the rest of the Acropolis. Among other things, he created the statue Pallas Athene (Athene Parthenos) in gold and ebony. Peidias had his own

studio in Olympia (map nr. 22, p. 18), with assistants to help him complete these enormous projects. In the Hellenistic period (323–30 B.C) a temple of Zeus and the Peristyle of Eumenes II were built, the latter as a kind of foyer to the Dionysian Theatre. During the time of Imperial Rome too, additions were made to the Acropolis – a Roman theatre and, typically, a Roman bath.

The Acropolis of Athens – the city's fortress – is one of Athens' greatest attractions, even today.

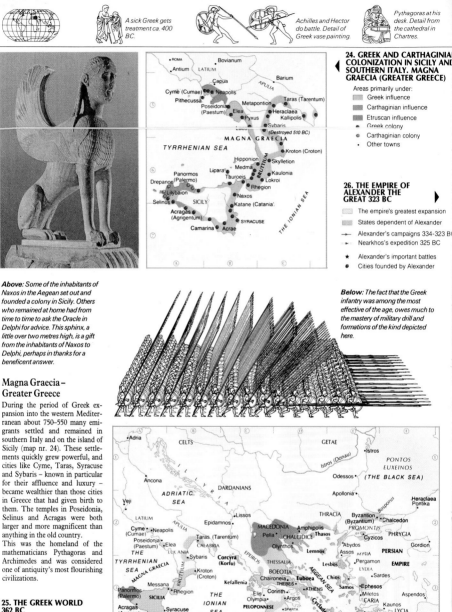

Top illustrations captions:

A sick Greek gets treatment ca. 400 BC.

Achilles and Hector do battle. Detail of Greek vase painting.

Pythagoras at his desk. Detail from the cathedral in Chartres.

24. GREEK AND CARTHAGINIAN COLONIZATION IN SICILY AND SOUTHERN ITALY. MAGNA GRAECIA (GREATER GREECE)

Areas primarily under:

Greek influence
Carthaginian influence
Etruscan influence
- Greek colony
○ Carthaginian colony
· Other towns

26. THE EMPIRE OF ALEXANDER THE GREAT 323 BC ▶

The empire's greatest expansion
States dependent of Alexander
→ Alexander's campaigns 334-323 BC
⇢ Nearkhos's expedition 325 BC
★ Alexander's important battles
● Cities founded by Alexander

Above: Some of the inhabitants of Naxos in the Aegean set out and founded a colony in Sicily. Others who remained at home had from time to time to ask the Oracle in Delphi for advice. This sphinx, a little over two metres high, is a gift from the inhabitants of Naxos to Delphi, perhaps in thanks for a beneficent answer.

Below: The fact that the Greek infantry was among the most effective of the age, owes much to the mastery of military drill and formations of the kind depicted here.

Magna Graecia – Greater Greece

During the period of Greek expansion into the western Mediterranean about 750–550 many emigrants settled and remained in southern Italy and on the island of Sicily (map nr. 24). These settlements quickly grew powerful, and cities like Cyme, Taras, Syracuse and Sybaris – known in particular for their affluence and luxury – became wealthier than those cities in Greece that had given birth to them. The temples in Poseidonia, Selinus and Acragas were both larger and more magnificent than anything in the old country.

This was the homeland of the mathematicians Pythagoras and Archimedes and was considered one of antiquity's most flourishing civilizations.

25. THE GREEK WORLD 362 BC

Athens and the Second Attic Maritime League
Sparta and her allies
Boeothia and its allies
Carthaginian territory

Alexander the Great

When Philip II had fallen at the hands of an assassin, the twenty-year-old Alexander – the son of Philip's fourth wife, Olympias – became king of the Macedonians. The Greeks hoped this would mean an end to Macedonian hegemony, but it soon became evident that the «pup», as he was called, was in fact a young «lion», and after a time the Greeks accepted their new ruler.

Only two years after his ascension to the throne, in 334, Alexander led an army of 35 000 men in a campaign of vengeance against the

Below: One who learned much from the geometry of Euclid was Eratosthenes from Cyrene (ca. 275–194 BC), who used Euclidean theories in measuring distances when developing his world map. The axis of the world passed through the Pillars of Hercules (Gibraltar), Rhodes and Issos, and along the Taurus Mts. to the Himalayas.

Right: In late December the Greeks honoured the god of wine and fertility, Dionysus. It was believed that by working themselves into a state of ecstasy, members of the cult could be possessed by the god, thereby sharing in his divinity. It was in particular women who took part in these orgiastic rituals during the feasts of Dionysus. From a vase, ca. 380 BC.

Persian Empire (map nr. 26). The first battle took place near the river Granikos the same year, and here, for the first time, the Greek riders were victorious against the Persian cavalry. In 333 Alexander defeated the Persian king Darius III at Issos, and following the assassination of the Persian king two years later, Alexander laid claim to his throne. He married the Bactrian princess Roxane and made Babylon the seat of his empire. In 323 the 33-year old king died of fever during preparations for new expeditions, this time into Sicily, Italy and Africa.

Above: This statue of a horseman depicts the Macedonian king Alexander the Great (356–323 BC). The horse is no doubt the famous warhorse Bukéfalos, which then prince Alexander managed to tame after all others had given up trying. Bukéfalos served his master right up until it was killed during a battle in India in 326 BC. In honour of his horse, Alexander named a city near the site of the battle Bukéfala (map nr. 26). The bronze statue was cast during the Roman period, but is likely a copy of a much older original.

Below: This enlargement of a portrait on a gold coin shows Alexander the Great's father, Philip II of Macedonia (382–336 BC). He ascended the throne in 359 and was a ruthless but very able ruler. He gained control over the gold mines in Thrace and raised a professional army that became the most effective in the world. Philip II united the Greeks in one kingdom.

Etruscan wagon. From grave painting at Volterra.

Etruscan wrestling match. Mural in Tarquinii from about 530 BC.

She-wolf nurses the founders of Rome, Romulus and Remus, at the Capitolium.

27. THE APENNINES (ITALIAN) PENINSULA AROUND 300 BC

Celtic from ca. 400 BC
Celtic advances
Etruscan territory
Romans and their allies
Samnitic League
Greek influence
Carthaginian territory
Important road

The Punic Wars

The Carthaginians – or **punici** – as the Romans called them, had possessions in the western part of Sicily, but by an ancient treaty, the Strait of Messina was to form a boundary between Roman and the Carthaginian spheres of interest. When Carthage carried out naval exercises of Tarentum in Calabria, many in southern Italy saw an excuse to take the rich island of Sicily. The Senate resisted for some time, but in 264 **The First Punic War** broke out.

After 23 years of war, both parties were exhausted, but Rome emerged victorious, and Sicily became a Roman province.

In 218 **The Second Punic War** erupted, and the Carthaginians' famous general, Hannibal, led an army of 40 000 men from Spain, over the Alps and down the entire length of Italy. Yet, in 201 Carthage had to sue for peace.

In 149 **the Third Punic War** began, ending three years later when North Africa too became a Roman province (maps nrs. 28 and 32, p. 24).

Below: The fertility god Demeter (and an armed servant), who, says the Sicilian poet Theocritus (ca. 300–260 BC), is carrying «poppys red, and sheaves of flowering grain in his generous hands». From an Etruscan tomb painting from the 5th century BC, found in Caere.

The Roman Empire 753 – ca. 300 BC

Monarchy

753 According to legend, Romulus and Remus found Rome.

750–575 Latins, Sabines and Etruscans form the *city-state* of Rome, ruled by kings, a senate, clerics and a popular assembly.

Ca. 550 The state is divided into administrative districts for the collecting of taxes and military organization. The society is further divided, according to class: patricians and plebeians.

Republic

The Early Rep. ca. 510–300 BC

Ca. 510 The king is expelled. Executive power is granted to elected officials who serve one year terms, governing in tandem so that *one* man cannot usurp power. Official posts and admission to the Senate are reserved for patricians.

494 Plebeians threaten to leave Rome; patricians forced to accept plebian civil servants and a plebian assembly. The plebeians have won their first victory in the struggle between the estates.

Ca. 493 Rome forms league with the Latin city-states, based on

principles of equality.

451–450 The plebeians win greater protection under the law with the introduction of the 'law of the twelve tablets'.

396 Veii, the most powerful of the Etruscan cities, is conquered. Rome's territory is nearly doubled. Way open to the north.

Ca. 390 Gauls burn Rome.

366–300 Plebeians gain access to patrician civil posts.

340–338 Rome wins a war against alliance of Latin states and Campania. Latins gain all the rights of Roman citizenship – the other defeated allies only half of these.

Etruscan warrior with helmet and sword.

Gallic armor in hammered bronze from time of Caesar.

Roman warrior from time of the Republic. Relief from 4th century BC.

28. THE PUNIC WARS

- ···→ Roman campaigns 218-201 BC
- ──→ Hannibal's campaigns 218-203 BC
- ···→ Hasdrubal's campaign 208-207 BC

Roman 264 BC
Expansion to 218 BC
Expansion westward 218-121 BC
Carthaginian 264 BC
Carthaginian expansion 238-218 BC
Controlled by Massilia

Below: It was against soldiers like those shown here that the Romans had to fight in neighbouring states. Their armour was apparently not much different than that of the Romans themselves. In fact many modern historians point to the fact of Rome's superior numbers as the most likely reason for her success against opponents on the Italian peninsula.

Below: Two stages in the battle of Cannae, where the Roman consul Terrentius Varro engaged the Carthaginian commander Hannibal – during the Second Punic War – in august, 216 BC. Hannibal routed the Romans.

First stage

Second stage

29. THE BATTLE OF CANNAE 216 BC

Hannibal's divisions: 1 and 5: Cavalry divisions. 2 and 4: African infantry. 3: Spanish/Gallic infantry. 6: Lightly armed Carthaginians.

Varro's Roman divisions: 7 and 9: Infantry. 8 and 10: Cavalry divisions.

30. ASIA MINOR 188 BC THE KINGDOM OF PERGAMON

Pergamon 218 BC
Pergamon 218-188 BC
Pergamon 188 BC
The Seleucid Kingdom
Free Greek cities

Roman wagon. The men rode. Woman, children and old people travelled by wagon.

 Houses in an Italian city, 1st century AD. Detail from a relief.

 Roman carpenter at work. Detail from mural in Pompeii.

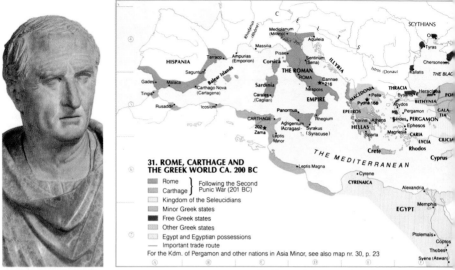

31. ROME, CARTHAGE AND THE GREEK WORLD CA. 200 BC

Rome ⎫
Carthage ⎬ Following the Second Punic War (201 BC)

Kingdom of the Seleucidians
Minor Greek states
Free Greek states
Other Greek states
Egypt and Egyptian possessions
— Important trade route

For the Kdm. of Pergamon and other nations in Asia Minor, see also map nr. 30, p. 23

Above: A very famous orator of the Roman period, Marcus Tullius Cicero (106–43 BC). Many of Cicero's orations, letters and philosophical treatises are preserved. Together they give an impression of a lively personality, with a sense of wit and rhythmic diction.

32. THE ROMAN EMPIRE AT THE DEATH OF CAESAR 44 BC

Roman provinces
Independent states

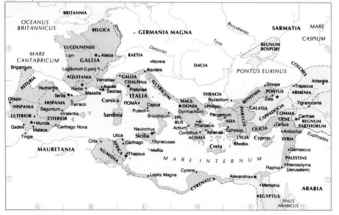

The Roman Empire Ca. 200–44 BC

The Late Republic

200–197 BC War with Macedonia to «liberate» the Greek city-states.
171–168 Macedonia becomes a Roman province. Booty and tribute such that the Romans themselves need not pay taxes.
149–146 Following the Third Punic War, Carthage becomes a Roman province.
133 Tribune Tiberius Gracchus recommends giving state lands to peasants. Because this would make Gracchus a leader of the small farmers, the **optimi**, the party of the nobles, are against the proposal. Gracchus is murdered.
123 Gaius, brother of Tiberius Gracchus, attempts unsuccessfully to push through agrarian reform by forming an alliance of the agrarian proletariat, the **eques** or «knights» and other members of the Latin League. G. killed during armed uprising.

113–101 Cimbrians and Teutons, threaten Rome. Consul Gaius Marius drafts proletariat creating a loyal professional army, whose members expect to be rewarded following each campaign.
88 Mithradates VI of Pontus has 80 000 Romans murdered in the cities in Asia Minor. Senate gives command of the army to Sulla; popular assembly withdraws this post and gives it to Marius. Sulla occupies Rome, and his enemies flee. After Sulla's departure, Marius again takes power.
82–79 Sulla returns after having defeated Mithradates. Marius and his supporters (**populares**) defeated. Sulla becomes dictator, reinstates the power of the Senate.
73–71 Thracian gladiator Spartacus leads a slave revolt that spreads across all of Italy; put down by Crassus.
60 Pompey, Crassus and Caesar form the first **triumvirate**, and so control both the Senate and the Popular Assembly.
58–51 Caesar conquers Gaul. He establishes an army with loyal soldiers.
49 Caesar crosses the Rubicon into Italy. War with the Senate and Pompey, ends with Caesars victory at Farsalos. Pompey flees to Egypt.
48 Pompey is murdered. Caesar makes Cleopatra queen of Egypt. Caesar continues his campaigns in Asia Minor, Africa and Spain.

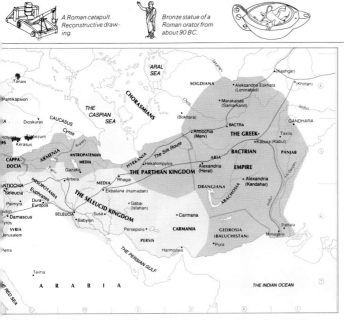

A Roman catapult. Reconstructive drawing.

Bronze statue of a Roman orator from about 90 BC.

46 Caesar crushes all opposition and becomes dictator for life. He introduces the Julian Calendar.
44 Caesar is murdered by conspiratorial senators.

Below: *All roads in the ancient world led to Rome, and all remain today. Here we see one of the most beautiful – the road from Ostia, Rome's seaport.*

Map nr. 33: *In 58–51 Caesar subjugates Gaul. The population is Romanized as Latin becomes the language of the people. In 55/54 Caesar invades Britain.*

Above: *This statuette of a Roman legionnaire shows, among other things, that the legionnaires wore coats of mail, constructed of overlapping bands of metal.*

33. GAUL AND BRITAIN
Roman provinces
Conquered by Caesar 58-51 BC
Controlled by Massilia
Caesar's invasion of Britain 55 and 54 BC
Roman province 43-71 AD

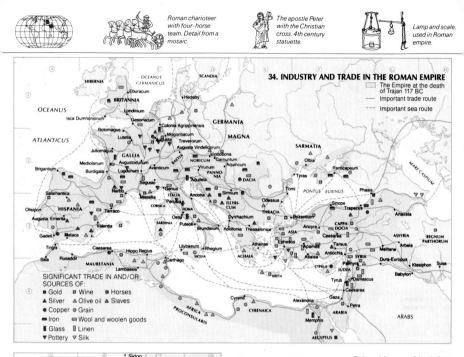

Roman charioteer with four-horse team. Detail from a mosaic.

The apostle Peter with the Christian cross. 4th century statuette.

Lamp and scale, used in Roman empire.

34. INDUSTRY AND TRADE IN THE ROMAN EMPIRE

The Empire at the death of Trajan 117 BC
— Important trade route
--- Important sea route

OCEANUS GERMANICUS
SCANDIA
HIBERNIA
OCEANUS
Eburacum
BRITANNIA
Isca Dumnoniorum
Hedeby
Londinium
GERMANIA
Gesoriacum
Colonia Agrippinensis
MAGNA
ATLANTICUS
Rotomagus
Lutetia
Mogontiacum
Treverorum
SARMATIA
Juliomagus
GALLIA
Augusta Vindelicorum
Vindobona
Augustodunum
Aventicum
Carnuntum
NORICUM
Olbia
Mediolanum
Lugdunum
Virunum
Aquincum
PANNO-
NIA
DACIA
Panticapeum
Brigantium
Burdigala
Segusio
Aquileia
MARE CASPIUM
Salamantica
Narbo
Genua
ITALIA
Ancona
Sirmium
Tyras
PONTUS EUXINUS
Phasis
HISPANIA
CORSICA
Perusia
Odessus
Sinope
Trapezus
Artaxata
Olisipo
ROMA
ILLYRI-
CUM
Tomi
THRACIA
Byzantium
CAPPA-
DOCIA
ASSYRIA
Augusta Emerita
Tarraco
Ostia
Dyrrhachium
Ancyra
Caesarea
REGNUM
PARTHORUM
Tingis
Caesarea
SARDINIA
Puteoli
Apollonia
Thessalonice
ASIA
Tarsus
Melitene
Arbela
Gades
Malaca
Valentia
Brundisium
ACHAIA
Ephesus
Apamea
Antiochia
SYRIA
Dura-Europus
Ktesiphon
Susa
Sala
Rusaddir
Lilybaeum
Rhegium
Athenae
Attalea
Palmyra
Babylon
MAURETANIA
SICILIA
CYPRUS
JUDEA
Damascus
Lambaesis
Hippo Regius
Carthago
KRETA
Tyrus
Caesarea
SIGNIFICANT TRADE IN AND/OR
SOURCES OF:
Cyrene
Alexandria
Gaza
Petra
■ Gold   ● Wine   ■ Horses
▲ Silver △ Olive oil ⊠ Slaves
● Copper ● Grain
AFRICA PROCONSULARIS
CYRENAICA
ARABIA
ARABS
➖ Iron   ⬜ Wool and woolen goods
▮ Glass ▯ Linen
Memphis
▼ Pottery ▽ Silk
AEGYPTUS

Palestine at the Time of Christ

Jesus was born in Bethlehem in Judah, which by this time had become an independent Roman district, separate from Galilee, Samaria and Perea. However, he grew up in Galilee, which together with Perea was governed by the Roman **tetrarch** Herod Antipas. When Jesus was crucified in Jerusalem, Pontius Pilate was «procurator», i.e., Roman governor, in Judea.

Below: A fragment of the gladiator mosaic in the Villa Borghese in Rome. The first known duels between gladiators in Rome took place in 264 BC, and after a time the barbaric custom became a popular diversion. Even Augustus brags that he has ordered 5 000 pairs of gladiators into life-or-death combat. The gladiators were often prisoners of war, or violent criminals who could serve out their punishment by performing in the arena for a specified number of years.

35. PALESTINE IN THE TIME OF CHRIST

The Roman province of Syria from 64/63 BC, incl. free states and cities under the Syrian governor

Kgd. of Judea under the vassal prince Herod the Great 40-4 BC

SIDON
Sarepta
Tyros
Dan
Cæsarea Filippi
PHOENICIA
SYRIA
PANEAS
GAULA-
Corasin
NITIS
Rafana
Ptolemais (Akka)
Betsaida
Kapernaum
GALILEA
Sea of
Galilee
BATANEA
TRAKONITIS
Cana
Tiberias
Hippos
Dion
Carmel
Nazareth
Tabor
Yarmuk
Abila
AURANITIS
Dora
Nain
Gadara
Cæsarea
Skytopolis
DEKA-
MEDITER-
Ginea
Pella
Gerasa
RANEAN
SAMARIA
POLIS
Samaria
Sikem
Gilead
Apollonia
Garisim
PEREA
Gadara
Joppe
(Jaffa)
Antipatris
Fasælis
Philadelphia
Arkelais
Lydda
Ephraim
Betania
Jamnia
Emmaus
Betania
Jericho
Asdod
JERUSALEM
Betlehem
Qumran
(The Dead Sea Scrolls)
Askalon
JUDEA
THE DEAD SEA
(398 m below sea level)
Gaza
Hebron
Masada
Beersheba

Galilee - Perea, Herod Antipas governed 4 BC-33 AD

Governed by tetrarch Philipus 4 BC - 33 AD

Samaria - Judea, governed by procurator Pontius Pilate 26-36 AD

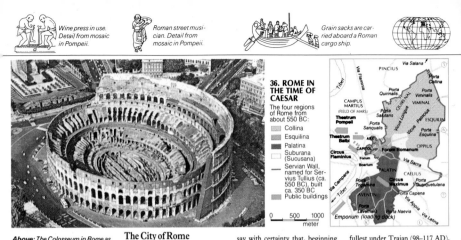

Wine press in use. Detail from mosaic in Pompeii.

Roman street musician. Detail from mosaic in Pompeii.

Grain sacks are carried aboard a Roman cargo ship.

36. ROME IN THE TIME OF CAESAR

The four regions of Rome from about 550 BC:

- Collina
- Esquilina
- Palatina
- Suburana (Sucusana)
- Servian Wall, named for Servius Tullius (ca. 550 BC), built ca. 350 BC
- Public buildings

0   500   1000
meter

Above: The Colosseum in Rome as it stands today with the Amphitheatre. The building takes its name from the colossal statue of emperor Nero, Colossus Neronis, which stood nearby. The Amphitheatre, which held an audience of about 50,000, was used primarily for combat, whether it be pairs of gladiators or pairs of wild beasts. It was dedicated in the year 80 BC, one year after Vespasian's death. The length axis of the building is 188 m and the cross axis is 156 m.

37. THE IMPERIAL MARKETS (FORA) IN ROME

Buildings and other structures from:

- Time before Caesar
- Time of Caesar, to 44 BC
- Augustus (43 BC - 14 AD)
- Tiberius - Vespasian (14 - 79 AD)
- Nerva - Trajan (96 - 117)
- Adrian - Antonius Pius (117 - 161)
- Constantine (306 - 337)
- Other periods

The City of Rome

South of the Tiber river lay the area known as Latium. North of the Tiber was Etruria (map nr. 27, p. 22). Commerce between the two regions was carried on via an island in the river (map nr. 36), and east of here it was – on the Pallatium, one of Rome's seven large hills – that the seeds of what was to become the city of Rome first germinated in the 14th century BC. According to legend, however, it was the twin sons of the war god Mars, Romulus and Remus, who founded the city in 753 BC. We can say with certainty that, beginning in about the year 550, Rome was a growing urban area. And the site on which the Forum Romanum stands today was an important centre even then. Several temples were built, of which the temple of Jupiter, dedicated in 509 BC, was the most magnificent.

In the time of Caesar, the Forum was greatly expanded. He constructed, among other things, the first Imperial market, the Forum of Caesar (Forum Julium). Later several new fora were established, one after the other: Augustus' Forum, Vespasian's Forum (Forum Pacis), Neva's (Domitian's) Forum and Trajan's Forum.

Not only did Rome extend its geographical boundaries to the fullest under Trajan (98–117 AD), but also became the radiant centre of the ancient world. The inhabitants – over a million – could take pleasure in well furnished baths, libraries and athletic facilities. They could divert themselves with theatre, chariot races and/or gladiatorial combat in the Colosseum.

*Below: Arch of Titus, raised in honour of the emperor Titus in 81 AD (map nr. 37: L 4). The triumphal processions in Imperial Rome began on **Campus Martius**, the «plain of Mars», went via Circus Flaminius, through the Arch of Titus and on along Via Sacra to Capitol, where the general or emperor placed his laurel wreath at the throne of Jupiter.*

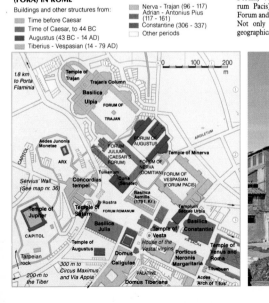

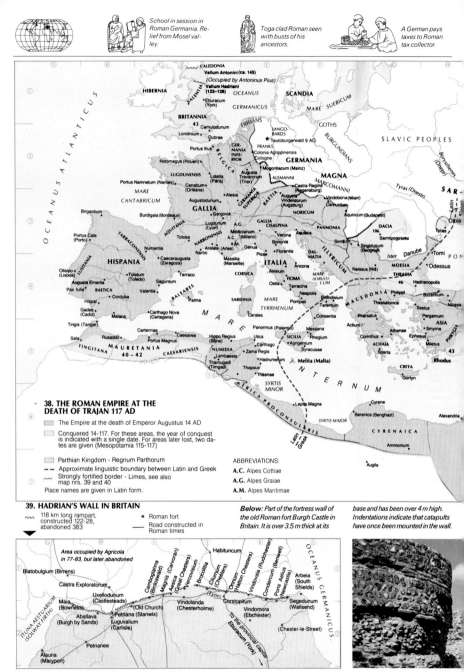

School in session in Roman Germania. Relief from Mosel valley.

Toga clad Roman seen with busts of his ancestors.

A German pays taxes to Roman tax collector.

CALEDONIA
Vallum Antonini (ca. 145)
(Occupied by Antoninus Pius)
Vallum Hadriani (122–128)
HIBERNIA
VALENTIA
Eburacum (York)
OCEANUS
GERMANICUS
SCANDIA
MARE SUEBICUM
BRITANNIA
43 Camulodunum
FRISIANS
GOTHS
Londinium
Dubrae
LANGO-
BARDS
Teutoburgerwald 9 AD
SLAVIC PEOPLES
Portus Itius
GERMANIA INFE-RIOR
Colonia Agrippinensis
Cologne
FRANKS
BURGUNDIANS
Borysthenes (Dnepr)
Rotomagus (Rouen)
BELGICA
Mogontiacum (Mainz)
GERMANIA
MAGNA
Tyras (Dnestr)
SAR-
OCEANUS ATLANTICUS
LUGDUNENSIS
Lutetia (Paris)
Augusta Treverorum (Trier)
ALEMANN
Castra Regina (Regensburg)
MARCOMANNI
Portus Namnetum (Nantes)
Cenabum (Orléans)
GERMANIA SUPERIOR
Augusta Vindelicorum (Augsburg)
Vindobona (Wien)
Carnuntum
Latin
Olbia
MARE CANTABRICUM
GALLIA
Alesia
Gergovia
RAETIA
NORICUM
Aquincum (Budapest)
DACIA
Tyras
Brigantium
Burdigala (Bordeaux)
AQUITANIA
Lugdunum (Lyon)
A.G.
GALLIA CISALPINA
Mediolanum (Milano)
Verona
Aquileia
PANNONIA
Sirmium
Singidunum (Beograd)
106
Sarmizegetusa
Tomi
PON-
Portus Cale (Porto)
TARRACONENSIS
Tolosa
NARBONENSIS
A.C.
A.M.
Bononia
Genua
Florentia
Pisae
ILLIRICUM
Naissus (Niš)
MOESIA
Odessus
Olisipo (Lisboa)
LUSITANIA
Numantia
Caesaraugusta (Zaragoza)
Arelate (Arles)
Narbo
Massilia (Marseille)
ITALIA
Ancona
DAL-MATIA
Ister
THRACIA
Hadrianopolis
Byzantium
Nicaea
HISPANIA
Toletum (Toledo)
Tarraco
CORSICA
Aisisium
ROMA
MARE ADRIATI-CUM
46
Philippi
ASIA
Pax Iulia
Augusta Emerita
BAETICA
Saguntum
Ostia
Tarracina
Neapolis
Brundisium
Tarentum
MACEDONIA
Thessalonice
Pharsalus
Pergamum
Sestus
Smyrna
Ephesus
PHRYG
Hispal
Corduba
Valentia
BALEARES
Palma
SARDINIA
Pompeii
MARE TYRRHENUM
Consentia
Rhegium
Actium
ACHAIA
Corinthus
Athenae
Sparta
Miletus
Rhodus
43
Gades (Cadiz)
Malaca
Carthago Nova (Cartagena)
Carales
SICILIA
Panormus (Palermo)
Messana
Agrigentum
Syracusae
CRETA
Gortyn
Tingis (Tanger)
Rusaddir
Cartennae
Caesarea
Portus Magnus
MARE
Utica
Hippo Regius (Bône)
Carthago
Zama Regia
Melita (Malta)
Sala
TINGITANA
MAURETANIA
40 – 42
CAESARIENSIS
NUMIDIA
Lambaesis
Thamugadi (Timgad)
Hadrumetum
Thapsus
Thaenae
INTERNUM
Sala
AFRICA PROCONSULARIS
SYRTIS MINOR
Leptis Magna
Cyrene
Berenice (Benghazi)
Alexandria
SYRTIS MAJOR
CYRENAICA
Ammonium
Augila

38. THE ROMAN EMPIRE AT THE DEATH OF TRAJAN 117 AD

The Empire at the death of Emperor Augustus 14 AD

Conquered 14–117. For these areas, the year of conquest is indicated with a single date. For areas later lost, two dates are given (Mesopotamia 115–117)

Parthian Kingdom - Regnum Parthorum

– – Approximate linguistic boundary between Latin and Greek

Strongly fortified border - Limes, see also map nrs. 39 and 40

Place names are given in Latin form.

ABBREVIATIONS:
A.C. Alpes Cottiae
A.G. Alpes Graiae
A.M. Alpes Maritimae

39. HADRIAN'S WALL IN BRITAIN

118 km long rampart, constructed 122–28, abandoned 383

■ Roman fort

— Road constructed in Roman times

Area occupied by Agricola in 77–83, but later abandoned

Blatobulgium (Birrens)
Castra Exploratorum
Habituncum
Camboglanna (Birdoswald)
Magnis (Carvoran)
Aesica (Great Chesters)
Vercovicium
Brocolitia
Cilurnum (Chesters)
Onnum (Halton Chesters)
Vindovala (Rudchester)
Condercum (Benwell)
Pons Aelius (Newcastle)
Arbeia (South Shields)
OCEANUS GERMANICUS
Uxellodunum (Castlesteads)
Maia (Bowness)
Aballava (Burgh by Sands)
Petriana (Stanwix)
(Old Church)
Luguvalium (Carlisle)
Vindolanda (Chesterholme)
Corstopitum
Vindomora (Ebchester)
Segedunum (Wallsend)
ITUNA AESTUARIUM (SOLWAY FIRTH)
To the provincial capital Eburacum (York)
(Chester-le-Street)
Alauna (Maryport)
Petrianea

Below: Part of the fortress wall of the old Roman fort Burgh Castle in Britain. It is over 3.5 m thick at its base and has been over 4 m high. Indentations indicate that catapults have once been mounted in the wall.

Roman basilica with free-standing bell tower, campanile.

Watch tower from the border with Germania. Reconstructive drawing.

Roman aqueduct – a bridge that transports water – from around 50 AD.

The Roman Empire 31 BC –117 AD

The Principate

Rome is still a republic, but the head of state – *princeps* – becomes the most powerful man in the empire, since he is commander in chief of the military – *imperium* – and has the largest personal fortune.

30 BC–14 AD Octavian receives the honourary title 'Augustus'. He is caesar, i.e., emperor. Augustus expands the provinces in Spain, Gaul and along the Donau (map nr. 38) and creates peace in the Empire, *Pax Romana*, The Roman Peace.

37 Tiberius' adopted son, Caligula, as the new emperor. Four years later he is murdered by members of the Praetorian Guard.

54–68 Nero becomes an increasingly despotic, murdering several members of his own family. Rome burns in 64. The generals rebel, and Nero commits suicide.

68–69 The Year of the Four Emperors. Generals in the outlying areas of the Empire declare themselves «Caesar» and advance on Rome.

98–117 The Empire is at the height of its expansion following Trajan's conquest of Dacia (Romania), Arabia, Armenia, Assyria and Mesopotamia (map nr. 38).

Britain 55 BC–128 AD

55 and 54 B.C The Roman proconsul in Gaul, Julius Caesar, crosses the Channel and attacks the Celtic tribes in the south (map nr. 33, p. 25).

43–128 AD Emperor Claudius initiates the conquest of the country. This is completed by governor Agricola in approx. 80 AD, and the island is incorporated into the empire as the imperial province of Britannia (map nr. 38). Agricola builds a breastwork between Forth and Clyde as a defense against the Scottish Picts. Under Emperor

Above: Two officers of the Imperial Guard. From a marble relief from the time of Hadrian, i.e., the beginning of the 1st century AD.

Hadrian this line of defense is pulled back to Solvay and Tyne where a 118 kilometre long fortification, Hadrian's Wall (*Vallum Hadriani*), is constructed between 122 and 128 AD (map nr. 39). The Romans are forced to abandon the wall in 383.

40. THE ROMAN EMPIRE'S BORDER (LIMES) WITH GERMANIA CA. 100

ᴧᴧᴧ Limes   — Trade route to Scandinavia
■ Fort

Colonia Agrippinensis (Cologne)
Bonna (Bonn)   GERMANIA
Confluentes (Koblenz)   MAGNA
Mogontiacum (Mainz)
Augusta Treverorum (Trier)   ALEMANNI
Castra Regina (Regensburg)
BELGICA   Rhenus (Rhein)   Danuvius (Donau)
Aquae (Baden-Baden)   Augusta Vindelicorum (Augsburg)
GERMANIA SUPERIOR   RAETIA
Turicum (Zürich)   Lacus Venetus

Right: The fortified 6.5 km long wall surrounding Constantinople, built in the time of

the East Roman emperor Theodosius II, 401–450, son of emperor Arcadius.

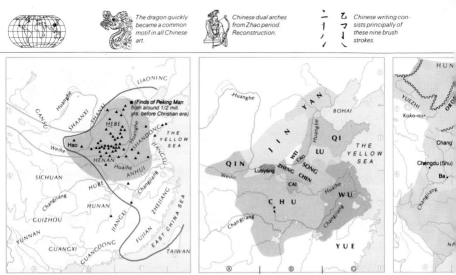

The dragon quickly became a common motif in all Chinese art.

Chinese dual arches from Zhao period. Reconstruction.

Chinese writing consists principally of these nine brush strokes.

41. CHINA CA. 4000-1600 BC

— Extent of the Yangshao culture ca. 4000-3000 BC

— Extent of the Langshao culture ca. 1600 BC

▦ Approximate extent of the Shang Empire 1600-1000 BC

▲ Archaeological finds from Shang period

Names of modern provinces

China ca. 1600–206

Approx. 1600–1027 BC China's historical period begins with the Shang Dynasty, a slave-society at the height of China's bronze age (map nr. 41). A written language is developed for use by the oracular priests. A very highly advanced technique is used in the production of bronze vessels. Ancestor worship demands large numbers of human sacrificial victims.

1027 The Shang Empire is conquered by the Chou, a people from the Wei river valley in Shan Xi.

1027–771 Under the Chou Dynasty China's emperors take the title *Tian-Zi*, Son of Heaven. Slave society is succeeded by feudalism. The kings confer fiefdoms on clan

42. CHINA CA. 500 BC. THE EASTERN CHOU.

▨ Areas retained by the Chou princes around Luoyang

Not all small states are marked

and tribal leaders in return for military support. The first canals and irrigation systems are built, and new agricultural implements of iron are used. The copper coin becomes the standard of exchange. On the whole, there is a high level of cultural activity.

771–221 The eastern Chou. The period sees a bitter and bloody power struggle between rival princes. This continues until the kingdom is once again united under the first emperor of Ch'in. Most of the period covers the age of Spring and Autumn, *chunqiu*, 722–481 BC (map nr. 42) and the 'Epoch of the Warring States', *chan kuo*, 481–221 BC. The periods are named after two chronicles describing their histories.

221 After the Ch'in ruler in the years 230–221 BC has subjugated the other states, he takes the title Ch'in Xi Huangxi – the First Emperor of Ch'in.

221–206 Under the Ch'in Dynasty, the systems of writing, and weights and measures are standard-

Left: Cheng Xi Huangzi, the first emperor of Ch'in (map nr. 43), ruled China's first empire from 221–210 BC. The extent of his power is demonstrated by the 'imperial guard', life-size terra cotta figures, 7 000 strong that were placed in his mausoleum. This army was discovered during the digging of a well in 1974 and is one of the most sensational archaeological finds of this century. The terra cotta army had originally stood under a wooden construction, covered with earth, but after this collapsed around 207 BC, the entire imperial guard lay hidden for over 2 000 years. The figures were originally painted red, green and brown. The soldiers are all facing east, toward areas conquered by the first emperor. The warriors were fully armed, but everything made of wood, such as spear shafts and bows, have all rotted away. .

Chinese symbols for
the 5 elements:
wood, fire, earth,
metal, water.

Sacred bronze ves-
sel, 36.5 cm high,
from the Shang
period.

43. FIRST CHINESE EMPIRE

░░░ Extent under the Ch'in 221 BC

▒▒▒ Expansion during Han Dynasty
(see also map nr. 44)

∿∿ The Great Wall, begun in the
4th century BC

ized. The Great Wall (see illust.
below) is built. All books in the
empire are to be burned. This
calamity befalls the writings of
Confucius as well, the individual
who played the greatest role in the
development of Chinese culture.
Yet it seems the book burnings
were not as effective as emperor and
his officials had hoped. In 210 the
First Emperor dies during a tour of
inspection.
206 Four years after Cheng's
death, general Liu Bang, seizes
power. Becomes the first emperor
of the western Han Dynasty, as Gao
Tzu.

*Above: A bronze statuette of two
wrestlers, crafted in China during
the Chou Dynasty, i.e., in the last
millennium BC. The statuette is now
in the British Museum, London.*

*Left: Part of the ca. 2400 km long
fortification begun in China in the
4th century BC to defend against
the Huns (maps nrs. 43 and 44).
The Great Wall was completed by
Cheng Xi Huangxi near the end of
the 3rd century BC. The world's
largest construction. Much reduced
in size in the 14th and 15th
centuries, it is now 6–10 m high,
4–6 m thick at the top, and has some
24000 watchtowers.*

Chinese warrior, dressed in trousers and short-waisted jacket.

Chinese clash in the Zhou period. Decoration on vase.

Silk production in the Tang period. Here raw silk is processed.

Top map (Ancient World):

ICELAND
ATLANTIC OCEAN
KOLA
WHITE SEA
Ob
SITONES (FENNI)
FENNI (SAMID- Lapps)
Ladoga
GOTHS
'The Roman fleet reached here in 4-5 AD'
CALEDONIA
ANGLES
BALTIC
URAL MTS
Tobol
Irtych
HIBERNIA (IRELAND)
Eburacum (York)
FRISIANS
SAXONS
GOTER
Dnepr (Borysthenes)
Volga
Ural
SCYTHIANS
KHIRGIS STEPPES
BRITANNIA
BELGICA
Londinium
Fectio
Colonia Agrippinensis (Köln)
GERMANIA MAGNA
BURGUNDIANS
Don
LAKE BALKHAS
Lutetia (Paris)
GALLIA
Castra Regina
Vindobona (Wien)
Olbia
REGNUM BOSPORI
Tartais
'Patrocles reached here ca. 285 BC'
THE ARAL SEA (Syr-Daria)
Jaxartes (Syr-Daria)
Onos
Aksu
Lugdunum
RAETIA
NORICUM
Aquileia
Istros
Tyras
Tomi
THE CASPIAN SEA
KUSHANA (Amu-Daria)
Marakanda (Samarkand)
Kashgar
Burdigala (Bordeaux)
Genua
Pisae
ILLYRI-
Salonae (Split)
MOESIA
THRACIA
Panticapaeum
Phasis
SOGDIANA
Yarkand
Narbo
Massilia
ITALIA
Roma
CUM
Byzantium
Sinope
PONTUS EUXINUS
Trapezus
PONTUS
ARMENIA
PARTHIAN EMPIRE
Alexandria (Merv)
Bactra
Aleksandria (Herat)
Kabura (Kabul)
Taxila
EMPIRE
Khot
Portus Cale (Oporto)
HISPANIA
Tarraco
Thessalonice
Ancyra
ASIA
Antiochia
Arbela
Ekbatana
Indus
Hydaspes
Valentia
SICILIA
Rhegium
Tarentum
Athenae
Ephesus
Pergamum
Damascus
Ktesifon
Susa
Persepolis
Indraprastha (Delhi)
Olisipo (Lisboa)
Carthago-Nova
Creta
Cyprus
Jerusalem
THE PERSIAN GULF
Mathu
Gades (Cadiz)
Carthago
MARE INTERNUM
Petra
Aelana
Harmozeia (Hormuz)
GEDROSIA
Bharukaccha
Tingis (Tanger)
Rusaddir
Syracusae
CYRENE
Alexandria
Memphis
AEGYPTUS
Germa
Barbaricon
MAURETANIA
Lixus
Leptis Magna
Cyrene
Thebae
Cryptus
Simylla
ANDHRI
MAGHREB
(Marrakech)
Sijilmasa
FEZZAN
Hauara
Jathrib (Medina)
THE RED SEA
Ain Salah
Murzuk
Syene
Mekka
Mosha
Musir
Ghat
Petronius reached Napata ca. 23 BC
Napata
Kerma
Adane
SAHARA
Audagost
Lake Chad
'Julius Maternus reached here ca 100 AD'
KUSH (NUBIA)
Meroë
Adulis
Aksum
Aromata
GHANA
Timbuktu
Gao
TUAREGS
SONGHAI
Sokoto
Kuka
Niger
ETHIOPIA
Avalites
Malao
Opone
GULF OF GUINEA
'Hannon of Carthage reached here ca. 525 BC'
Benin
Congo
CAMEROON
'Two Roman centurions reached here in 60 AD'
THE INDIAN OCEAN

Bottom map (China):

KHIRGISIANS
TARTARS
SEA OF JAPAN
JAPAN
Edo (Tokyo)
THE CASPIAN SEA
Aral Sea
To the Caliphate
751
HUNS
Lake Balkhash
Kara Balgasun
(MONGOLIA)
KGD. BOHAI
Heian (Kyoto)
Heijo (Nara)
SOGDIANA
751
Talas
751
Chinese protectorate 715–66
UIGHUR KINGDOM
To Silla 755
Han-Zhou
SILLA (KOREA)
KARA-KUM
Samarkand
Balasagun
791
EASTERN TURKS
Yuzhou (Peking)
Anpei
(Occupied by China 668–76)
THE YELLOW SEA
WESTERN TURKS
Fergana
Chinese 640–70 and 692–791 Tibetan 670–82
Suzhou
Wei
Baktra
Oxos
Kashgar
Kucha
Dunhuang
Huanghe
Luoyang
Yangzhou
AFGHANI-STAN
Gilgit
Lanzhou
CHANG'AN
Hsüan
EAST CHINA SEA
THE CALIPHATE
Purusapura
TOUFAN
TANG-HSIANG
Chiang-ling
CHINA
Hangzhou
Indus
Ganges
Lhasa
Brahmaputra
Changsha
Nanchang
Fuzhou
NEPAL
Pataliputra
Cheng-chiang
Guangzhou (Canton)
Taiwan
SIND
KAMARUPA
Dali 751
NAN-ZHAO
Annan (Chiao)
SOUTH CHINA SEA
ARABIAN SEA
MAGADHA
Pagan
THAI
CHEN-LA
Hainan
The Philippines
INDIAN

The Parthian Empire

was founded by an Iranian-Scythian nomadic people under king Arsaces in the middle of the 3rd century BC. By about 100 AD they had conquered most of present-day Iran and Afghanistan and areas of northwestern India (map nr. 44). In the middle of the 3rd century BC Parthia became part of the Sasanid Empire (map nr. 50, p. 36).

45. CHINA AROUND 750 (TANG DYNASTY)

The Empire of China under the Sui and Tang

Chinese protectorates

The Turkish kingdom (Eastern and Western Turks). Chinese vassal states.

TOUFAN Chinese vassal state

Horseman from the Han dynasty. Ceramic figure from 1st century AD.

Model of a gatehouse from the Han dynasty, found in a grave.

Camel carrying silk along the Silk Road. Statuette from the Han dynasty.

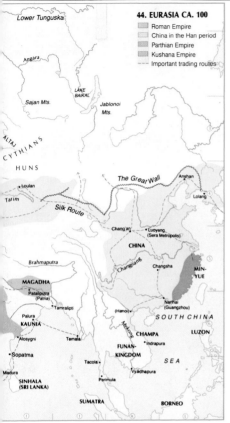

44. EURASIA CA. 100

- Roman Empire
- China in the Han period
- Parthian Empire
- Kushana Empire
- - - - Important trading routes

China 206 BC–907 AD

206 BC–220 AD Under the Western and Eastern Han Dynasties, Confucianism emerges victorious, and civil servants must pass examinations in Confucian literature. The caravan routes to the west are opened up, and internal trade is greatly increased. In the year 65 AD Buddhism comes to China and gradually becomes a strong influence on Chinese art. In about 100 AD paper is invented, and in 110 the first Chinese dictionary is completed.

220–289 The Time of the Three Kingdoms (Wei, Wu, Shu). The kingdom is divided. Nomadic tribes settle in the vicinities of the cultural centres and adopt Chinese culture and manners. The most important written teachings of Buddhism are translated into Chinese, again greatly influencing Chinese artists.

262 For the first time tea is drunk at court.

311 The Huns return to China's borders. Due to internal struggles within the empire, they manage to conquer all of northern China.

569–618 China is united again under the Sui Dynasty. Extensive construction is begun on canals, irrigation systems and roads. One million workers dig a canal from the river Chang-yang to the capital city of Lo-yang near the Huang-ho. Strong Chinese cultural influence is felt in Japan.

Below left: Ladies of the Chinese imperial court, as depicted in a mural from the Tang period. The artists of this time showed an impressive ability to capture individual character in portraits.

Above: Tai Zong, one of the greatest emperors in Chinese history, governed 626–49. Seen here with ladies of his court, contemp. painting of emperor during an audience.

618–907 Tang Dynasty aims to reestablish and expand the old empire (map nr. 45). Chang'an (map nr. 46) is a powerful cultural and political centre with two million inhabitants. An age of greatness for most branches of the arts. It is, among other things, the first period of blossoming in the art of calligraphy.

Below: The capital of the Sui and Tang emperors, Chang'an in N. China. The imperial palace with its harem is in the North part of the city. To the South are government offices.

46. CHANG'AN IN THE TANG PERIOD

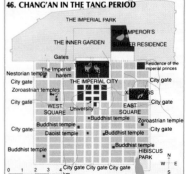

THE IMPERIAL PARK

THE INNER GARDEN

THE EMPEROR'S SUMMER RESIDENCE

Gates

Residence of the imperial princes

The Imperial harem

Nestorian temple

City gate

Zoroastrian temples

City gate

THE IMPERIAL CITY

City gate

XING QING PALACE

City gate

WEST SQUARE

University

EAST SQUARE

Zoroastrian temple

City gate

Buddhist temple

Buddhist temple

Buddhist temple

Daoist temple

Buddhist temple

Buddhist temple
HIBISCUS PARK

City gate   City gate City gate

0 1 2 3 4 km

N W E S

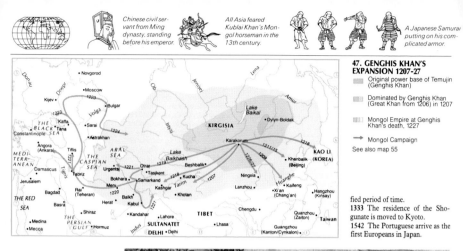

Chinese civil servant from Ming dynasty, standing before his emperor.

All Asia feared Kublai Khan's Mongol horseman in the 13th century.

A Japanese Samurai putting on his complicated armor.

47. GENGHIS KHAN'S EXPANSION 1207-27

▨ Original power base of Temujin (Genghis Khan)

▨ Dominated by Genghis Khan (Great Khan from 1206) in 1207

▨ Mongol Empire at Genghis Khan's death, 1227

→ Mongol Campaign

See also map 55

fied period of time.

1333 The residence of the Shogunate is moved to Kyoto.

1542 The Portuguese arrive as the first Europeans in Japan.

Mongolia 1196–1227

1196–1206 The chieftain Temujin unites the Mongolian tribes, chooses Karakorum as capital and as supreme ruler takes the name Genghis Khan.

1207–1227 Western Hsia and the Jin kingdom in China are conquered. Beijing (Peking) becomes Khanbalik. Khorezm on the Caspian Sea is also taken.

1227 Genghis Khan dies. The kingdom is divided among four sons under Oghotai in Karakorum. He continues the conquest of China. The other sons push on to Russia and Eastern Europe, Iran and Mesopotamia.

China 907–1644

907–960 The Five Dynasties. Political strife and dissolution.

960–1279 Song Dynasty. China is reunited and Kai-feng becomes the capital. Gun powder is used for military purposes. Contact with countries to the west is broken off. The empire is threatened by nomadic tribes, invading from the north.

1126 N. China is conquered by the Tungu and Khitan peoples. The Song Dynasty remains intact in the south.

1251–1280 The Mongols led by Kublai Khan conquer the Song, and from 1280 he is recognized as emperor of China.

1280–1368 The Mongols now make up only a small ruling class.

1307 Foreign religions gain a foothold. The first Roman Catholic archiepiscopal see is established in Beijing (Peking).

1355 Growing dissatisfaction with Mongolian rule leads to rebellion.

1368 Mongolian rule ends.

1368–1644 The Ming Dynasty. Trade relations with Russia and countries in the west are reestablished. The Great Wall is restored (illust. p. 31) and the aqueducts repaired.

1421 Rebuilt Beijing new capital (p. 35).

1514 The first Portuguese ship arrives in China.

1557 Portuguese in Macao granted trade monopoly.

1629 The Manchus breech the Great Wall and occupy the Liaotung peninsula.

1644–1912 The Qing Dynasty.

Manchus expand their rule to Mongolia, Turkistan, Tibet and Burma. Economy is growing while the population is rising quickly.

Japan ca. 1000–1542

Ca. 1000 Height of the Fujiwara Period. Warrior-aristocracy.

1185 Minamoto Yorimoto formed a military rule with headquaters in Kamakura. The age of the Samurai commences. The emperor in Kyoto loses all real political influence.

1192 Minamoto becomes *shogun*, supreme commander, and is given dictatorial powers for an unspeci-

Above: This section from a miniature of the 1200s is probably meant to represent the Mongol lord Genghis Khan (1161–1227), who built up one of the world's most effective military forces. The mobility of the Mongol cavalrymen allowed them to suprise opponents.

Right: Torii at the Itsukushima temple, symbol of a 1000 year-old trad. According to tradition, pilgrims sail through the torii, under water at high tide. On an island southwest of Hiroshima.

Large animals guard the tombs of the Ming emperors. Here a resting elephant.

Chinese floor vase from the Ming period. 70 cm high.

Three boon companions. Detail from a 16th century Chinese painting.

China's New Capital

In 1421 Emperor Yung Lo moved China's capital from Nan-king to Beijing (Peking) to bring his administration nearer to the border with Mongolia.

In the struggles against the Mongols, much in Beijing, or Khanbalik as it was known then, was destroyed. Now a number of new and magnificent buildings were constructed, both in the Forbidden City, where only the emperor and his attendants were allowed, and in the Imperial City.

On the site of the city's sacrificial alter the Temple of Heaven was erected. **The picture at the left** shows the core of this complex. Because the temple is roofed with blue tile, it is also referr to as the «Blue Temple». In spring the emperor sacrificed and prayed for a good harvest. This remnant of China's prehistory was revived during the Ming Dynasty and practised right up until the Revolution in 1911/12. Today the temple complex is a great tourist attraction.

Following a period of restoration in the 1420s, Beijing consisted of four walled cities, one inside the other. Innermost was «The Forbidden City», then «The Imperial City», which housed the administration, then the «Tartar City» and, finally, the «Chinese City». The perimeter wall was 20 m high and 30 km long.

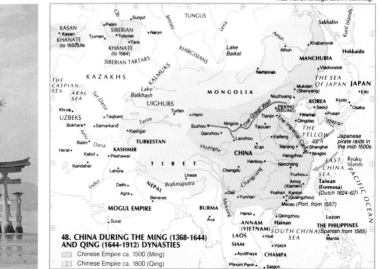

48. CHINA DURING THE MING (1368-1644) AND QING (1644-1912) DYNASTIES

☐ Chinese Empire ca. 1500 (Ming)
☐ Chinese Empire ca. 1800 (Qing)

CHINA UNDER THE MING AND CH'IN 35

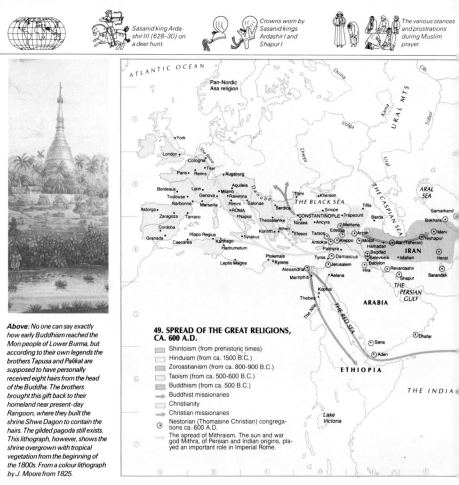

Sasanid king Ardashir III (628–30) on a deer hunt.

Crowns worn by Sasanid kings Ardashir I and Shapur I.

The various stances and prostrations during Muslim prayer.

ATLANTIC OCEAN

Pan-Nordic Asa religion

Above: No one can say exactly how early Buddhism reached the Mon people of Lower Burma, but according to their own legends the brothers Tapusa and Palikat are supposed to have personally received eight hairs from the head of the Buddha. The brothers brought this gift back to their homeland near present-day Rangoon, where they built the shrine Shwe Dagon to contain the hairs. The gilded pagoda still exists. This lithograph, however, shows the shrine overgrown with tropical vegetation from the beginning of the 1800s. From a colour lithograph by J. Moore from 1825.

49. SPREAD OF THE GREAT RELIGIONS, CA. 600 A.D.

- Shintoism (from prehistoric times)
- Hinduism (from ca. 1500 B.C.)
- Zoroastrianism (from ca. 800-900 B.C.)
- Taoism (from ca. 500-600 B.C.)
- Buddhism (from ca. 500 B.C.)
- Buddhist missionaries
- Christianity
- Christian missionaries
- Nestorian (Thomasine Christian) congregations ca. 600 A.D.
- The spread of Mithraism. The sun and war god Mithra, of Persian and Indian origins, played an important role in Imperial Rome.

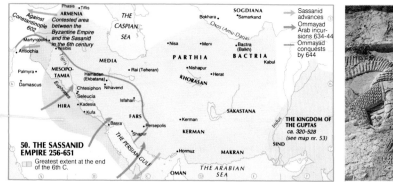

50. THE SASSANID EMPIRE 256-651

- Greatest extent at the end of the 6th C.

Sassanid advances
Ommayad Arab incursions 634-44
Ommayad conquests by 644

THE KINGDOM OF THE GUPTAS
ca. 320-528
(see map nr. 53)

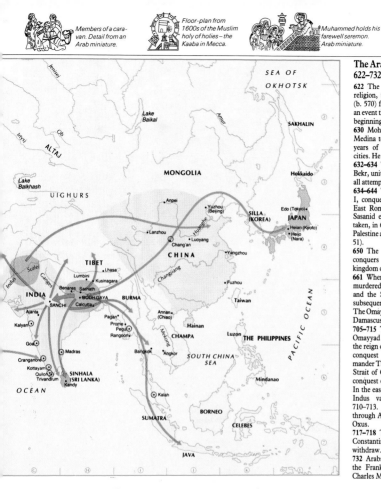

At the top of the page, illustrations with captions:

Members of a caravan. Detail from an Arab miniature.

Floor-plan from 1600s of the Muslim holy of holies – the Kaaba in Mecca.

Muhammed holds his farewell seremon. Arab miniature.

The Arabian Empire
622–732

622 The founder of the Islamic religion, the prophet Mohammed (b. 570) flees Mecca for Medina – an event that later came to mark the beginning of the Islamic calendar.

630 Mohammed returns from Medina to Mecca following many years of strife between the two cities. He dies two years later.

632–634 The first caliph, Abu Bekr, unites Arabia and puts down all attempts at division.

634–644 The second caliph, Omar I, conquers large portions of the East Roman (Byzantine) and the Sasanid empires. In 635 Syria is taken, in 637 Mesopotamia, in 640 Palestine and in 642 Egypt (map nr. 51).

650 The third caliph, Othman, conquers the remainder of the kingdom of the Sasanid (Persia).

661 When the fourth caliph, Ali, is murdered, the unity of Islam is lost, and the Shi'ites refuse to accept subsequent caliphs as legal rulers. The Omayyad clan comes to power. Damascus becomes the new capital.

705–715 The caliphate of the Omayyad reaches its zenith during the reign of Walid I. Following the conquest of North Africa, commander Tarik Ibn Ziyad crosses the Strait of Gibraltar and begins the conquest of the Iberian Peninsula. In the east, the western part of the Indus valley is conquered in 710–713. The Arabs push on through Afghanistan and cross the Oxus.

717–718 The Arabs lay siege to Constantinople, but are forced to withdraw.

732 Arabs defeated at Poitiers by the Frankish ruler of Austrasia, Charles Martel.

The Sasanid Empire

In the beginning of the 3rd century AD the powerful Parthian Empire (map nr. 44, p. 32) was on the verge of dissolution. A clan that had originally come from Fars in southwest Iran – the Sasanid - managed in a very short time to create another Persian great-power (map nr. 50).

The first leader of note of the Sasanid dynasty was king Ardashir I, who reigned from 224 to 241. A picture of him is carved out in a cliff relief in Firuzabad (see illust. left). The Sasanid epoch in Iran (256–651) was a rich one for the nation, both politically and culturally, and Zoroastrianism became the official state religion.

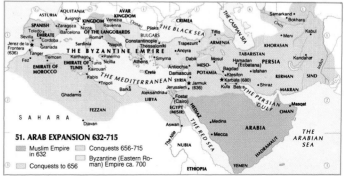

51. ARAB EXPANSION 632–715

- Muslim Empire in 632
- Conquests to 656
- Conquests 656–715
- Byzantine (Eastern Roman) Empire ca. 700

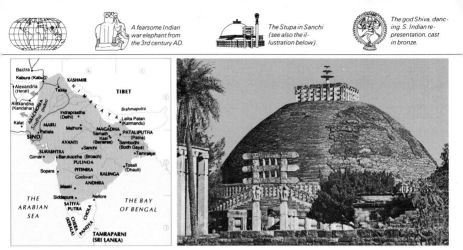

At top of page, left to right:

A fearsome Indian war elephant from the 3rd century AD.

The Stupa in Sanchi (see also the illustration below).

The god Shiva, dancing. S. Indian representation, cast in bronze.

52. THE MAURYA KINGDOM IN INDIA

▨ Greatest extent ca. 250 B.C.

— Alexander the Great's campaign 329-325 B.C. (see map 26)

*Below: In 1817 in Ajanta in western India (map nr. 53), British soldiers found several monasteries and temples that had been carved into the side of a mountain. Originally there had been only **one** cave, dedicated to the serpent god Naga, but several more were added, until today there are twenty-eight in all. Most are decorated with murals. A section of one of them is reproduced here – a religious, erotic art form, which influenced Asian art for centuries.*

India 329 BC–646 AD

329–325 BC The kings in the greater empire are engaged in internal struggle, and when Alexander the Great pushes into India from Afghanistan in 326, he meets no unified resistance. Some actually become his allies, while others are vanquished. In 325 Alexander's troops refuse to follow him any farther east. He is forced to return home (see also p. 21). At Alexander's death in 323 the Hellenic colonies he has founded revert to Seleukus I of Syria.

Ca. 320 The Maurya Dynasty, led by Chandragupta Maurya, comes to power and quickly regains control of the areas Alexander had conquered.

Ca. 305 Seleukus I campaigns in India in order to protect his possessions, but is defeated by Chandragupta.

Ca. 270 The Maurya Dynasty's greatest ruler, Ashoka, comes to power under bloody circumstances. Legend tells that he had first to dispose of ninety-nine brothers!!

Ca. 261 Ashoka attacks and conquers the state of Kalinga. The knowledge that the battles have cost the lives of 150 000 men puts the king in a state of despair. He becomes a believing Buddhist and proponent of non-violence, commanding his subjects to show moderation, friendliness, tolerance and piousness. He sends Buddhist missionaries to Greece, Syria, Egypt, Sri Lanka and Indo-China.

Ca. 235 Ashoka dies. The kingdom gradually splits up into several smaller states.

Ca. 320–528 AD The Gupta Dynasty. Northern India is united again under Chandragupta I in 320. The dynasty holds power for two hundred years, with the empire reaching the limits of its expansion under Chandragupta II (map nr. 53). The period is a golden age in art and literature.

606–647 After the country has been severely weakened during an attack by the White Huns in the middle of the 400s, king Harsha manages for a short time to hold together a kingdom in the north (map nr. 53). He makes Kanauj his capital and assembles scholars and poets at his court.

53. INDIA UNDER GUPTA DYNASTY AND HARSHA

▱ Gupta Empire 385-414

⟶ Attack by White Huns, mid-5th C.

▨ Harsha's kingdom 606-46

Woman from the Khmer kingdom. Detail of relief from the 12th century.

Representation of the Buddha from the Khmer kingdom. From the 12th century.

Detail depicting mythological beast – a makara – from central Vietnam.

Left: Shortly after the Buddha's death in 485 BC, he was revered as a god. His corpse was burned, his ashes kept as holy relics. Stupas were built over these relics. This picture shows a stupa in Sanchi in India, erected in the last century BC. It is 36 m in diameter and 16.5 m high. The stupas later became more like East-Asiatic temples. The tops of the mounds were built out so that the stupas became pagoda-shaped (illus. p. 36).

Right: At the zenith of the Khmer Empire this beautiful head of the Buddha was created. It was carved in sandstone in the 1100s and is now in the Musée Guimet, Paris.

Cambodia (the Khmer Kingdom) 600–1200

Approx. 600 The Khmer people from the highlands in the north advance into Funan and take power there.

The 700s The kingdom is for a time a dependency of Shailendra – a larger kingdom, centred in Java and Sumatra.

802–850 Jayavarman II liberates the Khmer Kingdom from Javan domination and makes Angkor the religious centre of the kingdom.

The 1100s The Khmer Kingdom's period of greatness. Under Suryavarman II (1113–1150) attains its greatest expansion (map nr. 54), and it is in his day that work on the mighty Angkor Vat is begun (see illus.). Near the end of the century Jayavarman VII, who governs the kingdom 1181–1218, erects Angkor Thom, a huge fortress, built around a temple.

Approx. 1200 Following continuous attacks from the Thai people and internal strife, the kingdom is in a state of disarray.

Right: Angkor Vat is the largest of the many temples in the Khmer Kingdom's capital of Angkor. It is thought that construction on the temple complex was begun by king Suryavarman II and completed later. It covers an area that is roughly rectangular, with a front side 185 m long. The main tower in the centre is 65 m high, and surrounded by four smaller towers, one in each corner. Angkor Vat is considered one of the most important surviving architectural structures from the Khmer Age in Cambodia.

54. INDOCHINA AND THE KHMER KINGDOM DURING THE ANGKOR DYNASTY

CHINA

• Pagan
LANNA
VIETNAM (ANNAM)
Independent from 939
Hanoi

TOUNGOO
• Prome
Chiang Mai
Hainan

Pegu
Menam
Vien Chang

Thaton
• Sukhothai
Indrapura

Andaman Islands
KHMER KINGDOM (KAMPUCHEA)
CHAMPA

Ayutthaya
• ANGKOR
Vijaya

FUNAN
Phan Rang

Phnom Penh
SOUTH CHINA SEA

Nicobar Islands

Samudra

Perlak•
PAHANG

SUMATRA

☐ Kingdom ca. 800
▨ Greatest extent under Suryvarman II (1113-50)

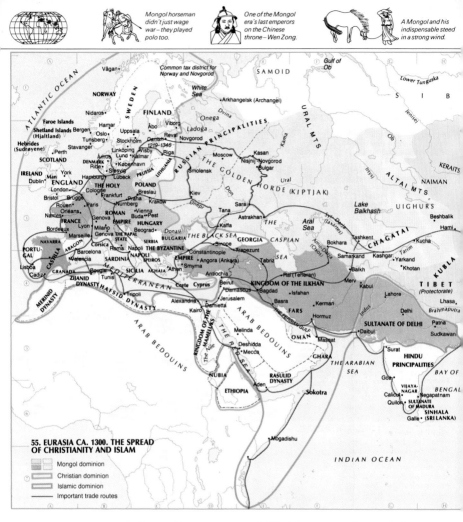

Mongol horseman didn't just wage war – they played polo too.

One of the Mongol era's last emperors on the Chinese throne – Wen Zong.

A Mongol and his indispensable steed in a strong wind.

55. EURASIA CA. 1300. THE SPREAD OF CHRISTIANITY AND ISLAM

▦ Mongol dominion
▢ Christian dominion
▢ Islamic dominion
— Important trade routes

Mongol Domination 1227–1405

1227 The Mongol Empire is divided, becoming four smaller kingdoms under the supreme command of the Great Khan Oghotai (see p. 34): The Golden Horde, north of the Black and Caspian Seas, the kingdom of the Il-khan in Iran and Afghanistan, the Chagatai-khanate and the kingdom of the Great Khan. Most Russian fiefdoms too come under Mongol control, the so-called «yoke of the Tartars».

The Kingdom of the Great Khan

1229–1241 Genghis Khan's son, the Great Khan Oghotai, insures the dominion of Northern China and makes Karakorum the capital.
1267–1279 Kublai-Khan, Oghotia's nephew, conquers the Song Empire in southern China, moves the capital to Dadu (Beijing) and calls it Khanbalik (city of the Khan). He becomes emperor of China in 1280.
1280–1368 Kublai-Khan attacks Toungoo (Burma) and conquers Pagan (1287), but the Mongols are

eventually driven back.

The Golden Horde 1237–1241
Genghis Khan's grandson, Batu, regent in the khanate of the Golden Horde, attacks Europe. Kiev is conquered, Moscow is sacked and burned. The Mongols are victorious in sixtyfive battles, and in Europe it is feared that it is only a matter of time until the plundering hordes from the East have conquered the entire continent. In 1241 it is Vienna's turn, but right in the middle of the siege, Batu receives word of Oghotai's death. He breaks

off at once so that he can return to take part in the succession question in Karakorum.

The Khanate of Chagatai
1227 Genghis Khan's second son, Chagatai, becomes khan and makes his own khanate the political centre of the Mongol kingdoms.

The Empire of the Ilkhans Approx. 1237–1258
The Mongols get a foothold in Iran, and in 1258 Genghis Khan's grandson, Hulagu, sacks Baghdad. The caliph is killed. For almost two

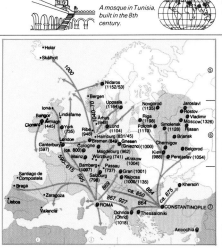

Timur-lenk on the throne. Copied from Persian miniature from the 1600s.

Mosque lamp of glass with quotations from the Koran. From the 1300s.

A mosque in Tunisia, built in the 8th century.

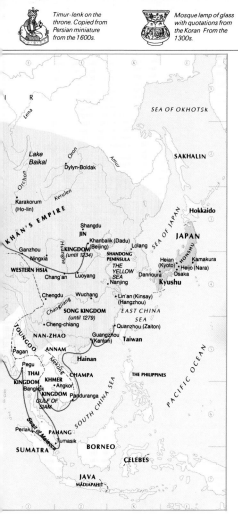

SEA OF OKHOTSK

Lena

SAKHALIN

Lake Baikal

Dylyn-Boldak

Oron

Orchon

Kerulen

Amur

Hokkaido

Karakorum (Ho-lin)

KHAN'S EMPIRE

Shangdu

Huanghe

JIN KINGDOM (until 1234)

Khanbalik (Dadu) (Beijing)

Lolang

SHANDONG PENINSULA

Heian (Kyoto)

Kamakura

Heijo (Nara)

JAPAN

HONSHU

Ganzhou

Ningxia

WESTERN HSIA

Chang'an

Luoyang

THE YELLOW SEA

Dannoura

Osaka

Kyushu

Chengdu

Wuchang

Lin'an (Kinsay) (Hangzhou)

EAST CHINA SEA

Changjiang

SONG KINGDOM (until 1279)

Cheng-chiang

Quanzhou (Zaiton)

NAN-ZHAO

Guangzhou (Kanton)

Taiwan

YOUNGOO

ANNAM

Mekong

Hainan

PACIFIC OCEAN

Pagan

CHAMPA

THE PHILIPPINES

Pegu

KHMER

THAI KINGDOM

Bangkok

Angkor

KINGDOM

Panduranga

GULF OF SIAM

SOUTH CHINA SEA

Perlak

Strait of Malacca

PAHANG

Tumasik

SUMATRA

BORNEO

CELEBES

JAVA

MADIAPAHIT

Holar

Skálholt

Nidaros (1152/53)

Bergen

1000

Uppsala (1164)

Novgorod (1135)

Jaroslavl

Iona

Bangor

Lindisfarne

Clonard (445)

York (735)

Árhus (948)

Lund (1104)

Ribe (948)

Riga (1198)

Polotsk (1119)

Smolensk (1128)

Rostov

Vladimir

Moscow, 1326)

Rjasan

Canterbury (597)

London (831/45)

Hamburg

Bremen (849)

Cologne (ca. 800)

Gnesen (Gniezno) (1000)

Chernigov

Belgorod

Santiago de Compostela

Mainz

Magdeburg (962)

Würzburg (741)

Bamberg (1007)

Passau

Krakow (1004)

Kiev (988)

Perejaslav (1054)

Braga

Salzburg (798)

Gran (1001)

Kalocsa (1000/1135)

Kherson

Lisboa

Zaragoza

ROMA

Ochrida (Ohrid) (1018)

Thessaloniki

CONSTANTINOPLE

Valencia

Antiochia

56. THE SPREAD OF CHRISTIANITY IN EUROPE

→ Missionaries

Greek Orthodox area

Roman Catholic area

Anglo-Saxon area

● Archbishopric with year of establishment

Islamic area

Below: Islam extended itself in the 1200s (map nr. 55), and Arab traders were common in both the East and the West. Here two travellers on camels are received at the city gate. From an Arab miniature from 1237.

---

hundred years the Ilkhans hold power in Iran, Iraq, Afghanistan and parts of Asia Minor.

The Dissolution of the Mongol Empire 1369–1405 Timur-lenk attempts to establish a new empire. From his base in Samarkand, his troops invade the kingdoms of the Ilkhans, which they conquer. He then pushes into the khanate of the Golden Horde and into northern India, but the newly founded great kingdom unravels quickly when Timur-lenk dies in 1405.

Spread of the World's Major Religions

Map nr. 56 Boundaries of the Catholic faith in early medieval times. Missionizing from Christendom's two great centres, Rome and Constantinople, from 1054 divided in a Roman Catholic and a Greek Orthodox Church.

Map nr. 55 shows the areas claimed by the Christian church by about 1300, and how far Islam had spread at the same point in time.

Today only Christianity has more adherents than Islam.

Byzantine fishermen. From a 6th century mosaic.

The Byzantine Imperial Palace in Constantinople in the 6th century.

Byzantine warrior from the beginning of the 7th century.

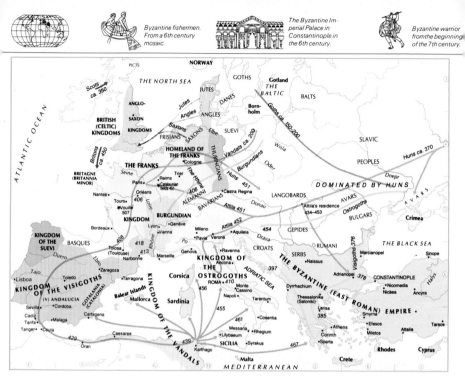

The map shows the Mediterranean lands ca. 600. Labels include:

PICTS · NORWAY · GOTHS · Gotland · THE BALTIC · BALTS · THE NORTH SEA · JUTES · DANES · Bornholm · Scots ca. 350 · ANGLO-SAXON · Angles · ANGLES · SUEVI · SLAVIC · Goths ca. 150-200 · BRITISH (CELTIC) KINGDOMS · SAXON KINGDOMS · Saxons · Elbe · Vandals ca. 200 · Wisla · Huns ca. 370 · Britons ca. 450 · FRISIANS · HOMELAND OF THE FRANKS · Cologne · THURINGIANS · Burgundians · Oder · PEOPLES · Dnepr · BRETAGNE (BRITANNIA MINOR) · THE FRANKS · Seine · Trier · Rhine · Huns 451 · DOMINATED BY HUNS · AVARS · Nantes · Paris · Reims · 406 · Donau · LANGOBARDS · Attila's residence 434-453 · Ostrogoths · Crimea · Orléans · Castra Regina · Attila 451 · BAVARIANS · BULGARS · Tours · Vouillé 507 · ALEMANNI · 406 · Catalaunian fields 451 · Loire · BURGUNDIAN KINGDOM · Lyon · Genève · Milano · Attila 452 · Aquileia · 454 · GEPIDES · RUMANI · Visigoths 376 · THE BLACK SEA · KINGDOM OF THE SUEVI · BASQUES · Bordeaux · 408 · Vienna · Po · Pavia · Verona · Drava · CROATS · SERBS · Naissus · Marcianopel · Sinope · Lisboa · Toledo · 418 · Tolosa (Toulouse) · Narbonne · Genova · Ravenna · Ancona · 397 · Adrianopel · 378 · CONSTANTINOPLE · Halys · Zaragoza · Tarragona · Corsica · KINGDOM OF THE OSTROGOTHS · ROMA · 410 · 456 · Monte Cassino · Dyrrhachium · Thessalonike (Saloniki) · Nicomedia · Nicaea · Ancyra · KINGDOM OF THE VISIGOTHS · (V) ANDALUCIA · Córdoba · GOTHANIA (CATALUNIA) · Balear Islands · Mallorca · Sardinia · Napoli · Tarentum · 455 · Larisa · 385 · Smyrna · Elesos · Miletos · Attalia · Tarsos · Sevilla · Cádiz · Tarifa · Tánger · Ceuta · Caesarea · 429 · 439 · Karthago · SICILIA · Lilybaeum · Syrakus · Messana · Rhegium · 461 · Cosentia · Athens · Corinth · Sparta · 467 · Rhodes · Cyprus · Oran · Malta · Crete · MEDITERRANEAN · THE BYZANTINE (EAST ROMAN) EMPIRE · ATLANTIC OCEAN

58. MEDITERRANEAN LANDS CA. 600

— The Byzantine Empire at the death of Justinian the Great in 565

    The Byzantine Empire ca. 600

    Kingdom of the Lombards from 568

    The Suevi Kingdom, lost to Visigoths in 585

The Byzantine (East Roman) empire 395–626

395 Emperor Theodosius dies, and as Rome's size makes it difficult to administrate from one central point, his sons each become emperor of one half of the empire: Eight-year-old Honorius in the West Roman Empire, his seven-year older, and equally ungifted, brother, Arcadius, in the East Roman

(Byzantine) Empire. Constantinople becomes the capital in the east, with Roman law and administration, but Greek language and culture.

527–565 Under Emperor Justinian I, North Africa, Italy and southern Spain are conquered (map nr. 58).

568 The Langobards take most of Italy, and Byzantine outposts in Ravenna.

626 Constantinople is attacked by Sasanidians and Slavs.

Below: The wife of Emperor Justinian I, Theodora surrounded by clergymen and ladies in waiting. From a mosaic in the church of San Vitale in Ravenna. The costume of the Byzantine church and court is embroidered with gold and decorated with jewels and pearls.

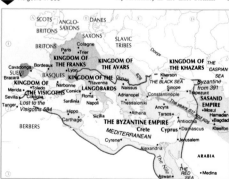

The second map labels include: SCOTS · ANGLO-SAXONS · DANES · BRITONS · Cologne · Paris · Trier · SLAVIC TRIBES · Dnepr · KINGDOM OF THE FRANKS · KINGDOM OF THE AVARS · KINGDOM OF THE KHAZARS · CASPIAN SEA · Cavadonga · Bordeaux · Lyon · Kherson · Byzantine from 391 · SUEVI · Bracara · BASQUES · KINGDOM OF THE LANGOBARDS · Danuv · THE BLACK SEA · Sinope · SASANID EMPIRE · KINGDOM OF THE VISIGOTHS · Merida · Toledo · Narbonne · Ravenna · Naissus · Constantinople · Ancyra · Tarsos · Mosul · Sevilla · Córdoba · Lost to the Visigoths 568 · Sardinia · Corsica · Roma · Napoli · Adrianopel · Thessaloniki · Hamadan · Bagdad · Tánger · Lost to the Visigoths 584 · Hippo · Sicilia · Athens · Antiochia · Damascus · Ktesifon · BERBERS · Carthage · THE BYZANTINE EMPIRE · Crete · Cyprus · Jerusalem · Cyrene · MEDITERRANEAN · The years 619-629 · ARABIA · Alexandria · THE NILE · THE RED SEA · Aswan · Medina

German knight from the 700s with short sword and long lance.

Frankish warrior from the 600s reaching for his dagger.

Gilded helmet from the middle of the 7th century, found in East Anglia.

57. GERMANIC MIGRATIONS AND THE GERMAN KINGDOMS 526

⇒ Vandals
⇒ Goths
⇒ Ostrogoths
⇢ Jutes, Angles and Saxons
⇒ Visigoths
⇒ Burgundians
⇒ Huns

Right: From the imperial palace in Constantinople there was a direct passageway to the imperial loge in the Hippodrome, where not only horse racing, but also mystery plays, mock hunts and acrobatics could be seen. This section of a palace mosaic from the latter half of the 6th century shows two athletes attacking a wild animal.

The Germanic Migrations

The Goths are the first to migrate, from Scandinavia, around 150 AD, reaching the coast of the Black Sea around the end of the century. At about the same time, the Burgundians and Vandals move westward. The former establish the Burgundian Kingdom in southeastern France in about 400. The Vandals found a kingdom in Spain, (V)Andalusia, at about the same time, but continue on to North Africa. The Goths in the vicinity of the Black Sea, who by the end of the 3rd century had separated into Visigoths (Western Goths) and Ostrogoths (Eastern Goths), also migrate toward the rich areas in the west. In Spain and the southernmost part of France the Visigoths establish their kingdom near the end of the 5th century. The Ostrogoths found a kingdom in Italy (493–553).

Kingdom of the Franks

Ca. 350 Franks migrate into Gaul.
486 King Clovis defeats the Roman governor Syagrius at Soisson, putting an end to Roman rule.
507 Clovis subjugate Visigoth territory north of the Pyrenees.
508 Capital moves from Soisson to Paris.
567 Kingdom divided into Autrasia, Neustria and Burgundia.
714–717 Charles Martel, grandson of Pipin completes the unification of the kingdom, begun by Pipin.
732 At Poitiers, Charles Martel puts a stop to the Moorish invasion over the Pyrenees.

59. WESTERN EUROPE CA. 750

Kingdom of the Franks in 741
Territories allied with the Franks
Kingdom of the Lombards in 744
Byzantine possessions
The Muslim Empire

Vendel
RINGE-RIKE
ROME-RIKE
UPPLAND
Uppsala
SVEAR
Birka
Skiringssal

PICTS
THE NORTH SEA
GOTES
SKÅNE
Lejre
THE BALTIC
Gotland
PRUSIANS
Wisla

Iona
NORTHUMBRIA
+ Lindisfarne
BERNICIA
+ Jarrow
DEIRA
York
Hedeby
Danevirke
OBODRITES

Armagh
Dublin
Man
IRELAND

WALES
MERCIA
EAST ANGLIA
ESSEX
Sutton Hoo
KENT
London
Canterbury
Cologne
FRISIANS
Utrecht
SAXONS
Dorestad
Paderborn
HESSEN
Fulda
THÜRINGEN
Elbe
Oder
SLAVS
SLOVAKS

CORNWALL
WESSEX
Isle of Wight

Seine
Soissons
Paris
Reims
Orléans
Loire
KINGDOM OF
THE FRANKS
BURGUND
AUSTRASIA
ALEMANNIA
St. Gallen
BAVARIA

BRETAGNE
NEUSTRIA
Nantes
Tours
Poitiers 732
AQUITANIA
Bordeaux
Garonne
Cahors
Lyon
Rhône
Milano
Torino
Genova
Pavia
KINGDOM OF THE LANGOBARDS
Ravenna
Firenze
Pisa
Siena
Spoleto
Roma
Monte Cassino
Capua
Benevento
Napoli
Bari
Taranto
THE ALPS
Aquileia
Drava
Sava
ADRIATIC SEA

Santiago de Compostela
ASTURIA
Duero
Segovia
Tajo
SPANISH
Toledo
Guadiana
EMIRATE
Cordoba
Sevilla
Granada
Cadiz
Gibraltar (Djebel al-Tarik)
Tanger
Ceuta
Pamplona
Toulouse
Narbonne
PROVENCE
Marseille
Lerina
Zaragoza
Barcelona
Tarragona
Ebro
Balear Islands
Corsica
Sardinia
Palermo
Sicilia
Messina
Reggio
Taormina
Syracuse
MEDITERRANEAN
Hippo
Carthage
Kairouan

ATLANTIC OCEAN

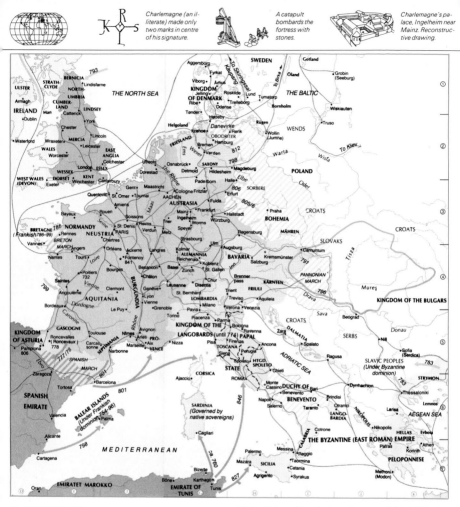

Charlemagne (an il-
literate) made only
two marks in centre
of his signature.

A catapult
bombards the
fortress with
stones.

Charlemagne's pa-
lace, Ingelheim near
Mainz. Reconstruc-
tive drawing.

---

60. CHARLEMAGNE'S EMPIRE 814

- The empire in 768
- At Charlemagne's death in 814
- Arab states in 814
- The Byzantine Empire
- Kingdom of the Bulgars 802-14
- Kingdom of the Avars to 796
- Carolingian advances
- Arab incursions
- Byzantine advances
- Viking raids (see also map 63)
- Important trade routes

The Kingdom of the Franks (France) 768–843

768 Pipin the Small dies. His son, Charles (Charlemagne), succeeds him.

773–774 Charles defeats the Langobards in Italy and incorporates their kingdom. A short time later, Saxony and Friesland are also conquered (map nr. 60).

777–778 Prominent Arabs in Spain ask Charles for help, and the Franks advance all the way to the Ebro, but are forced to return.

788 Bavaria is incorporated.

800 On Christmas Day, Charles the Great is crowned Holy Roman Emperor by Pope Leo III.

814 Charles dies in January in his favourite city of Aachen and is buried in the cathedral there. Charlemagne's eldest son has died, and a younger son, Louis the Pious, assumes the office.

817 Louis the Pious' eldest son, Lothar I, becomes co-emperor.

830 Following a rebellion, Louis the Pious cedes the rank of emperor to Lothar. In the years that follow there is serious feuding between Lothar, his brother Louis the

German, and his half brother Charles the Bald.

843 Following the Treaty of Verdun, the Frankish kingdom divided in three (map nr. 62). The West Frankish Kingdom is governed by Charles the Bald, the East Frankish Kingdom by Louis the German, and the Middle Kingdom by Emperor Lothar I. This division would give rise to the three nation-states of France, Germany and Italy.

A monk at his desk. From an ivory relief.

Cavalryman from the 900s, with saddle, but no stirrups.

11th century war ship with high stem in the Mediterranean.

The Byzantine (East Roman) Empire 673–1054

673–677 The Arabs lay siege to Constantinople, but are put to flight by «Greek fire» – a kind of early flame-thrower, consisting of sulphur, pitch, naphtha, lime and saltpetre.

726 Emperor Leo III bans «idolatry» (*ikonoduli*) and decrees that the «holy» images be removed from the churches. The great iconoclastic dispute rages for more than a hundred years.

751 Ravenna is conquered by the Langobards.

860 Constantinople is attacked by vikings (map nr. 63, p. 46).

907–976 Several Russian attacks on the Balkans and Asia Minor. Emperor John I Zimisces expels them in 971, retakes Syria and Palestine from the Arabs and annexes the eastern parts of Bulgaria (see next column).

976 Emperor Basil II, nicknamed «Slayer of the Bulgarians», also leads successful campaigns against the Arabs and the Bulgarians. The empire reaches the height of its power.

1054 The final break with the western church (The Great Schism).

Bulgaria 893–1018

893–927 Emperor Simon rules over most of the Balkan peninsula, with the exception of Greece, Croatia, Dalmatia and the district around Constantinople.

917–970 Under Peter I much territory is lost. The western portions of the empire become an independent Serbian kingdom in 963.

971 The eastern territories are conquered by Byzantium. The capital is moved to Ochrida (Ohrid) in Macedonia, and in **1018** the remainder of the country is incorporated in the Byzantine Empire.

61. SOUTHEASTERN EUROPE CA. 1050

☐ Byzantine Empire at death of Constantine IX in 1054
Greek Orthodox see (archbishopric red)
Roman Catholic see (archbishopric blue)
STRYMON Byzantine thema (province)

☐ Arab possessions

Below: *In addition to contemp. history, Charlemagne also encouraged scribes to copy older manuscripts. Here the emperor is receiving a copy of the Ten Commandments from Moses. From a miniature (ca. 850).*

62. DIVISION OF CHARLEMAGNE'S EMPIRE 843

☐ West Frankish Kingdom
☐ East Frankish Kingdom
☐ The Middle Kingdom

Stem of a Norwegian viking ship from Oseberg. Built around 800.

Ship builders in Normandy. Detail from Bayeux tapestry.

Anglo-Saxon axe-head and sword point from viking times.

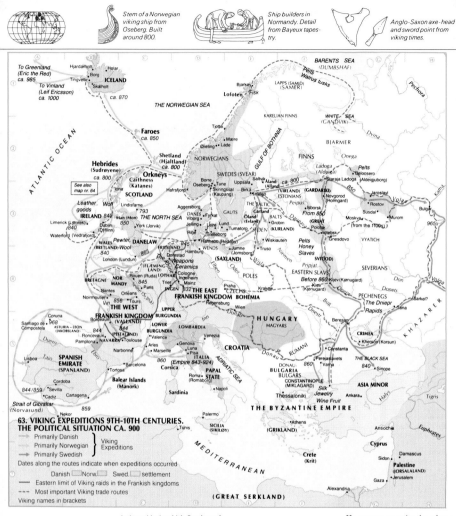

BARENTS SEA (DUMBSHAF)

To Greenland (Eric the Red) ca. 985

To Vinland (Leif Ericsson) ca. 1000

Hjardarholt • Holar
Tingvelli • Borg
Skalholt
ICELAND
ca. 870

Walrus tusks
Bjarkøy
LAPPS (SAMID) (SAMER)
Lofoten • Fisk

THE NORWEGIAN SEA

Faroes
ca. 850

KARELIAN FINNS

WHITE SEA (GANDVIK)

ATLANTIC OCEAN

Shetland (Hjaltland) ca. 800
Hebrides (Sudrøyene) ca. 800
Orkneys (Orknøene)
Caithness (Katanes)
SCOTLAND

Tiøtta
Mære
Øreting • Lade
NORWEGIANS

GULF OF BOTHNIA

BJARMER

Dvina

FINNS
Ladoga (Aldeigja)
Staraja Ladoga (Aldeigjuborg)

Onega
Pelts
Beloosero

Kama

Iona
Hafrsfjord
Borre • Oseberg
Tune (Kaupang)
Saltvik
Uppsala
Åland (Alland) ca. 800
SWEDES (SVEAR)
Birka
Helgö

Novgorod (Holmgard)
Isborsk
Rostov
Susdal • Murom
Jaroslavl
Volga
Bulgar
965

THE BALTIC
Gotland
Öland (Eyland)
Grobin (Kurland)

Peipus
(VIRLAND)
ESTONIANS
BALTS
From 860

Moskva •
(from the 1100s)

Leather goods
Wolf
IRELAND 840
Limerick (Hlymrek) 840
Dublin (Dyflinn)
Waterford (Vedrafjord)

Lindisfarne • 793
Man (Mön) 850
York (Jorvik)

Aggersborg
DANES • Fyrkat
Viborg
Jelling • Leirs
Ribe • Trelleborg

Lund
Tumaterp
SKÅNE

Wiskiauten
Truso (Jomsborg)

Gnesdovo
Polotsk
Vitebsk

VYATICH

Pelts
Honey
Slaves

SVITJOD

WALES (Bretland)
Wool 840
London (Lundun)

DANELAW
865
FRISLAND
846
Dorestad
(FLEMING-LAND)
LOTHAR

Hedeby (Hathebu)
Hamburg

WENDS
Jumne (Jomsborg)

Oder
Elbe
SAXLAND
Weser

Wisla
Niemen

EASTERN SLAVS
Before 860 Kiev (Kiønugard)
Kiev (Kiønugard)

Dniepr

SEVERIANS

Pripjat

Bug

Don
Volga

NOR-MANDY
BRETAGNE
Rouen (Ruda)
Paris
845

Pewter
Weapons
Ceramics
Cologne
Ingelheim
Trier
INGEN 832

Praha
CZECHS
BOHEMIA

Krakow

POLES

Donets
PECHENEGS
The Dniepr Rapids
Tana

Noirmoutier
Nantes
Orleans
857
Vin 856
• Tours

THE EAST FRANKISH KINGDOM
Regensburg
Wien

HUNGARY
MAGYARS

Beresan
CRIMEA
Kherson (Korsun)

KHAZARER

Coruna
Santiago de Compostela • 968
Bordeaux
ASTURIA – LEON (JAKOBSLAND)
844
Roncevaux
Pamplona •
NAVARRA (PETTALAND)

THE WEST FRANKISH KINGDOM (VALLAND)
UPPER BURGUNDIA
844
LOWER BURGUNDIA
Valence
Toulouse
Narbonne

Inn
Donau

LOMBARDIA
Genova
Venezia
• Luna
860 (Empire 843–924)
Arles
Marseille
Pisa
Corsica

CROATIA

Donau
RUMANI
RUMANI

Constanta

Perejaslavets
860
Varna

THE BLACK SEA
840
• Sinope

Lisboa
Tajo
SPANISH EMIRATE (SPANLAND)
Duero
Ebro
Tortosa
• Barcelona
Balear Islands (Manork)

Corsica
ITALIA
Roma • (Romaborg)
PAPAL STATE
• Napoli
Sardinia

ADRIATIC SEA

BULGARIA
BULGARS
CONSTANTINOPLE (MIKLAGARD)
Thessaloniki

Silk
Jewelry
Wine Fruit

ASIA MINOR

Tigris

844/859
Cordoba
• Sevilla
• Cadiz
Cartagena
Nekor
859

Strait of Gibraltar (Norvasund)

Palermo
SICILIA (SIKILØY)
• Tunis

MEDITERRANEAN

THE BYZANTINE EMPIRE

Athens
(GRIKLAND)

Crete (Krit)

Antiochia
Cyprus
Sidon •
Halis
Euphrates
Damascus
Palestine (JORSALALAND)
• Jerusalem
Gaza •

Alexandria

(GREAT SERKLAND)

63. VIKING EXPEDITIONS 9TH-10TH CENTURIES. THE POLITICAL SITUATION CA. 900.

⟶ Primarily Danish
⟶ Primarily Norwegian } Viking Expeditions
⟶ Primarily Swedish

Dates along the routes indicate when expeditions occurred

▢ Danish ▢ Norw. ▢ Swed. settlement

── Eastern limit of Viking raids in the Frankish kingdoms

--- Most important Viking trade routes

Viking names in brackets

The Vikings

We are not certain of the exact origin of the word 'viking', but we do know that from about 800 AD they ravaged with fire and sword along the coast of Europe in their newly developed seagoing vessels. The first expedition we know of went from western Norway to Wessex in 789. Four years later the monastery at Lindisfarne in Northumbria was attacked. All the inhabitants were killed, the cattle butchered and the cloister looted for everything of value before it was burned to the ground. These pillaging raids, in which Swedes and Danes also took part, evolved later into trading voyages, the conquest of outposts and the founding of settlements.

Around 900 there were Danish settlements in eastern England (the Danelaw), Normandy, Friesland and northern Germany. In Greenland, Iceland, the Faroe Islands, the Hebrides and the Orkneys, there were Norwegian colonies. So too in parts of Scotland and Ireland, on the Isle of Man and in Wales (Bretland) the Swedes established a number of colonies in Russia (map nr. 63).

England and Normandy 829–911

829 King Egbert of Wessex (802–839) subjugates the other minor kingdoms and becomes the first king of England. The viking attacks become more numerous and the viking fleet larger. From the middle of the 9th century large areas of England and Normandy are intermittently occupied by vikings (map nr. 64). 876 The vikings begin taking land in Northumbria, and establish themselves as settlers in the Danelaw. 871 Alfred the Great of Wessex becomes king.

He manages to unite the other tribes in a common struggle against the vikings. In 878 he defeats them at the Battle of Edington. The ensuing peace leaves only the Danelaw to the Scandinavians, while the Kingdom of Wessex now becomes the leader of a free England. 911 Charles III of France is forced to cede a large portion of Normandy as an independent duchy to the viking chieftain Rollo.

Right: Danish vikings on their way to England. From a miniature painting in an English manuscript from the 9th century.

The cathedral in Mainz, in the beginning of the 11th century.

Man with scythe. Drawing from beginning of the 10th century.

Otto the Great of Germany accepts humble tribute from the vanquished.

The German Empire under Otto the Great 936–973

936 Otto I of Saxony, nicknamed the Great, is made king.

939 Otto puts down a rebellion among his dukes and gives the duchies to members of his own clan.

951 Having defeated the Langobard king Berengar II, and after marrying the widow of the Frankish king Lothar, Otto is crowned king of the Langobards.

955 The Magyars are defeated in the Battle of the Lechfield.

962 Otto I is crowned Holy Roman Emperor by Pope John XII in Rome. Italy is united with the German Empire.

Right: William the Conqueror's Norman vikings on horseback, attacking the newly installed Harald Godvinsson's bodyguard during the Battle of Hastings on October 14, 1066. King Harald was killed, and William became king of England. From the Bayeux Tapestry, which according to tradition was woven by William's queen, Mathilde and her ladies in waiting in the 1080s.

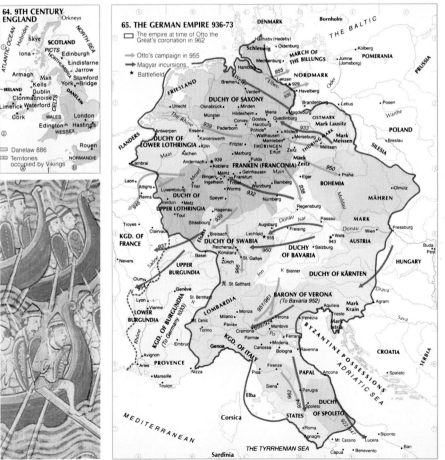

64. 9TH CENTURY ENGLAND

- Danelaw 886
- Territories occupied by Vikings

65. THE GERMAN EMPIRE 936-73

- The empire at time of Otto the Great's coronation in 962
- Otto's campaign in 955
- Magyar incursions
- ★ Battlefield

THE GERMAN EMPIRE IN THE 900s   47

«Centre of the world» – Church of the Holy Sepulchre. Christ at centre.

Even monks and nuns could land in the pillory.

A crusader takes a Muslim prisoner. Miniature from the 1200s.

66. EUROPE CA. 1100. THE FIRST THREE CRUSADES 1096-1192

Arab, mainly muslim, states

Christian lands:
 Roman Catholic
 Greek Orthodox

First Crusade 1096-99
Godfrey of Bouillon, Raymond of Toulouse, Robert of Normandy, Bohemund of Taranto

Second Crusade 1147-49 Conrad III (Holy Roman Emperor), Louis VII of France

Third Crusade 1189-92 Richard the Lionheart, Phillip II Augustus of France, Frederick Barbarossa (Holy Roman Emperor)

Left: Pope Urban II proclaims the First Crusade against the Seljuks – who had retaken the Holy Land. The concilium decided enthusiastically that on August 15, 1096 – when the year's crops had been harvested – the crusaders would leave their respective homelands and be reunited in Constantinople. 4000–5000 knights and approx. 30000 foot soldiers set out. In the spring of 1097 those who hadn't died of hunger or sickness, or been killed in battles with the Hungarians and Bulgarians on the way, were evacuated over the Bosporus.

The Crusaders

The First Crusade (1096–1099)
There were four main points of departure. Raymond of Toulouse, who due to his wealth and skill as a commander demanded to lead the entire crusade, began in Toulouse. The pious and unselfish Duke of Lower Lothringen, Gotfried of Bouillon, set out from Stenay in northern France.

Robert of Normandy led the adventurous Normans, who made up such a large share of the crusaders that the procession nearly resembled a Christian viking expedition.

He started in Lyon.
During the siege of a city in southern Italy, the stocky Norman, Bohemund of Taranto caught sight of Robert's column as it marched past. He saw at once that this offered his adventurous spirit a much larger field of play. Breaking off the siege, Bohemund joined one of the four great columns of army of crusaders from Brindisi.

A half century later Abbot Bernhard of Clairvaux called for a new crusade, in order to come to the aid of the Christians in Syria. The **Second Crusade** (1147–1149) was led by the deeply religious

Crusader Richard the Lionheart (I) doing battle with a dangerous foe.

A soldier cocks his crossbow, an effective and accurate weapon.

An English farmer on his way to the landlord's mill to mill his grain.

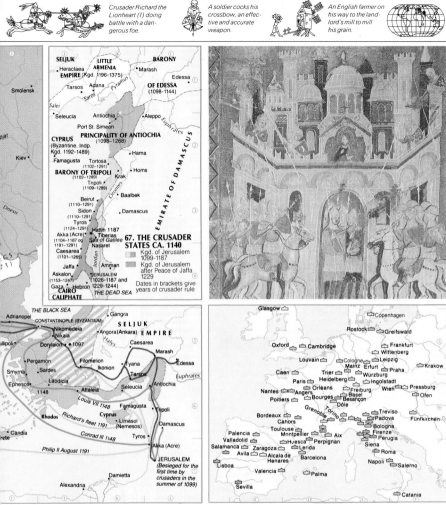

67. THE CRUSADER STATES CA. 1140

Kgd. of Jerusalem 1099–1187

Kgd. of Jerusalem after Peace of Jaffa 1229

Dates in brackets give years of crusader rule

JERUSALEM (Besieged for the first time by crusaders in the summer of 1099)

68. UNIVERSITIES IN THE MIDDLE AGES

- Founded before 1250
- 1251–1350
- 1351–1450
- 1451–1506

Louis VII of France, and Conrad III of Germany, and ended with a failed attempt to take Damascus.

The Third Crusade (1189–1192) was led by Richard the Lion-heart of England, the French king Philip II August, and the Holy Roman Emperor, Frederick I (Barbarossa). Many English and French soldiers were this time transported by sea. Although the crusade was led by the three most powerful men in the West, it ended in nothing more than small bands of unarmed Christians making pilgrimages to the Holy Sepulchre.

Right: Students following a lecture at the university in Bologna. From a miniature from the beginning of the 1400s. This university was founded as early as 1088, and during the 1100s was renowned as a school of law. In the Middle Ages the University of Bologna had as many as 2000 students from every corner of Europe. It is also from this period it has its nickname, la dotta, the learned one.

The map above right shows the founding dates of European universities in the Middle Ages.

Top: During the First Crusade, 1200–1300 cavalrymen and over 10000 foot soldiers reached Jerusalem on June 7, 1099, and on June 15 the city fell. Christendom had control of the city once again, and could guard the Holy Sepulchre. From a Venetian miniature from the 1200s.

UNIVERSITIES IN THE MIDDLE AGES 49

Scandinavian fisher-
man hauls in his
catch in the Baltic
in the 1200s.

Man drives his wife
home from the
fields, tempted by
her liquor.

The baker and his
wife shove bread
into 2 m deep oven.

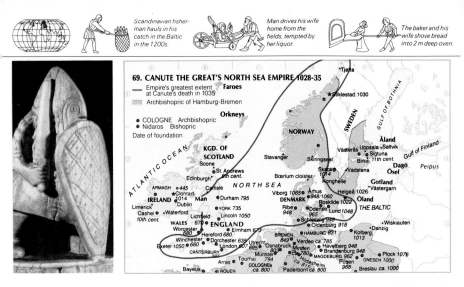

69. CANUTE THE GREAT'S NORTH SEA EMPIRE 1028-35

— Empire's greatest extent **Faroes**
at Canute's death in 1035
▨ Archbishopric of Hamburg-Bremen

● COLOGNE Archbishopric
● Nidaros Bishopric
Date of foundation

Above: A French soldier from the 11th or 12th century, armed with sword and shield. A chess piece in ebony, now in the Bibliotheque Nationale, Paris.

The North Sea Empire 1028–1035

In 1002 king Ethelred II (the Unready) of England decreed that all Danes in the kingdom were to be killed. Sven Forkbeard, and future Norwegian King Olav Haraldsson, king of Denmark from 983, and Norway from 1000, took revenge

by setting out year after year to plunder England. London was attacked in 1013, Ethelred fled the country, and Sven claimed the throne.

Sven's son, Canute the Great, became king in 1016, and conquered the whole of England. He dissolved the viking army and gave rich gifts to the Anglo-Saxon church.

In 1018 Canute succeeded his brother in Denmark, and ten years later was himself proclaimed Norway's king. His North Sea empire had become a European great-power (map nr. 69).

Frederick II von Hohenstaufen

Frederick, son of Henry VI, grew up in Sicily and spent the greater part of his life there. His foremost political ambition was to create a strong state in Italy. During the decade of the 1220s he reestablished the strong royal power of the Normans in southern Italy and on the island of Sicily, which had both seen periods with short-lived, weak governments. His attempts to accomplish something similar in northern and central Italy led to a

long struggle with the pope and the Italian cities. He was excommunicated, and in Germany faced open rebellion. Frederick II had strong intellectual interests, and his court in Palermo was the cultural centre of southern Europe during the time of his reign, and a meeting place for intellectuals from far and wide.

Below: Frederick II (1194–1250), king of Sicily 1197, German king 1212, Holy Roman Emperor 1220. From a miniature in his book on falconry, now in the Vatican Museum.

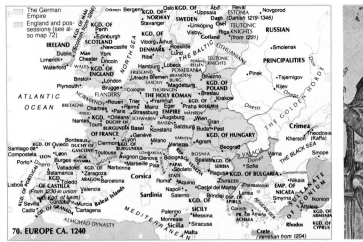

70. EUROPE CA. 1240

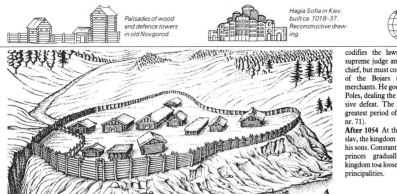

Palisades of wood and defence towers in old Novgorod.

Hagia Sofia in Kiev, built ca. 1018–37. Reconstructive drawing.

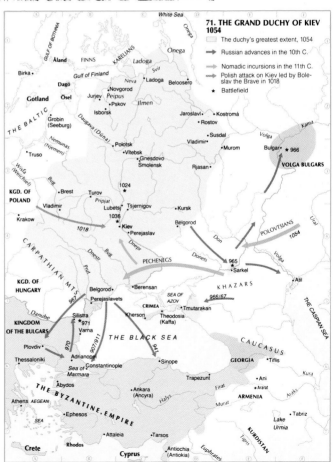

Above: A Russian village as it probably looked in the 9th and 10th century. Drawing by P.N. Tretjakov.

Russia 862–1054

862 According to tradition, the **væring**, i.e., viking, Rurik and his brothers seized power in northwest Russia. Rurik founds Novgorod (Holmgard).

880 Oleg (Helge) the Wise of Novgorod conquers Smolensk and Kiev. Thus, he controls all trade between Constantinople and the Baltic. Kiev (Great Svitjod) becomes the capital of Russia (kingdom of the **Rus**).

907–911 Oleg leads a fleet against Constantinople (Miklagard), resulting in a trade agreement.

944 Igor of Novgorod forces a new trade agreement on the Byzantine Empire. In return he promises to open Russia (Kievan Rus) to Christian missionaries.

965–967 Sviatoslav crushes the Volga Bulgars and Khazars around the mouth of the Don.

967–971 Sviatoslav attempts to conquer the Donau Bulgars, but in 971 Emperor John I Zimisces drives the Russians from the Balkans.

980 Vladimir the Great wins the power struggle with his brothers in 972. He marries the Byzantine emperor's sister and converts to Christianity in 998. Decrees that all idols are to be burned, and orders all his subjects to let themselves be baptized. Centralization of the kingdom's administration is begun.

1018 Boleslav Chrobry (= the Brave) of Poland attacks Kiev, but is beaten back.

1034–1054 Yaroslav the Wise is absolute monarch in the Grand Duchy of Kiev. He makes the city of Kiev a **metropolis**, subject only to the Patriarchy in Constantinople, organizes the church, and codifies the laws. The duke is supreme judge and commander in chief, but must consider the wishes of the Bojars (noblemen) and merchants. He goes to war with the Poles, dealing the Patzinaks a decisive defeat. The kingdom has its greatest period of expansion (map nr. 71).

After 1054 At the death of Yaroslav, the kingdom is divided among his sons. Constant warring between princes gradually reduces the kingdom to a loose confederation of principalities.

71. THE GRAND DUCHY OF KIEV 1054

The duchy's greatest extent, 1054

➡ Russian advances in the 10th C.

➡ Nomadic incursions in the 11th C.

➡ Polish attack on Kiev led by Boleslav the Brave in 1018

★ Battlefield

Nursing in a cloister in the 1300s. From a French miniature.

An English woman in a linen scarf is milking. 12th century miniature.

The Fall of Man as depicted in French manuscript from the 1200s.

72. ENGLAND AND FRANCE 1154–1328

— Scottish border in 1157
— Eastern limit of Henry II's French possessions in 1154
— Eastern limit of English possessions in France a century later
▨ Norwegian possessions until 1266-1469, thereafter Scottish
▨ French royal lands in 1180

France at death of Charles IV in 1328
▨ Ruled directly by King of France
▨ English rule
▨ Other French rulers

France 1154–1314

1154 Count Henry of Anjou becomes king of England (Henry II), and Duke of Normandy.
1202–1206 Philip II August takes all of the English fiefdoms, except Gascogne.
1294–1304 War with England over Gascogne and Flanders.
1301–1303 Philip IV wins his struggle with Pope Bonifatius VIII.
1312–1314 Bonifatius VIII is forced by Philip IV to dissolve the Knights Templars in 1312.

Knights Templars

In 1119 a clerical order of knighthood was established in Jerusalem to defend the Holy Land. The name Templars comes from the fact that they had their headquarters on the supposed site of Solomon's temple. By around 1300 the order had approximately 20000 knights and had acquired a great deal of worldly power. The order came to an end when Jacques de Molay, and his next in command, were burned at the stake as heretics in Paris in 1314 (see section from a contemporary miniature **below**).

Francis of Assisi

Francis was born in the village of Assisi in 1182. His father was a rich merchant, and Francis made the most of his position. He dreamed of becoming a knight and troubadour, but at the age of twenty-five he underwent a spiritual crisis, deciding to dedicate his life to the service of God, through acts of charity to the poor and sick. **The picture at the left** is from Giotto's painting: «Francis preaches to the birds».

England 1106–1328

1106 Henry I Beauclerc conquers Normandy.
1154–1189 Henry II strengthens the monarchy and reforms the legal system. The king, who has enormous possessions in France (map nr. 72), begins the conquest of Ireland in 1171.
1215 John Lackland issues the Magna Carta, securing the rights of the barons.
1284 Edward I conquers Wales and lays claim to Scotland.
1314 Robert I (Bruce) drives the English from Scotland following the Battle of Bannockburn.
1328 Of the French fiefdoms, only Britanny and Aquitaine remain English.

Harvesting grain with a sickle. From German 12th century miniature.

Mistreatment of prisoners. Miniature from an English manuscript.

German church, built in 800s and modeled on the church in Jerusalem.

Left: In the beginning of the 15th century Spinello Aretino, with the help of his son, painted sixteen large frescos in the Palazzo Publico (town hall) in Siena. His assignment was to depict the Lombardian cities' struggle against Frederick Barbarossa in the 1170s. The detail shown here shows Italian warriors aboard a galley. This type of vessel was already in use in Roman times. It was normally rowed, but in a strong wind it might also carry one or more sails. The galley was in use throughout the Middle Ages, especially in the Mediterranean, but also in the Baltic.

The German Empire 1024–1250

1024–1039 Conrad II, Holy Roman Emperor from 1027, grants his vassals hereditary rights to their fiefs.

1056–1106 Henry IV, emperor from 1084, employs the gentry and the middle class in his administration instead of the nobility proper. From 1076 he is fighting with Pope Gregory VII over the right to install bishops – the so-called Investiture Struggle. At the Synod of Worms in 1076, Henry is excommunicated. Begs the pope to lift the ban. This is done, but when Pope Gregory again excommunicates him in 1080, Henry drives the pope from Rome. Compromise reached.

1125–1137 Lothar II of Saxony, emperor from 1133, carries out a campaign of expansion north to the Baltic.

1152–1190 Frederick I Barbarossa becomes emperor in 1155. The northern Italian city-states (Lombardian League) defeat Frederick Barbarossa at Legnano in 1176, but the emperor manages to put down the rebellion. Frederick Barbarossa drowns while on the way to the Holy Land in 1190 (the Third Crusade).

1194–1250 Frederick II (see p. 50) rules nearly all of Italy, treats Germany as a dependency and establishes a modern, unified state in southern Italy. In 1227 Frederick II too is at odds with the pope, because the emperor has broken off a crusade. Frederick is excommunicated, but a year later he goes on a crusade anyway, and in 1230 the pope lifts his ban.

Map nr. 73 shows the Holy Roman Empire at the time of Frederick's death in 1250.

73. HOHENSTAUFFEN POWER IN EUROPE
— Boundary of the Holy Roman Empire at the death of Frederick II in 1250

 Two-wheeled English cart. Miniature in a 14th century manuscript.

Wine grapes being picked. French relief from beginning of the 1200s.

Grapes being trampled. French relief from beginning of the 1200s.

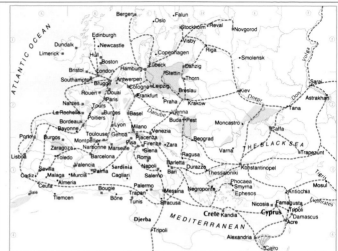

Above: Genoa's harbour at the end of the 1400s. Section from a contemporary woodcut. Genoa was just as wealthy and powerful as Venice and had hegemony at sea over an equally large area, but the city never experienced the same cultural blossoming as Venice and other Italian economic centres. The wealthy traders of Genoa preferred money to culture.

Below: A 15th century woman about to give birth. At left bath water is prepared for the newborn. Thereafter the child will be swaddled, and have its legs wrapped, so that they will grow straight.

Right: Washing and personal hygiene were not given high priority in the Middle Ages. That is **one** reason why the great epidemics could spread so quickly. In addition, a general lack of cleanliness led to an obtrusive stench of body odour. Now and then – and in any case at Christmas – people would climb into the tub, as in the scene shown here, where a man and wife seem to be enjoying their bath. From a German woodcut from the early 1500s. In the following centuries, members of the upper classes attempted to make body odour less noticeable by the generous application of perfumes.

74. INDUSTRY AND TRADE IN 13TH CENTURY EUROPE

Major production areas for:
- Grain
- Wine
- Olive oil
- Important trading centres and markets
- --- Important trade routes

75. SPREAD OF THE BLACK DEATH, MID-14TH CENTURY

Areas hit by the plague in:

1346   1347   1348

1349   1350   1351-53

Areas with little or no plague

The roasting of fish. English minia-ture from around 1330.

Plague doctor in prescribed garb. «Beak» on mask was to stop contagion.

Tilling the soil with a harrow. English miniature from around 1340.

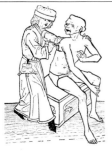

The Black Death

Ca. 1345 rumours spread of epidemics killing people by the hundreds of thousands in the East. In the West people at first took a certain satisfaction in the knowledge that the unbelievers were being punished. Not until 1347, when some sailors in Genoa had been infected, did they see that the sickness was not discriminating between non-believers and Christians.

Bubonic plague is caused by a bacillus in the blood of certain animals, especially rats. Humans were infected by fleas that infested both animal and human hosts, or through direct human contact. **The woodcut above** shows a physician lancing a bubo, or boil, unaware that countless bacteria were carried further in the many folds of his clothing.

In Paris there were eight hundred deaths per day. On the whole, cities were the hardest hit. As much as a third of the population died in areas affected by the plague (map nr. 75).

76. EUROPE CA. 1400

☐ Genoa and possessions
■ Venice and possessions

Venice and Genoa

Throughout the 14th century Venice and Genoa struggled for control of the Mediterranean. The two city-states had each established strategic outposts, both close to home, and in the Greek areas near the Black Sea (map nr. 76).

The entrance to the Black Sea was of special importance. Venice had acquired a trade monopoly in Constantinople, while Genoa held the fort of Pera north of the city.

Switzerland 1315–1499

1315 The original cantons of Uri, Schwyz and Unterwalden, which since 1291 have been united in the Swiss Confederation, having sworn 'Eternal Union', defeat Duke Leopold of Austria at the Battle of Morgarten. The other Swiss cantons then join, one after the other, the Eternal Union.

1389 Peace with the Hapsburgs, who time and again have attempted unsuccessfully to subjugate the cantons.

1499 Maximilian I recognizes the Swiss Confederation's political independence at the Peace of Basle. Switzerland remains only formally a part of the German Empire.

77. THE SWISS CONFEDERATION 1315-1536

☐ The original cantons
☐ Confederation 1481
■ Confederation 1536
☐ Protected by the confederation
☐ Subject to one or more cantons

The plague reached Crimea from the area around Lake Balkhash

English soldier with longbow at Battle of Azincourt in 1415.

Style-conscious young man with doublet and long stockings. 1400s.

Threshing grain with a swingle. From a calendar page from the 1400s.

The Hundred Years' War between England and France

The war actually lasted 116 years (1337-1453). At the outbreak there was no clear distinction between the two countries. The upper classes spoke French, and the Channel was at that time not a natural border.

The greatest victory for the English in the Hundred Years' War was won at Azincourt in 1415. The highpoint for the French was Joan of Arc's rescue of Orléans in the summer of 1429 (see column 4).

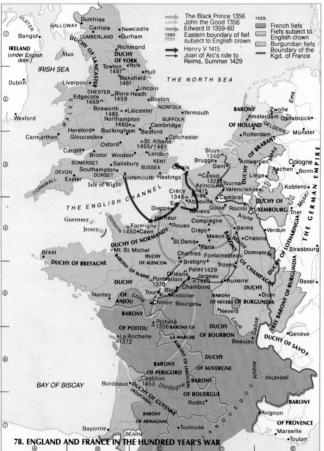

78. ENGLAND AND FRANCE IN THE HUNDRED YEAR'S WAR

The Hanseatic League

was actually formed by a «hansa» – a German merchant guild – in Wisby on the Swedish island of Gotland. Through the years, however, the organization strengthened its position and economic power, so that by around 1400, it controlled all trade in the North Sea, Skagerrak, Kattegatt and the Baltic (map nr. 79). Hamburg and Lübeck were the Hansa traders most important towns. **The picture above** – from a miniature in Hamburg's municipal laws from 1497 – shows lively traffic in Hamburg's harbour.

The Maid of Orléans

In the summer of 1429, seventeen-year-old Jeanne d'Arc led a division of French soldiers from one victory to the next. It wasn't until May of the following year that the English managed to capture her. She was put on trial as a heretic and witch, and on May 30, 1431 the legendary maiden was burned at the stake in Rouen. The **picture below** shows her being tied to the stake.

Town hall – Palazzo Vecchio – in Firenze, built at the end of the 13th century.

A generous amount of wine is drunk at the inn. Italian minia-ture from the 1300s.

Lady of the castle hauls in her lover. German miniature from the 1300s.

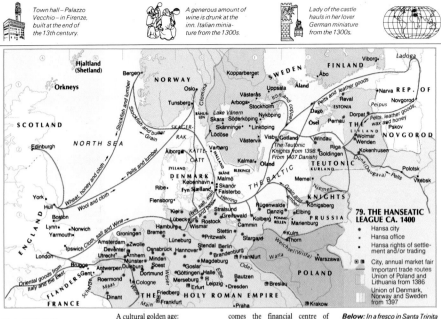

79. THE HANSEATIC LEAGUE CA. 1400

- Hansa city
- Hansa office
- Hansa rights of settle-ment and/or trading
- City, annual market fair

Important trade routes
Union of Poland and Lithuania from 1386
Union of Denmark, Norway and Sweden from 1397

Italy 1250–1454

1250 At the death of Frederick II, the Hohenstaufens rule almost the entire peninsula (map nr. 73, p. 53).
Around 1300 The northern Italian city-states gain independence, as bishops and imperial civil servants are pushed aside.

A cultural golden age:
Dante Alieghieri (1265–1321)
Francesco Petrarca (1304–1374)
Giovanni Boccaccio (1313–1375)
Giotto di Bondone (approx. 1266–1337)

Around 1450 Florence (Firenze), ruled by the Medici family, be-comes the financial centre of Europe. It is the time of the Early Renaissance.
In 1454, at the so-called Treaty of Lodi, Cosimo de' Medici the Elder, and Francesco Sforza, succeed in bringing about peace in Italy (map nr. 80).

Below: In a fresco in Santa Trinita in Florence, painted by Dominico Ghirlandaio, the mightiest of all the Medicis – Lorenzo de' Medici il Magnifico (1449–1492) – is placed between two prelates. The lad in the foreground is probably Lorenzo's son, Giovanni, who would later become Pope Leo X.

80. RENAISSANCE ITALY AFTER THE PEACE OF LODI 1454

Lecture in progress at a German university around 1500.

A carrier pigeon being sent off. 15th century woodcut.

Emperor Charles V, presiding over the Parliament in Worms in 1521.

81. SPREAD OF THE REFORMATION TO ABOUT 1550

- Protestantism established by 1550
- Catholic majority, reformatory advances
- Catholic majority never under threat
- Universities and colleges under strong reformatory influence
- 1537 Date when protestantism officially adopted

Boundaries refer to the situation in 1589, see also map 96

ses the patron saint of miners, St.Anna, that he will become a monk if she spares his life.

1507 Luther, now a monk, is ordained in the cloister of the Augustinian hermits in Erfurt.

1508 Transfers to the monastery in Wittenberg.

1517 Angered at the Dominican monk Johan Tetzel's tasteless peddling of indulgences in Saxony, Luther, on October 31, tacks his ninety-five theses against the traffic in indulgences to the door of the Castle Church of Wittenberg.

1520 Pope Leo X (Giovanni de' Medici) excommunicates Luther, but the papal bull threatening excommunication is thrown on a bonfire in Wittenberg. In the same year Luther publishes several programmatic essays.

Below: Alter piece by Lucas Cranac the Elder, painted in 1547, the year after Luther's death. Between the reformer in the pulpit, and the congregation, hangs the crucified Christ – according to Luther, man's only guarantee of salvation.

The Reformer Martin Luther

1483 Mine worker Hans Luther and Margarethe Ziegler have a son, and name him Martin.

1484–1501 The family moves from the town of Martin's birth, first to Magdeburg and then to Eisenach. Martin is strictly disciplined by his mother and father, and school is a place of rote learning and whippings.

1501 Martin is sent to Erfurt to study law.

1505 Student Martin Luther experiences a tremendous thunder storm during a journey and promi-

Dutch bride and groom from 1434. From painting by Jan van Eyck.

Two chastity belts. One on left from the 1400s, the other from the 1500s.

A gentleman negotiating with a money-lender. German woodcut from 1486.

Above: *Prince John Frederick of Saxony, and leading Reformation figures. From yet another painting by Lucas Cranach the Elder from around 1530. Luther is seen standing at left. On the other side of the prince stands the Swiss reformer Ulrich Zwingli (1484–1531), and farthest to the right we see Luther's melancholy friend, Philip Melanchton.*

82. THE SCHISM IN THE CATHOLIC CHURCH 1378-1417

▨ Adherents of Rome
▨ Adherents of Avignon
▨ Loyalties divided
Boundaries refer to the situation in ca. 1400

Left: *The movement led by the Frenchman Jean Calvin (1509–1564) opposed anything that distracted the worship service. This section of a painting from 1564 depicts the interior of a church in Lyon, furnished in a style both Calvinist and Spartan, in which the pulpit, not the alter, is central.*

1521 Professor Luther refuses to retract his earlier statements. He is made an outlaw, but by now he is already under the protection of Prince Frederick of Saxony at Wartburg. There, under the name of Junker Jürgen, Luther works on his translation of the New Testament.

1525 Marries former nun Katharine von Bora, who bears him six children.

1529 The Diet of Speyer reaffirms the judgment of 1521, but a minority lodges a formal protest. They are hereafter referred to as *protestants*.

1530 Luther's good friend, Philip Melanchton (see illust. above) formulates the «Augsburg Confession». In December of the same year the protestants form the Schmalkaldic League. Its purpose is to defend the teachings of Luther against the emperor by force of arms.

1546 Martin Luther dies on February 18 and is buried in the cemetery of the Castle Church in Wittenberg. Reformation established in Northern Europe.

83. THE CHURCH IN EUROPE CA. 1500

+ Archbishopric
▨ Under papal administration

▨ The Ottoman Empire
Other colours used to depict archbishoprics

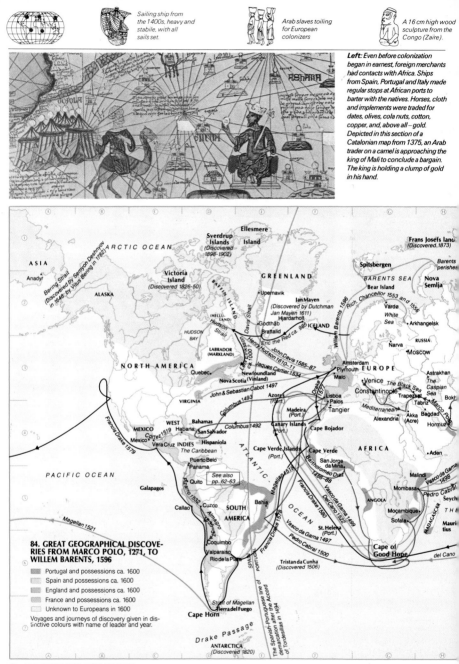

Sailing ship from the 1400s, heavy and stabile, with all sails set.

Arab slaves toiling for European colonizers

A 16 cm high wood sculpture from the Congo (Zaire).

Left: Even before colonization began in earnest, foreign merchants had contacts with Africa. Ships from Spain, Portugal and Italy made regular stops at African ports to barter with the natives. Horses, cloth and implements were traded for dates, olives, cola nuts, cotton, copper, and, above all – gold. Depicted in this section of a Catalonian map from 1375, an Arab trader on a camel is approaching the king of Mali to conclude a bargain. The king is holding a clump of gold in his hand.

84. GREAT GEOGRAPHICAL DISCOVE-RIES FROM MARCO POLO, 1271, TO WILLEM BARENTS, 1596

Portugal and possessions ca. 1600
Spain and possessions ca. 1600
England and possessions ca. 1600
France and possessions ca. 1600
Unknown to Europeans in 1600

Voyages and journeys of discovery given in distinctive colours with name of leader and year.

Spaniard Diego de Almagro, who discovered and conquered Peru.

 Kangaroo hunt in Australia. Cliff painting from Kimberley.

 Spanish conquistador beating an «uppity» indian in Mexico.

Explorations and Discoveries 1271–1596

1271–95 Marco Polo sets out from Venice and explores China.

1486–88 Portuguese captain **Bartholomeo Diaz** discovers the sea route around the southern tip of Africa.

1492–93 Christopher Columbus (illus. right) reaches the Lesser Antilles in Central America and names the island San Salvador.

1497 English-Italian explorer **John Cabot** and son **Sebastian** reach Virginia, which they claim for England.

1497–99 Portuguese **Vasco da Gama** (illus. right) finds the sea route to India.

1500 Portuguese **Pedro Alvares Cabral** reaches the land that will one day become Brazil, but hurries on to Portuguese East Africa and India.

1519 Spaniard **Fernando (Hernando) Cortez** leaves Cuba, which he helped to conquer in 1511–12, and conquers Mexico, defeating king Montezuma II (see also map nr. 87, p. 63).

1519–22 Portuguese **Fernando Magellan** is the first to circumnavigate the globe. In 1521 he is killed on the island of Mactan in the Philippines. **Juan Sebastian del Cano** sails his vessel home. **1531–37** The uncouth and brutal Spaniard **Francisco Pizarro** conquers Cuzco and the Inca Empire. His companion, **Diego de Almagro** crosses the Andes, where he discovers and conquers Chile.

1534–42 Frenchman **Jacques Cartier** undertakes three journeys to North America, primarily in search of a new route to India.

1553 and 1556 Francis Drake completes the world's second circumnavigation (map nr. 84).

1585–87 Englishman **John Davis** explores the coasts of Greenland, Baffin Island and Labrador.

1594 and 1596 Dutchman **Willem Barents** discovers Nova Zemlya, Spitsbergen and Bear Island.

Top right: Christopher Columbus (1451–1506), son of a weaver from Genoa, who, without knowing it himself, discovered America. From a painting in Museo Curco in Como.

Middle: Vasco da Gama (ca. 1460–1524), left Lisbon on July 8, 1497 for India. On May 20, 1498 he landed in Calcutta, and in July of 1499 he was back in Lisbon. In 1524, shortly before his death, he was made viceroy of India.

Bottom: Marco Polo (ca. 1255 – ca. 1325), his father and uncle are received Kublai Khan in Khanbalik (Beijing) in 1275. The journey to China had taken 3½ years, and Marco remained 17 years in the service of the Khan.

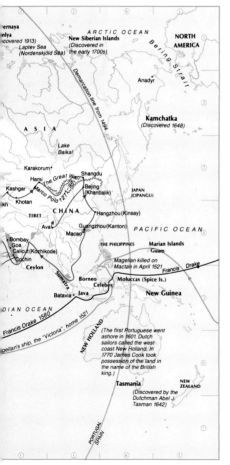

ARCTIC OCEAN

NORTH AMERICA

ernaya
nlya
covered 1913)
Laptev Sea
(Nordenskjöld Sea)

New Siberian Islands (Discovered in the early 1700s)

Bering Strait

Demarcation line from 1494

Anadyr

Kamchatka (Discovered 1648)

A S I A

Lake Baikal

Karakorum

Hami

Kashgar

Khotan

ikh

TIBET

Ava

Shangdu

Beijing (Khanbalik)

The Great Wall

Marco Polo 1271–95

C H I N A

Hangzhou (Kinsay)

Guangzhou (Kanton)

Macao

JAPAN (CIPANGU)

PACIFIC OCEAN

Bombay
Goa
Calicut (Kozhikode)
Cochin

Ceylon

Sumatra

Borneo

Celebes

Batavia

Java

THE PHILIPPINES

Marian Islands
Guam

Magellan killed on Mactan in April 1521

Moluccas (Spice Is.)

New Guinea

Francis Drake

DIAN OCEAN

Francis Drake 1580

gellian's ship, the "Victoria", home 1521

NEW HOLLAND

(The first Portuguese went ashore in 1601. Dutch sailors called the west coast New Holland. In 1770 James Cook took possession of the land in the name of the British king.)

Tasmania

(Discovered by the Dutchman Abel J. Tasman 1642)

NEW ZEALAND

PORTUGAL
SPAIN

 Reconstruction of a birch bark canoe from Canada.

 French courtesans on their way to New Orleans by order of Louis XIV.

 Tent ('wigwam') used by the American Plains Indians.

Left: *The terraced pyramid of Chichén Itza was erected during the time of the so-called Northern Mayan Culture on the Yucatàn Peninsula (map nr. 87). Stairways lead up to a temple at the top.*

North and South America 1620–1775

North America

1620 «The Pilgrim Fathers» arrive in Massachusetts on the «Mayflower». British colonization is accelerated. The Spanish have been established since 1535 in the viceroyalty of New Spain (map nr. 85).
1626 New Amsterdam (New York) is founded as the capital of the Dutch possessions.
1664 England conquers the Dutch colonies and occupies New Amsterdam. **1756–63** The British-French Colonial War over control of the North American territories. England wins, and at the Peace of Paris in 1763, all of North America became Anglo-Saxon (map nr. 85).
1774 Representatives of «The Thirteen Colonies» meet. The First Continental Congress adopts a Charter of Rights and votes to continue the boycott of English goods.
1775 The American War of Independence (see pp. 92–93).

South America

1650 Spain has control in two viceroyalties: Peru and La Plata. The Portuguese have occupied large areas on the east coast.
1775 Both Spain and Portugal have expanded their possessions in the interior of the continent.

85. THE EUROPEAN COLONIZATION OF THE AMERICAS TO 1775

European possessions in North and Central America:

- French until Peace of Paris, February 1763
- British after Peace of Paris
- Spanish after Peace of Paris

European possessions in South America: 1650   1775

- Spanish
- Portuguese
- French
- Dutch

➤ Important exports

The Spanishs tortured the Incas as well. Here one of them has his eyes gouged out.

Two Aztec chieftains surrender to Hernán Cortez.

Aztec woman weaving with loom made fast to a tree.

86. THE INCA EMPIRE

▨ Chimu Kgd. before 1470
▧ Empire's greatest extent 1530
– – – Regional border
—— Inca highways
Some modern names given for purposes of orientation

Bottom of the previous page:
Mayan warrior from the 700s armed with some imaginative weapons. Until a group of researchers found pictures like this – in a ceremonial building in Bonampák in the state of Chiapas in 1946 – the Mayans were thought by most to have been an almost pacifistic people.

Above: The Incan capital of Cuzco as sketched by a Spanish artist in the 1600s. Spanish/European influence has already made itself felt, not least in the Sun Temple, Coricancha, seen at the left. The plan of the city itself, however, with its straight streets, is from the Inca period.

87. AZTEC AND MAYAN CIVILIZATION

▨ Aztec heartland in 1486
▨ Aztec Kingdom ca. 1520
▨ Southern Mayan Civilization ca. 300-900
▨ Northern Mayan Civilization ca. 900-1200
▨ Mayan mountain kingdoms ca. 1500
→ Cortéz' route 1519-20
---- Present-day boundaries

Below: Toltec warrior from the temple in Tula in present-day Mexico. Originally this and others like it functioned as supporting columns for the temple's roof construction. They are carved out of basalt and are over 4.5 m high.

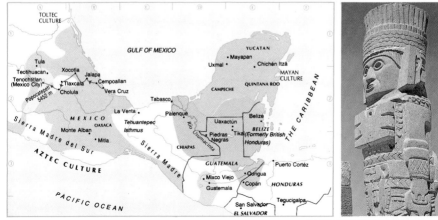

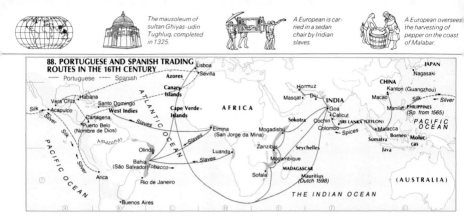

The mausoleum of sultan Ghiyas-udin Tughluq, completed in 1325.

A European is carried in a sedan chair by Indian slaves.

A European oversees the harvesting of pepper on the coast of Malabar.

88. PORTUGUESE AND SPANISH TRADING ROUTES IN THE 16TH CENTURY

— Portuguese ---- Spanish

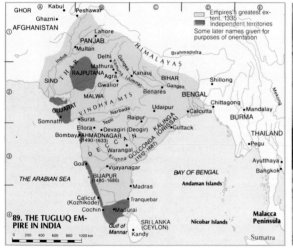

89. THE TUGLUQ EMPIRE IN INDIA

Empires's greatest extent, 1335

Independent territories

Some later names given for purposes of orientation

0 200 400 600 800 1000 km

India in the 14th Century

Sultan Ghiyas-ud-din Tughluq founds the Tughluq Dynasty in 1320, which retains power in India for almost eighty years. Under his son, Mohammed bin Tughluq (1325–51) the kingdom sees its greatest expansion (map nr. 89). His nephew, Firuz Shah cannot hold the empire together; and from 1398 it begins to dissolve.

90. THE MAJAPAHIT EMPIRE. DUTCH CONQUESTS IN INDONESIA

Empire ca. 1400

17th C.   18th C.

Dutch conquests

Above: The Mogul emperor Akbar the Great, who governed most of northern India 1556–1605, was an active participant in the cultural life of the kingdom, and showed great tolerance for other religions. This section of a contemporary miniature shows him in conversation with a Jesuit priest (in black) and Muslim philosophers. Akbar claimed that the various religions in reality did not differ from one another beyond the point of using different names for one and the same almighty, monotheistic divinity.

Left: Portuguese colonizer Affonso d'Albuquerque (1453–1515) sailed to the East in 1503, and 6 years later was made governor general of the Portuguese possessions in India, with headquarters in Goa on the west coast.

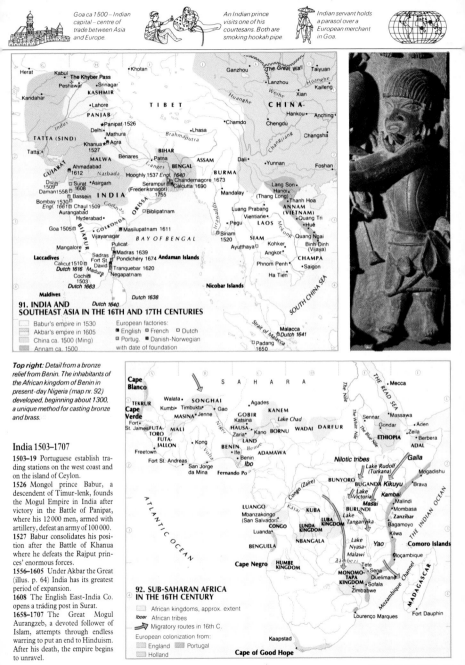

Goa ca 1500 – Indian capital – centre of trade between Asia and Europe.

An Indian prince visits one of his courtesans. Both are smoking hookah pipe

Indian servant holds a parasol over a European merchant in Goa.

91. INDIA AND SOUTHEAST ASIA IN THE 16TH AND 17TH CENTURIES

- Babur's empire in 1530
- Akbar's empire in 1605
- China ca. 1500 (Ming)
- Annam ca. 1500

European factories:
- ■ English ■ French □ Dutch
- □ Portug. ■ Danish-Norwegian
with date of foundation

Herat, Khotan, Ganzhou, Taiyuan, The Great Wall, Lanzhou, Huanghe, Kaifeng, Kabul, The Khyber Pass, Peshawar, Srinagar, KASHMIR, Xian, Weihe, Lahore, TIBET, CHINA, Kandahar, PANJAB, Hankou, Anching, Panipat 1526, Delhi, Mathura, Lhasa, Chamdo, Chengdu, Changsha, TATTA (SIND), Khanua 1527, Agra, Brahmaputra, Tatta, Benares, BIHAR, Patna, ASSAM, Chang-Kiang, Yunnan, Dali, Foshan, MALWA, Ahmadabad 1612, BENGAL, BURMA, GUJARAT, Narbada, Asirgarh, Hooghly 1537 Engl. 1640, Chandernagore 1673, Serampur (Frederiksnagor), Calcutta 1690, Mandalay, Lang Son, Hanoi (Thang Long), Thanh Hoa, ANNAM (VIETNAM), Diu 1509, Surat 1608, Daman 1558, Bassein, INDIA, Godavari, ORISSA, Biblipatnam, Luang Prabang, Vientiane, Quang Tri, Hué, Bombay 1530 Engl. 1661, Chaul 1509, Aurangabad, Hyderabad, GOLKONDA, Masilupatnam 1611, Pegu, LAOS, Siriam 1520, SIAM, Mekong, Quang Ngai, Binh Dinh (Vijaya), Goa 1505, BIJAPUR, Vijayanagar, BAY OF BENGAL, Pulicat, Kohker, Ayutthaya, Angkor, CHAMPA, Saigon, Mangalore, Laccadives, Sadras, Madras 1639, Fort St. David, Pondichéry 1674, Andaman Islands, Phnom Penh, Ha Tien, Calicut 1510, Dutch 1616, Madura, Tranquebar 1620, Negapatnam, Cochin 1503, Dutch 1663, Nicobar Islands, Maldives, Dutch 1638, Dutch 1640, SOUTH CHINA SEA, Malacca Dutch 1641, Padang 1650

Top right: Detail from a bronze relief from Benin. The inhabitants of the African kingdom of Benin in present-day Nigeria (map nr. 92) developed, beginning about 1300, a unique method for casting bronze and brass.

India 1503–1707

1503–19 Portuguese establish trading stations on the west coast and on the island of Ceylon.

1526 Mongol prince Babur, a descendent of Timur-lenk, founds the Mogul Empire in India after victory in the Battle of Panipat, where his 12 000 men, armed with artillery, defeat an army of 100 000.

1527 Babur consolidates his position after the Battle of Khanua where he defeats the Rajput princes' enormous forces.

1556–1605 Under Akbar the Great (illus. p. 64) India has its greatest period of expansion.

1608 The English East-India Co. opens a trading post in Surat.

1658–1707 The Great Mogul Aurangzeb, a devoted follower of Islam, attempts through endless warring to put an end to Hinduism. After his death, the empire begins to unravel.

92. SUB-SAHARAN AFRICA IN THE 16TH CENTURY

- African kingdoms, approx. extent
- *Iber* African tribes
- Migratory routes in 16th C.

European colonization from:
- England
- Holland
- Portugal

Cape Blanco, Cape Verde, SAHARA, Mecca, The Nile, THE READ SEA, Walata, SONGHAI, Agades, TEKRUR, Kumbi, Timbuktu, Gao, GOBIR, KANEM, Lake Chad, Fort St. James, FUTA-TORO, FUTA-JALLON, MALI, Jenne, MASINA, KATSINA, HAUSA, Kano, ZARIA, LAND, BORNU, WADAI, DARFUR, Sennar, Massawa, Gondar, Aden, Zeila, Berbera, ETHIOPIA, ADAL, Freetown, Kong, Volta, BENIN, ADAMAWA, Galla, Nilotic tribes, Fort St. Andreas, San Jorge da Mina, Ife, Benin, Ibo, Fernando Po, Lake Rudolf (Turkana), Mogadishu, BUNYORO, BUGANDA, Kikuyu, Brava, Congo (Zaïre), Lake Victoria, Kambai, Masai, Malindi, LUANGO, Kasai, KUBA, LUBA KINGDOM, BURUNDI, Lake Tanganyika, Mombasa, Zanzibar, Mbanzakongo (San Salvador), CONGO, LUNDA KINGDOM, Bagamoyo, Kilwa, Luanda, NBANGALA, Lake Nyasa-Malawi, Yao, Comoro Islands, BENGUELA, Zambezi, MONOMO-TAPA KINGDOM, Tete, Sena, Quelimane, Sofala, Zimbabwe, Moçambique, Cape Negro, HUMBE KINGDOM, Mozambique Channel, MADAGASCAR, Lourenço Marques, Fort Dauphin, ATLANTIC OCEAN, THE INDIAN OCEAN, Kaapstad, Cape of Good Hope

93. THE DUTCH REVOLT 1559-1648

- Spanish campaign in the North 1572-74
- Boundary of the Catholic Union of Arras 6 January 1579
- The United Provinces after Union of Utrecht 23 Jan. 1579
- **Gent** Towns that briefly joined the United Provinces
- Became part of United Provinces in 1648

The Spanish Netherlands:

- in 1579   in 1648
- Church lands
- ♦ Protestant } universities
- ♦ Catholic }

The Netherlands 1559–1648

1559 The Spanish king Philip II leaves the country, making his half-sister, Margaret of Parma, governor. She continues the persecution of the protestants.

1566–67 Protestant riots due to famine. Philip II sends the Duke of Alba with an elite force of 20 000 to the provinces. Courts of the Inquisition are established, and mass executions are carried out.

1573–74 Spanish campaigns against rebels in the north (map nr.

93). The Duke of Alba resigns as governor in 1573. Leyden, under seige by the Spanish, is liberated by William of Orange in 1574.

1579–81 Provinces in the north form the Union of Utrecht in 1579; later The United Netherlands. An assembly of the seven estates deposes Philip II in 1581.

1648 At the Peace of Münster, Spain recognizes the United Netherlands. Estates General (map nr. 93) united with the northern provinces. Spanish Netherlands (Belgium) remain under the rule of the Hapsburgs.

The Great Fire in London in 1666

Londoners had scarcely begun to recover from a terrible outbreak of bubonic plague that claimed 70 000 lives in 1665, when a massive fire broke out on Sept. 2, 1666.

It started in a street in City where warehouses were used to store jute and tar. The fire moved quickly through the wooden structures. The Stock Exchange, St. Paul's Cathedral, eighty-eight other churches and some 13 000 houses burned in 5 days. Some 100 000 people were left homeless.

Above: Children at play in a Dutch town. From a painting by Pieter Brueghel the Elder (approx. 1525–69). The children are turning cartwheels and playing leapfrog.

94. LONDON IN SHAKE-SPEARE'S AND PEPYS' TIME

- Extent ca. 1600 (200 000 inh.)
- London Wall
- Extent of the Great Fire 1666

London Bridge was the capital's only one across the Thames until Westminster Bridge was built in 1750

Solider with musket around 1600. To aim the gun was laid in the cradle (left).

Musketeer fills the barrel of his musket with powder from a powder horn.

Goods being transported by sled on a winter's day in Amsterdam ca. 1600.

Various forms of insult might lead to a duel.

Prince James (later James II) playing tennis around 1625.

Sir Walter Raleigh, who brought back tabacco from the Americas.

Above: Queen Elizabeth I of England as she is portrayed in the so-called Armada Portrait from the end of the 1530s, i.e., after the Spaniards' «Invincible Armada» (top left) had been crushed in 1533. The Virgin Queen was the daughter of Henry VIII and Anne Boleyn, who was accused of infidelity and executed at the age of twenty-nine. Elizabeth was herself twenty-five when she ascended England's throne, and when she died in 1603 she had ruled her country for nearly forty-five years and lent her name to an entire epoch in European history.

England and Scotland
1553–1673

1553–58 Struggles between religious factions, and an attempt to reintroduce Catholicism during the reign of Mary Tudor (Bloody Mary). England becomes involved on the side of Spain in the war with France.

1558–1603 Under Elizabeth I both the monarchy and the Anglican church see greater stability. In 1584 Walter Raleigh is given the task of claiming new lands in America. He calls the coastal region north of Florida «Virginia» – after the «Virgin Queen» – and sends colonists to the area. The execution of Scottish-French queen Mary Stuart in

1587 leads to war with Spain. The «Invincible Spanish Armada» is annihilated in 1588. The East India Company is established in 1600.

1603–25 James VI, Mary Stuart's son with Lord Darnley and King of the Scots from 1567, is from 1603 also King of England, taking the name of James I. He persecutes the Puritans and, following a Catholic assassination attempt (The Gunpowder Plot) in 1605, also Catholics. Religious minorities begin emigrating to North America.

1625 James I's son, Charles I, becomes king. He governs without a parliament from 1629 to 1640

because of a dispute about taxation. Convocation of *The Long Parliament* leads to civil war in 1642.

1642–49 Charles I is taken captive by the Parliamentary Army. Oliver Cromwell defeats the Catholics (the Scots) at Preston in 1648 (map nr. 95). He removes all of his opponents in the Parliament, and has Charles I executed in 1649.

1653–58 Oliver Cromwell governs without parliament, as absolute ruler with the title of *Lord Protector*. War with Spain 1654–58.

1660–73 Charles I's son, Charles II, is elected king. London burns in 1666 (see p. 66). To counteract Charles II's Catholic sympathies,

96. THE RELIGIOUS POSITION IN EUROPE CA. 1560

- Roman catholics
- Orthodox cathol.
- Lutherans
- Calvinists
- Hussites
- Anglicans
- Muslims

95. THE BRITISH ISLES IN THE MID-17TH CENTURY

Civil War between King (K.) and Parliament (P.) 1642-49

- Controlled by P. end of 1643
- Controlled by K. end of 1643
- Under P.'s control 1645
- Cromwell's campaign 1649-51
- Reserved for Cromwell's protestant veterans
- Reserved for banished Irish
- ★ Major battlefield with date

the Test Act is passed, requiring all civil servants to receive Holy Communion in accordance with the Anglican rite.

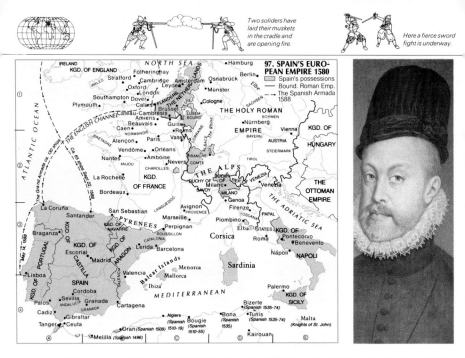

Two soldiers have laid their muskets in the cradle and are opening fire.

Here a fierce sword fight is underway.

97. SPAIN'S EURO-PEAN EMPIRE 1580

Spain's possessions
— — Bound. Roman Emp.
The Spanish Armada 1588

Spain under Philip II 1556–98

In contrast to his father, Charles V, Philip II was a genuine Spaniard, fanatically Catholic, dutiful and industrious. The picture of him – **top of this page** – is from Alonzo Sachez Coello's contemporary portrait. One might easily think this a clergyman or monk, rather than the ruler of the dominant great- power of the day.

Philip II had no real interest in life at court, with grand balls and hunts. His favourite place was sitting behind his desk. Nor was he a warrior, but when Elizabeth I had Mary Stuart executed in 1587, Philip sent «The Great Armada» to crush England. This ended in tragedy for Spain.

98. GERMANY IN THE THIRTY YEAR'S WAR 1618-48

Habsburg Lands:

  Austrian   Spanish
→ Christian IV's campaign to Lutter am Barenberge 1625-26
→ Gust. Adolphus' camp. 1630-32
→ Tilly's most important campaigns
--→ Wallenstein to Lützen 1632
★ Major battlefield with date
  Church lands
  France and French possessions in Germany
Bavaria, Brandenburg and Saxony are shown in distinctive colours

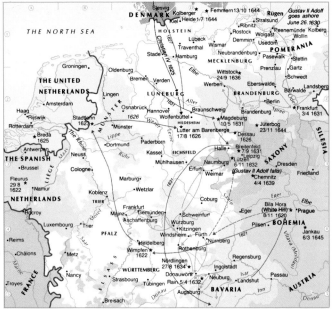

One soldier uses his sword, while the other swings his musket.

 Here fighting is hand-to-hand.

 They even go at each other with their musket cradles. Drawings from 1600s.

Above: Christian IV of Denmark-Norway. Painting by Peter Isaacsz, 1610. Christian IV was made king at the death of his father in 1588, but did not actually govern the country until his 19th year, in 1596.

99. SWEDEN IN THE 17TH CENTURY. CHARLES XII'S CAMPAIGNING 1700-1718

▨ Sweden in 1560
▨ Annexed from Denmark-Norway 1645-60
▨ Other conquests 1561-1660
→ Campaign against Copenhagen 1657-58 (Charles X)
→ Charles XII's camp. 1700-1718
⇢ Charles' ride to Stralsund 1714
★ Major battlefield with date

The Thirty Years' War 1618-1648

The Thirty Years' War, even though there is evidence that it began as early as 1609, ended 1659. This was mainly a struggle between the Hapsburgs and France for supremacy in Europe. Fighting on the side of the Hapsburgs was the Catholic League, supported by Spain. France got support from the Protestant League, incl. Christian IV (see above) of Denmark and Gustavus II Adolphus of Sweden.

Sweden 1617-1718

1617 Peace of Stolbova. Sweden receives Keksholm and Ingermanland (map nr. 99).
1629 Sweden receives Livonia and Riga at the Peace of Altmark.
1630-48 Thirty Years' War. Gustavus Adolphus falls at Lützen (1632).
1643-45 War with Denmark-Norway. Sweden receives Jämtland, Härjedalen, Halland, Gotland and Ösel.
1700-21 Great Northern War. Charles XII falls at Fredriksten (1718).

Right: Queen Christina of Sweden. From a painting by Sebastien Bourdon, 1653. She was keenly interested in French intellectual life, and as reigning queen from 1644, she wanted to make Sweden a cultural great-power, in keeping with the country's political position. In 1654 Christina abdicated, and on Christmas Eve of the same year she secretly converted to Roman Catholicism. Later she lived mostly in Rome, and was buried in The Church of St. Peter in the Vatican in 1689.

Dispatch rider brings news of the Peace of Westphalia in 1648.

Child in a walker. Drawn from an engraving from 1636.

Print shop in 1568. At right the type is being inked, at left a finished sheet.

The Peace of Westphalia 1648

Politically, the conditions of the peace of 1648 were disastrous for the German Empire. Of the in all 234 states and 51 cities that had been subject to the emperor, most were now granted sovereignty. The emperor's influence after 1648 was based solely on his position as ruler of Bohemia, Hungary and the Hapsburgs' hereditary lands in Austria. Of the sovereign states, Brandenburg became one of the most powerful (see illust. below).

The most important clause, from a religious viewpoint, was that which upheld the right of the governments themselves to decide religious matters. The distribution of Catholicism and Protestantism in the German areas was, therefore, roughly that of the present day.

The relative positions of Sweden and France too were strengthened by the War. Both received territory previously held by the German emperor. France got portions of the Alsace. Sweden was given Hither Pomerania, with Stettin, Wismar and Ren, and the Duchy of Bremen and Verden. Both countries were also given status as «protectors of the peace», giving them the formal right to intervene in German internal affairs.

Below: In 1618 East Prussia was united through succession with Brandenburg, and from 1648 Further Pomerania was also part of the kingdom.
Brandenburg-Prussia's leader Frederick Wilhelm is seen here accepting the homage of the Prussian Estates on October 18, 1663. In the background at the right is the Castle Church where his son, Frederick I, was crowned in 1701, making Prussia a sovereign kingdom (see also p. 75).

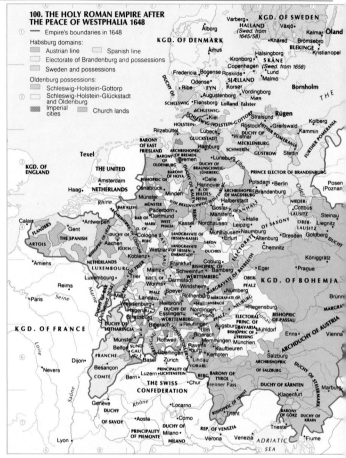

100. THE HOLY ROMAN EMPIRE AFTER THE PEACE OF WESTPHALIA 1648

- Empire's boundaries in 1648

Habsburg domains:
- Austrian line
- Spanish line
- Electorate of Brandenburg and possessions
- Sweden and possessions

Oldenburg possessions:
- Schleswig-Holstein-Gottorp
- Schleswig-Holstein-Glückstadt and Oldenburg
- Imperial cities
- Church lands

The Ottoman (Turkish) Empire 1360–1683

1360–89 Under Murat I the empire expands greatly in Asia Minor (map nr. 102).

1389–1402 Bajasid I Jildirim conquers large areas of the Balkans. Bulgaria is annexed in 1393.

1451–81 Mohammed (Mehmet) II captures Constantinople in 1453, making it the capital of the Osman Empire. Serbia, Bosnia, Albania and Greece become Turkish provinces.

1512–20 Selim I conquers the northern parts of Mesopotamia,

Tent encampment outside Vienna during Turkish siege in 1529.

Soldier with a hand mortar in Peter the Great's guard.

A host of crippled veterans were forced to beg for a living.

101. RUSSIAN EXPANSION 1300–1795

- Muscovy ca. 1300
- Muscovy 1462
- Lands conquered before 1689
- Peter the Great's conquests 1689-1725
- Conquered 1725-95

See also maps 120 and 126

The Russia of Peter the Great

Peter the Great, seen **above** in the battle against the Swedish king Charles XII at Poltava in 1709, was born in 1672, the son of Tzar Alexis by his second marriage. Following Alexis' death in 1676, there was a struggle for the throne among family members. Peter was proclaimed tzar when only ten years old, but he had no real power before 1689. During the nearly thirty years that Peter the Great governed the country, he opened Russia to western technology and customs. He had only been governing on his own one year when he undertook a lengthy period of travel in Western Europe, to learn ship building and other trades. And he brought western experts back with him to his backward country.

In the Great Northern War (1700–21) he took part on the side of Poland and Denmark against Sweden. The prize was Livonia, Estonia, Ingermanland and portions of Karelia (map nr. 101).

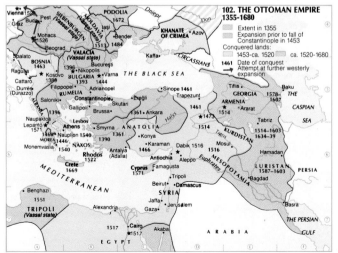

102. THE OTTOMAN EMPIRE 1355–1680

- Extent in 1355
- Expansion prior to fall of Constantinople in 1453

Conquered lands:
- 1453-ca. 1520
- ca. 1520-1680.

1461 Date of conquest
★ Attempt at further westerly expansion

W. Kurdistan, Syria and Egypt.
1520–66 Under Suleyman II the Ottoman Empire takes Beograd (1521), Rhodes (1522) and most of Hungary. In 1529, 300 000 Turks lay siege to Vienna, but the city is able to withstand the assault. Siebenbürgen, Moldavia, Georgia, Armenia and Tripoli become vassal states.

From 1567 Gradual disintegration of the empire. In the naval battle at Lepanto in the same year, however, Spanish and papal forces are victorious.

1683 Vienna is once again under siege.

English pillory, used at the beginning of the 1700s.

Condemned man is drawn and quartered in the square of a French town in 1757.

The Tower of London, 1641. Built in 1078 king's residence until 1509.

Above: Child portrait of Maria Theresa, painted in 1726 by the Dane Andreas Møller. Maria Theresa was then only nine years old. Fourteen years later she became a reigning empress, and governed her Catholic kingdom with strength and wisdom for another forty years.

Austria 1740–80

Following the death of Charles VI in 1740, there was a struggle over the lands of the Hapsburgs. Only after the War of Succession (1740–48), in which Prussia, France, Bavaria, Saxony and Spain were involved, was Maria Theresa (see above) finally able to draw the longest straw.

She abolished torture during interrogation, limited the power of the nobles and regulated the legal rights of farmers vis-à-vis the landed proprietors.

103. EUROPE 1721

Austria and possessions

Great Britain and possessions

Prussia and possessions

BARBARY COAST

Sweden and possessions

Boundary of the Hole Roman Empire

Left: A meeting in the British lower house in London in 1710, i.e., three years after England and Scotland were united as Great Britain. From a contemporary painting by the Dutch painter Peter Tillemans. At this point the House of Commons had 558 members, and there were actually not enough seats for everyone many had to stand during legislative sessions. Fortunately, it was rare to find everyone present at once. Nearly half the representatives belonged to the landed nobility, the Gentry. Seated in the centre is The Speaker.

Great Britain 1707–42

1707 England and Scotland are united as *The United Kingdom of Great Britain.* Following the Spanish War of Succession, Great Britain receives Gibraltar, Menorca, Newfoundland and Nova Scotia.

From 1714 Parliamentary system evolves. Industrial Revolution begins in the textile industry (map nr. 109, p. 77).

1742 Walpole forced to step down as PM due to failure in Austrian War of Succession.

 Team of horses pulls wheeled plow, an 18th century invention.

Conscription of soldiers in the early 1700s.

Right: Road construction in France. From a painting by Joseph Vernet, now in the Louvre, Paris. The 18th century was a period of vast road building projects in France, and it was for the most part the peasants, obliged to provide the crown with day-labour, who shouldered the construction and maintenance of the royal highways. In addition, the state collected a toll from everyone who used roads and bridges. With the establishment of École des ponts et chaussées ('school of bridges and roads') technical standards rose enormously, and French highways were considered the best in Europe.

Poland 1764–95

1764 Catherine the Great of Russia secures the Polish throne for her former lover, Stanislav Poniatowsky.

1772 The first partition of Poland. Russia takes the territories east of the Daugava (Da) and the upper part of the Dnieper. Austria takes Galicia and Lodomeria. Prussia receives West-Prussia, with the exception of Danzig (Gdanzk) and Thorn (Torun) (map nr. 104).

1791 The Polish parliament – *sejm* – adopts a new constitution, making Poland a hereditary monarchy, and abolishing the right of free veto.

104. THE PARTITIONS OF POLAND 1772, 1793, 1795

Ceded to:	1772	1793	1795
Russia			
Austria			
Prussia			

----- Poland before third partition
------- Poland's boundary 1991

1792 In order to «reestablish order», Prussia and Russia undertake the second partition of Poland. Russia gets vast areas west of the Daugava and Dnieper. Prussia takes Danzig, Thorn, Poznan and South-Prussia (Kalisz).

1794 Tadeusz Kosciuszko leads a large rebellion, which is, however, put down by Russian and Prussian troops.

1795 The third partition of Poland. The country is obliterated as a nation, and is not declared an independent state again until 1917. Poland's final borders are not established until 1921.

The Russia of Catherine the Great 1762–96

Catherine the Great, shown here from a portrait by Alexander Roslin **below right**, was born Sophia Augusta, daughter of prince August of Anhalt-Zerbst. Born in Stettin in 1729, she was married at the age of sixteen to Grand Duke Karl Peter Ulrik of Gottorp. He was a nephew of the Russian empress Elizabeth, and succeeded her as Peter III when Elizabeth died in January of 1762.

In July of the same year, however, Catherine seized power in a coup,

and only a few days later, Peter III died mysteriously.

In the course of her thirty-four year reign Catherine turned the country into a great-power. After a number of wars against the Ottoman Empire (Turkey) – 1768–74, 1783 and 1787–92 – Russia conquered the Khanate of the Crimean, and the coast of the Black Sea to the Dnestr (map nr. 120, p. 83). With the three partitions of Poland, Russia expanded her territory even more. Catherine wanted to be seen as a great friend of the philosophers of the Enlightenment, but seldom took their advice.

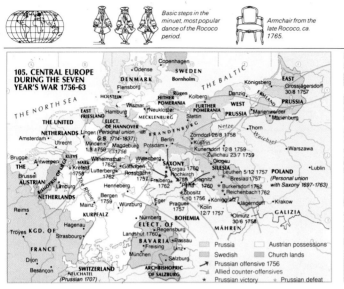

Basic steps in the minuet, most popular dance of the Rococo period.

Armchair from the late Rococo, ca. 1765.

Rococo woman of the upper classes, dressed in skirted gown, 1766.

105. CENTRAL EUROPE DURING THE SEVEN YEAR'S WAR 1756–63

THE NORTH SEA
THE BALTIC
Copenhagen
• Odense
SWEDEN
DENMARK
Bornholm
Flensborg
Rügen
Königsberg
EAST
PRUSSIA
HOLSTEIN
Kolberg
Danzig
Grossjägersdorf
30/8 1757
Wismar •
HITHER
POMERANIA
WEST
PRUSSIA
Neukloster
FURTHER
POMERANIA
Marienwerder
Hamburg
Stettin
Marienburg
EAST
FRIESLAND
MECKLENBURG
THE UNITED
ELECT.
Netze
Thorn
NETHERLANDS
Linger (Personal union with G.B. 1714–1837)
BRANDENBURG
Weichsel
Amsterdam •
Utrecht
Minden •
Magdeburg
Potsdam •
Berlin
Zorndorf 26/8 1758
Küstrin
• Warszawa
1/8 1759
1756
Brugge •
KLEVE
Wilhelmsthal
Wittenberg
Glogau
• Lublin
THE
Antwerpen
1762
Krefeld
Lutterberg •
Gröningen
SAXONY
SILESIA
Liegnitz
Leuthen 5/12 1757
POLAND
Brussel
1758
1762
Rossbach •
Torgau 1760
Kochkirch
Breslau 1757
(Personal union with Saxony 1697–1763)
AUSTRIAN
Limburg
Henneberg
1757
Freiberg
1762
Pirna
1759
Burkersdorf 1762
NETHERLANDS
Bergen
1759
Würzburg
Eger
Prague
Lobositz
1/10 1756
Königgratz
Reichenbach 1762
• Krakow
Reims •
Mainz •
KURPFALZ
1757
Kolin
18/6 1757
Jägerndorf
GALIZIA
• Nürnberg
Regensburg
BOHEMIA
Olmütz
30/6 1758
MÄHREN
Troyes
KGD. OF
Hagenau
Landshut 1760 •
ELECT. OF
FRANCE
Strasbourg •
• Freising
• Passau
Linz •
BAVARIA
Dijon •
München •
Salzburg •
Besançon •
SWITZERLAND
NEUCHATEL
(Prussian 1707)
ARCHBISHOPRIC
OF SALZBURG

Prussia
Austrian possessions
Swedish
Church lands
Prussian offensive 1756
Allied counter-offensives
★ Prussian victory
☆ Prussian defeat

The Musical Life of the 18th Century

The entire century was a period of flourishing musical activity. One of the greatest names was Wolfgang Amadeus Mozart (1756–91), who during his short life created music that still today is as alive, airy and life-affirming as when it was written over 200 years ago. Wolfgang Amadeus was the son of Austrian violinist and composer Leopold Mozart, and composed his first pieces of music at the age of six or

seven. His best known large works are «Abduction from Seraillet» (1782), «Figaro's Weddings» (1786), and «Don Giovanni» (1787).
Other leading composers from this rich period were Johan Sebastian Bach (1685–1750) and Joseph Haydn (1732–1809).
In Italy were Antonio Vivaldi (1678–1741) and Domenico Cimarosa (1749–1801) were active. And in Great Britain, the German-born composer, Georg Friedrich Händel wrote one large oratorium after the other. In Sweden Carl Michael Bellman (1740–95) was writing and performing his «Fredman's Epistles» and «Fredman's Songs».

The Seven Years' War 1756–63

For some years already there had been confrontations between British and French troops in America, and between naval units at sea, when in 1756 Great Britain declared war on France. The French had at this time allied themselves with the Austrians, while Great Britain had a mutual defense pact with Frederick the Great of Prussia. Later, Russia, Spain, Saxony and Sweden were drawn into the conflict on the side of France in the war on the European continent, in which the largest battle was fought between Prussia and Austria-Russia.

Great Britain's greatest contribution to the clashes in Europe was its subsidizing of Prussia, who began the struggle with a surprise attack on Saxony in the autumn of 1756. One of the most famous battles of the war was fought at Rossbach in Saxony, on November 5, 1757, where Prussia's 21 600 man army was attacked by a combined force of 43 000 Germans, Austrians and Frenchmen. By a surprise manoeuvre the Prussians managed to surround the allies, who fled in panic into the biting cold of the winter's night. Frederick the

Below: Family concert in the palace of Renescure (18th century). Painting by an unknown artist. Musée des Beaux Arts, Lille.

Below: Wolfgang Amadeus Mozart. From a contemporary painting by an unknown artist.

Man and wife harvesting together in 1675.

Harvest wagon, ca. 1750.

Wheelbarrow ca. 1750.

Left: *From the battle of Prague, May 6, 1775. Contemporary copperplate engraving. The Austrians could not stop Frederick the Great's crack Prussian troops. They were driven back into the strongly fortified city of Prague. Still, Frederick paid a high price for victory. Nearly 18000 of his men lost their lives, and the loss of four hundred officers – among them his able general, Kurt von Schwerin – was very nearly catastrophic «Schwerin was worth 10000 men,» the king was heard to sigh.*

Great's losses were 156 dead and 376 wounded. Losses to the allies numbered in the thousands.
Map nr. 105 shows Prussia's most important charges with red arrows, allied counterattacks in blue. Red stars indicate Prussian victories, blue stars those of the allies.
The most significant effects of the Seven Years' War, however, came about as a result of battles between

Below: *Uniforms from Frederick the Great's army. From a small-scale placque drawn by von Muhlen.*

the British and the French that were fought out on battlefields far from Europe, and at the Peace of Paris in 1763, France was forced to cede her colonies in North America to Great Britain (map nr. 85, p. 62). The French possessions in India were also lost.

Frederick the Great

Frederick II, who was later given the nickname «The Great», was in his youth – to his father's dismay – greatly influenced by French Enlightenment philosophy. His command of French surpassed that of his own mother-tongue, and he corresponded regularly with the greatest author of the Enlightenment in France, François Voltaire, and others. He wrote poetry in French, and composed around 120 pieces for the flute. .
When Frederick II took the reins of government in Prussia in 1740, he further bolstered the country's military so that Prussia became the fourth largest military power on the continent.

Above: *Frederick the Great of Prussia, the king who divided his energies between war and philosophy. Painting by J.G. Glume.*

Brandenburg-Prussia 1415–1795

1415 Brandenburg comes under the Royal House of Hohenzollern.
1525 End of the rule of the Teutonic Knights, and East-Prussia becomes a duchy under Polish hegemony.
1539 The Lutheran religion is introduced.
1618 Prussia is united with Brandenburg (map nr. 101, p. 70).
1640–88 Under «the Grand Electoral Prince» – Frederick Wilhelm – both Further Pomerania and West-Prussia are placed under Brandenburg, and East-Prussia no longer Polish fief.
1701 Electoral Prince Frederick III of Brandenburg is proclaimed king of Prussia as Frederick I.
1720 Peace of Stockholm. Sweden cedes Pomerania to Prussia.
1742 Under Frederick II (the Great) Austria cedes Silesia.
1756–63 During the Seven Years' War, Prussia is on her way to becoming a great-power.
1772–95 Following the three partitions of Poland (map nr. 104, p. 73), Prussia receives large territories.

106. EXPANSION OF BRANDENBURG-PRUSSIA 1415–1797

THE NORTH SEA
THE BALTIC

Brandenburg 1415
Added 1415-1535
Added 1608-19
Added 1640-88
Added 1688-1740
Added 1740-86
Added 1786-97
1648 Year of annexation

★ Battlefield
— Boundary of the Holy Roman Empire

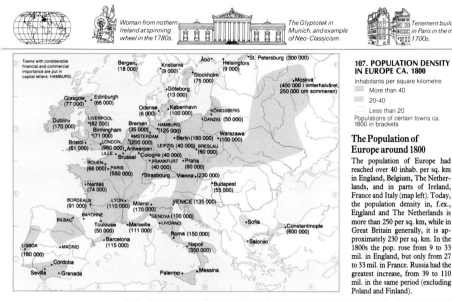

Towns with considerable financial and commercial importance are put in capital letters: HAMBURG

Bergen (18 000)
Kristiania (9 000)
Åbo
Helsingfors (9 000)
St. Petersburg (300 000)
Stockholm (75 000)
Göteborg (13 000)
Moskva (400 000 i vinterhalvåret, 250 000 om sommeren)
Glasgow (77 000)
Edinburgh (66 000)
Odense (6 000)
København (100 000)
KÖNIGSBERG
Dublin (170 000)
LIVERPOOL (82 000)
Bremen (35 000)
HAMBURG (125 000)
DANZIG (50 000)
Birmingham (71 000)
AMSTERDAM
Berlin (160 000)
Warszawa (100 000)
Bristol (61 000)
LONDON (980 000)
Antwerpen
LEIPZIG (40 000)
BRESLAU (60 000)
LILLE
Brussel
Cologne (40 000)
ROUEN (66 000)
PARIS (550 000)
FRANKFURT (40 000)
Praha (60 000)
Strasbourg
Vienna (230 000)
Nantes (74 000)
Budapest (55 000)
BORDEAUX (91 000)
LYON (110 000)
Milano (170 000)
VENICE (135 000)
BAYONNE
BILBAO
Toulouse (50 000)
Marseille (111 000)
LIVORNO
GENOVA (100 000)
Roma (150 000)
Sofia
Constantinople (600 000)
LISBOA (180 000)
MADRID
Barcelona (115 000)
Napoli (350 000)
Saloniki
Cordoba
Palermo
Messina
Sevilla
Granada

107. POPULATION DENSITY IN EUROPE CA. 1800

Inhabitants per square kilometre

More than 40

20-40

Less than 20

Populations of certain towns ca. 1800 in brackets

The Population of Europe around 1800

The population of Europe had reached over 40 inhab. per sq. km in England, Belgium, The Netherlands, and in parts of Ireland, France and Italy (map left). Today, the population density in, f.ex., England and The Netherlands is more than 250 per sq. km, while in Great Britain generally, it is approximately 230 per sq. km. In the 1800s the pop. rose from 9 to 33 mil. in England, but only from 27 to 33 mil. in France. Russia had the greatest increase, from 39 to 110 mil. in the same period (excluding Poland and Finland).

London ca. 1800

The most densely populated districts in England around 1800 were the industrial areas around Liverpool, Manchester and Leeds (map nr. 109). But London, with almost a million inhabitants, was by far the country's largest city. **The picture below**, by Pugin and Rowlandson, shows a fire in London in 1808. The city's first fire brigade was sponsored by insurance companies, but in 1833 the London Fire Brigade was organized. St. Paul's Cathedral is seen in the background.

108. POPULATION DENSITY IN ENGLAND 1801

Populations of larger towns in brackets

Inhab. per square km

151-300
101-150
76-100
61- 75
41- 60
21- 40
20 and less

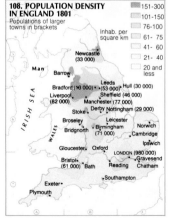

Man

Newcastle (33 000)
Barrow
IRISH SEA
Bradford (13 000)
Leeds
Hull (30 000)
Liverpool (82 000)
Sheffield (46 000)
Manchester (77 000)
Stoke
Derby
Nottingham (29 000)
Broseley
Leicester
Norwich
Bridgnorth
Birmingham (71 000)
Cambridge
WALES
Ipswich
Gloucester
Oxford
LONDON (980 000)
Bristol (61 000)
Bath
Reading
Gravesend
Chatham
Southampton
Exeter
Plymouth

The street-lamp is lit in a London street in 1800.

A handcart on the waterfront in Philadelphia in 1800.

A European enjoys a clay pipe of Virginia tobacco. ca. 1800.

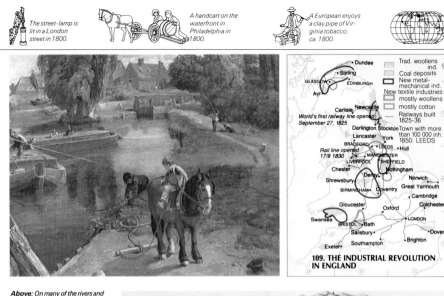

109. THE INDUSTRIAL REVOLUTION IN ENGLAND

Trad. woollens ind.
Coal deposits
New metal-mechanical ind.
New textile industries: mostly woollens
mostly cotton
Railways built 1825-36
Town with more than 100 000 inh. 1850: LEEDS

World's first railway line opened September 27, 1825

Rail line opened 17/9 1830

Dundee, Stirling, GLASGOW, EDINBURGH, Ayr, Carlisle, Newcastle, Darlington Stockton, Lancaster, York, BRADFORD, LEEDS, Hull, MANCHESTER, LIVERPOOL, SHEFFIELD, Chester, Derby, Nottingham, Shrewsbury, Norwich, BIRMINGHAM, Coventry, Great Yarmouth, Cambridge, Gloucester, Oxford, Colchester, Swansea, BRISTOL, Bath, LONDON, Salisbury, Dover, Exeter, Southampton, Brighton

Above: On many of the rivers and canals in England, barges were drawn by horses, following a path along the bank. From a painting by the famous landscape painter John Constables from around 1800.

Left: The two largest cities on the European continent around 1800 were Constantinople, with around 600 000 inhabitants, and Paris, with approximately 550 000. This detail from a plan of Paris by Minister of Finance Turgot from the last half of the 18th century shows central portions of Paris, with the Tuileries (tile works) and Pont Royal in the foreground.

Roads and Transport

During the fifteen years between 1765 and 1780, something of a transportation revolution occurred in France. As shown in map nr. 110, a journey from Brussels to Toulouse took nineteen days in 1765, as did a trip from Strasbourg to Rennes. Following a period of highway improvements, and the introduction of regularly scheduled diligence routes (see Charles Rossiter's painting, below left), the trip from Brussels to Toulouse was reduced by 1780 to only eleven days, with stops. From Rennes to Strasbourg it now only took 8 days.

Above: George Stephenson's steam locomotive – invented 1813/14 – pulling a row of coal cars. This invention was crucial to the transport needs of the new industrial areas in northern England.

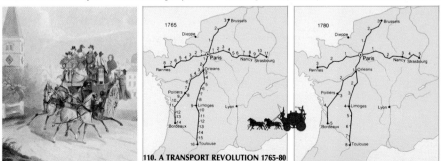

110. A TRANSPORT REVOLUTION 1765-80

IRELAND
Nationalist uprising against the British, led by Wolfe Tone

THE UNITED NETHERLANDS (1784)

THE AUSTRIAN NETHERLANDS (1787)
Paris

FRANCE
The French Revolution Storming of the Bastille July 14, 1789.
Madrid **SPAIN**
A popular revolt against French rule leads in 1808 to a broadly based guerilla war.

Budapest **TYROL**
Uprising in 1808/09, led by Andreas Hofer after Bavaria had occupied Tyrol.
Beograd

POLAND
Rebellion against the Russians in 1794, led by general Tadeusz Kosciuszko
Warszawa ★ Maciejowice
★ Raclawice

HUNGARY
Ignac Martinovics heads a Jacobin-Republican conspiracy against the monarchy in 1794.

SERBIA
Peasant rebellion against the Turks in 1804, led by Karajordje (Black George)

SOUTHEAST RUSSIA
Peasant uprising 1773-75, led by the Cossack J.I. Pugachev, who disguised himself as the dead Tzar, Peter III.
Saratov

Tsaritsyn

111. REVOLUTION AND FREEDOM IN EUROPE CA. 1800

Above: The actor Chinard in the sans-coulottes costume. The petty bourgeoisie, the radical force of the Revolution, wore long trousers, in contrast to those worn by the bourgeoisie proper. They were sans coulotte, i.e., without knee breeches. Painting by Louis-Léopold Boilly.

European Revolutions

1773–74 Yemelyan I. Pugachev leads a peasant uprising in southern Russia (see also p. 83).

1789 The French Revolution (see next column).

1794 Ignac Martinovich heads a conspiracy against the monarchy in Hungary.

1794 General Tadeusz Kosciuzko leads a rebellion against the Russians in Poland (see p. 73).

1796–98 The Irish nationalist, Wolfe Tone directs an unsuccessful war of independence.

1804 In Serbia, prince George Petrovich (Black George) leads uprising against the Turks.

1808 An uprising in Spain leads to a protracted guerilla war against the army of Napoleon.

1808–09 The Tyrolean freedom fighter Andreas Hofer drives the French from Tyrol.

Below: In 1788 censorship was abolished in France. The presses were spewing out newspapers and pamphlets.

The French Revolution 1789–95

1789

May 5 The Estates General meet for the first time since 1614. Louis XVI has been forced to convene the assembly because of an economic crisis.

June 17 The Third Estate forms a constituent national assembly (the **Constituante**), and three days later they pledge to separate until France has a new constitution (the Tennis Court oath).

July 14 Storming of the Bastille (see illust. on the following page).

July 20 – August 5 Peasant uprisings throughout most of France. Rumours that bands of robbers are plundering the country cause the uprisings to be referred to as «The

Great Terror» (map nr. 113, p. 79). The clergy and the nobility relinquish their privileges.

October 5 Because of the lack of food in Paris, a procession of market woman head to the palace of Versailles, chanting «Bread for Paris!» (illust. following page).

1791 Fall of the monarchy. Louis XVI and Marie Antoinette flee, but are stopped.

1793–95 The royal couple is executed (January 21 and October 17, 1793). Uprising of royalists and federalists (map nr. 114, p. 79). The «Committee of Public Safety» organizes mass executions. Nine states form a coalition and declare war. France wins key victories. Among the foremost military leaders is Napoleon Bonaparte.

112. PARIS AT THE OUTBREAK OF THE FRENCH REVOLUTION 1789

0   500   1000   1500   2000 m

A woman and man of the Third Estate toast the Revolution in 1789.

Representatives of Paris' light-hearted leisure class in the 1790s.

Louis XVI is executed by guillotine in Paris, on January 21, 1793.

Right: On October 5, 1789 between five and six thousand women walked the 30 km from Paris to Versailles to demand bread.

Below: Storming of the Bastille, July 14, 1789. From a contemporary colour lithograph. When the commandant saw the mass of people approaching, he gave the order to open fire. Then, following a short but hectic battle, he raised the white flag, and the people stormed in. The prisoners, seven in all, most of them criminals, were freed, and the crowd marched in triumph through the streets of Paris, carrying the head of the commandant on a pike. July 14 became France's national celebration (Bastille Day).

113. FRANCE UNDER THE TERROR

- ⬤➡ Where the uproar started
- ⬜ Unaffected areas

Brussel • Cologne
ARTOIS • Koblenz ①
Amiens • Meas • Moser • Worms
PICARDIE • Sedan
Le Havre • Estrées
Jersey • Rouen • PARIS • Valmy
BRETAGNE • NORMANDIE • Versailles • Romilly
Rennes • Laferté • Troyes • Saint-Florentin
ANJOU • Orléans
Nantes • POITOU • BERRY • NIVERNAIS • FRANCHE-COMTÉ • Bern ②
La Rochelle • MARCHÉ • Louhans
Ruffac • AUVERGNE • Lyon • Torino
Bordeaux • DAUPHINÉ
GIRONDE • Dordogne • Rhône
Bayonne • Pau • Toulouse • Avignon • PROVENCE • Nizza (Nice)
Carcassonne • Marseille • Toulon
⬜ Peasant revolts, July 1789 Ⓐ • MEDITERRANEAN Ⓒ

114. REVOLT IN THE PROVINCES

- ⬜ Royalist, Summer 1793
- ⬜ Federalist, Summer 1793
- — France's boundaries 1792
- ⬜ Conquered 1794-95

• Haag • Nijmegen ①
Dunkerque • Antwerpen
Brussel • Neerwinden
Boulogne • Fleurus • Koblenz
THE ENGLISH CHANNEL • Arras • Valenciennes • BELGIUM • Mainz
Amiens • Le Quesnoy
• Brest • Rouen • Varennes
BRETAGNE • NORMANDY • Saint-Denis • PARIS • Valmy
Quiberon • Rennes • Versailles • Seine
Savenay • Orléans • Chattilon • Basel
Nantes • Loire • Dijon • Montbeillard ②
VENDÉE • Bourges • FRANCHE-COMTÉ
La Rochelle • Nevers • Genève
SAVOIA
Bordeaux • Lyon
Garonne • Mende • Valence • KGD. OF SARDINIA ③
Bayonne • Dax • Nîmes • Avignon • PROVENCE
Toulouse • Montpellier • Marseille • Nice
SPAIN • Foix • ROUSSILLON • THE MEDITERRANEAN • Toulon
Ⓐ • Perpignan Ⓑ • Ⓒ

Emperor Napoleon in a characteristic stance.

French canon from the 1760s. Used during the Napoleonic Wars.

Empress Joséphine, whom Napoleon divorced in December 1809.

WÜRTTEM-BERG
FD. NEUENBURG (NEUCHÂTEL) (Prussian)
The Rhine
Donau • Vienna
KGD. OF BAVARIA (From 1808)
Konstanz
Zürich
HELVETIAN REPUBLIC (1798–1803)
Genève
Martigny
SALZBURG
STEIERMARK
AUSTRIA
Buda •• Pest
SAVOY (Occupied by Fr.) 1792
Great St. Bernhard
BARONY OF TYROL To Kgd. of Italy 1810
PIEMONTE To Fr. from 1796
Campoformio Peace Treaty Oct. 18 1797
Udine
KÄRNTEN
Sardinia 1798
Milano
Novare
Lodi 10/5 1796
LOMBARDIA
Rivoli 14/1 1797
Arcole 17/11 1796
Bassano 8/9 1796
Trieste
KRAIN
Drava
Sava
Torino
Piacenza
DUCHY OF PARMA
Venezia
Mantova (Besieged June 1796 – Feb. 1797)
ISTRIA
CROATIA
Marengo 14/6 1800
Guastalla
Ferrara
THE CISALPINE REPUBLIC
Pola
REPUBLIC OF VENEZIA
BOSNIA
SERBIA
Mondovi 22/4 1796
Genova
Modena
Parma
Bologna
Rimini
Zara
DALMATIA
THE OTTOMAN EMPIRE
Millesimo 13/4 1796
LIGURIAN REP. (1797–1805)
SAN MARINO
HERCE-GOVINA
Sarajevo
Nizza (Nice) • Monaco
Pisa
LUCCA
TOSCANY
Firenze
Ancona
THE ADRIATIC SEA
Livorno
KGD. OF ETRURIA (1801–08)
Siena
Perugia
Assisi
PAPAL STATES
REP. OF RAGUSA
MONTE-NEGRO
Corsica (French from 1768)
Elba
Piombino
Orbetello
Opvieto
Spoleto
(THE ROMAN REPUBLIC 1798–99)
Ajaccio
Roma
PONTECORVO
KGD.
Barletta
Bari
Napoleon arrives with his army March 26. 1796
Gaeta
Capua
BENEVENTO
Napoli
Salerno
OF NAPOLI
Brindisi
KGD. OF SARDINIA
(THE PARTHENOPEAN REP. 1799)
Otranto
TYRRHENIAN SEA
Cagliari

115. NAPOLEON'S ITALIAN CAMPAIGNS 1796–1800 AND FRENCH DOMINATION IN ITALY CA. 1800

Liparian Islands
Palermo
Messina • Reggio
Marsala
KGD. OF SICILY
Catania
Syracuse (Syrakus)
Malta (French 1798–1800)

French territory:
- France 1792
- Piedmont, taken from Sardinia 1798
- Duchy of Parma, annexed 1803
Under French control:
- Cisalpine 1797–02, Italian 1802–05
- Ligurian 1797–05
- Papal States, Roman Rep. 1798–99
- Luccan Rep. 1799–1805
- Kgd. of Naples. Parthenopean Rep. 1799
- Kingdom of Etruria 1801–08
- Duchy of Piombino 1801
— Kingdom of Italy 1808
Napoleon's campaigns:
➡ 1796–97 ➡ 1800
— Venetian Republic, Austrian 1797–1805

Napoleon 1796–1800

1796–97 In March 1796 the twenty-six-year old Napoleon Bonaparte marries Joséphine de Beauharnais, six years his senior, with whom he is passionately in love. The fact that he had good political connections did nothing to lessen his passion.

A few weeks later he is placed in command of the French army, which was set to attack the Austrians in northern Italy. He departs from Nice and crosses the border into Piemonte, and in April and May of 1796 he defeats the Austrians in a series of battles: Millesimo, Dego, Mondovi, Lodi (map nr. 115). After victories at Bassano in September, Arcole in November, and the fall of Mantova in February 1797 peace is negotiated in Campoformio. Lombardy becomes The Cisalpine Republic.

1798 Having given up plans to break Great Britain with an attack across the Channel, Napoleon moves against British Egypt in May. On July 21 he defeats the Mameluks and captures Cairo, but when Admiral Nelson gives the British a victory in a naval battle at Aboukir (illust. p. 81), Napoleon and his army are trapped in Egypt. He pushes on toward Syria to defend against a Turkish offensive, but is forced to return to Egypt.

1799 N. leaves Egypt, arriving in Paris at the end of October. Carries out a coup d'etat, and is made First Consul with very nearly dictatorial powers.

1800 French forces are trapped in Genoa, and Napoleon decides to go to their rescue. In May he leads an army of 60 000 men over the Alps (illust. above), and following his victory at Marengo on June 14, he can boast «Italy's fate is sealed.» (cont. p. 82)

Above: The Corsican, Napoleon Bonaparte, who had become a lieutenant in the artillery in 1785 at the age of 16, is, in this portrait from 1796, a general, leading the French forces to victory in a battle against the Austrians at Arcole northwest of Venice on November 17, 1796. It was here that he inspired his troops by charging ahead of them into the fray with a raised banner. From a painting by Jean Gros.

Empress Joséphines bed in the palace of Malmaison.

Mens' and ladies' dress in Napoleon's time.

Fontainebleau where Napoleon said farewell to his soldiers in 1818.

116. EUROPE AFTER THE PEACE OF LUNÉVILLE 1801

- France and the four "republics"
- Habsburg domains
- Prussia and possessions
- Boundary of Holy Roman Empire

Above: Napoleon's army crossing the Alps, May 15–20, 1800. The troops have reached San Bernadino, where they dismantle their canons and pack them in hollowed out tree trunks for transport through the pass. From a contemporary painting by Charles Thévenin.

The Battle of Austerlitz 1805

On the anniversary of his coronation as emperor, December 2, 1805, Napoleon defeated Tzar Alexander I's forces, and what was left of the Austrian army, at Austerlitz. This was the crushing blow for Austria.

The Peace of Lunéville 1801

Following Napoleon's victory at Marengo (see p. 80) Franz II of Austria sued for peace. It was concluded in Lunéville February 9, 1801, and stated among other things that the Rhine would form France's eastern border, from Switzerland to The Netherlands. Austria was also forced to recognize the four sister republics, the Ligurian, the Cisalpine, the Helvetian, and the Batavian (map nr. 116). France had thus consolidated her power in Europe, as had First Consul Napoleon in France.

Right: England's famous admiral, Horatio Nelson, Napoleon's nemesis at Aboukir in 1798, and at Trafalgar in 1805.

Napoleon in Spain and Portugal 1808–14

In 1807 Napoleon occupied Portugal. In May 1808, he deposed the Spanish king and placed his own brother, Joseph, on the Spanish throne. Only a short time later, however, all of Spain was in revolt. The Duke of Wellington came to the rescue with 8 000 British soldiers. (map nr. 118).

117. BATTLE OF AUSTERLITZ 1805

- French forces
- Russians and Austrians
- Marsh

118. THE FRENCH CAMPAIGNS IN IBERIA 1808–14

- Napoleon's thrust
- British counter-offensives
- Battlefield

William Pitt and Napoleon compete for the largest slice of the globe.

Napoleon's simple throne is in the Neo-Classical style – 'Empire'.

Napoleon returning to Paris after defeat in Russia in 1812.

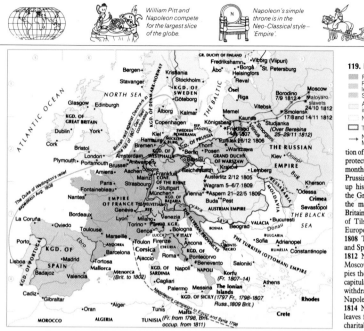

119. EUROPE IN 1812

- French territory
- Ruled by members of Napoleon's family
- States under French control
- Allies of France against Russia in 1812
- Neutral states
- The Rhine Confederation
- → Napoleon's Moscow campaign, May-December 1812

tion of the Rhine, with Napoleon as protector (map nr. 119). Three months later Napoleon marches on Prussia, and on October 27 he sets up his headquarters in Frederick the Great's Potsdam. On Nov. 21 the mainland blockade of Great Britain is initiated. After the Peace of Tilsit in July 1807, France is Europe's most powerful state.

1808 The French occupy Portugal and Spain (see p. 81).

1812 Napoleon marches toward Moscow (map nr. 119) and occupies the city, but without any final capitulation. During the French withdrawal, great numbers of Napoleon's troops perish.

1814 N. abdicates on April 7, and leaves for Elba, left to him by the charitable victors (below).

Napoleonic France 1801–14

1801 Peace is concluded with Austria at Lunéville on February 9 (see p. 81). On July 15 Napoleon signs a concordat with Pope Pious VII, stating that Catholic mass would once again be allowed, following a ten-year ban.

1802 The Peace of Amiens, March 27, puts an end to the war with Great Britain. The results of a plebescite make Napoleon First Consul for life.

1803 On May 16 Great Britain again declares war on France.

1804 Napoleon is elected emperor in May, and on December 2 the coronation takes place in Notre Dame in Paris. Spain joins France in the war against Great Britain.

1805 Great Britain, Russia, Austria, Sweden and the Kingdom of Napoli (Naples) form the Third Coalition against France. The goal of the alliance is to force France back behind its former borders. On October 20 the French defeat the Austrians at Ulm, but the very same day Admiral Nelson defeats the French fleet at Trafalgar. On November 13 Napoleon enters Vienna. The battle of Austerlitz takes place on December 1–2 (see p. 81).

1806–07 On July 16, 1806 sixteen German states form the Confedera-

From a Russian village at the beginning of the 1800s.

Russian coach from around 1800.

Russian serfs get a taste of the whip around 1800.

Russia 1796–1812

1796 Tzar Paul I – a bitter, introverted man, totally unsuited to rule his vast empire – succeeds his mother, Catherine the Great (see p. 73). In the nearly four years of his reign, Paul I wavers back and forth from one ally to the other.

1801 In March Tzar Paul is deposed in a coup d'état and killed. His son, Alexander I Paulovitch (illust. left), who has consented in the coup, takes over.

1805 Russia joins the Third Coalition against Napoleon, but suffers defeat at Austerlitz (see p. 81).

1807–09 Following yet another defeat at Friedland in June 1807, Alexander I makes peace with Napoleon in Tilsit. Russia must promise to join the mainland blockade, and cede territories to Napoleon's dependency, the Grand Duchy of Warsaw (map nr. 119, p. 82). On the other hand, the Russians are given a free hand in Finland, which is conquered in 1808–09 and made a Grand Duchy.

1812 Bessarabia is taken from the Ottoman Empire (map nr. 105). Napoleon attacks Russia after Tzar

Alexander has resumed trade with a deserted Great Britain. The French reach Moscow on September 14, and Napoleon sets up headquarters in the Kremlin. The following day the Muscovites set fire to the city, where 80 percent of Moscow's 9 000 buildings are made of wood. Napoleon offers the Tzar a ceasefire, but the offer is rejected. On October 18 Napoleon orders his army to pull out. Of the 610 000 men who began the campaign in June, only 85 000 make it home.

Above: Alexander I, Russian Tzar 1801–25. From James Walker's portrait. Alexander I was at first a liberal monarch, but became increasingly conservative – not least after Napoleon's invasion in 1812.
Left: Napoleon says farewell to his officers and men in the palace square outside Fontainebleau before his departure for Elba, April 20, 1814. From a painting by Horace Vernet, in Fontainebleau.
Below: The Don Cossack Yemelyan Pugachev, masquerading as the murdered Tzar Peter III, led an uprising in southern Russia in 1773–74 (map nr. 120). Here Pugachev is being transported in a cage to Moscow, where he was eventually executed.

120. THE RUSSIAN EMPIRE 1762–1812

- Russia in 1762
- Conquests 1762–96
- Russia in 1812
- Affected by Pugachovs revolt 1773–74

RUSSIA 1762–1812 83

Napoleon at the head of his army in 1814.

  British visiting an occupied Paris in the summer of 1814. Caricature.

 Louis XVIII has returned to Paris after fleeing in 181

Napoleon Will Not Surrender

He had been allowed to retain the title of emperor, and a force of 1 200 men, which he still drilled regularly. But Napoleon was suffering from boredom on Elba.

At the end of February 1815 – more than five months after the Congress of Vienna had convened (see p. 85) – an opportunity for further dramatics presented itself. Leading his men, he managed to reach Antibes undetected. March 10 he reached Lyon. Three days later the Congress declared him an outlaw, and a large number of countries vowed that they would not lay down their arms until he had been rendered harmless.

On March 19 Louis XVIII fled Paris (illust. p. 85), and the next day – cheered by his veterans – Napoleon once more occupied the Tuileries. On June 1 he was sworn in, promising a new, more liberal constitution.

Seventeen days later he was defeated at Waterloo (see p. 85). Napoleon was transported to Great Britain on July 15, 1815 (**illus. above**), and then on to St. Helena, where he ended his days on May 5, 1821.

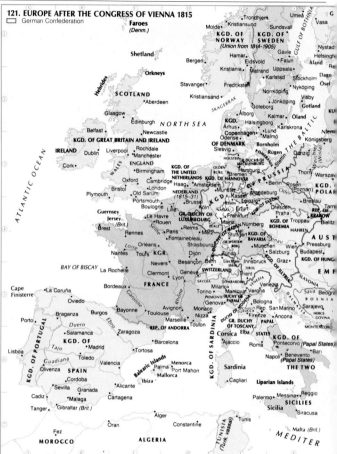

121. EUROPE AFTER THE CONGRESS OF VIENNA 1815
German Confederation

Left: Some of the delegates to the Congress of Vienna, 1814–15. In the left foreground sits Prussia's negotiator, Karl August von Hardenberg. The gentleman to his right, in front of the chair, is Austria's chief negotiator, Prince Metternich. Russia's Carl Vasilyevitch von Nesselrode is seen standing just to the right of Metternich. The man with his legs crossed – in the centre of the picture – is the British foreign minister, Lord Castlereagh. Farthest right – with his arm on the table – is France's foreign minister, Talleyrand.

Delegates to Congress of Vienna «dance and dance, but get nowhere.»

280 kg of silver were used to make the cradle for Napoleon's son.

Parisian girls of the «light guards getting ready for the evening.

DUCHY OF FINLAND
Onega
Ladoga
Viborg (Vipuri)
Fredrikshamn
Schlusselburg
GULF OF FINLAND
St. Petersburg
Vologda
Narva
Novgorod
Peipus
Lake Ilmen
Jaroslavl
ESTONIA
Ostrov
Tver
LIVONIA
Riga
Moscow
LAND
THUANIA
Vitebsk
Smolensk
Kaunas
Vilnius
Mogiljov
Orel
Minsk
Desna
Bialystok
Brest-Litovsk
Pripjat
Tsjernigov
VOLHYNIA
Kijev
Dnepr
Lublin
Lemberg (Lvov)
Russian 1809-15
KGD. OF GALICIA AND LODOMERIA
PODOLIA
Dnestr
Bug
Dnepr
IAN
BUKO- VINA
Iasi
BESSARABIA
Debrecen
MOLDAVIA
Odessa
Krim
TRANSILVANIA (SIEBENBURGEN)
Donau delta (Russian 1829-56)
RE
VALACIA
BLACK SEA
ANATE
Bucuresti
Donau
Varna
SERBIA
BULGARIA
THRACIA (THRACE)
Bosporus
THE
Adrianopel
Constanti nople
OTTOMAN EMPIRE
Sea of Marmara
Kütahya
ACEDONIA
Saloniki
Lemnos
Mytilene
THESSALY
AEGEAN
Chios
Smyrna
Missolonghi
SEA
Cephallenia
Athen
GREECE (Indep. 1829/30)
Navarino
Rhodes
Cetigo
Crete
RANEAN

The Congress of Vienna 1814-15

From the French Revolution in 1789 until the Congress of Vienna convened September 16, 1814, the political situation in Europe had changed drastically. In Germany and Italy over 250 city-states and principalities had been dissolved and replaced by new ones. It was these conditions that the Congress of Vienna was supposed to put in order.

The delegates were all men, but in the evenings the ladies took the spotlight. Among emperor Franz's guests at Hofburg were **one** Tzar, four kings, and a number of princes, each with his own entourage. Forty tables were set for dinner, which was followed by dancing. It has been said of the Congress of Vienna that «it danced and danced, without forward progress,» and that the atmosphere was marked as much by erotic as by political conflicts.

When the congress was concluded on July 11, 1815, the delegates felt they had established the balance of power which both Britain's Lord Castlereagh and Austria's Prince Metternich had been ardently promoting. France was forced to withdraw back behind her old borders, and Belgium was thrown together with Holland in The United Netherlands (map nr. 121). Russia received three fourths of the Grand Duchy of Warsaw, the so-called «Congress Poland», with Tzar Alexander as king. Prussia was also expanded, although divided in two along religious lines. The many German states were joined in a loose federation – The German Confederation (Deutscher Bund).

Right: On March 19, 1815 Louis XVIII, now sixty years old, is again forced to flee. This time he is accompanied by his and Louis XVI's younger brother, who would become Charles X (farthest left). The royal pair are making a hasty retreat with the crown jewels. Anonymous French caricature from 1815.

The battle of Waterloo 1815

On March 6, 1815 the members of the Congress of Vienna received word of Napoleon's return from Elba (see p. 84). They reacted immediately. In less than an hour a coalition had resolved to carry out another military campaign against him.

The final clash took place at Waterloo, a small village in Belgium, on June 18, 1815. In spite of the emperor's gifts as a tactician, Napoleon's 125 000 men were forced to surrender to Wellington and Blücher's 220 000 man force.

Above: Following Napoleon's abdication on April 7, 1814 (see p. 83), an interim peace treaty was signed in Paris on May 30, 1814. One result of this peace was that the British forces could immediately return home. The peace was celebrated with a huge fireworks display in Hyde Park in London, August 1, 1814. This hand-painted copperplate commemorating the event was issued only a couple of weeks after the festivities. A month later the Congress of Vienna was convened to work out the details of the peace treaty of May 30.

A «petroleuse» – arsonist – during the uprising in Paris in the spring of 1871.

A crinoline clad lady putting a letter in a Paris post box, from 1850.

Three pupils before their headmaster. Silhouette from the 1800s.

122. UNIFICATION OF GERMANY 1865-71

Prussia 1865

Added to Prussia 1866

North German Confederation 1867

Attacks on Denm., Austria, France

The German Empire 1871

tion (map nr. 121, p. 84).

1864 Prussia and Austria attack Denmark in January, taking Schleswig and Holstein (map nr. 123).

1866–67 Disagreement over the administration of Schleswig-Holstein leads to war between Prussia and Austria in the summer of 1866. Following Prussia's victory, the German Confederation is dissolved, and in 1867 the North German Confederation is formed, under the leadership of Otto von Bismarck (map nr. 122).

1870 Bismarck arms the country (see illus. bottom) and provokes the French under Napoleon III, until on July 19 France declares war on Prussia. Following a humiliating defeat at Sedan, Napoleon III surrenders to Bismarck. In France the imperial dynasty is abolished. The Republic is reintroduced. The war continues.

1871 On January 28 the French capitulate. By this time king William of Prussia has already become German emperor, and Bismark chancellor (illus. below). At peace negotiations in May, France has to cede Alsace-Lorraine (Elsass-Lothringen).

The German Empire 1859–71

1859 In a war with France and Sardinia (map nr. 124) Austria loses Lombardy and Parma. At the same time, Prussia is gaining influence in the German Confedera-

123. SCHLESWIG-HOLSTEIN

Danish areas in Schleswig 1864

Areas ceded to Denmark, Treaty of Vienna Oct. 1864

Austro/Prussian attack- in all 51000 troops

Schleswig's northern boundary:
1864 --- after 1864

Boundary of German Confederation 1815-66

Denm.'s south boundary 1920

Above: William I is proclaimed emperor of Germany at Versailles on January 18, 1871. The picture's central figure is Prussia's formidable prime minister, Otto von Bismarck. Beside him stands Field Marshal General Helmuth von Moltke. From a painting by Anton von Werner from 1876.

Left: Prussian soldiers test new canons from the Krupp Munitions Works at a firing range outside Berlin. At the right, Otto von Bismarck is seen on horseback. The man in the top hat is presumably Alfred Krupp. Woodcut in «L'Univers Illustré» from January 2, 1869.

Garbaldi helps Victor Emanuel II put on the «Italian boot».

Sofa for two persons, a so-called «vis-à-vis» from the 1860s.

A French student and his «grisette» – a self-employed woman.

The Apennines (Italian) Peninsula 1815–61: Italian Unification

1815 Following the Congress of Vienna, French hegemony is transferred to Austria, led by Metternich. The kingdom of The Two Sicilies comes into being (map nr. 124).

1830 The despotic Ferdinand II, a close relative of the Austrian emperor, becomes king.

1831 Giuseppe Mazzini founds the revolutionary liberation organization *Giovine Italia*, Young Italy, whose political goal is a united Italian republic.

1848–49 Uprisings in Naples and Palermo lead to a new and more liberal constitution. Sardinia, the Papal States and Toscany follow suit, and after the revolution in Vienna in 1848, Milano and Venice break with Austria. Only a year later, however, the Italian states are again brought to heel.

1859 France and the Kingdom of Sardinia form an alliance against Austria. After the Battle of Solferino (see below) Lombardy and Parma fall to Sardinia.

1860 Giuseppe Garibaldi (see illust. at right) and his armed volunteers, the «Red Shirts», who carried out the «Campaign of the 1000», go ashore in Sicily in May (map nr. 124), and in September they take Naples.

1861 Garibaldi's men advance northward, as Sardinia's forces push southward. Central Italy falls, and on March 17 the Kingdom of Italy is proclaimed, with Sardinia's Victor Emanuel II as its first king.

Above: Following the French February Revolution in 1848, Napoleon I's nephew, Louis Napoléon Bonaparte was elected president. In 1852 he became Emperor Napoleon III, shown here as a prisoner in the castle of Wilhelmshöhe following his defeat at Sedan in 1870. Bismarck is the consoling victor.

Below: On June 24, 1859 Napoleon III led combined French and Sardinian forces against the Austrians at Solferino. With a total of 30 000 killed and wounded in one day, the battle was one of the bloodiest of the 19th century, and gave rise to the establishment of the International Red Cross.

Above: Freedom fighter Giuseppe Garibaldi. From an unsigned Italian painting. Garibaldi struggled all his life for freedom and justice, as in South America, where he led the defense of Montevideo against an Argentinean attack in 1843. During the unification of Italy in 1860-61, he was Victor Emanuel's most important supporter.

124. UNIFICATION OF ITALY 1859-61

- Sardinia 1859
- Austrian 1859
- Sardinia in May 1860
- Added to Sardinia Autumn 1860
- Garibaldi's expedition 1860

A newspaper reader in Paris around 1830.

Women of a harem in a Turkish bath. From at painting by Ingres from 1862.

A taste for things Oriental made an impact on men's fashion too.

125. GREEK WAR OF INDE-PENDENCE 1821-29

Turkish in 1821

Ionian Islands, republic under British protection 1815-63

Kingdom of Greece, recognized by great powers 3/2 1830

Below: Euge Delacroix' famous revolutionary painting «July 28. Liberty leads the people» from 1830 – now in the Louvre – symbolizes one of the 19th century's characteristic features: The people's desire for national liberation. This was certainly the case in France, Italy and Greece.

Above: George Noel Gordon, from 1798: Lord Byron (1788–1824). From a painting by Thomas Phillios. Byron's poetry, and his ardent belief in political freedom, was a source of inspiration for poets and liberation movements alike, not least in Greece. Fired by his enthusiasm for heroic deeds, the romantic Lord Byron travelled to Greece to take part in the struggle against the Turks. A few months after his arrival, however, he came down with rheumatic fever, and died on April 24, 1824. The unusually handsome poet became a symbol of idealism, courage and unselfishness.

Greece 1821–29

1821 An uprising against Turkish rule is countered with hard resistance and great brutality. Thousands of Greeks are massacred or sold into slavery.

1827 An allied fleet of British, French and Russian naval forces annihilate the Turkish-Egyptian fleet at Navarino. Thus Turkey is forced to give up Greece.

1828 The former Russian foreign minister, Count Kapodistrias, becomes the country's interim president.

1830 Great Britain, France and Russia recognize Greece as an independent state.

Russian Expansion
1689–1860 (map nr. 126, p. 89)

1689–1725 The reign of Peter the Great (see p. 71).

1762–96 Catherine the Great makes Russia a European great-power (see p. 73). Rebellion led by the Cossack Pugacev (see p. 83).

1814–15 Following the Congress of Vienna, Russia gets three fourths of the Grand Duchy of Warsaw (see p. 85). Tzar Alexander I (see p. 83) calls for the establishment of a «Holy Alliance», directed against the forces of revolution and liberalism. When the alliance is formally established in September 1815, most of Europe's princes join the cause.

1816–17 Serfdom is abolished in the Baltic provinces, but the peasants receive no land, remaining dependent on wealthy estate owners.

1825 Alexander I dies with no heir at the age of forty-seven, and his brother, Constantine Pavlovitch, viceroy of Poland, is proclaimed Tzar. However, Constantine has two years earlier renounced his claim to the throne in favour of his younger brother Nicholas. During the period of uncertainty that results, a secret society of officers demands a new and more liberal constitution and system of government. In St. Petersburg they refuse

A Russian girl carries buckets of water with a yoke. Ca. 1850.

Russian peasants dancing a ring dance in the 1850s.

A soldier in Tzar Nicholas I's imperial guard.

to swear loyalty to Nicholas, proclaiming Constantine instead. The coronation of Nicholas I takes place in December (Russian: *decabr*), and the rebels are therefore referred to as the *Decabrists*. Nicholas I orders the use of artillery against them, and the Decabrist revolt is quickly crushed.

1825–31 Nicholas I's reactionary policies are met with growing opposition. A war with Iran makes portions of Armenia Russian. The country gives aid to the war of liberation in Greece in 1828. Poland becomes a Russian province following a Polish uprising in 1830–31.

1853–56 Crimean War (see column 4).

126. RUSSIAN EXPANSION 1689–1860

Russian territory in 1689, real control in the east only in patches

Conquests:
- 1699-1725
- 1725-1800
- 1800-1815
- 1815-1860

For Western Russia see also maps 101 and 120

Below: An allegorical colour print offers a satirical explanation for the Crimean War: The Tsarist eagle is putting Turkey in its cage.

Below right: The Scottish Guard charges at Alma in the first battle of the Crimean War, September 20, 1854. The allies – Turkey, France and Great Britain – had only limited forces at their disposal, but defeated the Russians all the same.

Left: The promenade along the Neva in St. Petersburg, Russia's capital 1712–1918. From a painting by Carl Beggrow from the middle of the 1800s. In the foreground is the old Hermitage Museum, built 1771–81, in the background the Hermitage Theatre from 1783–87.

The Crimean War 1853–56

In 1853 the Russians moved into Moldavia and Wallachia (map nr. 141, p. 101). Turkey declared war on Russia in October, and in March of 1854, Great Britain and France entered the war on the side of Turkey. The war was the first to get broad press coverage, and one figure to receive well deserved notice was the British nurse, Florence Nightingale for her contribution. Russia had to capitulate, and March 30, 1856 a peace was reached in Paris.

THE CRIMEAN WAR 1853–56 89

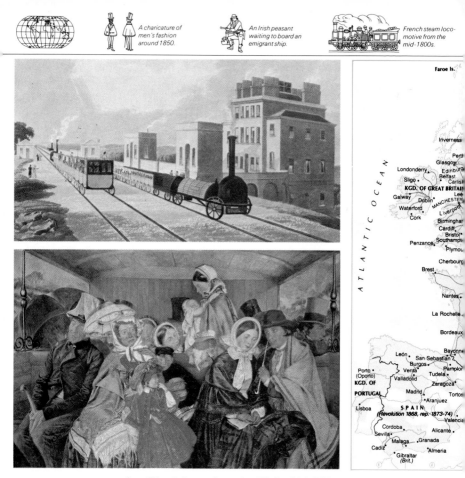

Faroe Is.

ATLANTIC OCEAN

Inverness

Perth
Glasgow
Londonderry, Edinburg
Sligo, Belfast
Galway KGD. OF GREAT BRITAIN
Dublin MANCHESTER Lee
Waterford Liverpool
Cork Birmingham
Cardiff
Bristol
Penzance, Southampton
Plymouth

Cherbourg

Brest

Nantes

La Rochelle

Bordeaux

Bayonne
León San Sebastián
Burgos Pamplor
Porto Venta Tudela
(Oporto) Valladolid Zaragoza
KGD. OF Madrid Tortos
PORTUGAL ,Aranjuez
Lisboa SPAIN
(Revolution 1868, rep. 1873-74) Valencia

Cordoba Alicante
Sevilla, Almeria
Malaga, Granada
Cadiz Gibraltar
(Brit.)

The Railways

must be seen as one of the most revolutionary innovations of the 19th century. But like so many other inventions, it too had an evolution. For a long time it had been common to use wagons pulled on tracks of wood or iron in the mines, and in the 1770s the Frenchman Joseph Cugnot had constructed a steam-driven wagon. In England, George Stephenson combined these two systems, and in 1814 he had constructed a steam-driven wagon that could pull eight ore cars (see illus. p. 77). The invention was at first not an unqualified success. However, in 1825 Stephenson demonstrated a new locomotive, and showed that it was the transportation system of the future. This took place on a short stretch of track between Stockton and Darlington.

The picture at the top of the page shows the first trains on the Liverpool-Manchester run, which was opened in 1830. During the construction phase a contest had been announced for builders of locomotives. And in the famous trial at Rainhill, George Stephenson won the prize with his locomotive, «The Rocket».

Freight transport on the canal between Liverpool and Manchester took thirty-six hours; the stage coach could cover the distance in 4 1/2 hours. «The Rocket» covered the same distance in under two hours!

In the beginning only short, point-to-point lines were built, but from about 1860, Great Britain, Belgium and some German states began construction of interconnected railway systems. Fifteen years later areas of Austria-Hungary, Italy, Spain and France were also linked to the railway systems in the German Empire, Russia and Romania (map nr. 127).

In 1830 Europe had 316 km of tracks, 279 km of these in Great Britain. In 1865 this had increased to a total of 75 882 km, and ten years later, 142 494 km.

The picture below, from Charles Rossiter's painting «Brighton and Back for 3/6» from 1859, shows a crowded, but inexpensive third class car. Railroad cars of the time had three classes. The least expensive were used by the petty bourgeoisie and the working class.

Right: The world's largest iron-hulled ship at the end of the 1850s, the «Great Eastern», drawn and constructed by British engineer Isambard K. Brunel. Construction of the 207 m long ship – driven by paddle-wheel, propeller and sail – was begun in 1852. September 9, 1859 marked her maiden voyage, which, however, ended in tragedy. An overheated boiler blew up, killing six machinists, and destroying the bow section of the ship. Brunel himself died of a heart attack only days later. The «Great Eastern», which was built to carry 4000 passengers on voyages to India and Australia, was an economic fiasco. Because of the vessel's huge size, it was difficult to fill. Nor did it help matters that the ship was extremely unstable at sea.

American Robert
Fulton's steamship
«Clermont» from
1807.

*Poor children in one
of London's slum
districts in the
1860s.*

*Women's liberation.
German caricature
from 1848.*

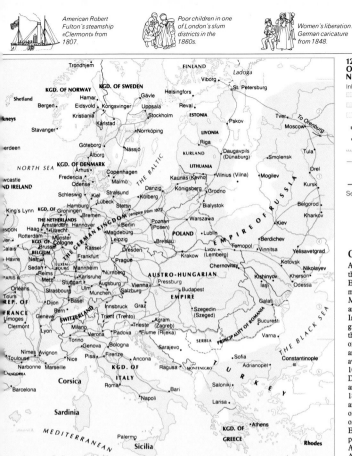

Inhabitants per square kilometre:

More than 100

20-100

Less than 20

- City with more than 1 million inh.: PARIS

· City with 500 000-1 million inh.

Important canal

Railway built 1827-70 (the most important in British Isles and C. Europe are shown).

Frontier

See also map 107

Changes in Population

As seen from the map at the left, there were only four cities in Europe in 1870 with more than a million inhabitants: London and Manchester in Great Britain, Paris and Constantinople (Istanbul).

In Europe – which had by far the greatest population density of all the continents – it was only in parts of Great Britain and Italy, and in areas of Central Europe, that the average density was greater than 100 inhabitants per sq. km.

Due to emigration to the Americas and Australia at the end of the 1800s, the populations of these areas were growing faster than that of Europe. Research has shown that on average the population of Europe grew by 50 percent, 90 percent in South and Central America, 220 percent in North America, and a whopping 300 percent in Australia and Oceania.

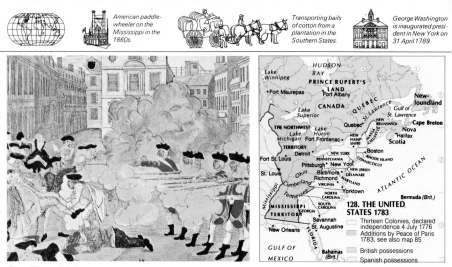

American paddle-wheeler on the Mississippi in the 1860s.

Transporting bails of cotton from a plantation in the Southern States.

George Washington is inaugurated president in New York on 31 April 1789.

Above: The so-called «Boston Massacre», May 5, 1770. From a contemporary copperplate engraving by Paul Revere. Like other illustrators of his day, Revere has dramatized the event in order to strengthen opposition to the British. It began with some youngsters throwing snowballs at two British sentries. The sergeant of the guard was summoned, several adults arrived, a soldier was pushed to the ground, and suddenly shots rang out – five colonists were killed and six wounded. To increase the effect of the picture, Revere has written Butchers Hall over the entrance to the British customs house.

128. THE UNITED STATES 1783

Thirteen Colonies, declared independence 4 July 1776
Additions by Peace of Paris 1783, see also map 85
British possessions
Spanish possessions

The United States Of America (USA) 1783–1867

1783 The final peace treaty following the American war of independence is signed in Paris. The independence of the colonies is recognized, and their territories are expanded (map nr. 128).
1787 A constitutional convention in Philadelphia works out a new constitution.
1789 The constitution is in effect. George Washington becomes the union's first president (see illus. below).
1792 The political parties are formed. Alexander Hamilton and John Adams are in favour of a

strong federal state and form the Federalist Party. Thomas Jefferson, an avid opponent of centralization, founds the Democratic-Republican Party (later the Democratic Party).
1801 Thomas Jefferson takes the oath of office in the new capital of Washington.
1803 The USA purchases Louisiana from France for 80 million francs (map nr. 130, p. 93).
1812–14 War with Great Britain. British Canada's friendly attitude to the indians, who oppose the American government and clash regularly with American settlers moving westward, is one of the reasons for the war. In 1814 the

Below: George Washington (1732–99) was commander of the colonial army from 1775 in the American war of independence, and made such a favourable impression – in Europe as well – that Frederick II of Prussia sent him his portrait with the dedication: «From Europe's oldest general to the world's greatest». After serving as chairman of the committee that was to write a new constitution for the union, Washington was elected first president of the United States of America in 1789. He was reelected in 1792, but firmly refused to run for a third term. This portrait of Washington is from James Sharples' contemporary painting.

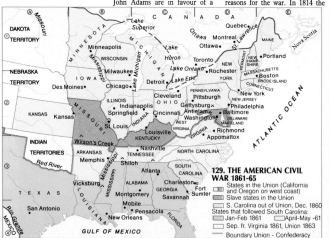

129. THE AMERICAN CIVIL WAR 1861-65

States in the Union (California and Oregon on west coast)
Slave states in the Union
S. Carolina out of Union, Dec. 1860
States that followed South Carolina:
Jan-Feb 1861 / April-May -61
Sep. fr. Virginia 1861, Union 1863
Boundary Union - Confederacy

Slave auction in the
Southern States in
the mid-1800s.

Indian lodge from
the 1790s, built of
logs.

General George
Meade leading the
Northern army at
Gettysburg in 1863.

*Above: The first shots of the
American Civil War were fired by
Confederate forces from
Charleston, South Carolina at Fort
Sumter, which was situated on an
island in the harbour, and manned
by ten Union officers and sixty-five
men. The attack began at dawn on
April 12, 1861, and the next
afternoon – after 3000 shells had
been fired at the fort – the company
surrendered. Only one soldier was
killed at Fort Sumter, but in the four
years the Civil War raged, 650 000
Americans lost their lives, out of a
total population of 30 million. This
is approximately 150 000 more than
America lost during the Second
World War.*

British set fire to the city of Washington. The war ends with old borders still intact.

1819 Spain sells Florida to the USA for five million dollars.

1823 President James Monroe issues the so-called Monroe Doctrine, which states that the USA will consider any attempt on the part of European states to colonize or otherwise interfere in the affairs of the North American continent to be an act of aggression.

1846–48 War with Mexico. Mexico cedes New Mexico and California to the USA.

1860–61 Abraham Lincoln, who

has run on a platform that would abolish slavery, is elected president. Six weeks later – in December of 1860 – South Carolina leaves the union. In the course of the spring, ten other states secede from the union. The eleven states that have seceded form their own union, The Confederate States of America.

1861–65 On April 12 the first shots are fired (see illus. above). In the early years of the war the Southern States are better armed and win important victories, but the North-

ern States have far greater resources. In September 1862 the northern army wins a key victory at Antietam. The following year general George Meade defeats the famous general of the Southern States, Robert E. Lee, at the Battle of Gettysburg. April 9, 1865 Lee surrenders to the Northern States' Ulysses S. Grant at Appomattox.

1867 The USA purchases Alaska from Russia for 7.5 million dollars.

130. THE UNITED STATES 1783-1912

The Thirteen States in 1776

Ceded by Britain 1783

Spain to France 1800, sold to U.S. 1803

Independence from Mexico 1836, annexed by U.S. 1845 Incorporated 1846

Ceded by Mexico 1848

United States (Union) 1861-65,

Confederacy 1861-65

First transcontinental railway, completed 10 May 1869

Dates are year when state was incorporated in the union

A partially veiled peasant girl from South America in the 1830s.

Sout American indians around 1830.

A Mexican military policeman in President Diaz' guard.

Liberation of Spanish America

Beginning in about 1810, Simon Bolivar (1783–1830) was actively engaged in the Latin American struggle for independence. He joined a group in New Granada (map nr. 131), and in 1819 he was made president of Venezuela – the eastern part of New Granada. The same year the western part was also incorporated, and the country of «Gran Colombia» proclaimed (map nr. 132), with Bolivar as its president. In 1822 he liberated present-day Ecuador, which also became a part of Gran Colombia. He then took part in Peru's struggle for liberation, and the northern part of the country – Bolivia – is named after him. In 1824 Spanish hegemony in South America came to an end. **The picture** of Bolivar, **top left**, is from a contemporary painting.

United States Intervention in Cuba 1898

Because the United States wanted to strengthen its Pacific fleet in the 1890s, it wanted to take on the construction and administration of the Panama Canal. To accomplish this, the U.S. would also have to control the Caribbean. Just such an opportunity presented itself in 1895 when Cuba rebelled against Spanish rule. There was an immediate cry to «come to the aid of Cuba,» and in 1898 the U.S. declared war on Spain. Within a few months the Spanish had been driven out of Cuba. **The picture below** shows Theodore (Teddy) Roosevelt, leading his «Rough Riders». In 1900 he became vice president, and following the assassination of president William McKinley in 1901, Roosevelt became president.

131. SPANISH - PORTUGUESE AMERICA 1790

Colony of: Spain, Portugal, France, Netherl., Gr. Britain

Argentinian «gau-chos», drovers, at the beginning of the 1800s.

A female Mexican revolutionary soldier from the end of the 1800s.

French officers in Mexico in 1863.

Mexico 1519–1911

1519–21 N. part of Spanish America, the Viceroyalty of New Spain (map nr. 131) is taken from the Aztecs and Toltecs (see p. 63).

17th and 18th centuries Growing unrest between Spanish civil servants and the Spanish colonists.

1810–24 The War of Independence against the Spanish begins in 1810. In 1821 Augustin de Iturbide proclaims himself emperor, but has to step down in 1823. The following year Mexico becomes a federal republic.

1845–58 Following a war of liberation Texas declares its independence, and is incorporated by the U.S. in 1845 (map nr. 130, p. 93). American activities in the northwestern territories lead to war with the U.S. The Americans take Mexico City in 1848. California becomes an American state in 1850, and three years later the Americans purchase a small area in present-day Arizona (map nr. 130, p. 93). The indian Benito Juarez becomes president of Mexico in 1858.

1861–67 Sends French troops to Mexico. The Austrian archduke Maximilian is installed as emperor in 1864, but when the French have withdrawn, he is shot on June 19, 1867. Juarez becomes the country's leader again, and remains so until his death in 1872.

1877–1911 President Porfirio Diaz – who in the **picture top right on the previous page** is seen in the company of money-grubbing captains of industry during a dance recital – is supported by the army and the estate owners, and gives foreign capital a free hand. Following a revolution in 1911, Diaz goes into exile in Paris.

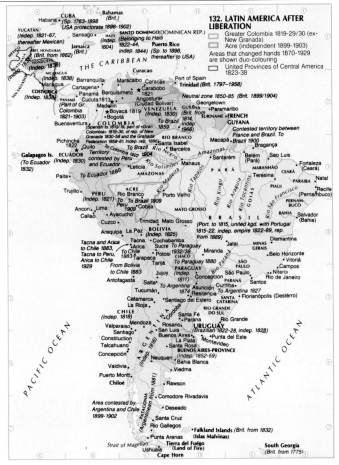

132. LATIN AMERICA AFTER LIBERATION

☐ Greater Colombia 1819-29/30 (ex-New Granada)
☐ Acre (independent 1899-1903)
Areas that changed hands 1870-1929 are shown duo-colouring
☐ United Provinces of Central America 1823-38

Argentina 1776–1842

1776 Spain establishes the viceroyalty of Rio de la Plata (map nr. 131, p. 94).

1806–07 A British force of 10 000 men occupies Montevideo and advances toward Buenos Aires. They are stopped and forced to withdraw.

1810 The province of Buenos Aires refuses to submit to Spanish rule.

1816 The province of Rio de la Plata declares its independence.

1826 Argentina a republic.

1842 Spain recognizes the country's independence.

Brazil 1549–1822

1549 A Portuguese colony since 1500, gets governor general. Bahia (Sao Salvador) becomes governor's residence. The Jesuits begin missionizing among the indians.

1750–77 The Jesuits are driven from the country. Rio de Janeiro becomes the new capital in 1762.

1815 Independent monarchy, governed by Portuguese crown regent John VI, whom Napoleon has exiled.

1822 John's son, Pedro I, becomes emperor of an independent Brazil.

Right: German naturalist and geographer Alexander von Humboldt (1769–1859). From a contemporary painting. From the summer of 1799 to early 1804 Humboldt made an epoch-making journey in South America together with Aimé Bonpland. And in 1805 started work on a thirty volume work, «Voyage aux régions équinoxiales du nouveau continent», which it took thirty years to complete. Humboldt undertook several voyages of exploration later, and there are over a thousand geographic locations around the world that he named.

British cavalryman in wood, made by an African in the 1800s.

Woman with child is put on the auction block in Marrakesh in 1905.

Livingstone (at left) and Stanley meet in Ujiji in the spring of 1871.

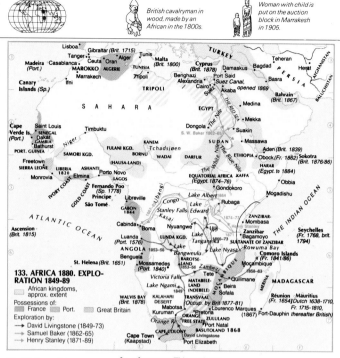

133. AFRICA 1880. EXPLORATION 1849-89

African kingdoms, approx. extent

Possessions of:
France   Port.   Great Britain

Exploration by:
→ David Livingstone (1849-73)
→ Samuel Baker (1862-65)
→ Henry Stanley (1871-89)

The Nations of the Barbary Coast,

or the **Pirate States**, as they were also known, was an older name for Morocco, Algeria, Tunisia and Libya (map nr. 103, p. 72). They made their living, quite simply, through piracy, and the tribute paid for safe passage. This continued until the French drove the Turks from the area.

Algeria was conquered in the 1830s, but as the map below indicates, it was some time before the French gained control over the whole country. **Tunisia** was a French protectorate from 1881, and **Morocco** was slowly subjugated by the French in the period 1906-34. **Libya** became an Italian colony in 1912.

The influx of Europeans was great, especially in Algeria, where in 1906 there were already 450 000 Frenchmen.

Livingstone and Stanley

The Scottish physician and missionary David Livingstone (1813-73) travelled as a missionary at age twenty-seven to Southern Africa.

In 1841 he reached Bechuanaland, where he practised as doctor and missionary for eight years before beginning his long trek northward. He established a number of mission stations and began his struggle against the extensive slave trade in the interior of Africa.

In 1852 he sent his family home and set off alone on his first great exploration westward. The map above shows his next two expeditions as well (1858-64 and 1866-73). It was during this last journey, to the area around Lake Tanganyika in search of the source of the Nile, that contact with Livingstone was lost. In 1869 the English-born American journalist Henry Morton Stanley (1841-1904) was ordered by his editor in chief to find Livingstone, «no matter what the cost.» In March 1871 he started out from Zanzibar, and in early November Stanley reached Ujiji. It was there he caught sight of a man who looked as though he could be Livingstone and uttered the line of the century: «Dr. Livingstone, I presume.» The missionary's strength was failing, and he died on May 1, 1873.

Stanley, who remained with Livingstone for four or five months, later explored the upper Congo River, founded the Free State of the Congo and stayed on as its governor. The portrait of him at the **top of the page** was painted by his wife in 1893.

134. FRENCH CONQUEST OF ALGERIA 1830-1902

Conquests in:
1830-35   1871-1900
1836-47   After 1900
1848-70   — Present-day boundary

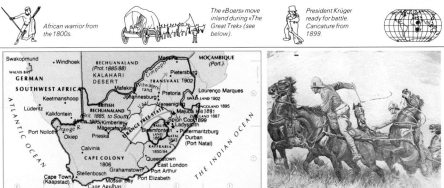

African warrior from the 1800s.

The «Boers» move inland during «The Great Trek» (see below).

President Krüger ready for battle. Caricature from 1899.

135. SOUTHERN AFRICA 1899–1910

- British colony or protectorate 1899
- Boer republic
- — Union of South Africa, 1910
- → The Great Trek, 1836
- ★ Battlefield

Dates indicate year of British occupation

The Sudan Becomes British

The northern Sudan was occupied by Egypt in 1821. In spite of African resistance, Egyptians and Europeans carried on an extensive slave trade in the years that followed. But in 1881 the Islamic people under the Mahdi rebelled and ousted their foreign rulers. At the end of the century British and Egyptian troops advanced southward to retake the Sudan. **The picture below** shows a scene from the decisive battle at Omdurman, September 2, 1898. Ca. 20 000 Englishmen, led by general Herbert Kitchener, and armed with modern weapons, including machine guns that could shoot nearly 700 rounds per minute, met 50 000 tribal warriors, armed with spears and old rifles. In just a few short hours, the «executions» were over. Around half of the natives had been cut down, with 11 000 dead. The British lost 386 men.

The Boers and the Boer War 1899–1902

After the Cape Colony had changed hands from Dutch to British in 1806, the white farmers, who in Dutch were called «Boers», began to leave. In 1836 began the «Great Trek» northeastward into the interior. There they established the two Boer republics: Transvaal in 1852, and the Orange Free State in 1854 (map nr. 135).

The British hoped to include the Boers in a South African union under British dominion, but the Boers were not interested. The rich gold deposits discovered in Transvaal in 1886 did nothing to reduce the British appetite for the territories. In the autumn of 1899 the British increased troop strength in South Africa, and when they rejected an ultimatum from Transvaal president Paul Krer to withdraw these forces, the Boers attacked. Both Mafeking and Kimberley in British Bechuanaland were besieged. Great Britain sent large numbers of reinforcements to South Africa, and in the summer of 1900 the British took Johannesburg, Pretoria and Bloemfontain.

Some months later the two states were annexed, but the Boers continued a guerilla war that led the British to take very unconventional countermeasures. They established concentration camps in which conditions were so appalling that it even aroused disgust at home in Britain. As a condition of the peace in 1902, the Boers were forced to recognize British hegemony.

The picture at the top of the page shows horses, pulling a canon into position during the war. From a contemporary painting by George Scott.

136. AFRICA 1914

Colony of:
- Belgium
- France
- Italy
- Portugal
- Spain
- Great Britain
- Turkey
- Germany

Dates indicate year of occupation
- Independent state

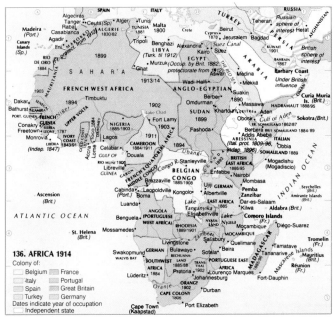

Little girl from the mid-1800s, fashionably dressed.

Two British soldiers during a parade for Queen Victoria.

Unemployed British worker around 1850.

137. IMPERIALISM IN ASIA AND AUSTRALIA 1850-1914

- Russia 1850
- Russian conquests 1850-1914
- Colony of:
  - Great Britain
  - France
  - Japan
  - United States
  - Netherlands
  - Germany
- **1859** Dates indicate year of occupation
- Railway
- Shipping route (Suez Canal opened 1869)

Two of the British Empire's foremost figures. Top: Queen Victoria, reproduced from a portrait in «The Times» on the day that marked her 60th year on the British throne, June 21, 1897. Not only did Victoria lend her name to the zenith of British imperial history, but also to the period style in architecture, art and literature. She was a strong-willed regent, who often protested against the decisions of her prime ministers. This was especially bothersome for William Ewart Gladstone, seen below. He served four terms as prime minister between 1864 and 1894.

Imperialism

The maps on this placard illustrate the colossal European expansion in other parts of the world at the end of the 19th century.

At the time of Queen Victoria's diamond anniversary, for example, the British Empire included a quarter of the world's population. It was four times larger than the Roman Empire had been.

138. THE BRITISH EMPIRE 1815-1914

- 1815
- 1914

Colonies in 1815 lost before 1914 are not shown

British troops employed elephants during battles in India.

Disraeli hands Victoria the imperial crown of India.

India got its first railway in the 1850s. constructed by the British.

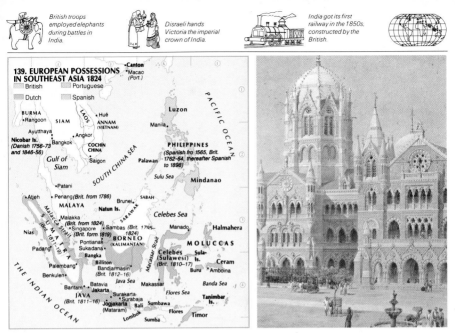

139. EUROPEAN POSSESSIONS IN SOUTHEAST ASIA 1824

- British
- Portuguese
- Dutch
- Spanish

•Canton
•Macao (Port.)

BURMA
•Rangoon   SIAM   LAOS   •Hué   ANNAM (VIETNAM)   Luzon
Ayutthaya   •Angkor   COCHIN CHINA   Manila   •   PACIFIC OCEAN
Nicobar Is. (Danish 1756-73 and 1846-56)   •Bangkok
Gulf of Siam   Saigon   Palawan   PHILIPPINES (Spanish fro 1565, Brit. 1762-64, thereafter Spanish to 1898)
•Patani   Sulu Sea   Mindanao
•Atjeh   •Penang (Brit. from 1786)   Brunei   SABAH
MALAYA   Natun Is.   SARAWAK   Celebes Sea
Nias   Malakka (Brit. from 1824)   •Singapore (Brit. form 1819)   •Sambas (Brit. 1795-1824)   Manado   Halmahera
Padang   Pontianak   BORNEO (KALIMANTAN)   MOLUCCAS
Palembang•   Sukadana   Celebes (Sulawesi) (Brit. 1810-17)   Sula Is.   Ceram
Bangka   Bandjarmasin (Brit. 1812-16)   Buru   •Amboina
Benkulen•   Billiton   Makassar   Banda Sea
Bantam•   Batavia   Jakarta   Java Sea   Flores Sea   Tanimbar Is.
JAVA (Brit. 1811-16)   Surakarta•   •Surabaja   Sumbawa
Jogjakarta (Mataram)   Bali   Flores   Timor
Lombok   Sumba

SUMATRA (Brit. 1811-91)
THE INDIAN OCEAN

THE COLONIZING OF INDIA 99

Top right: Bombay's magnificent and luxuriously decorated Victoria Station from 1877–87. Looking more like a cathedral than the headquarters of the Indian Railways, it is an impressive symbol of British hegemony in India.

India 1756–1885

1756–63 Robert Clive drives the French out of India. The British East India Company takes power in many parts of the country.

1857–59 An Indian uprising, the Sepoy Rebellion (known to Indians as the First War of Liberation), is put down. The administration of India is transferred from the East India Company to the British Crown.

1877 India becomes an empire, with Victoria as empress.

1885 The Indian Congress Party is formed and advances the struggle for India's liberation.

140. THE COLONISATION OF INDIA 1765-1914

- British colonies in 1765
- Additions 1765-1858
- British colonies in 1914
- British subject states 1914, under Viceroy or Indian administration
- Boundary of British India 1914 (Indian Empire from 1877)
- **1883** Dates indicate year of colonisation

RUSSIA
Balkh   CHINA
Herat   AFGHANISTAN   Hindukush   1893   Kabul   Peshawar   KASHMIR 1846
Kandahar   Khyber Pass   Rawalpindi   Srinagar   TIBET (Chinese protectorate from 1720)
1893   1890   PANTAR 1849   •Amritsar   Lahsa
BALUCHISTAN   1876   •Multan   Lahore   1815   NEPAL   Brahmaputra
Gwador (Oman)   Shikarpur   Bikaner   1803   •Delhi   Kathmandu   Darjeeling   SIKKIM   BHUTAN   Contested area   •Sadva
Ormara   SIND   Hyderabad   1843   Jodhpur   RAJPUTANA   Jaipur   Agra   OUUH   Lucknow   Buxar 1764   ASSAM   •Kohima
Karachi   Ajmer   Gwalior   Kanpur   1856   Benares•   Patna   BIHAR   1765   Shillong   IMPHAL   MANIPUR   Bhamo
MAHRATS   Ahmadabad   Chamba   1757   Plassey   BENGAL   Dacca   Chittagong   BURMA 1886   Mandalay
GUJRAT   Narbada   Chandernagore (Fr.)   Calcutta   Akyab   Ava
Diu (Port.)   Surat   1854   Rajpul   ORISSA   Cuttack   PEGU 1852
Daman (Port.)   Baroda   BERAR 1860   Nagpur   Rangoon   SIAM
Bombay 1661   Poona   Godavari   BASTAR   •Visakhapatnam   Bassein   Moulmein
Satara   HYDERABAD (NIZAM)   Yanaon (Yanam) (Fr.)
Goa (Port.)   Hyderabad   1800   Krishna   •Masulipatnam   BAY OF BENGAL
Penner   Nellore   COROMANDEL COAST   Andaman Is. (Brit. 1789-96 and from 1858)
Mangalore•   MYSORE   1800   •Madras
Laccadives   Bangalore•   •Mysore   Pondichéry (Fr.)
(Brit. 1791/1855)   Mahé (Fr.)   Calicut   Trichin-opoly   Tranquebar (Danish 1620-1845)
MALABAR COAST   Cochin   1801   •Madura   Karikal (Fr.)   Nicobar Is. 1869
Cape Comorin   TRAVAN-CORE   Trincomalee   MALACCA PENINSULA
Maldives   Kandy   CEYLON (SRI LANKA)
(Brit. 1796/1815)   Colombo   (Dutch 1658-1795, Brit. from 1802/15)   Galle

THE ARABIAN SEA
THE INDIAN OCEAN

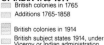

THE COLONIZING OF INDIA 99

Many Russian soldiers froze to death during the campaign in the Balkans.

A flower girl in London in 1888.

Two telegraphists a the main telegraph station in London in 1872.

Above: *Otto von Bismarck (1815–98). From a contemporary painting by Franz von Lenbach. Prince Bismarck, who created the first unified German state in 1871, held on to his position of power for almost twenty years.*

Below: *November 21, 1783 marked the first flight of an untethered hot-air balloon with passengers on board. The event, reproduced in this lithograph, took place in the Boulogne Forest in Paris. It was the brothers Joseph and Étienne Montgolfier who had constructed the balloon, later known as the Montgolfier.*

Unrest in the Christian States of the Baltic in the 1870s

In the summer of 1875 the people of Herzegovina rebelled against their Turkish overlords. The unrest soon spread to Bosnia, and in the spring of 1876 the Bulgarians joined the revolt. In response the Turks murdered in all 12 000 of the country's men, women, and children.

On June 30 Serbia declared war on Turkey, and a few days later Montenegro followed suit. By September 1 they had been defeated by Osman Pasha's forces. The following week William Gladstone wrote his sharp and angry pamphlet: «The Bulgarian Horrors and the Question of the East».

Tzar Alexander II decided to come to the rescue of the Balkan states, but first he let Austria know he would not oppose an Austrian occupation of Bosnia and Herzegovina. In April 1877 Russia declared war on Turkey.

Surprisingly, on the way to Constantinople the Russians were stopped by the Turks near Plevna. 14 000 Turks held off a superior Russian-Bulgarian force from July 20 to December 10, 1877.

After a hard winter in the Balkan Mountains the Russians were able to make it over the Shipka Pass and advance on Constantinople.

Then, on February 15, 1878, divisi-

141. SOUTHEASTERN EUROPE AFTER THE CONGRESS OF BERLIN 1878

— Ottoman Empire's boundary before prel. Peace of San Stefano in March 1878

---- Northern boundary of Ottoman tributary states

▨ Ottoman Empire after Congress of Berlin
Greater Bulgaria after preliminary Peace of San Stefano in March 1878

▨ Occupied by Austria-Hungary 1878

······ Boundaries before 1878. Areas duo-coloured changed hands by Congress of Berlin

ons of the British navy arrived in Constantinople, which meant that the Russian supply lines could now be interrupted at short notice. Both the Turks and the Russians now preferred to make peace. It was concluded in San Stephano in March 1878. At the insistence of Russia, one result of the war was the establishment of Greater Bulgaria (map nr. 141). The fact that this gave Russia access to the Aegean was equally troubling to both Great Britain and Austria. Bismarck took on the role of mediator and summoned all the relevant parties to

The Congress of Berlin

It was assembled for a month, beginning June 13 1878, and resulted in Greater Bulgaria being divided in three parts. Macedonia was once again Turkish, and Bulgaria and East Rumelia were under Turkish dominion. The Russians got Bessarabia and Batum. Yet, the fact that Austria's occupation of Bosnia and Herzegovina was accepted, sowed the seeds of the conflict that would throw the entire world into war in the summer of 1914 (see p. 103).

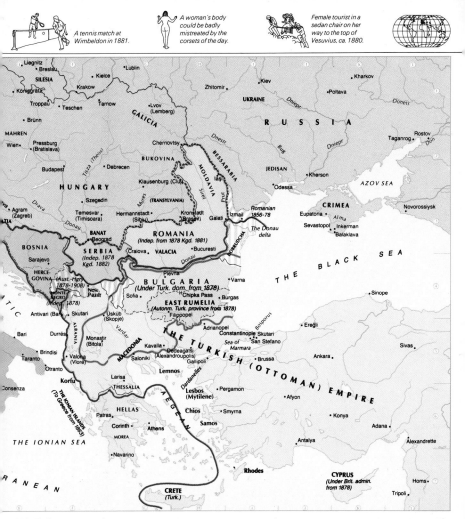

A tennis match at Wimbeldon in 1881.

A woman's body could be badly mistreated by the corsets of the day.

Female tourist in a sedan chair on her way to the top of Vesuvius, ca. 1880.

Liegnitz
Breslau
SILESIA
Königgrätz
Troppau · Teschen
MÄHREN
Wien ·
Pressburg
(Bratislava)

Lublin
Kielce
Krakow
Tarnow
Lvov
(Lemberg)

GALICIA

Zhitomir

Kiev

UKRAINE

Kharkov

Poltava

Dniepr

R U S S I A

Dnestr

Bug

Dniepr

Donets

Taganrog

Rostov

Don

Chernovtsy

BUKOVINA

BESSARABIA

JEDISAN

Kherson

AZOV SEA

Novorossiysk

Brünn

Budapest

Debrecen

Klausenburg (Cluj)

MOLDAVIA

Iaşi

H U N G A R Y

Szegedin

(TRANSYLVANIA)

Mureş

Sirei

Prut

Odessa

CRIMEA

Eupatoria

Alma

Temesvár (Timişoara)

Hermannstadt (Sibiu)

Kronstadt (Braşov)

Galati

Izmail

Romanian 1856-78

Sevastopol

Inkerman

Balaklava

Sinope

Agram (Zagreb)

Drava

Donau

BANAT

Beograd

ROMANIA

(Indep. from 1878 Kgd. 1881)

Bucuresti

DOBRUDCHA

The Donau delta

Craiova

VALACIA

BOSNIA

Sarajevo

SERBIA

(Indep. 1878 Kgd. 1882)

Donau

Plevna

Varna

T H E   B L A C K   S E A

HERCE-GOVINA

(Aust.-Hgry. 1878-1908)

MONTE-NEGRO

(Indep. 1878)

Nov. Pazar

BULGARIA

(Under Turk. dom. from 1878)

Sofia

Chipka Pass

Burgas

Antivari (Bar)

Skutari

EAST RUMELIA

(Autonm. Turk. province from 1878)

Filippopel

Durrës

ALBANIA

Uskûb (Skopje)

Adrianopel

Constantinople Skutari

Ereğli

Sivas

Bari

Brindisi

Taranto

Valona (Vlore)

MACEDONIA

Vardar

Monastir (Bitola)

Kavalla

Saloniki

Oedeagatsi (Alexandroupolis)

Gallipoli

Sea of Marmara

San Stefano

Brussa

Ankara

Otranto

Korfu

THESSALIA

Larisa

Lemnos

Dardanelles

T H E   T U R K I S H   (O T T O M A N)   E M P I R E

Consenza

THE IONIAN ISLANDS

(To Greece from 1863)

HELLAS

Patras

Corinth

Athens

MOREA

Samos

Navarino

Pergamon

Lesbos (Mytilene)

Chios

Smyrna

Afyon

Konya

Adana

Alexandrette

A E G E A N

THE IONIAN SEA

RANEAN

Rhodes

CYPRUS

(Under Brit. admin. from 1878)

Antalya

Homs

CRETE

(Turk.)

Tripoli

Right: *The foremost statesmen in Europe met in 1878 at the Congress of Berlin, led by Otto von Bismarck, seen here sitting with his back to the centre window. In front of the window at the left sits the British foreign minister, Lord Salisbury, and Prime Minister Benjamin Disraeli, who together with Bismarck played the most important role in the congress. The Russian delegation is sitting at the end of the table on the left, with the Turks opposite at the table on the right. Members of the delegation from Austria-Hungary are sitting on Bismarck's right, and the French on his left.*

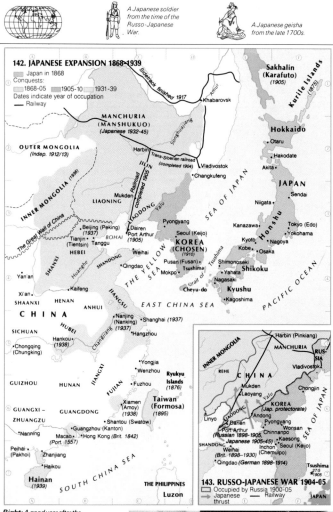

142. JAPANESE EXPANSION 1868-1939

- Japan in 1868
- Conquests:
  - 1868-05
  - 1905-10
  - 1931-39
- Dates indicate year of occupation.
- — Railway

Sakhalin (Karafuto) (1905)

Kurile Islands (1875)

Sibirisk finished 1917

Khabarovsk

MANCHURIA (MANSHUKUO) (Japanese 1932-45)

Songhuajiang

Amur

Hokkaido

Otaru

Hakodate

Akita

OUTER MONGOLIA (Indep. 1912/13)

Harbin

Trans-Siberian railroad (completed 1904)

Vladivostok

JILIN

Changfengeng

JAPAN

SEA OF JAPAN

Sendai

INNER MONGOLIA (1936)

LIAODONG Railroad completed 1905

Mukden

LIAONING

The Great Wall of China

Beijing (Peking) (1937)

Tianjin (Tientsin) Tanggu

Dairen Port Arthur (1905)

Yalu

Pyongyang

Seoul (Keijo)

Kanazawa

Niigata

Tokyo (Edo)

Yokohama

HEBEI

Weihai

Kyoto

Nagoya

Kobe

Osaka

Honshu

SHANXI

Qingdao

SHANDONG

Huanghe

THE YELLOW SEA

KOREA (CHOSEN) (1910)

Pusan (Fusan)

Tsushima

Shimonoseki

Yahata

Shikoku

Yan'an

Kaifeng

JIANGSU

Mokpo

Nagasaki

Strait of Tsushima

Kyushu

Xi'an

SHAANXI

HENAN

ANHUI

EAST CHINA SEA

Cheju-do

Kagoshima

PACIFIC OCEAN

CHINA

HUBEI

Nanjing (Nanking)

Shanghai (1937)

SICHUAN

Hankou (1938)

Hangzhou

Chongqing (Chungking)

Changjiang

JIANGXI

Yongjia

Wenzhou

Ryukyu Islands (1876)

GUIZHOU

HUNAN

FUJIAN

Fuzhou

GUANGXI – ZHUANGZU

GUANGDONG

Xiamen (Amoy) (1938)

Taiwan (Formosa) (1895)

Shantou (Swatow)

Nanning

Guangzhou (Kanton)

Macao (Port. 1557)

Hong Kong (Brit. 1842)

Peihai (Pakhoi)

Zhanjiang

Haikou

SOUTH CHINA SEA

Hainan (1939)

THE PHILIPPINES

Luzon

143. RUSSO-JAPANESE WAR 1904-05

- Occupied by Russia 1900-05
- → Japanese thrust
- — Railway

Harbin (Pinkiang)

INNER MONGOLIA

MANCHURIA

RUSSIA

Vladivostok

REHE

CHINA

Mukden

Laoyang

Yalu

LIAODONG

Chongjin

Linyo

Port Arthur

Dairen

KOREA (Jap. protectorate)

Andong

Pyongyang

Wonsan

Chinnanpo

Kaesong

SEA OF JAPAN

SHANDONG

Weihai (Brit. 1898-1930)

Korea 1905-45

Inchon (Chemulpo)

Seoul (Keijo)

Qingdao (German 1898-1914)

Tsushima 27.5 1905

JAPAN

Japan 1867–1939

1867–69 The Shogunate is abolished and replaced by a strong imperial system with Meiji Mutsuhito (1852–1912) on the throne. End of feudalism. The Damyos (noblemen) voluntarily transfer their territories to the emperor.

1875–76 Russia recognizes Japan's rights to the Kuriles (1875) and the Ryukyu Islands (1876).

1889 New constitution, based on Prussian model, but real power is retained by the emperor.

1894–95 China forced to cede Taiwan (Formosa).

1904–05 Japan declares war on Russia February 10, 1904. Russians suffer enormous losses. Following the battle in the Strait of Tsushima (illus. below), Russia has to capitulate. Japan gains hegemony over Port Arthur and Sakhalin.

1910 Korea (Chosen) becomes Japanese province.

1914–18 During WW1, the country takes part on the side of the Entente powers (Great Britain/ France).

1919 At Versailles, Japan receives the German possessions on the Shandong Peninsula, and the German islands in the Pacific that Japan occupied during the war. Occupied territories in China and Russia must be abandoned.

1931–33 Manchuria is taken and made the Protectorate of Mandshukuo (1931–32). When the League of Nations condemns the action, Japan withdraws its membership in the League (1933).

1936 Japan signs anti-Comintern pact with Germany. Later, Italy also joins the pact.

1937 Japan attacks China again, with great success, but in spite of military superiority, Japan is unable to crush Chinese resistance.

1939 The USA revokes its trade agreement with Japan.

Right: A good year after the outbreak of the Russo-Japanese War – May 27, 1905 – the Russian fleet, having sailed halfway round the world, was nearly annihilated in the Strait of Tsushima. It was all over in less than an hour. Of a combined Russian force of twenty-nine ships, only two destroyers and a light cruiser managed to escape. The Japanese lost a total of three torpedo-boats, and had only 117 casualties, compared to the Russians' 4830. Seen here is a Japanese cruiser. That a small Asiatic people had crushed an arrogant, white colossus, was a shock to many.

144. SOUTHEASTERN EUROPE AFTER THE BALKAN WARS 1912-13
—— Ottoman Empire's western boundary in 1912

The Balkan Wars 1912–13 and the Assassination in Sarajevo 1914

October 8, 1912 Montenegro declared war on Turkey. Within a week, Serbia, Bulgaria and Greece had been drawn into the war. By December 3 a cease-fire had already been reached, after the Balkan states had been victorious on all fronts. At the peace of London on May 30, 1913, Turkey was forced to give up all her European territories, with the exception of those nearest Constantinople. Albania became an independent state.

Bulgaria was dissatisfied with her acquisitions, and only a month after the peace went to war against a Serbian and Greek alliance. Romania joined on the side of Greece and Serbia. Turkey attacked Bulgaria as well.

In August 1913 a peace agreement was reached in Bucharest. Turkey broadened her European bridgehead, Romania received a smaller Bulgarian territory on the Black Sea, while Greece and Serbia divided the greater part of Macedonia between them (map nr. 144). Austria was worried that a stronger Serbia had become a focal point for Slavic nationalism.

In June of the next year the Serbian ambassador in Vienna warned the Austrian government against a visit by Arch-Duke Franz Ferdinand to Bosnia. He suspected that Serbian nationalists had planned an assassination. The warning was ignored, and on June 28 the Austrian crown prince and his wife were shot by a Bosnian student, Gavrilo Princip, in the capital of Sarajevo (illus. at left), triggering the First World War.

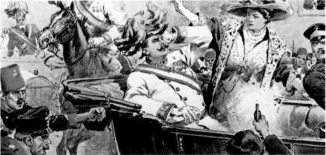

The Near East 1907–14

1907 After years of bitter struggle between Russia and Great Britain in **Persia (Iran)** the country is partitioned into spheres of influence (map nr. 145). Russia also accepts Brit. hegemony in Afghanistan, with India overseeing its foreign policy.

1908 In a coup d'etat in the **Turkish (Ottoman) Empire** students and officers («young Turks») depose the sultan.

1911–12 In the war with the Turks, the Italians occupy **Libya**, which after the peace of Ouchy at Lausanne (1912) becomes an Italian colony.

1912 Egypt, which has been occupied by the British since 1882, becomes a British protectorate.

145. MIDDLE EAST 1914
The Ottoman Empire
British
French

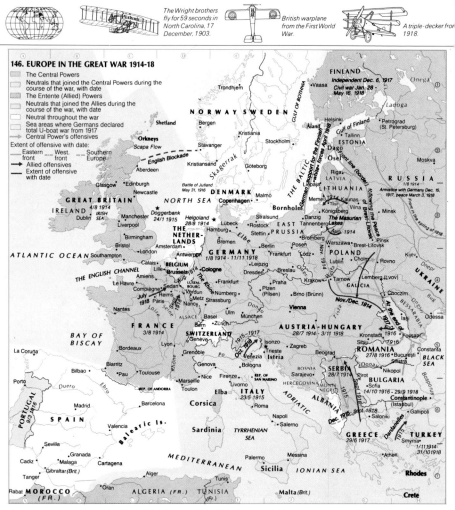

The Wright brothers fly for 59 seconds in North Carolina, 17 December, 1903.

British warplane from the First World War.

A triple-decker from 1918.

146. EUROPE IN THE GREAT WAR 1914-18

- The Central Powers
- Neutrals that joined the Central Powers during the course of the war, with date
- The Entente (Allied) Powers
- Neutrals that joined the Allies during the course of the war, with date
- Neutral throughout the war
- Sea areas where Germans declared total U-boat war from 1917
- Central Power's offensives

Extent of offensive with date:
- Eastern front
- West. front
- Southern Europe
- → Allied offensives
- — Extent of offensive with date

FINLAND
Independent Dec. 6, 1917
Civil War Jan. 28 – May 16, 1918

NORWAY SWEDEN

GULF OF BOTHNIA

German support for the Finnish white forces April 1918

Onega

Ladoga

Trondhjem

Vaasa

Åland

Helsinki

Gulf of Finland

Petrograd (St. Petersburg)

ESTONIA

Tallinn

Dagö Ösel new line (border)

Moskva

Bergen

Kristiania

Stockholm

Riga

LATVIA

Liepāja

RUSSIA

1/8 1914

Armistice following peace Dec. 15, 1917, peace March 3, 1918

Front in the spring of 1917

Shetland

Orkneys
Scapa Flow

Stavanger

Kristiansand

Göteborg

THE BALTIC

Skagerrak

Memel

LITHUANIA

1914 Kaunas

Vilna

Minsk

Glasgow • Edinburgh

Battle of Jutland
May 31, 1916

DENMARK

Malmö

Bornholm

Königsberg

The Masurian Lakes

Aug. 1914

Front at the end of Peace of Brest-Litovsk

English Blockade

Newcastle

NORTH SEA

Copenhagen

GREAT BRITAIN

IRELAND
4/8 1914

IRISH SEA

Dublin

Manchester • Liverpool

Doggerbank
24/1 1915

Heligoland
28/8 1914

EAST PRUSSIA

Danzig

Tannenberg

Aug. 1914

Bromberg

Warszawa

Brest-Litovsk

Pinsk

Kijev

UKRAINE

Birmingham

THE NETHER-LANDS

Stralsund

Rostock

Lübeck

Hamburg

Stettin

Poznań

Łódź

POLAND

Lublin

Chołm

Rovno

Bristol • London

Southampton

Amsterdam

Bremen

Berlin

Frankfurt

Breslau

1914

Kraków

Tarnow

Lemberg (Lvov)

GALICIA

ATLANTIC OCEAN

THE ENGLISH CHANNEL

Calais

BELGIUM

Brussels

1914

Cologne

THE Rhine

Frankfurt

Dresden

Leipzig

Praha
(Prague)

Plzeň
(Pilsen)

Brno (Brünn)

Nov./Dec. 1914

Choczim

Dnjestr

Odessa

Iaşi

BESSARABIA

Le Havre

Lille

Amiens

LUXEM-BOURG

Aug.

Sedan

Compiègne

Reims

Verdun

Metz

Strassburg

Nürnberg

Donau

Vienna

Tisza

Nantes

July 1918

Paris

Seine

Nancy

ALSACE

Basel

Ulm

München

AUSTRIA-HUNGARY
28/7 1914 – 3/11 1918

Nov./Dec. 1914

Kronstadt 1916

Sibiu

1916

Focşani

Constanţa

FRANCE
3/8 1914

Loire

SWITZERLAND

Genève

Bern

Zürich

1915–1917

Isonzo

Istria

Trieste

Zagreb

Beograd

ROMANIA
27/8 1916

Bucureşti

Smîrdan

BLACK SEA

BAY OF BISCAY

Lyon

Grenoble

Oct. 1918

Po

Venezia

Bologna

BOSNIA

Sarajevo

SERBIA
28/7 1914

Nikopol

Sofia

Constanţa

Bordeaux

Biarritz

Pau

Toulouse

Rhône

Marseille

Nice

Firenze

Livorno

Roma

HERCEGOVINA

MONTE-NEGRO

1915

Pirot

BULGARIA
14/10 1916 – 29/9 1918

Sofia

Constantinople
(Istanbul)

Bosporus

Gallipoli

La Coruña

Bilbao

Porto

Duero

Madrid

Barcelona

Valencia

REP. OF ANDORRA

Toulon

Elba

Corsica

ITALY
23/5 1915

Napoli

Salerno

ADRIATIC

ALBANIA

Dec. 1915

Sept. 1918

Saloniki

Dardanelles
1915

GREECE
29/6 1917

TURKEY
1/11 1914 – 31/10 1918

Smyrna

PORTUGAL
9/3 1916

SPAIN

Balearic Is.

Sardinia

TYRRHENIAN SEA

Roma

Sevilla

Granada

Malaga

Cartagena

Palermo

Messina

Sicilia

IONIAN SEA

Athen

Rhodes

Cadiz

Gibraltar (Brit.)

Tanger

MEDITERRANEAN

Malta (Brit.)

Crete

Rabat MOROCCO
(FR.)

Oran

ALGERIA (FR.)

TUNISIA
(Fr.)

Tunis

Alger

The First World War

A month after the assassination of Franz Ferdinand in Sarajevo on June 28, 1914 (see p. 103) Austria-Hungary declared war on Serbia. The map above shows at which points and on which side the other European countries became involved.

The war was the first conflict in history to involve the entire world (map nr. 149). The war was fought in several countries, on all the oceans, and, for the first time, aircraft were used extensively. **The water colour** by Marcel Jeanjean **at the top of the following page** shows a training camp in France. After a lightning offensive by the Germans in the summer and autumn of 1914 (map nr. 147), the troops dug in, in trenches on both the Western and Eastern fronts. A portion of Paul Nash's **painting at left** depicts conditions in a British trench on the Western Front. They gradually became fortified field positions, with bomb shelters, connecting passageways, etc., and with complicated technical equipment like periscopes, listening devices, and the like.

But large battles were also fought, both on land and at sea. The first of these on the Western Front, which took place September 5–12, 1914 on the Marne between German and combined French and British forces, halted the German offensive and saved Paris. In the first battle on the Eastern Front, at Tannenberg, August 30, 1914, the Germans handed the Russians a decisive defeat. **The caricature above** shows German crown prince Frederick Wilhelm and his father, Emperor Wilhelm II, peering toward Verdun from atop a pile of corpses, and agreeing that they will need more of these before they are

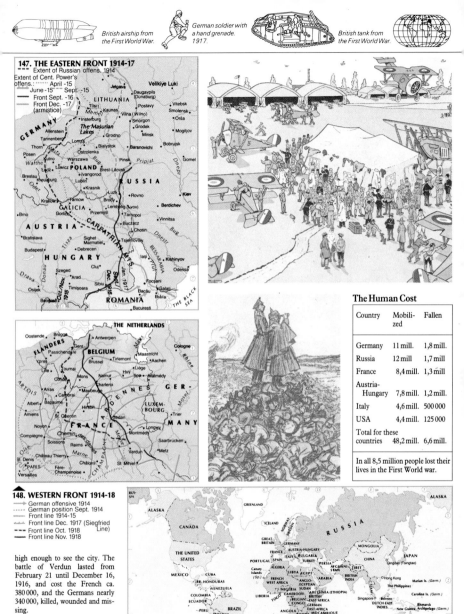

British airship from the First World War.

German soldier with a hand grenade. 1917.

British tank from the First World War.

147. THE EASTERN FRONT 1914-17

- Extent of Russian offens. 1914
- Extent of Cent. Power's offens. ... April -15
- June -15 — Sept. -15
- Front Sept. -16
- Front Dec. -17 (armistice)

GERMANY · Jelgava · Velikiye Luki · Daugavpils (Dunaburg) · Vitebsk · LITHUANIA · Tilsit · Postavy · Smolensk · Memel · Kaunas · Vilna (Wilno) · Orša · Interburg · Smorgon · Mogiljov · The Masurian Lakes · Grodno · Minsk · Allenstein · Tannenberg · Lomza · Baranovichi · Bobrujsk · Thorn · Ostrolenka · Bialystok · Gomel · Posen · Kutno · Warszawa · Pinsk · Pripjat · Dnepr · Wartha · Lowicz · POLAND · Bug · Breslau · Kreuzburg · Ivangorod · Brest-Litovsk · Oder · Lublin · RUSSIA · Krakow · Krasnik · Luzk · Kiev · Tarnow · Brody · GALICIA · Lemberg (Lvov) · Rovno · Berdichev · Gorlice · Przemysl · Tarnopol · Brno · Bratislava · CARPATHIAN MTS. · Dnestr · Buczacz · Vinnitsa · AUSTRIA · Sighet · Chotin · Bug · Marmaties · BESSARABIA · Budapest · Debrecen · Iasi · Kishinyov · Tisza · HUNGARY · Cluj · Odessa · Drava · Szeged · Arad · Focsani · Donau · Timisoara · Bacau · Galati · Osijek · Sibiu · Braila · THE BLACK SEA · Beograd · ROMANIA · Bucuresti

148. WESTERN FRONT 1914-18

- German offensive 1914
- German position Sept. 1914
- Front line 1914-15
- Front line Dec. 1917 (Siegfried Line)
- Front line Oct. 1918
- Front line Nov. 1918

THE NETHERLANDS · Oostende · Brugge · Antwerpen · FLANDERS · Gent · BELGIUM · Maastricht · Cologne · Passchendaele · Tienen · Aachen · Rhine · Ypres · Brussel · Lille · Tournai · Namur · Huy · Spa · Malmédy · ARTOIS · Mons · Charleroi · GER- · Arras · Cambrai · ARDENNES · Albert · Bapaume · Hirson · LUXEM- · Amiens · St. Quentin · Sedan · BOURG · Trier · MANY · Noyon · Longwy · Compiègne · Chemin des Dames · Montmédy · Mosel · Soissons · Reims · Saarbrücken · Oise · Château Thierry · Marne · Metz · St. Denis · Fère- · Châlons · St. Mihiel · PARIS · Champenoise · Verdun · CHAMPAGNE · Versailles · FRANCE · Maas

high enough to see the city. The battle of Verdun lasted from February 21 until December 16, 1916, and cost the French ca. 380 000, and the Germans nearly 340 000, killed, wounded and missing.

At eleven o'clock on November 11, 1918 a armistice went into effect. The Central Powers had been defeated. **Map nr. 151, p. 107** shows some of the consequences of the Treaty of Versailles in 1919.

The Human Cost

Country	Mobilized	Fallen
Germany	11 mill.	1,8 mill.
Russia	12 mill	1,7 mill.
France	8,4 mill.	1,3 mill
Austria-Hungary	7,8 mill.	1,2 mill.
Italy	4,6 mill.	500 000
USA	4,4 mill.	125 000
Total for these countries	48,2 mill.	6,6 mill.

In all 8,5 million people lost their lives in the First World war.

149. ALLIANCES IN THE GREAT WAR 1914-18

RUSSIA · ALASKA · GREENLAND · ICELAND · RUSSIA · ALASKA · CANADA · NORWAY · SWEDEN · FINLAND · GREAT BRITAIN · GERMANY · AUSTRIA-HUNGARY · MONGOLIA · THE UNITED STATES · FRANCE · ITALY · BULGARIA · TURKEY · PERSIA · AFGHANISTAN · TIBET · CHINA · JAPAN · MEXICO · PORTUGAL · SPAIN · ALGERIA · LIBYA · EGYPT · ARABIA · Qingdao (Tsingtao) · CUBA · Canary Islands (Sp.) · FRENCH WEST AFRICA · ANGLO-EGYPTIAN SUDAN · BR. HONDURAS · Hong Kong · Marian Is. (Germ.) · VENEZUELA · NIGERIA · ABESSINIA (ETHIOPIA) · The Philippines · COLOMBIA · LIBERIA · TOGO · CAMEROON · BRITISH EAST AFRICA · Caroline Is. (Germ.) · ECUADOR · BELGIAN CONGO · GERMAN EAST AFRICA · Singapore · Borneo · DUTCH EAST INDIES · New Guinea · Bismarck Archipelago (Germ.) · PERU · BRAZIL · BOLIVIA · ANGOLA · RHODESIA · MOCAMBIQUE · MADAGASCAR · PARAGUAY · GERMAN SOUTHWEST AFRICA · UNION OF SOUTH AFRICA · CHILE · URUGUAY · AUSTRALIA · ARGENTINA · Falklands Is. (Brit.)

Central Powers and allies
Allied Powers Jan. 1917
Allies at war's end
Neutral states

Top illustrations (left to right):
French field ambulance from the First World War.

A revolutionary soldier speaking to workers in Petrograd in July 1917.

Members of the women's Bolshevik «Death Battalion» in 1917.

Map labels:

NORWAY

THE Allied fleet March 1918

BARENTS SEA

SWEDEN

Murmansk

Kandalaksha

Mesen

March 1920

White Sea   Aug. 1918

Arkhangelsk

Kem

Gulf of Bothnia

Vaasa

FINLAND

Febr. 1920   Dvina

Jarensk

Syktyvkar

Solikamsk

URAL MTS.

Nystad

Petrosavodsk

Pudosj

Onega

Vytegra

Velsk

Kai

Yekaterinburg

Åland

Helsinki   Kronstadt

Ladoga

Belosersk

Nikolsk

Totma

Nolinsk

Sarapul

Admiral Koltshak 1918

Royal family shot by Bolsheviks July 1918

Admiral Koltshak 1918 retreat in the summer of 1919

Perm

Vyatka

Ufa

British fleet 1918

Gulf of Finland

General Yudenitsj 1919

Petrograd (Leningrad)

Tikhvin

Vologda

Galich

Kostroma

Varnavino

Kasan

ESTONIA

Novgorod

Kornilov's march on Petrograd Sept. 1917

Valdai

Yaroslavl

Ivanovo

Nizhniy Novgorod

Simbirsk

Orenburg

THE BALTIC

Riga   Germans

LATVIA

Pskov   Ostaskov

Reshev   Moscow

Oka

Murom

Saransk

Samara

Uralsk

Memel

LITHUANIA

Lithuanians

Velikiye Luki

Vyazma

Polotsk

Kaluga

Serpukhov

Tula

Morshansk

Pensa

White Cossacks

Vilna

Vitebsk

Orsa   Smolensk

Tambov

Saratov

Engels

Kalmykovo

Guryev

Aug. 1920

Minsk   Mogilev

Bryansk

Orel

Jelez

Balashov

Kamysjin

Warszawa

Bialystok

Poles

Gomel

Kursk

Voronezh

Pavlovsky

Saritsyn (Stalingrad)

Volga

POLAND

Brest-Litovsk

March 1921

Mosyr

Chernigov

General Denikin 1919

Belgorod

General Krasnov 1918

Astrakhan

Kielce

Rovno

Zhitomir

Kiev

Poltava

Kharkov

Jan. 1920

Don

Tarnow

Lvov

Berdichev

Tsjerkassy

Dnieper

General Denikin 1919

Ungvar

Vinnitsa   UKRAINE

July-Aug. 1920

Kirovograd

Yekaterinoslav

Saporosye

Rostov

Taganrog

THE CASPIAN SEA

BESSARABIA

Balta

Nikolayev

Kherson

Nikopol

Mariupol

1920

Dniester

Odessa Dec. 1918

General Wrangel 1920

Sea of Azov

Armavir

Krasnodar

Piatigorsk

Makhatsjkala

March 1920

CRIMEA

Sevastopol   Simferopol

Majkop

Novorossisk

Grosnyj

Sochi

Sukhumi

GEORGIA

Tbilisi

THE BLACK SEA

Batum

ARMENIA

Kars

Yerevan (Erivan)

Bosporus

Samsun

TURKEY

150. CIVIL WAR IN RUSSIA 1918–21

The Empire in 1914
After the Peace of Brest-Litovsk, March 1918
Towns taken over by Bolsheviks, Oct.-Nov. 1917   Smolensk
Empire's boundary 1914
Front line at outbreak of October Revolution
Russia's boundary after Brest-Litovsk
Boundary of area under Bolshevik control, Oct. 1919
White Russian offensive and anti-Bolshevik attacks
Bolshevik counter-offensives

Above: Bolshevik leader Vladimir Lenin, and Joseph Stalin, in Petrograd, April 16, 1917.

Civil War in Russia 1918–21

After famine had led to the Feb. Revolution and when Nicholas II abdicated, there was chaos in the old Russian empire, leading to civil war in 1918. The opponents of the Bolsheviks formed an anti-Bolshevik government in 1918 in Samara on the Volga. In September this provisional government joined another, strongly conservative one in Omsk, under admiral Alexander Koltshak.

In the south, general Anton Denikin had assembled an anti-Bolshevik army, and south of the Gulf of Finland the «White» forces under general Nicolai Yudenitch were standing ready. The White Army made great progress in 1919, and Denikin's successor, general Piotr Wrangel advanced from the south again in January 1920. But by now the Bolshevik counter-offensives were in full swing. By August 1920 the Red Army was victorious.

Right: The Russian imperial family, photographed in the park at the summer palace of Tzarskoye Selo, southeast of Petrograd, in January 1916. From left: the tzar's adjutant, Tzar Nicholas II, followed by his daughters, Grand Dutchess Tatyana, Olga, Maria and the lively Anastasia. Farthest right, in naval uniform, Crown Prince Alexei (b. 1904). The boy in the foreground, and the three in the background, are sons of the Tzar's eldest sister. In July 1918 Nicholas, his wife, his four daughters and Prince Alexei were shot by the Bolsheviks at Yekaterinburg.

Italian Fiat from 1936.

Woman's fashion – «La Garçonne» style – from end of the 1920s.

General Foch leads the sisters Alsace and Lorraine back to France.

The Peace of Versailles 1919

Germany, held chiefly responsible for the war, lost all colonies, Alsace-Lorraine, and Northern Schleswig (Dan. 1920). Saarland under the control of the League of Nations forced to cede large territories to the newly reconstituted Polish state (map nr. 151). Danzig a free state. Memel region to Lithuania. Austria-Hungary was completely dissolved (see map).

Above: Croydon outside London. Painting by Kenneth McDonough from the 1920s. There was rapid technical development during WW1 but passenger traffic grew just as rapidly after the war. In 1919 the first London–Paris route was opened.

Italian Imperialism

1889–90 Italy acquires Somaliland (1889) and Eritrea (1890) (map nr. 152).

1896 Italian troops defeated at Adua. Ethiopia, then an Italian protectorate, gains independence.

1911–12 Libya and the Dodecanese Is. (incl. Rhodes) are conquered.

1919–24 Tyrol, Istria, Zara and Lagosta are annexed.

1936 Ethiopia is occupied, emperor Haile Selassie flees to Great Britain.

1939 Albania is occupied.

1941 The Italians in Ethiopia surrender to the British. Haille Selassie returns home.

151. CENTRAL AND EASTERN EUROPE AFTER THE GREAT WAR *(From 1925.)*

1914 boundaries of:
- — Germ. – Russia
- — Austro-Hungary
- -- Curzon Line
Year of accession given

152. MUSSOLINI'S EMPIRE
- Colonies 1880's - 90's
- Protectorate 1889-96
- Conquests 1912-24
- Mussolini's conquests 1936-41

Radio with speaker from around 1925.

Adolf Hitler chose the swastika as his magic symbol.

Distribution of food to the unemployed in the period between the wars.

Germany 1918–39

Following defeat in the First World War the radical left hopes for a development along Soviet lines, but elections in January 1919 confirm that a majority of Germans are in favour of a non-socialist democratic republic. A new constitution is adopted at Weimar. Friedrich (Fritz) Ebert becomes the first president of the Weimar Republic, and Philip Scheidemann becomes chancellor. The harsh penalties imposed by the Treaty of Versailles have created a desire for revenge in the country, and Scheidemann leaves office in protest.

1920 Adolf Hitler becomes propaganda chief in a new political party: The National-Socialist German Workers' Party (Nazis).

1923 French and Belgian troops enter the Ruhr region to put pressure on Germany, which is having trouble meeting payments on its colossal war reparations debt. The country is experiencing an absurd rate of inflation. Just before the government puts a stop to it through devaluation in November, the rate of exchange in U.S. dollars is climbing at a rate of 613 000 marks per second on the stock exchange! Adolf Hitler carries out an unsuccessful coup d'etat in Munich and is imprisoned.

1929 Mass unemployment and social unrest provide ideal conditions for the Nazis' rise to power.

The Near East 1917–26

1917 Hidyaz gains independence.
1918 **Yemen**, **Armenia** and **Georgia** gain independence.
1920 **Palestine** and **Trans-Jordan** come under British mandate. French mandate over **Lebanon**

and **Syria**. **Kuwait** gains independence. **1921** **Iraq** gains independence. **Georgia** becomes part of the Soviet Union.
1922 **Egypt** becomes an independent kingdom.
1923 At the Peace of Lausanne,

Armenia, the **Izmir** region and a portion of the peninsula west of Istanbul are accorded Turkey, which becomes a republic.
1926 **Saudi-Arabia** becomes an independent kingdom, including **Asir** and **Hidyaz**.

Above: *«Peace in our time,» prime minister Chamberlain said when he returned to London following his meeting with Adolf Hitler in Munich on September 29, 1938. The Sudetenland was to be sacrificed and annexed by Germany. When Chamberlain announced the declaration of war against Germany on September 3, 1939, he admitted his error in judgment.*

Nazi Germany used the old Germanic «Heil!» salute.

From the field hospital, 110 m deep on the French Maginot Line.

1933 Hitler is elected chancellor, and quickly has all other political parties dissolved.

1934 Aging president Paul von Hindenburg dies. Hitler assumes his office as well, calling himself «Führer and Chancellor of the Reich».
Political opponents are sent to concentration camps. Jews are singled out for especially brutal treatment (illus. bottom of page).

1935 In contradiction to the Treaty of Versailles, universal military service is introduced.

1936 In March German troops advance into the demilitarized Rhineland (map nr. 155). In July, civil war breaks out in Spain (map nr. 156). Francisco Franco gets support from the German air force and Italian troops. In October Hitler visits Benito Mussolini in Rome, where they reach a secret agreement on a parallel foreign policy (illus. right).

1938 In March Hitler annexes Austria, and in October the Sudetenland, both moves allowed by Munich Agreement (illus. p. 108).

1939 In March Germany takes the remainder of Czechoslovakia, and in August signs a non-aggression pact with Russia (illus. right). On September 1 German troops invade Poland. Two days later the Second World War is underway.

Bottom: Jews on their way to a concentration camp. From a book from 1935, intended to teach children that Jews were rabble.
*Farthest right: A meeting between Hitler and Mussolini. **The caricature** of Stalin and Hitler carries the caption: «How long will the honeymoon last?»*

155. ANNEXATION AND DIPLOMACY IN CENTRAL EUROPE 1936-39

German, Polish and Hungarian annexation, with dates

Anti-COMINTERN pact with Japan Nov. 25, 1936

156. THE SPANISH CIVIL WAR

Nationalist control 1936   Republican control Feb. 1939
Conquests up to:
Oct. 1937   Nationalist stronghold
July 1938   Republican stronghold
Febr. 1939   Dates indicate when captured

Nazi stormtrooper.

Mother and child watch nervously for bombers over Madrid.

German Stuka on the attzok in WW2.

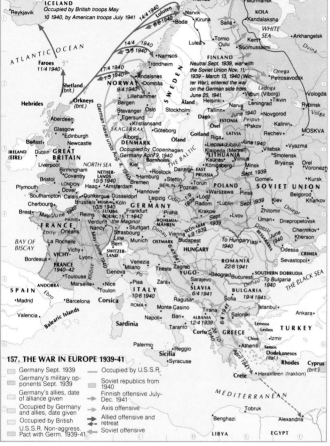

157. THE WAR IN EUROPE 1939–41

Germany Sept. 1939

Germany's military opponents 1939

Germany's allies, date of alliance given

Occupied by Germany and allies, date given

Occupied by British

U.S.S.R. Non-aggress. Pact with Germ. 1939–41

Occupied by U.S.S.R.

Soviet republics from 1940

Finnish offensive July-Dec. 1941

Axis offensive

Allied offensive and retreat

Soviet offensive

May 10 Germans invade The Netherlands and Belgium. British occupy Iceland.

June 10 Italy enters the war on German side.

June 14 Paris falls.

June 22 France signs an armistice. Most of the country is occupied. Southern France becomes in effect a German dependency.

June–September «Battle of Britain», with massive German air attacks. Huge German losses. Plans for an invasion of England have to be abandoned.

1941: June 22 Hitler attacks the Soviet Union.

Map nr. 157 shows when other European countries entered the war.

Top of next page: In 1939 there were already six concentration camps in Germany with 20000 political prisoners. Map nr. 158 shows some of the larger camps during the war, and how many Jews from each were liquidated by the Nazis. It is estimated that over eight million people lost their lives in camps like these.

The picture next to it shows what the British found when they entered the concentration camp at Bergen-Belsen on April 17, 1945.

Bottom of next page: Those responsible for the attack on Pearl Harbor on December 7, 1941. From a caricature in «Fortune». The man with the glasses is Japan's prime minister, general Hideki Tojo, with admiral Chuichi Nagumo. Tojo was judged to bear individual responsibility for the war and hanged in November 1948.

Below, this page: Tower Bridge near the London docks during the blitz of 1940. From a painting by Charles Pears.

Europe 1939–41

1939 September 1 German troops invade Poland from the west and from East Prussia.

September 3 Great Britain and France declare war on Germany.

September 17 The Soviet Union occupies the eastern part of Poland.

November 30 The Soviet Union attacks Finland.

1940 March 12 The Finns capitulate. The «Winter War» comes to an end.

April 9 Denmark and Norway attacked.

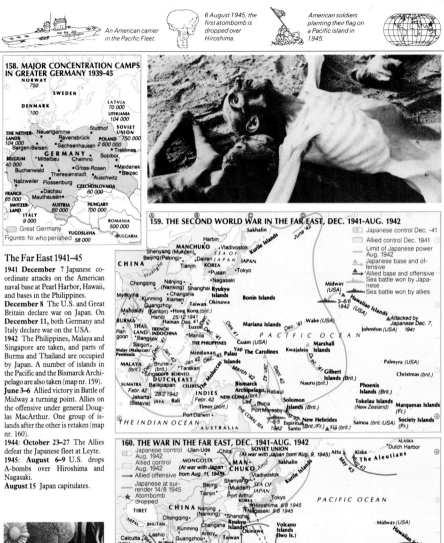

An American carrier in the Pacific Fleet.

6 August 1945, the first atombomb is dropped over Hiroshima.

American soldiers planting their flag on a Pacific island in 1945.

158. MAJOR CONCENTRATION CAMPS IN GREATER GERMANY 1939-45

NORWAY 750
SWEDEN
DENMARK 100
LATVIA 70 000
LITHUANIA 104 000
SOVIET UNION 750 000
THE NETHER-LANDS 104 000
Neuengamme
Ravensbrück
Stutthof
Bergen-Belsen
Sachsenhausen
Treblinka
GERMANY
BELGIUM 40 000
Mittelbau
Chelmno
Sobibor
Buchenwald
Gross-Rosen
Maidanek
Natzweiler
Theresienstadt
Auschwitz
Belzec
Flossenbürg
FRANCE 65 000
Dachau
Mauthausen
CZECHOSLOVAKIA 60 000
SWITZER-LAND
ITALY 9 000
AUSTRIA 60 000
HUNGARY 700 000
ROMANIA 500 000
YUGOSLAVIA 58 000
BULGARIA

Great Germany
Figures: Nr. who perished

The Far East 1941-45

1941 December 7 Japanese co-ordinate attacks on the American naval base at Pearl Harbor, Hawaii, and bases in the Philippines.
December 8 The U.S. and Great Britain declare war on Japan. On **December 11**, both Germany and Italy declare war on the USA.
1942 The Philippines, Malaya and Singapore are taken, and parts of Burma and Thailand are occupied by Japan. A number of islands in the Pacific and the Bismarck Archipelago are also taken (map nr. 159).
June 3-6 Allied victory in Battle of Midway a turning point. Allies on the offensive under general Douglas MacArthur. One group of islands after the other is retaken (map nr. 160).
1944: October 23-27 The Allies defeat the Japanese fleet at Leyte.
1945: August 6-9 U.S. drops A-bombs over Hiroshima and Nagasaki.
August 15 Japan capitulates.

159. THE SECOND WORLD WAR IN THE FAR EAST, DEC. 1941-AUG. 1942

Japanese control Dec. -41
Allied control Dec. 1941
Limit of Japanese power Aug. 1942
Japanese base and offensive
Allied base and offensive
Sea battle won by Japanese
Sea battle won by allies

Sakhalin
Harbin
MANCHUKO
Vladivostok
Kurile Islands
June '42
Shenyang (Mukden)
Beijing (Peking)
Dairen
SEA OF JAPAN
JAPAN
CHINA
Huang
Tianjin
KOREA
Pusan
Tokyo
Midway (USA)
Chongqing
Nanjing (Nanking)
Shanghai
Nagasaki
Ryukyu Islands
3-6
Myitkyina
Changsha
Taiwan
Okinawa
Bonin Islands
1942 (USA)
Hawaiian Islands
Kunming
Xiamen
Guangzhou
Hong Kong (brit.)
Wake (USA)
Attacked by Japanese Dec. 7.
Mandalay
Hanoi
Hainan
Des. 41
Luzon
Mariana Islands
Dec. '41
Johnston (USA) 1941
BURMA
25/12 1941
Des. 41
Dec. 41
PACIFIC OCEAN
Ran goon
THAI-LAND
FRENCH INDOCHINA
Manila
Guam (USA)
Yap
The Carolines
Bangkok
THE PHILIPPINES
Marshall Islands
Saigon
Mindanao
Palau
Kwajalein
Malay (Malaccan) Peninsula
Jan. 42
Dec. 41
Moluccas Islands
March 42
Palmyra (USA)
MALAYA (brit.)
Brunei (brit.)
Tarakan
Sept. 42
Gilbert Islands (Brit.)
Christmas (brit.)
Singapore
BORNEO
Jan. 42
DUTCH EAST
Nauru (brit.)
Phoenix Islands (Brit.)
SUMATRA
Balikpapan
CELEBES
Bismarck Archipelago
Rabaul
Febr. 42
INDIES
Febr. 42
NEW GUINEA (brit.)
Solomon Islands (Brit.)
Tokelau Islands (New Zealand)
Marquesas Islands (Fr.)
Jakarta (Batavia)
28/2 1942
Bali
Lae
Buna
Port Moresby
7-8.5
Timor (port.)
Espiritu Santo
New Hebrides (Brit./Fr.)
Samoa (brit./USA)
Society Islands (Fr.)
Port Darwin
1942
THE INDIAN OCEAN
AUSTRALIA
THE CORAL SEA
Fiji (brit.)

160. THE WAR IN THE FAR EAST, DEC. 1941-AUG. 1942

Japanese control Aug. 1942
Allied control Aug. 1942
Allied offensive
Japanese at surrender 14/8 1945
Atombomb dropped

SOVIET UNION
(At war with Japan from Aug. 9, 1945)
ALASKA
Dutch Harbor
Ulan-Ude
Chita
Attu
Kiska
The Aleutians
MONGOLIA (At war with Japan from Aug. 11, 1945)
MAN-CHUKO
Sakhalin
May 43
Shenyang (Mukden)
Vladivostok
Kurile Islands
Beijing
SEA OF JAPAN
Tianjin
Port Arthur
KOREA
Tokyo
PACIFIC OCEAN
TIBET
Hiroshima 6/8 1945
Nagasaki 9/8 1945
CHINA
Nanjing (Nanking)
Shanghai
NEPAL
BHUTAN
Chongqing
Changsha
Ryukyu Islands
Midway (USA)
Kunming
Amoy
Okinawa
Volcano Islands (Iwo Is.)
Calcutta
Lashio
Guangzhou
Taiwan
Hawaiian Islands
INDIA (brit.)
BURMA
Hanoi
Hong Kong (brit.)
19/6 1944
Wake (USA)
Jan. 44
Hawaii (USA)
Rangoon
THAILAND
FRENCH INDO-CHINA
Hainan
Lingayen
Mariana Islands
Saipan (Allied airbase from July 1944)
Johnston (USA)
Nov. 43
Andaman Islands (brit.)
Bangkok
Corregidor
THE PHILIPPINES
Manila
Guam
Tinian
June '44
Marshall Islands
Ceylon
Nicobar Islands (brit.)
Saigon
Leyte
23-27/10 1944
AUG 44
Eniwetok
Kwajalein
Palmyra (USA)
June 45
Mindanao
Caroline Islands
SOUTH CHINA SEA
Singapore
Brunei
Tarakan
Morotai
Tarawa
Gilbert Islands (Brit.)
Howland (USA)
SUMATRA
MALAYA
BORNEO
CELEBES
Moluccas
Febr. 43
Bismarck Archipelago
Nauru
Baker (USA)
Christmas (brit.)
DUTCH EAST INDIES
Diajapura (Hollandia)
Rabaul
Phoenix Islands (Brit.)
Djakarta (Batavia)
JAVA
NEW GUINEA
Bougainville
Ellice Islands (Brit.)
Tokelau Islands (New Zealand)
Makassar
Timor
Lae
Solomon Islands
Tulagi
Santa Cruz Islands (Brit.)
Port Darwin
Port Moresby
Guadalcanal
CORAL SEA
AUSTRALIA
Espiritu Santo
New Hebrides (Brit./Fr.)
Samoa (Brit./USA)
INDIAN OCEAN

German para-troopers over The Netherlands, 10 May 1940.

A British «desert rat» in North Africa.

A German V2 rocket, ready for launching.

161. THE WAR IN EUROPE 1942-45

- The Axis Powers 1942
- Joined the Allies, with date
- German control 1942
- Allied control Nov. 1942
- Neutrals that joined Allies
- Neutral throughout war
- → Allied offensive
- Front line: — Oct. 1943
- —Dec.-44 — March -45

Kirkenes • Petsamo
Narvik • Murmansk
Kiruna **Kola Peninsula**
Salla
Rovaniemi WHITE SEA • Arkhangelsk

Trondheim

FINLAND
Armistice with the Soviet Union Sept. 4, 1944. At war with Germany Sept. 9, 1944 - April 25, 1945

Shetlands
NORWAY
Bergen Oslo Helsinki Petrosavodsk
Stavanger SWEDEN Ladoga Onega
Glasgow Stockholm Tallinn Schlüsselburg Leningrad Dago ESTONIA
Edinburgh Göteborg Narva Novgorod Kasan
NORTH SEA Peipus • Pskov • Demjansk • Gorki
GREAT DENMARK Riga LATVIA Velikiye Luki • Rsjev Moscow
BRITAIN Copenhagen Malmö THE BALTIC Memel LITHUANIA Vitebsk • Vyazma Oka
Königsberg Kaunas Vilnius Smolensk SOVIET
THE NETHER- Hamburg Danzig Goldap Minsk Mogilev • Orel Voronezh
London LANDS Amsterdam Stettin Bialystok UNION
Southampton Arnhem Berlin Warszawa Brest-Litovsk Gomel • Kursk
Antwerpen GER- Oder Kiev Belgorod Don
Brussels BELGIUM MANY Torgau Breslau Kharkov Stalingrad
Caen Dieppe LUXEM- Dresden Prague BOHEMIA- Lvov Tarnopol Dnjepr Nov. 1942- febr. 1943
Paris Reims BOURG Frankfurt MÄHREN Baranov Nikopol • Saporosye • Rostov
FRANCE Nürnberg SLOVAKIA Bug Dnestr
Loire Strasbourg Linz Vienna HUNGARY Iasi SEA OF AZOV
Oradour München OSTMARK Budapest 31/12 1944 Odessa Crimea • Kerch • Krasnodar
Vichy Bern Zagreb ROMANIA 25/8 1944 Sevastopol • Jalta
Lyon SWITZER- Trieste Jajce Beograd Bucuresti Ploiesti THE BLACK SEA
LAND Milano CROATIA SERBIA Donau
Po Bologna Ravenna Sarajevo BULGARIA 8/9 1944
Marseille La Spezia Pisa MONTE- Sofia Istanbul
Toulon Rhône ITALY 13/10 1943 NEGRO Ankara
SPAIN Corsica Roma Anzio Armistic Tirana ALBANIA Saloniki TURKEY 23/2 1945
Barcelona Nettuno Napoli Sept. 8, 1943 (Thessalonike) Alexandrette
Balearic Sept. 3, 1943 Taranto GREECE Haleb (Aleppo) SYRIA
Islands Sardinia Bizerte Messina Reggio Athens Rhodes (Ital.) Cyprus (Brit.) Beirut LEBANON
American and British Sicilia Catania British troops Oct. 1944 Damascus
troops Tunis Gela Siracusa (Syracuse) Crete PALESTINE TRANSJORDAN
ALGERIA British troops July 1943 Malta (Brit.) MEDITERRANEAN Jerusalem Port Said SAUDI
TUNISIA Gabès ARABIA 1/3 1945
Tripoli Jan. 1943 Benghazi Nov. 1942 CYRENAICA Tobruk Alexandria EGYPT Port Said
LIBYA El Alamein Okt. 1942 Cairo • Suez

Above: In the winter of 1942–43 Russian and German troops battled for Stalingrad. The Russians were stubborn, and on January 31 German general Friedrich von Paulus and 90 000 men had to surrender. Walter Molina's drawing shows a German tank in Stalingrad.
Below: Bernard Law Montgomery, who with his 8th Army defeated the Germans at El Alamein in 1942, continued through North Africa, on to Sicily in July 1943, and then to southern Italy in September (maps nrs. 161 and 162). From a painting by Sir Oswald Birley.

8/11 1942 A Algiers Bougie Bône Bizerte Messina Reggio D Athens E TURKEY
12/11 1942 B 7/5 1943 Sicily GREECE
Tunis Cyprus (Brit.)
Biskra Kasserine TUNISIA Syracuse
18/2 1943 Malta (Brit.) Crete
ALGERIA Gabès MEDITERRANEAN
16/2 1943 Medenine
162. THE ALLIES' CAMPAIGNS NOV. 1942- MAY 1943 OPERATION TORCH Tripoli Tarhuna 19/1 1943 Benghazi 19/11 1942 Tobruk 12/11 1942 Port Said
Sirte CYRENAICA Sidi Barrani Alexandria
Allied advance, date of Axis surrender 21/12 1942 El Agheila 16/12 1942 9/11 1942 El Alamein Suez
British forces in Operation Torch LIBYA EGYPT 2/11-5/11 1942 Cairo

American infantry-
man with gas mask.

American bomber – a
Boeing B-17.

American landing-
craft in Normandy
6 June 1944.

163. THE EASTERN FRONT 1942–45

- ☐ Greater Germany
- ☐ Germany's allies
- German control Nov. 1942

Front line:
- ▲▲ Spring 1943 ▲▲ Autumn -44
- ▲▲ Autumn 1943 ▲▲ May 1945

©THE BLACK SEA

Western and Eastern Europe 1942–45

1942
November 2–5 General Rommel's German troops are defeated by the British at El Alamein.
November 8 Allies land in Morocco and continue eastward.
November 11 The remainder of France occupied by Germany.

1943
January 31 Germans capitulate at Stalingrad. **July** 10 British land in Sicily (map nr. 161).
July 25 Mussolini is deposed and replaced by Pietro Badoglio.
September 3 Allied invasion in southern Italy. Cease-fire from September 8.
September 12 Mussolini is freed by German paratroopers and becomes head of a northern Italian fascist republic.
October 13 Italy declares war on Germany. The country is occupied by German troops.

1944
March 19 Germany occupies Hungary.
June 4 The allies take Rome.
June 6 «D-day». Allies invade Normandy (map nr. 165).
July 20 Rebel German officers carry out an unsuccessful assassination attempt against Hitler.
August 24 Paris is liberated.
August 25 Romania declares war on Germany.
September 4–19 Armistice between Finland and the Soviet Union.
September 8 Bulgaria declares war on Germany.
September 11 The Western allies invade Germany.
October 4 British invade Greece.
October 19 Soviet troops enter East Prussia.

1945
February 11 The Russians take Budapest.
March 7 American forces cross the Rhine.
April 7 Russians take Vienna.
April 29 The Germans capitulate in Italy.
April 30 Hitler commits suicide.
May 7 Unconditional German capitulation.

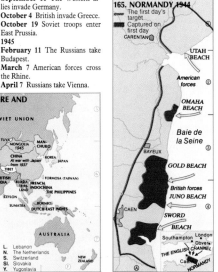

165. NORMANDY 1944
- ☐ The first day's target
- ☐ Captured on first day

CARENTAN

UTAH BEACH

American forces

OMAHA BEACH

Baie de la Seine

BAYEUX

GOLD BEACH

British forces

JUNO BEACH

SWORD BEACH

CAEN

Southampton London
THE ENGLISH CHANNEL Dover
Caen NORMANDY

164. POWER GROUPINGS IN THE SECOND WORLD WAR, BEFORE AND AFTER PEARL HARBOR

Germany, Italy, Japan and allies:
- ☐ bef. Dec. 7, -41
- ☐ after Dec. 7, 1941

The Allies:
- ☐ bef. Dec. 7, 1941
- ☐ after Dec. 7, 1941

Date of joining Allies given

☐ Neutral throughout war

A.	Albania	L.	Lebanon
B.	Belgium	N.	The Netherlands
Bu.	Bulgaria	S.	Switzerland
D.	Denmark	Sl.	Slovakia
H.	Hungary	Y.	Yugoslavia

THE SECOND WORLD WAR 1942–45 113

British medical team carrying a casualty to safety.

Soviet citizens, hanged by the Germans before their withdrawal.

Emaciated prisoners in a German concentration camp.

166. GERMANY AFTER THE SECOND WORLD WAR

SWEDEN
DENMARK
NORTH SEA
SCHLESWIG-
HOLSTEIN
Kiel
Bremerhaven
THE NETHER-
LANDS
Amsterdam
BELGIUM
Brussel
LUXEM-
BOURG
Bonn
Essen
Düsseldorf
NORDRHEIN
RHUR
Under international
control 1948-52
WESTPHALIA
RHEINLAND-
PFALZ
SAAR
(Indep. 1946-57)
Saarbrücken
Mainz
Frankfurt
Wiesbaden
HESSEN
Freiburg
BADEN
Stuttgart
Tübingen
WÜRTTEMBERG-
HOHENZOLLERN
WÜRTTEMBERG-
BADEN
SWITZERLAND
Bremen
Hamburg
Schwerin
MECKLENBURG
Rostock
THE BALTIC
Bornholm
Danzig
POMERANIA
Stettin
GERMAN
BRANDEN-
BURG
DEMOCRATIC
REPUBLIC (DDR)
(EAST GERMANY)
SACHSEN-
ANHALT
Potsdam
Berlin
(See map nr. 167)
Halle
Leipzig
Dresden
THÜRINGEN
Erfurt
SACHSEN
Prague
CZECHOSLOVAKIA
Nürnberg
Regensburg
BAVARIA
Munich
AUSTRIA
Vienna
Hannover
FEDERAL REPUBLIC
OF GERMANY (BRD)
(WEST GERMANY)
EAST
PRUSSIA
Polish from 1945
Russian
from 1945
SOVIET
UNION
POLAND
Warszawa
Polish
from 1945
SILESIA
Oder
Neisse
Elbe
Main
Donau
Schwerin

Zones of occupation 1945-54
British
American
French
Russian
Zones of admin. after 1945
Germany's boundaries 1937
Oder/Neisse Line
Boundary East - West Germ.
Land boundary W. Germ.
district boundary in East
Bremen Capital of Land/district

Right: A 15-year-old in a
Luftwaffe uniform sobs after
hearing the announcement of the
German surrender in May 1945.
When military reserve strength in the
final months of the war had become
practically nonexistent, young boys
– not least members of the youth
corps «Hitlerjugend» – were drafted
to defend the Fatherland.
Below: Three representatives of
the allies in Berlin – a British private,
a Russian woman from the Red
Army and an American corporal –
offer one another their hands in joy
upon hearing the report of Japan's
capitulation on August 15, 1945.
The war had finally come to an end.

The Human Cost of WW2

It is estimated that nearly 40 mill.
perished in WW2, i.e., over four
times as many as in World War 1.
And this time many more civilians
had been killed: approximately half
of all casualties in Europe. Ca. 8
million of these died in concentration
camps (see p. 110). Estimated
war-dead in some of the countries
involved:

The Soviet Union	ca. 20 mill.
Germany	ca. 6 mill.
Poland	ca. 5 mill.
Japan	ca. 2 mill.
Yugoslavia	ca. 1,7 mill.
France	ca. 0,6 mill.
Romania	ca. 0,6 mill.
Italy	ca. 0,4 mill.
Great Britain	ca. 0,4 mill.
USA	ca. 0,3 mill.

Peace Negotiations and the Division of Germany

At war's end it had already been
decided that Poland was to get the
eastern half of the old Germany as
far west as the Oder-Neisse (map
nr. 166). East Prussia was to be
divided between Poland and the
Soviet Union. The rest of Germany
was to be divided into four occupied
zones: one American, one British, one French and one Russian.
From 1949 on the Soviet zone was
an independent state under the
name Deutsche Demokratische
Republik (East Germany). In the
same year the three other zones
became the state of the Bundesrepublik Deutschland (West
Germany).

AIRLIFT 26/6 1948 - 12/5 1949. The Allies answer on Sovjet blockade
of the supply-lines.

EAST GERMANY

FRENCH
SECTOR
French HQ
Tegeler
See
Tegel
SPANDAU
REINICKEN-
DORF
PANKOW
WEISSENSEE
CHARLOTTEN-
BURG
WEDDING
PRENZLAUBERG
LICHTENBERG
British HQ
BRITISH
SECTOR
TIERGARTEN
WILMERS-
DORF
FRIEDRICH-
MAIN
KÖLN
RUSSIAN
SECTOR
Russian HQ
Gatow
KREUZ-
BERG
NEU-
KÖLLN
TREPTOW
STEGLITZ
SCHÖNE-
BERG
ZEHLEN-
DORF
American HQ
The Allied
Command
Tempelhof
AMERICAN SECTOR
KÖPENICK
Müggel See
Spree
Glienicker
Brücke
Schönefeld

167. BERLIN AFTER THE SECOND WORLD WAR
The Berlin Wall
with checkpoints
SPANDAU Districts (Bezirke)
Railway — Major road

KEY TO NUMERALS:
① Brandenburg Gate
② Checkpoint Charlie
③ Free University of Berlin
④ Allied Administrative Council
⑤ Humboldt University

Parisian woman looking for food in a garbage cart.

The Berlin Wall at the Brandenburg Gate in 1961.

168. ECONOMIC ALLIANCES IN EUROPE AFTER 1945

Members of COMECON, Council for Mutual Economic Assistance, founded Jan. 1949. Year and map text indicate later member country, associate country or ex-member country.

Members from outside Europe: MONGOLIA (joined 1962), CUBA (joined 1972) and VIETNAM (joined 1978).

Members of OECD, Organization for Economic Co-operation and Development, founded Sept. 1961 by reorganization of OEEC founded 1948.

Members from outside Europe: AUSTRALIA, JAPAN, CANADA, N. ZEALAND and USA.

Members of Council of Europe, founded May 1949.

EFTA Members of EFTA, European Free Trade Association, founded May 1960.

EEC Members of EC, The European Community, founded July 1967 through union of Coal and Steel Union (1952), European Economic Community (1958) and EURATOM, European Atomic Energy Commission (1958)

Members of Benelux, founded Jan. 1948.

ICELAND Members of The Nordic Council, founded 1952. Finland joined in 1955.

Berlin, which lay in the Soviet zone, was also to be divided among the four occupying nations. The «Cold War» between East and West, however, led to Russian construction of a wall right through the city in 1961 (map nr. 167). The wall did not come down again until 1989.
Japan. Just after the capitulation in August 1945, American forces occupied Japan until April 28, 1952. The Japanese had agreed to revoke all claims to territories outside Japan proper.

The United Nations (UN)

Even in the early stages of the war the allies had agreed that the peace to follow would best be preserved through the establishment of an international organization of all the world's free nations.
The idea was discussed during the war, and on April 25, 1945 representatives from fifty countries assembled in San Francisco to outline rules for the formation of the United Nations. Two months later they had reached agreement, and October 24, 1945 (UN-day) the organization was formally inaugurated.
The UN has six main bodies, of

which the General Assembly and Security Council are the most important. The organization has its headquarters in New York, and **the picture below** shows the UN Building, built there in 1952.

De Gaulle's France

General Charles de Gaulle (1890–

1970) managed to get out of the country when France capitulated in June 1940, and following the liberation in 1944, he returned to France as head of the provisional government. When, however, his suggestion to give the president extended powers in a new constitution met with stiff opposition, he left

the government in 1946.
When in 1958 France found herself on the brink of civil war and chaos, he again took over responsibility for the administration of the country. France's and Europe's strong man for more than a decade (**picture below**).

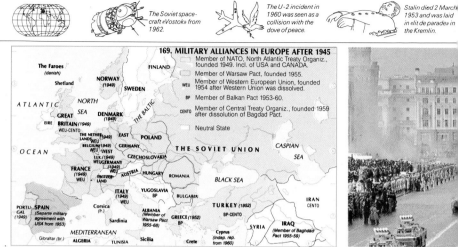

The Soviet space-craft «Vostok» from 1962.

The U-2 incident in 1960 was seen as a collision with the dove of peace.

Stalin died 2 March 1953 and was laid in «lit de parade» in the Kremlin.

169. MILITARY ALLIANCES IN EUROPE AFTER 1945

- Member of NATO, North Atlantic Treaty Organiz., founded 1949. Incl. of USA and CANADA.
- Member of Warsaw Pact, founded 1955.
- WEU Member of Western European Union, founded 1954 after Western Union was dissolved.
- BP Member of Balkan Pact 1953-60.
- CENTO Member of Central Treaty Organiz., founded 1959 after dissolution of Bagdad Pact.
- Neutral State

The Faroes (danish)
Shetland
FINLAND
NORWAY (1949)
SWEDEN
ATLANTIC
NORTH SEA
DENMARK (1949)
GREAT BRITAIN (1949)
EIRE
WEU-CENTO
THE NETHERLANDS (1949)
BELGIUM (1949)
LUX. (1949)
WEU
GERMANY
EAST GERMANY
POLAND
CZECHOSLOVAKIA
THE SOVIET UNION
CASPIAN SEA
OCEAN
FRANCE (1949)
WEU
SWITZER-LAND
AUSTRIA
HUNGARY
ROMANIA
BLACK SEA
ITALY (1949) WEU
YUGOSLAVIA BP
BULGARIA
PORTU-GAL (1949)
SPAIN (Separate military agreement with USA from 1953)
Corsica (fr.)
Sardinia
ALBANIA (Member of Warsaw Pact 1955-68)
GREECE (1952) BP
TURKEY (1952)
BP-CENTO
IRAN CENTO
SYRIA
IRAQ (Member of Baghdad Pact 1955-59)
MEDITERRANEAN
Gibraltar (br.)
ALGERIA
TUNISIA
Sicilia
Crete
Cyprus (Indep. rep. from 1960)

Nato and the Warsaw Pact

The Western powers began shortly after the war to make plans for a common defense alliance, and when the U.S. Senate in 1948 gave its approval for the government to enter into an agreement with Western Europe, a draft agreement was ready in January of 1949.

On April 4, 1949 the Atlantic Treaty was signed by the USA, Canada, Great Britain, France, the Benelux countries, Portugal, Denmark, Norway and Iceland. Since then several other nations have joined the alliance (map nr. 169). Each member nation will treat an attack on another member nation as an attack on itself.

A military and intelligence defense organization was formed which came to be known as NATO (the North Atlantic Treaty Organization).

The Eastern Bloc formed a corresponding military alliance, the so-called **Warsaw Pact**. It was signed in Warsaw on May 14, 1955 by the Soviet Union, Albania, Bulgaria, Hungary, Poland, Romania, Czechoslovakia and East Germany. Albania pulled out of the pact in September of 1968 after having broken with the Soviet Union the previous year and orienting itself more in the direction of China politically.

Right: Relative military strength between NATO and the Warsaw Pact at the beginning of the 1980s. Source: «Le Point», Paris, April 18, 1986.

Soviet Union 1945–85

1945–47 The country has become a great-power, but faces massive problems of reconstruction. The cult of personality surrounding Stalin reaches new heights. Poland, East Germany, Czechoslovakia, Hungary, Romania, Yugoslavia and Bulgaria are controlled from Moscow. Ideological conformity has been achieved.

1948 Berlin Crisis. The Russians block all roads leading to West Berlin. The Western powers carry out an airlift (map nr. 167, p. 114). The «Cold War» heats up.

1949 The country acquires nuclear weapons and is considered a super-power. The arms race has begun.

1953 Stalin dies. Collective leadership, with Nikita Khrushchev as the dominant figure.

1955 The Warsaw Pact is formed.

1956 Uprising in Hungary is put down.

1957–62 Soviet Union gets headstart in the Space-race. Break with China. Crises between the superpowers: Berlin (1958-59), U-2 (1960), Cuba (1962).

1964 Leonid Breshnev takes over.

1968 Intervention in Czechoslovakia.

1970–75 Detente with the West.

1977–80 Somewhat cooler relationship with the USA. The Soviet Union intervenes in Afghanistan (1979). Crisis in Poland following Lech Walesa's founding of the labour union Solidarity (1980).

1982–84 Breshnev dies in November 1982 and is succeeded by Andropov, and after him Chernenko.

1985 Michail Gorbachev is installed as General Secretary of the Communist Party and, in reality, leader of the Soviet Union.

Above: The Anniversary of the Revolution – November 7 – has for many decades been celebrated with military parades in Red Square.
Right: Defense minister Dmitri Ustinov and Leonid Breshnev, during the military parade on Revolution Day 1979.

China 1934–80

1934–35 The first communist state in China – formed in Jiangxi with Mao Tse-tung as foreman in 1931 – is surrounded by forces of the nationalist government, i.e., Chiang Kai-shek's troops. In October 100 000 members of the Red Army succeed in breaking out. Led by Mao, they begin the «Long March» to Shaanxi, which from 1935 becomes the communists' headquarters (map nr. 170).

1937 Japan attacks China. Chiang Kai-shek and the communists make

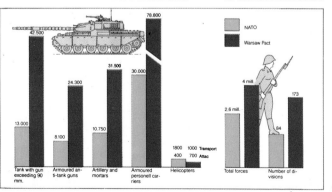

42.500
78.800
31.500
24.300
30.000
13.000
8.100
10.750
1800 1000 Transport
400 700 Attac
4 mill.
2.6 mill.
173
84

NATO
Warsaw Pact

Tank with gun exceeding 90 mm.
Armoured anti-tank guns
Artillery and mortars
Armoured personnel carriers
Helicopters
Total forces
Number of divisions

Chinese women in a rice paddy.

Young Chinese girls receiving military training.

After Mao, Chinese young people began dancing to Western rhythms.

Above: In 1966, 72-year-old Mao was venerated as an almost divine figure. As the Cultural Revolution did away with the last vestiges of old-fashioned «bourgeois ideology», it also turned most everything else upside-down. Even down to the traffic lights, where a green light now meant «stop»!

Left: In three years, 350 million copies of chairman Mao's sayings from 1964, the «Little Red Book», had been printed, and became the basis for every aspect of Chinese life.

civil peace to stand united against the aggressor (map nr. 142, p. 102).

1940–45 During WW2 the Chinese receive allied support against Japan (maps 159 and 160, p. 111).

1945 Mao Tse-tung goes on the attack against Chiang Kai-shek and his regime.

1949 The People's Republic of China, with Mao as leader, is proclaimed on October 1, Chiang and his forces withdraw to Taiwan, where in December he establishes his own state – Nationalist China (map nr. 170).

1958 The republic is organized in people's communes. At the same time the «Great Leap Forward» is initiated, an attempt to dramatically increase production.

1963 Conflict with Soviet Union.

1966–70 The «Cultural Revolution» uncovers deeply rooted differences in the party leadership and leads to bloody clashes.

1976 Mao Tse-tung dies and is succeeded by Hua Kuo-feng.

1980 Hua meets severe criticism and is replaced by Hu Yaobang.

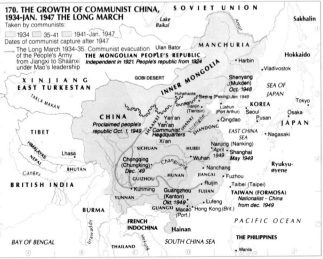

170. THE GROWTH OF COMMUNIST CHINA, 1934–JAN. 1947 THE LONG MARCH

Taken by communists:

☐ 1934 ☐ 35-41 ☐ 1941-Jan. 1947
Dates of communist capture after 1947

→ The Long March 1934-35. Communist evacuation of the People's Army from Jiangxi to Shaanxi under Mao's leadership

THE MONGOLIAN PEOPLE'S REPUBLIC
Independent in 1921. People's republic from 1924

SOVIET UNION
Lake Baikal
Amur
Sakhalin
Ulan Bator
MANCHURIA
Hokkaido
• Harbin
• Vladivostok
Shenyang (Mukden) Oct. 1948
SEA OF JAPAN
Tokyo
XINJIANG EAST TURKESTAN
GOBI DESERT
INNER MONGOLIA
Huhehote
Beijing (Peking) Jan. 1949
Tianjin (Tientsin)
Lüshun (Port Arthur)
KOREA
Seoul
Pusan
Osaka
JAPAN
TAKLA MAKAN
CHINA
Proclaimed people's republic Oct. 1, 1949
Yan'an
Communist Headquarters
Xi'an
Qingdao
SHANDONG
EAST CHINA SEA
Nagasaki
TIBET
Lhasa
HIMALAYAS
NEPAL
Ganges
BHUTAN
SICHUAN
Chongqing (Chungking) Dec. 49
Changjiang
HUBEI
Wuhan
Nanjing (Nanking) April 1949
Shanghai May 1949
Ryukyu-øyene
BRITISH INDIA
GUIZHOU
HUNAN
JIANGXI
Nanchang
Ruijin
• Fuzhou
FUJIAN
TAIWAN (FORMOSA) Nationalist - China from dec. 1949
BURMA
YUNNAN
• Kunming
Guangzhou (Kanton) Okt. 1949
Macao (Port.)
GUANGXI
• Lufeng
Hong Kong (Brit.)
Taibei (Taipei)
FRENCH INDOCHINA
Hainan
PACIFIC OCEAN
BAY OF BENGAL
THAILAND
SOUTH CHINA SEA
THE PHILIPPINES
• Manila

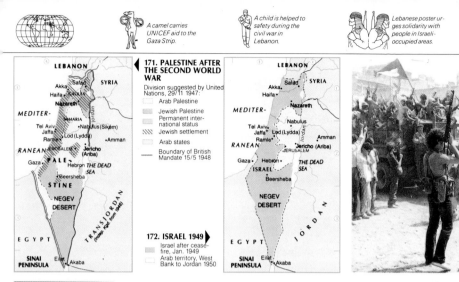

A camel carries UNICEF aid to the Gaza Strip.

A child is helped to safety during the civil war in Lebanon.

Lebanese poster urges solidarity with people in Israeli-occupied areas.

171. PALESTINE AFTER THE SECOND WORLD WAR

Division suggested by United Nations, 29/11 1947:

- Arab Palestine
- Jewish Palestine
- Permanent international status
- Jewish settlement
- Arab states
- Boundary of British Mandate 15/5 1948

172. ISRAEL 1949 ▶

- Israel after cease-fire, Jan. 1949
- Arab territory, West Bank to Jordan 1950

---

back, and win large areas of land.

1956–57 Egypt's president Nasser (illus. left) blocks Israeli shipping through the Suez Canal in 1956. The Israelis occupy the entire Sinai Peninsula. Bowing to strong international pressure, Israel pulls out of the Sinai, Gaza and the Strait of Tiran the following year.

1967 Egypt expels the UN troops and closes the Strait of Tiran to Israeli ships. Israel strikes back with great force. In the course of the Six Day War Israel occupies the Sinai Peninsula, Old Jerusalem, the West Bank of the Jordan, and the Golan Heights (map nr. 173).

Right: PLO leader Yassir Arafat (b. 1929), who from 1965 was the leader of the Palestinian resistance organization al-Fatah. Three years later, Arafat was also made leader of the PLO (Palestinian Liberation Organization). Its goal is the establishment of an independent state for the Palestinians. In 1982 the PLO was forced to leave Beirut, but Arafat managed to keep the organization together. *The picture at the top of the page* shows the departure of the PLO's soldiers from Beirut. They dispersed to Tunisia, Syria, the Sudan, Cyprus, Greece and Jordan.

Above: Colonel Gamal Abdel el Nasser (1918–70) was the mastermind behind the coup against Egypt's King Farukh in July 1952. Two years later he became the country's president.

Palestine-Israel 1947–67

1947 A UN-resolution, which has Jewish support, proposes the division of Palestine in a Jewish and an Arab state (map nr. 171).

1948–49 Palestine, which has been under British mandate since 1920, is given up by the British in May 1948. The state of Israel is proclaimed. The Arab countries attack immediately, but the Israelis strike

173. THE SIX DAY'S WAR, JUNE 5-10, 1967 ▶

- UN forces give way May 21
- Airfields bombed by Israelis June 5
- → Israeli armoured thrusts
- Israel's opponents in Six Day's War
- Members of the Arab League
- Occup. by Israel in Six Day's War

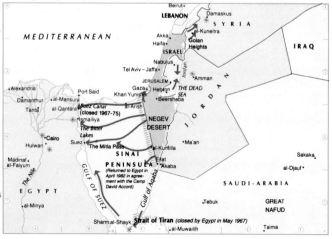

Oil platform in the North Sea.

Armed Iranian woman in traditional Shiite Muslim garb.

World's first atomic powered submarine. The American «Nautilus» (1954).

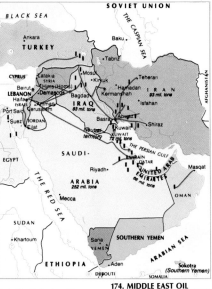

Korea 1945–53

1945 Korea occupied by Russian and American troops (map nr. 175). N. of the 38th Parallel, communist government was established.

1946–47 A UN commission is set to prepare for free elections.

1948 Commission is refused access to the north, but elections are held in the south. Republic of Korea proclaimed on Aug. 15. On Sept. 9 the People's Republic of Korea is proclaimed in the north. On December 12 the UN recognizes the South Korean regime as the country's only legitimate government.

1950–53 North Korean troops attack South Korea (map nr. 175). Armistice in 1953. Korea remains divided.

Left: The Muslim Ayatollah Khomeini, who from exile in Paris led opposition forces in Iran against Shah Mohammed Reza Pahlavi's regime. When the shah fled the country in January 1979, Khomeini returned in triumph to Iran, where he proclaimed the Islamic Republic, with himself as leader. This was the beginning of a period of internal terror and thousands of executions. The following year war broke out with Iraq. There were ferocious tank battles, and many casualities.

174. MIDDLE EAST OIL COUNTRIES

I Important oilfield
● Major oil refinery
— Oil pipeline

Each country's production of crude petroleum in 1986 given in mill. tons

The Oil States of the Mid-East

In **Bahrain** oil was discovered in 1932. **Egypt** has since the 1960s had a steady increase in oil production.

The **United Arab Emirates** have rich oilfields, both on land and offshore. In **Iraq** the first oil deposits were found at Kirkuk in 1927. From here oil pipelines have been stretched to the Mediterranean and the Persian Gulf (map nr. 174). In 1972–73 the internationally owned Iraq Petroleum Co. was nationalized. **Iran** (Persia) nationalized the British oil company Anglo-Iranian Oil Co. in 1951. In **Kuwait** oil production wasn't begun until 1946, but the rich deposits have made the country, which didn't gain independence until 1961, one of the world's wealthiest. In **Oman** the first oil discovery was made in 1964. **Qatar.** British protectorate from 1916 to 1971. Oil discovered in 1939. Production from 1949. **Saudi-Arabia** began extracting oil in 1933, and increased production drastically after 1945.

175. THE KOREAN WAR 1950-53

◄ A. 25/6 - 25/11 1950

→ North Korean offensive July-Aug. -50
— Pusan Bridgehead, 5/8-16/9 -50
→ South Korean and UN offensive Oct.-Nov. 1950
— Limit of greatest advance

▼ B. 26/11 1950 - 27/7 1953

→ Chinese - N. Kor. offens. fr. 16/11 -50
— Southernmost limit in Jan. 1951
→ South Korean and UN counter-offensive, Summer 1951
— Demarcation Line 27/11 1951, confirmed by armistice 27/7 1953

A starving child
from Biafra in
1970.

Slum district in
South Vietnam's
capital of Saigon.

The first human
lands on the moon
in July 1969.

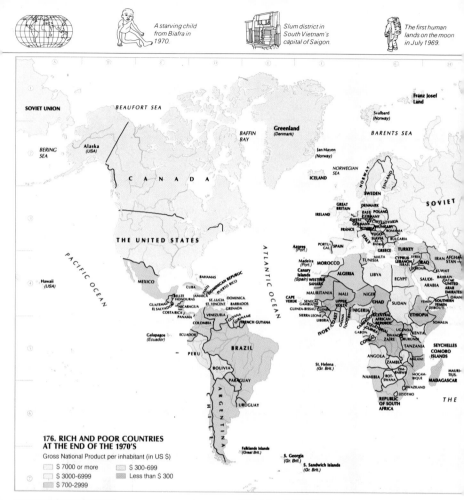

SOVIET UNION

BEAUFORT SEA

BAFFIN
BAY

Greenland
(Denmark)

BARENTS SEA

Franz Josef
Land

Svalbard
(Norway)

BERING
SEA

Alaska
(USA)

C A N A D A

Jan Mayen
(Norway)

NORWEGIAN
SEA

ICELAND

NORWAY

FINLAND

SWEDEN

SOVIET

PACIFIC
OCEAN

Hawaii
(USA)

T H E   U N I T E D   S T A T E S

ATLANTIC
OCEAN

DENMARK

IRELAND

GREAT
BRITAIN

EAST POLAND
GERMANY
WEST CZECHOSLOVAKIA
GERMANY
FRANCE AUSTRIA HUNGARY ROMANIA
SWITZERLAND YUGO-
ITALY SLAVIA BULGARIA

GREECE TURKEY

SYRIA IRAN AFGHA-
CYPRUS LEBANON IRAQ STAN

MEXICO

BAHAMAS
CUBA JAMAICA HAITI DOMINICAN REPUBLIC
PUERTO RICO
BELIZE
HONDURAS DOMINICA
GUATEMALA ST. LUCIA
EL SALVADOR NICARAGUA ST. VINCENT BARBADOS
COSTA RICA PANAMA GRENADA
VENEZUELA
COLOMBIA GUYANA
SURINAME
FRENCH GUYANA

Azores
(Port.)
Madeira
(Port.)
Canary
Islands
(Spain) WESTERN
SAHARA

PORTU-
GAL SPAIN

MALTA

MOROCCO
TUNISIA

ALGERIA LIBYA

EGYPT

SAUDI
ARABIA

QATAR
BAHRAIN
UNITED
ARAB
EMIRATES
OMAN

YEMEN SOUTHERN
YEMEN

MAURITANIA MALI NIGER

CHAD SUDAN

CAPE
VERDE SENEGAL
GAMBIA
GUINEA-BISSAU GUINEA UPPER
VOLTA
SIERRA LEONE
LIBERIA
IVORY COAST
GHANA
TOGO
BENIN
NIGERIA
CAMEROON
CENTRAL
AFRICAN
REPUBLIC

ETHIOPIA

SOMALIA

Galapagos
(Ecuador)

ECUADOR

PERU

BRAZIL

BOLIVIA

PARAGUAY

CHILE

ARGENTINA

URUGUAY

COLOMBIA
EQUATORIAL
GUINEA
GABON
CONGO
ZAIRE

UGANDA
RWANDA
BURUNDI

KENYA

TANZANIA

SEYCHELLES

COMORO
ISLANDS

St. Helena
(Gr. Brit.)

ANGOLA

ZAMBIA
MALAWI

MOZAM-
BIQUE

MAURI-
TIUS

MADAGASCAR

NAMIBIA

ZIM-
BABWE

BOT-
SWANA

SWAZILAND

LESOTHO

REPUBLIC
OF SOUTH
AFRICA

T H E

Falkland Islands
(Great Brit.)

S. Georgia
(Gr. Brit.)

S. Sandwich Islands
(Gr. Brit.)

176. RICH AND POOR COUNTRIES AT THE END OF THE 1970'S

Gross National Product per inhabitant (in US $)

- $ 7000 or more
- $ 3000-6999
- $ 700-2999
- $ 300-699
- Less than $ 300

Left: Fidel Castro (b. 1927), from 1959 Cuba's prime minister, and from December 1976 the country's president as well. After intensive preparations in Mexico, he came to Cuba in 1956 with 80 men to topple dictator Fulgencio Batista's corrupt regime. The charismatic Castro won the sympathy of the people, and in 1959 he and his guerilla force entered Havana in triumph after Batista had fled. The USA welcomed Castro until he drew closer to the communists (see next page). **Right:** Harvesting sugar cane in Cuba, which is the world's largest producer of sugar.

An American chromeplated gas-guzzler from the 1950s.

A German television set from the early 1950s.

American nuclear power plant in 1979.

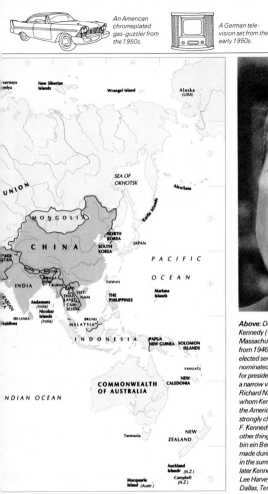

Above: Democrat John Fitzgerald Kennedy (1917–63) represented Massachusetts in the Congress from 1946. Six years later he was elected senator, and in 1960 was nominated as the party's candidate for president. In the election he won a narrow victory over Republican Richard Nixon. Like Castro – with whom Kennedy quickly clashed – the American president too had a strongly charismatic character. John F. Kennedy is remembered, among other things, for the statement: «Ich bin ein Berliner» – I am a Berliner – made during his visit to West Berlin in the summer of 1963. Six months later Kennedy was shot and killed by Lee Harvey Oswald during a visit to Dallas, Texas.

Cuba 1960–63

1960 Fidel Castro initiates close cooperation with the Soviet Union.

1961 A force of 1 500 Cuban exiles, supported by the USA, go ashore at the Bay of Pigs, but are quickly defeated (map nr. 178). Khrushchev promises Castro support. President Kennedy declares that the USA will counter any Soviet military intervention.

1962 Americans discover Soviet bases for medium distance rockets in Cuba. U.S. naval blockade of Cuba.

1963 Soviet Union gives in. 22 000 Soviet soldiers leave the island. All bases and equipment removed. The Cuban Missile Crisis ends.

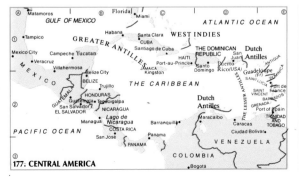

177: CENTRAL AMERICA

178. THE CUBA CRISIS, OCTOBER 1962

▲ Russian rocket bases, removed in 1962
⌖ American base
▷ Invasion by Cuban exiles, April 1961

Woman at a farming collective in Nyerere's Tanzania.

Man carrying ammunition on his head during the Biafran War.

Young boy in Angola armed with modern automatic weapons.

A

EGYPT 1922

ABESSINIA (Ital. 'colony' 1936–41)

LIBERIA 1847

COMMONWEALTH OF SOUTH AFRICA 1910

1939

B

MOROCCO 1956

TUNISIA 1956

LIBYA 1951

SUDAN 1956

GUINEA 1958

GHANA 1957

ETHIOPIA 1941

1958

C

ALGERIA 1962

MOROCCO TANIA 1960

MALI 1960

NIGER 1960

CHAD 1960

SENEGAL 1960

NIGERIA 1960

CENTRAL AFRICAN REP. 1960

IVORY COAST 1960

TOGO 1960

CAMEROON 1960

CONGO STATE From 1971 ZAIRE

KENYA 1963

SOMALIA 1960

MALAWI 1964

RHODESIA 1965 (Not recognized)

TANZANIA 1964

MADAGAS-CAR 1960

1. UPPER VOLTA 1960
2. DAHOMEY 1960
3. GABON 1960
4. SIERRA LEONE 1961
5. BURUNDI 1962
6. RWANDA 1962
7. UGANDA 1962

1965

The pictures at the top of this and the next page show, from the left: **1** Archbishop Desmond Mpilo Tutu (b. 1931), who received the Nobel Peace Prize in 1984 for his leadership of the non-violent protest movement against Apartheid. **2** Kenya's colourful leader, Yomo Kenyatta (1891–1978) **3** Julius Nyerere (b. 1922), Tanzania's president 1965–85. He and Kenyatta were among the most outspoken proponents of pan-Africanism and African socialism. **4** Anwar Sadat (1918–81), who became Egypt's leader following president Nasser's death in 1970. **5** Colonel Muammar al-Gaddaffi (b. 1942) came to power in Libya in coup in 1969. Most radical representative of pan-Arabic nationalism. **6** President of the Congo (Zaire), Joseph Kasavubu (1910–69), on the right, and general Sése-Seko (Joseph-Désiré) Mobutu (b. 1930). Kasavubu, who was the Republic of the Congo's first president from 1960 to 1965, was succeeded by Mobutu following a coup d'etat (see Congo Crisis, p. 123).

D

1965–90

179. AFRICAN INDEPENDENCE 1939–90

Sovereign state and year of independence

Map A states independent in 1939, map B independent 1939-58 and map C the 25 states that achieved indep. 1959-64. Map D dates show indep. after -64.

Belgian dependency

British dependency

French dependency

Italian colony

Portuguese colony, Portuguese province after 1971

Spanish dependency

League of Nations mandate, later United Nations

Racial rioting in the Johannesburg suburb of Soweto in 1976.

'A political prisoner in Ghana reunited with his wife after five years in prison.

An animal is left dying following a drought in Ethiopia.

RISK OF DESERTIFICATION

Desert

Very high risk

High risk

Moderate risk

African Liberation 1951–90

1951 Libya (24/12). **1956** Sudan (1/1), Morocco (2/3), Tunisia (20/3). **1957** Ghana (6/3). **1958** Guinea (2/10). **1960 The Great Year of Liberation**: Cameroon (1/1), Togo (27/4), Somalia (26/6), the Congo (Zaïre) (30/6), Benin (1/8), Niger (3/8), Upper Volta (Burkina Faso) (5/8), Ivory Coast (7/8), Chad (11/8), Central African Republic (13/8), Republic of the Congo (15/8), Gabon (17/8), Senegal (20/8), Madagascar (21/9), Mali (22/9), Mauritania (28/11), Nigeria (1/10). **1961** Tanzania (1/5) **1962** Burundi (1/7), Rwanda (1/7), Algeria (3/7), Uganda (9/10). **1964** Malawi (6/7), Zambia (24/10), Kenya (12/12). **1965** Gambia (18/2). **1966** Botswana (30/9), Lesotho (4/10). **1968** Swaziland (6/9), Equatorial Guinea (12/10). **1973** Guinea-Bissau (24/9). **1975** Comoro Islands (6/7), São Tomé and Principe (12/7), Moçambique (25/6), Angola (11/11). **1977** Djibouti (27/6). **1980** Zimbabwe (Rhodesia) (18/4). **1990** Namibia (21/3)

Below: The Congo's first prime minister, Patrice Lumumba (1925–61).

The Congo crisis 1960–65

The Congo, formerly the Belgian Congo, became an independent republic on June 30, 1960. The Belgians turned over the government to a coalition, with Patrice Lumumba (illus. below) as prime minister and Joseph Kasavubu as president (illus. above). Conditions quickly became chaotic, however, and Belgian troops entered the country again. In July the mineral-rich province of Katanga (Shaba) seceded under the leadership of Moise Tshombe, as did the southern part of Kasai, led by Albert Kalondshi (map nr. 179). Lumumba asked the UN for help, but when he wasn't satisfied with the efforts of the UN troops, he asked the Soviet Union for assistance. A displeased Kasavubu forced Lumumba out of office in early September 1960.

Shortly afterward, the army, under general Sése-Seko Mobutu seized

power in a coup. But Lumumba's deputy, Antoine Gizenga, formed a strong counter-regime in Stanleyville a few months later. In February 1961 the Tshombe government announced that Lumumba had been found murdered in Katanga. The Soviet Union placed responsibility for the killing on UN secretary Dag Hammarskjöld, who was killed in an unexplained air crash on September 18, 1961 while on his way to a meeting with Tshombe. UN troops were again sent into the country – in all 20 000 men from eighteen countries. In 1964 provinces of Katanga and Kasai gave up their opposition to being incorporated into the Congo.

Order restored when general Mobutu for the second time seized power in 1965. From 1971 on, the Congo is officially known as Zaïre.

The map above illustrates the threat of desertification in Africa. Irresponsible logging of the forests, intensive cultivation of the land and overgrazing, combined with almost perpetual drought, turns large areas of land each year into barren wasteland. The same phenomenon represents a threat to certain areas of North and South America, Asia and Australia.

180. THE CONGO CRISIS 1960-65

Areas giving support in 1961 to:

░ Kasavubu and Mobutu

▓ Albert Kalondshi in Kasai

▒ Lumumba and Gizenga

▓ Moïse Tshombe

● UN forces bases 1960-64

Revolts in 1964:
— Limits of Simba revolt
— Limits of Mulélé revolt

⚲ Landings by Belgian paratroops, Nov. 1964
--- Provincial boundary

At the top of the page, small illustrations with captions:
Vietnamese with child fleeing during the Tet Offensive in 1968. 
Farming with ancient methods in South Vietnam. 
Woman fleeing the war in Laos.

Map labels (map nr. 181):
BURMA, CHINA, Nanning, Lao Kay, Cao Bang, Song Bo (Black R.), Song Koi (Red R.), TONKIN, Dien Bien Phu (French defeat after 55 day siege March 13 – May 7, 1954), Hanoi, Haiphong, Zhanjiang, Sam Neua, Nam Dinh, Thanh Hoa, Luang Prabang, Xieng Khouang, L A O S (Proclaimed indep. Kingdom autumn of 1945), GOLF OF TONKIN, Hainan, Haikou, Vinh, V I E T -, Vientiane, Dong Hoi, Vinh Linh, Tengchiao, Udon Thani, Savannakhet, Hué, Phu Bai, T H A I L A N D (Called Siam until 1939 and from 1945 to may 11, 1949), Da Nang, Chu Lai, Pakse, N A M (Proclaimed indep. rep. Sept. 2, 1945), Bangkok, Battambang, Stung Treng, Binh Dinh, Qui Nhon, Tonlé Sap, CAMBODIA (Proclaimed indep. rep. March 9, 1945), Kompong Cham, Dalat, Nha Trang, GULF OF SIAM, Phnom Penh, Saigon, Phan Rang, Long Xuyen, COCHIN-CHINA, Bac-lieu, Mekong Delta, SOUTH CHINA SEA

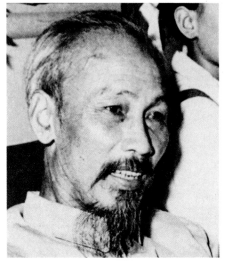

181. INDO-CHINA 1945-54

- Members of French Indo-China Union 1949 (Vietnam from -46)

Controlled by Viet Minh:
- 1946-50
- 1950-54
- After armistice in July 1954
- Partition of Vietnam after armistice (17th parallel)

Occupation forces from:
- Nationalist China
- United Kingdom
- France

French Indochina 1945–54

Cambodia

1945 Because Vichy-France (map nr. 143, p. 110) has allowed Japan and Thailand to establish bases in the country during the Second World War, king Norodom Sihanouk, with Japanese approval, proclaims Cambodia's independence in March. British, Indian and French troops enter the country, and in October they occupy the capital of Phnom Penh (map nr. 181). French rule is established.

1949 France recognizes Cambodia as an independent state within the French Union. The French retain control of the military and foreign policy.

1953 May 9 an agreement is signed with France, insuring Cambodia's full sovereignty in military, judicial, and economic affairs.

1954 The Geneva Convention confirms the country's independence.

Laos

1945 Declared an independent state on April 15. Sisavang Vong is made king. In August the Chinese invade, occupying most of the country (map nr. 181).

1946 In March French troops enter and retake the country. The government flees to Bangkok. France promises independence.

1947 Laos gets a new constitution. Parliamentary monarchy.

1949 Laos an associate nation in the French Union.

1953 Laos given full independence within the French Union.

1954 Vietminh enter Laos. According to the Geneva Convention, the country is forbidden to form alliances with any country. The government attempts to pacify the procommunist party, Pathet Lao, which is supported by both the Vietminh and North Vietnam. The French pull out of Laos.

Vietnam

1945 Japanese disarm the French troops and turn over control of the country to a puppet government under emperor Bao Dai. Shortly after the Japanese capitulation, the Vietminh, led by Ho Chi Minh, seize power.

1946 French move toward Hanoi (map nr. 181). An accord is reached, stating that the country will become a free state, but within the French Union. On Nov. 20, exchange of fire between French and Vietnamese soldiers in Haiphong. Three days later a French cruiser bombards a division of Vietnamese soldiers, resulting in a horrendous bloodbath. Vietnamese go on the attack on December 19. The **First Vietnam War** is underway.

1954 Following more than seven years of guerilla warfare – in which from 1950 on France had received considerable support from the USA – the French provoke the Vietnamese into attacking their base at Dien Bien Phu (map nr. 181). After a fifty-five day seige, the French are forced to surrender on May 7. The Geneva Convention negotiates a cease-fire. Vietnam is to be divided at the seventeenth parallel. Ho Chi Minh is elected leader of the Democratic Republic of Vietnam in the north. Bao Dai becomes chief of state in South Vietnam.

Left: When the American war in Vietnam was presented in images like this on television screens in the USA, demands for war-crimes trials were heard, even at home.

An FN soldier moving into Saigon, 30 April 1975. The war is over.

American bomber dropping its load over North Vietnam.

American soldier comforts a North Vietnamese woman.

Left: Vietnamese politician, Ho Chi Minh (1890–1969). After many years in Europe, where, among other things, he had helped to found the French Communist Party in 1920, Ho Chi Minh came to Hong Kong. Here he served as Comintern representative from 1930, and it was here that he laid the groundwork for a communist party in French Indochina (Vietnam). From 1941 he headed the liberation organization Vietminh, and in 1954 he became president of North Vietnam.

Below right: Hanoi is in ruins following the American bombing attack at Christmas 1972.

Vietnam 1955–76

1955 Bao Dai is toppled in South Vietnam. Ngo Dinh Diem is made president. 800 000 North Vietnamese flee south.
1956 Local uprisings in North Vietnam. South Vietnam is supported by USA.
1960 North Vietnamese infiltration of the south. The National Liberation Front (FNL) and its guerilla army are supplied from the north, via the Ho Chi Minh Trail. North Vietnam is supported by China and the Soviet Union.
1964 Purported clashes between American and North Vietnamese

naval vessels in the Gulf of Tonkin open the way for increased American involvement. The United States bombs North Vietnam. The total number of bombs dropped is greater than during all of WW II.
1967 450 000 American soldiers are fighting in Vietnam. In this one year, 9 000 of them lose their lives. Massive demonstrations against the war in the U.S. and in other countries.
1968 The Tet Offensive (70 000 men) against the regime in the south is a turning point.
1969 In November president Nixon announces that all American

ground troops are to be withdrawn.
1972 North Vietnam carries out a new offensive. U.S. bombing in the north is resumed.
1973 Negotiations in Paris lead to a cease-fire in January, but the armed struggle continues. At this point, three million Americans have taken part in the war, with nearly 54 000 casualties.
1975 South Vietnam's army is in disarray. North Vietnamese and FNL troops take Saigon on April 30. The city is renamed Ho Chi Minh City.
1976 North and South Vietnam are officially reunited on July 2.

182. THE VIETNAM WARS 1954-77

— Partition Line (17th parallel)
— Ho Chi Minh Trail, supply line
→ 7th US Fleet   to FNL
— American air raids
ı American bombing, dates indicate when most intense

A. 1954–69
FNL control 1965-66
Controlled by Pathet Lao
→ Weapons and troops to FNL
• Main US air bases 1969
→ Tet Offensive, Jan. 30 1968

B. 1969–73
FNL control 1973
Controlled by Pathet Lao
⊤⊤⊤ Amer. blockade May-Dec. -72
///// FNL base areas in Cambodia

C. 1973–77
FNL and North Vietnamese Final Offensive, March 1975
★ Border incidents 1975-78

Hanoi in ruins after the US bombattack at Christmas 1972

Temple of Borobudur in Indonesia is quadratic at the base. 515 × 515 feet.

Colossal statue of Philippine president (1965–86) Ferdinand Marcos.

A girl from Bali dancing the traditional Garuda dance.

183. INDONESIAS INDEPENDENCE

Indonesia 1976. A Dutch colony before independence, union with Netherl. 1949-56.
Federation of Malaysia, formed from British dependencies Sept. 16 1963
Earlier boundary

1963 Tense relations with Malaysia. The congress appoints Sukarno president for life.

1965 A communist coup attempt is put down. Tens of thousands of communists, and people of Chinese extraction, are murdered.

1967 Sukarno is forced to transfer all of the functions of the president and the prime minister to general Ibrahim Suharto. Friendly relations with China are replaced by a pro-Western policy.

1969 Following a plebescite, Irian Jaya (map nr. 183) becomes part of Indonesia, which has administered the area since 1963.

1975–76 Civil war in the Portuguese area of Timor. Indonesian forces invade and occupy the territory (map nr. 183).

within the framework of a Dutch-Indonesian union.

1950 Local uprisings and continued guerilla activity. On August 17 the Republic of Indonesia is proclaimed, with a strong central government, led by president Sukarno.

1956 On August 11 the union with the Netherlands is formally dissolved. **1957** Military coups, communist infiltration, and rising unrest in several provinces demanding self-rule. President Sukarno declares a state of emergency. Dutch property is confiscated and Dutch citizens expelled from the country.

Above: President Achmed Sukarno (1901–70) in Manila's bazaars in the Philippines in 1949. Sukarno, an engineer, was one of the founders of the Indonesian Nationalist Party, PNI, and was imprisoned several times by the Dutch in the inter-war period. The Japanese set him free, and after the Japanese surrender, Sukarno and Mohammed Hatta proclaimed Indonesia an independent republic August 17, 1945. Sukarno president. In the 1950s he abolished parliamentary democracy in the country, instituted what he called «guided democracy», and governed the country in almost dictatorial fashion. A conflict with the military led to his political demise in 1967.

Indonesia 1942–76

1942–45 Dutch East Indies is occupied by the Japanese. An anti-Dutch nationalist organization, led by Achmed Sukarno (illus. left), serves the Japanese in an advisory role.

1945 Sukarno and Mohammed Hatta proclaim Indonesia an independent republic on August 17. In September/October British and Dutch troops arrive to disarm the Japanese. Within a short time they are exchanging fire with Indonesian freedom fighters.

1949 After four years of intense fighting between Indonesians and Dutch government forces, both sides agree to the establishment of the United States of Indonesia,

Below: Jawaharlal Nehru's daughter, Indira Gandhi (1917–84), put her stamp on Indian political life for twenty years – both during the many years she governed India, and as leader of the opposition. Her strong personality made her a natural leader, but made her many enemies as well.

Left: Indira Gandhi was shot and killed on October 31, 1984. The pyre was lit by her son, Rajiv, who also succeeded her as prime minister.

Bangladesh 1947–84

1947 The eastern region of former British India becomes part of the dual state of Pakistan (East Pakistan).

1970 The Awami League, which is agitating for independence for East Pakistan, wins the December elections.

1971 Pakistani government forces enter East Pakistan in February. The Awami leader, Mujibur Rahman, is arrested, and all political activity is banned. In December Indian troops enter the country in support of the liberation forces, and on December 17 the war is over. East Pakistan becomes the state of Bangladesh. 1972 Rahman is set free in January and becomes head of the Government.

1975–77 Rahman is killed in a coup d'état. Zia Rahman seizes power and becomes president (1977).

1981–84 Zia Rahman is murdered. The country is under military rule until General Hussein Muhammed Ershad becomes president in 1984.

India 1939–91

1939–45 British India is automatically involved in the Second World War. Over two million Indians, drafted by the British, take part in the war. Demands for independence are growing steadily.

1947 The huge gap separating Hindus and adherents of Islam is a major obstacle to the creation of an independent, unified India. The country is, therefore, split in two, Hindu India, and Islamic Pakistan (map nr. 184), with the status of dominions. The division leads to the uprooting of many people, and much unrest. Pakistan resists the inclusion of Kashmir, largely Islamic, in the Indian state. Jawaharlal Nehru becomes India's first prime minister.

1948 Mahatma Gandhi, who led the struggle for independence, dies at age 78.

1950 On January 26 India becomes an independent republic with ties to the Commonwealth.

1952 The first election with universal suffrage gives the Congress Party and prime minister Jawaharlal Nehru a resounding victory.

1955 Moscow promises India economic and technical aid.

1959 Border disputes with China, which continue until 1967 (map nr. 184).

1964 Nehru dies and is succeeded by Lal Bahadur Shastri.

1965 August 5, Indian troops enter Pakistan. Cease-fire on September 22, following Soviet meditation, but the situation in the area remains extremely tense.

1966 Indira Gandhi becomes leader of the Congress Party and prime minister.

1971 Civil war in Pakistan. India intervenes actively on the side of East Pakistan, which separates from Pakistan (see col. 4).

1975 Indira Gandhi declares a state of emergency in order to crush a growing, albeit disorganized, opposition. Thousands are executed.

1977 Indira Gandhi loses the election and is succeeded by Morarji Desai of the Janate Party coalition.

1980 The Congress Party makes an impressive comeback. Indira Gandhi becomes prime minister.

1984 Indira Gandhi is shot and killed by two of her own Sikh bodyguards. Gandhi's son, Rajiv, is sworn in as India's new prime minister.

1989 The Congress Party loses the election and Gandhi is succeeded by V. P. Singh.

1991 Rajiv Gandhi is assassinated during the General Elections campaign.

184. DECOLONIZATION OF INDIA, PARTITION

Pakistan, formed 1947 of areas with muslim majority

Disputed areas from 1947, provisionally divided 1949 between India and Pakistan.

● Portuguese colonies to India, Dec. 18 1961

◉ French territory incorporated Aug. 16 1962

/// Border clashes between India and China

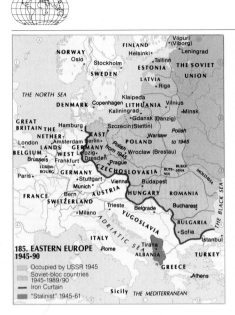

185. EASTERN EUROPE 1945-90

Occupied by USSR 1945
Soviet-bloc countries 1945-1989/90
— Iron Curtain
"Stalinist" 1945-61

Revolution Eastern Europe 1989–90 – communist dictatorships collapse

On Nov 9 1989 the East German authorities opened the Berlin Wall. For first time since its erection in 1961 East Germans were free to cross over into West Berlin. Its demolition both climaxed and symbolized the revolutions which in the fall of 1989 had brought down all the communist dictatorships, Moscow's allies.

All the east European revolutions were peaceful except in Romania. This meant an end to the Iron Curtain which for over 40 years had divided Europe.

The Soviet Union's former satellites began moving toward western-

style democracy and a market economy.

In Poland the anti-communist revolt had shown omens as early as 1980, when Lech Walesa had founded the free trade union Solidarity, at the same time as a wave of strikes paralyzed the country. Though Gen. Jaruzelski banned the movement and proclaimed martial law in 1981, Solidarity remained a powerful political force. After a new strike wave in 1988 the communist government opened negotiations which in 1989 led to partially free elections and Solidarity's great victory at the polls and majority in the new government (Aug. 1989). Though the communist party dissolved itself in Jan. 1990, Jaruzelski, the old régime's leader, remained president until Dec. 1990, when Poland's first democratic presidential election since World War II replaced him with Lech Walesa.

In Hungary growing dissatisfaction forced the communist leader, Janos Kadar, in power since 1956, to resign (1988). In Oct. 1989 the communist party dissolved itself and in March 1990 the first democratic elections were held since 1945, and led to the formation of a

Left: Mikhail Gorbachev, General Secretary of the USSR from 1985, and President from 1988.

non-socialist conservative coalition government.

In Czechoslovakia peaceful mass demonstrations led by students and intellectuals brought down the communist dictatorship in Nov–Dec. 1989. The party leadership, headed by Milos Jakes, resigned; and in Dec. Vaclac Havel, playwright and critic of the régime, was elected president. In June 1990 democratic elections gave a great victory to the Citizens Forum, the main force behind the revolution.

Romania had been ruled since 1948 by a grim communist dictatorship. In 1965 Nikolai Ceausescu had assumed power and made himself the object of an ever more grotesque personality cult, where his Securitate (secret police) exerted a reign of terror. Many people died in the revolution of Dec. 1989, when he was overthrown. A provisional government, the National Salvation Front, took over, and in May 1990 parliamentary elections were won by the Front, whose leader, Ion Iliescu, became president. But the opposition, claiming electoral fraud, accused the Front of being dominated by ex-communists who were sabotaging democratic developments. The atmosphere became even more bitter after the government (June 1990) had violently unleashed miners against a demonstration, killing five people.

Bulgaria, too, was affected. In Nov. 1989 Todor Zjivkov, the country's communist dictator since 1954, was overthrown. Reforming itself as a 'democratic socialist party', the Communist party won the first free elections (June 1990). But the opposition refused to accept this new government and in

Below: The hated Berlin Wall, erected in 1961 (see :nap 167), was opened 9–10 November, 1989, and later torn down.

Lech Walesa

Vaclav Havel

GERMANY from Oct. 3 1990

the fall of 1990 the country was paralyzed by strikes and demonstrations. In Dec. a coalition government was formed, with the communists (now calling themselves the Socialist party) in a minority. This meant the end of 45 years of communism in Bulgaria.

In East Germany (DDR) a mass flight of east Germans to the west began in the spring of 1989. At the same time the country was paralyzed by pro-democracy demonstrations. As a result of the crisis Erich Honecker, the communist leader, was deposed; and shortly afterwards the Berlin Wall was opened. A month later the forced resignation of Honecker's successor, Egon Krentz, put an end to the communist dictatorship. The country's first democratic elections (March 1990) were won by the anti-socialist Christian Democrats on a platform of reunion with West Germany. Economic collapse hastened the progress. In July the D-mark was introduced through monetary union with West Germany, and on Oct 3 the two German states were politically reunited, the former DDR becoming a member of the NATO alliance and of EEC.

The east European revolutions also reached the other two communist dictatorships on the Balkan peninsula. Ever since World War II YUGOSLAVIA had been ruled by a communist party, but since 1948, under president Josip Tito (d. 1980), it had reserved its right to find its own national path to socialism. From 1989 demands for democratic reforms fused with growing clashes between different ethnic groups. This resulted in a crisis which in 1991 came close to bursting the country apart. After democratic multi-party elections in 1990, power in four federal

republics went to non-socialist or nationalist parties. But in Serbia and Montenegro the socialists (i.e., the reformed Communist party) retained power. Slovenia and Croatia declared themselves sovereign states, with their own laws taking precedence over those of the federation. Both threatened to secede. While tension between Slovenes/Croats and Serbs came ever closer to flashpoint, the country was also shaken by a severe economic crisis, and there were sanguinary outbreaks of violence in Kosovo, a Serbian province whose Albanian majority demanded greater autonomy.

Since 1945 ALBANIA had been governed by a ruthless communist dictatorship. In 1990 the country was shaken by pro-democracy demonstrations demanding the citizen's right to go abroad. Thousands of Albanians began fleeing the country. In Dec. 1990 the communist president Ramiz Alia accepted a multi-party system.

The Communist party, now on a platform of democratic socialism, renamed itself Worker's Party. In March 1991 democratic elections gave it the victory. The democratic opposition showed considerable discontent with election results and violence occurred in many parts of the country.

A factor crucial to these east European rebellions was the reforms introduced by the Soviet leader Michail Gorbachev. Coming to power in 1985, he had tried to liberalize the Soviet Union's political and economic system and at the same time had encouraged reformist movements in eastern Europe, and rescinded the doctrine of military intervention against any threat to any communist state's political system. A withdrawal of military support by Big Brother which spelt

the east European satellite regimes' death-knell.

Union and Economic Strength from the West

Simultaneously with eastern Europe's ever more obvious decay during the 1980s, the west European economy went from strength to strength. This development played, and is still playing, an important role in the great transformation of Europe that began in 1989. The organizations for east European collaboration collapsed. The Warsaw Pact, created in Moscow in 1955, began to dissolve, and Soviet troops started withdrawing from Hungary, Czechoslovakia, Poland and the former DDR. In the spring of 1991 the pact's military collaboration came to an end. Comecon, the east European economic organization (cf. map 168) also lost all practical significance and western Europe's political and economic institutions - above all EEC - became the model for the economic reforms aimed at by the new east European governments. Several aimed at integration in west European collaboration. But the road into EEC is a long one. As a first step toward the west, Hungary and Czechoslovakia were accepted as members of the Council of Europe. In 1985–91 EEC took important measures to strengthen its internal collaboration. It was decided to create a free internal market by 1992, and negotiations began for a future political union.

EUROPE at beginning of 1991

- Member of EEC
- Member of EFTA
- Member of NATO
- Belongs to Council of Europe 1990–91

With the military threat to Europe from the Warsaw Pact now almost nil, NATO, too, lost its original motivation. Instead, it became the guarantor of European stability and a bridge for collaboration with the USA.

The USSR, a Disintegrating Empire

1. Estonia
2. Latvia
3. Lithuania
4. Belorussia
5. Ukraine
6. Moldavia
7. Georgia
8. Armenia
9. Azerbaijan
10. Turkmenistan
11. Uzbekistan
12. Tadzhikistan
13. Kirgizia

● Areas where ethnic and/or political conflicts have caused loss of life since 1986.

By early 1990 all 15 Soviet republics had declared their sovereignty, with their own laws taking precedence over those passed by the Soviet parliament. Esthonia, Latvia, Lithuania and Georgia went furthest in striving for complete autonomy. They had expressed a desire to leave the Union altogether.

THE DISCORDANT YUGOSLAVIA

Ethnic Moslems
Serbs
Croats
Slovenes
Monte-negrins
Albanians
Macedonians
Hungarians
International boundary
Republic boundary
Regional boundary

USA – the World Power

After World War II the USA was seen to be one of the world's two superpowers. It abandoned the isolationism which had long determined its policies toward the rest of the world outside the American continents. More than anything else it had been USA's economic and military strength which had secured the Allies' victory over Germany and Japan. The American nation became conscious of its own power and of having a global mission: to defend western-style democracy against communism.

Through the NATO alliance, led by USA, a barrier was raised against the military threat from the USSR, the other superpower. By a chain of alliances and military bases USA also tried to create guarantees against communist expansion

elsewhere. By intervening in the Korean War (1950–53) it repulsed communist aggression (see p. 119). USA's next major military effort was in Vietnam (Indochina), where it fought a sanguinary war 1964–73, the first not to end in an American victory. After the US army's withdrawal, South Vietnam was conquered by North Vietnam, and communist régimes also took power in the rest of Indochina. This defeat shook American self-confidence. Though USA retained its leading role among democracies, its total dominance here had shrunk. A factor here was that the USA's relative weight in world economy dwindled as new economic forces made themselves felt – primarily Japan and EEC. This development has continued in the early 1990s. At the same time revo-

lutionary events have reinforced USA's relative global weight and prestige.

The fall of communism in eastern Europe and the USSR's threatened economic collapse have left USA as the sole remaining military super-power – a position even more

obvious after the liberation of Kuwait by a total American-Allied victory over Irak in early 1991. The alliance, sanctioned by the UN, was dominated and led by USA, which also contributed 80 % of the war effort. The US global military presence can be seen from the map.

USA IN THE WORLD

● Air base   ▲ US military force (over 10,000 all arms) outside contiguous USA.
× Naval base

LATIN AMERICA

1. GUATEMALA
2. BELIZE 1981 x
3. HONDURAS
4. EL SALVADOR
5. NICARAGUA
6. COSTA RICA
7. PANAMA
8. JAMAICA 1962 x
9. BAHAMAS 1973 x
10. ST. KITTS-NEVIS 1983 x
11. ANTIGUA-BARBUDA 1981 x
12. DOMINICA 1978 x
13. ST. VINCENT 1979 x
14. BARBADOS 1966 x
15. ST. LUCIA 1979 x
16. GRANADA 1974 x
17. TRINIDAD-TOBAGO 1962 x

(1981 = year of liberation, x = member of CARICOM)

Members of:

LAIA, Latin American (economic) Inte-gration Association, 1981, successor of Latin American Free-Trade Area founded 1960.

CARICOM, Caribbean Community for co-operation in economic, foreign policy and other areas, founded 1973.

CACM, Central American Common Market, founded 1960.

Production of Narcotics

△ Cocaine   ◻ Marijuana
○ Opium
● Important Centre of Narcotics Refining

US Intervention in Central America:

Guatemala, military intervention leading to establishment of conservative regime in 1954;
EL SALVADOR, many years of military and economic aid to government fighting left-wing insurgency;
HONDURAS, financing of bases for 'contras' gerillas in 1980's;
NICARAGUA, military and economic aid to 'contras' fighting the left-wing regime, until 1990;
PANAMA military intervention to overthrow the dictator Noriega in 1989;
GRENADA, military intervention following power struggle within the Marx-ist regime in 1983. US-friendly interim government installed.

Latin America was largely decolo-nialized in the early 19th century (see pp. 94–95). The 1960–1990 period brought a new anti-colonial wave: 12 Brit. colonies and the formerly Dutch Surinam became independent. The map dates the independence of each country since

1960. The Latin-American countries have set up several organizations for economic (and to some extent also political) collaboration. But trade within the region is still poorly deve-loped. Only 14 % of Latin-American trade is internal to the region (1989) – the rest mainly with USA and Europe.

Democracy on the March

In the late 1970s most Latin-American countries had been overt or indirect military dictatorships. But the 1979–1990 period has seen a major change. Most of the dicta-torships have been replaced by elected civilian governments. This re-democratization process began in Ecuador, where the military régime was dismantled, with democratic elections in 1979. Since then democracy has been establish-ed in Peru (1980), Bolivia (1982), Argentina (1983), Brazil, Guate-mala and Uruguay (1985), Panama (1989), Chile, Haiti and Nicaragua (1990). After the dictator Stroess-ner's fall in 1989 Paraguay, too, has begun to become more democratic. For many decades Central America has been ravaged by civil wars and sanguinary political violence, con-flicts aggravated by great power interference. USA's traditional policy of naked power politics, together with its immense econo-mic influence, has determined much of the region's development. Up to the late 1980s USSR, helped by Cuba, was aiding and abetting left-wing revolutionary move-ments. Since then there has been more reason for optimism. In 1987 the Central-American countries agreed on a peace plan that made possible the 1990 transition to democracy and an end to civil war in Nicaragua. But the civil wars in El Salvador and Guatemala were still going on in early 1991, albeit with greater hope of peace, not least as a result of the end of the Cold War.

Democracy under threat

The military still exerts great in-fluence in Latin America. Many of its democracies must take its inte-rests into account to avoid new military coups. A concern which e.g. has half-paralyzed attempts to bring to trial earlier military dicta-torships' criminal infringements of human rights. One of the great problems has been the burden of debt incurred by so many Latin-American governments in the 1970s. Ill-judged investments and the 1979 oil crisis helped lay the foundations for a growing crisis of indebtedness in the 1980s. Latin-America has a total foreign debt of $400-bill., the world's heaviest per capita. Many Latin-American countries are tied to restrictive economic policies often also demanded by the World Bank and by the International Monetary Fund, as a condition for further loans. A crisis aggravated in many Latin-American countries by massive inflation and flight of capital, with risk of social unrest and a latent threat to democracy.
The drug traffic is another threat. Cocain, opium and marijuana are produced in large areas of Latin America (see map). Colombia has become a centre for their refine-ment, exporting drugs from all over South America and containing the most ruthless drug syndicates, threatening democracy, law and order by their corruption and murders.
Left-wing revolutionary move-ments are still a problem – mainly in Peru and El Salvador.

The Middle East

The Middle East is still the world's most conflict-ridden region. In 1988 the eight-year war between Iran and Iraq ended with a suspension of hostilities. Neither side had gained anything. The war had cost both countries a million lives and immense material devastation. Yet Iraq was still militarily powerful. And its president Saddam Hussein did not relinquish his aggressive policies. Kuwait became his next target. He hope by control of this small but oil-rich neighbour to solve his economic problems and realize his dream of becoming the Arab world's leader.

On Aug 2 1990 Iraq occupied Kuwait. But world reactions were much stronger than Saddam Hussein had anticipated. In UN the great powers agreed to apply economic sanctions. Forming a military alliance, USA sent big military forces to the Persian Gulf area. The UN Security Council empowered the alliance to attack Iraq unless it had evacuated Kuwait by Jan 15 1991. On Jan. 17 the allies launched devastating air attacks on Iraq's industrial, military and communications system, lasting for six weeks. A final land offensive, based on total command in the air and an outflanking movement, liberated Kuwait. On Feb 28 hostilities were suspended. The brief war had cost Iraq more than half her army. Despite this total defeat, Saddam Hussein remained in power, with enough forces to suppress a revolt by Shiite

THE MIDDLE EAST
The Political Scene in the Middle East after the Gulf War

- Arab countries that joined US-led alliance against Iraq. Post-war security cooperation makes them the leading political bloc in the region
- Gulf Cooperation Council, an economic and political organization dominated by Saudi Arabia.
- Turkey. US-ally through membership of NATO.

Defeated Iraq:
- Occupied by allies in February 1991
- Revolts in March 1991, controlled at times by Shia Muslims (in south) and Kurds (in north)
- Countries sympathetic to Iraq during war
- Shiite and Kurdish refugees (March-April 1991)

Muslims in the south and Kurds in the north. This civil war unleashed a further catastrophe. Half of Iraq's 3.5 mill. Kurds fled toward Iran and Turkey.

Kuwait had been liberated; but Israel remains in occupation of the West Bank and Gaza strip, where the Arab population has been in revolt since 1987, demanding an independent Palestinian state. After the Kuwait war, USA has launched a diplomatic offensive to seek a peaceful solution to this conflict. If it fails, new wars threaten the Middle East.

South Africa

Great changes occurred in southern Africa in the years 1989–91. In 1989 South Africa accepted a UN plan, under which it gave up its control of Namibia, which in 1990 became an independent state, with a democratically elected black government.

At the same time South Africa moved swiftly toward equal rights for its black majority. Politically, socially and economically the black population had been discriminated against by race laws, first introduced in 1948. As the oppression became worse in the 1970s and 80s,

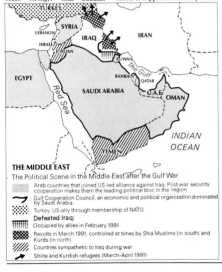

South Africa was formed in 1910 by a fusion of the British colonies of Natal, Cape Province, the Orange Free State and Transvaal. The country remained in the British Commonwealth until 1961.

Of South Africa's 32 million inh. 68 % are black, 18 % white, and the rest Indians or «coloured» half-breeds.

many countries decided to exert pressure on South Africa in the form of economic sanctions. When widespread unrest broke out among the black population in 1985, the governing Nationalist party realized the system must be reformed. But not until F.W. de Klerk became president in 1989 did such reforms really begin. In 1990 the government released the ANC leader Nelson Mandela from his long imprisonment. ANC became legal, and peace negotiations were opened with Mandela for the abolition of apartheid.

In early 1991 de Klerk promised to abrogate the last remaining racial laws as soon as possible. Negotiations are under way for a new constitution with democratic elections and a black franchise. But this peace movement is being disturbed by violence and bloodshed between the ANC and rival black groups.

Oceania

Oceania consists of 25 000 islands, scattered over a region equal to one-tenth of the earth's surface. Here the domination of the western colonial powers persisted longer than in any other part of the world. Australia and New Zealand apart, all Oceania's independent states have come into existence in the last 25 years.

For a long while Oceania remained politically stable. Only in recent years have its islands experienced troubles, often related to ethnic conflicts. A revolt broke out among

the Kanakas in French Caledonia in the late 1980s; Fiji was hit by two military coups in 1987; and the island of Bougainville, in Papua-New Guinea, has been in a state of revolt demanding its independence since 1989. The South Pacific Forum (founded 1971) is the region's organ for political and economic collaboration among all its 11 countries. In 1985 SPF declared the whole region a non-nuclear zone, thus defying France, which since 1966 had been carrying out nuclear bomb tests on Mururoa.

Boundary of proclaimed 'Nuclear weapon-free zone'
1970 The year of independence

ABBREVIATIONS USED IN MAPS AND TEXT

Aug.	*August*	Fr.	*French, France*	PR	*Principality*
Beg.	*Beginning*	GR DUCHY	*Grand Duchy*	Nov.	*November*
Brit.	*British*	indep.	*independent*	Port.	*Portugal,*
Ca.	*Circa*	internat.	*international*		*Portuguese*
Chin.	*Chinese*	Ital.	*Italian*	Pruss.	*Prussian*
Denm.	*Denmark*	Jan.	*January*	Prot.	*Protectorate*
Dec.	*December*	Jap.	*Japan*	REP	*Republic*
DSP	*Despóty*		*Japanese*	Russ.	*Russia, Russian*
Egypt.	*Egyptian*	KGD.	*Kingdom*	Sept.	*September*
ELECT.	*Electorate*	LGR	*Landgravate*	Sp.	*Spain, Spanish*
EMP.	*Empire*	MGR	*Margravate*	Sw.	*Swedish*
Febr.	*February*	Oct.	*October*	Turk.	*Turkey, Turkish*

MAP INDEX

The index contains all names found in the maps. The number in italics show page number, while the bold figure refers to the map number. The letters and number which then follow refer to the grid plan on the map.

A

Aachen *44* **60** G3, *45* **62** K6, *56* **78** E3
Aare *55* **77** C5
Aargau *55* **77** C5
Abadan *108* **153** DE5, *119* **174** C5
Abakan *98* **137** C3
Aballava (Burgh by Lands) *28* **39** H2
Abbeville *56* **78** D3
Abdera, Spain *16* **19** B2, *23* **28** B3
Abdera, Thrace *16* **19** DE2, *17* **21** D1
Åbenrå *86* **123** AB6
Aberdeen *58* **81** AB2, *81* **116** B1
Abessinia (Ethiopia) *97* **136** E3, *98* **137** A5, *105* **149** D2
Abidjan *122* **179** B5
Abila, Decapolis *26* **35** C2
Abila, North Africa *23* **28** A3
Abka *14* **15** A7
Åbo (Turku) *81* **116** D1, *83* **120** A2, *107* **151** D1
Abu Dhabi *108* **153** E6
Abu Simbel *14* **15** AB7
Abusir *14* **15** A2
Abydos *44* **60** L6, *51* **71** AB6
Abydos, Egypt *11* **10** B5, *14* **15** B4
Abyle *16* **19** A2
Acapulco *64* **88** A6
Accra *97* **136** B3, *122* **179** B5
Acdes Caesarum, Rome *27* **37** L4
Acerenza *45* **61** B6, *59* **83** D7
Achaia, principality *50* **70** E7
Achaia, province *24* **32** D6, *28* **38** G5
Achaia, region *16* **20** B5, *17* **21** B3

Acholla *16* **19** C3
Acre (Akka), town *54* **74** F4
Acre, region in South America *95* **132** C3
Actium *24* **32** D6, *28* **38** G5
Adal *65* **92** F2
Adalia (Antalya) *71* **102** BC6, *83* **120** AB7
Adamawa *65* **92** C2
Adana *49* **67** K1
Adane (Aden) *32* **44** F6
Adda *55* **77** E7
Addis Abeba *97* **136** DE2, *98* **137** A5
Adelaide *98* **137** EF7
Aden *36* **49** E6, *40* **55** E6, *96* **133** E4, *103* **145** D7, *108* **153** D7, *122* **179** EF4
Aden, Gulf of *97* **136** EF2
Adige *55* **77** F6
Adigrat *98* **137** A5
Adria (Hadria) *16* **19** C1, *22* **27** C2
Adrianople (Edirne) *45* **61** E5, *48* **66** I5, *51* **71** B6, *55* **76** E3, *81* **116** E3, *103* **144** DE3
Adriatic Sea (Mare Adriaticum) *22* **27** D3–4, *44* **60** I5, *81* **116** CD3, *87* **124** C2, *107* **151** C5–6
Adua *97* **136** E2, *98* **137** A5
Aduatuca *25* **33** BC2
Adulis *32* **44** EF6
Aedes Junonis Monetae, Rome *27* **37** I2
Aedui *25* **33** B3
Aegadian Isles *22* **27** C6
Aegates Insulae (The Aegean Islands) *22* **27** C6
Aegean Sea *17* **21** D2–3, *81* **116** E4
Aegium *16* **20** B5
Aegyptus (Egypt) *24* **32** E7, *26* **34** F4, *28* **38** I7
Aelana *28* **38** IJ6, *32* **44** E5
Aella Capitolina (Hierosolyma, Jerusalem) *28* **38** IJ6
Aemilia *22* **27** BC2
Aerø *86* **123** B6
Aesica (Great Chesters) *28* **39** I1
Afghanistan *64* **89** A91, *99* **140** DE6, *120* **176** HI4, *127* **184** AB1

Afinani *16* **20** F5
Africa *71*, *60* **84** G4, *65* **92**, *96* **133**, *97* **135**, *97* **136**, *120* **176**, *122* **179**
Africa Proconsularis *26* **34** CD4, *28* **38** EF6
Africa, Roman province *23* **28** E3, *24* **32** BC6–7
Afrodítopolis *14* **15** B2, *21* **26** AB3
Afyon *101* **141** J6
Agades *65* **92** C1
Agadir *97* **136** AB1
Agartala *127* **184** E3
Agathe *16* **19** B1, *23* **28** C1
Agedincum *25* **33** BC3
Aggersborg *44* **60** G1, *46* **63** D3
Agnagni *47* **65** D7
Agora, Olympia *18* **22** E6
Agra *35* **48** B3, *64* **89** B2, *65* **91** H2, *99* **140** C2
Agram (Zagreb) *50* **70** D6, *91* **127** IJ5, *101* **141** E3, *107* **151** C5
Agrigento (Agrigentum, Akragas) *53* **73** DE7, *101* **151** C5
Agrigentum (Agrigento, Akragas) *22* **27** D6, *23* **28** E3
Agulhas, Cape *97* **135** CD7
Ah-hsi *13* **13** E1
Ahmadabad *65* **91** H2, *83* **120** B3, *127* **184** B3
Ahmednagar *64* **89** B3, *65* **91** H3
Ahwaz *119* **174** C5
Aigaion *45* **61** D6
Aigeira *16* **20** C5
Aigina, island *16* **20** E6, *17* **21** C3
Aigina, town *16* **20** B5
Aigospotamoi *17* **21** DE2
Aigun (Heiho) *89* **126** K6
Aihun *35* **48** E1
Ain Salah *32* **44** B5, *96* **134** BC2, *122* **179** BC3
Ain Sefra *96* **134** B1
Ainos *16* **19** E2, *17* **21** E1
Aire *56* **78** D4, *66* **93** B5
Aitolia *16* **20** AB4, *17* **21** B3
Aix *44* **60** F5, *59* **83** C6
Aix-la-Chapelle, see Aachen
Ajaccio *44* **60** G6, *80* **115**

AB4, *81* **116** C4, *87* **124** A2
Ajan *98* **137** E2
Ajanta *36* **49** G5, *38* **53** B2
Ajmer *99* **140** BC2
Akaba *97* **136** DE1, *108* **153** C5, *118* **173** CD6
Akaba, Gulf of *118* **173** C7
Akarnania *17* **21** A3
Akbar, kingdom of 1605 *65* **91**
Akhet-Aton (El Amarna) *11* **10** B4, *13* **13** AB3
Akita *102* **142** EF2
Akka (Acre, Ptolemais) *15* **17** AB5, *48* **66** L7, *49* **67** J3, *60* **84** G4, *118* **173** C4
Akkad *10* **8** A1, *11* **10** E3, *12* **11** C2–3
Akrae *20* **24** B7
Akragas (Agrigentum) *16* **19** C2, *20* **24** A7, *20* **25** A3
Aksai Chin *127* **184** C1
Aksu *32* **44** H4
Aksum *30* **41** EF6
Aktion (Actium) *17* **21** A3
Akvitania (Aquitania) *28* **38** C3, *47* **65** J7, *50* **70** B6, *52* **72** CD6
Akyab *99* **140** E3
Åland (Aaland) *57* **79** F1, *69* **99** C4, *81* **116** D1, *83* **120** A2, *104* **146** F2, *106* **150** A3, *110* **157** D2
Al Mina *16* **19** F2
al-Arish *118* **173** C6
al-Djauf *118* **173** F6
Al-Fustat (old Cairo) *37* **51** J2
Al-Kuntilla *118* **173** C6
Al-Mansura *118* **173** AB5
al-Minya *118* **173** A7
al-Murvailih *118* **173** D7
al-Qantara *118* **173** C6
Alabama *92* **129** C3, *93* **130** E3
Alalakh *11* **10** CD3
Alalia (Aleria) *16* **19** C2, *22* **27** B4
Alam *108* AB2, *11* **10** F4, *12* **11** D2–3, *12* **12** F3
Alaska *60* **84** B2, *120* **176** B2
Alauna (Maryport) *28* **39** G2
Alba Longa *38* **52** CD4
Albacete *109* **156** E2
Albania *75* **76** E6, *72* **103** G6,

84 **121** C3, *92* **129** C3, *107* **151** CD6, *107*, **152** A1, *108* **154** E4, *110* **157** D6, *112* **161** C6, *115* **168** D4, *116* **169** C7, *120* **176** G3, *128* **185** C5
Albany, Australia *98* **137** E7
Albany, USA *92* **128** K2
Albert *95* **132** IJ2
Albert, Lake *96* **133** D5, *123* **180** F1
Albertville *97* **136** D3, *123* **180** F2
Albi *55* **77** DE7, *53* **73** A4–5
Albis (Elbe) *28* **38** EF1
Ålborg *57* **79** CD2, *70* **100** D1, *81* **116** C1
Albuera *73* **104** AB6
Alcala *83* A6
Alcala de Henares *49* **68** C7
Alcibiades' campaign to Sicily 415–413 BC *17* **21** B5
Aldabra *97* **136** EF4, *122* **179** F6
Aldeiga (Ladoga) *46* **63** F2
Aldeigjuborg (Staraja Ladoga) *46* **63** F2
Aleksandrovsk *98* **137** EF2–3
Alemanni *28* **38** E2, *29* **40** B6, *42* **57** H5
Alemannia *43* **59** D4, *44* **60** G4, *45* **62** K6
Alençon *56* **78** C4, *68* **97** B2
Aleppo (Haleb) *11* **10** D3, *36* **49** DE4, *71* **102** D6
Aleria (Alalia) *22* **27** B4
Alesia *25* **33** BC3, *28* **38** D3
Aleuteian *111* **160** E4, *120* **176** L2–3
Alexander the Great's campaign 334–232 BC *21* **26**
Alexandrette *108* **153** C4
Alexandria *21* **26** B2–3, *26* **34** F4, *28* **38** H6, *36* **49** CD4, *40* **55** CD4, *103* **145** B6, *112* **162** F2
Alexandria (Ghasni) *21* **26** EF2
Alexandria (Herat) *21* **26** E2, *24* **31** JK5, *32* **44** G5, *38* **52** J1
Alexandria (Kandahar) *21* **26** EF2, *24* **31** K5, *38* **52** J1
Alexandria Eskhata (Leninabad) *21* **26** F1, *24* **31** K4

Alexandria, Babylonia *21 26* CD3
Alexandria, Bactria *21 26* F2
Alexandria, Carmania *21 26* E3
Alexandria, Egypt *21 26* B2–3, *26* 34 F4, *28* 38 H6, *36* 49 CD4, *40* 55 CD4
Alexandria, Gedrosia *21 26* F3
Alexandria, Syria *21 26* BC2
Alexandropol (Leninakan) *108* 153 D4
Alexandropolis, Partia *21 26* E2
Alexandroupolis (Dedeagatsj) *101* 141 GH5
Alfeios *16 20* B6
Algeciras *97* 136 B1
Alger *68* 97 C4, *81* 116 B4, *96* 134 BC1, *122* 179 BC3
Algeria *96* 134 BC2, *97* 136 B1, *112* 162 A1, *120* 176 F4, *122* 179 BC3
Alicante (Lucentum) *81* 118 C7, *84* 121 C6, *91* 127 F7, *109* 156 F2
Aljubarrota *55* 76 A3
Alkmaar *66* 93 BC2
Alland (Åland) *46* 63 E2–3
Allenstein *70* 100 H2, *105* 147 J5
Aller *68* 98 D2
Allstedt *47* 65 D2
Alma *101* 141 K3
Almagros, Diego, campaign to Chile 1535–37 *60* 84 D5–6
Almanza *72* 103 B6
Almeria *54* 74 AB3, *91* 127 F7, *109* 156 E3
Almohad, dominion of ca. 1240 *50* 70 BC7
Almoravides, dominion of ca. 1100 *48* 66 CD5–6
Alpes Cottiae (A.C.) *28* 38 D3
Alpes Graiae (A.G.) *28* 38 E3
Alpes Maritimae (A.M.) *28* 38 DE3
Alps *43* 59 D4–5, *68* 97 CD2
Als *86* 123 B6
Alsace (Elsass) *68* 97 C2, *104* 146 D3
Alsace-Lorraine (Elsass-Lothringen) *107* 151 AB4
Alstahaug *72* 103 D2
Altai (mountains) *34* 44 I3, *36* 49 G2–3, *40* 55 GH2–3
Altamira *9* 7 A2
Altdorf *55* 77 D6
Altenburg *70* 100 E4
Altis (festival square), Olympia *18* 22 E6
Altmark *53* 73 CD1, *75* 106 C2
Altranstädt *69* 99 A6
Amalfi *53* 73 E6
Amanus *12* 11 B2
Amaseia *23* 30 C5, *45* 61 G5

Amastris *45* 61 F5
Amazon (Rio Amazonas) *62* 85 DE5, *63* 86 C1–2, *95* 132 D3
Amazonas, province *95* 132 C3
Amboina *99* 139 L4
Amboise *56* 78 C5, *68* 97 BC2
Ambracia *17* 21 A2
Ambrona *9* 7 A2
Ameland *66* 93 CD1
Amida *11* 10 DE2
Amiens (Samarobriva) *45* 62 J6, *48* 66 D4, *56* 78 D4, *68* 97 BC1, *79* 113 B1, *79* 114 B1, *81* 116 B2, *105* 148 I2, *107* 151 A3
Amirante Islands *97* 136 F3, *98* 137 B6, *122* 179 F6
Amisos (Amisus) *23* 30 D5, *28* 38 I4
Amiternum *23* 28 EF1
Amman *49* 67 K4, *108* 153 C5, *119* 174 A5
Ammon, region *15* 17 C5, *15* 18 F5
Ammonion (oracle of A-mon) *21* 26 A3, *28* 38 GH7
Amorgos *17* 21 E4, *88* 125 D3
Amorion *45* 61 F6
Amoy (Xiamen) *35* 48 E3, *45* 61 B6
Amphipolis *17* 21 C1, *20* 25 D2
Ampurias (Emporion) *24* 31 C4
Amri *8* 3 E6, *108* E3
Amritsar *99* 140 C1
Amsterdam *66* 93 C2, *72* 103 C4, *68* 97 C1, *76* 107 C5, *79* 114 C1, *81* 116 BC1, *91* 127 GH5, *107* 151 A3, *110* 157 BC4
Amu-Darja (Oxos) *32* 45 A2, *40* 55 F3–4
Amur *40* 55 K2, *89* 126 K6, *98* 137 E3, *117* 170 E4
Amur Railway *98* 137 DE2–3
Amur, province *89* 126 K6, *98* 137 E3
Anadyr *60* 84 A2, K2, *98* 137 F1
Anaiza *108* 153 D6
Anaphe *17* 21 DE4
Anas (Guadiana) *23* 28 A2
Anatolia *6* 2 C3, *71* 102 C6
Anatolikon *45* 61 F6
Anazarbos *45* 61 G6
Anching *65* 91 L1
Ancon *95* 132 B4
Ancona *22* 27 D1, *44* 60 H5, *45* 61 A5, *57* 80 K2, *80* 115 D3
Ancyra (Angora, Ankara) *12* 12 C1, *21* 26 B2, *26* 34 F3, *28* 38 I4, *45* 61 F6
Andalsnes *110* 157 C2
Andalucia *48* 66 B6, *68* 97 A4, *109* 156 DE3
Andaman Islands *64* 89 D3,

65 91 J4, *99* 140 EF4, *127* 184 EF4·
Andernach *47* 65 B3
Andes (mountains) *63* 86 B2–3
Andhra *32* 44 H6, *38* 52 K2, *38* 53 B3
Andhra Pradesh *127* 184 C4
Andisjan *98* 137 B3–4
Andong *102* 143 E6
Andorra *81* 116 B3, *81* 118 D5, *84* 121 CD6
Andros *17* 21 D3, *88* 125 C3
Andrussov *71* 101 J6, *72* 103 F2
Angara *32* 44 I2, *98* 137 C2
Angers *44* 60 E4, *49* 68 D6
Angkor *36* 49 IJ6, *39* 54 BC6
Angler *32* 44 C3, *42* 57 H4
Anglesey *52* 72 BC3
Anglo-Egyptian Sudan *97* 136 D2, *98* 138 E7, *103* 145 B7, *105* 149 D2, *108* 153 AB7, *113* 164 D6
Anglo-Saxon kingdoms *42* 57 G3–4
Anglo-Saxons *42* 58 B1
Angola *60* 84 G5, *96* 133 C6, *97* 136 C4, *105* 149 CD2, *113* 164 C7, *120* 176 G5, *122* 179 CD6, *123* 180 DE3
Angora (Ankara, Ancyra) *34* 47 A5, *40* 55 D4, *48* 66 K5
Angostura (Ciudad Bolivar) *95* 132 CD2
Angouleme *44* 60 E4
Anguiletum *42* 57 E2
Anhalt *70* 100 DE4, *86* 122 C2
Anhui *30* 41 C6, *102* 142 B4
Ani *51* 71 E6
Aniba *14* 15 B6
Anju *119* 175 B2
Ankara (Ancyra, Angora) *11* 10 C2, *28* 38 I4, *45* 61 F6, *71* 102 C5, *112* 161 EF6
Annam (Vietnam) *40* 55 IJ5, *65* 91 L3, *99* 139 J1–2, *124* 181 C5
Annan (Chiao) *32* 45 E3, *36* 49 IJ5
Anpei *32* 45 D2, *36* 49 IJ3
Ansbach *70* 100 D5, *75* 106 B3
Anshan, China *32* 44 L4
Anshan, Iran *10* 8 B2, *12* 11 DE3
Ansina (Adalia) *71* 102 B6, *103* 144 EF4
Antarctica *60* 84 DE7, *120* 176 EF7
Antigua *121* 177 E4
Antilles, Dutch *121* 177 D2, E1
Antilles, Greater *121* 177 BC1
Antilles, Lesser *121* 177 DE2

Antinoopolis *28* 38 I7
Antiochea, se Antiochia
Antiochia (Antiochea) *24* 31 G5–6, *24* 32 F6, *26* 34 F3, *28* 38 I5, *36* 49 D4, *36* 50 A2, *41* 56 L7, *45* 61 G6, *48* 66 L6, *49* 67 K2, *54* 74 F3
Antiochia (Merv) *24* 31 J5
Antiochia, Byzantine thema *45* 61 G6–7
Antiochia, principality *49* 67 K2
Antiochia, town *23* 30 CD7
Antipatris *26* 35 B3
Antisuyu *63* 86 BC3
Antium *20* 24 A4
Antivari (Bar) *45* 61 BC5, *101* 141 EF4, *103* 144 B3
Antofagasta *95* 132 BC5
Antung *119* 175 A1
Antwerpen *54* 74 BC2, *56* 78 DE3, *66* 93 BC3, *70* 100 B4, *76* 107 C5, *79* 114 C1, *107* 151 A3
Anxur (Tarracina) *22* 27 CD4
Anzio *112* 161 B5
Aosta *70* 100 C7, *101* 141 B3
Apamea (Apamea) *23* 30 B6, *26* 34 F3
Aperantia *16* 20 A4
Apollonia, Cyrene *9* 6 F7, *16* 19 E3
Apollonia, Illyria *16* 19 D2, *24* 31 DE5, *26* 34 D3
Apollonia, Israel *26* 35 A3
Apollonia, Thrace *16* 19 E2, *55* 77 E2
Appenzell *55* 77 E5
Appomattox *92* 129 D3
Aptara *17* 21 C5
Apulia *22* 27 E4, *45* 61 B5–6
Aquae (Baden-Baden) *29* 40 A7
Aquae Sextiae *24* 32 B6, *25* 33 C4
Aquae Sulis (Bath) *25* 33 A2
Aquileia *22* 27 D1, *28* 38 F3, *43* 59 E4, *45* 61 A4, *48* 66 F4, *59* 83 D6
Aquincum (Budapest) *26* 34 DE2, *28* 38 F3
Aquino *50* 70 D7, *57* 80 K3
Aquitania (Aquitania) *24* 32 B5, *25* 33 AB4, *28* 38 C3, *37* 51 H1, *43* 59 BC5, *44* 60 EF4, *45* 62 J7, *50* 70 B6, *52* 72 CD6, *55* 76 B3
Arabian Sea *37* 51 L2–3, *40* 55 FG5, *64* 89 A3
Arabs, Arabia, see also Saudi-Arabia *24* 31 GH7, *28* 38 I6, *36* 49 E5, *37* 51 K2, *71* 102 DE7, *97* 136 E1–2, *103* 145 CD6
Arachosia *13* 14 EF6, *24* 31 K5–6, *38* 52 J1
Arad *105* 147 J7, *109* 155 D6
Aragon *48* 66 C4, *50* 70 B6–7, *55* 76 B3, *56* 78 C7, *59* 82 B3, *68* 97 B3, *109* 156 E2

Arakan *99* 140 EF3
Araks *51* 71 F6
Aral Sea *13* 14 D5, *32* 44 G4
Aralsk *89* 126 H7
Aram *15* 18 F4
Aranjuez *81* 116 AB4, *81* 118 C6, *91* 127 F6, *109* 156 E2
Ararat *11* 10 E2, *51* 71 E6, *71* 102 E5
Arctic Ocean *60* 84 BC1, JK1
Ardennes *105* 148 KL2
Arelate (Arles) *25* 33 BC4, *28* 38 D3
Arensburg *69* 99 CD4
Arequipa *62* 85 CD5, *63* 86 B3, *95* 132 BC4
Arezzo *49* 68 E6–7, *57* 80 J2
Argentina *63* 86 C2, *95* 132 C5–6, *105* 149 B3, *113* 164 B7, *120* 176 D6
Argentoratum (Strasbourg) *29* 40 A7
Argiletum, Rome *27* 37 L2
Arginusai *17* 21 E3
Argolis *16* 20 D6
Argolis, Gulf of *16* 20 D7
Argos *16* 20 D6, *17* 21 B4, *20* 25 D3, *88* 125 B2
Argurokastron (Gjirokaster) *88* 125 A2
Århus *50* 69 D3, *55* 76 C1, *81* 116 C1, *86* 123 B5, *107* 151 B2
Aria *13* 14 E6, *24* 31 JK5
Ariba (Jericho) *118* 171 B2, *118* 172 F2
Arica *64* 88 AB7, *95* 132 C4
Ariere *13* 13 D2
Ariminum (Rimini) *22* 27 CD2
Arios *24* 31 J5
Arizona *93* 130 B3
Arkansas *92* 129 B3, *93* 130 C3
Arkansas River *92* 129 A2–3, *93* 130 C3
Arkelais *26* 35 C4
Arkhangelsk, city *60* 84 GH2, *83* 120 C2
Arkhangelsk, province *83* 120 CD2
Arles (Arelate), town *44* 60 F5, *47* 65 A6, *53* 73 B5
Arles (Burgundy), kingdom *53* 73 B4
Armagh *41* 56 I6, *43* 59 AB3, *47* 64 A1, *50* 69 A2

Armagnac 52 72 D7, 56 78 C7
Armavir 106 150 E6
Armenia 12 12 DE1, 13 14 C5–6, 21 26 C2, 23 30 DE6, 24 31 GH5, 24 32 F6, 28 38 JK4, 32 44 F4, 36 50 AB5, 37 51 JK1, 46 63 H5, 50 70 F7, 51 71 E6, 71 102 E5, 106 150 F7, 108 153 CD4, 115 168 F4
Armeniakon 45 61 G5
Armentières 66 93 A4
Arnhem 57 79 C4, 66 93 D2, 110 157 AB3–4
Arnhem Land 98 137 EF6
Arnus (Arno) 22 27 BC3
Arpi 22 27 E4
Arras 50 69 B4, 56 78 D3, 66 93 A4, 79 114 B1, 105 148 J2
Arretium 22 27 C3
Arta 88 125 A2
Artaxata 26 34 G3, 28 38 K4
Artemision 16 19 B2
Artemision (Artemesion), promontory 17 21 C3
Artois 52 72 C6, 66 93 A4, 70 100 A4, 79 113 B1, 105 148 I1–2
Aru Islands 15 17 B6
Arunachal Pradesh 127 184 EF2
Arundel 52 72 CD4
Arusha 122 179 E5
Arvad 12 12 C2
Arverni 25 33 B3–4
Arx, Rome 27 36 K6, 27 37 I2
Arxon 36 49 E4
Ascension 96 133 A6, 97 136 A3, 122 179 AB6
Aschaffenburg 68 98 C4
Asclepius, temple of, Acropolis 19 23 CD2
Asculum 22 27 D3 ·
Ashdod 11 57 A6, 15 18 D6
Ashkelon (Ashqelon) 8 5 E4, 15 17 A6, 15 18 D6, 26 35 A4, 49 67 J4
Ashqelon (Ashkelon) 8 5 E4, 15 17 A6, 15 18 D6, 26 35 A4, 49 67 J4
Asia Minor 46 63 G6
Asia, Roman province 23 30 E6, 26 34 EF3, 28 38 H5
Ashkhabad 98 137 B4
Asine 16 20 D6
Asir 108 153 CD6–7
Asirgarh 65 91 H2
Asisium 28 38 E4
Askra 16 20 D5
Aspadana 13 14 D6
Aspendos 20 25 F3, 23 30 B7
Aspern 82 119 D3
Assab 107 152 BC3
Assam 65 91 J2, 99 140 E2, 127 184 H2
Assen 66 93 D1

Assisi 53 73 D5, 80 115 C4
Assiut 14 15 AB4, 108 153 B5
Assos 20 25 E2
Assur 8 5 F3, 10 8 A1, 11 10 E3, 12 11 C2, 12 12 E2
Assyria 11 10 E3, 12 12 D2, 13 14 BC6, 26 34 G3, 28 38 K5
Astakos 17 21 F1
Astapus 32 44 I1
Astorga 36 49 A3, 81 118 B5
Astrakhan 40 55 E3, 71 101 L7, 83 120 DE5
Astrakhan Khanate 71 101 KL6, 83 120 D5
Asturia-Leon 46 63 AB5
Asturias 24 32 A5–6, 37 51 G1, 43 59 A5, 44 60 D5, 109 156 D1
Asturias-Leon 46 63 AB5
Astypalaia 88 125 D3
Asunción 63 86 C4, 95 132 D5
Aswan (Syene) 37 51 J2, 42 58 D3, 108 153 B6
Atandros 17 21 E2
Athens (Athenae) 17 21 C3, 19 23, 20 25 D3, 28 38 G5, 55 76 EA, 81 116 E4, 107 151 D7, 112 162 E1
Atholone 52 72 AB3
Athos 17 21 CD2, 88 125 C2
Atil 46 63 H4, 51 71 F5
Atjeh 64 90 H5, 65 91 JK4, 99 139 HI3
Atlantic Ocean (Oceanus Atlanticus) 28 38 AB1–3, 60 84 EF4–5
Atlanta 92 129 C3, 93 130 F3
Atropatenean Media 24 31 H5
Attaleia (Attalea) 45 61 F6, 50 70 F7
Attica 16 20 EF5, 17 21 C3
Attigny 47 65 A3
Attila's residence 434–53, 42 57 J5
Attu 111 160 E4
Auckland Islands 120 176 L7
Audagost 32 44 A6
Aufidus 23 29
Augila 28 38 G7
Augsburg (Augusta Vindelicorum) 28 38 E3, 44 60 GH4, 55 76 C2, 58 81 CD5
Augusta Emerita 26 34 AB3, 28 38 B4
Augusta Taurinorum (Torino) 22 27 A2
Augusta Treverorum (Trier) 28 38 D2, 29 40 A6
Augusta Vindelicorum (Augsburg) 28 38 E3, 29 40 B7
Augustenborg 70 100 D2, 86 123 B6
Augustodunum 26 34 C2, 28 38 D3
Aulis 16 20 E5

Aulona 48 66 GH5
Aurangabad 65 91 H3
Aurantis 26 35 D2
Auschwitz 111 158 B2
Ausculum 23 28 F2
Austerlitz 81 116 D2, 81 117, 82 119 D2
Australia, Commonwealth of 60 84 K5, 98 137 EF7, 98 138 F7, 105 149 EF3, 113 164 F7, 120 176 K5–6
Austrasia 43 59 CD3, 44 60 G3
Austria 53 73 DE3, 68 97 DE2, 69 99 B7, 70 100 F5–6, 72 103 D5, 80 115 EF2, 81 116 CD2, 82 119 DE3, 84 121 FG4–5, 87 124 BC1, 107 151 BC4, 108 154 D3, 109 155 C6, 115 168 C3
Austria-Hungary 91 127 JK4–5, 101 141 DF2–3, 103 144 AC1, 104 146 FG5, 105 147 JK6–7
Austrian Netherlands, The 72 103 C4, 74 105 A2–3, 78 111 BC1
Autun 81 116 B3
Auvergne 52 72 E6, 56 78 D6, 79 113 B2
Auxerre 44 60 F4, 56 78 D5, 79 113 B2
Ava 35 48 CD4, 64 84 IJ4, 99 140 F3
Avalites 32 44 F7
Avanti 38 52 K2
Avar Kingdom 35 48 I1, 42 58 JK1, 44 60
Avaricum (Bourges) 9 6 D6, 25 33 B3
Avars 42 57 K5, L5
Aventicum 26 34 C2
Aventin, Rome 27 36 K7
Aversa 45 61 A6
Avignon 47 65 A6, 49 68 DE6, 55 76 D3, 56 78 E7, 59 82 B2, 59 83 C6, 68 97 C3, 79 113 BC, 79 114 C3, 81 116 BC3
Avila 48 66 B5, 49 68 C7
Ayacucho 95 132 BC4
Ayodhya 38 53 BC1
Ayr 77 109 D5
Ayutthaya 35 48 D4, 39 54 B6, 64 89 K5, 65 91 K3
Azerbaijan 36 50 B5
Ashanti 96 133 B5
Azincourt 56 78 D3
Azores 60 84 E3, 120 176 F3
Azov (Voronesj), province 83 120 C4–5
Azov, Sea of 45 61 F4, 101 141 KL2, 113 163 E4
Azov, town 71 101 K7, 83 120 C5, 89 126 G6
Aztec culture 63 87 AB3

B

Ba 31 43 A6

Baalbek 45 61 G7, 49 67 K3
Babylon 8 5 F4, 10 8 A2, 11 10 E4, 12 11 C3, 12 12 E3, 13 14 C7, 21 26 C2, 24 31 H6, 28 38 K5
Babylonia 8 5 F3–4, 11 10 EF3, 12 12 E2, 13 14 C6, 21 26 CD3
Bacau 105 147 KL7
Bactra (Balkh) 21 26 E2, 24 31 K5
Bactria 13 14 E6, 21 26 F2, 36 50 E6
Badajoz 82 119 A4
Baden, city 55 77 D5
Baden, principality 55 77 C5, 84 121 DEA, 114 166 B4
Baden-Baden 29 40 A7
Bae-lieu 124 181 B5
Baecula 23 28 B2
Baetis (Guadalquivir) 28 38 B4
Baffin Bay 120 176 E2
Baffin Island 60 84 D2, 98 138 D6
Bagamoyo 65 92 EF3, 96 133 E6
Baghdad 11 10 E3, 36 49 E4, 40 55 E4
Baghdad caliphate 46 63 H6
Bagradas 22 27 B7
Bahamas (Lucayas) 54 75 D4, 62 85 CD3, 92 128 J3, 95 132 J1, 120 176 D4, 121 177 CD1, 121 178 BC1
Bahia (Sao Salvador) 62 85 EF5, 64 88 B7
Bahia, province 95 132 F4
Bahrain 12 11 DE4, 97 136 F1, 103 145 D6, 119 174 C6
Båhuslen 57 79 D1–2, 69 99 E3
Baie de la Seine 113 165 B3
Bailén 81 118 BC7
Bajkal, Lake 40 55 I2
Baker, island 111 160 F7
Baker, Samuel, W., explorer in Africa 1862–65 86 123 D4
Bakongo 123 180 D2
Baku 83 120 E6
Bala-Kot 108 E3
Balaklava 101 141 K3
Balasagun 32 45 B2
Balashov 106 150 DE5
Balaton 70 100 G6
Balearic Islands 24 31 B5, 23 28 C2, 28 38 CD4, 42 57 G6, 43 59 G6, 44 60 EF6, 68 97 BC3
Bali 64 90 K7, 99 139 JK4, 111 159 B3
Balikpapan 111 159 AB3
Balkh (Bactra) 32 45 A2, 40 55 F4, 60 84 H3–4
Balkhash, Lake 40 55 G3
Balta 73 104 P3, 106 150 C6

Baltic Bronze Age 8 5 D1–2
Baltic, The 43 59 E2, 50 69 E3, 55 76 D1, 104 146 F2–3, 107 151 C2, 113 163 AB2
Baltimore 92 128 JK2, 92 129 D2
Balts 42 57 J3, 46 63 EF3
Baluchistan (Gedrosia) 99 140 A2, 127 184 A2
Bamako 122 179 AB4
Bamberg 41 56 J6, 47 65 D3, 53 73 D2
Banat, agricultural region 72 103 E5, 84 121 G5, 101 141 F3
Banda Sea 99 139 L4
Bandar Abbas 108 153 EF5
Bandjarmasin 98 137 E6, 99 139 J4
Bangalore 99 140 BC4, 127 184 C4
Bangi 123 180 D1
Bangka 64 90 J6, 99 139 J4
Bangkok (Krung Thep) 47 65 I6, 111 160 AB6, 125 182 A3, D2–3, A6
Bangladesh 127 184 E2–3
Bangor 41 56 I6, 56 78 A1
Bangul 122 179 D5
Bangweulu, Lake 54 D6
Banjarmasin 64 90 K6–7
Banjuwangi 98 137 DE6
Banningville 123 180 DE2
Bannockburn 52 72 DE2
Banpo 8 3 F4
Bantam 64 90 J7, 99 139 I4
Bapaume 105 148 IJ2
Bar (Antivari), town on the Adriatic 103 144 EF4
Bar, duchy 70 100 B5
Bar, town in Podolia 73 104 E3
Baranov 112 161 D4
Baranovichi 105 147 K5
Barbados 94 131 D7, 120 176 DE4, 121 177 E2
Barbaricon 32 44 G6
Barbary Coast 108 153 E6
Barbary States 72 103 BC7
Barbastro 48 66 CD5
Barcelona (Barciano), city 23 28 C2, 43 59 C6, 55 76 B3, 68 97 C3, 76 107 B7, 81 116 B4, 109 156 F2
Barcelona, county (hist.) 48 66 D4–5
Barcelos 62 85 D5, 95 132 CD3
Barciano (Barcelona) 23 28 C2
Barda 36 49 E3–4
Barents Sea (Dumbshaf) 46 63 FG1, 60 84 G2
Barents', Willem, journey 1596–97 60 84 F2–3, H1
Barfleur 52 72 CD4
Bari (Barium) 22 27 F4, 43 59 E6, 44 60 I6, 45 61 B6, 48 66 G5, 55 76 D3, 87 124 C2

Baria *23* **28** B3
Barium (Bari) *22* **27** F4
Barka *37* **51** I2
Barletta *45* **61** B6, *59* **83** E6
Baroda *99* **140** B3
Baros *64* **90** HI6
Barquisimeto *95* **132** BC2
Barranquilla *95* **132** B2, *121* **177** C2
Barrow *76* **108** AB5
Bärwalde *68* **98** F2
Barygaza (Bharukaccha, Broach) *32* **44** H6, *38* **53** A2
Basan *15* **17** C5
Basel *45* **62** K6, *49* **68** E6, *53* **73** BC3, *55* **76** C2, *56* **78** E5, *68* **97** D2, *79* **114** C2, *81* **116** BC3, *107* **151** B4
Basilica Aemilia, Rome *27* **37** K3
Basilica Constantini, Rome *27* **37** L3
Basilica Julia, Rome *25* **33** J3
Basilica Ulpia, Rome *25* **33** J1
Basques *42* **57** F6, *42* **58** AB1
Basra *37* **51** K2, *40* **55** E4, *119* **174** B5
Bassano *80* **115** C2
Bassein *65* **91** H3, *99* **140** EF4
Bass Strait *98* **137** F7
Bastar *99* **140** C3
Bastia *101* **141** B4
Bastille, Paris *78* **112** F6
Basutoland *97* **135** E7
Bata *122* **179** C5
Batanea *26* **35** CD2
Batavia (Djakarta) *64* **90** J7, *99* **139** J4
Batavian Republic, The *81* **116** BC2
Bath *25* **33** A2, *52* **72** C4, *77* **109** E7
Bathurst, Africa *97* **136** A2
Bathurst, Australia *98* **137** F7
Battambang *124* **181** AB6
Batticaloa *65* **91** I4
Batum *106* **150** E7
Baturin *69* **99** F6
Baudouinville *123* **180** F2
Bautzen *57* **79** E4
Bavaria *43* **59** D4, *44* **60** H4, *45* **62** KL6, *50* **70** CD6, *68* **97** D1, *68* **98** DE5, *72* **103** D5, *106* **150** C4, *81* **116** C3, *107* **151** B4
Bavaria, duchy *47* **65** D4, *53* **73** D3
Bavaria, electoral principality *70* **100** E5, *74* **105** C3
Bavaria, kingdom *80* **115** C1, *82* **119** CD3, *84* **121** E4, *86* **122** C3–4
Bavarians *42* **57** H5
Bay of Pigs *121* **178** A2
Bayeux (Augustodurum) *44* **60** E3, *47* **64** B2, *50* **69** B4, *113* **165** AB3

Bayonne *52* **72** C7, *54* **74** AB2, *56* **78** B7, *76* **107** B6, *79* **113** A3, *79* **114** A3, *81* **116** B3, *81* **118** C5
Bayreuth *70* **100** E5, *75* **106** C3
Bear Island *60* **84** G2
Béarn *52* **72** D7, *56* **78** C7
Beaufort Sea *120* **176** BC1
Beaujeu *56* **78** D6
Beauvais *68* **97** BC1
Bechuanaland *97* **135** D6, *97* **136** D4
Bedford *56* **78** C2
Beersheba *15* **17** AB6, *118* **171** AB2
Behistun *13* **14** D6
Beijing (Peking), see also Khanbalik *60* **84** J3, *102* **142** B3, *117* **170** DE5
Beira *97* **136** DE4
Beirut *71* **102** C6, *103* **145** C6, *119* **174** A5
Belaja *83* **120** E3
Belém (Nossa Senhora de Belém, Para) *62* **85** EF5, *95* **132** E3
Belfast *72* **103** B3, *91* **127** F3
Belfort *70* **100** B6
Belgian Congo *97* **136** D3, *123* **180** E1
Belgium (Belgica) *24* **32** B3, *25* **33** BC5, *28* **39** B3, *51* **72** C7, *81* **114** C7, *91* **127** G4, *104* **146** D4, *105* **148** JK1, *107* **151** A3, *108* **154** C2, *110* **157** B4, *111* **158** A2, *112* **161** A4, *113* **164** C6, *115* **168** B3, *116* **169** B6, *120* **176** F3
Belgorod, on the Dnestr *45* **61** E4, *51* **71** B5
Belgorod, on the Donets *41* **56** L6, *51* **71** B4, *112* **161** E4, *113* **163** E3
Belize City *62* **85** C4, *63* **87** E2, *121* **177** B2
Belize, country *63* **87** E2, *120* **176** C4
Bellinzona *57* **80** IJ1
Belo Horizonte *95* **132** EF4
Beloozero *46* **63** G2, *51* **71** CD2, *71* **101** K5
Belozersk *106* **150** C3
Belzec *111* **158** C2
Benares (Kasi, Varanasi) *36* **49** GH5, *38* **52** K2, *64* **89** C2, *65* **91** I2, *99* **140** D2
Bender *69* **99** E7, *71* **102** BC4, *81* **116** E3
Benelux Economic Union *115* **168**
Benevento (Beneventum, Malventum) *43* **59** E6, *44* **60** I6, *68* **97** E3, *80* **115** DE5, *84* **121** F6, *87* **124** C2
Bengal *64* **89** D2, *65* **91** IJ2, *99* **140** E3
Bengal, Bay of *64* **89** CD3, *65* **91** IJ3
Benghazi (Berenice) *28* **38**

F6, *71* **102** A7, *97* **136** CD1, *112* **161** C7, *112* **162** D2
Benguela *65* **92** C3, *96* **133** C6
Beni Hassan *14* **15** AB3
Benin, country *65* **92** BC2, *122* **179** B5, *120* **176** F4
Benin, town *32* **44** BC7, *65* **92** B3
Benkulen *64* **90** I7
Benue *65* **92** C2
Benwell (Condercum) *28* **39** K1
Beograd (Singidunum) *28* **38** G3, *45* **61** C4–5, *55* **76** D3, *71* **102** A4, *101* **141** F3, *107* **151** D5, *110* **157** D5, *113* **163** B4
Berar *99* **140** C3
Berber *97* **136** D2, *108* **153** B7
Berbera *65* **92** F2, *97* **136** E2
Berbers *42* **58** A2
Berdichev *91* **127** KL4, *106* **150** BC5
Berenice (Benghazi), on the Mediterranean *28* **38** F6
Berenice, on the Red Sea *28* **38** I6
Beresan *46* **63** G5, *51* **71** C5
Beresina *81* **116** E1–2, *82* **119** E2
Berg, duchy *70* **100** C4
Bergamo *53* **73** CD4
Bergen (Mons), Belgium *66* **93** B4
Bergen, Germany *74* **105** B3
Bergen, Norway *55* **76** C1, *57* **79** C1, *76* **107** BC4, *81* **116** AB1, *110* **157** C2
Bergen-Belsen *111* **158** A2
Bering Sea *120* **176** A2
Bering Strait *71* **6, *80* **84** AB1–2, L1
Berlin *57* **79** D4, *68* **97** D1, *74* **105** D2, *75* **106** C2, *76* **107** CD5, *81* **116** C2, *91* **127** CD4, *107* **151** BC3, *109* **155** C5, *112* **161** BC5, *113* **163** A2, *114* **167**
Berlin Wall *114* **167** E1–2
Bermondsey, London *66* **94** DE7
Bermuda *92* **128** L3
Bern, Canton *55* **77** C6
Bern, city *55* **77** C6, *79* **113** C2, *101* **141** B2, *107* **151** B4
Bernicia *43* **59** BC2, *44* **60** E1
Berry *52* **72** DE6, *79* **113** B2
Berwick *56* **78** B1
Berytus, see also Beirut *28* **38** I5
Besançon *49* **68** E6, *53* **73** B3, *59* **83** C5, *70* **100** B6
Beshbalik *34* **47** D6, *40* **55** H3
Bessarabia *72* **103** F5, *83* **120** A5, *106* **150** B6, *107* **151** E4, *113* **163** C4
Betania, Judea *27* **37** B4
Betania, Perea *27* **37** C4

Bethel *15* **18** E5–6
Bethnal Green, London *66* **94** E6
Bethlehem *26* **35** B4
Bethsaida *26* **35** C2
Béziers *52* **72** E7
Bhagalpur *99* **140** DE2
Bhagatrav *10* **8** F4
Bhamo *99* **140** F3
Bhopal *127* **184** C3
Bhubaneswar *127* **184** D3
Bhutan *99* **140** E2, *127* **184** E2
Biafra *122* **179** C5
Bialystok *73* **104** D2, *83* **120** A4, *112* **161** D3, *113* **163** BC2
Biarritz *104* **146** C5
Biberach am Kinzing *70* **100** C5–6
Biberach an der Riss *70* **100** D6
Biblipatnam *65* **91** I3
Bibracte *25* **33** B3
Bielefeld *74* **105** B3
Bielitz *84* **121** F4
Bihar *64* **89** C2, *65* **91** I2, *99* **140** D2, *127* **184** D2–3
Bijapur *64* **89** B3, *65* **91** H3
Bikaner *99* **140** B2
Bila Hora (White Mountain) *68* **98** F4
Bilbao *55* **76** B3, *76* **107** A6, *109* **156** E1
Billiton *65* **99** J7, *99* **139** J4
Billungs, March of the *47* **65** D1
Bingen *47* **65** B3
Binh Dinh (Vijaya) *65* **91** L3, *124* **181** CD6, *125* **182** F3
Bioko (Macias Nguema) *122* **179** B5
Birdoswald (Camboglana) *28* **39** I1
Birka *43* **59** E1, *46* **63** E3, *50* **69** E2
Birmingham *76* **107** B5, *76* **108** BC6, *77* **109** E6, *91* **127** F4
Birrens *28* **39** H1
Biscay, Bay of *55* **76** AB3, *72* **103** AB5
Biskra *96* **134** C1, *112* **162** A1
Biskupin *9* **6** EF5
Bismarck Archipelago *105* **149** F2, *111* **159** C3, *111* **160** D7
Bistum *55* **77** B5
Bithynia *23* **30** B5–6, *24* **31** F5, *24* **32** E6
Bithynia et Pontus *28* **38** HI4
Bitola (Monastir) *88* **125** AB1, *103* **144** C3
Bitter Lakes *118* **173** B6
Bizerte *68* **97** D4, *96* **134** C1, *112* **161** B6, *112* **162** B1
Bjarkøy *46* **63** E1
Bjarmi, people (Old Norse name) *46* **63** FG2
Björneborg *69* **99** C3
Black River (Song-Bo) *124* **181** B4
Black Russia *73* **104** DE2

Black Sea, The (Pontus Euxinus) *28* **38** HI3–4, *46* **63** CD2, *55* **76** EF3
Blagoveshchensk *98* **137** E3
Blanco, Cape *65* **92** A1
Blatobulgium (Birrens) *28* **39** GH1
Blekinge *57* **79** E2, *69* **99** B5, *70* **100** F1
Blenheim *72* **103** D5
Bloemfontein *97* **135** DE7
Blois *52* **72** D5, *56* **78** C5
Blore Heath *56* **78** BC2
Blue Nile *65* **92** E1–2
Bo Hai, kingdom *32* **45** E1
Bo Hai, sea *30* **42** F1, *102* **142** BC3
Bo Hai, town *31* **43** C5
Bobrujsk *105* **147** L5
Bodensee (Lacus Venetus) *29* **40** B7, *55* **77** E5
Bodh Gaya *36* **49** H5, *38* **53** C2
Bodø *110* **157** D1
Boeotia *16* **20** DE5, *20* **25** CD3
Bogazköy, see Hattushash
Bogense *70* **100** D2
Bogota *62* **85** C4, *63* **86** B1, *95* **132** B2
Bohemia *44* **60** H3, *47* **65** DE3, *50* **70** D5, *53* **73** DE2, *67* **96** CD2, *68* **98** F4, *70* **100** EF5, *72* **103** D4, *84* **121** F4, *101* **141** DE1
Bohemia and Moravia *109* **155** C6, *110* **157** CD4, *112* **161** C4
Bohemund of Tarentum's crusade 1096 *48* **66** G5
Boiai *17* **21** C4
Bojador, Cape *60* **84** F4
Bokhara *34* **47** BC7, *36* **49** F4, *37* **51** L1, *40* **55** F3
Bolivia *63* **86** C3, *95* **132** C4
Bolobo *123* **180** D2
Bologna (Bononia) *22* **27** C2, *47* **65** D6, *49* **68** E6, *55* **76** C3, *80* **115** C3, *87* **124** B1, *107* **151** B5
Bolsena *57* **80** J2
Bolsward *66* **93** C1
Boma *96* **133** C6
Bombay *64* **89** A3, *65* **91** G3, *99* **140** B3, *127* **184** B3
Bona *68* **97** D4
Bône (Bona, Hippo Regius) *28* **38** D5, *48* **66** E6, *96* **134** C1, *112* **162** B1
Bonin Islands *111* **159** C2
Bonn (Bonna) *29* **40** A6, *56* **78** E3, *114* **166** AB3
Bononia (Bologna) *22* **27** C2
Bordeaux (Burdigala) *25* **33** A4, *43* **59** BC5, *44* **60** E5, *49* **68** C5, *52* **72** CD6, *55* **76** B3, *56* **78** B6, *68* **97** B2, *76* **107** B6, *79* **113** A3, *79* **114** A3, *81* **116** AB3
Borg *46* **63** D1
Börglum cloister *50* **69** CD2

Borgundarholm, see Born-
holm

Borgå *82* 119 E1

Borneo (Kalimantan) *60* 84
J5, *63* 90 K6, *99* 139 J3

Bornholm (Borgundarholm)
50 69 B5, *69* 99 C5, *81* 116
CD1, *107* 152 BC2

Bornu *65* 92 C1, *96* 133 C4

Borodino *82* 119 F1

Borre *46* 63 D2

Borysthenes (Dniepr), river
28 38 H2

Borysthenes, (Olbia), town
28 38 H3

Bosnia *71* 102 A5, *87* 124 C1,
101 141 E3, *103* 144 B2

Bosporus *20* 25 EFZ, *101* 141
I5

Boston, Great Britain *54* 74
B1–2, *56* 78 C2, *57* 79 A3

Boston, USA *62* 85 D2, *92*
129 E2, *93* 130 G2

Bostra *28* 38 IJ6

Bosworth *56* 78 B2

Bothnia, Gulf of *69* 99 CD3

Botswana *122* 179 D7

Bouganville *111* 160 D7

Bougie *54* 74 B3, *68* 97 C4, *96*
134 C1, *112* 162 A1

Bouillon *66* 93 C5

Boulogne *79* 114 B1, *81* 116
B2, *84* 121 BC4

Bourbon *56* 78 D5

Bourges (Avaricum) *25* 33
B3, *45* 62 J6, *49* 68 D6, *56*
78 CD5, *79* 114 B2

Bouvines *52* 72 E4

Bovianum *20* 24 B4

Bowness *28* 39 GH2

Boyacá *95* 132 BC2

Brabant *52* 72 E4, *56* 78 DE3,
66 93 BC4

Bracara *42* 58 A1–2

Bradford *76* 108 B5, *77* 109
E5

Braga *41* 56 I7, *59* 83 A6

Bragança, Brazil *95* 132 E3

Braganza, Spain *68* 97 A3, *84*
121 AB5

Brahestad *83* 120 E2

Brahmaputra *64* 89 CD1, *65*
91 IJ2

Braila *105* 147 L7

Brandenburg Gate, Berlin
114 167 E2 (1)

Brandenburg, city *50* 69
DE3, *53* 73 D2, *57* 79 D4,
68 98 E2

Brandenburg, margravate,
later principality and state
53 73 D2, *68* 98 E2, *70*
100 EF3, *74* 105, *75* 106,
83 120 CD, *86* 122 D2

Brasov (Kronstadt) *101* 141
H3

Brassempouy *9* 7 AB2

Bratislava (Pressburg) *107*
152 C4

Bratsk *89* 126 J6

Brattalid *60* 84 E2

Braunsberg *69* 99 C5, *70* 100
GH2

Braunschweig, city *57* 79
CD4

Braunschweig, state *86* 122
C2

Braunschweig-Lüneburg *70*
100 D3

Braunschweig-Wolfenbuttel
70 100 CD3–4

Brauron *16* 20 F6

Brava *65* 92 F2

Brazil *62* 85 DE5, *63* 86 C2,
94 131 KL6, *95* 132 DE4,
105 149 BC2, *113* 164 B7,
120 176 DE5

Brazzaville *97* 136 C3, *122*
179 C5

Breda *66* 93 C3, *68* 98 A3

Breisach *47* 65 B4, *68* 98 BC5

Breisgau *70* 100 C4

Breitenfeld *68* 98 E3

Bremen, archbishopric *70*
100 CD3

Bremen, city *47* 65 C2, *50* 69
CD3, *55* 76 C2, *57* 79 C3,
59 83 CD4, *76* 107 C5, *81*
116 C2, *107* 152 B3, *114*
166 B2

Bremerhaven *114* 166 B2

Brenner Pass *44* 60 H4, *53* 73
CD4

Brescia *53* 73 CD4

Breslau (Wroclaw) *50* 69 E4,
53 73 E2, *57* 79 E4, *74* 105
E2, *76* 107 D5, *81* 116
CD2, *107* 151 C3, *112* 161
C4, *128* 185 C3

Brest (Brest-Litovsk) *51* 71
AB3, *73* 104 DE5, *84* 121
G3, *107* 151 D3, *113* 163
C3

Brest, France *52* 72 BC5, *56*
78 A4, *79* 114 A2, *81* 116
A2, *110* 157 A4

Brest-Litovsk, front after the
peace in March 1918 *104*
146 G3

Bretagne (Britannia Minor)
42 57 F4–5, *43* 59 B4, *44*
60 D3, *46* 63 B4, *47* 64 B2,
50 70 B2, *52* 72 C5, *55* 76
B2, *56* 78 B4, *66* 93 B2, *79*
113 A1, *79* 114 A2, *81* 116
AB2

Brétigny *56* 78 CD4

Bretland (Wales) *46* 63 B3–4

Breton, Cape *62* 85 DE2, *92*
128 L1

Brieg *70* 100 G4

Brielle *66* 93 B2

Brigantium (La Coruna) *24*
32 A5, *26* 34 A2

Brighton *77* 109 F7

Brihuega *109* 156 E2

Brindisi (Brundisium) *28* 38
F4, *45* 61 BC6, *48* 66 G5,
59 83 E7, *87* 124 C2

Brisbane *98* 137 F7

Bristol *56* 78 B3, *76* 107 B5,
76 108 B7, *77* 109 E7

Britannia *25* 33 AB1, *26* 34
BC1, *28* 38 CD1, *32* 44 B3

Britannia Minor (Bretagne)
42 57 F4–5

British East Africa (Kenya)
97 136 E3, *122* 179 E5

British Eritrea *98* 138 E7

British Guyana *98* 138 CD7

British Honduras (Belize) *95*
132 A1

British India *98* 137 C4, *105*
149 E2

British North America *94*
131 J4

British North Borneo (Sa-
bah) *98* 137 E5, *126* 183
CD6

British Somaliland *98* 137
A5, *97* 136 EF2, *107* 152
C3

Brittany, March of *44* 60 E4

Bridgnorth *76* 108 B6

Brno (Brünn) *70* 100 F5, *103*
144 E1, *104* 146 F4, *107*
152 C4

Broach (Barygaza, Bharoch)
32 44 H6, *38* 52 JK2, *38* 53
A2

Broach (Bharukaccha, Barygaza) *32* 44 H6, *38* 53 A2

Brocolitia (Carrawbrough)
28 39 J1

Brody *105* 147 K6

Bromberg (Bydgoszcz) *70*
100 G3, *104* 146 F3

Bromley, London *66* 94 F6

Brompton, London *66* 94 A7

Broseley *76* 108 B6

Brugge *54* 74 B2, *56* 78 C4, *56*
78 D3, *57* 79 B4, *66* 93 B3

Brundisium (Brindisi) *22* 27
F4, *28* 38 F4

Brunei *98* 137 DE5, *111* 159
AB3, *126* 183 C6

Brunete *109* 156 E2

Brussa *55* 76 E3, *9* 102 B5

Brussel *66* 93 B4, *68* 97 C1,
79 113 C1, *79* 114 B1, *107*
151 A3, *112* 161 AB4

Bruttium *20* 24 C6, *22* 27
E5–6

Bryansk *41* 56 L6, *83* 120 B4,
106 150 C4

Brömsebro *70* 100 F1

Brünn (Brno) *70* 100 F5, *103*
144 E1

Bubastis *14* 15 B1

Bucharest *71* 102 B5, *81* 116
E3, *83* 120 A6, *91* 127
KL5, *101* 141 H3, *107* 151
DE5, *113* 163 E6, *128*
185 D4

Buchenwald *111* 158 A2

Buckingham House, London
66 94 B7

Buckinham *56* 78 B2

Buczacz *105* 147 K6

Budapest (Aquincum, Buda
and Pest) *28* 38 F3, *48* 66
G3, *55* 76 D2–3, *71* 102
A4, *76* 107 D6, *107* 151
CD4, *113* 163 B4, *128* 185
C3

Buenaventura *95* 132 B2

Buenos Aires, city *62* 85 D6,
63 86 C4, *95* 132 CD6

Buenos Aires, province *95*
132 CD6

Bug, tributary of the Vistula
73 104 D2, *107* 151 D3

Bug, river running into Black
Sea *73* 104 F3, *81* 116 E2,
84 121 H1, *113* 163 D4

Buganda *65* 92 E2

Buhen *14* 15 AB7

Bukavo *123* 180 F2

Bukefala *21* 26 F2

Bukellarion *45* 61 F5–6

Bukovina *54* 104 E3, *84* 121
G4, *101* 141 G2, *128* 185
D3

Bulawayo *97* 136 D4

Bulgar kingdom (Volga-Bul-
gars) *51* 71 F3

Bulgar kingdom, north of the
Donau *44* 60 K4

Bulgar, town *34* 47 B5, *46* 63
H3, *51* 71 EF3

Bulgaria *45* 61 CD5, *50* 70
E6, *51* 71 A5, *71* 102 B5,
81 116 E3, *84* 121 GH5,
101 141 GH4, *103* 144 D2,
104 146 GH6, *105* 149 D2,
107 151 DE5, *108* 154 F4,
110 157 E5, *111* 158 C5,
112 161 D5, *113* 163 BC4,
115 168 DE4, *116* 169 D7,
120 176 G3, *128* 185 D4

Bulgars *42* 57 K5, *37* 51 I1

Bulun *98* 137 D1

Bumba *123* 180 E1

Buna *111* 159 C4

Bunyoro *65* 92 DE2

Burdigala (Bordeaux) *25* 33
A4, *28* 38 C3

Burgas *103* 144 E2

Burgh by Sands *28* 39 H2

Burgos *54* 74 A3, *55* 76 A3, *56*
78 AB7, *81* 118 B5, *109*
156 E1–2

Burgund, barony *56* 78 E5

Burgundian kingdom *42* 57
G5

Burgundians *28* 38 F2, *32* 44
CD3

Burgundy, duchy *50* 70 BC6,
56 78 DE5

Burgundy, kingdom (Arles)
43 59 C4, *47* 65 AB5, *53* 73
B4

Burkersdorf *74* 105 E2

Burkina *122* 179D B4

Burma *64* 89 DE2, *99* 139 F3,
111 159 A2, *111* 160 AB6,
120 176 J4, *127* 184 F3

Burma Road *105* 148 A2

Buru *99* 139 KL4, *126* 183
D7

Burundi *65* 92 E3, *122* 179 F2
(5), *120* 176 G5, *123*
180 F2

Bushir *108* 153 E5

Busiris *14* 15 B1

Buxar *99* 140 D2

Byblos *1* 10 C3, *12* 12 C3, *15*
17 B4, *16* 19 F2

Bydgoszcz (Bromberg) *109*
155 CD5

Byzantine (East Roman)
Empire *37* 51 HI1, *42* 57
JK6–7, *42* 58 BC2, *44* 60
I–K7, *45* 61 DE6, *46* 63
E–G6, *51* 71 AC6–7, *59* 82
D3

Byzantium (Byzantion,
Constantinople, Istanbul,
Miklagard) *13* 14 B5–6, *16*
19 E2, *17* 21 F1, *20* 25 E2,
21 26 B1, *23* 30 AB5, *24* 31
F5, *26* 34 F3, *28* 38 H4, *42*
57 K6, *45* 61 E5, *46* 63 F6,
48 66 IJ5, *51* 71 B6, *71* 102
B5, *76* 107 EF6, *91* 127 L6

C

Cabinda *97* 136 C3, *122* 179
C6

Cabot's, John & Sebastian,
journey 1497 *60* 84 DE3

Cabrais, Pedro, emperor
1500, *60* 84 F6, H5

Cadiz (Gades) *16* 19 A2, *28*
38 B4, *43* 59 A7, *46* 63 A6,
55 76 A4, *68* 97 A4, *81* 116
A4, *81* 118 B7

Caecaraugusta (Zaragoza) *28*
38 C4

Caecarea (Mazaka), Asia Minor *23* 30 CD6, *45* 61 G6

Caecarea, Africa *23* 28 C3, *28*
38 C5

Caecarea, Israel *28* 38 I6, *45*
61 G7

Caelius, Rome *27* 36 L7

Caen *49* 68 D5, *56* 78 C4, *68*
97 B1, *79* 114 B1, *112* 161
A4, *113* 165 A4

Caere (Cerveteri) *22* 27 C4

Caesarea Filippi *26* 35 C1

Caesarea, Samaria *26* 35
AB3

Cagliari (Carales) *24* 31 C5,
44 60 G6, *81* 116 C4, *87*
124 A3

Cahors *43* 59 C5, *49* 68 D6,
52 72 D6

Cai *30* 42 E3

Cairns *98* 137 F6

Cairo (Fustat) *54* 74 E4, *74*
105 C7, *97* 136 D1, *112*
162 F2, *118* 173 A6

Cajamarca *63* 86 AB2

Calabar *97* 136 C3

Calabria *22* 27 F5, *44* 60 I6–7, *45* 61 B6

Calah (Nimrud) *11* 10 E3

Calais *52* 72 D4, *56* 78 C3, *68* 97 BC1, *104* 146 C4

Calcutta *64* 89 D2, *65* 91 IJ2, *99* 140 E3

Caledonia *28* 38 D1

Cali *95* 132 B2

Calicut (Kozhikode) *40* 55 G6, *60* 84 I4, *64* 89 B4, *65* 91 H4, *99* 140 B4, *127* 184 B4

California *93* 130 A3

California, Gulf of *93* 130 B4

Caliphate, The ca. 750 *32* 45 A2–3

Callao *60* 84 CD5, *95* 132 B4

Callatis *24* 31 F4

Callipolis *20* 24 C5

Calvinia *97* 135 C7

Calydon *16* 20 AB5

Calydon, Gulf of *16* 20 AB5

Camaracum *25* 33 BC2

Camarina *20* 24 AB7, *20* 25 A3

Camarina (Kamarina) *20* 24 B7, *22* 27 DE7

Cambodia (see also Khmer Kingdom) *39* 54 BC6, *98* 137 D5, *124* 181 BC6, *125* 182 AB3

Cambodunum (Kempten) *29* 40 B7

Camboglana (Birdoswald) *28* 39 I1

Cambrai *53* 73 B2, *56* 78 D3, *66* 93 B4

Cambridge *49* 68 D5, *52* 72 D4, *56* 78 C2, *68* 97 BC1

Camerino (Camerinum) *22* 27 D3, *45* 61 A5

Cameroon (Kamerun) *97* 136 C3, *122* 179 E2, C5, *123* 180 D1

Cammin *57* 79 E3, *59* 83 D4

Campania *22* 27 D4

Campbell *120* 176 L7

Campeche *63* 87 DE2, *121* 177 AB1

Camperdown *81* 116 B2

Campoformio *80* 115 C2, *81* 116 CD3

Campos *95* 132 F5

Campus Martius (Field of Mars), Rome *27* 36 K6

Camulodunum (Colchester) *25* 33 B2, *28* 38 D2

Can Tho *125* 182 B3

Cana *26* 35 B2

Canada *92* 128 JK1, *92* 129 CD1, *98* 138 C6, *105* 149 AB1, *113* 164 AB5, *120* 176 B–D2

Canary Islands *60* 84 F4, *62* 85 F3, *105* 149 C2, *122* 179 A3

Canberra *98* 137 F7

Candia (Iraklion, Heraklei-

on) Crete *45* 61 DE7, *54* 74 DE4

Candia (Kandia) *48* 66 I6

Cannae, Battle of *22* 27 E4, *23* 28 F2

Canos, Juan Sebastian del, journies 1521–22 *60* 84 F5, HI6

Canossa *53* 73 C4

Canterbury *43* 59 C3, *47* 64 B2, *50* 69 B3, *52* 72 D4

Canton (Kuang Chou) *64* 88 G6, *98* 137 D4

Cao *30* 42 E2

Cao Bang *124* 181 C4

Cape Canaveral (Cape Kennedy) *121* 178 AB1

Cape Colony, The *97* 135 CD7, *97* 136 CD5

Cape Kennedy (Cape Canaveral) *121* 178 AB1

Cape Town (Kaapstaden) *96* 133 C7, *97* 135 C7

Cape Verde Islands *60* 84 EF4

Capernaum *26* 35 BC2

Capitol, Rome *27* 36 K6, *27* 37 I3

Capitol, Rome *27* 37 H12

Cappadocia *12* 12 CD1, *23* 30 CD6, *28* 38 I4

Capsa *28* 38 DE5

Capua, commune *22* 27 D4, *43* 59 E6, *53* 73 E5–6

Capua, province *45* 61 A6

Capuchin Monestary, Paris *78* 112 C4

Carabobo *95* 132 C2

Caracas *94* 131 K5, *95* 132 C2, *121* 177 DE2

Carales (Cagliari) *22* 27 AB5, *24* 31 C5

Caralis *16* 19 C2

Carbisdale *67* 95 E5

Carcassonne *52* 72 DE7, *79* 113 BC3

Cardiff *56* 78 B3, *91* 127 F4

Cardigan *52* 72 B3

Carentan *113* 165 A1

Caria *23* 30 A7, *24* 31 F5

Caribbean Sea, The *62* 85 C4, *95* 132 BC1, *121* 177 CD2

Carlisle (Luguvalium) *28* 39 H12, *56* 78 B1, *67* 95 E6

Carmana *24* 31 J6

Carmania *24* 31 J6

Carmarthen *56* 78 AB2

Carmel *26* 35 B2

Carnac *8* 3 A5

Carnak-Luxor, see Thebes

Carnuntum *28* 38 F3, *44* 60 I4

Caroline Islands *98* 137 F5, *111* 159 C3

Carpathian Mts. *51* 71 AB4–5, *105* 147 K6–7

Carpatho-Ukraine (Ruthenia) *109* 155 DE6

Carpentaria, Gulf of *98* 137 F6

Carrawbrough, see Brocolitia

Carrhae *24* 32 F6, *28* 38 J5

Cartagena (Carthago Nova), Spain *23* 28 BC3, *43* 59 B7, *68* 97 B4, *81* 116 B4, *81* 118 C7, *109* 156 EF3

Cartagena, Colombia *62* 85 CD4, *95* 132 B2

Cartenna *23* 28 BC3, *28* 38 C5

Carthage (Carthago) *16* 19 C2, *24* 31 C5, *28* 38 E5, *42* 57 H7, *43* 59 D7, *44* 60 G3

Carthago (Carthage) *16* 19 C2, *24* 31 C5, *28* 38 E5, *42* 57 H7, *43* 59 D7, *44* 60 G3

Carthago Nova (Cartagena) *23* 28 BC3

Carthusian Monestary, Paris *78* 112 C6

Cartier's, Jaques, journey 1534 *60* 84 E3

Carvoran (Magnis) *28* 39 I1–2

Carystus (Karistos) *17* 21 C6

Casablanca *97* 136 AB1, *122* 179 AB3

Cashel *50* 69 A3, *59* 83 A4

Caspian Sea, The *12* 11 D1, *32* 44 F4, *40* 55 E3, *83* 120 E6

Cassel *56* 78 CD3

Castel del Monte *50* 70 DE7

Castelfidardo *87* 124 BC2

Castellum Caesaris *25* 33 C2

Castilla *40* 55 A4

Castilla *48* 66 B4, *50* 70 A6–7, *55* 76 A3, *56* 78 A7, *59* 82 A2–3, *68* 97 A3

Castillon *56* 78 C6

Castlebar *67* 95 D6

Castlesteads *28* 39 I1

Castor and Pollux, Temple of, Rome *27* 37 JK3

Castra Exploratorum *28* 39 H1

Castra Regina (Regensburg) *28* 38 F2, *29* 40 B6

Catal Hüyük *6* 2 C3, *11* 10 C2

Catalaunian Fields, The *42* 57 G5

Catalonia *42* 57 F6, *68* 97 BC3, *81* 118 D5–6, *109* 156 F2

Catamarca *95* 132 C5

Catana (Catania) *20* 24 BC7

Catania (Katane) *20* 24 B7, *22* 27 E6

Cateau-Cambrésis *68* 97 BC1

Cattaro *71* 102 A5 *81* 116 D3

Catterick *44* 60 E2

Cattigara *13* 13 E2

Caucasoid peoples *13* 13 C2

Caucasus *51* 71 EF6, *83* 120 D6, *113* 163 EF4

Caulonia *20* 24 C6

Cavadonga *43* 59 A1

Cavenne *62* 85 E4, *95* 132 E2

Cayenne *62* 85 E4

Ceará (Fortaleza), town *62* 85 E5, *95* 132 F3

Ceará, province *95* 132 F3

Cefalu *53* 73 E7

Celebes (Sulawesi) *64* 90 L6, *99* 139 K4, *111* 159 B3, *111* 160 BC7

Celebes Sea *64* 90 L6, *99* 139 K3

Celistin cloister, Paris *78* 112 E6

Celtica *25* 33 B3

Celts *24* 31 C–E4, *47* 64 B2

Cempoallan *63* 87 B2

Cenabum (Orléans) *25* 33 B3, *28* 38 D2

CENTO, Members of *116* 169

Central African Rebublic *122* 179 F1–2, D5

Central America *121* 177

Central and Eastern Europe *107* 152

Cephalonia *45* 61 C6

Ceram *99* 139 L4

Cerigo (Kithira) *84* 121 GH7

Cerinthos *16* 20 E4

Chalcedon *16* 19 EF2, *23* 30 B5

Chalcidice *17* 21 C1

Chaldea *11* 10 F4, *12* 12 E3

Chaldea *45* 61 G5

Chalkis *17* 21 C3

Châlon-sur-Saône *44* 60 F4, *101* 141 A2

Châlons-sur-Marne *52* 72 E5, *56* 78 DE4, *105* 148 JK3

Chalukya *38* 53 AB3

Chambal *38* 53 B2, *99* 140 C2

Chambord *56* 78 CD5

Chamdo *65* 91 JK1

Champa, Vietnam *32* 44 K6, *39* 54 C6, *40* 55 J5

Champagne *52* 72 E5, *56* 78 DE4, *79* 113 BC1, *105* 148 K2–3

Champs de Mars (Field of Mars), Paris *78* 112 A5

Champs Elysées, Paris *78* 112 A4

Chancellor's, Rich., journeys 1553–56 *60* 84 G2

Chanchan *63* 87 B5

Chandernagore *65* 91 IJ2, *99* 140 D3, *127* 184 DE3

Chandigarn *127* 184 BC1

Chang'an (Xi'an) *32* 44 K5, *32* 45 DE2, *33* 46, *40* 55 IJ4

Changjiang *40* 55 IJ4

Changkufeng *102* 142 D2

Changsha *31* 43 BC6, *32* 44 L5

Changujo-Daro *10* 8 E3

Channel Islands *81* 116 AB3

Charleroi *105* 148 K1

Charleston *92* 129 CD3, *93* 130 F3

Charlottenburg, Berlin *114* 167 D2

Charolles *68* 97 C2

Charsianon *45* 61 G5

Charter House, London *66* 94 CD6

Chartres *45* 62 J6, *52* 72 D5, *56* 78 CD4

Château Gaillard *52* 72 DE5

Château Thierry *105* 148 J3

Chatham *76* 108 C7

Chattanooga *92* 129 BC3

Châttilon *79* 114 BC2

Chaul *65* 91 G3

Chavin *63* 86 B2

Checkpoint Charlie, Berlin *114* 167 E2 (2)

Chelmno *111* 158 B2

Chelsea *66* 94 AB7

Chelyabinsk *98* 137 B3

Chernaya *83* 120 B5

Chemin-des-dames *105* 148 J2

Chemmis (Panopolis) *14* 15 B4

Chemnitz *68* 98 E3, *70* 100 E4

Chemulpo (Inchon) *102* 143 EF7

Chen *30* 42 E3

Chen-La (Khmer) *32* 45 D4

Cheng-chiang *32* 45 D3, *40* 55 IJ5

Chengdu (Shu) *31* 43 A6, *35* 48 D3, *40* 55 IJ4

Cheops, Pyramid of *15* 16 F6

Chephren's pyramid *15* 16 EF7

Chera (Kerala) *38* 52 K3

Cherbourg *72* 103 B4, *81* 116 B2, *91* 127 F4

Cherente *97* AB1

Chernigov *41* 56 K6, *106* 150 C5

Chernovtsy *101* 141 GH2

Chersonesus, *16* 19 F1, *24* 31 F4

Chester *25* 33 A2, *56* 78 B2, *77* 109 E6, *81* 116 B2

Cheyu-do *102* 142 D4

Chiang Mai *39* 54 AB5

Chiang-ling *32* 45 E3

Chiao (Annan) *32* 45 E3

Chiapas *63* 87 D3

Chicago *92* 129 B2, *93* 130 E2

Chichén Itzá *63* 87 E1

Chieti *44* 60 H5

Chile *63* 86 B4, *94* 131 K6, *95*

132 C5, *105* *149* B3, *113* *164* B7, *115* *168* D6

Chiloé *95* *132* BC6

Chimukingdom *63* *86*

China *31* *43* B6, *32* *44* K5, *32* *45* E2–3, *35* *48* D5, *113* *164* E6, *117* *170* BC5

China, The Great Wall of *31* *43*, *102* *142* A3

Chinese states under the Chou *13* *13* F1

Chinju *119* *175* B3

Chinnampo *102* *143* EF6

Chinon *56* *78* C5

Chios *17* *21* D3, *20* *25* E3, *45* *61* DE6, *88* *125* CD2, *103* *144* D4, *107* *151* E6

Chita, USSR *98* *137* D3

Chittagong *64* *89* D2, *99* *140* E3

Choczim *104* *146* GH4

Chola *38* *52* K3, *38* *53* B3

Cholm *104* *146* G4

Cholula *87* AB2

Chongjin *102* *143* F6, *119* *175* C1

Chongju *119* *175* B3

Chongqing (Chunking) *102* *142* A5, *117* *170* C6

Chonju *119* *175* B3

Chorasmia *13* *14* DE5

Chorasmians *23* *31* 14–5

Chosen (Korea) *102* *142* D3–4

Chotin *105* *147* K6

Chotusitz *75* *106* D3

Chou-Kou-Tien, see Zhou-koudian

Christiania (Oslo after 1925) *69* *99* B4, *76* *107* C4, *107* *151* B1

Christiania (Oslo) *81* *116* C1

Christmas, atoll in the Pacific *111* *159* F3

Chu *30* *42* DE3

Chu Lai *124* *181* CD6, *125* *182* C2

Chunchon *119* *175* F3

Chungju *119* *175* B3

Chunking, see Chongqing

Chur *45* *62* K6, *55* *77* E6

Cienfuegos *121* *178* B2

Cilicia *12* *12* CD2, *23* *30* C7

Cilurnum (Chesters) *28* *39* J1

Cimon's Wall, Acropolis *19* *23* D2

Cincinnati *92* *129* C2

Cintra *81* *118* A6

Cipangu (Japan) *60* *84* K3

Circassia *73* *104* F3, *106* *150* C5

Circassians *71* *102* D4–5, *83* *120* C6

Circus Flaminius, Rome *27* *36* JK6

Circus Maximus, Rome *27* *36* KL7

Cirta (Constantine) *23* *28* D3, *24* *32* B6

Cisalpine Republic *80* *115* BC3, *81* *116* C3

City, London *66* *94* D6

Ciudad Bolivar (Angostura) *95* *132* CD2, *121* *177* DE3

Ciudad Real *81* *118* BC6

Ciudad Rodrigo *81* *118* B6

Civitavecchia *57* *80* J2

Clairvaux *48* *66* D3

Clepsydra's Spring, Acropolis *19* *23* AB1

Clermont *48* *66* D4, *52* *72* E6

Cleveland *92* *129* C2, *93* *130* F2

Clonard *41* *56* I6

Clonmacnoise *47* *64* A2

Clonmel *67* *95* D6

Clontarf *50* *69* AB3

Clovis *3* F1

Cluj (Klausenburg) *101* *141* G2, *107* *151* DE4

Clunia (Feldkirch) *29* *40* B7

Cluny *47* *65* A5

Cnidus (Knidos) *17* *21* F4

Cobija *95* *132* C4

Cochabamba *95* *132* C4

Cochin *60* *84* I5, *64* *89* B4, *65* *91* H4

Cochin China *99* *139* J2, *124* *181* BC7

Coimbra *49* *68* B7, *81* *118* A6

Colchester (Camulodunum) *8* A1, *25* *33* B2, *28* *38* D2, *44* *60* F2, *56* *78* C2, *67* *95* F6, *71* *109* F4

Colesberg *97* *135* D7

Collasuyu *63* *86* BC3

Colmar *70* *100* C6

Colofon *17* *21* EF3

Cologne (Köln, Colonia Agrippinensis) *41* *56* J6, *43* *59* D3, *49* *68* E5, *50* *69* C4, *55* *76* C2, *56* *78* E3, *57* *79* C4, *59* *83* C5, *76* *107* C5, *79* *113* C1, *107* *151* B4

Cologne, archbishopric *70* *100* C4

Colomb Béchar *96* *134* B1

Colombia *63* *86* B1, *95* *132* BC2–3, *105* *149* B2, *113* *164* B6, *120* *176* D5, *121* *177* CD3

Colombo *64* *88* F6, *99* *140* C5

Colonia Agrippinensis (Cologne) *26* *34* C7

Colorado, river *93* *130* B3

Colorado, state *93* *130* C3

Columbia, river *93* *130* A1

Columbus's journey 1492 and 1493 *60* *84* DE4

Columnae Herculis (Pillars of Hercules, Gibraltar) *23* *28* AB3

Comana *23* *30* D6

COMECON, members of *115* *168*

Commagene *24* *32* F6, *28* *38* IJ5

Commander Islands *98* *137* F2

Como *57* *80* I1

Comodoro Rivadavia *95* *132* CD7

Comorin, Cape *99* *140* BC5

Comoro Islands *96* *133* E6, *97* *136* E4 *120* *176* H5, *122* *179* EF6

Compiègne *56* *78* D4, *104* *146* CD4, *105* *148* IJ2, *107* *151* A3

Comum *22* *27* B1–2

Conakry *97* *136* A2, *122* *179* A5

Concepción, Chile *95* *132* BC6

Concepción, Paraguay *95* *132* D5

Concordia, Temple of, Rome *27* *37* IJ2–3

Condé (-sur-L'Escaut) *105* *148* J1

Condercum *28* *39* K1

Confederate States, The Southern States *93* *130*

Confluentes (Koblenz) *29* *40* A6

Congo Free State *122* *179* F2, D5, *123* *180* E1–2

Congo Republic *122* *179* EF2, C5, *123* *180* D1–2

Congo, from 1971 Zaïre *65* *92* C3, *123* *180*

Congo, People's Republic of the *122* *179* D5

Connaught *67* *95* D6

Connecticut *92* *128* K2, *92* *129* DE2, *93* *130* G2

Constanta *103* *144* E2

Constantine (Cirta) *23* *28* B6–7, *96* *134* C1

Constantinople (Byzantium, Miklagard) *41* *56* KL7, *45* *61* E5, *48* *66* J5, *55* *76* EF3, *81* *116* E3, *104* *146* HI6

Constitution *95* *132* BC6

Conway *52* *72* E4

Copán *63* *87* E3

Copenhagen *49* *68* EF5, *69* *99* B5, *76* *107* CD5, *81* *116* C1, *82* *119* CD2, *9* *127* I3, *107* *151* BC2

Coptus (Coptos, Qift) *14* *15* C4, *36* *49* D5

Coptus (Koptos) *28* *38* I7

Coquilhatville *123* *180* DE1

Coquimbo *62* *85* D6, *95* *132* BC6, *63* *86* BC4

Coral Sea *111* *159* CA, *111* *160* D7

Corbridge, see Corstopitum

Corbridge *56* *78* D4

Corasin *26* *35* C2

Cordelier Club, Paris *78* *112* D6

Cordoba (Corduba), Spain *23* *38* BA4, *37* *51* G1, *42* *58* A2, *43* *59* A7, *50* *70* A7, *55* *76* A3, *68* *97* A4, *81* *116* A4, *81* *118* B7, *109* *156* DE2

Cordoba, Argentina *62* *85* D6, *95* *132* CD5

Corfinium *22* *27* D4

Corfu (Kerkyra, Korkyra) *81* *116* D4, *82* *119* E4, *88* *125* A2, *101* *141* F5–6, *107* *151* D6

Corinth (Corinthus) *16* *20* D6, *42* *57* J7, *45* *61* D6

Corinth, Gulf of *16* *20* C5, *17* *21* B3

Corinthus (Corinth) *28* *38* G5

Cork *47* *64* A2, *52* *72* A3, *67* *95* D7, *81* *116* A2

Cornwall *43* *59* AB3, *52* *72* BC4, *56* *78* A3

Coromandel Coast *99* *140* C4

Corregidor *111* *160* B6

Corsica (Kyrnos) *16* *19* C2, *23* *28* D2, *24* *31* C4, *42* *57* GH6, *43* *59* D6, *44* *60* G6, *46* *63* C5, *53* *73* C5, *55* *76* C3, *57* *80* I2, *68* *97* D3, *72* *103* CD6, *80* *115* B4, *81* *116* C3, *87* *124* A2, *107* *151* AB6

Corstopitum (Corbridge) *28* *39* JK1

Cortez', Fernando (Hernán), expedition 1519–20 *63* *87*

Coruna *46* *63* A5

Corvey *47* *65* C2

Cosa *22* *27* BC3

Cosentia *42* *57* I7

Cossura (Pantelleria) *22* *27* C7

Costa Rica *95* *132* A2, *113* *164* AB6, *120* *176* C4, *121* *177* BC3

Cotentin *56* *78* B4

Cotrone (Croton, Kroton) *22* *27* F5, *44* *60* I6

Cottbus *70* *100* F4, *75* *106* D2

Cotyora *23* *30* D5

Courland *67* *95* D6

Courtrai *52* *72* E4

Covent Garden, London *66* *94* BC6

Coventry *52* *72* CD3

Craiova *101* *141* G4

Cranganore *36* *49* G6

Crécy *52* *72* E4

Cremona *22* *27* B2, *47* *65* C5–6

Crépy *56* *78* D4

Crete (Creta, Krit) *17* *21* D5, *26* *34* E4, *38* *52* K5, *54* *61* E4, *54* *74* C4, *55* *76* E4, *71* *102* B6, *72* *103* F7, *81* *116* E4, *88* *125* C4, *101* *141* GH7, *103* *144* CD4, *107* *151* E7, *112* *162* E1

Crete, Sea of *17* *21* CD5

Crimea *71*, *46* *63* G5, *54* *75*

L6, *55* *76* F3, *106* *150* CD6, *112* *161* E5, *113* *163* D4

Crimea, khanate *71* *101* JK7, *71* *102* CD4, *83* *120* BC6

Crimean Coast *99* *140* C4

Cro-Magnon *7* 1

Croatia *48* *66* G4, *80* *115* DE3, *101* *141* DE3, *107* *151* C5, *112* *161* C5, *113* *163* A4

Croatia, kingdom *45* *61* B5

Croatians *42* *57* I6, *44* *60* I3, I5, K3

Cromwell's, Oliver, campaign against the Catholics in Ireland 1649–51 *67* *95* E6

Croton (Cotrone, Kroton) *24* *31* F5

Cryptus *32* *44* G6

Ctesiphon *13* *14* C6, *26* *34* GH4, *32* *44* GH5

Cuaibà *62* *85* D5

Cuba *59* *83* C4, *94* *131* JK5, *95* *132* B1, *105* *149* B2, *113* *164* B6, *120* *176* D4, *121* *177* C1, *121* *178* BC2

Cuba *65* *92* D3

Cucuta *95* *132* B2

Cumae (mod. Cuma; Cyme) *20* *24* A5, *22* *27* D4

Cumana *62* *85* D4

Cumberland, Great Britain *44* *60* E1, *52* *72* C3, *56* *78* B1

Cumberland, river in USA *92* *128* J2

Cunaxa *13* *14* C6

Cuntisuyu *63* *86* B3

Curaçao *62* *85* D4, *95* *132* C1–2

Curitiba *95* *132* E5

Custozza *87* *124* AB1

Cuttack *64* *89* CD2, *99* *140* D3

Cuxhaven *86* *123* A7

Cuzco *60* *84* D5, *63* *86* B3

Cyclades *17* *21* D4, *88* *125* C3

Cyme (Cumae), Italia *16* *19* CD2, *20* *24* A5

Cyme, Asia Minor *17* *21* E3

Cyprus (Krip) *8* E4, *109* A2, *16* *19* F2, *23* *30* C7, *28* *38* I5, *48* *66* K6, *49* *67* J2, *50* *70* F7, *54* *74* E4, *55* *76* F4, *71* *102* C6, *96* *133* DE, *97* *136* D1, *101* *141* K7, *103* *145* BC6, *108* *153* B4, *112* *161* EF6, *112* *162* F1, *115* *168* E5, *116* *169* DE7

Cyrenaica *21* *26* A2, *24* *31* E6, *96* *134* DE1, *107* *152* A2

Cyrenaica (Kyrenaika) *28* *38* G6, *112* *161* CD7, *112* *162* DE2

Cyrene *13* *14* A6, *16* *19* E3

Cyrene (Kyrene) *28* *38* G6

Cyrus (Kyros, Kura) *28* *38* K4

Cyzikus *17* *21* F1, *23* *30* A6, *45* *61* E6

Czechoslovakia *107* 151 CD4, *109* 155 CD6, *115* 168 CD3, *116* 169 C6, *128* 185 BC3
Czechs, people *46* 63 E4

D

Da Lat *124* 181 C7
Da Nang (Tourane) *124* 181 CD6, *125* 182 C2
Dabik *71* 102 D6
Dacca *99* 140 E3, *127* 184 E3
Dachau *111* 158 A3
Dacia *24* 32 D5, *28* 38 G3
Dadu (Khanbalik, Beijing) *40* 55 J3–4
Dagö *57* 79 F1, *69* 99 D4, *104* 146 G2, *107* 151 D1
Dahomey *97* 136 B2, *122* 179 CE2
Daibul *40* 55 G5
Dakar *96* 133 A4, *122* 179 A4
Dacians *59* 6 F6
Dakota Territory *92* 129 A1
Dali *32* 45 D3, *63* 91 K2
Dallas *93* 130 D3
Dalmatia *28* 38 F3, *55* 76 D3, *80* 115 E3, *81* 116 D3, *84* 121 F5, *87* 124 C1–2
Dalälven *57* 79 E1
Daman (Damao) *65* 91 G2, *99* 140 B3, *127* 184 B3
Damanthur *118* 173 A5
Damao (Daman) *127* 184 B3
Damascus, city *109* B3, *12* 12 D2, *13* 14 BC6, *15* 17 C4, *21* 26 BC2, *24* 31 G6, *24* 32 F7, *26* 34 F4, *36* 49 DC4, *37* 51 J2, *45* 61 G7, *71* 102 D6, *108* 153 C5, *118* 173 DE4, *119* 174 A5
Damascus, emirate *49* 67 L2–3
Damietta *40* 55 D4, *48* 66 K7
Dan *15* 17 B4, *26* 35 C1
Danelaw (Danelagh) *46* 63 C3, *47* 64 B2
Danes *42* 57 H3, *42* 58 B1, *46* 63 D3
Danevirke *44* 60 GH2, *86* 123 A6
Danevirke (border) *43* 59 D2–3
Dannoura *40* 55 K4
Danuvius (Donau, Ister) *24* 32 C5
Danzig (Gdansk) *54* 74 D1, *57* 79 EF3, *69* 99 C5, *73* 104 C2, *76* 107 D5, *82* 119 D2, *107* 151 C2, *109* 155 C5, *113* 163 B2, *128* 185 C2
Dar-es-Salaam *97* 136 E3, *122* 179 E6
Dardanelles *101* 141 H5, *104* 146 H6, *107* 151 E4
Dardanians *20* 25 C1
Darfur *65* 92 D1, *96* 133 D4
Darién (Lüta) *102* 142 C3, *102* 143 E6, *119* 175 A2

Darjeeling *99* 140 DE2
Darlington *77* 109 E5
Darmstadt *70* 100 CD5
Darthmouth *48* 66 C2
Đashur *15* 16 A2
Daugava (Düna) *46* 63 F3, *81* 116 DE1, *84* 121 G2
Daugavpils (Dünaburg) *91* 127 K3, *105* 147 KL4
Dauphiné *52* 72 EF6, *56* 78 E6, *79* 113 C2–3
Davis Strait *60* 84 E2
Davis', John, journey 1585–87 *60* 84 EF3
Davos *55* 77 EF6
Dawenkou culture *8* 3 F5
Dax *79* 114 A3
Dead Sea *15* 17 B6, *26* 35 B4
Debrecen *101* 141 F2, *107* 151 D4
Decapolis *26* 35 C3
Decca *64* 89 B3
Dede Agach (Alexandroupolis) *88* 125 D1
Deir el Bahri *14* 15 B5
Deira *43* 59 B2
Delaware *92* 128 K2, *92* 129 D2, *93* 130 G2
Delft *66* 93 B2
Delhi (Indraprastha) *38* 52 K1, *38* 53 B1, *40* 55 G4, *64* 89 B1, *65* 91 H2, *99* 140 C2, *127* 184 C2
Delhi, Sultanate of *40* 55 G5
Delos *17* 21 E4
Delphi *17* 21 B3
Demjansk *112* 161 E3
Demmin *68* 98 E1
Denmark *40* 55 C4–5, *44* 60 G1, *50* 69 D3, *55* 76 C1, *57* 79 CD2, *68* 98 CD1, *70* 100 D1, *70* 101 C1, *84* 121 E2–3, *86* 122 C1, *86* 123 AB5, *91* 127 H3, *104* 146 E3, *107* 151 B2, *108* 154 D1, *110* 157 C3, *112* 161 B3, *113* 163 A1, *115* 168 C2, *116* 169 B5, *120* 176 G3
Denmark Strait *72* 103 AB1
Denmark-Norway *58* 81 C2–3, *67* 96 C1, *69* 99 A4–5, *72* 103 C2–4, *81* 116 C1–2, *82* 119 C1
Denver *93* 130 C2
Deogiri *64* 89 B3
Deptford, London *66* 94 E7
Derbent *83* 120 E6
Derby, Australia *98* 137 E6
Derby, England *44* 60 K3
Derna *96* 134 E1, *107* 151 A1
Dertosa *23* 28 BC2
Des Moines *92* 129 B2, *93* 130 E2
Desalpar *10* 8 E3
Deseado *95* 132 CD7
Deshidda *40* 55 E5
Desna *73* 104 F2, *81* 116 E1–2, *84* 121 H3
Dessau *68* 98 E3

Desterró (Florianópolis) *95* 132 E5
Detmold *44* 60 G2
Detroit *92* 129 C2, *93* 130 F2
Deva (Chester) *25* 33 A2, *28* 38 D1
Devagir (Deogir) *64* 89 B2
Deventer *57* 79 BC4, *66* 93 D2
Devon *56* 78 AB3
Dhafar *36* 49 F5
Dhauli (Tosali) *38* 52 L2
Dhaka (Dacca) *99* 140 E3, *127* 184 E3
Diamantina *95* 132 EF4
Diaz', Bartholomeo, journey 1486–88 *60* 84 F4–5
Dickson *98* 137 B1
Didyma *17* 21 E4
Die *58* 81 BC5
Dien Bien Phu *124* 181 AB4, *125* 182 B1
Dieppe *56* 78 C4, *67* 95 F7, *112* 161 A4
Dijon *52* 72 E5, *56* 78 DE5, *79* 114 C2, *81* 116 B3, *84* 121 D4, *107* 151 A4
Dili *98* 137 E6
Dilmun (Bahrain) *10* 8 A3, *12* 11 DE4, *112* 161 A2
Dinant *57* 79 B4
Dion *26* 35 D2
Dionysus, Theatre of, Athens *19* 23 EF3
Dioritt *14* 15 B6
Dioscurias *28* 38 J3
Dipaia *16* 20 BC6
Disentis *44* 60 G4
Ditmarsh *86* 123 A7
Diu *64* 88 F6, *65* 91 G2, *99* 140 AB3, *127* 184 B3
Diyarbakir *108* 153 CD4
Djajapura (Hollandia) *111* 160 C7
Djakarta (Batavia) *99* 139 J4, *111* 159 A3, *111* 160 B7, *121* 178 B7
Djambi *64* 90 IJ6
Djavan *37* 51 H2
Djebel al-Tarik *43* 59 B7
Djerba *48* 66 J4, *54* 74 C4
Djibouti *107* 152 C3, *122* 179 EF4
Djidda *101* 141 I3–4, *103* 144 E2, *107* 151 E5
Djokjakarta (Mataram) *99* 139 J4
Dnepropetrovsk *110* 157 F4
Dnepr (Borysthenes) *28* 38 H2, *103* 144 IK1–2, *107* 151 E3, *113* 163 D3
Dniepr Rapids *46* 63 G4
Dniestr (Tyras) *28* 38 GH3, *101* 141 H2, *107* 151 E4, *113* 163 C3
Dobrudja *101* 141 I3–4, *103* 144 E2, *107* 151 E5
Dodecanese *103* 144 DE4, *107* 151 E7
Dodoma *122* 179 E6
Dodona *17* 21 A2
Dogger Bank *104* 146 CD3

Dôle *49* 68 DE6
Dolni Vestonice *6* 2 B2
Dombås *110* 157 C2
Dominica *119* 176 DE4, *121* 177 E1–2
Dominican Republic *120* 176 D4, *121* 177 D1
Domrémy *56* 78 D4
Domus Caligulae, Rome *27* 37 J4
Domus Tiberiana, Rome *27* 37 K4
Don (Tanais) *32* 44 E3, *51* 71 D4, *55* 76 F2, *113* 163 E2
Don Cossacks *83* 120 CD5
Don Manag *125* 182 A2
Donau (Danube, Danuvius, Ister, Istros) *24* 31 EF4, *28* 38 G4, *55* 76 E3, *107* 151 B4, *113* 163 A3
Donau Bulgars *46* 63 EF5
Donau delta *84* 121 HI5, *101* 141 I3
Donauwörth *68* 98 D5
Donets *51* 71 D4, *113* 163 E3
Dong Hoi *124* 181 C5, *125* 182 B2
Dongola *97* 136 D4, *108* 153 E6
Dor *15* 17 A5, *15* 18 DE5
Dora *26* 35 B2
Dorchester *50* 69 B3
Dordogne (Duranius) *52* 72 D6, *79* 113 B2–3
Dordrecht *66* 93 C3
Dorestad *43* 59 C3, *44* 60 F2, *46* 63 CD4
Dorpat *57* 79 G1, *69* 99 DE4
Dorset *44* 60 E3, *52* 72 C4, *56* 78 B3
Dortmund *57* 79 C4, *70* 100 C4
Dory leion *48* 66 J5
Douai *54* 74 B2, *66* 93 AB4
Douala *97* 136 C3, *122* 179 C5
Dover *64* 89 B2, *72* 103 B4, *77* 109 F7
Down *67* 95 EF7
Downpatrick *52* 72 B3
Drake's, Francis, journeys 1577–79 og 1580 *60* 84 F3
Drake Strait (Drake Passage) *60* 84 DE7
Drama *88* 125 C1
Drangiana *24* 31 J5–6
Drava (Dravus) *81* 116 D3, *101* 141 E3, *107* 151 C4, *113* 163 A4
Dravidians *13* 13 D2
Dravus, see Drava
Drenthe *59* 83 D1
Drepanum (Trapani) *20* 24 A6
Dresden *53* 73 D2, *70* 100 EF4, *81* 116 C2, *86* 122 D2–3, *104* 146 E4, *107* 151 C3, *113* 163 A3
Drogheda *67* 95 DE6
Drury Lane Theatre, London *66* 94 BC6
Duan *67* 95 DE5

Dublin (Dyflinn) *43* 59 AB3, *46* 63 B3, *47* 64 A2, *50* 69 AB3, *55* 76 B1, *56* 78 A2, *67* 95 D6, *76* 107 A5, *81* 116 A2
Dubrae *28* 38 D2
Dubrovnik *109* 155 D7
Dudinka *98* 137 B1
Duero (Durius, Douro) *43* 59 A6, *81* 118 A6, *84* 121 B6
Duisburg *57* 79 BC4
Dulcigno (Ulcinj) *88* 125 A1
Dumbshaf *46* 63 FG1
Dumfries *56* 78 B1, *67* 95 E6
Dumnoniorum *26* 34 B1
Düna (Daugava, Dvina) *51* 71 B2, *57* 79 G2
Dünaburg (Daugavpils) *73* 104 E1, *81* 116 DE1, *83* 120 AB3
Dünamünde *69* 99 CD5
Dunbar *52* 72 C2, *67* 95 E5
Dundalk *54* 74 AB1
Dundee *77* 109 E4
Dunhuang *32* 45 CD2
Dunkerque *66* 93 A3, *79* 114 B1, *110* 157 B4
Dunvegan *67* 95 DE5
Dur-Sharrukin (Khorsabad) *12* 12 E2
Dura-Europos (Dura-Europus) *24* 31 G6, *26* 34 G4
Duranius (Dordogne) *28* 38 GH7
Durazzo (Dyrrhachion, Dyrrhachium, Durrës) *28* 38 F4, *44* 60 J6, *54* 74 D3, *101* 141 F5
Durban (Port Natal) *97* 135 E7, *122* 179 DE7
Durham *50* 69 B3, *52* 72 CD3, *56* 78 BC1
Durius (Duero) *23* 28 A2
Durocortorum (Reims) *25* 33 BC3
Durrës (Durazzo, Dyrrhachion, Dyrrhachium) *71* 102 A5, *88* 125 A1
Düsseldorf *86* 122 B2, *114* 166 B2
Dutch India (Dutch East Indies) *98* 137 DE5–6, *105* 149 E2, *111* 159 AB3, *111* 160 A–C7
Düva *81* 116 E1
Dvina (Düna, Daugava), Estland *69* 99 DE5
Dvina, Soviet Union *36* 49 D1, *83* 120 C2
Dyarbakir *12* 11 C2
Dybbol *86* 123 C1, *86* 123 A6
Dyflinn (Dublin) *46* 63 B3
Dylyn-Boldak *34* 47 EF6, *40* 55 J2
Dyme *16* 20 AB5
Dyrrhachion (Dyrrhachium, Durrazzo, Durrës), seaport *28* 38 F4, *42* 57 J6, *45* 61 C6

Dyrrhachion, thema *45* **61** C5–6

E

East Anglia *43* **59** C3, *44* **60** F2, *47* **64** B2
East China Sea *40* **55** K4, *102* **142** CD4
East Franconia *45* **62** K6
East Frankish Empire, The *45* **62**, *46* **63** D4
East Friesland *70* **100** C3, *74* **105** B1, *75* **106** AB1
East Germany (DDR), see also German Democratic Republic *114* **167** F1, *115* **168** C3, *116* **169** BC6, *120* **176** Q3, *128* **185** B2–3
East Goths (Ostrogoths) *42* **57** K5
East Hall, Olympia *18* **22** D4
East London *97* **135** E7
East Prussia *74* **105** F1, *75* **106** F1, *104* **146** F3, *109* **155** D5, *110* **157** D3, *114* **166** F1
Eastern Front, The 1942–45 *113* **163**
Eastern Galicia *107* **151** DA4
Eastern Locris *16* **20** DE4
Eastern Rumelia *101* **141** GH4
Eastern Siberia *89* **126** JK6
Eastern Slavs *46* **63** F4
Eastern Turkistan (Xinjiang) *117* **170** AB3
Eastern Turks *32* **45** D2
Ebchester (Vindomora) *28* **39** K2
Ebeltoft *86* **123** B5
Eberswalde *68* **98** EF2
Ebla *12* **11** B2
Ebro (Iberus) *23* **28** B1–2, *43* **59** B5
Eburacum (York) *25* **33** A1, *26* **34** BC1, *28* **38** D1
Ecbatana (Hamadan) *12* **11** D2, *12* **12** F2, *13* **14** D6, *21* **26** D2, *24* **31** HI6, *28* **38** L5
Ecole Militaire, Paris *78* **112** AB6
Ecuador *63* **86** A1, *95* **132** B3, *105* **149** B2, *113* **164** B6–7, *120* **176** CD5
Edessa *28* **38** J5, *36* **49** D4, *48* **66** L5
Edessa, county (hist.) *49* **67** L1
Edfu *14* **15** C5, *108* **153** B6
Edgecote *56* **78** B2
Edgehill *67* **95** EF6
Edinburgh *47* **64** B1, *52* **72** C2, *57* **79** A2, *81* **116** B1
Edington *47* **64** B1
Edirne (Adrianopel) *103* **144** E5
Edo (Tokyo) *36* **49** L3
Edom *15* **17** B7, *15* **18** E7

Edward, Lake *96* **133** D5
EEC, members of *115* **168**
Efesos (Ephesus) *17* **21** EF3, *28* **38** A6
Efraim *26* **35** B4
EFTA, members of *115* **168**
Eger (Cheb), city in Czechoslovakia *47* **65** D3, *68* **98** E4
Eger (Erlau), city in Hungary *45* **61** C4
Eger, river *68* **98** F3–4
Egersund *110* **157** C3
Egmond *66* **93** BC2
Egypt (Aegyptus, Misir) *6* **2** C4, *8* **3** B6–7, *11* **10** B4–6, *12* **11** A3, *12* **12** BC4, *13* **14** B7, *21* **26** B3, *24* **31** F7, *24* **32** E7, *32* **44** E5, *37* **51** J2, *42* **58** CD3, *71* **102** BC7, *96* **133** D4, *97* **136** D1, *103* **145** B6, *108* **153** B5–6, *112* **161** E7, *112* **162** F2, *118* **173** A7, *120* **176** G4
Eichsfeld *68* **98** D3
Eider *86* **123** A7
Eidsvold *84* **121** E1, *91* **127** H2
Eilat (Elath) *118* **172** E4, *119* **174** A5
Einsiedeln *55* **77** D6
Eion *17* **21** J4
Eire, see Ireland
Ekenäs *69* **99** D4
El Agheila *112* **162** D2
El Aiún *122* **179** AB3
El Alamein *112* **161** E7, *112* **162** F2
El Amarna (Akhet-Aton) *11* **10** BC4
El Ashmunejn (Hermopolis) *14* **15** A3
El Castillo *9* **7** A2
El Kharga oasis *14* **15** AB5
El Paso *94* **131** J4
El Salvador *113* **164** AB6, *120* **176** C4, *120* **177** BC3
el-Kuneitra *118* **173** D4
Elatea *16* **20** CD4
Elath (Eliath) *18* **22** C3
Elba (Ilva *22* **27** B3, *47* **65** C6, *57* **80** J2, *68* **97** D3, *80* **115** B2, *81* **116** C6, *87* **124** B1, *101* **141** C4, *107* **151** B5
Elbe (Albis), river *43* **59** D3, *44* **60** H2, *47* **65** CD2, *81* **116** C2, *107* **151** B2
Elbing *56* **78** F3, *69* **99** C5–6
Elche (Ilici) *23* **28** B3
Elea (Velia) *20* **24** B5, *22* **27** DE5
Elephantine (Filae) *14* **15** C6
Eleusis (Elevsis) *16* **20** E5
Elia, city *16* **20** A6
Elis, district *16* **20** A5–6
Elisabethville (Lubumbashi) *97* **136** D4, *122* **179** D6, *123* **180** F3
Ellesmere Island *60* **84** E1, *98* **138** D5–6

Ellice Islands *111* **160** E7
Ellora *64* **89** B2
Elmham *50* **69** BC3
Elmina (San Jorge da Mina) *64* **88** D6, *96* **133** B5
Elsass (Alsace) *45* **62** K6, *68* **98** B5, *101* **141** B1–2
Elsass-Lothringen (Alsace-Lorraine) *86* **122** B3–4
Ely *52* **72** D3
Embrun *52* **72** F6, *59* **83** C6
Emesa *28* **38** IJ5, *45* **61** G7
Emilia-Romagna *87* **124** B1
Emmaus *26* **35** B4
Emperor Nero's palace, Olympia *18* **22** F6
Emporion (Emporiae) *16* **19** B2, *23* **28** C2, *24* **31** C4
Ems *44* **60** G2, *56* **78** E2, *57* **79** C3
Engadin *57* **80** F6
Engels *106* **150** E4
Enghien *66* **93** B4
England (Britannia), see also Great Britain *31* **43**, *41* **56** I5–6, *42* **57** G3–4, *44* **60** E2, *46* **63** C3, *47* **64**, *50* **69** BC3, *52* **72** CD3, *55* **76** B2, *57* **79** A3–4, *58* **81** A3, *59* **83** B4–5, *67* **95** EF6, *68* **97** B1, *76* **108**, *77* **109**, *81* **116** B2
English Channel *47* **64** B2, *52* **72** CD4, *56* **78** BC3
Eniwetok *111* **160** D6
Enkhuizen *66* **93** C2
Enns *70* **100** F6
Entebbe *97* **136** DE3
Enugu *122* **179** C5
Epeiros (Epirus) *17* **21** A2, *20* **25** C2–3, *24* **32** D6, *50* **70** E7, *88* **125** A2
Ephesus (Efesos) *28* **38** H5
Epidamnos *16* **19** D2, *20* **25** BC2
Epidauros *16* **20** DE6, *88* **125** B3
Epinal *105* **148** L3
Epirus, see Epeiros
Equateur *123* **180** E1
Equatoria *96* **133** D5
Equatorial Guinea *122* **179** BC5
Erbil *12* **11** CD2
Erechtium (Erechteion), Athens *19* **23** CD1
Eregli *71* **102** C5, *101* **141** J5
Eresos *17* **21** D2
Eretria *16* **20** EF5, *17* **21** C3
Erfurt *47* **65** D3, *49* **68** E5
Eridu *11* **10** F4
Erie *62* **85** C2–3
Erik the Red's voyage ca. 985 *60* **84** EF2–3
Eritrea *97* **136** E2, *103* **145** C7, *107* **152** BC2, *108* **153** C7, *122* **179** E4
Erivan (Jerevan) *106* **150** F7
Erlau (Eger) *45* **61** C4

Ermland *70* **100** GH2, *74* **105** EF1
Erythrae *17* **21** E3
Esbjerg *86* **123** A5
Escorial, El *68* **97** A3
Eshnunna (Tell Asmar) *11* **10** EF3
Esna *14* **15** BC5
Espíritu Santo *111* **159** D4, *111* **160** DE7
Esquilin, Rome *27* **36** L6
Essen *47* **65** B2, *107* **151** B3, *114* **166** AB2
Essex *43* **59** BC3, *52* **72** D4
Esslingen *70* **100** CD5
Estates General (Netherlands) *66* **93** C3
Estonia *50* **70** E4, *57* **79** FG1, *67* **96** D1, *69* **99** D4, *71* **101** J5, *81* **116** D1, *83* **120** A3, *104* **146** G2, *106* **150** AB3, *107* **151** D1, *108* **154** EF1, *110* **157** E3, *112* **161** D2, *113* **163** C1, *115* **168** D2, *128* **185** C1
Estonians *46* **63** F3
Estrées *79* **113** B1
Esztergom (Gran) *45* **61** B4, *59* **83** E5
Ethiopia (Abessinia) *32* **44** EF7, *36* **49** E6, *40* **55** DE6, *65* **92** EF2, *96* **133** E4, *107* **152** BC3, *108* **153** C7, *113* **164** D6, *120* **176** GH4, *122* **179** D1, *125**
Etna *22* **27** E6
Etruria, Etruscans *16* **19** C2, *22* **27** BC3
Etruria, kingdom, province *80* **115** C3–4, *81* **116** C3, *82* **119** CD3
Eu *56* **78** C3
Euboea *16* **20** EF4, *17* **21** C3
Eupatoria *101* **141** J3
Euphrates *10* **9** B2, *12* **11** C2, *12* **12** D2, *28* **38** J5
Europe ca. 1400 *55* **76**
Europe in 1801 *81* **116**
European Council, members of *115* **168**
Eurotas *16* **20** C7
Evesham *52* **72** C3–4
Evland (Öland) *46* **63** E3
Evreux *52* **72** D5, *56* **78** C4
Evropos *17* **21** D2
Exeter *50* **69** AB3, *52* **72** C4, *56* **78** B3
Eziongeber *14* **15** D2, *15* **17** AB7

F

Faesulae (Fiesole) *22* **27** C3
Falasarna *17* **21** C5
Falkland Islands (Islas Malvinas/Iles Malouines) *62* **85** E7, *95* **132** D7
Falster *70* **100** E2, *86* **122** CD1
Falsterbo *57* **79** DE3

Falun *69* **99** C4, *72* **103** D3
Famagusta *48* **66** K6, *54* **74** EF4
Fano *86* **123** A6
Faris *16* **20** C7
Faroe Islands *46* **63** C2, *50* **69** BC1, *72* **103** B2, *110* **157** AB2, *115* **168** B1
Fars *36* **50** C7, *40* **55** F4
Farther Pomerania *70* **100** F2–3, *75* **106** D1
Fashoda (Kodok) *97* **136** D2
Faya (Largeau) *108* **153** A6–7
Fayum Oasis *14* **15** A2
Fectio *32* **44** B3
Fehmarn *68* **98** DE1, *86* **123** B6
Fehrbellin *69* **99** B6, *75* **106** C2
Feldkirch (Clunia) *29* **40** B7
Fenni *32* **44** CD2
Fère-Champenoise *105* **148** J3
Fergana *32* **45** B2
Ferma *57* **80** K2
Fernando Po *65* **92** BC2, *96* **133** BC5
Ferrara *49* **68** E6, *53* **73** D4
Fez *45* **61** G1, *96* **134** A1
Fezzan *45* **61** H2, *96* **134** C2
Field of Mars (Campus Martius), Rome *27* **36** K6
Field of Mars (Champs de Mars), Paris *78* **112** A5
Fiesole (Faesulae) *22* **27** C3
Fiji *111* **159** E4, *111* **160** E7
Filibé (Filippopel, Plovdiv) *58* **81** F4
Finisterre, Cape *84* **121** A5
Finland *58* **81** E1, *69* **99** D3, *71* **101** J4, *83* **120** AB2, *84* **121** G1, *91* **127** J1, *104* **146** G1, *106* **150** AB2, *107* **151** D1, *108* **154** E1, *110* **157** DE2, *112* **161** D2, *113* **163** C1, *113* **164** D5, *115* **168** D1, *116* **169** C5, *120* **176** G2
Finns (Samid) *46* **63** F1, F2, *51* **71** I3
Firat *51* **71** D6
Firenze (Florentia), by *28* **38** E4, *43* **59** D5, *45* **61** A5, *49* **68** E6, *54* **74** C5, *57* **79** C3, *68* **97** D3, *80* **115** C3, *84* **121** E5, *87* **124** B1, *107* **151** B5
Firenze, republic *57* **80** J2
Firenze, republic of *57* **80** J2
First Cataract *11* **10** B5, *14* **15** BC6
Fiume (Rijeka) *91* **127** I5, *107* **151** CB, *152* A1
Flæminghald *46* **63** C4
Flanders *47* **65** A2–3, *52* **72** DE4, *56* **78** D3, *59* **82** B5, *66* **93** AB3, *68* **97** C1, *70* **100** A4, *105* **148** IJ1
Flensborg (Flensburg) *70* **100** D2, *86* **123** AB6, *107* **151** B2

Fleurus 68 **98** A3, 79 **114** C1

Florentia (Firenze) 22 **27** C3

Flores 64 **90** L7, 99 **139** K4

Flores Sea 64 **90** L7, 99 **139** K4

Florianópolis (Destérro) 95 **132** E5

Florida 92 **128** J3, 93 **130** F4, 111 **159** C4, 121 **177** BC1

Flossenburg 111 **158** AB2

Focsani 104 **146** H5, 105 **147** L7

Föhr 86 **123** A6

Foix 79 **114** B3

Folsom 7 1

Fontainebleau 56 **78** D3, 81 **116** B2–3, 84 **121** D4

Fontenoy 44 **60** F4

Formigny 56 **78** C4

Formosa (Taiwan) 35 **48** EF3, 98 **137** E4, 113 **164** F6

Fort Albany 62 **85** CD2, 92 **128** J1

Fort Bourbon (Fort York) 62 **85** C1

Fort Caroline 62 **85** CD3

Fort Chippewan 62 **85** B1

Fort Churchill 62 **85** C1

Fort Edmonton 62 **85** B2

Fort Ellis 62 **85** B2

Fort Frontenac 92 **128** JK2

Fort Laperrine (Tamanrasset) 96 **134** C2

Fort Maurepas 62 **85** C2, 92 **128** IJ1

Fort Pontchartrain 62 **85** C2

Fort St. Andreas 65 **92** AB2

Fort St. Charles 62 **85** BC2

Fort St. David 65 **91** HI4

Fort St. James 65 **92** H4

Fort St. Louis 92 **128** IJ2

Fort Sumter 92 **129** D4

Fort York (Fort Bourbon) 62 **85** C1

Fort-Dauphin 97 **136** EF

Fort-Lamy (Ndjamena) 97 **136** C2, 122 **179** CD4

Fortaleza (Ceara) 95 **132** F3

Forum Boarium, Rome 27 **36** K6–7

Forum Julii 25 **33** C4

Forum Julium, Rome 27 **37** J2

Forum Pacis, Rome 27 **37** KL2

Forum Romanum, Rome 27 **36** KL6, 27 **37** JK3

Foshan 35 **48** E3, 65 **91** L2

Fotheringhay 68 **97** BC1

Fourth Cataract 11 10 B6

France (Gallia, Kingdom of the Frank) 9 7 B1, 42 **57** G4–5, 42 **58** AB1, 43 **59** CD4, 44 **60**, 45 **62**, 46 **63**, 50 **70** BC5, 52 **72** DE5, 55 76 B3, 58 **81** AB5, 59 **82** B2, 67 **96** B3, 68 **97** BC2, 72 **103** BC5, 74 **105** A3, 78 **111** B2, 79 **113**, 79 **114**, 81

116 B3, 82 **119** BC3, 84 **121** CD4, 86 **122** A4, 91 **127** G5, 104 **146** CD5, 105 **148** J2, 105 **149** C2, 107 **152** A4, 108 **154** BC3, 110 **157** AB4, 112 **161** A4, 115 **168** B3, 116 **169** AB6, 120 **176** F3

Franche-Comté 52 **72** EF6, 68 **97** C2, 70 **100** B6, 79 **113** C2, 79 **114** C2

Franeker 58 **81** BC3–4, 66 **93** C1

Franken (Franconia) 47 **65** C3, 53 **73** C3

Frankfurt (am Main) 53 **73** C2, 54 **74** C2, 55 76 C2, 57 79 C4, 68 **98** C4, 76 **107** C5, 81 **116** C2, 84 **121** E4, 107 **151** B3, 114 **166** B3

Frankfurt (an der Oder) 49 **68** EF5, 77 79 E4, 58 **81** D4, 68 **98** F2

Franks, homeland of 42 **57** GH4

Franks, kingdom of 42 **57** G4–5, 42 **58** AB1

Franks, people 28 **38** E2

Frans Josefs Land 60 **84** GH1

Fraustadt 69 **99** BC6

Fredericia 69 **99** D2, 91 **127** H3

Frederiksnagor (Serampur) 65 **91** I2

Frederiksstad, Slesvig 86 **123** AB6

Fredrikshald (Halden, Norway) 69 **99** AB4

Fredrikshamn 84 **121** G1

Fredriksten 84 **121** E2

Freetown 65 **92** A2, 96 **133** A5

Freiberg 74 **105** CD2

Freiburg (Fribourg), Switzerland 55 77 B6

Freiburg, canton 55 77 B6

Freiburg, Germany 49 **68** E6, 114 **166** B4

Freising, bishopric 70 **100** E3

Freising, city 47 **65** D4, 74 **105** C3

Fremantle 98 **137** D7

French Equatorial Africa 97 **136** CD3

French Guinea 97 **136** A2

French Guyana 95 **132** DE2

French Indochina 98 **137** D5, 111 **159** A2, 111 **160** B6, 113 **164** EF6

French Somaliland 97 **136** EF2, 103 **145** D7, 108 **153** CD7

French West Africa 97 **136** BC2

Friedberg 57 79 C4

Friedland, East Prussia 81 **116** D2, 82 **119** E2, 83 **120** A4

Friedland, Moravia 70 **100** G5

Friedrichsmain, Berlin 114 **167** E2

Friesland 44 **60** G2, 46 **63** CD3–4, 47 **65** B2, 53 73 BC1, 66 **93** CD1

Frisians 25 **33** C1, 28 **38** E1, 42 57 G4, 43 59 CD3

Fritzlar 44 **60** G3, 47 **65** C3

Friuli 44 **60** H4

Fujisan 102 **142** BC6, 117 **170** D6

Fulah kingdom 96 **133** BC4

Fulda 43 59 D3, 44 **60** G3, 45 62 K6, 47 **65** C3

Funan kingdom 32 44 K6, 39 54 BC6

Fünfkirchen (Pécs) 49 **68** F6, 58 **81** E5

Fürth 68 **98** D4

Fusan (Pusan) 102 **142** D4

Futa Jallon 65 **92** A2

Futatoro 65 **92** A1

Fuzhou 32 45 EF3, 102 **142** C6

Fyn 70 **100** D2, 86 **123** B6

Fyrkat 44 **60** G1

G

Gaba 26 **35** B2

Gabai (Isfahan) 21 26 D2, 24 **31** I6

Gaberone (Gaborone) 122 **179** D7

Gabès 48 **66** E7, 112 **161** B7, 112 **162** B1

Gabon 96 **133** C5, 97 **136** C3, 122 **179** EF2 (2), C5

Gadames 103 **145** A6

Gadara, Galilee 26 **35** C2

Gadara, Perea 26 **35** C3

Gades (Cadiz) 16 19 A2, 28 **38** B4, 32 44 AB5

Gaeta 80 **115** D5

Galapagos 95 **132** A3, 120 **176** H5

Galati 91 **127** KL5, 101 **141** H6

Galatia (Phrygia) 17 21 F2, 23 30 BC6, 24 **31** F5, 24 **32** E6, 28 **38** H5

Galatians 9 6 F6

Galich (Galicia) 106 **150** D3

Galicia 69 **99** D7, 81 **116** D2, 101 **141** G1–2, 104 **146** G4, 105 **147** J6

Galilee 26 **35** B2, 118 **171** AB1

Galilee 49 67 K3

Galilee, Sea of 26 **35** C2

Galle 40 55 GH6, 99 **140** C5

Gallia 24 **32** B5, 25 **33** B4, 28 **38** D3

Gallia Belgica 25 **33** B2

Gallia Celtica 25 **33** A3

Gallia Cisalpina 22 **27** AB1, 24 **32** C5–6, 28 **38** E3

Gallia Trans-Alpina 23 **28** C1

Gállivare 110 **157** D1

Gallipoli (Gelibolu) 71 **102** B5, 88 **125** D1

Galloway 55 76 **78** AB1

Galway 91 **127** E3

Gama's, Vasco da, journeys 60 **84** F5, F6, H4–5

Gambia 96 **133** A4, 97 **136** A2, 98 **138** D7, 120 **176** F4, 122 **179** A4

Gamla Karleby 69 **99** D3

Gamla 26 **35** B3

Gandhara (Kandahar), province 13 14 F6

Gandvik (White Sea) 46 63 FG2

Ganges 32 45 B3, 64 **89** B1–2, 99 **140** CD2

Gangra 23 30 C5–6, 48 **66** K5

Gansu 30 41 A5, 98 **137** CD3–4

Ganzhou 35 **48** CD3, 40 55 I3

Gao 32 44 B6, 65 **92** B3

Gardariki 46 63 F3

Garisim 26 **35** B3

Garonne 44 **60** E5, 79 **113** B3, 79 **114** B3

Garsaura 12 12 C1

Gartz 68 **98** F2

Gascony (Gascogne) 44 **60** E5, 50 **70** B6, 52 **72** CD7

Gatow, Berlin 114 **167** CD2

Gaugamela 13 14 C6, 21 26 C2

Gaulanitis 26 **35** C2

Gauts 46 63 DE3

Gävle 69 **99** C4, 84 **121** F1

Gaza 10 9 B3, 11 10 C4, 15 17 A6, 49 67 J4, 118 **173** C5

Gazaca 24 **31** H5

Gdansk, see Danzig

Gdynia 109 **155** CD4

Gedrosia (Baluchistan) 24 **31** K6, 32 44 G5

Gela 112 **161** B6

Gelderland 66 **93** D2

Geldern 56 **78** E2

Gelibolu (Gallipoli) 71 **102** B5

Gelnhausen 47 **65** C3, 53 73 C2

Gembloux 66 **93** C4

Gemena 123 **180** E1

Gemünden 68 **98** CD4

Geneva (Genève) 47 **65** B5, 55 76 C3, 55 77 A7, 56 **78** E5, 79 **114** C2, 81 **116** B3, 87 124 A1

Geneva, Lake of (Lacus Lemanus) 22 **27** A1, 55 77 AB7

Genova (Genua), seaport 28 **38** E3, 43 **59** D5, 53 73 C4, 55 76 C3, 68 **97** D2, 76 **107** C6, 81 **116** C3, 87 124 A1, 107 **151** B5

Genova, republic 57 **80** I2

Gent 56 **78** D3, 66 **93** B3, 105 **148** J1

Genua (Genova) 22 **27** AB2, 25 **33** C4, 28 **38** E3

Georgetown (Stabroek) 62 **85** DE4, 95 **132** D2

Georgia, on the Black Sea 51 71 E6, 71 **102** E5, 83 **120** D6, 92 **129** C4, 106 **150** EF7, 108 **153** D3, 115 **168** F4

Georgia, USA 92 **128** J3, 93 **130** F3

Gepides 42 57 J5

Gerasa (Jerash) 26 **35** CD3

Gergovia 25 **33** B4, 28 **38** D3

German Democratic Republic (DDR), East Germany 114 **166** CD2

German East Africa 97 **136** DE3

German Southwest Africa 97 **136** C4–5

Germani (Germanic tribes) 13 13 AB1

Germania 25 **33** C2

Germania Inferior 28 **38** DE2, 29 **40** A6

Germania Magna 24 **32** CD5, 26 34 D1–2, 28 **38** EF2

Germania Superior 28 **38** DE2–3, 29 **40** A7

Germany (BRD), see also West Germany 114 **166** BC3

Gerona 81 **118** DE5, 109 **156** F2

Gerrha 32 44 F5

Gesoriacum 26 34 BC1

Getes 20 25 DE1

Getes 43 59 D2

Gettysburg 92 **129** CD2

Geusen attack 1572 66 **93** B2

Ghadamis 8 5 H2, 107 **152** A2

Ghana 32 44 A6, 120 **176** F4–5, 122 **179** C1

Ghara 40 55 I3

Ghat (Gat) 32 44 C6, 96 **134** C2

Ghazni 21 26 EF2, 64 **89** A1

Ghor 64 **89** A1

Gibraltar (Djebel al-Tarik) 43 59 AB7, 68 **97** A4, 72 **103** A7

Gibraltar, Strait of 44 63 A6

Gilbert Islands 111 **159** DE3, 111 **160** E7

Gilead 26 **35** C3

Gilgit 32 45 B2

Ginea 26 **35** B3

Girnar Hills 38 52 J2

Gironde 79 **113** AB3

Gisjiga 98 **137** B2

Giza 14 15 A2, 15 16 A2, 15 16

Gjirokastër (Argurokastron) 88 **125** A2

Glarus, canton 55 77 DE6

Glarus, commune 55 77 DE6

Glasgow 76 **107** B5, 77 **109** D4, 81 **116** B1, 84 **121** C2

Glevnum (Gloucester) 25 **33** A2

Glienicker Brücke, Berlin 114 **167** CD2

Globe Theatre, London *66*
94 C6
Glogau *74* 105 DE2
Glomma *57* 79 D1
Gloucester *25* 33 A2, *56* 78
B2, *67* 95 E7, *76* 108 B6,
77 109 E6
Glücksborg *86* 123 A6
Glückstadt *74* 105 C1
Gmünd *70* 100 D5
Gnesdovo *46* 63 F3, *51* 71 C3
Gniezno (Gnesen) *41* 56 K6,
50 69 E3–4, *53* 73 E1–2, *59*
83 E5
Goa *36* 49 G5, *40* 55 G5, *64*
89 AB3, *65* 91 GH3, *99*
140 B4, *127* 184 B4
Gober *65* 92 C1
Gobi Desert *117* 170 CD5
Godavari *64* 89 BC3, *99* 140 C3
Godthâb *60* 84 E2
Golan Heights *118* 173 D4–5
Golconda *64* 89 C3, *65* 91 H13
Gold Beach (Normandy,
1944) *113* 165 B3
Gold Coast *96* 133 B5, *97* 136
B3
Goldap *112* 161 CD3
Goldberg *70* 100 F4
Golden Horde, The (Kip-
chak Empire) *40* 55
DE2–3, *55* 76 F2
Goldingen *57* 79 F2, *69* 99 C5
Gomel (Homel) *106* 150 C5,
113 163 D2
Gondar *65* 92 EF1
Gondokoro *96* 133 DE5
Good Hope, Cape of *60* 84
G6, *65* 92 CD5
Gordium (Gordion) *21* 26
B2, *23* 30 BC6
Gorki *112* 161 F3, *113* 163 F2
Gorlice *105* 147 J6
Gortyna *17* 21 D5, *28* 38 G5
Gorz *70* 100 EF7
Goshen *14* 15 B1
Goslar *47* 65 C2, *53* 73 C2
Gotalania (Catalonia) *42* 57
F6
Göta Canal *91* 127 I2
Göteborg (Gothenburg) *69*
99 B4, *76* 107 CD4, *81* 116
C1, *107* 151 BC1, *113* 163
A1
Goths *42* 57 HI3, *32* 44 C2,
CD3
Gotland *43* 59 E1, *57* 79 F2,
69 99 C5, *81* 116 D1, *107*
151 C2
Göttingen *57* 79 D4, *74* 105
C2
Gottorp *72* 103 CD4, *86* 123
A6
Grahamstown *97* 135 D7
Gran (Esztergom) *45* 61 B4,
41 56 K6, *70* 100 G6
Gran Colombia, earlier
NewGranada *95* 132
Granada, Central America *62*
85 C4

Granada, Spain, city *37* 51
G1, *43* 59 B7, *55* 76 A4, *68*
97 B4, *81* 118 C7, *109* 156
E3
Granada, Spain, kingdom,
bishopric *50* 70 AB7, *40* 55
A4, *58* 81 AB7, *59* 82 AB3
Grand Châtelet, Paris *78* 112
D5
Granicus (Granikos) *17* 21
E2, *21* 26 A2
Grasburg *55* 77 C6
Graubünden *55* 77 EF7
Gravesend *76* 108 C7
Gray's Inn, London *66* 94 C6
Graz *84* 121 F4, *91* 127 I5,
107 151 C4
Great Australian Bight *98*
137 E7
Great Bear Lake *62* 85 B1
Great Belt *86* 123 B5–6
Great Britain, see also Eng-
land *72* 103 BC3–4, *76* 107
B5, *81* 116 B2, *82* 119
B1–2, *84* 121 BC2–3, *91*
127 FG3, *104* 146 BC3,
108 154 BC2, *110* 157
AB3, *115* 168 B2–3, *116*
169 AB5–6, *120* 176 F3
Great Chesters (Aesica) *28* 39
IJ1–2
Great Mogul Empire *35* 48 B4
Great Nafud *118* 173 EF7
Great Sandy Desert *98* 137
E6
Great Serkland *46* 63 EF7
Great Slave Lake *62* 85 B1
Great Svitjod *46* 63 F3–4
Great Wall of China, The *30*
42 D2, *59* 82 J3
Great Yarmouth *77* 109 F6
Greater Germany (Germa-
nia Magna) *47* 65, *53* 73
CD2, *68* 98, *70* 100, *74*
105, *84* 121, *86* 122, *104*
146 DE4, *105* 147 IJ5, *105*
148 L1, *107* 151 BC3, *110*
157 CD4, *111* 158 AB2,
112 161 B4, *113* 163 AB3,
114 166
Greater Sunda Islands *126*
183 C7
Greco-Bactrian Kingdom,
The *24* 31 K5
Greece (Hellas) *16* 19 E2, *21*
26 A2, *24* 31 E5, *84* 121
G6–7, *88* 125 B2–3, *91* 127
K7, *104* 146 G6, *107* 151
D6, *108* 154 E4, *110* 157
E6, *112* 162 DE1, *115* 168
D4, *116* 169 CD7
Greenland *113* 164 C5, *120*
176 EF2
Greenwich *66* 94 F7
Greifswald *49* 68 EF5, *57* 79
DE3, *58* 81 D3
Grenada *120* 176 D4, *121* 177
E2
Grenoble *49* 68 D6, *81* 116
B3, *104* 146 D5

Grikland (Old Norse: Gree-
ce) *46* 63 EF6
Grimaldi *7* 1
Grobin (Seeburg) *46* 63 EF3,
69 99 C5
Grodek (Gorodok) *105* 147
K5
Grodno *69* 99 D6, *81* 118 JK3
Groningen, city *57* 79 BC3,
66 93 D1
Groningen, province *66* 93 D1
Grosnyj *106* 150 F6, *113* 163
F4
Grossjägersdorf *74* 105 F1
Gross-Rosen *111* 158 B2
Gruyères *55* 77 B6
Guadalajara *109* 156 E2
Guadalcanal *111* 159 D4, *111*
160 D7
Guadeloupe *62* 85 D4, *121*
177 DE2
Guadiana (Anas) *43* 59 A6, *48*
66 AB5
Guam *98* 137 F5, *111* 159 C3
Guanahani (Watling Island)
62 85 CD3
Guangdong (Kwangtung) *30*
41 B7, *102* 142 B6
Guangxi (Kwangsi) *30* 41
AB7, *117* 170 CD7
Guangxi-Zhuangzu
(Kwangsi Chuang) *102*
142 A6
Guangzhou (Kwang Chou,
Canton, Nanhai) *32* 45 E3,
40 55 J5, *60* 84 JK4, *102*
142 B6, *111* 160 B6
Guantanamo *121* 178 C2
Guastalla *80* 115 C3
Guatemala City *62* 85 BC4,
63 87 D3, *121* 177 B2
Guatemala, state *95* 132 A1,
120 176 C4, *121* 177 AB2
Guayaquil *63* 86 A2
Guernica *109* 156 E1
Guernsey *56* 78 B4, *84* 121
BC4
Guiana *113* 164 B6, *120* 176
E5
Guildhall, London *66* 94
CD6
Guinea *120* 176 F4, *122* 179
C1
Guinea Gabon *120* 176 G5
Guinea, Gulf of *32* 44 AB7,
97 136 B3
Guinea-Bissau *120* 176 F4,
122 179 A4
Guise *66* 93 B5, *68* 97 C1
Guizhou *114* 167 C6
Gujarat *64* 89 A2, *99* 140 B3,
127 184 B2
Gumla *108* EF2
Gundestrup *8* 4 B1, *9* 6 E5
Guptas, Kingdom of the *36*
50 F7
Guryev *89* 126 H6, *106* 150
F5
Gustrow *70* 100 E3
Guyana *94* 131 K5, *95* 132 D2

Guyenne (Aquitania), duchy
56 78 C6–7
Gwadur (Gwadar) *99* 140 A2
Gwalior *99* 140 C2
Gymnasium (Gymnasion),
Olympia *18* 22 D5
Gytheion *17* 21 B4

H
Ha Tien *65* 91 KL4
Haarlem *66* 93 BC2
Habana (Havana) *62* 85 C4,
121 177 B1, *123* 180 A2
Habituncum *28* 39 J1
Habsburg *55* 77 C5
Haderslev *86* 123 A6
Hadramaut *97* 136 F2, *98* 137
A5
Hadria (Adria) *22* 27 C2
Hadrianopolis *28* 38 GH4
Hadrumetum *28* 38 E5
Haeju *119* 175 B2
Hafrsfjord *46* 63 D3
Hafsids, Kingdom of the
1300 *40* 55 BC4, *55* 76 BC4
Hagenau *47* 65 BC4, *70* 100
C5
Hague, The *66* 93 BC2, *79*
114 BC1, *81* 116 B2, *84*
121 D3
Haifa *118* 171 A1, *119* 174 A5
Haikou *102* 142 A7, *124* 181
D5
Hainan *102* 142 A7, *124* 181
D5
Hainaut (Hennegouwen),
county (hist.) *66* 93 B4
Haiphong *124* 181 C4, *125*
182 BC1
Haithabu (Hedeby) *46* 63
J6, *32* 44 C5
Haiti *62* 85 D4, *95* 132 B1,
121 177 C1
Hakodate *102* 142 F2
Halberstadt, city *53* 73 D2,
86 122 C2
Halberstadt, state *75* 106 B2
Halden, see Fredrikshald
Haleb (Aleppo) *12* 12 D2
Halicarnassus (Halikarnas-
sos) *17* 21 F4
Halifax *92* 128 L2, *93* 130 H1
Hall *70* 100 D5
Hall of Echoes *18* 22 F5–6
Halland *57* 79 D2, *69* 99 B5
Halle *57* 79 D4, *75* 106 C2
Halles, Les, Paris *78* 112 D5
Hallstadt, University *44* 60 H3
Hallstatt Austria *8* 4 B1, *9* 6 E6
Halmahera *99* 139 L3, *126*
183 D7
Hälsingborg *84* 121 EF2
Halton Chesters *28* 39 JK1
Halys (Kizil Irmak) *10* 9 A1,
11 10 C2, *12* 11 AB1, *71*
102 CD5
Hama *49* 67 K2
Hamadan (Ecbatana) *36* 50
B6, *71* 102 EF6

Hamah (Hamath, Hama) *12*
12 D2
Hamar *69* 99 B3, *84* 121 E1
Hamath (Hamah) *12* 12 D2
Hamburg *50* 69 D3, *55* 76 C2,
57 79 CD3, *68* 97 D1, *76*
107 C5, *81* 116 C2, *104* 146
E3, *107* 151 B3, *110* 157
C3, *114* 166 C1–2
Hami *35* 48 C2, *60* 84 I3
Hammershus *69* 99 BC5
Han-Chou (Han-Zhou) *32*
45 EF2
Hanau *69* 99 A6
Hang-chou (Kinsai, Lin'an)
35 48 E3, *60* 84 JK4
Hangö *69* 99 D4
Hanhai *32* 45 D1
Hankou *35* 48 D3, *102* 142 B5
Hannon of Carthago's' voya-
ge to Africa *32* 44 AB7
Hannover, city *57* 79 CD4,
110 157 C4
Hannover, electoral princi-
pality *74* 105, C1–2, *81* 116
C2
Hannover, kingdom *84* 121
DE 3, *86* 122 BC2
Hannover, state *72* 103 CD4
Hanoi (Thang Long) *111* 159
A2, *125* 182 B1
Hao (Bow Island) *30* 41 M6
Hapsal *69* 99 D4
Harappa *8* 3 DE6, *108* F2
Harar *96* 133 EF5, *107* 152
BC3
Harbin (Pinkiang) *102* 142
C2, *117* 170 E4
Harfleur *56* 78 C4
Harmozeia (Hormuz) *24* 31
J6, *32* 44 G5
Harran *11* 10 D2, *12* 12 D2
Haryana *127* 184 BC2
Harzburg *47* 65 CD2
Härnösand *69* 99 C3
Hasa, Al *108* 153 D5–6
Hasor *15* 17 B5, *15* 18 E5
Hastenbeck *74* 105 C2
Hastings *47* 64 B2, *56* 78 C3
Hatra *11* 10 E3
Hatteras, Cape *62* 85 CD3, *93*
130 G3
Hatti (Hittite Empire) *8* 5 E3,
11 10 CD2
Hattin *49* 67 K3
Hattushash (Bogaz-Köy) *8* 5
E3, *11* 10 AB1, *11* 10 CD2,
12 11 B1
Hausaland *65* 92 C1–2, *96*
133 BC5
Havel, Berlin *114* 167 D1
Havelberg *47* 65 D2, *50* 69
D3
Hawaii *111* 160 F6, *120* 176
A4
Hawaiian Islands *111* 159 E2,
111 160 F6
Hawara *32* 44 E6
Hebe *30* 41 BC5
Hebei *102* 142 B4

Hebrides *46* 63 B2, *47* 64 A1, *50* 69 AB2
Hebron *26* 35 B5, *118* 173 C5
Hecatompylos *24* 31 IJ5
Hedeby, see also Haithabu *26* 34 CD1, *43* 59 D2, *44* 60 G2
Hedjaz *37* 51 J2, *108* 153 C5–6
Heian-kyo (Kyoto) *36* 49 L4, *40* 55 L4
Heidelberg *49* 68 DE6, *58* 81 C4
Heiho (Aigun) *89* 126 K6
Heijo (Nara) *36* 49 L4, *40* 55 L4
Heilbronn *70* 100 CD5, *86* 122 C3
Helena *16* 20 F6
Helgoland *86* 122 B1, *104* 146 D3
Helgö 63 E3
Helgå *50* 69 E3
Heliopolis *14* 15 B2
Hellespont *17* 21 DE2
Helluland 60 84 D2
Helsingfors (Helsinki) 69 99 D4, *76* 107 DE4, *81* 116 DE1, *83* 120 AB3, *107* 152 D1
Helsinki (Helsingfors) *58* 81 E2, *112* 161 D2, *113* 163 C1
Helvetian Republic, The *80* 115 AB2, *81* 116 C3, *82* 119 C3
Hemeroskopeion *16* 19 AB2
Henan *30* 41 B6, *102* 142 AB4
Henneberg *74* 105 BC3
Hennegouwen, se Hainaut
Heraclea (Herakleia), Italia *22* 27 F5, *23* 28 F2
Heraclea, Asia Minor *49* 67 J1
Heraclea, Italy *20* 24 C5
Heraclea, on the Black Sea *16* 19 EF2, *23* 30 B5
Heraion (Temple of Hera), Olympia *18* 22 EF5
Herakleia Pontika *20* 25 F2
Herakleion, department of Greece *16* 20 C4
Herakleopolis *14* 15 A2
Heraklion (Iraklion and Candia), Crete *17* 21 D5, *110* 157 EF6
Herakleion, Macedonia *17* 21 B2
Herat (Alexandria) *21* 26 E2, *34* 47 B7, *99* 140 A1
Hercegovina *84* 121 F5, *101* 141 E4, *103* 144 B2, *104* 146 F6
Herculaneum *23* 29 DE4
Hercules, Pillars of (Gibraltar) *23* 28 AB3
Hereford *50* 69 B3, *56* 78 B2
Héricourt *55* 77 B5
Herjedalen 69 99 B3
Hermannstadt (Sibiu) *72* 103 F5, *101* 141 G3

Hermione *16* 20 DE7, *17* 21 C4
Hermon *15* 17 B4
Hermopolis (El Ashmunejn) *12* 12 B3, *14* 15 A3
Hermos *17* 21 F3
Hermunduri *29* 40 B6
Herodes Atticus' Exedra, Olympia *18* 22 EF5
Herodes Atticus' Odeum (The Roman Theatre), Acroplis *19* 23 B2–3
Hesbon *15* 18 EF6
Hessen *43* 59 D3, *84* 121 E4
Hessen, grand duchy *86* 122 BC3
Hessen-Darmstadt *70* 100 CD4
Hessen-Kassel, landgravate *70* 100 CD4
Heuneburg *8* 4 B1, *9* 6 DE5
Hibernia (Ireland) *32* 44 A3, *36* 49 C1
Hierakonpolis *12* 11 A4, *14* 15 B5
Hierapetros *88* 125 D4
Hieron *16* 20 D6
Hierosolyma (Jerusalem) *24* 32 F7, *28* 38 J6
Hildesheim, bishopric 68 98 D2, *70* 100 D3
Hildesheim, city (episcopal see) *50* 69 D3
Hilmand *99* 140 A1
Himachal Pradesh *127* 184 C1
Himalaya, The *64* 89 BD1, *99* 140 CE2
Himera *20* 24 AB6, *22* 27 D6
Hindu Kush *99* 140 AB1
Hindu principalities in India *40* 55 GH5
Hinterrhein *55* 77 E6–7
Hippo *42* 58 B2
Hippo Diarrhytus *22* 27 AB6
Hippo Regius (Bône) *16* 19 BC2, *28* 38 D5, *43* 59 D7
Hipponium (Hipponion) *20* 24 BC6
Hippos *26* 35 C2
Hira *36* 49 E4, *36* 50 AB6
Hiroshima *111* 160 C5
Hirson *105* 148 B4
Hispal *28* 38 B4
Hispania (Spain) *23* 28 AB2, *26* 34 AB3, *28* 38 B4, *32* 44 AB4
Hispania Citerior *24* 32 A6
Hispania Ulterior *24* 32 A6
Hispaniola 60 84 D4
Hit *12* 11 C3
Hither Pomerania 69 99 B5, *70* 100 E2–3, *74* 105 CD1
Hititte Empire (Hatti) *10* 9 AB1, *11* 10 CD2
Hjaltland (Shetlands) *57* 79 B1
Hjardarholt *46* 63 B1, 60 84 F2

Hjortspring *9* 6 DE5
Ho Chi Minh City (Saigon) *125* 182 B2
Ho Chi Minh Trail *125* 182 B2–3
Ho-lin (Karakorum) *40* 55 HI3
Hochkirch *74* 105 D3
Hohenfriedberg *75* 106 D3
Hohenlinden *81* 116 C3
Hohenzollern *70* 100 CD6, *86* 122 C4
Højer *86* 123 A6
Hokkaido *98* 137 F3, *102* 142 F2
Holar *41* 56 I4, *46* 63 B1
Holborn, London 66 94 C6
Holland *52* 72 B3, *56* 78 DE2, *59* 82 B1, *66* 93 C2
Hollandia (Djaiapura) *111* 160 C7
Holmgard (Novgorod) *46* 63 F3
Holowezyn 69 99 E5
Holstein *53* 73 C1, *68* 98 CD1, *74* 105 BC1, *75* 106 108 C5, *81* 116 C5, *107* 152 A2
Holstein-Glückstadt *74* 105 C1
Holstein-Gottorp *74* 105 C1
Holy Roman Empire, The *47* 65, *48* 66 F2–3, *50* 70 CD5, *55* 76 C2–3, *57* 79 C–E4, *68* 97 DE1, *72* 103 CD4
Homs (Hims), Syria *49* 67 K2
Homs, Tripolitania *96* 134 D1
Hims (Homs), Syria *119* 174 B6
Honduras *95* 132 A1, *113* 164 B6
Hong Kong *98* 137 E4, *102* 142 B6, *111* 159 B2
Honiara *126* 183 F7
Honnstein *75* 106 B2
Honshu (Hondo) *40* 55 L3–4, *102* 142 EF3
Hooghly *65* 91 C2
Hoorn 66 93 C2
Hôpital de la Salpêtrière, Paris *78* 112 EF7
Hôpital St. Louis, Paris *78* 112 EF4
Hormuz (Harmozia) *40* 55 F5, 60 84 H4, *64* 88 EF6
Hormuz, Strait of *10* 8 BC3, *12* 11 EF4
Horn, Cape 60 84 D7, *95* 132 C7
Horsens *86* 123 AB5
Hôtel de Ville (City Hall), Paris *78* 112 E5
Hôtel National des Invalides, Paris *78* 112 AB5
Housesteads, see Vercovisium
Howland *111* 160 F7
Hoxton, London 66 94 D6
Hoya, county (hist.) *70* 100 CD3
Hsüan *32* 45 E2

Hué *65* 91 L3, *124* 181 C5, *125* 182 B2
Huaihe *30* 41 C6, *30* 42 EF3, *31* 43 C6
Huambo *122* 179 CD6
Huancapampa *63* 86 AB2
Huanghai, see Yellow Sea
Huanghe *32* 44 L4, *40* 55 IJ3
Hube *30* 41 B6
Hubei *102* 142 B5, *117* 170 D6
Hudiksvall 69 99 BC3
Hudson Bay 60 84 D2–3, *62* 85 C1
Hudson Strait 60 84 D2
Hudson's Bay Company *62* 85 B–D1
Hudson's, Henry, voyages 1610–11 60 84 E3
Huelva *109* 156 D3
Huesca *49* 68 D7, *109* 156 EF2
Huhehot (Huhohaote) *117* 170 D5
Huichon *119* 175 B1
Hull *54* 74 B1, *56* 78 C1, *76* 108 C5, *81* 116 C5, *107* 152 A2
Hulwan (Hilwan) *118* 173 A6
Humbe kingdom *65* 92 C3–4
Humboldt Universität, Berlin *114* 167 E2 (5)
Hummelshof 69 99 D4
Hunan *30* 41 B6–7, *98* 137 D4, *102* 142 B6, *117* 170 D6
Hungary *46* 63 EF5, *48* 66 H3, *55* 76 D3, *67* 96 D2, *69* 99 C7, *70* 100 G5–6, *72* 103 E5, *78* 111 FG4, *81* 116 D3, *84* 121 FG4, *107* 151 CD4, *108* 154 E3, *112* 161 CD4, *113* 163 B4, *115* 168 D4, *128* 185 C3
Hungnam *119* 175 BC1
Huns *32* 44 IJ4, *42* 57 KL5
Huron *62* 85 E7
Husi 69 99 E7
Huy *105* 148 K1
Hydaspes (Jhelum) *32* 44 H5
Hyde Park, London 66 94 AB6
Hyderabad (Nizam), state *99* 140 C3
Hyderabad, city *99* 140 C4, *127* 184 BC3
Hyderabad, Sind *99* 140 B2, *127* 184 AB2
Hydrea *16* 20 E7
Hyesan *119* 175 C1
Hühnerwasser *86* 122 D3
Hymettus (Hymettos) *16* 20 EF6
Hypata *16* 20 BC4
Hyrcania *24* 31 I5
Hyrmine *16* 20 A5

I

Iaşi *83* 120 A5, *84* 121 H4, *101* 141 H2, *107* 151 E4, *110* 157 E4

Ibadan *122* 179 BC5
Iberia *16* 19 A2
Iberians *9* 6 C6
Iberus (Ebro) *23* 28 B1–2
Ibiza *68* 97 C4, *81* 118 D6
Ibos *65* 92 C2
Ica *63* 86 B3
Iceland *46* 63 B1, 60 84 F2, *72* 103 AB1, *110* 157 A1, *113* 164 C5, *115* 168 B1
Iconium, Galatia *28* 38 I5
Icosium *24* 31 B5
Idaho *93* 130 B2
Ieper (Ypres) *66* 93 A4
Ife *65* 92 BC2
Ifni *97* 136 A1, *122* 179 AB3
Ijssel 66 93 D2
Ikaria *17* 21 E3–4, *88* 125 D3
Ikonion (Ikonium) *45* 61 F6, *48* 66 K6
Ikonion, sultanate *50* 70 170 D5
Ilas Malvinas (Falkland Islands) *62* 85 E7, *95* 132 D7
Ile de France *52* 72 DE5
Ilerda *24* 32 B6
Ilici (Elche) *23* 28 B3
Ilion (Troy) *17* 21 E2, *23* 30 A6
Ilipa *23* 28 A3
Ilkhan, Kingdom of the *40* 55 H–J3–4
Ilkhans, Empire of the *40* 55 EF4
Illinois *92* 129 B2, *93* 130 E2
Illyria (Illyricum) *17* 21 B1–2, *23* 28 F1, *24* 32 C6, *28* 38 F3–4, *32* 44 CD4
Illyria, kingdom *84* 121 F5
Illyrian provinces, De *82* 119 D3
Illyrians *9* 6 E6, *16* 19 D1
Ilmen *51* 71 C2, *84* 121 H2
Ilva (Elba) *22* 27 B3
Imphal *99* 140 EF2, *127* 184 EF3
Inca empire *63* 86
Inchon (Chemulpo) *102* 143 EF7, *119* 175 B2
India *36* 49 G5, 60 84 I4, *64* 88 F6, *120* 176 I4, *127* 184 BD3
Indian Ocean, The *36* 49 FG6, 60 84 HI5
Indian Territory *92* 129 A3
Indiana *92* 129 C2–3, *93* 130 EF2
Indianapolis *92* 129 C2
Indigirka *98* 137 E1
Indonesia *120* 176 JK5, *126* 183 CD7
Indraprastha (Delhi) *32* 44 HI5, *38* 53 B1
Indrapura, Champa *32* 44 K6, *39* 54 C5
Indrapura, Sumatra *64* 90 I6
Indus (Sindhu) *24* 31 L4, L6, *32* 44 H5, *65* 91 G2, *99* 140 B1, C1
Indus culture *8* 3 E6

Ingelheim *46* 63 D4, *47* 65 BC3

Ingermanland *69* 99 E4

Ingolstadt *49* 68 E6, *68* 98 D5

Inkerman *101* 141 K3

Inn *47* 65 C5, *53* 73 D3

Inner Mongolia *102* 142 AB3, *117* 170 DF5

Innsbruck *84* 121 E4–5, *101* 141 CD2

Insterburg *105* 147 JK4–5

Interlaken *55* 77 C6

Inverlochy *67* 95 E5

Inverness *52* 72 C1, *91* 127 F2

Ioànnina *88* 125 A6

Iona *41* 56 15, *43* 59 B2, *44* 60 D1, *47* 64 A1

Ionian Islands, The *72* 103 E6, *81* 116 D4, *82* 119 E4, *84* 121 G6–7, *88* 125 A3, *101* 141 F6

Ionian Sea (Mare Ionium) *20* 25 BC3, *101* 141 EF6

Ios *17* 21 D4

Iowa *92* 129 B2, *93* 130 DE2

Ipsus *23* 30 B6

Ipswich, Australia *98* 137 F7

Ipswich, England *57* 79 AB3, *76* 108 C6

Iraklion (Herakleion, Candia), Crete *88* 125 C4

Iran *21* 56 D2, *36* 49 F4, *113* 164 D6, *116* 169 F7, *119* 174 C5

Iraq (Irak) *108* 153 CD5, *113* 164 D6, *116* 169 F7, *119* 174 B5

Ireland (Eire, Hibernia) *43* 59 A3, *44* 60 D1–2, *47* 64 A1, *55* 76 AB1, *56* 78 A1, *59* 82 A1, *67* 95 D6, *78* 111 AB1, *81* 116 A2, *84* 121 B3, *104* 146 B3, *108* 154 AB2, *110* 157 A3, *115* 168 AB1, *104* 146 BC3

Irian Jaya *126* 183 D7

Irish Sea *47* 64 AB1, *56* 78 AB1, *104* 146 BC3

Irkutsk *89* 126 J7, *98* 137 D3

Iron mines in Egypt *14* 15 C2

Irrawaddy *65* 91 J3, *99* 140 F3

Irtysh *32* 44 H3, *36* 49 G2

Isar *47* 65 D4, *68* 98 E5

Isborsk *46* 63 F3, *51* 71 B2

Isca Dumnoniorum *26* 34 B1

Isfahan (Gabai) *36* 50 C6, *40* 55 F4, *119* 174 C5

Isla de Pinos *121* 178 A2

Isla de Santiago, see Jamaica

Islamabad *127* 184 B1

Islands Malvinas (Falkland Islands) *62* 85 E7, *95* 132 D7

Isle of Wight *43* 59 B2, *56* 78 BC3

Ismailia *118* 173 B6

Isonzo *104* 146 F5

Israel *15* 18 E5, *118* 172 E2, *118* 173 CD5

Issus (Issos) *13* 14 B6, *21* 26 BC2

Istanbul (Constantinople) *81* 116 E3, *107* 151 E6, *112* 161 E5

Isted *86* 123 A6

Ister (Istros, Donau, Danube) *28* 38 G4

Istria *80* 115 D2–3, *104* 146 F5, *107* 152 A1

Istros (Ister, Danuvius, Donau, Danube), river *20* 25 DE1

Istros, city *16* 19 E1, *20* 25 E1

Italian Somaliland *98* 137 A5, *97* 136 EF3, *107* 152 C3, *113* 164 DE6

Italians (anc.) *9* 6 E6

Italica, Spain *23* 28 A3

Italy *24* 32 C6, *45* 62 K7, *46* 63 D5, *59* 82 C2, *104* 146 D4, *110* 157 C5, *112* 161 B5, *115* 168 C4, *116* 169 BC7

Italy, kingdom *47* 65 C6, *53* 73 C4–5, *82* 119 D3, *93* 130 I6, *101* 141 CD4

Italy, Unification of, 1860 *87* 124

Itanos *23* 30 A7

Ithaca *17* 21 A3, *88* 125 A2

Ituna Aestuarium (Solway Firth) *28* 39 G2

Itzehoe *44* 60 G2, *86* 123 AB7

Ivangorod, Ingermanland *69* 99 E4

Ivangorod, Poland *105* 147 JK5

Ivanova *106* 150 D3

Ivory Coast *96* 134 AB5, *97* 136 AB3, *110* 157 E2, B5, *120* 176 F4–5

Iwo Jima *111* 160 C1

Iwon *119* 175 C1

Izmail *101* 141 I3

Izmir (Smyrna) *107* 151 E6, *108* 153 B4

J

Jacobin Club, Paris *78* 112 C4

Jadotville *123* 180 F3

Jaffa (Joppe) *10* 9 B3, *49* 67 J4, *71* 102 C7, *118* 171 A2

Jaffna *65* 91 H4

Jägerndorf *74* 105 E3, *75* 106 D3

Jaipur *99* 140 C2, *127* 184 C2

Jajce *112* 161 C5

Jalapa *63* 87 B2·

Jamaica (Isla de Santiago) *62* 85 C4, *95* 132 B1, *121* 177 C1·2

Jamestown *62* 85 CD3

Jammu and Kashmir *127* 184 C1

Jamnia *26* 35 A4

Jan Mayen *60* 84 F2, *120* 176 F2

Jankau *68* 98 F4

Japan (Cipangu) *36* 49 L3–4, *40* 55 L3, *60* 84 K3, *98* 137 F3, *102* 142 F3, *111* 159 C1

Japan, Sea of *40* 55 KL3, *102* 142 DE2

Japara (Djepara) *64* 90 J7

Japlonoi Mts. *32* 44 K3

Jardin des Plantes, Paris *78* 112 E6

Jarensk *83* 120 D2, *106* 150 D2

Jargeau *56* 78 D5

Jarmo *6* 2 E3

Jarmuk, battle field *37* 51 J2

Jarmuk, river *15* 17 C5, *26* 35 C2

Jaroslaw, Poland *69* 99 D7

Jarrow *43* 59 BC2, *47* 64 B1

Jatai *95* 132 E4

Java *60* 84 J5, *64* 90 J7, *98* 137 D6, *99* 139 J4, *111* 159 A3, *111* 160 B7, *126* 183 C7

Java Sea *64* 90 JK7, *99* 139 J4

Jaxartes (Syr-Darja) *13* 14 E5, *32* 44 E4

Jedisan *103* 144 IJ2

Jekabpils *105* 147 K4

Jelez *106* 150 D4

Jemdet Nasr *8* 3 CD5, *11* 10 EF4

Jemtland *69* 99 B3

Jena *58* 81 D4, *81* 116 C2

Jenné *65* 92 B1

Jerez de la Frontera *37* 51 G1

Jericho (Ariba) *26* 35 B4, *118* 172 F2

Jersey *79* 113 A1, *84* 121 C4

Jerusalem (Aella Capitolina, Hierosolyma) *10* 9 AB3, *12* 12 C3, *15* 18 E6, *26* 35 B4, *36* 49 D4, *49* 67 K4, *55* 76 F4, *118* 171 AB2

Jeufosse *47* 64 B2

Jews *42* 57 H3

Jhukar *10* 8 E2

Jiangsu *30* 41 C6, *102* 142 BC4

Jiangxi *117* 170 DE6

Jin *30* 42 J3

Jin kingdom *32* 45 J3

Joao Pessoa *95* 132 F3

Johannesburg *97* 135 DE6, *122* 179 D7

Johnston *111* 159 E2, *111* 160 B2

Jolo *64* 90 K7

Jomsborg, see Jumne

Jönköping *69* 99 B4

Joppe (Jaffa) *14* 15 D1, *15* 18 D5, *16* 19 F3, *26* 35 A3–4

Jordan, river *26* 35 C3, *110* 171 B1

Jordan, state *118* 173 DE5–6, *119* 174 A5

Jordhpur *99* 140 B2

Jorsalaland (Old Norse: Palestine) *46* 63 GH7

Jorvik (Old Norse: York) *46* 63 C3

Juàzeiro *62* 85 E5

Juda *15* 17 AB6, *15* 18 E6

Judea *26* 34 F4, *26* 35 B4

Judeae *28* 38 I6

Jüdich, duchy *70* 100 BC4

Jujuy *95* 132 C5

Juliomagus *26* 34 B2

Julius Cæsar's temple, Rome *27* 37 K3

Julius Maternus' journey ca. 100 AD *32* 44 CD6

Jumna *64* 89 B2, *127* 184 C2

Jumne (Jomsborg, Wollin) *46* 63 E3–4, *47* 65 E1

Juno Beach *113* 165 B3

Jupiter's temple, Rome *27* 37 I3

Jurjev *51* 71 B2

Jüterbog *68* 98 EF2

Jutland *70* 100 D1

Jutland, Battle of 31/3 1916 *104* 146 D3

K

Kaapstad (Cape Town) *65* 92 CD5

Kabis *37* 51 H2

Kabul (Kabura) *34* 47 C7, *40* 55 G4, *64* 89 A1, *99* 140 B1

Kabura (Kabul) *24* 31 K5

Kadesh *8* 5 E4, *10* 9 B3, *11* 10 D3

Kadesh-Barnea *15* 18 DE7

Kadesia (Kadisiya) *36* 50 B6

Kaesong *102* 143 F6, *119* 175 B2, E2

Kaffa (Theodosia), Crimea *54* 74 E2, *55* 76 F3, *83* 120 BC6

Kaffa, Africa *96* 133 E5

Kaffraria *97* 135 E7

Kagoshima *102* 142 E4

Kai *106* 150 E2

Kaifeng *35* 48 E3, *102* 142 B4

Kaimeiros *17* 21 F4

Kairouan *37* 51 H1–2, *43* 59 D7, *68* 97 D4, *96* 134 CD1

Kaiser Wilhelm Canal *35* 48 E2–3

Kaiser-Wilhelmsland *98* 137 F6

Kaiserslautern *86* 122 B3

Kaiserswerth *47* 65 B3

Kajana *69* 99 DE3, *72* 103 E2

Kalah *36* 49 I6

Kalahari Desert *96* 133 CD7, *97* 135 CD6

Kalamai (Kalamata) *88* 125 B3

Kalat *38* 52 J1

Kalibangan *8* 3 E6, *10* 8 F2

Kalimantan *126* 183 C7

Kalinga (Orissa) *38* 52 K2, *38* 53 BC2, *64* 89 C2

Kalinin *110* 157 F3, *113* 163 D1–2

Kaliningrad *128* 185 C2

Kalisz *86* 122 E2

Kalkfontein *97* 135 C6

Kalmar *69* 99 B5, *84* 121 F2

Kalmykovo *106* 150 F5

Kalmyks *35* 48 BC2

Kalocsa *41* 56 C4, *45* 61 K6, *59* 83 E6

Kaluga *106* 150 C4

Kalundborg *86* 123 B5

Kalyan *36* 49 G5

Kalymnos *17* 21 E4

Kama *46* 63 H3, *83* 120 E2, D3

Kamachos *45* 61 G5

Kamakura *40* 55 L4

Kamarupa *32* 45 C3

Kambai *65* 92 EF2

Kamchatka *60* 84 KL2, *98* 137 F2

Kamina *123* 180 E2

Kammin *70* 100 F3

Kampala *122* 179 E5

Kamysjin *106* 150 E5

Kanajj *38* 53 B1, *64* 89 BC2

Kanazawa *102* 142 E3

Kanchi *38* 53 B3

Kandahar (Alexandria) *65* 91 G1, *99* 140 AB1

Kandalaksha *106* 150 BC1, *110* 157 E1

Kandy *36* 49 H6, *64* 89 C4, *99* 140 C5

Kanem *65* 92 C1, *96* 133 C4

Kanesh (Kültepe) *8* 5 E3, *10* 9 AB2, *11* 10 CD2, *12* 11 B1

Kangaroo Island *98* 137 E7

Kanggye *119* 175 B1

Kangnung *119* 175 C2, F3

Kano *65* 92 C1, *122* 179 C4

Kanpur *99* 140 C2

Kansas *92* 129 A2, *93* 130 D3

Kansas City *92* 129 AB1, *93* 130 D3

Kansay (Hang Chou, Li-n'an) *40* 55 K4

Kao Li (Korea) *34* 47 F6

Kara Balgasun *32* 45 D1

Kara Kum *32* 45 A2

Karachi *99* 140 A2, *127* 184 A2

Karafuto (Sakhalin) *102* 142 EF1

Karakorum (Ho-lin) *34* 47 E6, *40* 55 HI3

Karaman *71* 102 C6

Karashahr *98* 137 C3

Karasjok *83* 120 B1

Karbala *37* 51 K2

Kardis *69* 99 D4

Karelia *71* 101 J1, *112* 161 E2

Karelians *51* 71 BC1

Karikal *99* 140 C5, *127* 184 C4

Karkemish *109* B2, *11* 10 D3, *12* 12 D2

Karl XII's withdrawal from Pitesti *109* CD7

Karlovci (Karlowitz) *72* 103 E5

Karlsbad *86* 122 D3

Karlskrona *69* 99 BC5, *81* 116 CD1, *84* 121 F2

Karlsruhe *91* 127 H5, *109* 155 B6

Karlstad *69* 99 B4, *84* 121 EF2

Karna *32* 44 F6

Karna Suvarna *38* 53 C2

Karnataka *127* 184 B4

Karnatik *99* 140 C4–5

Kärnten *44* 60 H4, *45* 62 L6

Kärnten, duchy *47* 65 DE5, *53* 73 D3–4, *70* 100 EF6

Karpathos *17* 21 EF5

Karpenision *88* 125 B2

Kars *106* 150 E7, *108* 153 CD4

Kasai, river *65* 92 D3, *96* 133 CD5

Kasai, state *123* 180 E2

Kasakher *35* 48 AB2

Kasan (Kazan), city *40* 55 E2, *106* 150 E3, *113* 163 F1

Kasan (Kazan), state *83* 120 DE4

Kasan, khanate *35* 48 A1, *71* 101 L5

Kasatsehe *89* 126 JK5, *98* 137 D1

Kasel *75* 106 E3

Kashgar *32* 44 H4, *40* 55 G4

Kashmir *65* 91 H1, *99* 140 C1

Kasi (Benares) *38* 52 K2

Kasimov *83* 120 C4

Kasos *17* 21 E5

Kassala *107* 152 B2, *108* 153 BC7

Kassel *68* 98 C3, *81* 116 C2, *107* 151 B3

Kasserine *112* 162 B1

Katabaru *98* 137 F6

Katanga (Shaba) *122* 179 D6, *123* 180 EF3

Katmandu (Lalita Patan) *99* 140 D2, *127* 184 D2

Katsina *65* 92 C1

Kattegatt *57* 79 D2

Kattura *41* 56 C3

Katyn *113* 163 D2

Kaufbeuren *70* 100 D6

Kaunas (Kovno) *105* 147 K4, *107* 151 D2, *110* 157 E3

Kaunia *32* 44 I6

Kaunos *17* 21 F4, *20* 25 F3

Kaupang *46* 63 D3

Kautokeino *83* 120 A1

Kavalla *88* 125 C1, *101* 141 G5

Keetmanshoop *97* 135 C6

Kefallenia (Cephalenia) *17* 21 A3, *84* 121 G6, *88* 125 A3

Keijo (Seoul) *102* 142 D3

Keksholm *69* 99 E3, *72* 103 F2

Keksholms len *69* 99 E3

Kells *47* 64 A1

Kem *106* 150 B2, *110* 157 E1

Kempten (Cambodunum) *70* 100 D6

Kensington Gardens, London *66* 94 A6

Kensington Palace, London *66* 94 A7

Kent *43* 59 BCC3, *44* 60 E3, *56* 78 C3

Kentucky *92* 129 C3, *93* 130 EF3

Kenya *120* 176 GH5, *122* 179 F2, GH5

Keos *16* 20 F6, *16* 20 CD4

Kerala (Chera) *64* 89 B4, *127* 184 B4–5

Kérasos (Karasus) *24* 31 G5

Kerch *112* 161 F5

Kerkyra (Corfu) *88* 125 A2

Kerma *11* 10 B6

Kerman, city *40* 55 F4, *103* 145 E6

Kerman, state *36* 50 D7, *37* 51 L2

Kermanshah *12* 11 D2, *119* 174 BC5

Kerulen *35* 48 E6, *40* 55 IJ3

Kesseldorf *75* 106 C3

Key West *121* 178 A2

Khabarovsk *98* 137 E3, *102* 142 DE1

Khaibar (Khyber) *108* 153 C6

Khan Yunis *118* 173 C5

Khanbalik (Dadu, Beijing, Yushou) *34* 47 EF6, *40* 55 JK3

Khania (Canea) *88* 125 C4

Khanua *65* 91 H2

Kharijites *40* 55 H2

Kharkov *83* 120 BC5, *106* 150 D5, *113* 163 DE3

Khartoum *97* 136 DE2

Khatanga *89* 126 J5, *98* 137 C1

Khazar kingdom ca. 600 *42* 58 D1

Khazars *46* 63 H4–5, *51* 71 DE5

Kherson (Korsun), city, Crimea *41* 56 L7, *51* 71 C5

Kherson, province *45* 61 F4

Kherson, seaport city on the Dniepr *71* 101 J7, *101* 141 J2

Khiva *108* 153 F4

Khmer kingdom *39* 54 B5, *40* 55 IJ5–6

Khon Kaen *125* 182 D2

Khorasan *36* 50 D6, *37* 51 KL1

Khorsabad, see Dur-Sharrukin

Khotan *13* 13 D1, *60* 84 I3–4

Khyber Pass, The *65* 91 H1, *99* 140 B1

Kibyra, city *23* 30 B6

Kibyrra, thema *45* 61 EF6

Kiel *57* 79 CD3, *69* 99 A5, *86* 123 B6, *107* 151 B2

Kiel Bay *86* 123 B6

Kielce *73* 104 CD3, *106* 150 A5

Kiev, city *41* 56 K6, *46* 63 F4, *51* 71 C4, *54* 74 E2, *55* 76 CD3, *106* 150 C5, *107* 151 E3, *112* 161 DE4, *113* 163 CD3

Kiev, state *83* 120 B4

Kiev, State of *45* 61 D3

Kikwit *123* 180 D2

Kikyu (Bantu tribe) *65* 92 EF2

Kilkenny *67* 95 D6

Killarney *67* 95 D6

Kilsyth *67* 95 E5

Kilwa *65* 92 F3, *97* 136 E4

Kimberley *97* 135 D6

Kindu *123* 180 EF2

King's Lynn *91* 127 G4

Kings, Valley of the *14* 15 B5

Kingston *121* 178 C3

Kinsay (Hang Chou) *34* 47 F7

Kinshasa (Leopoldville) *122* 179 CD6

Kipchak (The Golden Horde) *40* 55 DF2–3

Kipr (Kypros, Cyprus) *46* 63 EF6

Kir-Haraset *15* 17 B6, *15* 18 EF6

Kirensk *89* 126 J6

Kirghiz peoples *32* 45 C1, *35* 48 C1

Kirghiz Steppes *32* 44 GH3

Kirghizia *34* 47 DE6

Kirkjuvåg (Kirkwall) *52* 72 CD1

Kirkuk *119* 174 B4

Kirkwall (Kirkjuvåg) *50* 69 BC2, *52* 72 CD1

Kirovograd *106* 150 C6

Kiruna *110* 157 D1

Kisangani (Stanleyville) *122* 179 D5

Kish *12* 11 C3

Kishinyov *101* 141 I2, *105* 147 L7

Kiska *111* 160 E4

Kitzingen *68* 98 D4

Kivik *8* 5 C1

Kivu *123* 180 F2

Kjønguard (Kiev) *46* 63 F4

Kladeios *18* 22 C5

Klagenfurt *101* 141 DE2

Klaipeda (Memel) *105* 147 K4, *107* 151 D1, *110* 157 D1

Klaipeda (Memel) *105* 147 K4

Klaipeda (Memel) *105* 147 D4, *110* 157 D3, *128* 185 C2

Klarälven *57* 79 DE1

Klausenburg (Cluj) *101* 141 G2, *103* 144 D1, *107* 151 DE4

Kleitor *16* 20 B6

Kleve, city *66* 93 D3, *75* 106 A2

Kleve, county (hist.) *70* 100 BC4, *75* 106 A2

Kliszow *69* 99 C6

Klysma (Suez) *14* 15 BC2

Knäred (Knærød) *69* 99 B5

Knossos *8* 5 D4, *17* 21 D5

Kobe *98* 137 E4, *102* 142 E4

Koblenz (Confluentes) *47* 65 BC3, *56* 78 E3, *68* 98 B3, *79* 113 C1, *79* 114 C1

Kodok (Fashoda) *97* 136 D2, *122* 179 D5

Kohima *99* 140 F2, *127* 184 EF2

Kohker *65* 91 KL3

Kokenhusen *57* 79 G2, *69* 99 DE5

Koko Nor *31* 43 A5

Kola, city *83* 120 B1

Kola, peninsula *83* 120 C1, *110* 157 E1

Kolberg *50* 69 E3, *57* 79 D3

Kolberger Heide *68* 98 D1

Kolchaks retreat 1919 *106* 150 EF3

Kolding *69* 99 A5, *86* 123 A5

Kolin *74* 105 D3

Kolmar *44* 60 G4

Koloneia, episcopal see *45* 61 G5

Koloneia, thema *45* 61 G5

Kolwezi *123* 180 E3

Kolyma *98* 137 E1

Kompong Cham *124* 181 BC6–7

Kong *65* 92 B2

Kongeåen *86* 123 A6

Konghelle *50* 69 D2

Kongolo *97* 136 D3, *123* 180 F2

Kongsberg *69* 99 A4, *72* 103 C3

Konstanz *47* 65 C4, *55* 76 C3, *55* 77 E5, *58* 81 C5

Konya *71* 102 C6, *101* 141 K6

Kopais *16* 20 D5

Köpenick, Berlin *114* 167 EF2

Kopparberg *57* 79 E1

Korat (Nakhon Ratchasima) *125* 182 DE2

Koreë *88* 125 A1

Korea (Chosen, Kao-Li, Silla) *35* 48 EF2, *98* 137 E4, *102* 142 D3, *102* 143 F6, *111* 160 C5

Korea Strait *119* 175 C3

Korkyra (Corfu) *16* 19 D2, *20* 25 C3

Kornilov's march on Petrograd Sept. 1917 *106* 150 BC3

Korsum *46* 63 G5

Korsør *70* 100 DC2

Kos *17* 21 E4, *23* 30 B6 BC4, *75* 106 A2

Kosovo (Polje) *55* 76 DE3, *71* 102 A5

Kostenki *6* 2 D1

Knossos *8* 5 D4, *17* 21 D5

Kobe *98* 137 A2, *106* 150 D2

Kotovsk *91* 127 L4

Kottayam *36* 49 G6

Kovno (Kaunas) *69* 99 D5, *73* 104 D1

Kozhikode (Calicut) *64* 89 B4, *127* 184 B4

Krain *80* 115 D2, *101* 141 D3

Krain, duchy *70* 100 F7

Krain, margravate *53* 73 E4

Krak *49* 67 K2

Krakow *41* 56 K6, *46* 63 E4, *49* 68 F5, *55* 76 D2, *57* 79 F4, *69* 99 C7, *81* 116 D2, *91* 127 J4, *107* 151 D3, *113* 163 B3

Krakow, republic *84* 121 F4

Krasnik *105* 147 JK6

Krasnodar *105* 147 DE6, *112* 161 F5

Krasnov's advance in 1918 *106* 150 E5

Krasnovodsk *98* 137 C2

Krasnoyarsk *98* 137 C2

Krefeld *74* 105 B2

Kremsmünster *44* 60 H4

Kreutzberg, Berlin *114* 167 E2

Kreuzburg *105* 147 J5–6

Krishna *38* 53 AB3, *64* 89 B3, *99* 140 C4

Kristianople *70* 100 F1

Kristiansand *69* 99 A4, *110* 157 C3

Kristiansund *84* 121 DE1

Kristinestad (Kristiinankaupunki) *69* 99 CD3, *83* 120 A2

Kriti (Crete) *46* 63 F7

Kronborg *70* 100 E1

Kronstadt (Brasov), Hungary *101* 141 H3, *104* 146 GH5

Kronstadt, Soviet Union *106* 150 B3

Kroton (Croton) *16* 19 D2, *20* 25 B3, *20* 24 C6

Krung Thep (Bangkok) *125* 182 A3, D2–3, D6

Kucha *32* 45 C2, *40* 55 G3

Kufa *36* 50 B6

Kufra *107* 152 AB2

Kufra Oasis *108* 153 A5–6

Kuibyshev, see Samara

Kuka *32* 44 C7

Kuldja *98* 137 C3

Kulikovo *55* 76 F1, *71* 101 K6

Kulm *57* 79 F3

Kultepe *109* KB3

Kültepe (Kanesh) *109* AB2

Kumbi *65* 92 A1

Kumbi *65* 92 A1

Kumchon *119* 175 B3

Kumma *14* 15 AB7

Kunersdorf *74* 105 D2

Kungur *83* 120 E3

Kunming *111* 159 A2

Kunsan *119* 175 B3

Kur-Hessen *86* 122 C3

Kur-Sachsen *70* 100 E4

Kura 51 71 F6
Kurdistan 71 102 E7, 86 122
E6
Kuria Muria Islands 97 136
F2
Kurile Islands 98 137 F3, 102
142 F1, 111 159 C1
Kurland 57 79 F2, 69 99 D5,
71 101 I5, 73 104 D1, 81
116 D1, 83 120 A3, 84 121
G2
Kurpfalz 70 100 C5, 74 105 B3
Kursk 71 101 JK6, 91 127 L3,
113 163 E3
Kuruman 96 133 CD7
Kush (Nubia) 11 10 BC6, 14
15 C7, 30 41 E6
Kushana kingdom 32 44
GH4–5, 38 53 A1
Kusinagara 36 49 H5
Küstrin 74 105 D2, 75 106 D2
Kütahya 84 121 HI6
Kutno 105 147 J5
Kuwait, city 98 137 A4, 103
145 D6, 119 174 C5
Kuwait, state 97 136 E1, 108
153 D5, 119 174 BC5
Kven (Finno-Norwegians)
46 63 F1
Kwajalein 111 159 D3, 111
160 DE6
Kwangju 119 175 B3
Kyme, Hellas 16 20 F4
Kyoto (Heian) 98 137 EF4,
102 142 E3
Kyrnos (Corsica) 16 19 C2
Kyros 12 12 E1
Kythera (Cerigo) 17 21 BC5,
84 121 GH7, 88 125 B4
Kyushu 40 55 L4, 102 142 E4

L

La Charité, Paris 78 112 C5
La Cité, Paris 78 112 D5
La Conciergerie (prison),
Paris 78 112 D5
La Coruña 68 97 A2–3, 81
118 A5, 109 156 D1
La Ferrassie 9 7 AB1
La Macta 96 134 B1
La Madeleine, Paris 78 112
BC4
La Marche (county, hist.) 56
78 CD6
La Paz, New Spain 94 131
I5
La Paz, South America 94
131 K6, 95 132 C5
La Plata 95 132 D6, 121 178
BC2
La Rioja 95 132 C5
La Roche-aux Moines 52 72
D5
La Rochelle 54 74 AB2, 55 76
AB3, 56 78 BC6, 68 97 B2,
79 113 A2, 79 114 A2, 81
116 AB3, 110 157 AB4
La Spezia 112 161 B5
La Tène 96 D6

La Tène culture 8 4 B1, 9 6
DE5–6
La Venta 63 87 C2
Labach 84 121 F5
Labrador (Markland) 60 84
D3, 62 85 D2
Lac de Neuchâtel 55 77 AB6
Laccadive Islands 99 140 B4,
127 184 A4
Lacedaemon (Sparta) 45 61
D7
Laconia 17 21 B4, 20 25 D3
Lacus Benacus (Lago di
Garda) 22 27 BC1
Lacus Larius (Lago di Co-
mo) 22 27 B1
Lacus Lemanus (Lake Gene-
va) 22 27 A1
Lacus Trasimenus 22 27 C3
Lacus Venetus (Bodensee) 29
40 AB7
Lacus Verbanus (Lago Mag-
giore) 22 27 A1
Lade 46 63 DE2
Ladoga (Aldeiga), Lake 46 63
F2, 55 76 E1, 69 99 E3, 113
163 D1
Ladoga, city 51 71 C2
Ladysmith 97 135 E6
Lae 111 159 C3, 111 160 D7
Laferté 79 113 B1–2
Lagash 10 8 A2, 11 10 F4, 12
11 D3
Laghouat 86 122 C1
Lago de Nicaragua 121 177
B2
Lago di Como 22 27 B1, 55
77 E7
Lago di Garda, see Lacus
Benacus
Lago Maggiore 55 77 D7
Lagos 55 76 A4, 96 133 BC5,
122 179 BC5
Lagosta 107 152 A1
Lahore 64 89 B1, 65 91 H1,
99 140 C1
Lake Athabasca 62 85 BC1
Lake Erie 92 129 C2, 93 130
F2
Lake Huron 92 128 J2, 92 129
C1, 93 130 F2
Lake Michigan 92 129 J2, 92
129 C1–2, 93 130 E2
Lake Ontario 92 129 D1–2,
93 130 F2
Lake Superior 92 128 J1, 92
129 C1, 93 130 E1
Lake Turkana 7 1
Lake Winnipeg 55 76 C2, 92
128 I1
Lalita Patan (Katmandu) 38
52 L1
Lambaesis 26 34 BC4, 28 38
BC4
Lambeth, London 66 94 C7
Lamia 17 21 B3
Lampsacus (Lampsakos) 17
21 E2
Lan-chou 13 13 E1, 35 48 D3

Lancaster 52 72 C3, 56 78
B1–2, 77 109 E5
Landau 70 100 C5
Landsberg 69 99 B6
Landshut 68 98 E5, 74 105 C3
Lang Son 65 91 KL2
Langeland 86 123 B6
Langensalza 86 122 C2
Langobardia 44 60 IJ6
Langobards 28 38 E2, 42 57
IJ5
Langobards, Kingdom of the
42 58 B1–2, 43 59 DE5, 44
60 G5
Langport 67 95 E7
Langres 44 60 F4, 52 72 EF5
Languedoc 50 70 BC6, 52 72
DE7, 56 78 D6–7, 68 97
C2–3, 79 113 B3
Lanna 39 54 B5
Lao Kay 124 181 B4
Laodicea, Syria 23 30 D7
Laodikeia (Laodicea), Asia
Minor 45 61 EF6, 48 66 J6
Laon 47 65 A3
Laos, Asia 65 91 K3, 98 137
D5, 124 181 B5, 125 182
B2, DE1–2, A5
Laos, Italy 20 24 B5
Laoyang 102 143 E6
Lappland 71 101 J4
Laptev Sea (Nordenskjöld
Sea) 60 84 I1
Largeau (Faya) 108 153 A6–7
Largs 52 72 C2
Larisa, Greece 17 21 B2, 45
61 D6
Larisa, Lydia 17 21 E3
Larsa 11 10 EF4, 12 11 D3
Las Navas de Tolosa 48 66
B5
Las Palmas 122 179 A3
Lascaux 6 2 A1, 9 7 B1
Lashio 111 160 A6
Latakia 119 174 A4
Latium 20 25 A2, 22 27 C4
Latvia 104 146 G2, 106 150
AB4, 107 151 D2, 108 154
EF1, 110 157 E3, 113 163
C2, 128 185 C1
Latvians 106 150 A4
Lauenburg 75 106 DE1, 86
122 C1, 86 123 B7
Laus 22 27 C5
Lausanne 44 60 G4, 55 77 B6
Lausitz culture 8 5 CD2
Laussel 9 7 B1
Le Havre 79 113 AB1, 84 121
C4, 91 127 G4
León, city 55 76 A3, 56 78 A7,
81 118 B5, 91 127 E6
Le Puy 47 65, 101 141 A3
Le Quesnoy 79 114 BC1
Le Temple, Paris 78 112 EF5
Lebanon 108 153 BC5, 112
161 F7, 113 164 D6, 118
173 CD4, 119 174 A5
Lebus 47 65 E2, 48 66 F2
Lech, city 55 77 F5
Lech, river 55 77 F5

Lechfeld 47 65 C4
L'Écluse 52 72 DE4
Leeds 76 108 B5–6, 77 109
E5–6, 91 127 F3
Legnano 53 73 C4
Leicester 25 33 AB2, 56 78
C2, 67 95 F6
Leiden 66 93 BC2
Leine 68 98 D3
Leipzig 49 68 EF5, 54 74 C2,
55 76 CD2, 57 79 D4, 58
81 CD4, 69 99 B6, 76 107
CD5, 81 116 C2, 91 127
I4, 107 151 BC2, 109 155
B5, 114 166 CD3
Leiv Eiríksson's voyage ca.
1000? 60 84 E3
Lejre 43 59 D2, 46 63 D3
Lemberg (Lvov) 58 81 F4, 73
104 D3, 84 121 G4, 104
146 G4, 105 147 K6, 107
151 D3
Lemnos 17 21 D2, 101 141
GH5, 110 157 E6
Lena, river 40 55 I1, 98 137 D1
Leninabad 24 31 K4
Leninakan, (Alexandropol)
108 153 D6
Leningrad (Petrograd, St.
Petersburg) 110 157 E2,
112 161 DE2, 113 163 D1,
128 185 D1
Lenzen 47 65 D2
Leon, kingdom 48 66 AB4, 50
70 A6
Leonidaeum (Leonidaion),
Olympia 18 22 D6
Leontium 16 20 B5
Leopoldville (Kinshasa), city
97 136 C3, 123 180 D2
Leopoldville, state 123 180
DE2
Lepanto 55 76 D4, 71 102 A6
Lepenski Vir 6 2 BC3
Leptis Magna (Leptis Ma-
jor) 16 19 CD3, 24 32 C7,
28 38 F6, 32 44 C5
Leptis Minor 16 19 C3, 24 31
C5–6
Lerida 49 68 D7, 68 97 B3, 81
116 B3–4, 109 156 EF2
Lerina 43 59 D5
Lerna 16 20 C6
Les Carmes (prison), Paris
78 112 C6
Les Eyzies 9 7 B1
Les Gobelins, Paris 78 112
DE7
Les Trois Frères 9 7 B2
Les Tuileries, Paris 78 112
C5
Lesbos (Mytilene) 16 19 E2,
23 30 A6, 88 125 CD2, 101
141 H6, 103 144 D3, 107
151 E6
Lesotho 120 176 G6, 122 179
DE7
Lesser Sunda Islands 126
183 CD7
Leticia 95 132 C3

Letrini 16 20 A6
Leuthen 74 105 E2
Leuven (Louvain) 66 93
C3–4
Levadeia (Livadia) 88 125
B2–3
Levctra 16 20 D5
Levkas, island (see also Ioni-
an Islands) 17 21 A3, 88
125 A2
Lewes 52 72 D4
Lewis 52 72 BC1
Leyden 58 81 BC4, 68 97 C1
Leyte 111 160 C6
Lhasa 32 45 C3, 35 48 C3, 99
140 E2
Liao-tung 102 142 C3, 102
143 E6
Liaoning 30 41 C5, 102 142
BC3
Libau (Liepaja) 73 104 D1
Liberia 96 133 AB5, 97 136
A3, 113 164 C6, 122 179
A2, AB5
Libreville 96 133 C5, 122 179
C5
Libya (Tripoli) 37 51 I2, 96
134 D2, 97 136 C1, 103
145 A6, 107 152 A2, 108
153 A5, 112 161 BC7, 113
164 D6, 122 179 D1, CD3
Lichfield 50 69 B3
Lichtenberg, Berlin 114 167
E2
Liechtenstein, city 108 154
D3
Liechtenstein, principality
70 100 CD6, 84 121 E5,
107 151 B4
Liège (Lüttich), city 53 73
B2, 56 78 E3, 105 148 KL1
Liège, bishopric 66 93 C4, 68
97 C1, 70 100 B4, 74 105
A2
Liegnitz 53 73 E2, 74 105 D3
Liepaja (Libau) 110 157 D3
Lier 66 93 B3
Liesnaya 69 99 E6, 72 103 F4
Liger (Loire) 28 38 C2–3
Liguria 22 27
Ligurian Republic, The 80
115 B3, 81 116 C3
Ligurian Sea, The (Mare Li-
gusticum) 22 27 AB3
Ligurians 9 6 D6, 16 19 C5
Lille 66 93 A4, 104 146 CD4,
105 148 J1, 107 151 A3
Lillehammer 110 157 C2
Lilongwe 122 179 D6
Lilybaeum (Lilybaion, Mar-
sala) 20 24 A6, 22 27 C6,
23 28 E3, 26 34 CD3, 42 57
H17
Lima 63 86 AB2, 95 132 B4
Limasol (Nemesos) 48 66 K6
Limburg, county (hist.) 66 93
D4
Limerick (Luimneach) 46 63
AB3, 47 64 A2, 54 74 A1,
72 103 AB4

Limoges 52 72 D6, 91 127 G5
Limonum (Poitiers) 25 33 AB3
Limousin, county (hist.) 56 78 C6
Limpopo 65 92 DE4, 97 135 DE6
Limpurg 75 106 B3–4
Lin 'an (Kinsay, Hang-chou) 40 55 K4
Lincoln 44 60 KL3, 50 69 B3, 56 78 C2
Lincoln's Inn, London 66 94 C6
Lindau 70 100 D6
Lindisfarne 43 59 BC2, 44 60 E1, 46 63 C3, 47 64 B1
Lindos 17 21 F5
Lindsey 44 60 E1
Lindum 25 33 B2
Lingayen Gulf 111 160 C6
Lingen 74 105 B2, 75 106 B2
Linhua 31 43 C5
Linjiang 119 175 BC1
Linköping 57 79 D2, 69 99 BC4
Linyo 102 143 D6
Linz 102 143 D2, 109 155 C6
Lipara 20 24 B6
Lipareae Insulae (Lipari Islands) 22 27 DE5–6
Lipari Islands (Lipareae Insulae) 80 115 D6, 84 121 F6
Lippe, county (hist.) 86 122 BC2
Lippe, river 68 98 BC3
Lippespring 45 62 K5
Lisala 123 180 E1
Lisbon (Lisboa, Olisipo) 46 63 A5, 49 68 BC7, 54 74 A3, 59 83 A6, 60 84 F3, 68 97 A3, 81 116 A4, 82 119 A4
Lissus (Lissos) 20 25 C2
Lithuania 55 76 E1–2, 59 82 D1, 71 101 IJ5, 72 103 E4, 73 104 DE2, 83 120 A4, 84 121 G2, 91 127 J3, 104 146 G3, 105 147 K4, 106 150 AB4, 107 151 D2, 108 154 E1–2, 110 157 DE3, 112 161 D3, 113 163 BC2, 115 168 D2–3
Lithuanians 50 70 E5, 106 150 B4
Little Armenia 49 67 K1
Little Poland (Malopolska) 73 104 D3
Livadia (Levadeia), city 88 125 B2–3
Livadia (Levadeia), province 72 103 E6, 88 125 B2
Liverpool 55 76 E2, 76 107 B5, 76 108 AB6, 77 109 DE6, 91 127 F3
Livingstone 97 135 D6
Livingstone's journeys in Africa 96 133 D7
Livonia (Livland) 57 79 G2,

70 100 D4, 71 101 J5, 81 116 D1, 83 120 A3, 91 127 J2
Livorno 76 107 C6, 87 124 B2, 104 146 E6
Lixos (Lixus) 16 19 A2, 32 44 A5
Ljodhus (Lewis) 52 72 BC1
Llandaff 52 72 C4
Lobositz 74 105 D3
Locarno 55 77 D7
Lod (Lydda) 118 171 AB2
Lodi 54 75 IJ1, 80 115 B3, 87 124 A1
Lödöse 57 79 D2
Łódź 104 146 F4, 105 147 J5, 110 157 D6
Lofoten 46 63 E1, 110 157 CD1
Lögum cloister 86 123 A6
Loire (Liger) 56 78 D5, 79 114 B2, 84 121 C4
Lokroi 20 24 C6
Lolang 32 44 L4, 40 55 K3
Lolland 70 100 DE2, 86 122 BC5
Lombardia 44 60 G4, 47 65 BC5, 53 73 C4, 80 115 B2, 84 121 E5, 87 124 A1, 101 141 BC3
Lombok 64 90 KL7, 99 139 J4
Lome 97 136 B3
Lomza 105 147 J5
Londinium (Lundun, London) 25 33 AB3, 26 34 BC1, 32 44 B3
London (Londinium, Lundun) 41 56 I6, 43 59 BC3, 44 60 E2–3, 47 64 B2, 50 69 B3, 54 74 B1–2, 55 76 B2, 56 78 C3, 66 94 (detail), 68 97 BC1, 76 107 B5, 76 108 BC7, 81 116 B2, 91 127 G4
London Bridge, London 66 94 D6
Londonderry 67 95 D6, 91 127 EF
Long Xuyen 124 181 B7
Longwy 105 147 J3
Lorraine (Lothringen) 68 97 C1–2
Los Angeles 93 130 A3, 94 131 I4
Lothal 8 3 E6, 10 8 F3
Lotharingen 45 62 JK6, 46 63 CD4
Lothringen (Lorraine) 56 78 E4, 70 100 BC6, 72 103 C5, 86 122 B4
Louhans 79 113 C2
Louis VII's crusade 48 66 D3, DE3, G3–4, JK6
Louisiana 62 85 B2–3, 92 129 B4, 93 130 E4
Louisiana, state 93 130 E4
Louisville 92 129 C3
Loulan 32 44 I4
Lourenço Marques (Maputo) 65 92 E4, 96 133 DE7, 97 136 DE5

Louvain (Leuven) 49 68 D5
Louvre, Paris 78 112 D5
Lower Burgundy 47 65 A5
Lower Egypt 14 15 AB2
Lower Lorraine (Lothringen), duchy 47 65 AB3, 53 73 B2
Lower Tunguska 32 44 HI1
Lowicz 105 147 J5
Lu 30 42 E2
Lualaba (Congo), river 123 180 F2
Luanda 65 92 C3, 96 133 C6, 97 136 C4, 122 179 C6
Luang Prabang 65 91 K3, 124 181 B4, 125 182 A1, D1
Luango 65 92 C3
Luba kingdom 65 92 D3
Lubetsh 51 71 BC3–4
Lübeck 54 74 C1, 55 76 C2, 57 79 CD3, 68 98 D1, 81 116 C2, 107 151 B2, 109 155 B5
Lublin 69 99 D6, 73 104 D3, 110 157 E4
Lubumbashi (Elisabethville) 122 179 DE6
Luca 22 27 B3
Lucania 20 25 B2, 22 27 E5
Lucayas, see Bahamas
Lucca, city 53 73 D5, 57 80 IJ2
Lucca, republic 80 115 B3, 82 119 C3, 84 121 E5
Lucentum (Alicante) 23 28 B4
Luceria (Lucera) 22 27 DE4, 47 65 E7
Lucknow 99 140 CD2, 127 184 CD2
Lüderitz 97 135 B6, 97 136 C5
Luebo 123 180 E2
Lufeng 117 170 DE7
Lugano 55 77 DE7
Lugdunensis 28 38 CD2
Lugdunum (Lyon) 25 33 BC4, 26 34 BC2, 32 44 BC4
Lugo 81 118 B5
Luguvalium (Carlisle) 28 39 HI2
Luimneach (Limerick) 46 63 AB3
Luleå 69 99 D2, 110 157 D1
Lullubi (Sulaimanya) 12 11 CD2
Lulabourg 123 180 E2
Lumbini 36 49 H4
Luna 22 27 B2, 46 63 D5
Lund 41 56 J6, 50 69 D3
Lunda kingdom 65 92 D3, 96 133 D7
Lundehøj 8 3 B5
Lundun (London) 46 63 C4
Lüneburg 57 79 CD3, 68 98 CD2
Lunéville 81 116 B2–3
Luoyang (Sera Metropolis) 30 42 D2–3, 32 44 KL5, 40 55 J4

Lurewala-Ther 108 F2
Luristan (Lorestan) 11 10 F3, 71 102 EF6
Lusaka 122 179 D6
Lüshun (Port Arthur) 117 170 E5, 119 175 A2
Lusitania 23 28 A2, 28 38 AB4
Lüta (Dairen) 119 175 A2
Lutetia (Paris) 25 33 B3, 26 34 B2, 28 38 D2, 32 44 B3
Lutter am Barenberge 68 98 D2
Lutterberg 74 105 BC2
Lüttich (Liège) 53 73 B2, 105 148 KL1
Lützen 68 98 E3
Luxembourg 68 97 C2, 70 100 B5, 91 127 H4, 104 146 D4, 105 148 L2, 107 151 AB3, 108 154 C2–3, 42 57 B4, 45 61 B4, 115 168 B3
Luxembourg, city 47 65 B3, 70 100 B5
Luxembourg, duchy 56 78 E4, 66 93 D4–5
Luxembourg, grand duchy 84 121 D4
Luxor-Karnak 14 15 C5
Luzern 55 77 CD6, 101 141 B2
Luzk 105 147 K6
Luzon 36 49 K5, 99 139 K1, 111 159 B2, 111 160 B6, 126 183 C5–6
Lvov (Lemberg) 69 99 D7, 91 127 JK4, 107 151 DE3, 110 157 E4
Lycia, see Lykia
Lydda (Lod) 26 35 B4
Lydia 12 12 B1, 17 21 F3
Lykandos 45 61 G6
Lykia (Lycia) 23 30 B7, 24 31 F6, 24 32 E6
Lynn 57 79 A3
Lyon (Lugdunum) 43 59 C5, 44 60 F4, 54 74 B2, 59 82 B2, 76 107 B6, 79 113 C2, 79 114 C2, 81 116 B1
Lys 66 93 B4

M
Ma'an 118 173 D6
Maas (Meuse) 42 57 B3, 56 78 E3, 66 93 C3, 79 113 C1
Maastricht 66 93 D4, 105 148 KL1
Mabotsa 96 133 D7
Macan 108 E3
Macao 35 48 E4, 60 84 J4, 64 88 G6, 102 142 B6, 117 170 D7
Mâcon 52 72 E6
Macapà 95 132 DE3
Macapan 71
Macassar 99 139 K4, 111 160 BC7
Macedonia (Makedonia) 23 28 F2, 24 32 D6
Macedonians 9 6 F6–7

Machu Picchu 63 86 B2
Macias Nguema (Bioko) 122 179 B5
Maciejowice 78 111 C1
Macistus 16 20 B6
Mactan 60 84 K4–5
Madagascar 65 92 F4, 96 133 F6, 97 136 E4, 98 137 A6, 122 179 F2
Madang 98 137 F6
Madeira 60 84 F4, 97 136 A1
Madhya Pradesh 127 184 C3
Madinat al-Faiyum 118 173 A6
Madjapahit 40 55 J7
Madras 36 49 H6, 65 91 HI3, 64 89 C3, 98 137 C5
Madrid 68 97 B3, 76 107 AB7, 81 116 A4, 81 118 A5, 101 116 A4, 101 141 E2
Madura Sultanate 40 55 GH6
Madura, India 99 140 C5
Madura, Java 64 90 K7
Madurai 127 184 C5
Maere 46 63 E3
Mafeking 97 135 D6
Magadan 98 137 J2
Magadha 13 13 E2, 32 44 I5, 38 52 KL1
Magdala 98 137 A5
Magdeburg, archbishopric 41 56 J6, 50 69 D3–4, 59 83 D5, 70 100 DE3
Magdeburg, city 47 65 D2, 55 76 C2, 57 79 D4, 58 81 C4, 81 116 C2, 107 151 BC3
Magdeburg, state 75 106 C2
Magellan's voyage 1519 60 84 EF5, L5
Magellan's voyage 1521 60 84 AB5, K4
Magellan, Strait of 60 84 DE7
Magenta 87 124 A1
Magersfontein 97 135 D6–7
Maghreb 32 44 B6
Maginot Line 110 157 C4
Magna Graecia 20 24 BC6, 20 25 AB3, 22 27 E5
Magnesia 24 31 F5
Magnis (Carvoran) 28 39 I1–2
Mago 23 28 CD2
Magyars 46 57 B5
Maharashtra 127 184 BC3
Mahé 99 140 b 4, 127 184 B4
Mähren 44 60 I3, 45 62 L6, 47 65 EF3, 53 73 E3, 70 100 FG5, 72 103 D5, 74 75 I3, 84 121 F4, 86 122 E3, 101 141 E2
Maia (Bowness) 28 39 GH2
Maiandros 17 21 F3
Maidanek 111 158 C2
Main 114 166 C3
Maine, France 52 72 D5, 56 78 C5
Maine, state USA 92 129 E1, 93 130 G1
Mainz (Mogontiacum) 41 56

J6, *44* **60** G3, *48* **66** E3, *49*
68 E5, *55* **76** C2, *79* **114** C1
Maison de la Révolution, see
Palais Bourbon, Paris
Majkop *98* **137** A3, *106* **150**
E6, *113* **163** E4
Majuba Hill *97* **135** E6
Makassar Strait *99* **139** K3–4
Makedonia (Macedonia) *17*
21 B1, *20* **25** CD2, *21* **26**
A1, *24* **31** E5, *84* **121** G6,
101 **141** G5, *103* **144** C3,
107 **151** D6
Makhatsjkala *106* **150** F6
Makran *12* **11** F4, E7, *36* **50**
DE7, *37* **51** L2
Malabar Coast *99* **140** B4
Malacca (Malaka) *16* **19** A2,
26 **34** A3
Malacca, city *65* **91** KL5, *98*
137 D5, *99* **139** I3
Malacca, Strait of *99* **139** I3,
126 **183** B6–7
Malaga *65* **92** A4, *81* **116** A4,
81 **118** B7, *109* **156** E3
Malange *123* **180** D2–3
Malao *32* **44** F7
Mälaren *43* **59** D1
Malawi *110* **157** F2, E6
Malawi, Lake *122* **179** E6
Malay Peninsula (Malacca)
64 **89** E4, *64* **90** I3
Malaya *99* **139** I3, *111* **159**
A3, *111* **160** B6
Malaya, Union of *98* **137** D5,
98 **138** E7
Malaysia *120* **176** J5, *126* **183**
BC6
Maldives *99* **140** B5, *127* **184**
A5
Mali *65* **92** AB1, *122* **179** E1, B4
Maliakos, Gulf of *16* **20** C4
Malindi *60* **84** GH5, *65* **92** F3
Malines (Mechelen) *66* **93** C3
Mallorca *55* **76** B3, *68* **97** C3,
81 **116** B4, *82* **119** B4, *109*
156 F2
Mallos *16* **19** F2
Malmédy *105* **148** L1
Malmö *70* **100** E2, *91* **127** I3
Malo *60* **84** F3
Maloyaroslavets *82* **119** F1
Malplaquet *72* **103** D4
Malta (Melita) *45* **61** B7, *55*
76 CD4, *68* **97** E4, *72* **103**
E7, *80* **115** E7, *81* **116** D4,
82 **119** D5, *84* **121** F7, *87*
124 BC4, *94* **133** C5, *101*
141 D7, *104* **146** F7, *107*
151 C7, *112* **161** BC6, *112*
162 C7, *120* **176** C5, *122*
179 C3
Malventum (Beneventum)
22 **27** DE4
Malwa *38* **53** AB2, *64* **89** B2,
65 **91** H2
Malwan *10* **8** F4
Mameluke Empire ca. 1300
40 **55** D4–5, *55* **76** EF4
Man (Mon), island *43* **59**

B2–3, *46* **63** BC3, *47* **64**
AB1, *50* **69** B3, *56* **78** B1,
67 **95** E6, *76* **108** A5, *81* **116**
AB2
Man, kingdom *50* **70** B4, *52*
72 B1–2
Manado *99* **139** K3
Managua *95* **132** A2, *121* **177**
B2
Manaus *62* **85** D5, *95* **132** D3
Manchester *76* **108** B6, *77*
109 EF6, *104* **146** C3
Manchukuo (Manchuria)
111 **159** B1, *111* **160** C4–5,
113 **164** EF6
Manchuria (Manchow,
Manchukuo) *35* **48** EF1,
98 **137** DE3, *102* **142**
BC1–2, *117* **170** DE4
Mandalay *64* **89** E2, *65* **91**
JK3, *98* **137** CD4, *99* **140**
F3, *111* **159** A2
Mandasur *38* **53** A2
Mangalore *65* **91** GH3, *99*
140 B4
Manila *99* **139** K2, *111* **159**
B2, *126* **183** C6
Manipur *99* **140** F2, *127* **184**
EF2
Mannar, Gulf of *64* **89** B4
Mannheim *91* **127** H4
Manono *123* **180** F2
Manork (Balearic Islands) *46*
63 BC6
Mansfeld *70* **100** DE4
Mantineia *16* **20** C6, *17* **21** B4
Mantova (Mantua) *22* **27**
BC2, *47* **65** CD5, *80* **115**
C3
Manzikert (Malazgirt) *45* **61**
H5
Maputo (Lourenço Mar-
ques) *122* **179** E7
Maquarie Islands *120* **176** K7
Maracaibo *95* **132** C2, *121*
177 D2
Maracanda (Samarkand) *21*
26 F1, *32* **44** GH4
Maranhao, city *62* **85** E5
Maranhao, state in Brazil *95*
132 E3
Marash *48* **66** L5, *49* **67** KL1
Marathi *99* **140** BC2
Marathon *16* **20** F5
Marburg *47* **65** C3, *58* **81** C4
Marché *79* **113** B2
Marchfeld *53* **73** E3
Marcianople *42* **57** K6
Marcomanni *28* **38** F2
Mare Adriaticum (Adriatic
Sea) *22* **27** D–F3–4
Mare Cantabricum *28* **38** BC3
Mare Caspium *28* **38** KL3
Mare Internum (Mediterra-
nean) *24* **32** C–E7, *28* **38**
D–G4–5
Mare Ionium (Ionian Sea) *22*
27 F6–7
Mare Ligusticum (Ligurian
Sea) *22* **27** AB3

Mare Suebicum *28* **38** F1
Mare Tyrrhenum (Tyrrhe-
nian Sea) *22* **27** B–D5
Marengo *80* **115** AB3, *81* **116**
BC2
Mari *11* **10** E3, *12* **11** BC2
Marian Islands *60* **84** KL4,
98 **137** F5, *111* **160** CD6
Mariano *121* **178** A2
Marienburg, East Prussia *55*
76 D2, *74* **105** EF1
Marienburg, Livland *69* **99**
E5
Marienwerder (Kwidzyn) *70*
100 G3
Maritsa *108* **153** B4–5
Mariupol (Zhdanov) *106* **150**
D6
Mark Istria *47* **65** E5
Mark Krain *47* **65** E5
Mark Lausitz *47* **65** DE2
Mark Meissen *47* **65** E2–3
Mark Zeitz *47* **65** D3
Mark Österreich *47* **65** E4
Mark, county (hist.) *70* **100**
C4, *74* **105** B2, *75* **106** AB2
Markland (Labrador) *60* **84**
DE3
Marmara, Sea of *17* **21** F1, *55*
76 F2, *101* **141** I5, *103* **144**
E3
Marocco *96* **134** A1, *97* **136**
B1, *120* **176** F4, *122* **179**
C1, AB3
Marocco, emirate *37* **51** G1–2
Maroneia *17* **21** D1, *23* **30** A5
Marquesas Islands *111* **159**
F4
Marrakech *32* **44** A5, *96* **134**
A1
Marsala (Lilybaeum) *57* **80**
J4, *87* **124** B3
Marseille (Massilia) *43* **59**
CD5, *46* **63** C5, *54* **74** BC3,
56 **78** E7, *76* **107** C6, *79* **113**
C3, *79* **114** C3, *81* **116** B3,
91 **127** G6
Marshall Islands *111* **159** D3,
111 **160** E6
Marston Moor *67* **95** E6
Marstrand *52* **72** F1
Martapura *64* **90** K7
Martigny *80* **115** A2
Martinique *62* **85** D4
Martyropolis *36* **50** A5
Maru *38* **52** J1
Maryland, state *92* **128** K2,
92 **129** D2, *93* **130** F2
Marylebone, London *66* **94**
B6
Maryport (Alauna) *38* **39** G2
Masada *15* **17** B6, *26* **35** B5
Masai, people *65* **92** E3
Masan *119* **175** BC3
Mascarene Islands *97* **136** F4
Maseru *122* **179** D7
Masilupatnam *65* **91** HI3,
127 **184** CD4

Masina *65* **92** AB1
Maski *38* **52** K2
Masovia (Mazowsze) *73* **104**
D2
Masqat (Muscat) *40* **55** F5,
64 **88** E6, *98* **137** B4, *108*
153 F6, *119* **174** D6
Massachusetts *92* **128** K2, *92*
129 DE2, *93* **130** G2
Massagetae, people *21* **26** E1
Massawa *65* **92** EF1, *97* **136**
E2
Massilia (Marseille) *13* **13**
A1, *16* **19** B2, *23* **28** D1, *26*
34 C3, *32* **44** B4
Masulipatnam *99* **140** CD4,
127 **184** CD4
Masurian Lakes, The *105*
147 JK5
Maszowsze (Masovia) *73* **104**
D2
Matabeleland (Ndebele) *96*
133 D6
Matadi *123* **180** D2
Matamoros *121* **177** A1
Mataram (Jogjakarta) *99* **139**
J4
Matera *59* **83** D7
Mathura *32* **44** HI5, *38* **52**
K1, *64* **89** B1–2, *65* **91** H2
Mato Grosso, city *95* **132** D4
Mato Grosso, state in Brazil
95 **132** D4
Matrand *84* **121** E2
Matwy *70* **100** G3
Maubeuge *105* **148** JK2
Mauretania Caesariensis *28*
38 BC5
Mauretania Tingitana *28* **38**
BC5
Mauritania *97* **136** A2, *120*
176 F4, *122* **179** E1
Mauritius *64* **88** EF7, *96* **133**
F7, *98* **137** B6, *122* **179** F7
Mauthausen *111* **158** A3
Mayan culture *63* **87** F2
Mayapan *63* **87** E1
Mayfair, London *66* **94** B6
Maysar *10* **8** C3
Mazaca (Caesarea) *23* **30**
CD6
Mazara *20* **24** A6, *44* **60** H7
Mbanzacongo (San Salva-
dor), *65* **92** CD3
Mecca *32* **44** F6, *108* **153** C6
Mechelen (Malines) *66* **93** C3
Mecklenburg, city *47* **65**
CD1
Mecklenburg, duchy *70* **100**
E3, *75* **106** C1–2
Mecklenburg, grand duchy
84 **121** E3
Mecklenburg, state *68* **98**
DE1, *74* **105** CD1, *82* **119**
C2, *114* **166** CD1
Mecklenburg-Schwerin *86*
122 CD2
Medea *96* **134** C1

Medellin *96* **134** B2
Medenine *112* **162** B2
Media *12* **12** F2, *13* **14** D6, *24*
31 H5, *36* **50** B6
Media Atropatene *24* **31** H5
Medina (Jathrib) *40* **55** E5,
108 **153** C6
Medina de Rioseco *81* **118**
BC6
Mediolanum (Milano) *22* **27**
AB2, *23* **38** E3
Mediolanum, Gaul *26* **34** B2
Mediterranean (Mare Inter-
num) *46* **63** DE7, *112* **162**
C–F1
Medma *20* **24** B6
Megalithic culture *8* **3** AB5
Megalopolis *16* **20** BC7
Megara *14* **15** BC3, *16* **20**
DE5
Megaris *16* **20** D5
Meghalaya *127* **184** E2
Megiddo *10* **9** B3, *11* **10** C3,
15 **17** B5
Mehrgahr *10* **8** E2
Meissen *47* **65** DE3, *53* **73** D2
Meknes *96* **134** B1
Mekong *64* **89** E2, *124* **181**
A4, B5, *125* **182** B2, E2, B6
Mekong Delta, The *124* **181**
BC7
Melbourne *98* **137** F7
Melilla *68* **97** B4, *109* **156** E3,
122 **179** B3
Melinda *40* **55** E7
Melita (Malta) *16* **19** D3, *20*
25 AB4, *23* **28** F3, *28* **38** F5
Melitene *23* **30** D6, *36* **49**
DE4, *45* **61** DH4
Melos *17* **21** C4, *88* **125** C3
Meluhha *10* **8** E3
Memel (Klaipeda) *69* **99**
CD5, *104* **146** F3, *107* **151**
CD2, *109* **155** D4, *113* **163**
B2
Memel, river *70* **100** H2
Memleben *47* **65** D3
Memmingen *68* **98** CD5, *70*
100 D4
Memphis (Cairo), Egypt *10* **9**
A4, *11* **10** B4, *12* **11** A3, *14*
15 B2, *24* **31** F7, *26* **34** F4,
28 **38** H16, *36* **49** D4
Memphis, USA *92* **129** B3,
93 **130** B3
Menam *39* **54** AB5
Mende *79* **114** BC3
Mendoza, Argentina *62* **85**
D6, *63* **86** B4, *95* **132** C5
Menorca *53* **73** AB6, *68* **97**
C3, *72* **103** C6, *81* **116** B4,
81 **118** DE6
Merauke *98* **137** F6
Mercia *43* **59** B3, *44* **60** E2, *47*
64 B2
Mercurii *22* **27** A5
Merida (Augusta Emerita),
Spain *28* **38** B4, *42* **58** A2,
109 **156** D2
Merina *96* **133** E6–7

Merinid dynasty ca. 1300 *40* 55 A4, *55* 76 A4

Meroë *13* 13 C2, *32* 44 E6

Merowe *108* 153 B6

Merseburg *47* 65 D3, *57* 79 D4

Merv (Alexandria Margiane, Antiokia, from 1937 Mary) *13* 13 D1, *13* 14 E6, *21* 26 E2, *24* 31 J5, *36* 49 F4, *40* 55 F4, *98* 137 B4, *103* 145 E5, *108* 153 F4

Mesembria *45* 61 E5

Mesen *106* 150 D1

Meshed *108* 153 EF4

Mesolongion *88* 125 AB2

Mesopotamia *11* 10 DE3–4, *12* 11 C2, *21* 26 C2, *28* 38 JK5, *71* 102 DE6

Messana, see Messina

Messene, commune *16* 20 B7

Messenia *16* 20 B7, *17* 21 B4

Messina (Messana), Italy *43* 59 E6, *54* 74 D5, *55* 76 D4, *59* 83 D7, *81* 116 D4, *112* 161 BC6, *112* 162 C1

Messina, Transvaal *97* 135 E6

Metapontion (Metapontum) *20* 24 BC5, *22* 27 F5

Metaurus *23* 28 E1

Methone (Methoni, Modon, Modoni), Peloponnesus *17* 21 B4, *44* 60 JK7

Methone, Macedonia *17* 21 B1

Metroum (Metroon), Olympia *18* 22 F5

Metz *44* 60 F3, *86* 122 B3, *104* 146 D4

Meuse (Maas) *105* 148 K2

Mexico (Tenochtitlan), city *62* 85 B4, *94* 131 IJ5, *121* 177 A1

Mexico, Gulf of *62* 85 BC3, *92* 129 B4, *121* 177 AB1

Mexico, state *60* 84 C4, *63* 87 B2, *113* 164 A6, *120* 176 C4, *121* 177 A2

Miami *121* 177 C1, *121* 178 B1

Michigan *92* 129 C1, *93* 130 EF2

Middelfart *86* 123 B5–6

Middle Congo *97* 136 C3

Middle East, The 1400s *10* 9

Middlesex, London *66* 94 B–D5–6

Midian *15* 18 E7

Midway *111* 159 E2, *111* 160 EF5

Miklagard (Old Norse = Constantinople) *46* 63 F6

Milano (Mediolanum), city *22* 27 AB3, *43* 59 D5, *54* 74 C2, *55* 76 C3, *59* 83 CD6, *68* 97 D2, *76* 107 C6, *81* 116 C3, *87* 124 A, *107* 152 B

Milano, duchy *57* 80 IJ1, *68* 97 D2, *70* 100 CD7

Mile End, London *66* 94 EF5

Miletos (Miletus) *17* 21 EF4, *23* 30 A6, *45* 61 E6

Millesimo *80* 115 A3

Milwaukee *92* 129 B2

Min-Yue *32* 44 L5

Minagara *24* 31 L6

Minas Gerais *95* 132 E4

Mindanao *98* 137 E5, *99* 139 L2, *126* 183 D6

Minden, city *50* 69 D3, *57* 79 C4

Mindèn, state *74* 105 B2, *75* 106 B2

Minerva, Temple of, Rome *27* 37 K2

Minneapolis *92* 129 B, *93* 130 D2

Minnesota *92* 129 B1, *93* 130 D1

Minsk *55* 76 E2, *105* 147 L5, *106* 150 B4

Miranda *95* 132 D4

Misir (Egypt) *37* 51 J2

Miskolc *109* 155 D6

Mississippi Territory, The *92* 128 IJ3

Mississippi, river *92* 129 B1–2, *93* 130 E3

Mississippi, state *92* 129 B1–2, *93* 130 E3–4

Missolonghi *84* 121 G6

Missouri, river *92* 129 A1, *93* 130 E3

Missouri, state *92* 129 B2–3, *93* 130 E3

Mitanni *8* 5 F3, *10* 9 B2, *11* 10 DE2

Mitla *63* 87 B3

Mitla Pass *118* 173 B6

Mittelbau *111* 158 A2

Mixco Viejo *63* 87 B3

Mizoram *127* 184 E3

Moab *15* 17 B6, *15* 18 E6

Mobile *92* 129 BC4

Moçambique Channel *65* 92 EF4

Moçambique, city *60* 84 GH5, *98* 137 A6

Moçambique, state *96* 133 DE6–7, *97* 136 E4, *122* 179 E6–7

Modena (Mutina), city *47* 65 D6, *87* 124 AB1

Modena, state *75* 80 J1, *72* 103 D5, *84* 121 E5

Modon (Modoni), see Methone *48* 66 H6

Moeris, Lake *14* 15 A2

Moesia *28* 38 G4, *32* 44 D4

Mogadishu (Mogadiscio) *64* 88 E6, *65* 92 F2

Mogilev *69* 99 E5, *83* 120 B4, *113* 163 CD2

Mogontiacum (Mainz) *26* 34 C2, *29* 40 AB6

Mohács *71* 102 A4, *72* 103 E5

Mohenjo-Daro *8* 3 D6, *10* 8 E3

Mokissos *45* 61 F6

Mokp'o *102* 142 D4, *119* 175 B3

Moldau (Vltava) *47* 65 E3–4

Moldavia *55* 76 E2–3, *71* 102 B4, *72* 103 F5, *81* 116 E2–3, *84* 121 H4, *101* 141 H2–3, *128* 185 C3

Molde *84* 121 DE1

Mölln *53* 73 D1

Mollwitz *75* 106 E3

Molopo *97* 135 D6

Moluccas, The *99* 139 KL3, *111* 159 B3, *111* 160 C7, *126* 183 D7

Mombasa *65* 92 F3, *98* 137 A6

Mömpelgard *55* 77 B5

Mön *70* 100 E2, *86* 122 D1

Mon (Man) *46* 63 C3

Monaco *80* 115 A3, *87* 124 A1–2

Monastir (Bitola) *101* 141 F5

Moncastro *54* 74 DE2

Mondovi *80* 115 A3

Monembasia (Monemvasia) *59* 83 F7, *71* 102 A6

Mongolia *35* 48 CD2, *36* 49 J3, *111* 160 B4, *113* 164 E6, *120* 176 IJ3

Mongolian People's Republic *117* 170 B–D4

Monomotapa kingdom *65* 92 E4

Monreale *53* 73 DE7, *59* 83 D7

Monrovia *97* 136 A3, *122* 179 A5

Mons (Bergen), Belgium *66* 93 B4

Monsatir *48* 66 H5

Mont Carmel *7* 1

Mont Cenis *47* 65 B5

Mont Royal *62* 85 CD2

Mont-Ferrat *57* 80 I1

Montana *93* 130 BC1

Montauban *58* 81 AB6

Montbéliard *52* 72 B5, *79* 114 C2

Monte Alban *63* 87 B3

Monte Cassino *43* 59 DE6, *44* 60 H6

Montenegro *72* 103 E6, *82* 119 E3, *101* 141 F4, *103* 144 BC2, *104* 146 F6, *107* 151 CD5

Monterey *62* 85 B3

Montevideo *95* 132 D5

Montgomery *92* 129 C4

Montméday *105* 148 KL2

Montmartre, Paris *78* 112 CD4

Montpellier *49* 68 D6, *54* 74 B2, *79* 114 A3

Montreal *92* 129 D1, *93* 130 G1

Montrose's campaign against Scotland 1660 *67* 95 F4

Monza *47* 65 C5

Mook *66* 93 D3

Mora *69* 99 B3–4

Morea (Peloponnesus) *71* 102 A6, *72* 103 F6, *81* 116 E4

Morgarten *55* 77 D6

Morges *55* 77 A6

Morotai *111* 160 C7

Morshansk *106* 150 DE4

Moscow, city *41* 56 L6, *55* 76 E1, *76* 107 F4, *82* 119 F1, *106* 150 D4, *113* 163 E2

Moscow, principality *71* 101 K5, *83* 120 C4

Mosdok *83* 120 D6

Mosel (Mosella) *47* 65 B3, *56* 78 E3, *68* 98 B4, *79* 113 C1

Mossamedes *96* 133 C6

Mossel Bay *97* 135 D7

Mostar *55* 76 D3

Mosul *36* 49 E4, *54* 74 F3, *119* 174 B4

Mosyr *106* 150 BC5

Moulmein *99* 140 F4

Moutiers *59* 83 C6

Mt. St. Michel *56* 78 BC4

Mudanya *108* 153 B4

Müggel See, Berlin *114* 167 F2

Mühldorf *70* 100 E6

Mühlhausen *53* 73 CD2

Mukden (Shenyang) *35* 48 E2, *102* 142 C3

Multan *64* 89 AB1, *99* 140 D2

München *55* 76 C2, *68* 98 E5, *81* 116 C3, *101* 141 CD2, *107* 151 B4, *114* 166 C4

Münchengrätz *86* 122 DE3

Munda *24* 32 A6

Münster, bishopric *70* 100 C3–4

Münster, Lothringen, city *70* 100 BC6

Münster, Saxony, city *47* 65 B2, *50* 69 C3–4, *55* 76 C2, *56* 78 B2, *57* 79 C4, *68* 97 CD1

Münster, state *68* 98 BC2

Murat *51* 71 DE7

Murcia *50* 70 B7, *109* 156 E3

Mures *44* 60 J4, *101* 141 G3

Murman Coast *83* 120 C1

Murmansk *106* 150 B1, *110* 157 E1

Murom *46* 63 G3, *106* 150 D4

Murzuk *32* 44 C5, *96* 134 D2

Muscat, see Masqat

Musiris *32* 44 H7

Mutina (Modena) *22* 27 D6

Mwene Ditu *123* 180 E2

Mycenae *8* 5 D3, *11* 10 A2, *16* 20 D6

Mycerinus, Pyramid of *15* 16 EF7

Myitkyina *111* 159 A2

Mylae *22* 27 D6, *23* 28 F3

Myonia *16* 20 C4

Myos Hormos *14* 15 CD3

Myra *45* 61 F7

Mysia *17* 21 E2, *20* 25 E2

Mysore, city *99* 140 C4, *127* 184 BC4

Mysore, state *98* 137 C5, *99* 140 C4

Mytilene (Lesbos) *84* 121 H6

Mytilene, archbishopric *45* 61 DE6

N

Nabulus (Sechem) *118* 171 B2, *118* 172 F2, *118* 173 CD5

Nagada *12* 11 A4, *14* 15 BC4

Nagaland *127* 184 F2

Nagasaki *102* 142 DE4, *111* 160 C5

Nagoya *102* 142 EF3

Nagpur *99* 140 C3

Naiman *40* 55 H2

Nain *26* 35 B2

Nairobi *97* 136 E3

Naissus (Nis) *28* 38 G4, *42* 57 J6, *103* 144 C2

Nakhon Ratchasima (Khorat) *125* 182 DE2

Nalanda *38* 52 C2

Nam Dinh *124* 181 C4

Namibia (South-West Africa) *120* 176 G5, *122* 179 C6

Namsos *110* 157 D1

Namur *66* 93 C4, *91* 127 G4

Nanchang *35* 48 E3, *117* 170 DE6

Nancy *104* 146 D4, *110* 157 B4

Nanhai (Pan-yu, Guangchou) *32* 44 L6

Nanjing (Nanking) *35* 48 E3, *102* 142 C3

Nanning *102* 142 A6, *124* 181 D4

Nantes (Portus Namnetum) *43* 59 B4, *46* 63 B4, *49* 68 C6, *54* 74 B2, *56* 78 B5, *68* 97 B2, *76* 107 B6, *79* 113 A2, *79* 114 A2, *81* 116 B3, *91* 127 F5

Nanyue *31* 43 AB7

Nan-Zhao (Thai) *32* 45 D3, *40* 55 IJ5

Napata *11* 10 B6, *32* 44 E6

Naples (Napoli), city *43* 59 E6, *45* 61 A6, *49* 68 EF7, *55* 76 CD3, *59* 83 D7, *68* 97 E3, *76* 107 D7, *81* 116 C4, *87* 124 BC2, *91* 127 I6, *107* 151 BC6

Napoleon's campaign in Italy *80* 115

Napoleon's campaign to Moscow 1812 *82* 119

Napoleon's campaign in Spain and Portugal *108*–14 *81* 118

Napoli (The Parthenopian Republic 1799) *80* 115 E5

Napoli, kingdom *55* 76 D3, *58* 81 DE6–7, *59* 82 C3, *68*

97 E3, 72 103 DE6, 81 116
CD4, 82 119 D4
Nara (Heijo) 36 49 L4
Narbada 64 89 B2, 65 91 H2,
99 140 C3
Narbo 24 32 B6, 25 33 B4, 32
44 B4
Narbonne (Narbonensis) 25
33 C4, 28 38 D3, 43 59 C5,
46 63 C5, 52 72 E7, 59 83
BC6, 91 127 G6
Narva 66 99 D4, 81 116 D1,
110 157 E2
Narvik 110 157 D1, 112 161 C1
Naryn 35 48 B1
Nashville 92 129 C3, 93 130
EF3
Nassau, Bahamas 121 178
BC1
Nassau, Germany 70 100 C4,
84 121 E4, 86 122 B3
Nässjö 91 127 I3
Natal, Brazil 62 85 EF5, 95
132 F3
Natal, South Africa 97 135
E7
Natuna Islands 99 139 J3
Natzweiler 111 158 A2
Naucratis 14 15 A1, 16 19 F3
Naulochus 24 32 C6
Naumburg 68 98 DE3
Naupactus (Navpaktos) 16
20 B5, 45 61 CD5
Nauplia (Navplion) 71 102
AB6, 88 125 B3
Nauru 111 159 D3, 111 160
E7
Navara 87 124 A1
Navarino 84 121 G7, 88 125
A3
Navarra 40 55 A3, 46 63 B5,
48 66 BC4, 55 76 B3, 56 78
B7, 59 82 A2, 68 97 B3
Naxos, Greek colony in Si-
cily 20 24 B6
Naxos, island in the Aegean
17 21 D4, 71 102 B6
Nazareth 26 35 B2, 118 171
AB1, 118 172 EF1
Nazca 63 86 B3
Nbangala 65 92 D3
Ndebele (Matabeleland) 96
133 C3
Ndjamena (Fort Lamy) 122
179 CD4
Ndola 122 179 D6
Neanderthal 7 1
Neapolis (Napoli) 16 19
CD2, 20 25 A2, 20 24 B5
Neapolis, Africa 22 27 BC7
Neapolis (Anatolikon) in
Asia Minor 45 61 F6
Nebraska 93 130 D2
Nebraska Territory, The 92
129 A2
Nederland 58 81 B4, 59 114
C1, 86 122 AB2, 91 127
G4, 104 146 D3, 107 151
AB3, 110 157 B3, 112 161

AB3, 115 168 B3, 116 169
B6
Nedjed (Nejd) 108 153 D6
Neerwinden 79 114 C1
Negapatnam 65 91 HI4
Negev Desert, The 15 17
A6–7, 118 171 A3, 118 172
E3, 118 173 C6
Negro, Cape 65 92 C4
Negroponte 54 74 D3
Nekor 46 63 A6
Nellore 99 140 C4
Nemausus (Nîmes) 25 33 B4
Nemea 16 20 C6
Nemesos (Limasol) 48 66 K6
Nemunas (Neman) 51 71
A2–3
Nepal 99 140 D2, 120 176 I4
Nertshinsk 35 48 DE2
Nerva's (Domitian's) Fo-
rum, Rome 27 37 K2
Nesos 17 21 E2
Nesse 114 166 D2
Netherlands, The 68 97 C1
Nettuno 112 161 B5
Netze 74 105 B5
Neubrandenburg 68 98 E1
Neuburg 68 98 DE5
Neuchâtel (Neuenburg) 55
77 B6, 74 105 B4
Neuenburg, principality 80
115 A2
Neuengamme 111 158 A2
Neukloster 74 105 C1
Neu-Kölln, Berlin 114 167 E2
Neumark 75 106 D2
Neuquen 95 132 C6
Neuss 68 98 B3
Neustadt 86 123 B7
Neustria 43 59 EF3, 45 62 J6
Neva 51 71 C2
Nevada 93 130 AB2
Nevers, city 56 78 D5, 68 97
C2, 79 114 B2, 84 121 CD5
Nevers, province 52 72 E5, 56
78 D5
New Amsterdam (New
York) 62 85 D3
New Brunswick 92 128 KL1
New Caledonia 120 176 L5–6
New Delhi (see also Delhi
and Indraprastha) 127 184
C2
New Granada, Viceroyalty
of 62 85 CD4–5, 94 131
K5, 95 132 C2
New Grange 8 3 A5
New Guinea 98 137 F6, 111
159 BC3, 111 160 CD7,
120 176 KL5
New Hampshire 92 128 K2,
92 129 D1, 93 130 G2
New Hebrides 111 159 D4,
111 160 E7
New Jersey 92 128 K2, 92 129
D2, 93 130 G2
New Mexico 93 130 C3
New Orleans 92 129 BC4, 93
130 EF4, 94 131 J4

New Scotland (Nova Scotia)
62 85 DE2
New Siberian Islands 60 84
J1
New South Wales 98 137 F7,
98 138 F7
New Spain, Viceroyalty of 62
85 B3–4, 94 131 IJ4–5
New York (New Amster-
dam) city 62 85 D3, 92 129
DE2, 93 130 G2
New York, state 92 128 JK2,
92 129 D1–2, 93 130 F2
New Zealand 105 149 F3, 113
164 F7
Newburn 67 95 EF6
Newcastle 56 78 BC1, 67 95
EF6, 76 108 B5, 81 116 B1,
91 127 G3
Newfoundland (Tierra de los
Bacallaos, Vinland) 52 72
E3, 62 85 E2, 92 128 L12,
98 138 D6
Newington, London 66 94
CD7
Nezhin 105 147 L5
Ngami, Lake 96 133 CD6
Nha Trang 124 181 CD7
Nias 64 90 HI6, 99 139 H3
Niaux 9 7 B2
Nicaea (Nice) 22 27 A3
Nicaea (Nikaia), Asia Minor
28 38 H4, 36 49 D4, 42 57
K6
Nicaragua 95 132 A2, 120 176
CD4, 121 177 B2
Nicastro 53 73 E6
Nice (Nicaea, Nizza) 79 113
C3, 79 114 C3, 81 116
BC3, 91 127 H6, 110 157
B5
Nicobar Islands 64 89 D4, 99
139 I2, 99 140 F5, 111 160
A6, 127 184 C6
Nicomedia 42 57 KL6
Nicopolis, city in Greece 44
60 J6
Nicopolis, city on the Donau
(Danube) 55 76 DE3, 71
102 B5, 104 146 GH5
Nicopolis, province in Gree-
ce 44 60 J6, 45 61 C6
Nicosia 54 74 E4
Nidaros 41 56 J5, 50 69 D1
Nieder-Lausitz 70 100 F4
Niedersachsen 114 166 B2
Niger, river 65 92 B1–2, 97
136 AB2
Niger, state 120 176 G4, 122
179 EF1, 174
Nigeria 97 136 BC2, 122 179
EF1, C5
Nihavend 36 50 B6
Niigata 102 142 EF3
Nijmegen 66 93 D2, 79 114 C1
Nikaia (Nicaea), Asia Minor
45 61 EF5, 48 66 J5
Nikaia (Nicaea, Nice) 16 19
C1

Nikaia, Iran 21 26 F2
Nikaia, kingdom 50 70 F7
Nike, Temple of, Acropolis
19 23 B2
Nikephorion 21 26 C2
Nikolayev 83 120 B5, 106 150
C6
Nikolayevsk 98 137 EF2
Nikolsburg 86 122 E3
Nikolsk 106 150 DE3
Nikomedeia 23 30 B5, 45 61
EF5, 48 66 J5
Nikopol 106 150 CD6
Nile, The (Nilus) 14 15 B4,
108 153 B6
Nilots 65 92 E2
Nilus (Nile) 32 44 E6
Nimes (Nemausus) 25 33 B4,
52 72 E7, 58 81 B6, 91 127
G6
Nimrud (Calah) 11 10 E3
Nine Elms, London 66 94 C7
Ningbo 35 48 EF3
Ninghsia 35 48 D2, 40 55 I4
Ninive 11 10 E3, 12 11 C2, 12
12 E2
Nippur 8 3 C6, 11 10 E4, 12
11 CD3, 12 12 E3
Nis (Naissus) 44 60 J5, 103
144 C2
Nisa 36 50 CD5
Nisbis 36 50 A5
Nishapur 36 49 F4, 36 50 D6
Nishne-Kolymsk 98 137 EF1
Niteroi 95 132 EF5
Niuzhuang 35 48 E2
Nivernais 79 113 B2
Nizam (Hyderabad) 99 140
C3
Nizhniy Novgorod 40 55 N2,
71 101 K5, 106 150 DE3–4
Nizza (Nice), city 44 60 G5,
53 73 C5, 79 113 C3, 80
115 A3, 87 124 A1
Njemen (Nemunas) 81 116
DE2, 105 147 K4–5
Noirmoutier 46 63 B4
Nolinsh 106 150 E3
Nombre de Dios (Puerto Be-
lo) 64 88 A6
Nora 22 27 AB5
Nordenskjöld Sea (Laptev
Sea) 60 84 IJ1
Nordhausen 70 100 D4
Nördlingen 68 98 D5
Nordmark 47 65 D2
Nordrhein-Westfalen 114
166 B2–3
Noreia 24 32 C5
Norfolk, England 52 72 D3,
56 78 C2
Norfolk, USA 93 130 G3
Noricum 26 34 D2, 24 32 C4
Normandy 46 63 C4, 47 64
B2, 56 78 C4, 79 113 AB1,
79 114 AB2, 113 165
Normanni, Kingdom of the
48 66 FG6
Norrköping 84 121 F2, 91
127 I2

North Africa, campaign
1942–43 117 162
North America 60 84 CD3, L1
North Atlantic Treaty mem-
bers 116 169
North Borneo (Sabah) 126
183 C6
North Cape (Nordkapp) 69
99 D1
North Carolina 92 128 J2–3,
92 129 CD3, 93 130 F3
North Dakota 93 130 CD1
North Korea 119 175 B2,
EF2, 120 176 K3
North Sea, The 46 63 CD3,
50 69 C2, 55 76 BC1, 57 79
BC2, 104 146 D3, 110 157
B3
North Vietnam 125 182 B1,
EF2
Northampton 56 78 BC2
Northern Rhodesia (Zam-
bia) 122 179 F2, D6
Northern Spain, caves in 9 7
Northern Territory 98 137
EF7
Northumberland 52 72 CD2
Northumbria 43 59 B2, 47 64
B1
Northwest Territory, USA
92 128 J2
Norvasund (Norse = Strait
of Gibraltar) 46 63 A6
Norway (Norge) 46 63 D2, 50
69 D1, 55 76 C1, 84 121
E1, 91 127 H2, 105 149 C1,
110 157 C2, 112 161 B2,
113 164 CD5, 115 168 C2,
116 169 B5
Norwegian Sea 72 103 BC1
Norwich 52 72 D3, 76 108 C6
Nossa Senhora de Belém
(Belém) 62 85 EF5
Nöteborg 66 99 E4
Notre Dame, Paris 78 112
DE6
Nottingham 76 108 BC6
Nouakchott 122 179 A4
Nova Scotia (New Scotland)
60 84 DE3, 62 85 DE2, 92
129 E1
Novara 80 115 B2
Novaya Zemlya 60 84 H2, 98
137 A1
Novgorod (Holmgard) 54 74
E1, 55 76 E1, 81 116 E1,
106 150 BC3, 113 163 D1
Novgorod, region 71 101 J5
Novgorod, republic 57 79
GH1–2
Novgorod-Seversk 83 120
BC4
Novi Pazar 101 141 F4
Noviomagus (Speyer) 25 33
AB2, 29 40 AB6
Novorossisk 106 150 DE6
Novosibirsk 98 137 C3
Novotcherkassk 71 101 K6–7
Noyon 105 148 J2
Nubia (Kush) 40 55 D5

Numantia 23 28 B2, 28 38 C3
Numidia, state 24 32 B7, 28
38 D5
Numidians 16 19 B3
Nürnberg 47 65 CD3, 68 97
C2, 68 98 DE4, 81 116 C2,
104 146 E4, 107 151 B4,
114 166 C3
Nyasa (Malawi), Lake 65 92
E3
Nyasaland (Malawi) 97 136
DE4
Nyborg 86 123 B6
Nyenskans (St. Petersburg)
69 99 E4
Nyköping 69 99 C4, 84 121
F2
Nyslott 69 99 DE3
Nystad 69 99 CD4
Nyuangwe 96 133 D6

O
Oaxaca 63 87 B2
Ob 35 48 B1, 36 49 F1, GH2
Ob, Gulf of 98 137 B2
Obbia 96 133 F5, 97 136 F3
Ober-Geldern 66 93 D3, 75
106 A3
Ober-Lausitz 70 100 F4
Ober-Pfalz 70 100 E5
Ober-Wallis 55 77 C7
Obock 96 133 E4, 97 136 E2
Obodrites 43 59 D3, 44 60
GH2
Ocana 81 118 C6
Oceania 7 1
Oceanus Atlanticus 28 38
A1–3
Oceanus Britannicus 25 33
A2–3
Oceanus Germanicus 28 38
DE1
Ochrida (Ohrid) 41 56 K7, 45
61 C6
Odense 50 69 D3, 69 99 A5,
76 107 C5, 91 127 H3
Oder (Viadua) 44 60 I3, 68 98
F2, 86 122 D2, 104 146 F4,
107 151 C3, 113 163 A2,
114 166 D2
Oder-Neisse Line 114 166
Odessa 81 116 E2, 106 150
C6, 112 161 E5, 113 163
D4
Odessos (Odessus) 16 19 E1,
28 38 H4
Ofanto (Aufidus) 23 29
Ofen 49 68 F6
Ogden 93 130 B2
Ohio, river 93 130 F2
Ohio, state 92 129 C2, 93 130
F2
Ohrid (Ochrida) 88 125 A1
Oia 16 19 A5
Oiniadai 16 20 A5
Oise 105 148 I2–3
Oka 106 150 D4
Okhotsk 98 137 E2
Okhotsk, Sea of 98 137 EF2

Okiep 97 135 C7
Okinawa 111 159 B2, 111 160
C5
Oklahoma 93 130 D3
Öland (Evland) 46 63 E3, 57
79 E2, 69 99 C5
Olbia (Borysthenes), city 16
19 E1, 24 31 F4
Olbia, Sardinia 22 27 B4, 23
28 DC2
Old Church 28 39 I2
Old Sarum 84 121 C3
Oldenburg, city, Niedersa-
chsen 68 98 C2
Oldenburg, city, Schleswig-
Holstein 50 69 D3
Oldenburg, county (hist.) 70
100 C3, 84 121 E3, 86 122
B2
Olduvai 7 1
Olenek 98 137 C1
Olinda 62 85 EF5, 64 88 BC7
Olisipo (Lisboa) 23 28 A2, 28
38 A4
Oliva 69 99 C5, 75 106 E1
Olivenza 81 118 AB7
Ollantaytambo 63 86 BC3
Olmütz 45 62 F3, 74 105 E3
Olympia 16 20 AB6
Olympus (Olympos) 17 21
B2
Olynthus (Olynthos) 17 21
C2, 20 25 D2
Olyokminsk 81 137 D2
Olyutorskij 98 137 F2
Omaha (USA) 93 130 D2
Omaha Beach 113 165 B2
Oman 12 11 F4, 37 51 L2, 98
137 B5, 103 145 E7, 108
153 F6, 119 174 D6
Oman, Gulf of 12 11 F4
Omara 99 140 A2
Ombos 14 15 BC5
Omdurman 97 136 D2
Omo 7 1
Omsk 89 126 I6, 98 137 B3
Onega, lake 83 120 C2, 106
150 C2–3, 113 163 D1
Onega, river 51 71 D1
Onnum (Halton Chesters) 28
39 JK1
Onoba 23 28 A3 ·
Ontario 62 85 C2
Oostende 66 93 A3, 105 148
IJ1
Opis 12 11 C2–3, 13 14 C6
Opon 32 44 F7
Oporto (Porto, Portus Cale)
81 116 A3, 91 127 E6
Opos 16 20 D4
Oppius, Rome 27 36 L6
Opsikion 44 60 L6, 45 61 E6
Optimaton 45 61 EF5
Oradour 112 161 A4
Oran 68 97 B4, 96 133 B3, 96
134 B1
Orange 49 68 D6, 58 81 B6
Orange Free State (Oranje
Vrystaat) 96 133 D7, 97
· 135 DE6–7

Orange, river 97 135 C6
Orange, state 97 136 D5
Orbetello 80 115 BC4
Orchomenus (Orchomenos)
16 20 D4
Orchon 40 55 12–3
Ordos 31 43 B5
Örebro 69 99 B4
Oregon 93 130 A1–2
Orel 91 127 L3, 106 150 CD4
Orenburg 83 120 EF4, 98 137
AB3
Øresund 72 103 D3
Øreting 46 63 D2
Oriental 123 180 F1
Orissa 64 89 C2, 99 140 D3,
127 184 D3
Oristano 59 83 CD7
Orkney Islands 47 64 B1, 50
69 BC2, 81 116 B1, 110
157 B2
Orléans 25 33 B3, 43 59 C4,
46 63 C4, 49 68 D6, 56 78
C5, 68 97 C2, 79 113 B2,
79 114 B2, 91 127 G5, 110
157 B4
Oron 40 55 J2
Orontes 49 67 K3
Orsa 105 147 L4, 106 150 B4
Orthes 58 81 A6
Orvieto 53 73 D5, 80 115 C4
Pahang 39 54 B7, 40 55 1J6
Paita 95 132 AB3
Pakhoi (Pei-hai) 102 142 A7
Pakistan 120 176 HI4, 127
184 AB1
Paksë 124 181 C6
Palais Bourbon (Maison de la
Révolution), Paris 78 112
B5
Palais de Justice, Paris 78 112
D5
Palais du Luxembourg, Paris
78 112 C6
Palais Royal, Paris 78 112 D5
Palaistra, Olympia 18 22 D5
Palatina, Rome 27 36 KL7
Palatine, Rome 27 37 K4
Palau 98 137 F5, 111 159 C3,
111 160 C6
Palawan 99 139 K2
Palembang 64 90 IJ7, 99 139
I4
Palencia 49 68 C6
Palenque 63 87 CD2
Palermo (Panormos) 54 74
C3, 55 76 C4, 59 83 D7, 68
97 E4, 72 103 D6, 87 124 B3
Palestine (Norse: Jorsala-
land) 7 1, 109 B3, 24 32
· F7, 8 3 108 153 BC5, 112
161 H3, 111 161 A2
Pallava 38 53 B3
Palma 44 60 F6, 49 68 D7, 54
74 B3
Palmyra Island 111 159 F3,
111 160 F6
Palmyra, city, Syria 24 31
G6, 26 34 G4
Palos 55 76 A4, 60 84 F3–4,
68 97 A4

Ouagadougou 122 179 B4
Ouargla 96 134 C1
Oudh 99 140 C2
Oulu (Uleåborg) 110 157 E1
Outer Mongolia 98 137 CD3
Overijssel 66 93 D2
Oviedo 81 116 A3, 84 121 B5,
109 156 D1
Oxford 49 68 CD5, 56 78 B3,
58 81 A4, 68 97 B2
Oxos, see Amu Darja

P
Pachacamac 63 86 AB2
Pacific Ocean 111 159 C–E2,
120 176 AC3–5, KL4
Padang 65 91 K5, 98 137
D5–6
Paddington, London 66 94 A6
Paderborn 43 59 D3, 47 65
C2, 50 69 CD4
Padova (Patavium) 45 61 A4,
49 68 E6, 91 127 I5
Padus (Po) 22 27 C2
Paestum (Poseidonia, Posi-
donia) 20 24 B5, 22 27
DE5
Pagalu 122 179 BC5
Pagan 36 49 I5, 39 54 A5
Palura 32 44 I6
Pamir 103 145 F5
Pamplona 43 59 B5, 44 60
DE5, 91 127 F6
Panamá, city 60 84 D5, 95
132 B2, 121 177 C3
Panamá (part of Gran Co-
lombia) 95 132 B2
Panamá (part of Inca Empi-
re) 63 86 A1
Panama, state 113 164 B6, 121
177 C3
Panduranga 40 55 J6
Pandya 38 52 K3, 38 53 B4
Paneas 26 35 C1
Pankow, Berlin 127 184 E1
Panmunjom 119 175 B2, E3
Pannonia 26 34 D2, 28 38 F3
Pannonian March, The 44 60
I4
Panopolis (Khemmis) 14 15
BC4
Panormos (Panormus, Paler-
mo) 16 19 C2, 20 24 A6, 22
27 D6
Pantelleria (Cossura) 22 27
C7
Panthéon (St. Geneviève),
Paris 78 112 D6
Pantheon (temple), Acropo-
lis 19 23 E2
Pantikapaion (Panticapae-
um) 26 34 F2
Pan-yu (Nanhai) 13 13 EF2
Papal State 55 76 CD3, 68 97
D3, 81 116 C3, 87 124 B2
Paphlagonia 23 30 C5, 45 61
F5
Paphos 16 19 F2
Papua New Guinea 120 176
KL5, 126 183 E7
Papua, part of the Common-
wealth of Australia 98 137
F6
Pará (Belém) 95 132 E3
Paraguay 63 86 C3, 95 132
D5, 120 176 DE5
Paraiba 95 132 F3
Paraitonion 21 26 A2
Paramaribo 62 85 DE4, 95
132 DE2
Paraná, Brazil 95 132 E5
Parana, city, Argentina 95
132 D5
Paris (Lutetia) 25 33 B3, 43
59 C4, 46 63 C4, 54 74 B2,
56 78 D4, 68 97 C1–2, 76
107 B6, 78 112 (detail) 79
113 B1, 79 114 B2, 91 127
G5, 110 157 B4
Paristrion 45 61 D5
Parliament, London «St.
Stephen's Hall» 66 94
BC7
Parma, city 44 60 G5, 53 73
CD4

Parma, duchy *80* **115** B3, *84* **121** E5, *87* **124** A1

Parnassus (Parnassos) *16* **20** C4, *88* **125** B2

Paros *17* **21** D4, *88* **125** C3

Parthenon, Acropolis *19* **23** D2

Parthenopean Republic *80* **115** E5

Parthia *13* **14** D6, *21* **26** DE2, *36* **50** D6

Parthian Empire *24* **31** I5, *32* **44** FG5

Pasargadae *13* **14** D7, *21* **26** DE3

Pasei *64* **90** HI5

Pasewalk *68* **98** EF1

Passau *47* **65** DE4

Passau, bishopric *70* **100** DE5

Passohendale *105* **148** J1

Pasto *63* **86** AB1

Patagonia *94* **131** K7, *95* **132** C7

Pataliputra (Patna) *13* **13** E2 *32* **44** I5–6

Patani *64* **90** I5, *99* **139** I2

Patara *23* **30** A7

Patavium (Padova) *22* **27** C2

Patay *56* **78** D4

Patmos *17* **21** F5

Patna (Pataliputra) *99* **140** D2

Patrai (Patras) *88* **125** B3

Patras (Patrai) *16* **20** B5, *45* **61** CD6, *107* **151** D7

Pattala *38* **52** J2

Pau *79* **113** A4, *104* **146** C5

Paulis *123* **180** E7

Pavia *43* **59** D5, *47* **65** C5, *49* **68** E6

Pavlovskij *106* **150** DE5

Pax Iulia *28* **38** AB4

Pearl Harbor *111* **159** F2

Pech-Merle *9* **7** B1

Pechora *83* **120** D1

Pécs (Fünfkirchen) *45* **61** BC4, *49* **68** F6, *109* **155** D6–7

Peenemünde *68* **98** F1

Pegu, British colony *99* **140** F3

Pegu, city *36* **49** I5, *64* **89** E3, *98* **137** D5

Peihai (Pakhoi) *102* **142** A7

Peipus, Lake *51* **71** BC2, *55* **76** E1, *81* **116** DE1, *83* **120** B3, *107* **151** DE1, *113* **163** C1

Peitaland *46* **63** BC5

Peiting *32* **45** C2

Peking (Beijing, Yuzhou) *35* **48** E2

Pelagos *45* **61** E6–7

Pelim *35* **48** AB1

Pella, Decapolis *26* **35** C3

Pella, Macedonia *17* **21** B1, *21* **26** A1

Pelopeion, Olympia *18* **22** E5

Peloponnes (Morea) *55* **76** E4, *17* **21** B4, *88* **125** B3

Pelusion (Pelusium) *14* **15** C1, *21* **26** B3

Pemba *97* **136** E3

Penang *64* **90** I5, *99* **139** I3

Penner *99* **140** C4

Pennsylvania *92* **128** JK2, *92* **129** D2, *93* **130** F2

Pensa *83* **120** D4, *106* **150** E4

Pensacola *92* **129** C2

Penzance *91* **127** F4

Pera *55* **76** E3

Perak *64* **90** I6

Perea *26* **35** C3

Perevolotyna *69* **99** F7

Pereyaslav *41* **56** L6

Pereyaslavets *51* **71** B5

Pergamon (Pergamum), city *23* **30** A6, *32* **44** DE4, *101* **141** HI6

Pergamon, state *23* **30** AB6, *24* **31** F5

Périgord *56* **78** C6

Périgueux *52* **72** D6

Perimula *32* **44** JK7

Perlak *39* **54** AB7, *39* **54** I6

Perm *83* **120** E3, *106* **150** F2

Pernambuco (Recife) city *95* **132** F3

Pernambuco, region in Brazil *95* **132** F3–4

Pernau *57* **79** F–G2, *69* **99** D4

Perpignan *49* **68** D6–7, *68* **97** C3, *79* **114** BC3

Persepolis *12* **11** E3, *13* **13** CD2, *21* **26** D3

Persia (see also Iran) *37* **51** KL1, *108* **153** E5

Persian Empire *13* **13** CD1, *13* **14**

Persian Gulf, The *12* **11** D3–4, *32* **44** F5, *119* **174** C5–6

Persis *13* **14** D7

Perth, Australia *98* **137** E7

Perth, Scotland *52* **72** C2, *91* **127** F3

Peru *62* **85** CD5, *63* **86** B2, *94* **131** JK6, *95* **132** B3, *113* **164** B7, *120* **176** D5

Perugia *47* **65** D6, *49* **68** E6

Perusia *26* **34** C3

Pescara *57* **80** K2

Peshawar (Purushapura) *13* **13** D1, *64* **89** AB1, *99* **140** B1

Pessinus *23* **30** B6

Pest *55* **76** D2–3, *58* **81** E5, *72* **103** E5

Petra *26* **34** F4, *32* **44** E5

Petriana (Stanwix) *28* **39** H1–2

Petrianea *28* **39** H2

Petrograd (St. Petersburg, Leningrad) *106* **150** BC3, *107* **151** E1

Petronius' journey to Napata 231 f.Kr. *32* **44** D6

Petropavlovsk *89* **126** L5

Petrosavodsk *83* **120** BC2, *106* **150** BC3, *110* **157** EF2

Petrovsk *83* **120** E6

Petsamo *110* **157** E1

Petsheneger *48* **66** HI4, *51* **71** C4

Pfalz *84* **121** DE4, *86* **122** B3

Pfalz-Neuburg *70* **100** DE5

Phailaka *10* **8** AB2

Phaistos *17* **21** D5

Phaleron *16* **20** E6

Phan Rang *124* **181** CD7, *125* **182** C5

Phanagoreia *16* **19** F1

Pharae *16* **20** BC7

Pharsalus (Farsalos) *24* **32** D6, *28* **38** G4, *45* **61** D6

Pharsalus (Phàrsalos) *17* **21** B2, *45* **61** D6

Pharus *22* **27** E3

Phaselis, Palestine *26* **35** BC3

Phigalia *16* **20** B7

Philadelphia *26* **35** C4

Philadelphia *62* **85** D3, *92* **129** D2, *93* **130** G2

Philae, see Elephantine

Philippi *24* **32** D6, *28* **38** G4

Philippines *64* **88** G6, *98* **137** E5, *99* **139** KL2, *111* **159** B3, *111* **160** C6, *113* **164** F6, *120* **176** K4, *126* **183** CD6

Philippopolis (Plovdiv) *45* **61** D5, *58* **81** F6, *71* **102** AB5, *101* **141** GH4

Philistines *15* **17** A6, *15* **18** D6

Phillaphaugh *67* **95** EF5

Philomelion *48* **66** JK5

Phnom Penh *39* **54** C6, *124* **181** B7, *125* **182** AB3, DE3, AB7

Phocaea *17* **21** E3, *54* **74** E3

Phocis *16* **20** CD4

Phoenicia *11* **10** C3, *15* **17** B4, *16* **19** F2, *26* **35** B1–2

Phoenicia *28* **38** I5–6

Phoenix Islands *111* **159** EF3, *111* **160** F7

Phrygia *28* **38** H5

Phrygia (Galatia) *12* **12** BC1, *13* **14** B6, *17* **21** F2, *28* **38** H5

Phu Bai *124* **181** C5

Piacenza *60* **84** G5, *49* **68** E6, *54* **74** C2–3

Piatigorsk *106* **150** EF6

Piaui *95* **132** EF3

Piazza Armerina *22* **27** D6

Picardie *79* **113** B1

Picenum *22* **27** D3

Pichincha *95* **132** AB3

Picts, people *42* **57** G3, *43* **59** B2, *47* **64** AB1

Piedras Negras *63* **87** D3

Piemonte *70* **100** G7, *80* **115** AB2–3, *81* **116** BC3, *84* **121** DE5, *101* **141** B3

Pietermaritzburg *97* **135** E6

Pietersburg *97* **135** E6

Pieve di Cadore *57* **80** J1

Pilau *69* **99** C5

Pilsen (Plzeň) *68* **98** E4, *107* **151** C4, *108* **154** C4

Pinar del Rio *121* **178** A2

Pincius, Rome *27* **36** K5

Pindos *17* **21** B2

Pingyang *31* **43** B5

Pinkiang (Harbin) *102* **143** F5

Pinsk *69* **99** DE6, *104* **146** G3

Piombino, principality *57* **80** J2, *68* **97** D3, *80* **115** B4

Pirene *17* **21** EF3

Pireus *16* **20** E6, *17* **21** C3

Pirot *104* **146** G6

Pisa (Pisae) *43* **59** D5, *49* **68** E6, *59* **83** CD6, *91* **127** H6

Pisae (Pisa) *22* **27** B3, *23* **28** E1

Pisidia *12* **12** BC2, *23* **30** B6

Pistoriae *24* **32** C6

Piteå *69* **99** C2

Pithecussa *20* **24** A5

Pitinika *38* **52** K2

Pittsburgh *92* **128** J2, *92* **129** D2

Pityus *16* **19** F1

Pityusae *16* **20** DE7

Pizarros journey 1532 *60* **84** D5

Place de la Rèvolution, Paris *78* **112** B4

Place de Victoires, Paris *78* **112** D4–5

Place Royale, Paris *78* **112** EF5

Place Vendôme, Paris *78* **112** C4

Placentia *22* **27** B2

Plain of Jars *125* **182** DE1–2

Plassey *99* **140** D3

Plataea *16* **20** E5

Plei Ku *125* **182** BC3

Pleven (Plevna) *101* **141** GH4

Pliska *37* **51** I1, *44* **60** L5

Plock *50* **69** E3

Ploiesti *109* **155** E7, *112* **161** H3

Plovdiv (Filibé, Filippopel) *51* **71** A6, *88* **125** C1, *103* **144** D3

Pluron *16* **20** A5

Plymouth *60* **84** F3, *68* **97** AB1, *72* **103** B4, *81* **116** A2, *91* **127** F4

Plzen (Pilsen) *68* **98** E4, *104* **146** EF4, *107* **151** C4

Plön *86* **123** B7

Po (Padus) *43* **59** D5, *53* **73** C4, *101* **141** C3

Podolia *69* **99** E7, *71* **102** BC4, *73* **104** E3, *81* **116** E2

Pohang *119* **175** C3

Pöhlde *47* **65** C2

Poissy *58* **81** AB4

Poitiers (Limonum) *25* **33** AB3, *43* **59** C4, *44* **60** E4, *49* **68** CD6, *52* **72** D6, *54* **74** B2, *56* **78** C5

Poitou *52* **72** CD6, *56* **78** C4, *79* **113** AB2

Poland *48* **66** G2, *50* **70** DE5, *55* **76** D2, *72* **103** EF4, *74* **105** F2, *75* **106** E2, *78* **111** D1, *83* **120** A4, *84* **121** FG3, *104* **146** G4, *105* **147** JK5, *107* **151** CD3, *110* **157** E3–4, *115* **168** D3, *116* **169** C6

Poland-Lithuania *67* **96** DE2, *69* **99** DE6

Poles *46* **63** E4, *106* **150** B5

Polo's, Marco, explorations *60* **84** HI4, IJ3

Polotsk *41* **56** K6, *46* **63** F3

Polovtsians, people *46* **63** H4, *51* **71** EF4

Poltava *69* **99** F7, *106* **150** CD5

Pomerania *50* **70** D5, *53* **73** DE1, *68* **98** F1, *75* **106** C1, *81* **116** CD2, *84* **121** EF3, *86* **122** D1, *114* **166** D1

Pomerelia (Pommerellen) *50* **70** D5, *53* **73** E1, *57* **79** EF3

Pompadour *72* **103** BC5

Pompeii *22* **27** D4, *28* **38** F4

Pondichéry (Pondicherry) *65* **91** HI4, *98* **137** C5, *99* **140** CD4, *127* **184** C4

Pons Aelius (Newcastle) *28* **39** K2

Pont Neuf, Paris *78* **112** D5

Pont Royal, (bridge) Paris *78* **112** C5

Pontecorvo *68* **97** E3, *80* **115** D4, *81* **116** CD4, *84* **121** F6, *87* **124** B2, *101* **141** D5

Pontianak *64* **90** JK6, *99* **139** J3

Pontos (Pontus) *23* **30** CD5, *24* **31** FG5

Pontus Euxinus (Pontos Euxeinos, Black Sea) *28* **38** HI3–4

Pontvallain *56* **78** C5

Poona *99* **140** B3

Poplar, London *66* **94** F6

Popocatepetl *63* **87** A2

Populonium *22* **27** B3

Port Arthur (Lüshun), Manchuria *98* **137** C3, *102* **142** C3, *102* **143** E6, *111* **160** C5

Port Arthur, Kaffraria *97* **135** E7

Port Darwin *98* **137** E6

Port de France *121* **177** E2

Port Elizabeth *96* **133** D7, *97* **135** DE7

Port Francqui *123* **180** E2

Port Louis *122* **179** F7

Port Mahon *84* **121** D6

Port Maud *98* **137** D6

Port Moresby *98* **137** F6, *111* **159** C4, *126* **183** EF7

Port Natal (Durban) *96* **133** D7

Port Nolloth *97* **135** BC7

Port of Spain *95* **132** D2, *121* **177** E2

Port Royal (prison), Paris *78* **112** D7

Port Said *112 161* EF7, *112 162* F2, *118 173* B5
Port St. Simeon *49 67* K2
Port Stanley *95 132* D7
Port Sudan *108 153* C6, *122 179* E4
Port-au-Prince *121 177* CD1
Porta Capena, Rome *27 36* L7
Porta Collina, Rome *27 36* L5
Porta Esquilina, Rome *27 36* L6
Porta Lavernalis, Rome *27 36* K7
Porta Naevia, Rome *27 36* L7
Porta Querquetulana, Rome *27 36* L7
Porta Quirinalis, Rome *27 36* KL5
Porta Raudusculana, Rome *27 36* K7
Porta Salutaris, Rome *27 36* K6
Porta Sanqualis, Rome *27 36* K6
Porta Trigemina, Rome *27 36* K7
Porta Viminalis, Rome *27 36* L5–6
Porticus Neronis Margaritaria, Rome *27 37* KL4
Portland, England *72 103* B4
Portland, USA *92 129* E1, *93 130* K1
Porto (Oporto, Portus Cale) *54 74* A2–3, *91 127* E6
Porto Novo *96 133* BC5
Porto Velho *95 132* CD3
Portovecchio *57 80* IJ3
Portsmouth *52 72* C4, *56 78* C3, *81 116* B2, *82 119* B2
Portugal *55 76* A3, *67 96* A3, *68 97* A3, *81 116* A4, *104 146* A6, *105 149* C2, *108 154* A4, *113 164* C6, *115 168* A4, *116 169* A7
Portugal, county (hist.) *48 66* AB4–5
Portugal, kingdom *50 70* A6–7, *59 82* A2–3, *72 103* A6, *82 119* A3–4, *84 121* A6
Portuguese East Africa *97 136* DE4
Portuguese Guinea *96 133* A4, *97 136* A2, *113 164* C6
Portus Cale (Porto) *28 38* AB3
Portus Itius *28 38* D2
Portus Magnus *28 38* C5
Portus Namnetum (Nantes) *25 33* A3, *28 38* C2
Poseidonia (Paestum) *20 24* B5, *20 25* A2
Posekiær *8 3* B5
Posen (Poznan), city *50 69* E4, *73 104* C2, *81 116* D2, *107 151* C2
Posen, province *86 122* E2
Postavy *105 147* KL4

Poteidaia *17 21* C2
Potosi *63 86* C3, *95 132* C4
Potsdam *74 105* C2, *114 166* C2
Povyenetch *83 120* BC2
Poznan (Posen) *91 127* I4, *107 151* C2
Praeneste *22 27* CD4
Prague *47 65* E3, *55 76* D2, *59 83* D5, *74 105* D3, *76 107* D5, *81 116* CD2, *107 151* BC3, *113 163* A3, *128 185* B3
Praia *122 179* A4
Praisos *17 21* E5
Prasiai *16 20* D7, *17 21* B4
Prato *57 80* J2
Prayaga *38 53* B2
Prémontre *48 66* D3
Prenzlau *68 98* EF1–2
Prenzlauerberg, Berlin *114 167* E1
Pressburg (Bratislava) *49 68* F6, *70 100* G6, *81 116* D3, *101 141* EF2, *107 151* C4
Preston *67 95* E6
Pretoria *96 133* D7, *97 135* E6
Priene *21 26* B2, *23 30* A6
Prieska *97 135* D7
Principe *96 133* B5
Pripjat *51 71* B3, *81 116* E2, *107 151* E2, *113 163* C3
Pritzwalk *57 79* D3
Prome *36 49* I5, *39 54* A5
Propylaea, Acropolis *19 23* F1
Provence *43 59* CD5, *44 60* F5, *47 65* AB6, *53 73* B5, *56 78* E7, *68 97* C3, *79 113* C3, *79 114* C3
Prussia *55 79* F3, *58 81* E3
Prussia, duchy *70 100* H2
Prussia, kingdom *72 103* D4, *73 104* BC2, *81 116* CD2, *82 119* D2, *84 121* EF3, *86 122* B–E2
Prussians *43 59* E2
Prut *101 141* H3, *105 147* L7, *107 151* E4
Prytanaeum (Prytaneion), Olympia *18 22* B5
Przemysl *105 147* JK6
Psara *88 125* C2
Pskov *51 71* BC2, *106 150* B4, *107 151* E1, *113 163* CD1
Psofis *16 20* B6
Ptolemaios, on the Nile *24 31* F7
Ptolemais (Akka), Phoenicia *26 35* B2
Ptolemais, North Africa *36 49* C4
Pudosj *106 150* C2
Puerto Belo (Nombre de Dios) *60 84* D4, *62 85* C4, *64 88* A6
Puerto Cortéz *63 87* EF3
Puerto Montt *95 132* BC6
Puerto Rico *94 131* K5, *95 132* C4, *120 176* D4, *121 177* D1–2

Pulicat *65 91* H3
Pulinda *38 52* K2
Pultusk *82 119* E2
Puná *63 86* A2
Punjab, people *13 13* B3
Punta Arenas *95 132* C7
Punta del Este *95 132* D6
Pura *24 31* JK6
Purushapura (Peshawar) *17 53* A1
Pusan (Fusan) *102 142* D4, *102 143* F7, *111 159* B1–2, *119 175* C3
Puteoli *32 44* C4
Pydna *17 21* B2
Pygmies, people *13 13* B3
Pylos *17 21* AB4, *88 125* B3
Pyongyang *102 143* EF6, *119 175* AB2
Pyramus *49 67* K1
Pyrenèes *54 75* I6–7, *56 78* CD7, *68 97* BC3
Pyrgos *16 20* B7
Pyxus *20 24* B5

Q

Qatar *108 153* E6, *119 174* C6, *120 176* H4
Qi *30 42* D2
Qin *30 42* D2
Qingdao (Tsingtao) *35 48* E2, *98 137* E4, *102 143* DE7, *117 170* E5
Qinglian'gang culture, China *8 3* F5
Quanchou (Zaiton) *40 55* JK5
Quang Nam *65 91* L3
Quang Ngai *65 91* L3
Quang Tri *65 91* L3, *125 182* F2
Quay d'Orsay, Paris *78 112* B5
Quebec, city *92 128* K1, *92 129* D1
Quebec, province *92 128* K1
Quedlinburg *47 65* D2
Queensland *98 137* F6–7
Queenstown *97 135* DE7
Quelimane *96 133* E6
97 136 E4
Quentovic *44 60* EF3
Qui Nhon *124 181* CD6
Quiberon *79 114* A2
Quilon *36 49* G6, *40 55* G6
Quinghai *98 137* C4
Quintana Roo *63 87* E2
Quirinal, Rome *27 36* L6
Quito *63 86* A1, *95 132* B3
Qumran *26 35* C4
Qurigua *63 87* E3

R

Raab, city *70 100* G6
Raab, river *70 100* G6
Rabat *97 136* B1, *122 179* B3
Rabaul *111 159* CD3, *111 160* D7, *126 183* F7
Rabbat-Ammon *15 18* EF5

Radom *110 157* DE4
Raetia *26 34* C2, *28 38* E3, *29 40* B7
Rafana *26 35* D2
Rafia (Raphia) *12 12* C3, *15 18* D6, *24 32* EF7
Ragusa, city *45 61* BC5, *55 76* D3, *110 157* D5
Ragusa, republic *72 103* E6, *80 115* E4
Rai (Teheran) *36 49* EF4, *40 55* EF4
Raimond of Toulouses crusade *48 66* C4, EF4
Rain *68 98* D5
Rajasthan *127 184* B2
Rajpur (Raipur) *64 89* BC2, *99 140* C3
Rajputana *64 89* AB2, *99 140* BC2
Ramle *118 171* A2, *118 172* E2
Rangoon *98 137* CD5, *111 160* A6
Rangpur *108* F3–4
Rapallo *109 155* B7
Raphia (Rafia) *12 12* C3, *15 18* D6, *24 32* EF7
Ras Shamra, see Ugarit
Rasulid kingdom ca. 1300 *40 55* EF5
Ratae (Leicester) AB2
Ravenna *22 27* C2, *43 59* DE5, *45 61* A5, *101 141* CD3
Ravensburg *75 106* B2
Ravensbrück *111 158* B2
Ravensburg *53 73* CD3, *70 100* D6
Ravi *108* F2
Rawalpindi *99 140* BC1
Rawitz *69 99* C6
Rawson *95 132* CD6
Reading *76 108* B7
Reate *22 27* C3
Recife (Pernambuco) *62 85* E5, *95 132* F3
Red River *92 129* A3, *93 130* D3
Red River (Song-Koi) *124 181* B4
Red Russia *76 107* DE3
Red Sea (Sinus Arabicus) *12 11* AB4, *108 153* C6, *119 174* A6–7
Regensburg (Castra Regina) *46 63* D4, *48 66* F3, *70 100* E5, *81 116* C2, *114 166* CD4
Regent's Park, London *66 94* B6
Reggio (Rhegion), Calabria *43 59* E6, *45 61* B7, *59 83* G6, *112 162* C1
Reggio, Modena *49 68* E6
Regia, Rome *27 37* K3
Regnum Bospori *24 32* E5, *28 38* I3, *32 44* E4
Regnum Parthorum *24 32* F6, *28 38* KL4–5

Rehe *102 143* E5
Reichenau *44 60* G4, *47 65* C4
Reichenbach *74 105* E3
Reims *25 33* C3, *43 59* C4, *55 76* BC2, *56 78* DA4, *59 83* C5, *69 82* B2, *81 116* B2, *91 127* G4, *105 148* J2, *107 151* A4
Reinickendorf, Berlin *114 167* DE1
Rendsborg *86 123* B7
Rennes *52 72* C5, *79 113* A1–2, *79 114* A2, *84 121* C4
Rerik *44 60* H2
Reshev *113 163* D1
Resitencia *95 132* D5
Rethymnon *88 125* C4
Réunion *96 133* F7, *97 136* F4, *98 137* B6
Reutlingen *70 100* D5
Reval (Tallinn) *55 76* DE1, *57 79* FG1, *69 99* DA4, *81 116* D1, *107 151* D1
Revardashir *36 49* EF4
Reykjavik *72 103* A1
Rhagae *24 31* HI5
Rhamnus (Rhamnos) *16 20* F5
Rhegium (Rhegion, Reggio) *16 19* D2, *20 24* BC6, *22 27* E6
Rheinland-Pfalz *114 166* AB3
Rhenus (Rhine) *29 40* A7
Rhine (Rhenus), river *47 65* B2, *53 73* B2
Rhine, Confederation of the *82 119* CD2
Rhine, province *86 122* B3
Rhineland *109 155* AB5
Rhodanus (Rhône) *24 31* C4
Rhode Island *92 128* K2, *92 129* E2, *93 130* G2
Rhodes (Rhodos), bishopric *45 61* E6
Rhodes (Rhodos, Rhodus), *11 10* B3, *13 14* B6, *17 21* F4–5, *20 25* EF4, *23 30* A7, *24 31* F6, *42 57* K7, *50 70* L7, *55 76* E4, *71 102* B6, *81 116* E4, *84 121* H7, *101 141* I7, *103 144* E4, *104 146* HI7, *112 161* E6
Rhodesia (Zimbabwe) *71 5*, *97 136* D4, *105 149* D2–3, *113 164* D7, *122 179* F7
Rhône (Rhodanus) *24 31* C4, *52 72* E6, *56 78* E6, *79 113* C3, *79 114* C3
Ribe *50 69* D3, *55 76* C1, *69 99* A5
Ribla *15 17* C4, *15 18* F4
Ribnitz *68 98* E1
Richard the Lionheart's crusade *48 66*
Richmond, England *56 78* BC1
Richmond, USA *92 128* J2, *92 129* D3
Riga *41 56* K6, *55 76* D1, *57*

79 FG2, **59** 83 E3, **69** 99 D5, *81* 116 D1, *107* 151 D1, *113* 163 BC1, *128* 185 C1

Rijeka (Fiume) *91* 127 I5

Rijswijk *68* **98** A2

Rimini (Ariminum) *45* **61** A6, *53* 73 D5

Ringerike *43* 59 DE

Ringkøbing *86* 123 A5

Rio Amazonas *62* 85 DE5, *95* **132** D3

Rio Araguia *95* **132** E3

Rio Branco, city *95* **132** C3

Rio Branco, province *95* **132** CD3

Rio de Janeiro *62* 85 E6, *95* **132** EF5

Rio de la Plata, city *60* **84** D6

Rio de la Plata, river *62* 85 DE6

Rio de la Plata, viceroyalty *62* 85 D6, *94* 131 K6

Rio de Oro *97* 136 A1

Rio Gallegos *95* **132** C7

Rio Grande Do Sul, province *95* **132** DE5

Rio Grande, city South America *62* 85 E6, *95* **132** DE5

Rio Grande, river North America *62* 85 B3, *92* 129 A4, *93* **130** CD4

Rio Madeiro *95* **132** CD3

Rio Muni *97* **136** C3

Rio Negro *95* **132** C3

Rio Paranã *95* **132** DE4

Rio Sao Francisco *95* **132** EF3–4

Rio Solimoes *95* **132** C3

Rio Tapajos *95* **132** D3

Rio Tocantins *95* **132** E3–4

Rio Usumacinta *63* **87** D2–3

Rio Xingu *95* **132** D3

Ritzbüttel *70* **100** C2–3

Rivoli *80* 115 BC2

Riyadh *108* 153 D6, *119* 174 B6

Robert of Normandy's crusade *48* **66** D4, E4

Rochdale *84* 121 C3

Rochester *92* 129 D2

Rocroi (Rocroy) *56* 78 D3–4, *68* **98** A4

Rodez *56* 78 D7

Roer (Rur) *66* **93** D3

Roermond *57* 79 B4, *66* **93** D3

Rokitno Moors *105* 147 KL5

Roman Empire, The *24* 31 CD4–5, *23* 28, *24* 32, *28* 38

Romania (Rumenia) *91* 127 K5, *101* 141 GH3, *103* 144 D2, *107* 151 B4, *108* 154 EF3, *110* 157 E5, *112* 161 D5, *113* 163 B4, *114* 166 D6, *115* 168 D4, *116* 169 CD6

Romanians (see also Romania) *42* 57 J6, *46* **63** F5

Rome (Roma, Romaborg) *22* 27 C4, *23* 28 E2, *41* 56 J7, *45* 61 A5, *46* **63** D5–6, *55* 76 C3, *81* 116 C4, *87* 124 B2

Rome, (detail) *27* 36, *27* 37

Romerike *43* 59 D1

Romilly *79* 113 B1

Romulus, Temple of *27* 37 K3 (3)

Rømø *86* 123 A6

Roncevalles (Roncevaux) *44* **60** E5, *46* **63** B5

Røros *69* **99** B3

Rosario *95* **132** CD5

Rosetta *14* 15 A1

Roskilde *50* **69** D3

Ross *67* 95 D6

Rossano *59* 83 E7

Rossbach *74* 105 C2

Rostock *69* **99** E5, *57* 79 D3, *58* **81** CD3, *113* 163 A2

Rostov, Kiev *41* 56 L5, *46* **63** G3, *51* 71 D2

Rostov, on the Don *106* 150 DE6, *113* 163 EF4

Rostra, Rome *27* 37 J3

Rothenburg *53* 73 CD3, *68* **98** CD4

Rotomagus (Rouen) *25* 33 B3

Rotterdam *56* 78 DE2, *91* 127 G4, *107* 151 A3

Rottweil *70* **100** C6

Rouen (Rotomagus, Ruda) *46* 63 C4, *47* 64 B2, *50* **69** B4, *56* 78 C4, *59* 83 B5, *76* **107** B5–6, *79* 113 B1, *79* 114 B1

Rouergue *56* 78 D6

Rouffignac *97* AB1

Roundway *67* 95 EF7

Roussillon (Roussillon, Roussilon) *56* 78 D7, *68* **97** C3, *79* 114 B3

Rovaniemi *112* 161 D1

Rovno *104* 146 G4, *106* 150 B5

Rowuma Bay *96* 133 E6

Royal Road between Susa and Sardes *13* 14 BC6

Rsyev *106* 150 C4

Rub al-Khali *108* 153 DE6–7

Ruda (Rouen) *46* 63 C4

Rudchester *28* 39 K1

Rue de Seve, Paris *78* 112 B6

Rue St. Antoine, Paris *78* 112 E5

Rue St. Denis, Paris *78* 112 D4–5

Rue St. Honoré, Paris *78* 112 C4

Rue St. Jaques, Paris *78* 112 D6

Rue St. Martin, Paris *78* 112 DE5

Ruffac *79* 113 AB2

Rügen *69* 99 B5, *70* **100** E2, *74* 105 D1, *86* 122 D1

Rügenwalde *57* 79 E3

Ruhr *114* 166 B2

Ruhr, river *68* **98** C3

Ruijin *117* 170 DE6

Rumelia *71* **102** AB5, *82* 119 EF4

Rumindi *38* 52 K1

Rupar *8* 3 E6, *108* 8 F2

Rupert House, Canada *62* 85 D2

Rupert's Land *62* 85 CD2, *92* 128 JK1

Rusaddir *16* 19 A2, *23* 28 B3, *24* 31 A5

Russia (see also Soviet Union) *55* 76 F1, *81* 116 E2, *83* 120, *84* 121 GH2–3, *89* 126 H–J, *91* 127 KL3–4, *98* 137 BD2, *103* 144 EF1, *105* 149 DE1

Russian principalities (1200s and 1300s) *40* 55 C–E2, *50* **70** EF4

Rutenia (Karpato Ukraina) *109* 155 DE6, *128* 185 C3

Rütli *55* 77 D6

Rwanda *65* **92** DE3, *122* 179 F2 (6), DE5, *123* 180 F2

Ryazan *41* 56 L6, *83* 120 C4

Rybinsk *83* 120 C3, *110* 157 F2

Ryukyu Islands *98* 137 E4, *102* 142 D6, *111* 159 B2

S

Saale *68* **98** E3–4

Saar, region *107* 151 B4, *109* 155 AB6, *114* 166 B3

Saar, river *68* **98** B4

Saarbrücken *105* 148 L2, *114* 166 B3

Saba *13* 13 C2

Sabah (North Borneo) *99* 139 K3, *126* 183 C6

Sachsen-Anhalt *114* 166 C2

Sachsenhausen *111* 158 AB2

Sacramento *93* 130 A2

Sadiya *99* 140 F2

Sadowa *86* 122 DE3

Sadras *65* 91 H4

Safad *118* 171 B1, *118* 172 F1

Sagarthia *13* 14 E6–7

Sagua la Grande *22* 178 B2

Sagunto (Saguntum) *24* 31 B4, *28* 38 C4, *81* 118 C6

Sais *13* 13 B2, *14* 15 A1

Sakaka *108* 153 C5

Sakastana *36* 50 E6

Sakhalin (Karafuto) *35* 48 EF1, *98* 137 F3, *111* 160 D4

Sakkara *14* 15 A2

Sal *26* 34 A3, *28* 38 A5

Salamanca (Salamantica) *49* **68** BC7, *109* 156 D2

Salamantica (Salamanca) *26* 34 A3

Salamis, Cyprus *23* 30 C7

Salamis, Greece *16* **20** E6

Salé *54* 74 A3

Salef *49* 67 J1

Salekhard *98* 137 B2

Salerno (Salernum) *22* 27 DE4, *45* 61 AB6, *87* 124 C4

Salisbury (Harare) Zimbabwe *122* 179 E6

Salisbury, England *56* **78** BC3, *77* 109 E7

Salla *110* 157 E1, *112* 161 D1

Salomon Islands *111* 159 D3–4, *111* 160 DE7, *126* 183 F7

Salonae, see Split

Saloniki (Thessaloniki, Thessalonica) *81* 116 D4, *88* 125 B1, *103* 144 CD3, *107* 151 D6, *110* 157 E6

Salt Lake City *93* **130** B2

Salta *94* 131 K6, *95* **132** C5

Saltvik *46* **63** E2

Salvador (Bahia) *95* **132** F4

Salzburg, archbishopric *70* **100** E6, *74* 105 CD4, *80* 115 CD2

Salzburg, city *41* 56 J6, *59* 83 D5, *101* 141 D2, *107* 151 BC4

Samara (Kuybychev) *83* 120 DE4, *106* 150 F4

Samaria, city *26* 35 B3

Samaria, region *26* 35 B3, *118* 171 AB1

Samarkand (Marakanda) *34* 47 C5, *36* 49 F3, *40* 55 F4, *98* 137 B4

Sambas *99* 139 J3

Sambodhi (Bodh Gaya) *38* 52 KL2

Samchok *119* 175 C2, F3

Samid, people *46* **63** F1

Sam-Neua *124* 181 B4

Samnium *22* 27 D4

Samoa *111* 159 E4, *111* 160 F7

Samoid, people *83* 120 D1

Samori kingdom *96* 133 B4–5

Samos, city *17* 21 E3

Samos, island *23* 30 A6

Samosata *26* 38 J5

Samothrace *17* 21 D1

Samsun *55* 76 F3, *108* 153 C4

Samsø *86* 123 B5

Samudra *64* 90 HI6

San Antonio *92* 129 A4, *93* **130** D4

San Carlos *62* 85 CD7

San Francisco *93* **130** A2

San Jorge da Mina (Elmina) *60* **84** F4–5

San José *121* 177 B3

San Juan *121* 177 D1

San Luis *95* **132** C5–6

San Marino, republic *57* 80 JK2, *84* 121 EF5, *87* 124 B1, *104* 146 EF5–6

San Salvador, (Mbanzakongo), Congo *65* **92** E1

San Salvador, El Salvador, city *63* 87 E4, *121* 177 AB2
San Salvador, island *60* 84 D4
San Salvador, state *95* 132 A2, *121* 177 AB2
San Sebastian *109* 156 E1
San Stefano *101* 141 I5
Sana *36* 49 E5, *119* 174 B7
Sanchi *36* 49 GH5, *38* 53 B2
Sandomir *70* 100 H4
Sangarios *23* 30 B6
Sankt Gallen *43* 59 D4, *44* 60 G4, *55* 77 DE5
Sankt Gotthard *47* 65 C5
Santa Anna Goraz *62* 85 E5
Santa Catarina *95* 132 DE5
Santa Clara *121* 177 C1, *121* 178 B2
Santa Cruz Islands *111* 160 E7
Santa Cruz, Brazil *62* 85 EF5
Santa Cruz, Patagonia *95* 132 C7
Santa Cruz, Peru *62* 85 D5
Santa Fé, Argentina *95* 132 D5
Santa Fe, New Mexico *93* 130 C3
Santa Fe, New Spain *62* 85 B3
Santa Isabel *95* 132 CD3
Santa Rosa *95* 132 CD6
Santa Severina *45* 61 B6, *59* 83 E7
Santander *68* 97 AB3, *109* 156 E1
Santarém *95* 132 DE3
Santes *44* 60 E4
Santiago de Compostela *43* 59 A4, *59* 83 A6
Santiago de Cuba *95* 132 B1, *121* 177 C1, *121* 178 C2–3
Santiago del Estro *95* 132 CD5
Santiago, Chile *63* 86 BC4, *95* 132 B1
Santiago, Spain *81* 118 A5
Santo Domingo (Dominican Republic) *62* 85 D4, *64* 88 B6, *95* 132 C1, *121* 177 D1
Santos *95* 132 E5
Sanuago *81* 118 A5
Sao Luis *95* 132 EF3
Sao Luis do Maranhao *94* 131 L6
Sao Paulo, city *95* 132 E5
Sao Paulo, province *95* 132 E4–5
Sao Paulo (Bahia) *62* 85 E5, *64* 88 B7
Sao Tomé and Principe *122* 179 B5
Sao Vicente *62* 85 E6
Saône *52* 72 E5–6, *56* 78 E5
Saporosye *106* 150 E6, *112* 161 EF4, *113* 163 E4
Sarai *40* 55 E3, *71* 101 L6
Sarajevo *107* 151 C5, *110* 157 D5

Saransk *83* 120 D4
Sarapul *106* 150 F3
Saratov *71* 101 K6, *83* 120 D4
Sarawak *98* 137 DE5, *126* 183 C7
Sardes *13* 14 B6, *21* 26 B2, *45* 61 E6
Sardinia (Sardo) *43* 59 D6, *44* 60 G6, *55* 76 C3, *68* 97 D3, *72* 103 D6, *87* 124 A3, *107* 151 B6
Sardinia, kingdom *57* 80 I3, *79* 114 C3, *80* 115 B5, *81* 116 C4, *84* 121 D5–6, *87* 124 A1
Sardo (Sardinia) *16* 19 C2
Sarepta *26* 35 B1
Sarev *83* 120 D5
Sargans *55* 77 E6
Sargon, Kingdom of *12* 11 A4
Sarkel *51* 71 E4–5
Sarmatia *24* 32 F5, *26* 34 F2, *28* 38 H3
Sarmizegetusa *28* 38 G3
Sarnath *36* 49 H5, *38* 52 K2
Saronic Gulf, The *16* 20 E6
Saros *23* 30 C6–7, *49* 67 JK1
Sasanid Empire *38* 53 A1, *42* 58 DE2
Sassari *59* 83 C7
Satara *99* 140 B3
Satiyaputra *38* 52 K3
Sattaship *125* 182 A3
Saturn, Temple of, Rome *27* 37 J3
Saudi-Arabia (see also Arabs, Arabia) *108* 153 CD5–6, *113* 164 D6, *119* 174 AB6
Sault Sainte Marie *62* 85 CD2
Saumur *58* 81 AB5
Sava *43* 59 E5, *44* 60 E5, *81* 116 D3, *101* 141 E3, *107* 152 C5
Savannah *92* 129 CD4, *93* 130 F4
Savannakhet *124* 181 BC5
Savenay *79* 114 A2
Savoia (Savoy) *56* 78 E6, *57* 80 HI1, *68* 97 CD2, *72* 103 C5, *79* 114 C2, *80* 115 A2–3, *87* 124 A1
Savoy Palace, London *66* 94 C6
Savus *28* 38 F3
Saxon duchies *70* 100 DE4
Saxons (see also Saxony, Sachsen) *32* 44 C3, *42* 57 D2, *43* 59 D2
Saxony (Sachsen) *44* 60 G2, *47* 65 C2, *53* 73 DC2, *68* 97 D1, *68* 98 EF3, *69* 99 B6, *72* 103 D4, *74* 105 CD2, *81* 116 C2, *84* 121 EF4, *86* 122 D3, *114* 166 CD3
Sayan Mountains *32* 44 I3
Scallabis *23* 28 A2
Scandia *28* 38 EF1

Scapa Flow *104* 146 C2
Scardona *45* 61 B5
Schaffhausen *55* 77 CD5
Schelde *56* 78 D3, *66* 93 B4
Schleswig (Slesvig), duchy *47* 65 C1, *75* 106 B1, *86* 122 C1
Schleswig, city *50* 69 B3
Schleswig (Sardo) *43* 59 D6, *44* 60 G6, *55* 76 C3, *68* 97 D3, *72* 103 D6, *87* 124 A3, *107* 151 B6
Schleswig-Holstein; region *114* 166 BC1
Schleswig-Holstein-Glückstadt, duchy *70* 100 CD3–4
Schleswig-Holstein-Gottorp, duchy *70* 100 DE2
Schlüsselburg *112* 161 DE2
Schmalkalden (Smalkald) *58* 81 CD4
Schwedt *68* 98 F2
Schweidnitz *74* 105 E2
Schwerin *53* 73 D1, *70* 100 DE3, *114* 166 C2
Schwiebus *75* 106 D2
Schwyz *55* 77 D6
Schöneberg, Berlin *114* 167 DE2
Schönefeld, Berlin *114* 167 EF3
Scone *50* 69 B2
Scotland *47* 64 B1, *48* 66 CD1, *52* 72 C1–2, *55* 76 B1, *58* 81 A2–3, *72* 103 B3, *81* 116 B1
Scots *42* 57 F3
Scythians *32* 44 EF3, I3
Sea peoples *10* 9 A3
Seattle *93* 130 A1
Sebastia (Sebaste), city *45* 61 G5
Sebastia, thema *45* 61 G5
Second Cataract *11* 10 B6, *14* 15 B7
Sedan *58* 81 BC4, *79* 113 BC1, *86* 122 A3, *104* 146 D4, *105* 148 K2
Seeburg (Grobin) *51* 71 A2
Segeberg *86* 123 B7
Segedunum (Wallsend) *28* 39 L1–2
Segovia *43* 59 AB6, *48* 66 B5
Segusio *26* 34 C2
Seine (Signa, Sequana) *44* 60 EF2, *78* 112 A5, F7, *79* 114 B2
Sela *15* 17 B7, *15* 18 E7
Seleucia *28* 38 K5
Seleucia, Cilicia *23* 30 C7, *45* 61 G6
Seleucia, thema *45* 61 F6
Seleucia, Mediterranean *24* 31 G6
Seleucia, Tigris *24* 31 H6, *36* 49 E4
Seleucid Empire *23* 30 CD7, *24* 31 HI6
Selinus *20* 24 B6
Selja *50* 69 D1
Seljuk empire *48* 66 KL5, *49* 67 J1–2
Selle *70* 100 D3

Semgallen *73* 104 DE1
Semipalatinsk *89* 126 I7
Semna *14* 15 A7
Sempach *55* 77 C6
Sena (Sentinum), Italy *22* 27 C3, *24* 31 D4
Sena Gallica *22* 27 D3
Sena, Africa *65* 92 E4
Senate, The, Rome *27* 37 J2–3
Sendai *102* 142 F3
Senegal *97* 136 A2, *122* 179 E1, A4
Senia *22* 27 DE2
Senkursk *106* 150 CD2
Sennar *65* 92 E1
Sens *52* 72 E5, *59* 83 BC5
Sentinum (Sena), Italy *22* 27 C3, *24* 31 D4
Seoul (Keijo) *102* 142 D3, *119* 175 B2
Septimania *44* 60 F5, *45* 62 J7
Sera Metropolis (Luoyang) *32* 44 KL5
Serampore (Frederiksnagor) *65* 91 I2
Serbia *45* 61 BC5, *53* 73 F5, *72* 103 E5, *78* 111 CD2, *84* 121 G5, *101* 141 F3–4, *103* 144 C2, *104* 146 G5, *112* 161 C5, *113* 163 B4
Serbs (Serbians), people *42* 57 J6, *44* 60 J5
Serdika *111* 160 D5
Serkland (Norse = Bagdadh califate) *46* 63 H6
Serpukov *106* 150 D2
Servian Wall, Rome *27* 37 I2–3
Sestus *28* 38 GH4
Sevastopol *83* 120 B6, *106* 150 C6, *113* 163 D4
Severia *69* 99 F6
Severians *46* 63 G4
Severnaya Zemlya *60* 84 HI1
Sevilla *43* 59 A7, *49* 68 C7, *59* 83 A7, *68* 97 A4, *81* 116 A4, *109* 156 DE3
Sextiae *24* 32 B6
Seychelles *96* 133 F6, *98* 137 B6, *122* 179 F5
Sfakteria *17* 21 A4
Shaanxi *98* 137 D4, *117* 170 C5–6
Shaba (Katanga) *123* 180 DF3
Shan *32* 45 D2
Shangdu *40* 55 J3, *60* 84 J3
Shanghai *98* 137 E4, *102* 142 C5, *117* 170 E6
Shantou (Swatow) *102* 142 BC6
Shantung Peninsula *40* 55 K4, *102* 143 DE7, *117* 170 DE5
Shanxi *117* 170 D5
Shapur *36* 49 EF4
Shari-i Sokhta (Aratta?) *10* 8 CD2, *12* 11 F3
Sharm al-Shaykh *118* 173 BC7

Sharuhen *10* 9 AB3
Sheffield *76* 108 B6, *77* 109 EF6
Shenkursk *59* 83 C2
Shenyang (Mukden) *111* 160 C5, *117* 170 DE5
s'Hertogenbosch *66* 93 CD3
Shetlands (Hjaltland) *46* 63 CD2, *72* 103 B3, *81* 116 B1, *104* 146 CD2, *110* 157 B2
Shianoukville *125* 182 A3
Shikarpur *99* 140 B2
Shikoku *102* 142 E4
Shillong *64* 89 D2, *127* 184 E2
Shiloh *92* 129 E3
Shimonoseki *102* 142 E4
Shirax *37* 51 K2, *119* 174 C5
Shoreditch, London *66* 94 D6
Shrewsbury *77* 109 E6
Shu (Chengdu) *31* 43 A6
Siam (Thailand) *65* 91 K3, *98* 137 D5
Siam, Gulf of *40* 55 I6, *125* 182 A3, D3, A7
Siberia *40* 55 G–I1, *83* 120 EF3
Siberia, khanate *35* 48 B1
Siberian Khanate *35* 48 B1
Siberian Tartars *35* 48 AB1
Sibiu (Hermannstadt) *104* 146 G5, *105* 147 K7
Sichuan *98* 137 D4, *117* 170 C6
Sicilies, The Two, kingdom *84* 121 F6, *87* 124 C2–3
Sicily (Sicilia, Norse: Sikiløy) *22* 27 D6, *23* 28 EF3, *24* 31 D5, *28* 38 EF5, *43* 59 E7, *45* 61 D6, *46* 63 D6, *48* 66 F6, *68* 97 E4, *104* 146 F7, *112* 161 B6, *112* 162 C1
Sicily, kingdom *53* 73 E5–6, *55* 76 CD4, *59* 83 F4, *58* 81 D7, *80* 115 D6, *81* 116 CD4, *82* 119 D4, *87* 124 B3
Siddapura *38* 52 JK3
Side *16* 19 F2
Sidi Barrani *112* 162 E2
Sidon *10* 9 A3, *11* 10 C3, *15* 17 B4, *49* 67 JK3
Siebenbürgen (Transylvania) *71* 102 AB4, *72* 103 F5, *101* 141 GH3, *103* 144 D1
Siegfried Line, The *105* 148 J2–3
Siena, city *43* 59 D5, *45* 61 A5, *49* 68 E7, *55* 76 C3, *59* 83 D3
Siena, republic *57* 80 J2
Sierra Leone *97* 136 A2, *122* 179 E1–2 (4)
Sierra Madre *63* 87 CD3
Sierra Madre del Sur *63* 87 AB2–3
Sighet Marmatiei *105* 147 K6
Signa (Seine) *46* 63 C4

Sigtuna 50 69 E2
Sijilmassa 32 44 B5
Sikelia (Sicilia) 20 24 AB6
Sikem (Nabulus) 15 17 B5, 26 35 B3
Sikiløy (Norse = Sicilia) 46 63 D6
Sikkim 99 140 E2, 127 184 DE2
Sikyon (Sicyon) 16 20 C5
Silesia (Schlesien) 53 73 E2, 55 76 D2, 70 100 FG4, 74 105 DE2, 75 106 D3, 86 122 E2–3, 114 166 DE3
Silistra 45 61 B5, 51 71 B5
Silk Road (Silk Route), The 32 44 J4
Silla (Korea) 32 45 F2
Silsile 14 15 C5
Silves 48 66 A5
Simbirsk 83 120 D4, 106 150 EF4
Simferopol 106 150 D6
Simla 127 184 C1
Simplon 55 77 C7
Simylla 32 44 H6
Sinai 14 15 C3, 118 173 BC6–7
Sind 32 45 A3, 38 52 J2, 38 53 A2, 64 89 A2, 99 140 AB2, 127 184 A2
Sindhu (Indus) 38 52 J1
Singapore 64 90 J6, 99 139 I3, 111 159 A3, 111 160 B7
Singara 26 34 G3
Singidunum (Beograd) 28 38 G3
Sinhala (Ceylon, Sri Lanka) 36 49 H6
Sinope 16 19 F1, 46 63 G5, 55 76 F3, 71 102 CD5
Sinus Arabicus (Red Sea) 28 38 IJ7
Sinus Persicus 28 38 L6
Sipka Pass 101 141 H4
Siponto 45 61 B5, 59 83 DE6
Sippar 11 10 E3, 12 12 E2
Siracusa (Syracuse) 50 70 D7, 53 73 E7, 84 121 F7, 87 124 C4
Siret 101 141 H3
Siriam 65 91 J3
Sirmium, city 26 34 D2, 28 38 F3
Sirmium, thema 45 61 C5
Sirte 112 162 C2
Sitones (Fenni) 32 44 C2
Sivas 108 153 C4
Siwa 108 153 AB5
Sjælland 70 100 DE2
Skagerrak 104 146 E2
Skamlingsbanken 86 123 A6
Skanör 57 79 D2
Skara 50 69 D2, 57 79 D2
Skara Brae 8 3 B4
Skie, see Skye
Skiringssal (Kaupang) 43 59 CD1, 46 63 D3, 50 69 D2
Skodar (Skutari), Albania 45 61 C5

Skopje (Üsküb) 45 61 C5, 107 151 D6
Skutari, Albania 101 141 F4
Skutari, Turkey 71 102 BC5, 101 141 I5
Skye (Skie) 47 64 A1, 52 72 B1
Skylletion 20 24 C6
Skyros 17 21 CD3, 88 125 C2
Skytopolis 26 35 C3
Skänninge 57 79 E2
Skálholt 41 56 I5, 46 63 B1
Skåne 43 59 D2, 69 99 B5, 70 100 E1
Slavic peoples 42 57 K4, 42 58 C1, 43 59 E3, 44 60 JK5
Slavonia 84 121 F5, 103 144 B2
Slesvig (Schleswig), principality 86 123 A5
Slesvig, city 84 121 E3, 86 123 AB6
Sligo 67 95 D6, 91 127 EF3
Slovakia 109 155 D6, 110 157 D4, 113 163 F3
Slovaks 43 59 E4, 44 60 I4
Slovenia 107 151 C4–5
Sluys 56 78 D3
Smolensk, city 41 56 K6, 55 76 E1, 82 119 F1, 107 151 E2, 113 163 D2
Smolensk, province 83 120 B4
Smorgon (Smorgoni) 82 119 E2, 105 147 KL5
Smyrna (Izmir) 45 61 E6, 91 116 E4, 101 141 HI6
Sneek 66 93 CD1
Sobibor 111 158 BC2
Sochi 106 150 E6
Society Islands 111 159 F4
Socotra, Sokotra 96 133 F4, 119 174 D7
Söderköping 57 79 E2
Soest 57 79 C4
Sofala 65 92 E4, 97 136 DE4
Sofia, Sophia (Serdika) 72 103 F5–6, 101 141 G4, 107 152 D5, 128 185 D4
Sogdiana 32 45 A2
Soissons 44 60 E3, 55 76, 52 72 DE4, 105 148 J2
Sokoto 32 44 B6
Soldau 70 100 H3
Solferino 87 124 AB1
Solikamsk 83 120 E3
Soloi, Asia Minor 16 19 F2
Soloi, Cyprus 16 19 F2
Solothurn 55 77 BC5
Somalia 122 179 F1–2, F5
Somerset 52 72 C4, 56 78 B3
Somerset House, London 66 94 C6
Somme 66 93 A4, 105 148 I2
Somnath 64 89 A2
Somosierra 81 118 C6
Sønder Borg 8 3 B7
Sønderborg 86 123 B6
Song 30 42 E2
Song kingdom 40 55 J4
Song-Bo (Black River) 124 181 B4

Song-Koi (Red River) 124 181 B4
Songhai 32 44 B6, 65 92 B1
Songhuajiang 102 142 D2
Songjin 119 175 C1
Soor 75 106 D3
Sopara 38 52 J2
Sopatma 32 44 HI6
Sorbonne, Paris 78 112 D6
Sorek 26 35 A4
Sordavala 69 99 E3
Sorek 26 35 A4
Sorrento 59 83 D7
Sotka-Koh 108 D3
South Africa, Republic of 122 179 D7
South America 60 84 DE5
South Australia 98 137 EE7
South Carolina 92 128 J3, 92 129 CD3, 93 130 F3
South China Sea, The 40 55 JK5–6, 99 139 J2, 111 160 B6
South Dakota 93 130 CD2
South Korea 119 175 BC2, EF3
South Sandwich Islands 120 176 F7
South Shields (Arbeia) 28 39 L1
South Vietnam 125 182 C3, F3
South-East Russia 78 111 EF1
South-West Africa (Namibia) 122 179 CD7
Southampton 52 72 C4, 56 78 B3, 67 95 F7, 68 97 B2
Southern France, Caves in 7
Southern Georgia 95 132 EF7, 120 176 EF7
Southern Prussia 73 104 C2
Southern Yemen 119 174 C7, 122 179 F4
Soviet Union (USSR) 107 151 E1, 110 157 E4, 112 161 EF2–3, 113 163 EF2, 115 168 EF3, 116 169 DE6
Spa 105 148 L1
Spain (Spania, Iberia, Hispania, Spanland) 97 A2, 16 19 AB2, 23 28 AB2, 24 31 A4, 24 32 AB6, 26 34 AB3, 28 38 BC3–4, 37 51 G1, 42 57 EF6–7, 42 58 A1–2, 46 63 AB5, 49 68 C7, 50 70 AB6–7, 72 103 AB6, 78 111 A2, 81 116 A4, 81 118, 84 121 B6, 91 127 FE7, 104 146 AB6, 108 154 AB4, 109 156 DE2, 115 168 A4, 116 169 AB5
Spandau, Berlin 114 167 D1
Spanish Emirate (Spanland) 37 51 G1, 43 59 B6, 46 63 AB5

Spanish Empire 1580 68 97
Spanish Guinea 113 164 C6
Spanish March 44 60 E5–6
Spanish Marocco 109 156 DE3
Spanish Netherlands, The 70 100 AB4
Spanish Sahara 113 164 C6
Spanland 46 63 AB5
Sparta (Lakedaimonia) 17 21 B4, 20 25 D3
Spartalos 17 21 C2
Speyer 29 40 B6, 44 60 G3
Spina 16 19 C1
Spion Cop 97 135 E6
Spitsbergen 60 84 G1
Split (Salonae) 109 155 C7
Spoleto, city 43 59 DE5, 45 61 A5, 47 65 D7
Spoleto, duchy 45 61 A5, 47 65 DE7
Spree 68 98 F2, 114 167 F2
Springfield 92 129 BC2, 93 130 E2
Sredne-Kolymsk 98 137 EF1
Sri Lanka (Ceylon, Sinhala) 64 89 C4, 65 91 I4, 99 140 CD5, 127 184 C5
Srinagar 65 91 H1
St. Petersburg (Novgorod), region 83 120 B3
St. Petersburg (Nyenskans, Petrograd) 71 101 J5, 76 107 E4, 81 116 E1
Stabrok (Georgetown) 94 131 KL5
Stade 68 98 C1
Stadtlohn 68 98 B2
Stalingrad (Tsaritsyn) 112 161 F4, 113 163 F3
Stamford Bridge 47 64 B1
Stanley Falls 96 133 CD5
Stanley's, Henry, explorations in Africa 96 133 E6
Stanleyville (Kisangani) 97 136 D3, 122 180 F1
Stans 55 77 D6
Stanwix (Petriana) 28 39 H1–2
Staraya Ladoga (Aldeigjuborg) 46 63 F2
Stargard 57 79 E3
Stavanger 69 99 A4, 110 157 C2
Stavropol 83 120 D6
Steglitz, Berlin 114 167 D2
Steiermark 53 73 E3, 68 97 DE2, 70 100 F6, 80 115 D1–2
Steinau 70 100 F4
Steinheim 7 1
Steinviksholm 69 99 B3
Stellenbosch 97 135 CD7
Stenay 48 66 E3
Stendal 57 79 D4
Stepney, London 66 94 E6
Stettin (Szczecin) 57 79 DE3, 68 98 F1, 69 99 B6, 81 116 CD2, 86 122 D2, 107 151 BC3, 113 163 A2, 114 166 D2, 128 185 BC2

Stiklestad 50 69 DE1
Stirling 77 109 E4
Stockholm 55 76 D1, 69 99 C4, 76 107 D4, 81 116 D1, 107 151 C2, 113 163 B1
Stockton 77 109 EF5
Stoke 76 108 B6
Stolbova 69 99 EF4
Stolpe 70 100 F2
Stonehenge 6 2 A5
Storowice 83 120 A4
Stralsund 57 79 D3, 68 98 E1, 69 99 B5, 86 122 D1
Strasbourg (Strassburg, Argentorate) 47 65 B4, 53 73 BC3, 55 76 BC2, 56 78 E4, 58 81 BC5, 70 100 C5, 72 103 C5, 81 116 C2, 84 121 D4, 107 151 B4
Stratford 68 97 B1
Strathclyde 44 60 DE1
Stratos 16 20 A4
Strymon, river 17 21 C1
Strymon, thema 45 61 D5, 44 60 K6
Studjanka 82 119 EF2
Stung Treng 124 181 C6
Stuttgart 114 166 BC4
Stutthof 111 158 B2
Stymphalis 16 20 C6
Suakin 96 133 E4, 97 136 E2
Suchou 35 48 C2
Sucre 95 132 C4
Sudan 122 179 D1, D4, 123 180 F1
Sudetenland 109 155 B5
Sudkawan 40 55 HI5
Sudrøyene (Hebrides) 46 63 B2
Suez 103 145 C6, 112 162 F2, 118 173 B6
Suez Canal 96 133 DE3, 118 173 B6
Suez, Gulf of 118 173 B7
Suffolk 52 72 D3, 56 78 C2
Sukadana 99 139 J3
Sukhona 83 120 C3
Sukhothai, city 38 52 B5
Sukhumi 106 150 E7
Sula Islands 99 139 L4
Sulaimaniya (Lullubi) 12 11 CD2
Sulawesi (Celebes) 126 183 C7
Sulu Archipelago 64 90 L5–6
Sulu Sea 99 139 K2
Sumatra 64 89 E4, 64 90 I6, 99 139 I3, 111 159 A3, 111 160 AB7, 126 183 B7
Sumba 99 139 K5
Sumbawa 99 139 K4
Sumbra 64 90 I2
Sumer 11 10 F4, 12 11 D3
Sundgau 70 100 C6
Sundsvall 69 99 C3
Sungir 6 2 D1
Sunion, Cape 16 20 F6
Suomussalmi 110 157 E1
Surabaja 64 90 K7, 99 139 J4
Surakarta 99 139 J4

Surashtra *38* **52** J2
Surat *64* **89** B2, *99* **140** B3
Surgut *35* **48** B1
Surinam *95* **132** D2
Surparaka *38* **53** A2
Surrey, London *66* **94** D7
Susa *12* **11** D3, *13* **14** CB6, *21*
　26 D2
Susdal *51* **71** D2, *83* **120** C3
Sussex *52* **72** D4, *56* **78** C3
Sutkagen-Dor *108* **CD3**
Sutlej *36* **49** G4
Sutton Hoo *43* **59** C3
Svalbard *120* **176** G1
Svear, people (Swedes) *43* **59**
　D1
Sverdlovsk (Yekaterinburg)
　83 **120** EF3
Sverdrup Islands *60* **84** D1
Sviar *46* **63** E2
Svir *51* **71** C1, *84* **121** H1
Swabia (Schwaben) *47* **65**
　BC4, *50* **70** C6, *53* **73** C3
Swabian kingdom *42* **57** E5–6
Swabians *42* **57** HI4, *42* **58**
　A1
Swakopmund *97* **136** C4
Swanscombe *7* **1**
Swansea *77* **109** D7
Swatow (Shantou) *102* **142**
　BC6
Swaziland *97* **135** E6, *122* **179**
　DE7
Sweden (Sverige) *55* **76** D1,
　57 **79** EF1, *69* **99** C3, *70*
　100 EF1, *72* **103** DE2, *81*
　116 CD1, *82* **119** D1, *84*
　121 EF1, *104* **146** EF1, *107*
　151 C2, *110* **157** 83 CD2,
　113 **163** AB1, *114* **166** D1,
　115 **168** CD2
Swedish Pomerania *82* **119**
　D2
Swiss Confederation (Die
　Eidgenossenschaft) *55* **77**,
　70 **100** C6
Switzerland *75* **106** C5, *84*
　121 DE5, *87* **124** A1, *104*
　146 DE5, *107* **151** B4, *108*
　154 CD3, *115* **168** C3
Sword Beach *113* **165** B4
Sybaris *20* **24** C5, *20* **25** B3
Sydney *98* **137** F7
Syene (Aswan) *11* **10** C5, *14*
　15 BC6
Syktyvkar *106* **150** E2
Sylt *86* **123** A6
Syracuse (Syrakusai, Syra-
　cusae, Siracusa) *16* **19** C2,
　20 **24** B7, *22* **27** E7, *43* **59**
　E7, *45* **61** B7, *112* **162** C1
Syr-Darja (Jaxartes) *40* **55** F3
Syria *109* **82**, *12* **12** C2, *15* **18**
　F4, *21* **26** B2, *24* **31** G6, *24*
　32 F6, *28* **38** J5, *71* **102**
　CD7
Syros *17* **21** D4, *88* **125** C3
Syrtis Major *28* **38** F6
Syrtis Minor *28* **38** E5–6
Szczecin, see Stettin

Szeged (Szegedin) *91* **127** J5,
　101 **141** F3

T

Ta Khli *125* **182** A2
Tabaristan *37* **51** K1
Tabasco *63* **87** BC2
Tabor *26* **35** BC2
Tabriz *34* **47** B6, *71* **102** E5–6
Tacna *95* **132** C4
Tacola *32* **44** J7
Taegu *119* **175** C3
Taganrog *106* **150** DE6
Tagliacozzo *53* **73** DE5
Tagus, see Tajo
Taibei (Taipei) *99* **139** E4,
　117 **170** E6
Taillebourg *52* **72** D6
Taima *118* **173** E7
Taiwan (Formosa) *35* **48**
　EF3, *102* **142** C6, *111* **160**
　C6, *117* **170** E7
Taiyuan *35* **48** DE2
Tajmyr *98* **137** BC1
Tajo (Tagus) *42* **57** E6, *43* **59**
　A6, *84* **121** AB6
Takla Makan *117* **170** A5
Talas *32* **45** B2
Talavera *81* **118** B6
Talcahuano *95* **132** BC6
Tallinn (Reval) *107* **151** D1,
　110 **157** DE2, *113* **163** C1,
　128 **185** C1
Talmis *14* **15** BC6
Tamanrasset (Fort Laperri-
　ne) *96* **134** C2
Tamatave *97* **136** EF4
Tambov *106* **150** D4
Tamil Nadu *127* **184** C4–5
Tammerfors (Tampere) *83*
　120 A2
Tampa *62* **85** C3, *121* **178** A1
Tampico *62* **85** B3, *121* **177**
　A1
Tamralipti *38* **52** L2, *38* **53**
　C2
Tamraparni (Sri Lanka) *38*
　52 K3
Tana (Tanais) *34* **47** B6, *46* **63**
　G4, *55* **76** F2
Tanagra *16* **20** E5
Tanais (Don), river *28* **38** J2
Tanais (Tana), city *16* **19** F1,
　32 **44** E4
Tananarive *97* **136** EF4
Tanganyika (Tanzania) *122*
　179 F2, *123* **180** F2
Tanganyika, Lake *96* **133** D6,
　102 **142** DE6
Tanggu *102* **142** B3
Tang-hsiang *32* **45** D3
Tangiers (Tingis) *37* **51** G1,
　43 **59** A7, *55* **76** A4, *68* **97**
　A4, *81* **116** A4, *96* **134** A1,
　97 **136** B1, *104* **146** A7
Tanimbar Islands *99* **139** L4
Tanis *109* **A3–4**, *11* **10** BC4,
　14 **15** B1, *16* **19** F3
Tanjore *38* **53** B3

Tannenberg *105* **147** J5
Tanta *118* **173** A6
Tanzania (Tanganyika) *122*
　179 F2, E6
Taormina *43* **59** E5, *44* **60** I7
Tarabulus (Tripoli) *122* **179**
　C3
Tarakan *43* **59** E6, *111* **159**
　B3, *111* **160** BC7
Taranto (Taras, Tarentum)
　45 **61** B6
Tarapaca *95* **132** C4
Taras (Tarentum) *16* **19** D2,
　20 **24** C5, *22* **27** F4–5
Tarawa *111* **160** E7
Targowica (Targowitz) *73*
　104 F3
Tarhuna *112* **162** C2
Tarifa *42* **57** E7
Tarija *95* **132** C4
Tarim *35* **48** B2
Tarnopol *105* **147** K6
Tarnow *104* **146** G4, *105* **147**
　J6
Tarpeian Rock, Rome *27* **37**
　HI4
Tarquinii *22* **27** C4
Tarracina (Anxur) *22* **27**
　CD4
Tarraco *23* **28** C2, *32* **44** B4
Tarraconensis *28* **38** BC3
Tarragona *43* **59** C6, *59* **83**
　BC6, *109* **156** F2
Tarranova *57* **80** K4
Tarsus (Tarsos) *28* **38** I5, *36*
　49 D4
Tartars, people *32* **45** DE1
Tartessos *16* **19** A2
Tarut *108* **A3**
Tashkent *40* **55** G3, *98* **137**
　B3
Tasmania *60* **84** K6, *120* **176**
　K6
Tatarsk *83* **120** E2
Tatta (Sind), region in India
　65 **91** G2
Tatta, city *65* **91** G2
Tauroeis *20* **24** B6
Tauromenium (Tauromeni-
　on, Taormina) *22* **27** E6
Taurus *12* **11** B2
Tavastehus *69* **99** D4
Taxila *21* **26** F2, *38* **52** JK1
Tbilisi *106* **150** F7
Tchad (Chad) *122* **179** F1,
　CD4
Tchad, Lake *32* **44** CD6, *96*
　133 C4
Tebuk *108* **153** C5
Tegea *16* **20** C6
Tegel, Berlin *114* **167** D1
Tegeler See, Berlin *114* **167**
　D1
Tegucigalpa *63* **87** EF4, *121*
　177 B2
Teheran (Rai) *103* **145** D5
Tehuantepec, Isthmus of *63*
　87 C2
Teima *24* **31** G7
Tekrur *65* **92** A1

Tel Aviv *118* **171** A2, *118* **172**
　E2
Tel Aviv-Jaffa *118* **173** C5
Telamon *22* **27** BC3
Tell Abu Hureyra *6* **2** D3
Tell Asmar (Eshunna) *11* **10**
　EF3
Tell Halaf *6* **2** D3
Telmessos *23* **30** B7
Temala *32* **44** J6
Temesvar (Timisoara) *101*
　141 F3
Tempelhof, Berlin *114* **167**
　E2
Temple, London *66* **94** C6
Tengchiao *124* **181** D5
Tennessee, river *92* **128** J2–3
Tennessee, state *92* **129** BC3,
　93 **130** EF3
Tenochtitlan (Mexico) *63* **87**
　D4
Tenos *63* **87** D4
Teos *17* **21** E3
Teotihuacan *63* **87** A2
Tepe Hissar *108* **BC1**
Tepe Yahya *108* **C3**
Tepti *64* **89** B2
Teresina *95* **132** E3
Tergeste, see Trieste
Termessos *23* **30** B7
Termopylene *13* **14** A6, *16* **20**
　C4
Ternopol *91* **127** K4
Terranova *57* **80** K4
Terschelling *66* **93** C1
Teruel *55* **76** AB3, *109* **156**
　EF2
Teschen (Tesin) *101* **141** F1
Tete *96* **133** D6, *122* **179** DE6
Teutoburgerwald *28* **38** EF2
Teutonic Order, The *50* **70**
　D5, E4, *55* **76** DE1, *57* **79**
　F2–3, *59* **82** C1
Texas *92* **129** A4, *93* **130** D4
Texel *66* **93** C1
Teyat *9* **7** B1
Thaenae *28* **38** E5
Thai kingdom *40* **55** I5–6
Thailand (Siam) *64* **89** E2–3,
　111 **159** A2, *111* **160** AB6,
　124 **181** AB5, *125* **182** A2,
　DE2, A6
Thames *53* **73** A2, *66* **94**
　E6–7
Thamugadi (Timgad) *28* **38**
　D5
Thanesar *38* **53** B1
Thanesar *38* **53** B1
Thang Long (Hanoi) *65* **91**
　KL3
Thanh Hoa *65* **91** L3, *124* **181**
　C5
Thapsacus (Thapsakos) *23*
　30 DE7
Thapsus (Thapsos) *16* **19** C3,
　24 **32** C7
Thar *64* **89** A1–2
Tharros *16* **19** C2
Thasos *17* **21** D1, *20* **25** D2
Thaton *39* **54** A5

Théâtre Français, Paris *78*
　112 CD6
The German Empire *56* **78**
　E3–4, *58* **81** C5, *59* **82**
　BC2, *69* **99** AB7, *91* **127**
　HI4
Theatrum Balbi, Rome *27* **36**
　K6
Theatrum Pompeii, Rome *27*
　36 K6
Thebae *32* **44** E5–6
Thebae (Karnak-Luxor) *11*
　10 B5, *12* **11** A4, *14* **15** C5
Thebes *12* **20** E5, *17* **21** C3
Theiss (Tisza) *44* **60** J4, *107*
　152 D4
Themistocles' Wall, Acropo-
　lis *19* **23** CD1
Theocoleum (Theokoleion),
　Olympia *18* **22** D6
Theodosia (Kaffa) *28* **38** HI3
Theodosiupolis *45* **61** GH5
Thera *17* **21** D4, *88* **125** C4
Theresienstadt *111* **158** AB2
Therma, see Thessaloniki
Thermos *16* **20** B4
Thespiai *16* **20** DE5
Thessalia *17* **21** B2, *20* **25**
　CD3, *101* **141** G6, *103* **144**
　C3
Thessaloniki (Salonike,
　Therma), city *17* **21** B1, *41*
　56 K7, *45* **61** D6, *55* **76** D3
Thessaloniki, thema *45* **61**
　CD6
Thingvellir *46* **63** B1
Thinis *12* **11** A4
Thorikos *16* **20** F6
Thorn *55* **76** D2, *57* **79** F3, *84*
　121 F3
Thrace (Thracia) *21* **26** AB1,
　103 **144** D3, *107* **152** E6
Thracian Sea, The *17* **21**
　CD2
Thracians *9* **6** F6
Thrakesion *44* **60** L6, *45* **61** E6
Thun *55* **77** C6
Thurgau *55* **77** DE5
Thuria *16* **20** B7
Thüringen *42* **57** H4, *43* **59**
　D3, *45* **62** K6, *47* **65** CD3,
　53 **73** C2, *114* **166** C3
Thuringian March *47* **65**
　DE2–3
Thurii *22* **27** EF5
Thurso *67* **95** E4
Thusis *55* **77** C6
Thyreia *16* **20** C7
Tiahuanaco *63* **86** BC3
Tianjin (Tientsin) *35* **48**
　DE2, *102* **142** B3, *117* **170**
　B3, *111* **160** A5
Tiber, Rome *27* **36** JK5, *7*
Tiberias *26* **35** BC2
Tiberis (Tiber) *22* **27** C3, *27*
　36 K7
Tibet *35* **48** BC3, *99* **140**
　DE1, *111* **160** A5
Tientsin (Tianjin) *102* **142**
　B3, *111* **160** A5

Tiergarten, Berlin *114* 167 DE1

Tierra de los Bacallaos (Newfoundland) 62 85 EF2

Tierra del Fuego 95 *132* CD7

Tiflis *34* 47 B6, 71 102 E5

Tigranocerta *24* 32 F6, *28* 38 JK4

Tigris *12* 11 C2, *12* 12 E2, *28* 38 K5

Tikal 63 87 E3

Tikhvin (Tikvin) *106* 150 C3, *110* 157 F2

Tiksi 89 126 J5

Tiku 64 90 I6

Tilsit 70 100 H2, 81 116 D1, *105* 148 K4, *107* 151 D2

Timbuktu 65 92 B1, 97 136 B2

Timgad (Thamugadi) *28* 38 D5

Timian *111* 160 D6

Timor 99 *139* L4, *111* 159 B4, *111* 160 C7, *126* 183 D7

Tindouf 96 *134* A2

Tingis (Tangier) *32* 44 A5

Tipasa *16* 19 B2

Tippermuir 67 95 E5

Tiran, Strait of *118* 173 C7

Tirana *107* 151 CD6, *110* 157 D6, *128* 185 C4

Tirlemont *105* 148 K1

Tirnovo 45 61 D5

Tirol (Tyrol) 68 97 D2, 70 100 D6, 72 103 D5, 78 111 BC2, 80 115 C2, 81 116 C3, *84* 121 E5, *87* 124 B1, *101* 141 C2, *107* 152 A1

Tirsa *15* 18 E5

Tiryns *16* 20 D4

Tisza (Theiss) *101* 141 F2

Titicaca, Lake 63 86 BC3

Titus, Arch of, Rome *27* 37 L4

Tivoli *45* 61 A6, *57* 80 JK2

Tjøtta 46 63 B2

Tlaxcala 63 87 AB2

Tlemcen *37* 51 G1, 96 *134* B1

Tmutarakan *51* 71 D5

Tobol *36* 49 F2

Tobolsk *35* 48 B1, 98 *137* B2

Tobruk *112* 161 D7, *112* 162 E2

Togo 97 *136* B2–3, *122* 179 B5

Tokelau Islands *111* 159 E3

Tokyo (Edo) 98 *137* F4, *102* 142 F3

Toledo (Toletum) *23* 28 B2, *43* 59 AB6, *55* 76 A3, *59* 83 AB7, *81* 116 A4

Tollund *8* 4 B1, *9* 6 DE5

Tolosa (Toulouse) *25* 33 B4, *42* 57 G6

Toltec culture 63 87 A1

Tomebamba 63 86 AB2

Tomi *18* 38 B3, *32* 44 D4

Tomsk 98 *137* B2

Tønder *44* 60 G2, 86 *123* A6

Tongoland 97 *135* EF6

Tonkin 98 *137* D4, *124* 181 C4

Tonkin, Gulf of *124* 181 CD4–5

Tonlé Sap *124* 181 B6

Tønning 86 *123* A6

Tor Bay 67 95 E7

Tordesillas *55* 76 AB3, *81* 118 B6

Torgau 74 *105* D2, *112* 161 BC4

Torino (Augusta Taurinorum) *43* 59 CD5, *47* 65 B5, *49* 68 DE6, 79 *113* C2

Torneå (Tornio) 69 99 D2, *110* 157 DE1

Toronto 92 *129* CD1

Tortosa, Spain *46* 63 BC5, *82* 119 B4, *109* 156 F2

Tortosa, Tripoli 49 67 K2

Torun *110* 157 D4

Tosali (Dhauli) *38* 52 L2

Tothill Fields, London 66 94 B7

Totma *106* 150 D3

Toufan *32* 45 C3

Touggourt 96 *134* C1

Toul *47* 65 B4, *53* 73 B3

Toulon *47* 65 A6, *56* 78 E7, 79 *113* C3, 79 *114* C3, *81* 116 BC3, *82* 119 C3

Toulouse (Tolosa) *43* 59 C5, *48* 66 D4, *49* 68 CD6, *56* 78 CD7, *59* 83 B6, 76 *107* B6, 79 *113* B3, 79 *114* B3, *81* 116 B3, *81* 118 D5

Toumai *50* 69 O4

Toungoo *34* 54 A5, *40* 55 I5

Tourane (Da Nang) *82* 119 D5

Tournai *50* 69 C4, *56* 78 D3, *105* 148 J1

Tours *43* 59 C4, *46* 63 C4, *52* 72 D5, *56* 78 C5, *59* 83 B5

Tower, London 66 94 D6

Townsville 98 *137* F6

Towton *56* 78 D2

Trabzon *108* 153 C4

Trachonitis *26* 35 D2

Trafalgar *81* 116 A4

Trafalgar, Cape *81* 118 AB7

Tragurium *22* 27 E3

Trajan's Column, Rome *27* 37 J1

Trajan's Forum, Rome *27* 37 J1

Trajan, Temple of, Rome *27* 37 J1

Tranquebar 64 89 BC4, 65 91 HI4, 99 *140* C4

Transjordan *108* 153 C5

Trans-Siberian Railway 98 *137* D3

Transvaal 96 *133* DE7, 97 *135* E6

Transylvania (Siebenbürgen) *55* 76 DE3, *81* 116 DE3, *84* 121 G4–5

Trapan (Trapani) *54* 74 C3, *57* 80 J4

Trapezunt (Trapezus) *16* 19 F1, *45* 61 GH5, *54* 74 F3

Trasimenus (Trasimeno) *23* 28 E2

Travancore 99 *140* BC5

Traventhal 68 98 D1

Trebia *23* 28 D1

Trelleborg 46 63 DE3

Trento (Trient) *101* 141 C3, *102* 143 DE7

Treptow, Berlin *109* 156 E2

Treviso *44* 60 H4, *49* 68 E6

Tribur *47* 65 C3

Trichinopoly 99 *140* C4

Trient (Trento) *57* 80 J1, *101* 141 C3

Trient, bishopric 70 *100* DE7

Trier (Augusta Treverorum), city *47* 65 B3, *49* 68 DE5, *56* 78 E4, *59* 83 C5

Trier, archbishopric 68 98 B4, 70 *100* C5

Trieste (Tergeste) *87* 124 B1, *101* 141 D3, *107* 151 C5

Trikkala 88 *125* AB2

Trincomalee 99 *140* CD5

Trinidad and Tobago *121* 177 E2

Trinidad, Bolivia, city 95 *132* C4

Trinidad, state 95 *132* D2

Trinil *7* 1

Tripoli (Libya) 71 102 A7, 96 *133* C3

Tripoli (Tarabulus esh Sham), crusader stronghold 49 67 JK2

Tripoli (Tarabulus), city Libya *55* 76 F4, 96 *134* D1, *112* 161 B7, *112* 162 C2, *122* 179 CD1, C3

Tripoli, Syria, city 49 67 K3, *54* 74 F4

Tripolis, Greece 88 *125* B3

Tripolitania 96 *134* CD1, *107* 152 A1–2

Tripura 99 *140* E3, *127* 184 E3

Tristan da Cunha 60 84 E6

Trivandrum *127* 184 B5

Troizen *16* 20 DE6

Tromelin 97 *136* F4

Tromsø *110* 157 D1

Trondhiems len 69 99 AB3

Trondhjem (Trondheim) *84* 121 E1, *110* 157 CD2

Troppau *84* 121 F4, *86* 122 EF3

Troy, Troja (Ilion) *8* 5 D3

Troyes *52* 72 E5, *56* 78 D4, 79 *113* B1

Trujillo 95 *132* B3, *121* 177 B2

Trundholm *8* 4 B, *9* 6 E5

Truso 46 63 E3

Tsaritsyn (Stalingrad) 83 120 D5, *106* 150 E5

Tsingtao (Qingdao) 98 *137* E4, *102* 143 E7

Tsushima *102* 142 DE4, *102* 143 F7

Tsushima Strait *102* 142 D4

Tuam *50* 69 A3, 67 95 D6

Tuaregs, people *32* 44 C6

Tübingen *58* 81 C5, *114* 166 B4

Tucso (Tucson) 93 *130* B3–4, 94 *131* 14

Tucumán 63 86 BC4, 95 *132* C5

Tudela *81* 118 C5, *91* 127 F6

Tughluq (Tughlak) dynasty 64 89

Tuileries, Jardin des, Paris *78* 112 C5

Tula, Mexico 63 87 A1

Tula, Soviet Union 71 *101* K5

Tulagi *111* 160 DE7

Tullianum, Rome *27* 37 J2

Tumasik *40* 55 J6

Tumatorp 46 63 E3

Tumbez 62 85 C5, 63 86 A2

Tune 46 63 D3

Tunes (Tunis) *22* 27 B7

Tungashadra 64 89 B3

Tunguses, people *35* 48 CD1

Tunis, city *44* 60 G7, 68 97 D4, 96 *134* C1, 97 136 C1, *112* 161 B6, *112* 162 B1, *122* 179 CD1, C3

Tunis, emirate *37* 51 H1

Tunisia *82* 119 C5, *84* 121 E7, 96 *134* CD1, 97 136 C1, *112* 161 B7, *112* 162 B1, *122* 179 CD1, C3

Turkey *107* 151 E6, *108* 153 C4, *110* 157 F6, *112* 162 F1, *116* 169 DE7

Turkish (Ottoman) Empire, The *82* 119 EF3–4, *84* 121 GH5–6, *101* 141 G–J5–6, *103* 144 EF3–4, *103* 145 BC5

Turkmenians 83 *120* F6

Turkmenistan *103* 145 E5

Turov *51* 71 B3

Tuscany (Toscana) *44* 60 GH5, 68 97 D3, 72 103 D6, 80 115 C3–4, *84* 121 E5, *87* 124 B2

Tushpa 8 5 F3, *12* 12 E1

Tuttul *12* 11 C2

Tuva *113* 164 E5

Tuy Hoa *125* 182 C3

Tuyana *45* 61 G6, *48* 66 K5

Tyne *28* 39 J1–2

Tyras (Dniestr), river *28* 38 GH3

Tyras, city *16* 19 E1

Tyros (Tyrus), Syria *10* 9 A3, *12* 12 C2, *21* 26 B2, *48* 66 KL6, 49 67 J3, *55* 76 F4

Tyros, Peloponnes *16* 20 D7

Tyros, Phoenicia *11* 10 C3, *15* 18 E4, *26* 35 B1

Tyrrhenian Sea, (Mare Tyrrhenum) *57* 80 JK3, 87 124 B3

Tyumen *35* 48 AB1

U

Uaxactún 63 87 DE2

Ubangi 96 *133* C5

Überlingen 70 *100* C6

Ubon (Ubon Ratchathani) *125* 182 B2, D2

Ucciali *107* 152 BC3

Udaipur 64 89 C2

Udine 80 115 D2, *101* 141 D3

Udon Thani *125* 182 D2

Ufa 98 *137* A3, *106* 150 F3

Uganda 97 136 D3, *122* 179 F2(?), (Res, Damas) 83 F1

Ugarit (Ras Shamra) *8* 5 E3–4, *10* 9 AB2, *12* 12 C2

Uglitsj 71 *101* JK5

Uighur Empire (Mongolia) *32* 45 D2

Uighurs, people *36* 49 GH3, *40* 55 GH3

Uijij 96 *133* D6, 97 136 D3

Ujjain *38* 53 AB2

Uka 98 *137* F2

Ukraine (Ukraina) 71 *101* J6, *106* 150 C5–6, *107* 151 E3, *113* 163 CD3

Ulan Bator (Urga) 98 *137* D3

Ulan-Ude *111* 160 B4

Ulcinj (Dulcigno) *88* 125 A1

Uleåborg (Oulu) 69 99 D2

Ulm *53* 73 C3, 70 *100* D6, 81 116 C3

Ulster *56* 78 A1, 67 95 D6, *81* 116 A1

Uman *110* 157 F4

Umbria *22* 27 C3

Umeå 69 99 C3, 72 103 D2

Umma *12* 11 C3

Union of South Africa *122* 179 B2

United Arab Emirates *119* 174 CD6, *120* 176 H5, *122* 179 F4

United Netherlands, The (see also Netherlands) 66 93, 68 98 AB2, *84* 121 D3

United States of America 92 128, 92 129, 93 130, *113* 164, *120* 176

United States, The (USA) 93 130, *105* 149 AB2, *113* 164 AB6, *120* 176 BC3

Unter-Walhis *55* 77 B7

Unterwalden *55* 77 CD6

Upernavik 60 84 E2

Upper Burgundy *47* 65 BA4–5

Upper Egypt *11* 10 BC5, *14* 15 AB4

Upper Lorraine (Lotheringen), duchy *47* 65 AB4, *53* 73 BC3

Upper Volta 97 136 B2, 122 179 E1 (2), B4

Uppland E1

Uppsala 41 56 JK5, 43 59 E1, 49 68 EF4, 55 76 D1, 58 81 D2, 59 83 DE2, 81 116 C1

Ur 11 10 F4, 12 11 CD3, 12 12 E3

Ural Mountains 83 120 EF2

Ural, river 83 120 EF2

Uralsk, city 83 120 E4

Uralsk, region 83 120 F5

Urartu 8 5 F3, 12 12 E1

Urbillum (Erbil) 12 11 C2

Urbino 57 81 D2

Urga (Ulan Bator) 98 137 D3

Urgench 34 47 B6

Uri 55 77 D6

Urmia, Lake 51 71 EF7

Urnfield culture 8 5 BC2

Uruguay 95 132 D5, 113 164 · B7

Uruk (Warka) 11 10 E4, 12 11 C3

USA, see United States

Usedom 68 98 EF1

Ushuaia 95 132 C7

Üsküb (Skopje) 103 144 C3

Ust-Kamchatsk 98 137 D3

Ust-Olenjok 98 137 C1

Utah 93 130 B2

Utah Beach 113 165 B1

Utica 16 19 C2, 23 28 E3

Utrecht, bishopric 66 93 C2

Utrecht, city 43 59 C3, 50 69 C3, 66 93 C2

Uttar Pradesh 127 184 C2

Uxellodunum (Castlesteads) 28 39 I1

Uxmal 63 87 D1

Uzbeks 35 48 A2

V

Vaal 97 135 D6

Vaasa (Vasa) 106 150 A2

Väc (Waitzen) 45 61 C4

Vada Sabatia 22 27 AB2

Vadstena 50 69 E2, 55 76 D1

Vågan 69 99 BC1

Valacia 55 76 E3, 58 81 F5, 72 103 F5, 81 116 E3, 82 119 E3, 83 120 A5, 84 121 GH5, 101 141 G3, 103 144 D2

Valdai 106 150 C3

Valdivia 62 85 CD6, 95 132 BC6

Valence 49 68 D6, 52 72 EF6, 79 114 C3, 81 116 B3

Valencia (Valentia), city 23 28 B2, 49 68 C7, 55 76 B3, 59 83 B7, 68 97 B3, 81 116 B4, 81 118 CD6, 109 156 F2

Valenciennes 56 78 D3, 79 114 B1

Valentia, province 28 38 D1, 68 97 B3–4

Valladolid 49 68 C6, 81 116 A3, 81 118 B6

Valland, (West Frankish Kingdom) 46 63 C5

Vallum Antonini 25 33 A1, 28 38 D1

Vallum Hadriani (Hadrians Wall) 25 33 AB1, 28 38 D1, 28 39

Valmy 79 113 BC1, 79 114 C2, 81 116 B2

Valona (Vloré) 101 141 F5

Valparaiso 95 132 BC5

Vancouver 93 130 A1

Vandals, Kingdom of the 42 57 GH6–7

(V)Andalucia 42 57 EF6

Vänern (Wener) 57 79 DE1

Vannes 44 60 D4

Vanuatu 120 176 L5

Varanasi (Benares) 127 184 D2

Varberg 57 79 D2

Vardar 101 141 G5

Vardø (Vardøhus) 60 84 G2, 69 99 E1, 72 103 E1

Vardøhus len 69 99 C1–2

Varennes 79 114 C1, 81 116 BC2

Varna 55 76 E3, 71 102 B5, 101 141 I4, 107 151 E5

Varnavino 106 150 DE3

Vasa (Vaasa) 69 99 CD3

Vassy 68 97 C1–2

Västergarn 50 69 E2

Västervik 57 79 E2

Västerås 50 69 E2, 55 76 CD1, 69 99 C4

Vättern 57 79 DE2

Vaucelles 58 81 A4

Vauxhall, London 66 94 C7

Vaud 55 77 A6

Växjö 70 100 EF1

Veji 22 27 C4

Vejle 86 123 AB5

Veles 88 125 AB1

Velia (Elea) 22 27 E5

Veliki Ustyug 71 101 KL5

Velikiye Luki 106 150 BC4, 112 161 DE3

Velsk 106 150 D2

Veltin 55 77 E7

Vendée 79 114 A2

Vendel 43 59 E2

Vendôme 48 66 CD3, 68 97 B2

Venetian Republic 45 61 A5, 50 70 D6, 53 73 DE4–5, 57 80 J1, 68 97 B1, 72 103 D5, 80 115 CD3, 87 124 B1, 101 141 CD3

Venezuela 95 132 C2, 113 164 B6, 121 177 D3

Vengi 38 53 B3

Venice (Venetia, Venezia) 22 27 C1, 23 28 E1

Venice, city 47 65 D5, 55 76 C3, 57 80 JK1, 59 83 D6, 68 97 D2, 76 107 CD6, 81 116 C3, 87 124 B1, 107 151 B5

Venlo 66 93 D3

Venta 91 127 F6

Venus and Roma, Temple of, Rome 27 37 L3–4

Vera Cruz (Veracruz) 63 87 B2, 64 88 A6, 121 177 A1

Vercellae 22 27 A2, 24 32 C5

Vercelli 49 68 DE6

Vercovisium (Housesteads) 28 39 J1

Verde, Cape 60 84 F4, 122 179 A4

Verden 50 69 D3, 53 73 C1

Verdun 47 65 AB4, 56 78 E4, 104 146 D4, 105 148 K2

Vereeniging 97 135 E6

Verkhoyansk 98 137 DE1

Vermandois 52 72 E4

Vermont 92 129 D1, 93 130 G1–2

Verona, city 22 27 C2, 57 80 J1, 87 124 B1, 107 151 B5

Verona, county (hist.) 47 65 D5

Versailles 72 103 B5, 79 113 B1, 107 151 A4

Vesontio 25 33 C3

Vespasian's Forum (Forum Pacis) 27 37 KL2

Vesta, Temple of, Rome 27 37 K3

Vestal Virgins, House of the, Rome 27 37 K3

Vestprém (Weissbrunn) 45 61 B4

Vesuvius 22 27 D4

Vézelay 48 66 D3

Via Appia 22 27 F4, 27 36 L7 JK7

Via Campana, Rome 27 36 JK7

Via Flaminia 22 27 C3, 27 36 K5

Via Latina, Rome 27 36 L7

Via Nova, Rome 27 37 K4

Via Ostiensis, Rome 27 36 K7

Via Sacra, Rome 27 36 L7, 27 37 KL3

Via Salaria 27 36 L5

Viborg (Viipuri), Finland 69 99 F4, 71 101 J5, 83 120 B2–3, 107 151 DE1

Viborg, Denmark 50 69 D3, 69 99 A5

Vicenza 49 68 E6, 53 73 D4

Vichy 110 157 B5, 112 161 A4

Vichy-France 110 157 B5

Vicksburg 92 129 B4

Victoria Falls 96 133 CD6

Victoria Island 60 84 C2

Victoria, Commonwealth of Australia 98 137 F7

Victoria, Lake 96 133 DE5

Victoria, Seychelles 122 179 F6

Vicus Jugarius, Rome 27 37 I3–4

Vicus Longus, Rome 27 36 L6

Vicus Patricius, Rome 27 36 L6

Viedma 95 132 D6

Vien Chang 39 54 B5

Vienna (Vindobona) 47 65 F4, 49 68 EF6, 55 76 D2, 76 107 D6, 81 116 D2, 84 121 F4, 107 151 C4, 113 163 A3

Vienne (Vienna), city 45 62 K7, 59 83 C6

Vienne, river 44 60 E4

Vientiane 124 181 B5, 125 182 A2, DE2, AB5

Vierwaldstätter, lake 55 77 CD6

Vietnam (Annam) 39 54 BC4, 124 181 C5–6, 125 182 BC6

Vigo 109 156 D1–2

Viipuri (Viborg) 110 157 E2, 112 161 D2

Vijaya (Binh Dinh) 39 54 C6

Vijayanagar, city 65 91 H3

Vijayanagar, state 40 55 G6, 64 89 B3

Vilcas 63 86 B3

Villafranca 87 124 B1

Villahermosa 121 177 A2

Vilna (Vilnius, Wilno) 81 116 DE1, 82 119 E2, 105 147 K4, 107 151 D2, 113 163 C2, 128 185 C2

Vilyui 98 137 C2

Vilyuisk 98 137 D2

Vimeiro 81 118 A6

Viminal, Rome 27 36 L6

Vindhya Mountains 64 89 B2

Vindobona (Vienna) 28 38 F3

Vindolanda (Chesterholme) 28 39 J1–2

Vindomora (Ebchester) 28 39 K2

Vindovala (Rudchester) 28 39 K1

Vinh Linh 124 181 C5, 125 182 B2

Vinland (Norse = Newfoundland) 60 84 E3

Virginia, city 60 84 D3

Virginia, state 92 128 J2, 92 129 CD3, 93 130 F3

Virland 46 63 F3

Viroconium 25 33 A2

Virunum 26 34 D2

Visakhapatnam 99 140 D3

Visby 55 76 D1, 57 79 E2, 69 99 C4

Visigoth Kingdom 42 57 EF6, 42 58 A2

Visigoths (Western Goths) 42 57 B3

Vissingen 66 93 B3

Vitebsk 46 63 F3, 81 116 E1, 82 119 E1, 106 150 E2, 113 163 CD2

Viterbo 45 61 A5, 53 73 D5

Vitoria, Brazil 95 132 F4

Vitoria, Spain 81 116 AB3, 81 118 BC5

Vladimir, northeast of Moscow 41 56 L6, 83 120 C3

Vladimir, principality of Kiev 51 71 A4

Vladivostok 98 137 E3, 102 142 D2

Vlieland 66 93 C1

Vlorë (Valona) 88 125 A1

Vltava (Moldau) 68 98 F4

Volga 83 120 D5, 113 163 E1

Volga Bulgars 46 63 H3, 51 71 F3

Volhynia 73 104 E3, 84 121 GH3, 107 151 DE3

Vologda 83 120 C3, 110 157 F2

Volos 88 125 B2

Volsinii 22 27 C3

Volta 65 92 B2

Vorarlberg 70 100 D6

Vorder-Rhein (Rhine) 55 77 DE6

Vordingborg 69 99 B5

Voronezh (Asov), province 83 120 C4–5

Voronezh, city 83 120 C4, 106 150 D5, 113 163 E3

Vouillé 42 57 G5

Vulcan Islands 111 160 D5–6

Vulci 22 27 C3

Vung Tau 125 182 B3

Vyadhapura 32 44 K7

Vyatich 46 63 G3

Vyatka, city 71 101 KL5, 106 150 E3

Vyatka, river 83 120 D3

Vyazma 110 157 F3, 112 161 E3, 113 163 D2

Vytegra 106 150 C3

W

Waadt 55 77 B6

Wadai 96 133 C4

Wadi el-Allaki 14 15 D7

Wadi Halfa 103 145 B7, 108 153 B6

Wadi Maghara 14 15 CD3

Wadi Tumulat 14 15 C2

Wagram 82 119 D3

Waitzen (Väc) 45 61 C4

Wake 111 159 D2, 111 160 E6

Wakefield 56 78 BC2

Walata 65 92 AB1

Wales (Norse: Bretland) 43 59 B3, 47 64 B2, 52 72 C3, 56 78 B2, 68 97 B1, 76 108 A6

Wallhausen 47 65 CD2

Wallsend (Segedunum) 28 39 L1–2

Walvis Bay 96 133 C7, 97 135 C4, 122 179 C7

Walworth, London 66 94 D7

Warangal 64 89 B3

Warka (Uruk) 11 10 E4

Warsaw (Warszawa) 69 99 CD6, 76 107 DE5, 107 151 D3, 110 157 DE4, 113 163 B3, 128 185 C2

Warsaw (Warszawa), grand duchy 80 115 DE2

Warta 57 79 EF4
Wartburg 58 81 C4
Washington, city 92 129 D2, 93 130 C5
Washington, state 93 130 A1
Washukanni 109 B2, 11 10 DE3
Waterford (Vedrafjord) 47 64 AB2, 52 72 B3
Watling Island (Guanahani) 62 85 CD3–4
Wedding, Berlin 114 167 DE1
Wehlau 70 100 H2
Wei, city 32 45 E2
Wei, state 30 42 E2
Weichsel (Wisa) 74 105 EF2
Weihai 98 137 DE4, 102 143 E7
Weihe 65 91 KL1
Weimar 68 98 DE3, 107 151 B3
Weissbrunn (Vestprém) 45 61 B4
Weissenburg 70 100 C5
Weissensee, Berlin 114 167 E1
Wellington's campaign against Spain 1802 and 1808 81 118 A5–6, 82 119 AB3
Wels 47 65 E4
Wenchou 102 142 C5
Wenden 57 79 G2, 69 99 D5
Wends, people 44 60 I2, 46 63 D3
Werben 68 98 DE2
Werla 47 65 C2
Wernigerode 75 106 B2
Wessex 43 59 B3, 44 60 E2, 47 64 B2
West Bengal 127 184 DE3
West Frankish Kingdom, The (Valland) 46 63 BC4–5
West Frisian Islands 66 93 BC1
West Germany, see also Germany, Federal Republic of (BRD) 115 168 C3, 116 169 BC6, 128 185 B3
West Hsia 40 55 I4
West Indies, Federation of the 60 84 CD4, 121 177 CD1
West Indies, islands 64 88 B6
West Prussia 73 104 C2, 74 105 E1, 75 106 DE1–2
West Virginia 92 129 C2–3, 93 130 F3
West Wales (Devon) 44 60 D3

Western Australia 98 137 E7
Western Europe ca. 750 43 59
Western Galicia 73 104 D2, 107 151 D3–4
Western Goths (Visigoths) 42 57 K6
Western Locris 16 20 BC5
Western Sahara 122 179 A4
Western Siberia 89 126 I6
Western Turkistan 98 137 B3
Western Turks 32 45 A–C2
Westminster Abbey, London 66 94 C7
Westphalia 70 100 C4, 86 122 B2
Wetzlar 68 98 C3, 70 100 C4
Wexford (Veisufjord) 56 78 A2, 67 95 DE6
White Chapel, London 66 94 D6
White Cossacks 106 150 F5
White Nile 65 92 E1–2, 96 133 D4–5
White Russia 107 151 E2, 115 168 DE3
White Sea (Gandvik) 32 44 E2 46 63 FG1, 69 99 EF2, 106 150 C2
Whitehall, London 66 94 C7
Wiesbaden 114 166 B3
Wildeshausen 69 99 A6
Wildhaus 69 99 A6
Wilhelmsthal 74 105 B2
Wilmersdorf, Berlin 114 167 D2
Wilno (Vilna) 105 147 K4
Wilson's Creek 92 129 B3
Wimpfen 68 98 C4
Winceby 67 95 F6
Winchester 50 69 B3
Winchester House, London 66 94 D7
Windau 57 79 F2, 73 104 D1
Windhoek 122 179 C7
Windsheim 68 98 D4, 70 100 D5
Windsor 52 72 CD4, 56 78 BC3
Winnipeg 93 130 D1
Winterthur 55 77 D5
Wisa (Weichsel, Wisla) 75 106 E2, 81 116 D2, 107 152 C3, 113 163 B2
Wisconsin 92 129 B1, 93 130 E2
Wiskiauten 44 60 IJ1
Wismar 57 79 D3, 69 99 AB5, 74 105 C1, 81 116 D2, 107 151 C3, 113 163 B2

Wittenberg 49 68 EF5, 55 76 F4, 58 81 D4, 74 105 D2
Wittstock 68 98 E2
Witwatersrand 97 135 DE6
Wolfenbüttel 68 98 D2
Wolgast 68 98 E1, 69 99 B5
Wollin (Jumne) 44 60 H2, 68 98 F1
Wolmar 57 79 G2
Wonju 119 175 F3
Wonsan 102 143 F6, 119 175 BC2
Worcester 50 69 B3, 67 95 E6
Worms 47 65 C3, 55 76 C2, 58 81 C4, 79 113 C1, 81 116 C2
Wrangel Island 120 176 K1
Wraxeter 44 60 E2
Wroclaw, see Breslau
Wu, city 31 43 CD6
Wu, state 30 42 F3
Wuchang 40 55 J4
Wuhan 117 170 D6
Württemberg, duchy 68 98 C5, 70 100 CD5
Württemberg, kingdom 84 121 E4, 86 122 C3–4
Württemberg-Baden 114 166 BC3
Württemberg-Hohenzollern 114 166 BC4
Würzburg, bishopric 68 98 D4, 70 100 D5
Würzburg, city 47 65 C3, 49 68 E5–6
Wyoming 93 130 C2

X

Xerxes' campaign against Greece 480 BC 13 14 A6
Xi'an (Chang'an) 35 48 D3, 117 170 D6
Xiamen (Amoy) 102 142 C6, 111 159 B2
Xieng Khouang 124 181 AB5
Xinjiang (Eastern Turkistan) 98 137 C3, 117 170 AB5
Xocotla 63 87 AB2

Y

Yahata 102 142 E4
Yakutsk 89 126 K6, 98 137 D2
Yalta 112 161 E5, 113 163 D4
Yalu 102 142 C3, 119 175 B1
Yamuna (Jumna) 64 89 B1–2
Yan 30 42 E1
Yan'an 117 170 D5
Yana 98 137 D1

Yanam (Yanaon) 127 184 CD4
Yanaon (Yanam) 99 140 D3
Yang-Shao-culture 8 3 F5
Yangchou 32 45 EF2
Yangyang 119 175 EF2
Yao, tribe 65 92 E3
Yaoundé 122 179 C5
Yap 111 159 C3
Yarkand 32 44 H4, 40 55 G4
Yarmouth 56 78 CD2, 57 79 AB3
Yaroslavl, Russia 41 56 L5, 46 63 G3, 71 101 K5, 106 150 CD3
Yathrib (Medina) 32 44 EF6
Yekaterinburg (Sverdlovsk) 83 120 F3, 106 150 F2
Yekaterinoslav 71 101 JK6, 106 150 D5–6
Yelisavetgrad 91 127 L4
Yellow Sea (Hwang Hai) 35 48 E2–3, 102 142 C4
Yemen 37 51 K3, 108 153 D7, 119 174 B7
Yeniseisk 89 126 J6
Yenisey 32 44 H1, 40 55 GH1, 98 137 B2
Yerevan (Erivan) 106 150 F7
Yezd (Yazd) 108 153 E5
Yokohama 98 137 F4, 102 142 F3
Yongdok 119 175 C3
Yongjia 102 142 C6
York, city (Eburacum, Eporvik) 25 33 A1, 41 56 IJ6, 43 59 B3, 46 63 C3, 47 64 B2, 50 69 B3, 55 76 B1, 56 78 C1, 58 83 B4, 81 116 B2
York, duchy 56 78 B1
Yorkshire 52 72 D3
Yorktown 92 128 K2
Ypres (Ieper) 105 148 J1
Yucatan 63 87 E1, 95 132 A1, 121 177 B1
Yuchou (Beijing) 32 45 E2, 36 49 J3
Yudenich's advance in 1919 106 150 B3
Yue 30 42 F4
Yuezhi 31 43 A5
Yugoslavia 107 151 CD5, 108 154 E4, 110 157 D5, 115 168 CD4, 116 169 C7, 128 185 C4
Yunnan, city 35 48 D3
Yunnan, province 117 170 C7

Z

Zagreb (Agram) 107 151 C5, 110 157 D5

Zaire (Congo), river 122 179 D5
Zaire (Congo Free State) 122 179 F2, D5, 123 180 E2
Zaiton (Quanchou) 40 55 J5
Zakynthos (Zante) 17 21 A3
Zama 23 28 D3, 24 31 C5
Zama Regia 28 38 E5
Zambezi, river 96 133 D6
Zambia (Northern Rhodesia) 122 179 F2, D6
Zante, see Zakynthos
Zanzibar 65 92 F3, 97 136 E3, 122 179 E6
Zanzibar, sultanate 96 133 E5–6
Zara 45 61 B5, 59 83 D6
Zaragoza (Caecaraugusta) 43 59 B6, 49 68 C7, 59 83 B6, 81 118 C6
Zarandj (Sarandsh) 36 49 F4
Zaria 65 92 C1–2
Zeeland, county (hist.) 66 93 B3
Zehlendorf, Berlin 114 167 D2
Zeila 65 92 F
Zeitz 47 65 D3
Zela 23 30 D6, 24 32 E6
Zelea 21 26 B2
Zenta 55 76 D3, 72 103 E5
Zeus, Alter of, Olympia 18 22 E5
Zeus, Temple of, Acropolis 19 23 E1
Zhanjiang 102 142 A7
Zhejiang 30 41 C6–7
Zheng 30 42 E2–3
Zhenkursk 83 120 C2
Zhitomir 73 104 E3, 106 150 B5, 113 163 C3
Zhoukoudian (Chou-Kou-Tien) 7 1, 30 41 C5
Zienksee 66 93 B3
Zijanid dynasty 40 55 AB4, 55 76 B4
Zimbabwe (Rhodesia), state 122 179 D6
Zimbabwe, city 65 92 E4
Zomba 122 179 E6
Zorndorf 74 105 D2
Zug 55 77 D6
Zuider Zee 66 93 C2
Züllichau 74 105 DE2
Zululand 97 135 EF6
Zuni 62 85 B3
Zürich (Turicum) 55 77 D5, 107 152 B4
Zwing-Uri 55 77 D6
Zwolle 56 78 E2, 57 79 C3, 66 93 D2

INDEX (SUBJECT AND NAME)

Personal name entries include brief biographical information, so that the index can be used as a little «lexicon». References are to page and column. A reference to **37 A**, f.ex., means that the reference is to be found on page 37, in the column furthest to the left. The columns are *not* marked A, B, C and D, but to make locating entries easier, we have called column one 'A', column two 'B', etc., in the index. An asterisk ★ after the column letter means «illustration». The following abbreviations are used:

Afr. – African
Amer. – American
approx. – approximately
Arab. – Arabic, Arabian
Arg. – Argentinian
Ass. – Assyrian
Aus. – Austrian
aut. – author
Azt. – Aztec

Bab. – Babylonian
beg. – beginning
Belg. – Belgian
b. – born
Braz. – Brazilian
Brit. – British
Bulg. – Bulgarian
Burm. – Burmese
Byz. – Byzantine

ca. – circa
Chil. – Chilean
Chin. – Chinese
Cub. – Cuban
Czech. – Czechoslovakian

d. – died
Da. – Danish

Egypt. – Egyptian
Eng. – English
est. – established

Fin. – Finnish
Fr. – French

Ger. – German

hist. – historian, historically
Hung. – Hungarian
h. of – husband of

Ind. – Indian
Isr. – Israeli
Ital. – Italian

Jap. – Japanese

Kor. – Korean

Lat. – Latin

Mac. – Macedonian
Mex. – Mexican
Mes. – Mesopotamian

Nor. – Norwegian

org. – organization
orig. – originally

Pak. – Pakistan
Pal. – Palistinian
Pers. – Persian
p.m. – prime minister
pol. – politician Port.
       – Portuguese
pres. – president
Prus. – Prussian

r.n. – real name
Rom. – Roman
Rum. – Rumanian
Russ. – Russian

secr. – secretary
Serb. – Serbian
Sov. – Soviet
Sp. – Spanish
Sum. – Sumerian
Sw. – Swiss
Swed. – Swedish
Syr. – Syrian

Turk. – Turkish

U.S. – United States

Viet. – Vietnamese

w. of – wife of

Yug. – Yugoslavian

A

Aachen, 814, **44 C**
Abu Bekr (573–634), the first caliph **37 D**
Abukir, naval battle of (1798) **80 B, 81 D**
Acropolis **90 A–D★**
Adams, John (1735–1826), pres. in the U.S. 1797–1801 **92 B, D**
Adelheid (931–99), Holy Roman empress, w. of king Lothar and emperor Otto 1. **47 B**
Adua, Battle of (1896) **107 A**
Afghanistan, 100 AD **32 D**
–, 1907 **103A**
–, 1979 **116 C**
Africa's liberation 1951–90 **123 A**
Africa, 1300s **60 D★**
–, desertification **123 D**
Agricola, Rom. governer in Britannia ca. 80 AD **29 C**
Aigospotaimoi, Battle of (405 BC) **17 A** Ajanta, cave shrines **38 A★**
Akbar the Great (1542–1605), Great Mogul 1556 **64 D★, 65 A**
Akkad **12 B**
Akragas (Agrigento) **20 A**
al-Fatah, Pal.-Arab. lib. org., est. 1959 **118 C**
Alaska, 1867 **93 C**
Alba, Fernando Alvarez de Toledo, Duke of A. (1508–82), **66 A–B**
Albania, 1453 **70 D**
–, 1913 **103 D**
–, 1939 **107 A**
–, 1955 **116 A**
Albuquerque, Affonso d' (1453–1515), Port. colonizer **64 D★**
Aleksei Mikhailovich (1629–76), Russ. tzar 1645 **71 B**
Aleksei Nikolayevich (1904–18), Russ. heir apparent, son of Nicholas II **106 A★**
Alexander I Pavlovich (1777–1825), Russ. tzar 1801 **81 A, 83 A★, B–D, 85 B, 88 D**
Alexander II Nikolayevich (1818–81), Russ. tzar

1855 **100 B**
Alexander III, r.n. Orlando Bandinelli, pope 1159–81 **53 A**
Alexander the Great (356–323 BC), king of Macedonia, Asia and Egypt 21 **A–B, D★, 38 B**
Alfred the Great (849–99), king of Wessex 871 **46 C–D**
Algerie, 1830s **96 A–B**
–, 1962, **123 A**
Ali Ibn Talib (602–61), caliph 656 **37 D**
Alma, Battle of (1854) **89 B–C**
Almagro, Diego de (1475–1538), Sp. officer and conquistador **61 C**
Alsace (Elsass), 1648 **70 A**
–, 1871 **86 D**
–, 1919 **107 D**
Altmark, Peace of (1629) **69 B**
Amenemhet I, Egypt. king ca. 2000–1970 BC **15 A**
America, The Confederate States of, see also Southern States, The **93 B**
America, United States of, see U.S., USA
American Civil War (1861–65) **93 B–C**
American War of Independence (1776–83) **62 D**, **92 B**
Amiens, Peace of (1802) **82 A**
Amon–Ra, Egypt. god **15 A**
Amphiteatrum Flavianum, Colosseum **27 A**
Anastasia (1901–17), Russ. grand duchess, daughter of Nicholas II **109 A★**
Andalucia, (V)Andalucia **43 A**
Andrassy, Julius (1823–90) Austro-Hung. foreign min. **101 A★**
Andropov, Yuri (1914–84), Sov. general secratary **116 C**
Angkor **39 A**
Angkor Thom **39 A**
Angkor Vat **39 A★**

Angola, 1975 **123 A**
Anne Boleyn (1507–36), Eng. queen, w. of Henry VIII **67 A**
Anne, patron saint of miners **58 A**
Anti-Comintern Pact (1936) **102 D**
Antibes, (1815) **84 A**
Antietam, Battle of (1862) **93 C**
Antilles, The Lesser **61 A**
Appomattox, capitulation at (1865) **93 C**
Aquitania **52 C**
Arabia (Arabs), around the year 100 AD **29 C**
–, 622–732 **37 D, 45 A**
Arafat, Yasir (b. 1929), Pal. resistance leader **118 C★**
Arcadius (377–408), East Roman emperor 395 **42 B**
Archimedes (287–212 BC), mathematician and physicist from Syracuse **20 A**
Arcole, Battle of (1796) **80 B, D**
Ardashir I, Sasanid king 224–41 **37 A**
Aretino, Spinello (1332–1410), Ital. painter **53 D**
Argentina, 1776–1842 **95 A**
«Ark of the Covenant» **15 C**
Armada, The Great (Spanish) (1588) **67 A★, 68 A**
Armenia, around the year 100 **29 C**
–, 1500s **71 A**
–, 1820s **89 A**
–, 1908 **108 A**
–, 1923 **108 C**
Arshak (Arsakes) (d. 248 BC), Parthian king of the Seleucids **32 D**
Ashoka, Ind. prince ca. 269–228/229 BC **38 C**
Asir, 1926 **108 C**
Assyria, about the year 100 **29 C**
Astyages, Median king 584–550 BC **13 A**
Athene (Pallas Athene), Gr. goddess **19 A, C, D**
Athens, in Antiquity **13 A, 16 D, 17 A, 19 A–D**
Atlantic Treaty Organiza-

tion (1949) 116 A
Augsburg Confession (1530) 59 A
August von Anhalt-Zerbst, father of Catherine the Great 73 C
Augustus, r.n. Gaius Julius Cæsar Octavianus (63 BC–14 AD), Rom. emperor 30 BC 26 D, 29 C
Aurangzeb (1618–1707), Ind. Great Mogul 1658 65 A
Austerlitz, Battle of (1805) 81 A*, 82 A, 83 C
Austrasia 43 A
Austria, 1740–80 72 A, 73 A, 74 C
–, 1801 81 B, 82 A
–, 1805 81 A, 82 A
–, 1859 87 C
–, 1864 86 D
–, 1938 109 A
Austria-Hungary, 1914–18 104 B
–, 1919 107 D
Austrian War of Succession, The (1740–48) 72 A, D
Awami League 127 C
Azincourt, Battle of (1415) 56 A
Aztecs 95 A

B
Babur, r.n. Zahir-ud-din Mohammed, Great Mogul 1483–1530 65 A
Babylon 11 C, 13 A, 21 B
Babylonia 13 A
Babylonian Captivity, Jews' 13 A
Bach, Johann Sebastian (1685–1750), Ger. composer 74 B
Badoglio, Pietro (1871–1956), Ital. marshal, led government 1943–44, 113 A
Baffin Island 61 C
Baghdad 40 D
Bahia (Sao Salvador) 95 B
Bahrain 119 D
Bajasit I Jildirim (1347–1402), Turk. sultan 1389 70 D
Balkan Wars, The (1912–13) 103 D
Balkans, 900s 45 C
–, 1870s 100 B–D
Balloon 100 A*
Baltic states, 1989–90 128 C
Bangladesh 1947–72 127 D
Bannockburn, Battle of (1314) 52 C
Bao Dai (1913–), emperor of Annam 1925–45, S. Vietn. leader 1954–55 124 D, 125 B
Barbary Coast 1830–1910 96 A–B

Barents, Willem (1555–97), Dutch explorer 61 C
Basel, Peace of (1499) 55 D
Basil II, 'Slayer of the Bulgarians' (ca. 958–1025), Byz.. emperor 976 45 B
Bassano, Battle of (1796) 80 B
Bastille, Storming of the (1789) 79 A*
Batavian Republic 81 B
Batista, Fulgencio (1901–73), Cuban dictator 1933–59 120 B
Batu (d. 1256), Mongol. Tatarkhan 40 C
Batum, 1878 100 D
Bavaria, 1740–48 72 A
Bay of Pigs 121 D
Bayeux tapestry 47 B*
Bear Island 61 C
Beauharnais, Joséphine de, see Joséphine, Fr. empress
Bechuanaland 96 C, 97 C
Beggrow, Karl (1799–1875), Baltic born Russ. painter 89 D
Beijing (Peking, Dadu, Khanbalik) 34 A–B, 35 D*, 40 B, 61 C
Beirut 118 C*
Belgian Congo, see also Congo Free State
Belgium, 1648 66 B
–, 1815 85 B
–, 1940 110 D
Belgrade (1521) 71 A
Bellini, Giovanni (ca. 1430–1516), Ital. painter 57 C
Bellman, Carl Michael (1740–95), Swed. poet 74 B
Benin, 1300s 65 A
–, 1960 123 A
Berengar II (d. 966), Ital. margrave, Langobard king 47 A
Bergen-Belsen 110 D*
Berlin (1945) 114 A*, 115 A
Berlin Crises, The, (1948) 116 B
Berlin Wall, The (1961) 115 A, 128 C–D*
Berlin, Congress of (1878) 100 D, 101 A*
Bernhard av Clairvaux (1090–1153), Fr. philosopher and relig. leader 48 D
Bessarabia, 1812 83 C
–, 1878 100 D
Bethlehem 26 C
Biskupin, Poland 9 A*
Bismarck, Otto Eduard Leopold von (1815–98), Prus. p.m. 1862, Ger. chancellor 1871 86 D*, 87 A*, 100 A*, C, 101 A*
Bismarck Archipelago (1942) 111 A

Black Death, The 55 A
Black George, see Petrovic, Georg
Bloemfontein 97 D
Blue Temple, Beijing, see Temple of Heaven
Blücher, Gebhard Leberecht von (1742–1819), Prus. general 85 C
Boccaccio, Giovanni (1313–75), Ital. auth. 57 B
Boer War (1899–1902) 97 B–D
Bohemund of Taranto (ca. 1060–1111), Duke of Taranto, prince of Antiochia 48 D
Boilly, Louis-Léopold (1761–1845), Fr. painter 78 D
Boleslav Chrobry (the Brave) (967–1025), Polish king 992 51 A
Boleyn, Anne, see Anne Boleyn
Bolivar, Simon (1783–1830), hero of S. Amer. liberation 94 A
Bolivia, beg. of 1800s 94 B
Bologna, University of 49 B*
Bolsheviks 106 D
Bombay 99 A*
Bonampäk 63 A
Bonaparte, Joseph (1768–1844), brother of Napoleon I, king of Napoli 1806–08, of Spain 1808–13 81 D
Bonaparte, Louis Napoléon, see Napoleon III
Bonifatius VIII, r.n. Benedetto Gäetani, pope 1294–1303 52 D
Bonpland, Aimé Jacques Alexandre (1773–1858), Fr. botanist and explorer 95 C
Bora, Katharina von (1499–1552), w. of Martin Luther 1525 59 A
Bosnia, 1400s 70 D
–, 1870s 100 B, D
–, 1914 103 D
Boston Massacre, The (1770) 92 A*
Botswana (1966) 123 A
Botticelli, Sandro, r.n. Alessandro Filipepi (1444/45–1510), Florentine painter 57 C
Bourdon, Sébastien (1616–71), Fr. painter 69 C
Brömsebro, Peace of (1645) 69 B
Brandenburg-Prussia 1415–1795 70 A, 75 D
Brazil, 1500 61 B
–, 1549–1822 95 B
Bremen 70 A
Breshnev, Leonid Ilyitch (1906–82), Sov. gen. secr.

1964–82 116 C, D*
Bretagne 52 C
Bretland (Wales) 46 B
Britannia 55–128 29 C–D
British Bechuanaland 97 C
British India, 1939–45 127 A
–, 1947 127 D
Bruce, Robert, see Robert I, king of Scotland
Brueghel, Pieter the Elder (ca. 1525–69), Flemish painter 66 D
Brunel, Isambard Kingdom (1806–59), Brit. engineer 90 D
Bucephalus (Bukéfalos), Alexander the Great's war horse 21 D*
Bucharest, Peace of (1913), 103 D
Budapest 113 C
Buddha, r.n. Siddharta Gautama (ca. 565–485 BC), founder of Buddhism 36 A, 39 A*
Buddhism 33 C, 36 A
Buenos Aires 95 A
Bukéfala 21 D
Bulgaria, 893–1018 45 C
–, 1393 70 D
–, 1870s 100 B–D
–, 1912 103 D
–, 1944 113 C
–, 1945–47 116 B
–, 1955 116 A
–, 1989–90 128 B
Bulgars 51 A
Burgh Castle, Great Britain 28 C*
Burgundy 43 A
Burma, in the Middle Ages 34 C, 36 A
–, 1942 111 A
–, see also Toungoo
Burundi 123 A
Byron, George Noel Gordon, Lord B. (1788–1824), Brit. poet 88 C*
Byzantine (East Roman) Empire 395–626 42 B–C
–, 673–1054 45 A–B

C
Cabot, John, r.n.. Giovanni Caboto (1450–98), Eng. explorer 61 C
Cabot, Sebastian, r.n. Sebastiano Caboto (1472–1557), son of John C., Eng. seafarer and cartographer 61 C
Cabral, Pedro Alvares (ca. 1460–ca. 1526), Port. explorer 61 B
Cæsar, Gaius Julius (100–44 BC), Rom. statesman and fieldmarshal 24 D, 25 A, C, 29 C

Calais 67 A
Calicut 61 C
California, 1800s 93 A, 95 A
Caligula, Gaius Cæsar (12–41), Rom. emperor 37 29 C
Callicrates, Gr. architect around 450 BC 19 A
Calvin, Jean (1509–64), Fr.-Swiss Reformation figure 59 D
Cambodia (Khmer kingdom), 600–1200 39 A
–, 1945–54 124 A–B
Cameroon, 1960 123 A
Campaign of the 1 000 (1860) 87 C
Campania 22 C
Campoformio, Peace of 1797) 80 B
Canada, 1812–14 92 C
Cannae, Battle of (216 BC) 23 A
Cano, Juan Sebastian del (ca. 1460–1526), Sp. seafarer 61 B
Canossa 53 A
Cape Colony, The 97 B
Caporetto, Battle of (1917) 105 A
Caribbean Ocean, The 94 C
Cartier, Jacques (1491–1557), Fr. explorer 61 C
Castlereagh, Robert Stewart, Marquis of Londonderry, viscount C. (1769–1822), Brit. pol. 84 D*, 85 B
Castro, Fidel (b. 1927), Cuba's p.m. 1959–65, first secr. 1965–76, pres. 1976–120 B*, 121 D
Catherine League, The 69 A
Ceausescu, Elena (d. 1989), w. of Nicolae C. 128 B
Ceausescu, Nicolae (1918–89), Rum. leader 1965–89 128 B
Celts 9 D
Central African Republic, 1960 123 A
Ceylon (Sri Lanka), 1500s 65 A
Chagatai, Mongol khan in 1200s 40 D
Chagatai-khanate, The 40 A, D Dubcek, Alexander (1921–), Czech. pres. in national assembly 1989–128 B
Chaldea 12 C
Chamberlain, Arthur Neville (1869–1940), Brit. pol., p.m. 1937–40 108 A*, 109 A
Chamonix 18 D
Chancellor, Richard (d.

1556), Eng. seafarer 61 C

Chandragupta I, Ind. king ca. 320 38 D

Chandragupta II (d. 414), Ind. king 385–414 38 D

Chandragupta Maurya (d. ca. 297 BC), Ind. king from ca. 320 BC 38 B–C

Chang'an 33 C, D*

Charlemagne (742–814), Frankisk king 768, emperor 800 44 B–C, 45 D*

Charles (1600–49), king of England and Scotland 1625 67 B

Charles II (1630–85), king of England, Scotland and Ireland 1660 67 C

Charles II, the Bald (822–877), Frankish king 840, emperor 875 44 D

Charles III, the Simple (879–929), Fr. king 898 46 D

Charles Martell (ca. 688–741), Frankish ruler, Lord Governor from 719 37 D, 43 A

Charles V (1500–58), Sp. king 1516, Holy Roman emperor 1519–56 68 A

Charles VI (1685–1740), Holy Roman emperor 1711 72 A

Charles X (1757–1836), Count of Artois, Fr. king 1824–30 85 B*

Charles XII (1682–1718), Swed. king 1697 69 C, 71 B

Charleston, South Carolina 93 A

Cheops, Egypt. king 2575–2550 BC 14 C

Cheops, Pyramid of 14 D, 15 A*

Chephren, Egypt. king 2540–2515 BC 14 D

Chephren, Pyramid of 15 A*

Chiang Kai-shek, see Jiang Jieshi

Chichén Itza 62 D*

Chile, 1530s 61 C

China, ca. 1600–206 BC 31 A, D

–, 206 BC–907 AD 33 C–D

–, 907–1644 34 A–C, 35 D, 61 C

–, 1894–95 102 D

–, 1934–70 116 C, D, 117 A, 124 C, 127 A

China, Great Wall of 31 D*

Chinard, Fr. actor at the end of the 1700s 78 D*

Chosen, see Korea

Chou (Zhou) Dynasty, Age (1027–256 BC) 30 B–C, 31 D

Christian IV (1517–1648), king of Denmark-Norway 1588 69 A*

Christina (1626–89), reign. queen of Sweden 1644–54 69 C*

Churchill, Winston Spencer (1874–1965), Brit. p.m. 1940–45 and 1951–55 97 C

Cicero, Marcus Tullius (106–43 BC), Rom. consul and orator 24 A*

Cimarosa, Domenico (1749–1801), Ital. composer 74 B

Cimbrians 24 D

Cisalpine Republic 80 B, 81 B

Claudius, r.n. Tiberius Claudius Nero (10 BC–54 AD), Rom. emperor 41–54 29 C

Cleopatra (69–30 BC), Egypt. queen 24 D

Clive, Robert (1725–74), Baron of Plassey, Brit. field marshal and governor general of India 99 A

Clovis (Ludvig), Frankisk king 481 43 A

Coello, Alonso Sanchez (1515–90), Port. painter 68 A

«Cold War, The» 116 B

Colosseum, Rome 27 A*, D

Columbus, Christofer (1451–1506), Ital.-Sp. explorer 61 A, C*

Comoro Islands (1975) 123 A

Confucius (551–479 BC), Chin. philosopher 31 A

Congo (People's Republic of the Congo), 1960 123 A

Congo Crisis, The (1960–65) 123 B–C

Congo Free State 96 D

Congo, The (river) 96 D

Congolese Republic (from 1971: Zaire) 122 D, 123 A, B–C

Congress Party, India 99 A, 127 A, C

«Congress-Poland» 85 B

Conrad III (1093–1152), Ger. king 1138 49 A

Conrad of Franken (990–1039), Ger. king 1024, Lombard king 1026, Holy Roman emperor 1027 53 A

Concentration camps 97 D, 109 A*, 110 D*, 114 D

Constable, John (1776–1837), Brit. painter 77 A

Constantine Pavlovitch (1779–1831), Russ. grand duke, viceroy of Poland 1820 88 D, 89 A

Constantinople, 395 42 B–C

–, 673 and 860 45 A–B

–, 717–1837 D

–, 1054 41 B–, 1300s 55 B

–, 1453 70 D

Dalmatia 45 C

Damascus 37 D, 49 A

Danelaw, The 46 B, C

Dante Alighieri (1265–1321), Ital. poet 57 B

Danzig, 1772 73 A

–, 1919 107 D

–, see also Gdansk

Darius 3., Pers. king 336–330/331 BC 21 B

Darius I, Pers. king 522–485 BC 13 A

Darlington 90 B

Darnley, Henry Stuart, Lord D. (1545–67), Scottish nobleman, h. of Maria Stuart 67 B

Daun, Leopold Joseph von (1705–66), Austr. commander 75 A

David, king of Israel ca. 1015–972 BC 15 C

Davis, John (ca. 1550–1605), Eng. explorer 61 C

Decabrist Rebellion (1825) 89 A

Dego, Battle of (1796) 80 A

Delacroix, Eugène (1798–1863), Fr. painter 88 B

Delian League, The 17 A

Delos 17 A

Delphi 18 A*, 20 A

Demeter, Gr. goddess of fertility 22 D*

Democratic Party, USA 92 C

Democratic Republican Party (later: The Democratic Party), USA 92 C

Denikin, Anton Ivanovitch (1872–1947), Russ. general 106 D

Denmark, 1864 86 D

–, 1940 110 A

Denmark-Norway, 1643–45 69 B

Desai, Morarji Ranchhodji (b. 1896), Ind. pol., p.m. 1977–79 127 C

Desertification 123 D

Diaz, Bartholomeo (ca. 1450–1500), Port. explorer 61 A

Diaz, José de la Cruz Porfirio (1830–1915), pres. i Mexico 1877–80 and 1884–1911 95 A*

Dien Bien Phu (1954) 124 D

Dionysus Theatre, Athens 19 B, C

Dionysus, Gr. god of wine and fertility 21 B

Disraeli, Benjamin, from 1876 Earl of Beaconsfield (1804–81), Brit. statesman 101 A*

Djibouti, 1977 123 A

Dodecanese, 1911–12 107 A

Donatello, r.n. Donato di Nicollo de Betto Bardi (1386–1466), Ital. sculp-

tor 57 C

Drake, Francis (1540–96), Brit. seafarer 61 C

Dutch East Indies, 1942–45 126 B

E

East Germany (Deutsche Demokratische Republik) 114 D, 116 A, B, 128 C

East India Company, The British 67 B, 99 A

–, The French 65 A

East Pakistan, 1947 127 D

–, 1971 127 B

–, see also Bangladesh

East Prussia, 1525 75 D

–, 1618 70 A

–, 1944–45 113 C, 114 D

East Roman Empire, 673–1054 45 A–B

–, see also Byzantine Empire

Eastern Goths (Ostrogoths) 43 A

Eastern Rumelia, 1878 100 D

Ebert, Friedrich (Fritz) 1871–1925), Germ. chancellor 1918–19, pres. 1919–25 108 D

Ecuador, beg. of 1800s 94 B

Edington, (Ethandun) Battle of (878) 46 D

Edward I (1239–1307), Eng. king 1272 52 C

Egbert, king of Wessex 802–39 46 C

Egypt, in Antiquity 10–11, 14 C–D, 15 A

–, at the time of the Pers. Empire 13 A

–, 642 37 D

–, in 1500s 70 D

–, 1798–99 80 B–C

–, in 1900s 103 A, 108 B, 118 A, 119 D, 122 D

El Alamein, Battle of (1942) 112 D, 113 A

Elba, 1814 82 D, 84 A

Elisabeth I (1533–1603), Eng. queen 1558 67 A*, 68 A

Elisabeth Petrovna (1709–62), Russ. tzarina 1741 73 C

Elsass (Alsace), 1648 70 A

–, 1871 86 D

England, 829–911 46 B–D

–, 1028–35 50 A–B

–, 1106–1328 52 C

–, 1337–1453 56 A

–, 1553–1673 67 A

–, after 1707, see Great Britain

English Channel, The 29 C

Equatorial Guinea 123 A

Eratosthenes of Cyrene (ca. 275–194 BC), Gr. scientist 21 A

Erechtheus, Gr. god 19 C

Erechtium (Erechteion), Athens 19 C

Eretria 13 A

Eritrea, 1890 107 A

Ershad, Hussein Muhammed (1930–), pres. of Bangladesh fra 1984 127 D

Estates General, The 66 B

Estonia (Estland), 1721 71 D

–, 1989–90 128 C

Ethandun, see Edington

Ethelred II the Unready (ca. 968–1016), Eng. king 978–1013 50 A

Ethiopia, 1896 107 A

–, 1936 107 A

Euclid (Evkleides), mathematician and astronomer from Alexandria around 300 BC 21 A

Eumenes II's collonade, Athens 19 D

Europe, Population of ca. 1800 76 D

–, 1800s 91 D

F

Faroe Islands 46 B

Faruk (1920–65), Egypt. king 1936–52 118 A

«February Revolution» in Russia (1917) 106 D

Federalist Party, The, USA 92 C

Feidias (ca. 490–ca. 430 BC), Gr. sculptor 19 C

Ferdinand II, «King Bomba» (1810–59), king of the Two Sicilies 1830 87 C

Finland, 1808–09 83 C

–, 1939, 1941 and 1944 110 A, D, 113 C

Firenze 57 B

First World War, WW1 (1914–18) 104 B–D, 105 D

Firuz Shah, Ind. sultan 1351–88 64 C

«Five Dynasties, Time of the» (907–960), China 34 A

Flandern 52 D

Florida, 1819 93 A

FNL, National Liberation Front, Vietnam 125 B, D

Fontainebleau 83 A*

Formosa (Taiwan) 102 D

Fort Sumter 93 A*

Forum Julium, Rome 27 C

Forum Pacis, Rome 27 C

Forum Romanum, Rome 27 C

France, 1648 70 A

–, 1154–1314 52 D

–, 1337–1453 56 A

–, 1740–48 72 A

–, 1756 74 C, 75 A

–, 1788 78 A

–, 1789–95 78 B–C

–, 1801–15 81 B, 82 A–D, 85 B

–, 1853–56 89 D

–, 1859 86 A, 87 C

–, 1870–71 86 D

–, 1939 110 A

–, 1942 113 A

–, under de Gaulle, 1944–46 and 1959–69 115 C–D

–, in Indochina 124 B–D

Francis (Franz) II (1768–1835), Holy Roman Emperor 1792, from 1804 emperor of Austria as Francis II 81 B, 85 A

Francis Ferdinand (1863–1914), Austrian archduke, heir to Austro-Hungarian throne 103 D*, 104 B

Francis of Assisi (Franciscus the Holy) (1182–1226), founder of the Franciscan Order 52 B*

Franciscus the Holy, see Francis of Assisi

Franco, Francisco (1892–1975), Sp. general and dictator, «Caudillo» («Leader») fra 1937 109 A

Franks, Kingdom of (France), ca. 350–732 43 A

–, 768–843 44 B–D

Frederick I, Barbarossa (ca. 1123–90), Holy Roman emperor 1155 49 A, 53 A, D

Frederick I, (1657–1713), king of Prussia 1701, Elector Frederick III of Brandenburg from 1688 70 A, 75 D

Frederick II of Hohenstaufen (1194–1250), king of Sicily 1197, Ger. king 1212, Holy Roman emperor 1220 50 C–D*, 57 A

Frederick II, the Great (1712–86), king of Prussia 1740 74 C–D, 75 B, D*, 92 D

Frederick III, elector of Brandenburg, see Frederick I, king of Prussia

Frederick III, the Wise (1463–1525), elector of Saxony 1486 59 A

Frederick William (1688–1951), Ger. crown prince 104 D*

Frederick William I (1688–1740), king of Prussia 1713 75 B

Frederick William (1620–88) electoral prince of Brandenburg 1640, «the Great Elector» 70 A*, 75 D

Fredriksten, 1718 69 B

French Indochina 1945–54 124 A–D

French Revolution 1789–95

78 B–C

French Union, The 124 B–D

Friedland, Battle of (1807) 83 C

Friesland 46 B

Funan 39 A

G

Gabon, 1960 123 A

Gadaffi, Muammar al- (f. 1942), Libyan off., chief of state from 1969 122 D*

Gagarin, Yuri (1934–68), Sov. cosmonaut 116 C

Galilee 26 C

Galizia, 1772 73 A

Gama, Vasco da (ca. 1460–1524), Port. seafarer, viceroy of India 1519 61 B, C*

Gambia, 1965 123 A

Gandhi, Indira (1917–84), Ind. p.m. 1966–77 and 1980–84 126 D*, 127 A–D

Gandhi, Mohandas Karamchand (Mahatma) (1869–1948), Ind. philos. and nationalist leader 127 A

Gandhi, Priyanka, daughter of Rajiv G. 127 D*

Gandhi, Rajiv (b. 1944), Ind. p.m. from 1984, son of Indira G. 127 D*

Gange-Rolf (Rollo), see Rolf

Gao Zu (Liu Bang), first emperor of Han dynasty in China 206–195 BC 31 A

Garibaldi, Giuseppe (1807–82), Ital. freedom fighter 87 C, D*

Gascogne 52 D

Gaul, 58–51 BC 24 D, 25 C

–, ca. 350 43 A

Gaulle, Charles de (1890–1970), Fr. general and statesman, leader the Free France 1940–44, p.m. 1944–46 and 1958, pres., 1959–69 115 C–D*

Gdansk, see also Danzig 128 C

General Assembly, in UN 115 A

Geneva Convention (1954) 124 B–D

Genghis-Khan, orig. Temudjin (1161–1227), Mongol prince 34 A, D*

Genova, 1300- and 1400s 54 A*, 55 B

–, 1800 80 C

George Petrovich, see Petrovich

Georgia, 1500s 71 A

–, 1918 108 A

–, 1921 108 B

German Confederation, The (Deutscher Bund) 85 B, 86 D

German Democratic Republic (East Germany) 114 D, 128 C

German-Russian Non-aggression Pact (1939) 109 A

Germanic Migrations, The 43 A

Germany, Federal Republic of (West Germany) 114 D

Germany, German Empire, A, 110 A, D

–, 1941–45 111 A, 113 B, C, 114 D

–, 1989–90 128 C

Germany, German Empire, 843 44 D

–, around 900 46 B

–, 936–73 47 A–B

–, 1024–1250 53 A

–, 1648 70 A

–, 1814–15 85 A

–, 1859–71 86 A–D

–, 1914–18 104 B–D, 105 D

–, 1918–39 107 D, 108 D, 109 A

Gettysburg, Battle of (1863) 93 C

Ghana, 1957 123 A

Ghaza Strip, 1956–57 118 B

Ghirlandaio, Dominico, r.n. Dominico di Thomasso Bigordi (1449–94), Ital. painter 57 D

Ghiyas-ud-din Tughluq, Ind. sultan 1320–25 64 A

Gibraltar 72 D

–, see also Hercules, Pillars of

Giotto di Bondone (ca. 1266–1337), Ital. painter, sculptor and architect 52 B, 57 B

Giunea-Bissau, 1973 123 A

Giza 15 A*

Gizenga, Antoine (b. 1925), Congolese pol., deputy p.m. 1961–62 123 C

Gladiators 26 D*

Gladstone, William Ewart (1809–98), Brit. statesman 99 A*, 100 B

Godfrey of Bouillon (1061–1100), Duke of Lower Lothringen, «Protector of the Holy Seplechur» 48 C

Golden Horde, The 40 A–C

Gomulka, Wladyslaw (1905–82), Polish first secr. 1943–48, and 1956–70 128 A

Gorbachev, Mikhail (1931–) Sov. party chairman and chief of state from 1985 116 C, 128 A*, C

Gorchakov, Alexander (1798–1883), Russ. prince, chancellor 101 A*

Gordon, George, see Byron, Lord

Goths 43 A

Gotland 56 D, 69 B

Gracchus, Gaius Sempronius (ca. 154–121 BC), Rom. tribunal 24 C

Gracchus, Tiberius Sempronius (ca. 162–133 BC), Rom. tribunal 24 C

Granikos, Battle of (334 BC) 21 B

Grant, Ulysses Simpson (1822–85), Amer. general, pres. 1869–77 93 C

Great Britain, 1707–42 72 C, D

–, 1756 74 C, 75 A

–, 1803 82 A

–, 1812–14 92 C

–, 1853–56 89 D

–, 1939 110 A

–, 1941 111 A

–, Great Britain, see also Britannia, England and Scotland

«Great Eastern», Brit. steamship 90 D

Great Khan, kingdom of the 40 A–B

Great Svitjod (Norse: Kiev) 51 A

Greater Bulgaria 100 C–D

Greater Greece – Magna Graecia 20 A

Greece (Hellas), ca. 750–449 BC 13 A, 16 D, 17 A, 18 A–D, 19 A–D

–, 300s BC 21 D

–, beg. of 900s 45 C

–, 1453 70 D

–, 1821–29 88 C

–, 1912 103 D

–, 1944 113 C

«Greek fire» 45 A

Greenland, around 900 46 B

–, 1580s 61 C

Gregory VII, r.n. Hildebrand (ca. 1020–85), pope 1073 53 A

Gros, Antoine Jean (1771–1835), Fr. painter 80 D

Guinea, 1958 123 A

Gun Powder Conspiracy (1605) 67 B

Gupta Dynasty, Ind. royal line 38 C, D

Gustavus 2. Adolphus (1594–1632), Swed. king 1611 69 A–B, C

H

Hadrian's Wall (Vallum Hadriani) 29 D

Hadrian, r.n. Publius Aelius Hadrianus (76–138), Rom. emperor 117 29 D

Hagia Triada 8 A

Haile Selassie (1891–1975), Ethiop. emperor 1930–74 107 A

Haiphong, 1946 124 D

Halland 69 B

Hallstatt 8 C

Hamburg 56 D*
Hamilton, Alexander (1757–1804), Amer. pol. and general 92 B
Hammarskjöld, Dag (1905–61), Swed. pol., UN General Secr. 1953–61 123 C
Hammurabi, king of Babylon from 1848 BC 11 C
Händel, Georg Friedrich (1685–1759), Ger.-born composer, lived in England from 1712 74 B
Han Dynasty, The Western (206–8 BC) 31 A, 33 C
Han Dynasty, The Eastern (24–220) 33 C
Hannibal (249–183 BC), Carthaginian general 22 D, 23 A
Hanoi, 1946 124 D
–, 1972 125 A*
Hansa League, The 56 D
Harald Godvinsson (ca. 1022–1066), Earl of Wessex, Eng. king 1066 47 B
Harappa 10 A
Hardenberg, Karl August von (1750–1822), Ger. prince and pol. 84 D*
Harsha (Harshavadana), N. Ind. king 606–47 38 D
Hastings, Battle of (1066) 47 B*
Hatshepsut, Egypt. queen 1488–70 BC 10 C
Hatta, Mohammed (1902–80), Indonesian pol., p.m.1948 and 1949–50, vice-pres. 1950–56 126 A, B
Havel, Vaclav (1936–), Czech. dramatist, pres. from 1989 128 B, C–D*
Hawaii, 1941 111 A
Haydn, Joseph (1732–1809), Austrian composer 74 B
Hebrides, The 46 B
Hedjaz, 1917 108 A
–, 1926 108 C
Hekataios, Gr. scientist, middle of the 500s BC 19 D
Helsinki Accord (1975) 116 C
Helvetian Republic, The 81 B
Henry I Beauclerc (1068–1135), Eng. king 1100 52 C
Henry II Plantagenet (1133–89), Count of Anjou, Duke of Normandy, Eng. king 1154 52 C, D
Henry IV (1050–1106), Holy Roman emperor 1056–1105 53 A
Henry of Anjou, see Henry II, Eng. king
Henry VIII (1491–1547),

Eng. king 1509 67 A
Hercules, Pillars of (Gibraltar) 21 A
Herjedalen 69 B
Hermitage Museum, St. Petersburg 89 D*
Hermitage Theatre, St. Petersburg 89 D*
Herod (Herodes Antipas) (4 BC–39 AD), Rom. tetrarch in Galilee 26 C
Herzegovina 100 B, D
Hindenburg, Paul von (1847–1934), Ger. general, pres. 1925–33 109 A
Hindus 127 A
Hippodrome, Greece 18 B, D
–, Constantinople 43 A
Hiroshima (1945) 111 A
Hitittes, Kingdom of the (Hatti) 10 D
Hitler, Adolf (1889–1945), Ger. pol., «Führer» and chancellor from 1933 108 A, D, 109 A*, 110 D, 113 B, D
Hittites (Hatti) (Hittite Empire) 10 D
Ho Chi Mihn, r.n. Nguyen That Than (1890–1969), Vietn. pol., pres. of N. Vietnam from 1954 124 D, 125 A*
Ho Chi Minh City 125 D
Ho Chi Minh Trail 125 B
Hofer, Andreas (1767–1810), hero of Tyrolian liberation 78 A
Holland, 1815 85 B
–, 1940 110 D
–, in Indonesia 126 B–C
–, Netherlands, The United, 1815 85 B
Holmgard (Novgorod) 51 A
Holstein, 1864 86 D
Holy Alliance, The 88 D
Holy Land, The 52 D, 53 A
Holy Seplechur, The 49 A
Homo erectus 7 A
Honecker, Erich (1912–), E. Ger. first secr. 1971–89, 128 C
Honorius, Flavius (384–423), West Roman emperor 395 42 B
House of Commons, The British 72 C*
Hu Yaobang (1914–89), Chin. party chief 1981–86 117 A
Hulagu (d. 1264), Mongol prince and general, grandson of Genghis Khan 40 D
Humboldt, Alexander von (1769–1859), Ger. geografer and naturalist 95 C*
Hundred Years' War (1337–1453) 56 A

Hungary, 1526 71 A
–, 1794 78 A
–, 1944 113 B
–, 1945–47 116 B
–, 1955 116 A
–, 1989–90 128 C
Huns 31 D, 33 C
Husàk, Gustàv (1913–), Czech. pres. 1975–87 128 B
Hyde Park, London (1814) 85 D*

I
Iceland, ca. 900 46 B
–, 1940 110 D
Idris as-Sanusi (1890–1983), king of Libya 1950–69 122 D
Igor, Grand Duke of Novgorod 912–45 51 A
Iktinos, Gr. architect, second half of 400s 19 A
Ilkhans, Empire of the 40 A, D
Imhotep, Egypt. architect, physician and pol. around 2900 BC 14 C
Imperialism 98 B
Inca Empire 61 C
India, 329 BC–646 AD 32 D, 38 B–D
–, 1300s 64 A–C
–, 1497–98 61 C
–, 1500 61 B
–, 1503–1707 61 C, 65 A
–, 1756–1885 99 A
–, 1939–84 126 D, 127 A–D
Indian (Amer.) 92 C
Indochinese Confederation 124 D
Indonesia, 1942–76 126 A, B–D
Indus culture 10 A
Ingermanland, 1617 69 B
–, 1721 71 D
Investiture Struggle 53 A
Iran, 100 AD 32 D
–, 1826–28 89 A
–, 1951 119 D
–, 1979 119 C
–, see also Persian Empire and Persia
Iraq, 1921 108 B
–, 1972–73 119 D
Ireland, ca. 900 46 B
–, 1171 52 C
Irian Jaya, 1969 126 D
Isaacsz, Peter (1569–1625), Dan.-Dutch painter 69 A
Islam, Muslims 37 D, 41 B, D, 127 A
Islamic Republic, The (Iran) 119 C
Israel, Palestine, ca. 1030–931 BC 15 B–D
–, 1947–67 118 A
Issos, Battle of (333 BC) 21 B
Istanbul, see Constantinople
Istria, beg. of 1900s 107 A

Itúrbide, Augustine de (1783–1824), Mex. officer and hero of liberation, emperor of Mexico 1822–23 95 A
Italy, 843 44 D
–, 962 47 B
–, 1176 53 A
–, 1220s 50 C
–, 1250–1454 57 A
–, 1800 80 D
–, 1814–15 85 A
–, 1815–61 87 C–D
–, 1889–1941 107 A, 110 D, 111 A
–, 1943–45 113 B
–, see also Roman Empire Italy, Itsukushima Temple 34 D*
Ivory Coast 123 A
Izmir region, The, 1923 108 C

J
Jakes, Milos (1922–), Czech. pres. 1987–89 128 B
James I (1566–1625), Scottish king as James VI from 1567, Eng. king from 1603 67 B
Janate, Ind. pol. alliance 127 C
Japan, ca. 600 33 C
–, 1867–1939 102 D, 116 D, 117 A
–, 1941–45 111 A, 115 A, 124 A
Jaroslav the Wise (978–1054), Grand Prince of Kiev 1019 51 A–D
Jaruzelski, Wojchiech (1923–), Polish p.m. 1981–85, head of state from 1985 128 A
Jayavarman II, king of Khmer kingdom (Cambodia) 802–50 39 A
Jayavarman VII, king of Khmer kingdom 1181–1218 39 A
Jeanne d'Arc, Maid of Orléans (1412–31), Fr. saint and mil. leader 56 A, D*
Jefferson, Thomas (1743–1826), pres. of USA 1801–09 92 B
Jemtland 69 B
Jeroboam, Isr. rebel, king of Israel 931 BC 15 D
Jerusalem 15 C, 49 D*
Jesuits 95 B
Jesus Christ 26 C
Jews, during WW2 109 A*, 113 D
Jiang Jieshi (Chiang Kaichek) (1887–1975), Chin. statesman, pres. of Nationalist China (Taiwan)

1949–75 116 D, 117 A
Jin (Ch'in) kingdom, China 34 A
Johannesburg 97 D
John Frederick the Noble (1503–54), Elector of Saxony 1532–47 58 D*
John I Zimisces, Byz. emperor 969–76 45 B, 51 A
John Lackland (1167–1216), Eng. king 1199 52 C
John VI (1767–1826), Port. regent from 1792, king from 1816 95 B
John XII, r.n. Octavianus, pope 955–63 47 B
Joséphine de Beauharnais, b. Tascher de la Pagerie (1763–1814), Fr. empress w. of Napoleon I 1798–1809 80 A, D
Juarez, Benito (1806–72), pres. of Mexico 1858–72 95 A Juda 15 D
Judea 26 C
Julian calendar 25 A
Jupiter, Temple of, Rome 27 C
Jürgen, Junker, see Lùther, Martin
Justinian I (482–565), East Roman emperor 527 42 C

K
Kàdàr, Jànos (1912–), Hungarian first secr. 1956–88 128 C
Kadhafi, see Gadaffi
Kaifeng 34 A
Kalinga 38 C
Kalisz, see S. Prussia
Kalondshi, Albert, leader of liberation movement i Kazai, Zaïre 1960 123 C
Kambyses II, Pers. king 529–522 BC 13 A
Kanauj 38 D
Kapodistrias (Capo d'Istria), Johannes Antonius (1776–1831), count, Russ. foreign min., pres. of Greece 1828–31 88 C
Karadjordje, see Petrovich George
Karakorum 34 A, 40 B
Karelia, 1721 71 D
Karl Peter Ulrik of Gottorp, see Peter III
Karthago (Carthage) 16 A, 22 D
Kasai 123 B
Kasavubu, Joseph (1910–69), pres. of Zaïre 1960–65 122 D*, 123 B
Kashmir, 1947 127 A
Katanga (Shaba) province 123 B
Ka-aper, Egypt. regional prince 2000s BC 11 A*

Keksholms len 69 B
Kennedy, John Fitzgerald (1917–63), pres. of USA 1961–63 121 C*, D
Kenya, 1963–64 122 D, 123 A
Kenyatta, Jomo (1891–1978), p.m. of Kenya 1963, pres. from 1964 122 D*
Keswick 7 C*
Khanbalik (Beijing) 34 A, 35 D, 40 B, 61 C
Khanua, Battle of (1527) 65 A
Khazars 51 A
Khitan people 34 A
Khmer Kingdom (Cambodia) 39 A
Khomeini, Ruhallah (ca. 1900–89), Iran. ayatollah, leader from 1979 119 C
Khorezm Empire 34 A
Khruschev, Nikita Sergeyevitch (1894–1971), Sov. first secr. 1953–64, p.m. 1958–64 116 B, C, 121 D
Kiev (Norse: Svitjod) 40 C, 51 A–D
Kimberley 97 C
Kish 12 B
Kitchener, Horatio Herbert, Earl K. of Khartoum (1850–1916), Brit. general 97 A
Knights Templars 52 D
Knossos 8 A
Knut I (Canute), the Great (995–1035), king of England 1016, of Denmark 1018 and of Norway 1028 50 B
Koltchak, Alexander Vasilyevitch (1873–1920), Russ. admiral and polar explorer 106 D
Konon (d. 390 BC), Gr. general 17 A
Korea (Chosen), 1910 102 D
–, 1945–53 119 A
Kosciuszko, Tadeusz (1746–1817), Polish liberation hero 73 B, 78 A
Kronstadt 102 A
Krupp, Friedrich Alfred (1854–1902), Ger. captain of industry 86 D*
Krüger, Paul (Paulus) (1825–1904), pres. of Transvaal 1883–1900 97 C
Kublai Khan (1216–94), Mongol and Chin. Great Khan 34 A, 40 B, 61 C
Kurile Islands, 1875 102 D
Kush 10 A
Kuwait, 1920 108 B
–, 1946–61 119 D
Kyoto 34 D
Königsberg 70 A*

L
La Plata, see Rio de La Plata
La Tène 9 D
Labrador 61 C
Lagosta, beg. of 1900s 107 A
Lahore, 1965 127 A
Langobards 42 C, 44 B, 47 A
Laos, 1945–54 124 B–C
Lascaux cave 6 C*
Latvia, 1989–90 128 C
Lausanne, Peace of (1923) 108 B
Lebanon, 1920 108 B
Lechfeld, Battle of (955) 47 A
Lee, Robert Edward (1807–70), Amer. Confederate general 93 C
Leeds, around 1800 76 A
Legnano, Battle of (1176) 53 A
Lenbach, Franz von (1836–1904), Ger. painter 100 A
Lenin, Vladimir Ilyitch, r.n. Ulyanov (1870–1924), Sov. statesman 106 D*
Leo III (750–816), pope 795 44 C
Leo III, the Isaurian (ca. 675–741), Byz. emperor 717 45 A
Leo X, r.n. Giovanni de' Medici (1475–1521), pope 1513 57 D, 59 A
Leonidas (d. 480 BC), king of Sparta 489 13 A
Leopold I of Habsburg (ca. 1292–1326), Duke of Austria 55 C
Lepanto, Naval battle of (1571) 71 A
Lesotho, 1966 123 A
Leyden, 1574 66 B
Leyte, 1944 111 A
Libya (Tripoli), 500s BC 13 A, 19 D
–, 1911–12 96 A–B, 103 A, 107 A
–, 1951 123 A
–, after 1969 122 D
Ligurian Republic, The 81 B
Lincoln, Abraham, (1809–65), pres. in USA 1861–65 93 B
Lindisfarne 46 A
Lithuania, 1919 107 D
–, 1989–90 128 C
Liu Bang, see Gao Zu
Liverpool, 1800s 76 A, 90 B
Livingstone, David (1813–73), Scot. medical missionary and explorer 96 C–D
Livonia (Livland), 1629 69 B
–, 1721 71 D
Locomotive (1813–14) 77 D*
Lodi, Battle of (1796) 80 A
Lodi, Treaty of (1454) 57 C
Lodomeria, 1772 73 A
«Long Parliament, The» 67 B–C

Lombardia, 1797 80 B
–, 1859 86 A, 87 C
Lombardian Confederation, The 53 A
London, 1013 50 B
–, 1666 66 C, 67 C
–, around 1800 76 A
–, 1814 85 D*
–, 1870 91 D
–, 1940 110 D*
London, Peace of (1913) 103 D
London, the L. Blitz (1940) 110 D*
Long March, The, in China (1934–35) 116 D
Lorraine (Lothringen), 1871 86 D
–, 1919 107 D
Lothar I (ca. 795–855), Frankish emperor 823, emperor in the Middle Kingdom from 843 44 C–D
Lothar II of Saxony (1075–1137), Ger. king 1125–37, Holy Roman emperor from 1133 53 A
Lothringen, see Lorraine
Louis the German (ca. 805–876), king of E. Frankish kingdom 843 44 D
Louis the Pious (778–840), Frankish emperor 814 44 C
Louis VII, the Young (1120–80), Fr. king 1137 48 D
Louis XVI (1754–93), Fr. king 1774–92 78 B–C, 85 B
Louis XVIII (1755–1824), Fr. king 1814–15 and 1815–24 84 A, 85 B*
Louisiana, 1803 92 C
Lübeck 56 D
Lumumba, Patrice (1925–61), p.m. in Congo Republic 1960 123 B*
Lunéville, Peace of (1801) 81 B, 82 A
Luoyang 33 C
Luther, Hans (d. 1530), father of Martin L. 58 A
Luther, Martin (1483–1546), Ger. reformationist 58 A, D*, 59 A
Lützen, Battle of (1632) 69 B, D
Lydia 13 A
Lyon, 1815 84 A

M
MacArthur, Douglas (1880–1964), Amer. general, allied commander in Japan 1945–51 111 A
Macedonia, 512 BC 13 A
–, 300s BC 21 A
–, 200 BC 24 B
–, 971 45 C

–, 1878 100 D
–, 1913 103 D
Madagascar, 1960 123 A
Madjars 47 A
Mafeking 97 C
Magellan, Fernando, r.n. Fernao de Magalhaes (1480–1521), Port. seafarer 61 B
Magna Carta (1215) 52 C
Magna Graecia – Greater Greece 20 A
Mahdi Kingdom 97 A
Mainland Blockade, The (1806–14) 83 C–D
Malawi, 1964 123 A
Malaya, 1942 111 A
Malaysia, 1963–66 126 C–D
Mali, 1960 123 A
Mali, king of 60 D*
Man 46 B
Manchester, around 1800 76 A
–, 1830 90 B
–, 1870 91 D
Manchuria, 1629 34 B–C
–, 1931–33 102 D
Manchus 34 B–C
Mandshu-kuo, 1931–32 102 D
Mantova, 1797 80 B
Mao Zedong (Mao Tsetung) (1893–1976), Chin. revolutionary and statesman, foreman of People's Republic of China from 1949 116 D, 117 D*
«Mao's Little Red Book» 117 D*
Marathon, Battle of (490 BC) 13 A, 16 D
Marengo, Battle of (1800) 80 C
Margarete of Parma (1522–86), Sp. governor in the Netherlands 66 A
Maria (1899–1918), Russ. grand duchess, daughter of Nicholas II 106 A*
Maria Fedorova (b. Dagmar), (1847–1928), Russ. tzarina, w. of Alexander III 106 A
Maria Theresia (1717–80), Holy Roman empress, Archduchess of Austria, queen of Hungary and Bohemia 72 A*
Marie Antoinette, orig. Josephe Jeanne (1755–93), Fr. queen, w. of Louis XVI in 1770 78 C
Marius, Gaius (157–86 BC), Rom. consul and general 24 D
Marne, Battle of (1914) 104 C
Marocco, 1906–34 96 A–B
–, 1942 113 A
–, 1956 123 A

Marshall, sir John Hubert (1876–1958), Brit. archeologist 10 A
Martinovics, Ignac (1755–95), Hungarian philosopher and pol. 78 A
Mary I Tudor, (Bloody Mary) (1516–58), Eng. queen 1553, w. of Philip II of Spain 67 A
Mary Stuart (1542–87), Queen of Scots, 1543–67, Fr. queen in her marriage with Francis II from 1559 67 A, 68 A
Mathilde (d. 1083), Eng. queen, w. of William the Conqueror in 1053 47 B
Mauritania, 1960 123 A
Maurya dynasty 38 B–C
Maximilian Ferdinand Joseph (1832–67), emperor of Mexico 1864, orig. Archduke of Austria 95 A
Maximilian I (1459–1519), Ger. king 1486, Holy Roman emperor 1493 55 C
Mayan culture 62 D*, 63 A*
Mazowiecki, T. (f. 1927), Polish p.m. 1989–90 128 B
Mazzini, Giuseppe (1805–72), Ital. auth. and revolutionary 87 C
McKinley, William (1843–1901), pres. in USA 1897–1901 94 D
Meade, George (1815–72), Amer. general 93 C
Mecca 37 D
Medes, Kingdom of the 13 A
Medici, Cosimo de', the Elder (1389–1464), Florentine banker and statesman 57 C
Medici, Giovanni de', see Leo X
Medici, Lorenzo de', il Magnifico (1449–92), Ital. prince, patron and poet 57 D
Medina 37 D
Megalithic Age, The 7 C, 9 A
Mehmet, see Muhammed
Meiji (Mutsuhito) (1852–1912), Jap. emperor 1867 102 D
Melanchton, Philip (1497–1560), Ger. reformationist 58 D*, 59 A
Memel region, 1919 107 D
Memphis 14 C
Menorca 72 D
Mesopotamia, 3000 BC 11 A–C
–, around 100 29 C
–, 637 37 D
–, 1500s 70 D
Metternich, Clemens von (1773–1859), prince, Austrian foreign min. 84 D*,

Mexico City **95** A
Mexico, 1519–1911 **61** B, **95** A
–, 1846–48 **93** A
Midway, Naval battle of (1942) **111** A
Miklagard (Constantinople) **51** A
Milano, 1848–49 **87** C
Millesimo, Battle of (1796) **80** A
Miltiades (ca. 550–489 BC), Gr. statesman and general **13** A
Minamoto Yoritomo (1147–99), Jap. rebel leader, shogun 1192–99 **34** C–D
Ming Dynasty, Chin. imperial dynasty 1368–1644 **34** B
Mitanni **10** D
Mithradates VI Eupator (ca. 132–63 BC), king of Pontos from 120 **24** D
Mnesicles, Gr. architect in beg. of 400s BC **19** B
Mobutu, Sése–Seko, r.n. Joseph–Désiré (1930–), pres. in Zaire from 1965 **123** B
Moçambique, 1975 **123** A
Modrow, Hans (f. 1928), E. Ger. p.m. 1989–90 **128** FB
Mohacs, Battle of (1526) **71** A
Mohenjo–Daro **10** A, **11** B*
Molay, Jacques de (ca. 1250–1314), Grandmaster of the Templars **52** D*
Moldavia, 1500s **71** A
Møller, Andreas (1684–1762), Da. painter **72** A
Moltke, Helmuth von (1800–91), Da. count, later Pruss. officer **86** D
Mon, people **36** A
Mondovi, Battle of (1796) **80** A
Mongol dominion 1227–1405 **40** A–D, **41** A
Mongolia, 1196–1227 **34** A
Monroe Doctrine, The **93** A
Monroe, James (1758–1831), pres. in USA 1817–25 **93** A
Montenegro, 1876 **100** B
–, 1912 **100** B
Montevideo, 1806–07 **95** A
–, 1843 **87** D
Montezuma II (1468–1520), Aztec king from 1502 **61** B
Montgolfier, Étienne de (1745–99), Fr. inventor **100** A
Montgolfier, Joseph de (1740–1810), Fr. inventor **100** A
Montgomery of Alamein, Bernard Law, Lord Hind-

head (1887–1976), Brit. general, mil. governor in Germany 1945 **112** D
Morgarten, Battle of (1315) **55** C
Moscow, 1200s **40** C
–, 1812 **82** D, **83** D
–, 1970s **116** D*
Moses, traditionally the liberator of the Jews from bondage in Egypt (ca. 1225 BC) **45** D*
Mozart, Johann Georg Leopold (1719–87), Austrian violinist and composer, father of Wolfgang A. M. **74** A
Mozart, Wolfgang Amadeus (1756–91), Austrian composer **74** A, D
Muhammed (ca. 570–632), founder of Islam **37** D, **41** B
Muhammed (Mehmet) II the Conqueror (1429–81), Turk. sultan 1451 **70** D
Muhammed bin Tughluq, Ind. sultan 1325–51 **64** B
Muhammed Reza Pahlavi (1919–80), Shah of Iran 1941–79 **119** C
Munich (München), Coup d'Etat in, (1923) **109** A
–, Meeting in (1938) **108** A
–, Congress of (1938) **109** A
Münster, Peace of (1648) **66** B
Murat (Murad) I (1319–89), Turk. sultan 1360 **70** D
Mussolini, Benito (1883–1945), Ital. statesman, founder of Ital. fascism, «Duce» (Leader) from 1922 **108** A, **109** A*, **113** A
Mutsuhito, see Meiji
Mycerino, Pyramid of **15** A*

N

Naga, Ind. serpent god **38** A
Nagasaki, 1945 **111** A
Nagumo, Chuichi (1887–1944), Jap. admiral **110** D*
Namibia, 1990 **123** A
Nanjing **35** D
Napoleon Bonaparte (1769–1821), Fr. emperor 1804–14 and 20.3.–28.6 1815 **73** A, **78** C, **80** A, D*, **81** B, D, **82** A–D, **83** A*–D, **84** A, **85** C, D
Napoleon III, r.n. Charles Louis Napoléon Bonaparte (1808–73), Fr. pres. 1848–52, emperor 1852–70 **86** D, **87** A*, B, **95** A
Napoli, 1805 **82** A

–, 1848–49 **87** C
–, 1860 **87** C
Nash, Paul (1889–1946), Brit. painter **104** C
Nasser, Gamal Abd al (1918–70), Egypt. pres. 1956–70 **118** A*, B, **122** D
National Liberation Front, The, in Vietnam, see FNL
National Socialist Party (Nazis), The, in Germany **108** D
Nationalist China **117** A
NATO (North Atlantic Treaty Organization) **116** A
Navarino, Battle of (1827) **88** C
Naxos **20** A
Nazareth **26** C
Near East, The, 1907–14 **103** A
–, 1917–26 **108** A–C
Nehru, Jawaharlal (1889–1964), Ind. p.m. 1917–64 **127** A
Nelson, Horatio (1758–1805), Brit. admiral **80** B, **81** D*, **82** A
Nero, Lucius Domitius (37–68), Rom. emperor 54 **27** A, **29** C
Nesselrode, Karl Vasilyevitch von (1780–1862), Russ. diplomat, foreign min. **84** D*
Netherlands, The United **66** B
Netherlands, The, 1559–1648 **66** A–B
Neustria **43** A
New Amsterdam (New York) **62** D
New Granada **94** A
New Mexico **93** A
New Spain, 1500s **62** D, **95** A
New York (New Amsterdam) **62** D, **115** B*
Newfoundland **72** D
Ngo Dinh Diem (1901–63), S. Vietn. pres. 1955–63 **125** B
Nicholas I Pavlovitch (1796–1855), Russ. tzar 1825 **89** A
Nicholas II (1868–1918), Russ. tzar 1894–1917 **106** A*, D
Niger, 1960 **123** A
Nigeria, 1960 **123** A
Nightingale, Florence (1820–1910), Brit. nurse and philanthropist **89** D
Nile, sources of **96** D
Nixon, Richard Milhous (1930–), pres. in USA 1969–74 **121** C, **125** D
Normandy, 829–911 **46** B, C–D

–, 1106 **52** C
–, 1944 **113** B
Normanni, people **50** C
Norodom Sihanouk (1922–), king of Kampuchea 1941–55, head of government 1960–70 and 1975–76 **124** A
North America, 1620–1775 **62** D, **75** A
North Atlantic Treaty Organization, see NATO
North Korea, 1945–53 **119** A
North Sea Empire, The (1028–35) **50** A–B
North Vietnam, 1945–54 **124** C–D
–, 1955–76 **125** B–D
Northern Schleswig, 1919–20 **107** D
Northern States, The, USA **93** C
Northern War, The Great (1700–21) **69** B, **71** D
Norway, 1940 **110** A
Nova Scotia **72** D
Nova Zemlya **61** C
Novogorod (Holmgard) **51** A
–, 520s BC **13** A
Nubia, 1860 BC **15** A
Nyerere, Julius Kambarage (1922–), pres. of Tanzania 1964–85 **122** D*

O

Ochrida (Ohrid) **45** C
Oder–Neisse Line **114** D
Oghotai (ca. 1185–1241), Mongol Great Khan from 1229 **34** A, **40** A, C
Ohrid, see Ochrida
Olav II Haraldsson, the Saint (995–1030), Norw. king 1015–28 **50** A–B
Oleg (Helge) the Wise (d. 912), Kiev kingdom's leader from 880 **51** A
Olga (1895–1918), Russ. grand duchess, daughter of Nikolai II **106** A*
Olympia, Greece **18** A, B, D
Olympias (d. 316 BC), Macedonian queen, w. of Philip II **21** A
Olympic Games, Greece **18** B–D
Oman, 1964 **119** D
Omar I, Caliph 634–44 **37** D
Omayyads **37** D
Omdurman, Battle of (1898) **97** A
Orange Free State, 1854 **97** B
Orinoco **95** D
Orkneys **46** B
Ösel **69** B
Osman Nuri Pasja (1832–1900), Turk. general and pol. **100** B
Oswald, Lee Harvey (1939–

63), according to Warren Report, John F. Kennedy's murderer **121** C
Othman (d. 656), caliph 644 **37** D
Otto I the Great (912–73), Ger. king 936, Holy Roman emperor 962 **47** A–B
Ottoman (Turkish) Empire, 1360–1683 **70** D
–, end of 1700s **73** D
–, see also Turkish kingdoms
Ouchy at Lausanne, Peace of (1912) **103** A
Oxenstierna, Axel (1583–1654), Swed. chancellor **69** C
Oxus, treasures of **13** A*

P

Pagan **40** B
Pakistan 1947–71 **127** A, B, D
Palatine, Rome **27** B
Palermo **50** D
Palermo, 1848–49 **87** C
Palestine Liberation Organization, see PLO
Palestine, 1400s BC **10** D
–, 539 BC **13** A
–, at the time of Christ **26** C
–, 640 **37** D
–, 1920 **108** A
–, –Israel 1946–67 **118** A–C
Palikat, figure of legend in Mon kingdom **36** A
Pallas Athene (Athene Parthenos) **19** C
Pañama Canal **94** A
Panipat, Battle of (1526) **65** A
Papal State, The (1848–49) **87** C
Paris, 508 **43** A
–, around 1800 **77** A
–, 1870 **91** D
–, 1914 **104** D
–, 1940 **110** D
–, 1944 **113** D
Paris, Peace of (1763) **62** D, **75** A
–, (1783) **92** B
Parma, 1859 **86** A, **87** C
Parthenon, Athens **19** A, C, D*
Parthian empire **32** D, **37** A
Pathet Lao, Laotian Communist Party **124** C
Patrisians **22** B
Patzinaks **51** A, D
Paul I (1754–1801), Russ. tzar 1796 **83** B
Paulus, Friedrich von (1890–1957), Ger. general **112** D
Pearl Harbor (1941) **110** D, **111** A
Pedro I (1798–1834), emperor of Brazil 1822–31 **95** B
Peisistratos (d. 527 BC), ruler of Athens around 560 **16** D
Peking, see Beijing

Peloponnesian War, The 17 A

Pera 55 B

Perea 26 C

Pericles (ca. 500–429 BC), Athenian statesman 17 A, 18 A, C

Pericles' Odeion 19 B

Persepolis 13 A

Persia, 1907 103 A

–, see also Iran

Persian Empire, 559–479 BC 13 A, 16 D, 17 A

–, 334 BC 21 A–B

Persian Wars, The 16 D

Peru, 1650 62 D

–, beg. of 1800s 94 B

Peter I Alexeyevitch, the Great (1672–1725), Russ. tzar 1689 71 B*, 88 D

Peter I, king of Bulgaria 927–70 45 C

Peter III, r.n. Karl Peter Ulrik of Gottorp (1728–62), Russ. tzar 1762 73 C, 83 A

Petrarca, Francesco (1304–74), Ital. poet 57 B

Petrovich, Georg, called Karadjordje (Black George) (ca. 1766–1817), Serb. rebel leader, prince of Serbia 78 A

Philadelphia (1787) 92 B

Philip II (1527–98), Sp. king 1556 66 A–B, 68 A*

Philip I August (1165–1223), Fr. king 1180 49 A, 52 D

Philip II of Macedonia (382–336 BC), king 359 BC 21 A, D*

Philip IV the Fair (1268–1314), Fr. king 1285 52 D

Philippines, 1941–42 111 A

Phnom Penh 124 A

Phoenicia, Phoenecians 16 A

Picts 29 D

Pilatus, Pontius, Rom. governor in Judea 26–36 26 C

Pious VII, r.n. Barnaba Luigi Chiaramonti (1742–1823), pope 1800 82 A

Pipin (ca. 640–714), Frankish major domus 687–71 43 A

Pipin the Small (ca. 714–68), Frankish king from 751 44 B

Pizarro, Francisco (ca. 1475–1541), Sp. seafarer, Peru's conqueror 61 C

Plataiai, Battle of (479 BC) 13 A

Plebes, Plebians 22 B–C

Plevna 100 B

PLO (Palestine Liberation Organization) 118 C

PNI, Indonesian Nationalist Party 126 A

Poitiers, Battle of (732) 37 D, 43 A

Poland, 1764–95 73 A–B, 78 A

–, 1919 107 D

–, 1939 109 A, 110 A

–, 1945 114 D

–, 1948–90 116 A, 128 A–B

Poland, the three divisions of (1772, 1793 and 1795) 73 A–B, D

Polo, Marco (ca. 1255– ca. 1325), Venetian explorer 61 A, C*

Poltava, Battle of (1709) 71 B

Pomerania, 1720 75 D

Pomerania, Farther 70 A, 75 D

Pomerania, Hither 70 A

Pompeius, Gnaeus P. the Great (106–48 BC), Rom. consul 70 BC 24 D

Poniatowski, Stanislav August, see Stanislav II August

Port Arthur, 1904–05 102 D

Portugal, 1808–14 81 D, 82 D

Portuguese East Africa 61 B

Poseidon, Gr. god 19 C

Poseidonia 20 A

Posen (Poznan), 1792 73 B

–, 1956 128 A

Prague, Battle of (1757) 75 A

Prasad, Rajendra (1884–1963), Ind. pres. 1950–62 127 A

Preston, Battle of (1648) 67 C

Pretoria 97 D

Princip, Gavrilo (1894–1918), Serb. assassin 1914 103 D

Pronaia, Temple, Delphi 18 A*

Propylaea 19 B

Protestant League, The 69 A

Prussia (Preussen), 1415–1795 75 B, D

–, 1701 70 A

–, 1740–48 72 A

–, 1756–63 74 C–D, 75 A

–, 1772 73 A

–, 1806–07 82 D

–, 1815 85 B

–, 1859–64 86 A

Pugachev, Yemelyan Ivanovitch (1726–75), Don Cossack, Russ. rebel leader 83 A*, 88 D

Pugin, Auguste (1762–1832), Fr.-born Brit. painter and architect 76 A

Punic Wars, The 22 D

Pyramids, Battle of the (1798) 80 B

Pythagoras (ca. 570–500 BC), Gr. philosopher and mathematician 20 A

Pythia, priestess of the Oracle in Delfi 18 A

Q

Qatar, 1916–71 119 D

Qin dynasty, China (221–206 BC) 30 D, 31 A

Qin Shi Huangdi, first emperor of Qin 221–210 BC 30 D, 31 A, D

Qing dynasty, China (1644–1912) 34 C

R

Ra, Egypt. sun god 14 D

Rahman, Mujibur (1920–75), Pakist. pol., pres. in Bangladesh 1972–75 127 D

Rahman, Ziaur (Zia) (1936–81), general, pres. in Bangladesh 1977–81 127 D

Railways, 1800s 90 A–C

Rainhill, contest at (1829) 90 B

Raleigh, sir Walter (ca. 1552–1618), Eng. colonizer 67 A

Ravenna 42 C–D, 45 A

Raymond of Toulouse (1036–1105), Count of T., margrave of Provence, knight-crusader 48 C

Red Cross, The International 87 B

Rehaboam, king of Juda in beg. of 900s 15 D

Remus, according to legend, Rome's founder together with Romulus 22 A, 27 B

Renescure, Fr. palace 74 A*

Revere, Paul (1735–1818), Amer. patriot and engraver 92 A

Rhine, 1801 81 B

Rhine, Confederation of the 82 A

Rhineland, 1936 109 A

Rhodes (Rhodos), 1522 71 A

–, 1911–12 107 A

Rhodesia, see Zimbabwe

Richard I, the Liohheart (1157–99), Eng. king 1189 49 A

Riga 69 B

Rio de Janeiro 95 B

Rio de Plata La 62 D, 95 A

Road construction, 1700s 73 A*

Roads and Transport, at the end of the 1700s 77 A

Robert I, Robert Bruce (1274–1329), king of Scotland 1306 52 C

Robert III (1060–1134), duke of Normandie 1087 48 C

Rollo (Gange-Rolf, or Rolf) (d. 933), Normanni chieftain 46 D

Roman Empire, 753– ca. 300

BC 22 A–C

–, ca. 200–44 BC 24 B–D

–, 31 BC–117 AD 29 C

Romania, 1913 103 D

–, 1944 113 C

–, 1955 116 A

–, 1989–90 128 B

–, see also Dacia

Rome, 753 BC–117 AD 22 A–C, 24 D, 25 B*, 27 B–D, 29 C

–, 1054 41 D

–, 1944 113 B

Rommel, Erwin (1891–1944), Ger. panzer general 113 A

Romulus, see also Remus 22 A, 27 B

Roncevaux, Battle of (778) 44 B

Roosevelt, Theodore (Teddy) (1858–1919), pres. in USA 1901–09 94 D*

Roslin, Alexander (1718–93), Swed. painter 73 C

Rossbach, Battle of (1757) 74 D

«Rough Riders» 94 D*

Rowlandson, Thomas (1756–1827), Brit. artist 76 A

Roxane (d. ca. 310 BC), Pers. queen, w. of Alexander the Great 21 B

Rubicon 24 D

Ruhr region, 1923 108 D

Rurik (d. ca. 879), chieftain in Novgorod 862 51 A

Russia, 862–1054 51 A–D

–, 1689–1860 88 D, 89 A

–, under Peter the Great (1689–1725) 71 B–D

–, 1756–63 74 C

–, 1772–96 73 A, C–D, 78 A

–, 1796–1812 82 A, D, 83 B–D

–, 1815 85 B

–, 1853–56 89

–, 1870s 100 B–C

–, 1904–05 102 D

–, 1918–21 (Civil War) 106 D

–, see also Soviet Union, The

Russo-Japanese War (1905) 102 A

Rwanda, 1962 123 A

Ryukyu Islands, 1876 102 D

S

Saar region, 1919 107 D

Sadat, Muhammad Anwar al- (1918–81), Egypt. off. and pol., pres. from 1970 122 D*

Saigon, 1968 125 D

–, 1975 125 D

S(ain)t Bernhard, Great 81 A*

S(ain)t Helena, 1815 84 A

S(ain)t Paul's Cathedral,

London 76 A*

S(ain)t Petersburg 71 D

Sakhalin, 1904–05 102 D

Sakkara 11 A

Salamis, Battle of (480 BC) 13 A, 16 D

Salisbury, Robert Arthur Talbot Gascoyne-Cecil, III Marquis of S. (1830–1903), Brit. pol. 101 A*

SALT-(Strategic Arms Limitation Talks) Agreement (1972) 116 C

Samaria 26 C

Samarkand 41 A

Samurai 37 A

San Francisco, Congress of (1945) 115 A

San Salvador 61 A

San Stefano, Peace of (1878) 100 C

Sanchi 39 A*

Sanssouci, castle in Potsdam 75 B

Sao Tomé and Principe, 1975 123 A

Sarajevo, assassination in (1914) 103 D*, 104 B

Sardinia, 1848–49 87 C

–, 1854 89 D

–, 1859 86 A

–, 1961 87 C

Sargon I, king of Akkad 2382–2327 BC 12 B

Sasanids 32 D, 37 A, D

Saudi-Arabia, 1926 108 C

–, 1933–45 119 D

Saul, king of Israel ca. 1030–1015 BC 15 BC

Saxony, 1740–48 72 A

–, 1756 74 D

Scheidemann, Philip (1865–1939), Ger. social democrat, chancellor 1919 108 D

Schleswig, 1864 86 D

Schmalkaldic League, The 59 A

Schwerin, Kurt Christoph von (1684–1757), Pruss. count and general 75 A

Schwyz 55 C

Scotland, around 900 46 B

–, 1284 52 C–, 1553–1673 67 A–D

–, 1710 72 C

–, see also Great Britain

Scythians 13 A

Second World War (WW2) 109 A, 110 A, D, 111 A, 112 D, 113 A–D, 114 A, D

–, in China 117 A

Security Council, UN 115 B

Sedan, Battle of (1870) 86 D

Selevkos I Nikator (358–281 BC), Macedon. general, king of Syria 38 B

Selim I (1466–1520), Turk. sultan 1512 70 D

Selinus 20 A

Senegal, 1960 **123** A
Sepoy Rebellion (1857–59) **99** A
Serbia, 1453 **70** D
–, 1804 **78** A
–, 1870s **100** B
–, 1912 **103** D
–, 1914–18 **104** B
Sesostris III Khakaura, Egypt. king 1878–1840 BC **15** A
Seven Years' War (1756–63) **74** C–D, **75** A
Sforza, Francesco (1401–66), Ital. condottiere, duke of Milano 1450 **57** C
Shaba Province, see Katanga Province
Shailendra empire **39** A
Shandong Peninsula, 1919 **102** D
Shang kingdom **30** A–B
Sharples, James (ca. 1750–1811), Amer. painter **92** D
Shastri, Lal Bahadur (1904–66), Ind. p.m. 1964–66 **127** A
Shetlands **46** B
Shi'ites **37** D
Shipka Pass **100** C
Shwe Dagon pagoda, Rangoon **36** A*
Sicilies, The Two, 1815 **87** C
Sicily, 750–550 BC **20** A
–, 200s BC **22** D
–, 1220s **50** C
–, 1860 **87** C
–, 1943 **112** D, **113** A
Sidon **16** A
Siebenbürgen, 1500s **71** A
Silesia (Schlesien), 1742 **75** D
Simon (d. 927), Bulgarian emperor 893 **45** C
Sinai, 1956–57 **118** B
Singapore, 1942 **111** A
Singh, Viswanat Pratap (1931–), Ind. finance min. 1985–87 **127** C
Sisavang Vong, king of Laos 1945–59 **124** C
Six Day War, The (1967) **118** B
Smolensk **51** A
Sofia Fredrika Augusta of Anhalt-Zerbst, see Catherine the Great
Soisson, Battle of (486) **43** A
Solferino, Battle of (1859) **87** B*, C
Solidarity, Polish trade union **116** C, **128** A. B, C
Soliman, see Suleyman
Solomon, king of Israel ca. 972–931 BC **15** C
Solon (ca. 640–561 BC), Gr. philosopher and statesman **16** D
Somalia, 1960 **123** A
Somaliland, 1889 **107** A

Song dynasty (Empire), China (960–1279) **34** A, **40** B
Sophocles (496–406 BC), Gr. dramatist **17** A
South Africa, 1899–1902 **97** B–D
–, after WW2 **122** D
South America, 1650–1775 **62** D
–, in beg. of 1800s **94** A–B
South Carolina, 1860 **93** B
South Korea, 1945–53 **119** A
South Vietnam, 1954–76 **124** D, **125** B–D
Southern Prussia (Kalisz), 1792 **73** B
Southern States, The Confederate States of America **93** A, B
Soviet Union, The, 1939 **110** A
–, 1941 **110** D
–, 1944 **113** C
–, 1945–82 **114** D, **116** A, B–D
Space travel **116** C
Spain, 1556–98 **68** A
–, 1740–48 **72** A
–, 1804 **82** A
–, 1808–1478 **A**, **81** D, **82** D
–, 1898 **94** D
Spanish Civil War, The (1936–39) **109** A
Spanish Netherlands, The **66** B
Spanish War of Succession, The (1701–13) **72** D
Sparta **16** D, **17** A
Spartacus (d. 71 BC), leader of slave rebellion in Rome **73** BC–D
Spitsbergen **61** C
Sputnik 1 **116** C
Stalin, Josef Vissarionovich, r.n. Djugashvili (1879–1953), Sov. leader **106** D*, **109** A*, **116** B
Stalingrad (1942–43) **112** D*, **113** A
Stanislav II August, Poniatowski (1732–98), Polish king 1764–95 **73** A
Stanley, sir Henry Morton (1841–1904), Brit.–Amer. journalist and explorer **96** C–D
Stephenson, George (1781–1848), Brit. railway engineer **77** D, **90** A, B
Stephenson, Ronert (1803–59), Brit. railway engineer, son of George S. **90** B
Stockholm, Peace of (1720) **75** D
Stockton **90** B
Stolbova, Peace of (1617) **69** B
Stupas **39** A*
Sudan, end of the 1800s **97** A
–, 1956 **123** A

Sudetenland, 1938 **108** A, **109** A
Suez Canal, 1956 **118** B
Suharto, Ibrahim (1921–), Indonesian general and pol., pres. from 1968 **126** A, D
Sui dynasty (581–618) **33** C
Sukarno, Achmed (1901–70), indonesian pol., pres. 1945–67 **126** A*
Suleyman (Soliman) II (1496–1566), Turk. sultan 1520 **70** D
Sulla, Lucius Cornelius (ca. 138–78 BC), Rom. statesman **24** D
Sumer, Sumerians **11** C
Surat **65** A
Suryavarman II, king of Khmer kingdom 1113–50 **39** A
Susa **13** A
Svatjoslav, Russ. grand duke 945–72 **51** A
Sven Forkbeard (Tjugeskjegg) (ca. 960–1014), Da. king 983–1014, Norw. king 1000–1014 **50** A
Swaziland, 1968 **123** A
Sweden, 1617–1718 **69** B, **70** A
–, 1700–21 **71** D
–, 1805 **82** A
Swiss Confederation **55** C–D
Switzerland, 1315–1499 **55** C–D
Syagrius (430–87), Rom. governor in Gaul **43** A
Sybaris **20** A
Syracuse (Syrakus(ai)) **20** A
Syria, 1400s BC **10** D
–, 323 BC **38** B
–, 635 **37** D
–, 1500s **70** D
–, 1798 **80** B
–, 1920 **108** A
Syuvalov, Peter (1827–89), count, Russ. diplomat and general **101** A*

T
Tai Zong (Li Shimin), Chin. emperor 626–49 **33** D*
Taiwan (Formosa), 1894–95 **102** D–, 1949 **117** A
Talleyrand-Périgord, Charles Maurice de (1754–1838), Fr. bishop and pol. **84** D
Tang dynasty (618–906) **33** C
Tanganyika, Lake **96** D
Tanganyika, see Tanzania
Tannenberg, Battle of (1914) **104** D
Tanzania, after 1945 **122** D, **123** A
Tapusa, figure of legend in

Mon kingdom **36** A
Taras **20** A
Tarik Ibn Zijad (d. ca. 720), Arab.–Berber general **37** D
Tatyana (1897–1918), Russ. granduchess, daughter of Nicholas II **106** A*
Tchad (Chad), 1960 **123** A
Temple of Heaven, Beijing **35** D*
Temujin, see Genghis Kahn
Tennis Court Oath at Versailles (1789) **78** B
Termopylene, Battle of (479 BC) **13** A
«Terror, Reign of» (Frankrike 1789) **78** BC
Terty, Battle of (687) **43** A
Test Act, The (1673) **67** D
Tet offensive, in Vietnam (1968) **125** C
Tetzel, Johann (ca. 1465–1519), Ger. Dominican monk and peddler of indulgences **58** D
Teutonic Order **75** D
Teutons, people **24** D
Texas, 1845 **95** A
«The Great Leap Forward», China **117** A
Thévenin, Charles (1764–1838), Fr. painter **81** A
Thailand, 1942 **111** A, **124** A
Thebes, Egypt **15** A
Themistocles (ca. 525– ca. 460 BC), Gr. statesman and general **13** A
Theocritus (ca. 300–260 BC), Sicilian poet **22** D
Theodora (ca. 500–548), E. Roman empress, w. of Justinian I **42** D*
Theodosius I the Great (ca. 346–395), Rom. emperor 379 **18** C, **42** B
Thirty Years' War (1618–48) **69** A, **70** A
Thorn (Torun), 1772 **73** A
Thrakia (Thrace) **13** A
Thutankhamon Nebkheperura, Egypt. king 1346–1337 BC **14** B*
Thutmos III Menkheperra (1490–1438 BC), Egypt. king 1468 **10** B, C, D, **15** A
Tiberius Claudius Nero (42 BC–37 AD), Rom. emperor 14 AD **29** C
Tibet **34** C
Tillemans, Peter (1684–1734), Dutch painter and illustrator **72** C
Tilly, Jean Tserclaes (1559–1632), Ger. count, general **69** A
Tilsit, Peace of (1807) **82** D, **83** C
Timor, 1975–76 **126** D
Timur–lenk (1336–1405),

Tiran, Strait of, 1956–57 **118** B
Titus, Arch of, Rome **27** C*
Togo, 1960 **123** A
Tojo, Hideki (1884–1948), Jap. general, p.m. 1941–45 **110** D*
Toltec Wars **63** D*
Tone, Theobald Wolfe (1763–98), Irish jurist and pol. **78** A
Tonkin, Gulf of, 1964 **125** C
Torun, see Thorn
Toscana (Toscany), 1848–49 **87** C
Toungoo (Burma) **40** B
Tower Bridge, London, 1940 **110** D*
Trafalgar, Battle of (1805) **81** D, **82** A
Trajan, r.n. Marcus Ulpius Trajanus (53–117), Rom. emperor 98 **27** D, **29** C
Transjordan, 1920 **108** A
Transvaal, 1852 **97** B
«Trek, The Great», South Africa (1836) **97** B
Tripoli, 1500s **71** A
–, 1912 **96** B
–, see also Libya
Tsarskoje Selo **106** A*
Tshombe, Moise (1919–69), p.m. in Congo (now: Zaïre) 1964–65 **123** B
Tsushima, Strait of, naval battle in (1905) **102** A*, D
Tula **63** D
Tungus **34** A
Tunisia, 750–550 BC **16** A
–, 1800s **96** A–B
–, 1956 **123** A
Turgot, Anne Robert Jacques, Baron de l'Aulne (1727–81), Fr. finance min. **77** A
Turkey, 1827 **88** C
–, 1853–57 **89** A, D
–, 1870s **100** B
–, 1908 **103** A
–, 1912 **103** D
–, 1923 **108** C
Turkish (Ottoman) Empire, 1360–1683 **70** D
–, end of 1700s **73** D
Turkistan **34** C
Tutu, Desmond Mpilo (1931–), South-Afr. archbishop **122** D*
Tyrol, 1808–09 **78** A
–, beg. of 1900s **107** A
Tyros **16** A

U
Uganda, 1962 **123** A
Ujiji **96** D
Ulm, Battle of (1805) **82** A
UN Building, New York **115** B*

UN Day 115 A
UN forces 123 B–C
United Nations, The (UN) 115 A
United States see U.S. (USA)
University of Bologna 49 B★
Unterwalden 55 C
Upper Volta, 1960 123 A
Ur in Chaldea 12 C
Urban II, r.n. Odo de Lagny (ca. 1042–99), pope 1088 48 A★
Uri 55 C
Uruk 11 B, C
USA, United States of America, 1783–1867 92 B–C, 93 A–C
1898 94 C–D
–, 1941 111 A
–, after WW2 116 A
–, in Vietnam, 124 C★, 125 C–D
–, see also North America
Ustinov, Dmitri (1908–84), Sov. min. of defense 1976–84 116 D★
Utica 16 A
Utrecht, Union of (1579) 66 B

V
Vallum Hadriani (Hadrian's Wall) 29 D
Vandals 43 A
Varro, Gaius Terentius, Rom. consul 216 BC 23 A
Veji 22 C
Venezuela, beg. of 1800s 94 A

Venice, 1300s 55 B
–, 1848–49 87 C
Verden (an der Aller) 70 A
Verdun, Treaty of (843) 44 D
–, the Battle for (1916) 104 D
Vernet, Horace (1789–1863), Fr. painter 83 A
Vernet, Joseph (1714–89), Fr. painter 73 A
Versailles, 1789 79 A
Versailles, Peace of (1919) 107 D, 108 D
Vespasian, r.n. Titus Flavius Vespasianus (9–79), Rom. emperor 69 27 A, 29 C
Victor Emanuel II (1820–78), king of Sardinia–Piemonte 1849, Ital. king 1861–78 87 C, D
Victoria (1819–1901), queen of Great Britain and Ireland 1837, empress of India 1877 98 A★, 99 A
Victoria Station, Bombay 99 A★
Vienna, 1241 40 C
–, 1529 71 A
–, 1683 71 A
–, 1805 82 A
–, 1945 113 D
Vienna, Congress of (1814–15), 84 D★, 85 A–B
Vietminh, Vietn. liberation org. 124 C–D, 125 A
Vietnam, 1945–54 124 C★, A
Vikings 45 B, 46 A–B, C–D★, 47 B★, 50 A–B
Villa Borghese 26 D
Virginia 61 A, 67 A
Visby 56 D

Vivaldi, Antonio (1678–1741), Ital. composer 74 B
Vladimir I, the Great (ca. 956–1015), Russ. grand duke 980 51 A
Voltaire, François Marie Arouet de (1694–1778), Fr. auth. 75 B

W
Wales (Bretland), around 900 46 B
–, 1284 52 C, 128 A, C–D★
Walesa, Lech (1943–), Polish trade union leader pres. 1990 116 C, 128 A, D★
Walid I., caliph 705–15 37 D
Wallenstein, r.n. Waldstein, Albrecht von (1583–1634), Austrian general and pol., Duke of Friedland 69 A
Walpole, sir Robert (1676–1745), Earl of Orford, Brit. p.m. 1721–42 72 D
Warsaw Pact, est. 1955 116 A
Warsaw, Grand Duchy of, 1807–15 83 C, 85 B, 88 D
Wartburg 59 A
Washington D.C. 93 A
Washington, George (1732–99), pres. in USA 1789–97 92 B, D★
Waterloo, Battle of (1815) 84 A, 85 C
Weimar Republic, The 108 D
Wellington, Arthur Wellesley, Duke of W. (1769–1852), Brit. general and

pol. 81 D, 85 C
Werner, Anton von (1843–1915), Ger. painter 86 D
Wessex 64 C–D
West Germany (Bundesrepublik Deutschland) 114 D, 128 C
West Kennet 9 A
West Kurdistan, 1500s 70 D
West Prussia, 1600s 75 D –, 1772 73 A
West Roman Empire 42 B
Western Goths (Visigoths) 43 A
Western Xia 34 A
Westphalia, Peace of (1648) 70 A
White Sea 61 C
«Winter War, The», Finland (1939) 110 A
William (Vilhelm) I (1797–1888), king of Prussia 1861–71, Ger. emperor 1871–88 86 D★
William (Vilhelm) II (1859–1941), Ger. emperor 1888–1918 104 D★
William I, the Silent (1533–84), Prince of Orange, Count of Nassau, governor in the Netherlands 66 B
William the Conqueror (1027/28–87), king of England 1066 47 B
Wismar 70 A
Wittenberg 58 D, 59 A
Woolley, sir Leonard (1880–1960), Brit. archeologist 12 C

Worms, Concordat of (1122) 53 A
–, Parliament of (1521) 59 A
Wrangel, Piotr Nikolayevich (1878–1928), Ger.-Baltic baron and «white» general 106 D

X, Y, Z
Xerxes I (d. 465 BC), Persian king 485 13 A
Yemen, 1918 108 A
Yong Luo, Chin. emperor 1403–24 35 D
Young Italy, The – Giovina Italia 87 C
Yuan Dynasty (1280–1367) 34 A
Yudenitch, Nikolai (1862–1933), Russ. «White» general 106 D
Yugoslavia, 1945–47 116 B
Zaire (Republic of the Congo), 1960 123 A
Zambia, 1964 123 A
Zara, beg. of 1900s 107 A
Ziegler, Margarethe (d. 1531), w. of Hans Luther 58 A
Zimbabwe (Rhodesia), 1980 123 A
Zjivkov, Todor (1911–), Bulg. p.m. 1962–71, pres. 1971–89 128 B
Zoroastrianism 37 A
Zwingli, Ulrich (Huldrich) (1484–1531), Swiss reformationist 58 D★

HISTORICAL TIMELINE

Since the earliest beginnings in Africa, the evolution and spread of humankind has seen great variations.
For different reasons at different times highly developed cultures have evolved in one area of the world, while people in other areas were still living as hunters and gatherers. By the same token, it has often happened that geographically distant cultures have seen similar achievements in such areas as tool-making, art, architecture and music at approximately the same point in time.

With the aid of modern scientific methods archaeological finds can now be dated with great accuracy. However, there is often much disagreement over the conclusions to be drawn from these finds. And besides, archaeologists have yet to explore and research many areas of the globe. And that is why our knowledge of the earliest ages of human evolution are constantly changing and being reevaluated. The overview on the following pages shows, in chronological order, examples of historical events and human development at approximately the same moments in history around the world.

	UNITED STATES	AFRICA	ASIA	AUSTRALIA
		The earliest evidence of tool-making in Eastern Africa. Chopping and crushing tools.		
		Palaeolithic: Old Stone Age (Hunter-gatherer Stone Age).		
		Homo sapiens sapiens becomes the dominant species.		
180 million BC	During the Mesozoic Era, dinosaurs roam on the North American Continent.	Large areas of Africa inhabited.	Large areas of Asia inhabited.	Large areas of Australia inhabited.
10,000 BC	Groups of Paleo-Indians cross the Bering Strait from what is now Siberia to Alaska.	The total human population of the earth increases to ca. 2 million.		
8,000 BC	The Atlatl, or spear, is widely used in the Southwest. It revolutionizes hunting techniques.	Hunter-gatherer cultures evolve, having roughly the same characteristics in all parts of the world. During points, knives and scrapers), masters the controlled use of fire, and makes practical use of stored energy		
5,000 BC	Corn is domesticated in Mexico and spreads from there into the Southwest.	The Neolithic: New Stone Age (agricultural Stone Age). Also known as the Neolithic Revolution. The of food. In agricultural areas, the population grows rapidly. Man begins to cultivate and refine certain wild plants – the birth of our food grains. The taming and		
2500 BC	Agriculture and pottery-making begin in Eastern North America.	This gradual change in the method of food-production leads to a change in the nomadic life-style of and begin building permanent settlements. A consequence of grain production is the need for storage archaeologist.		
100 BC	Farming villages appear in the Southwest.	The more-or-less unilinear evolution of world culture is broken, as development quickly accelerates in		
		Evidence of food grain production in the Nile Valley	In the eastern Mediterranean and Mesopotamia people begin using copper and building houses of clay brick.	
			Irrigation of fields begins in Mesopotamian and Indo-Iranian areas. Advanced pottery-making. Fertility cults.	
		The beginnings of so-called high culture in various parts of the world. Increased agricultural production elite evolves, and develops the art of writing for administrative purposes. The wheel and the seal are applications. Religious beliefs find expression in monumental constructions.		
		Egypt – glazed ceramics. Bronze production. The first flutes and harps.	In the Tigris-Euphrates area the Sumerians invent the wheel and the cart. They also make use of the potter's wheel. China – cultivation of rice begins in Yang Xao. Thailand – copper tools.	Aborigines make use of musical instruments – «didgeridoos and *bullroarers».
		The first Egyptian dynasty ca. 3000–2810 BC. First Egyptian cities of brick.	The Sumerians develop writing – cuneiform symbols on clay tablets. Early Indus Valley culture from ca. 3000 BC. Cultivation of cotton and use of coloured textiles.	
		Ca. 2630 – The first pyramid at Saqqara-worlds oldest stone structure.	Large cities with high standards of hygiene. Bathrooms in villas and apartments. Utilization of metals.	
		Calendar with 365 days. Bantu tribes in West Africa begin migrating to the east and south.		

EUROPE	NORTH AND CENTRAL AMERICA	SOUTH AMERICA		
				2 500 000 BC
				35 000–8 000 BC
				35 000 BC
Large areas of Europe inhabited				
				25 000 BC
this hunter-gatherer Stone Age, mankind learns to make specialized tools (needles, arrow and harpoon (bow and arrow).				8 000–5 000 BC
most important technical advancement in human history takes place during this period – the cultivation		
Dwelling ca. 20 000 BC.	
raising of certain animal species is also begun (wild sheep, goats, oxen and boar).				
the hunter-gatherer cultures. In order to cultivate plants and animals, human societies stop wandering				
vessels. Pottery-making flourishes, and is an inestimable source of information for the modern				
agricultural areas.				
Artistic development: Cave paintings in Altamira (Spain) and Lascaux (France) Stone and bone sculpture (Venus of Willendorf) in Eastern and Central Europe. Cultivation of grain along the coast of the Mediterranean. The oldest Scandinavian rock carvings depicting animals. Stone chamber graves, monoliths and temples of stone in Scandinavia, Northern Germany, Holland, Belgium, France (Carnac), Portugal, Spain and Great Britain (Stonehenge) bear witness to a developing religious imagination.	North and Central America inhabited.

Evidence of maize growing in Mexico. | |
Venus of Willendorf.

Dwelling made of mammoth tusks. | |
due to irrigation makes it possible to feed the populations of growing cities. A political and religious				5 000 BC
invented. Commerce increases. The alloy we call bronze is used in artistic as well as practical				4 000 BC
Minoan culture begins on the island of Crete. Advanced tools and weapons of bronze. Cretan ships in the Mediterranean.		
Australians making music.	
The loom is invented. Early rock carvings in southern Norway. On Crete stone is used as building material.	Central America 3 372 BC – the first year in the Mayan calendar – devised by the priests.	Peru – the first cities and villages along the coast.

Cultivation of cotton begins. | | 3 100 BC |
| | | |
Sumerian chariot. | 2 630 BC |

	UNITED STATES	AFRICA	ASIA	AUSTRALIA
BC – 500 AD	Ceremonial earthworks and burial mounds are built in the Northeast.	Egypt – The Old Kingdom – 2665–2155. The hieroglyphs are already developed. All	The first Aryan invasion of the Indus Valley region. Bronze used in China.	
400 AD	Pottery is manufactured in the Southwest; Basket-making cultures also flourish in the Southwest.	power, both human and divine, is concentrated in the hands of Pharaoh – at the head of a religious and administrative		
950	Anasazi people construct the Mesa Verde cliff dwellings in the Southwest.	hierarchy. The characteristic relief and painting is highly developed.	1848 – Sumerian decline. The first Babylonian dynasty. The laws of Hammurabi reflect a carefully regulated economy.	
1000 – 1500	Temple mounds and towns are built in the Mississippi Basin.		Advanced system of counting, with 60 as its base – our hours, minutes and seconds. The day	
1000	Leif Ericsson explores the Atlantic Coast of North America.		is divided into two 12-hour periods. The zodiac devised. 1 800 – Aryans destroy the Indus cultures. Smelting of iron. The caste system develops.	
			1 400 – Use of iron reaches western Asia.	
		1290–1224 BC Egypt, under Ramses II expands into Asia. Temple built at Abu Simbel.	Ca. 1 230 – Moses leads the Jews out of Egypt – the Exodus. On Mount Sinai he receives the Ten Commandments from God.	
		Horse and wagon used on trade routes in the Sahara.	1 100 – The first Chinese lexicon.	
		Ca. 600 BC – Bantu people spread in East Africa.	Ca. 1 015–930 BC Palestine – Saul introduces monarchy. David and Solomon reign. Jerusalem becomes the capital of a united Israel. A temple is being built where the Arc of the Covenant with the	
1492	Christopher Columbus sails to the New World.		laws is kept.	
1513	Ponce de Leon explores what is now Florida.		Japan 600 BC According to tradition, the empire is founded.	
1539	Hernando de Soto travels in what is now Florida, Georgia and Alabama, reaching the Mississippi River.		586 – The Babylonians occupy Jerusalem, destroy the temple. The Arc disappears. Part of the population taken away – »the	
1540	Vasquez de Coronado explores what is now Arizona and New Mexico.		Babylonian Captivity.« The Phoenicians – a civilized trading people – found a	
1550	Great Plains Indians ride horses to hunt buffalo.		colonial empire in the Mediterranean (f.ex. Carthage). Develop written language.	
1607	Captain John Smith, an Englishman, helps establish Jamestown, VA.		565 – Buddha (Siddharta Gautama) is born and creates the first missionizing world	
1610	Henry Hudson reaches what is later called the Hudson Bay and River; Spanish settle Santa Fe.		religion of nonviolence. Buddhism's temple architecture develops.	
1619	The first Black slaves are brought to Virginia.		China – 6th century Confucius preaches reverence for ancestors, loyalty to authority	
1620	The Pilgrims arrive in Cape Cod, settle Plymouth Colony and draft the Mayflower Compact.		and respect for ancient customs.	

EUROPE	NORTH AND CENTRAL AMERICA	SOUTH AMERICA		
The Bronze Age commences in Europe. Crete – the first palace of Knossos.			Mural from Knossos.	2000 BC 1830 BC
2000–1400 – Crete dominates the Aegean. Minoan culture flourishes – cult of the bull and bare-breasted goddesses.			Hammurabi standing in front of the sun god.	
Ca. 1400 – Mycenae – local upswing. The «golden» Mycenae. Fortress with the Lion Gate. 1200–1100 The Trojan War. Earlier advanced cultures have meant little to recent developments. In the last millennium BC cultures arise in Greece and Italy which have a decisive influence on the development of the West. Greece – 776 The first Olympic games. Italy – 753 according to legend, Romulus and Remus founds the city of Rome. Ca. 700–500 The archaic age of Greece. Homer author of the Iliad and the Odyssey. Rise of the Greek city-states. Italy – 700–500 Etruscan civilization flourishes in present-day Toscany. Remarkable artworks – sculptures and murals in grave chambers. Greece – 500–338 The classical period. Art, science and philosophy flourish. 500–449 The Persian Wars: Greek victories at Marathon (490) and Salamis (480). 447–438 The Parthenon is built. Socrates 469–399 – sought by means of leading questions to guide men towards knowledge and proper behaviour. Sentenced to drink cup of hemlock at age 70. Plato 427–347 – The visible things are only reflections of the invisible, eternal ideas. Those who could see the ideas – the philosophers – should govern. Aristotle 384–322 Antiquity's most versatile thinker. The authority in nearly every area of the sciences.	Ca 800–400 Central America. The Olmec culture evolves west of Yucatan. Writing, and a system of counting which includes zero.		Dead man's heart is weighed. Olympic sprinter. Greek amphitheatre. The Acropolis in Athens.	1500 BC 1200 BC 1100 BC –400 BC

	UNITED STATES	AFRICA	ASIA	AUSTRALIA
			Ca. 300 – Construction begins on the Great Wall of China. China – **206 BC** Han dynasty comes to power initiates a period of intense expansion. Class of Mandarins develops. Confucianism spreads.	
1629	The Massachusetts Bay Colony is founded.			
1639	The first New World newspaper is printed in Cambridge, MA.			
			4?? – Jesus born. **30??** – The Crucifixion	
1649	Maryland Assembly grants religious freedom.			
			Ca. 50 – The early Christians decide that the teachings of Jesus are not meant for Israel alone. Christianity belongs to the world.	
1682	Sieur de LaSalle claims the Mississippi River area for the French.		**60–70** – The great missionary, Paul, dies after founding	
1692	At least 19 people (most of them women) are executed as witchcraft hysteria spreads through Salem, MA.		Christian communities in Asia Minor and Greece.	
1712	A revolt by slaves in New York leads to the execution of 21 Blacks; 6 slaves commit suicide.	Egypt **Ca. 150** Alexandrian philosopher Ptolemy publishes his great geographical work; the earth is the centre of the universe. The geocentric world-view.	**74–94** The Chinese open the Silk Route to the West.	
1732	Benjamin Franklin publishes Poor Richard's Almanac.		**325** – The Council of Nicea determines that even women have souls.	
1733	Georgia, the last of the original 13 colonies, is founded.	**200** – Camels introduced from Asia and become important means of transport.	Japan 400s: Immigration from China is major cultural influence.	
1741	13 Blacks are hanged, 13 burned and 71 deported after a second New York slave uprising.	**439** – The Vandals – a germanic tribe – invade Northern Africa via Spain (Andalusia). **455** – Vandals sack Rome. It is from them we have the term 'vandalism'.	**570–632** Mohammed, founder of the monolithic world religion Islam. M:s revelations, the Koran is Muslims' holy book.	
1770	British troops kill five townspeople in what became known as the Boston Massacre.		China **618–907** Tang dynasty. Political and cultural Golden Age.	
1773	East India Company's cargo of tea is thrown overboard at the "Boston Tea Party", a colonial revolt against taxes.		**622** Mohammed expelled from Mecca – point of reckoning for the Islamic era.	
1774	The first Continental Congress is held in Philadelphia, PA.		Holy war begun to spread teachings of Islam.	
1775	The American Revolution begins with battles in Lexington and Concord, MA.		8th century: Chinese landscape painting evolves. Golden Age of lyrical poetry; court poet Li Tai-po	
1776	The colonists adopt the Declaration of Independence.			
1777	General George Washington defeats Lord Cornwallis at Princeton, NJ; the 13 colonies unite under the Stars and Stripes flag said to have been designed by Betsy Ross.	**700** Bantu tribes cross the Limpopo into Southern Africa and introduce the use of iron. Arabs conquer Tunisia.	**711** Muslim empire from Spain in the west to China in the east. **750** The Arabs learn the art of paper-making from the Chinese.	
1778	British pull out of Philadelphia, PA; Congress prohibits importing slaves.	The Berbers are driven out of Ghana, and the country comes under black African rule.	Japan 880s: Japan becomes a feudal state with cultural blossoming (the novel, and philosophical texts, textiles and metallurgy, masterpieces in lacquer).	
1783	The British and the United States sign a peace treaty.	**800** – Trade develops across the Sahara between North and West Africa. Camels of major importance.		
1787	The US Constitution is adopted.	**850** – The Great Citadel in Zimbabwe is built.		

EUROPE	NORTH AND CENTRAL AMERICA	SOUTH AMERICA		

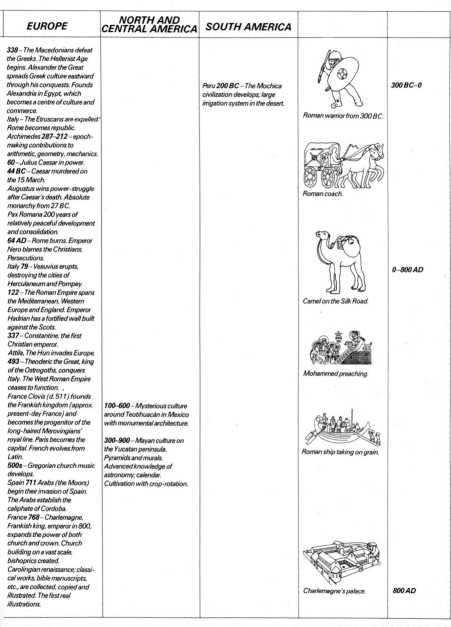

338 – The Macedonians defeat the Greeks. The Hellenist Age begins. Alexander the Great spreads Greek culture eastward through his conquests. Founds Alexandria in Egypt, which becomes a centre of culture and commerce.
Italy – The Etruscans are expelled. Rome becomes republic.
Archimedes 287–212 – epoch-making contributions to arithmetic, geometry, mechanics.
60 – Julius Caesar in power.
44 BC – Caesar murdered on the 15 March.
Augustus wins power-struggle after Caesar's death. Absolute monarchy from 27 BC.
Pax Romana 200 years of relatively peaceful development and consolidation.
64 AD – Rome burns. Emperor Nero blames the Christians. Persecutions.
Italy 79 – Vesuvius erupts, destroying the cities of Herculaneum and Pompeii.
122 – The Roman Empire spans the Mediterranean, Western Europe and England. Emperor Hadrian has a fortified wall built against the Scots.
337 – Constantine, the first Christian emperor.
Attila, The Hun invades Europe.
493 – Theoderic the Great, king of the Ostrogoths, conquers Italy. The West Roman Empire ceases to function.
France Clovis (d. 511) founds the Frankish kingdom (approx. present-day France) and becomes the progenitor of the long-haired Merovingians' royal line. Paris becomes the capital. French evolves from Latin.
500s – Gregorian church music develops.
Spain 711 Arabs (the Moors) begin their invasion of Spain. The Arabs establish the caliphate of Cordoba.
France 768 – Charlemagne, Frankish king, emperor in 800, expands the power of both church and crown. Church building on a vast scale, bishoprics created.
Carolingian renaissance; classical works, bible manuscripts, etc., are collected, copied and illustrated. The first real illustrations.

Peru 200 BC – The Mochica civilization develops; large irrigation system in the desert.

100–600 – Mysterious culture around Teotihuacán in Mexico with monumental architecture.

300–900 – Mayan culture on the Yucatan peninsula. Pyramids and murals. Advanced knowledge of astronomy; calendar. Cultivation with crop-rotation.

Roman warrior from 300 BC.

300 BC – 0

Roman coach.

Camel on the Silk Road.

0 – 800 AD

Mohammed preaching.

Roman ship taking on grain.

Charlemagne's palace.

800 AD

	UNITED STATES	AFRICA	ASIA	AUSTRALIA
1789	George Washington becomes the first US president; John Adams, vice president; Thomas Jefferson, secretary of state; and Alexander Hamilton, secretary of the treasury.			
1790	Congress meets in the temporary capital of Philadelphia, PA; the US Supreme Court holds its first session.			
1791	The Bill of Rights goes into effect.			
1792	Alexander Hamilton and John Adams form the Federalist Party.			
1793	Eli Whitney files for the patent on the cotton gin.	*961–1171* – The Fatimid caliphate in Egypt is at the centre of a Shiite attempt to take over Islam. The Fatimids gained control over the lucrative trade between southern and eastern Asia. Their dominance continues on until the Europeans begin sailing around Africa.	*960–1279* – China. The Sung dynasty comes to power and contact with the West is broken. Period of blossoming in the ceramic arts. Gun powder is used for military purposes.	
1797	John Adams becomes the second president.			
1800	Washington, D.C., is chosen as the United States capital.			
1803	The US buys the Louisiana Territory from France for approximately $15 million;			
1804	Lewis and Clark begin their expedition of the Northwest.			
1807	Robert Fulton makes the first steamboat trip from New York City to Albany, NY.			
1808	Slave importation is outlawed.			
1812	After the British seize US ships and give Native Americans guns to intensify border disputes, Congress declares war on Britain.			
1814	British soldiers invade Washington DC, and burn the capitol; Francis Scott Key writes the "Star Spangled Banner," which later becomes the US National Anthem.		*1096* – The first crusade. *1099* – Jerusalem is occupied and becomes a Christian kingdom. Several other Christian kingdoms are established in the Middle East.	
1820	Congress passes the Missouri Compromise, allowing slavery in that state.			
1821	Emma Willard founds Troy Female Seminary, the first women's college		*1187* – Saladin, Sultan of Egypt and Syria, retakes Jerusalem, giving rise to the third crusade, in which, among others, Richard the Lionheart of England takes part.	
1827	The first Black US newspaper, Freedom's Journal, is published.			
1828	The Democratic Party is established; first Native American newspaper, Cherokee Phoenix, is published.		*1192* – Japan – The Shogun (supreme commander) takes power from the emperor.	
1831	Black activist Nat Turner leads a rebellion of Virginia slaves.			
1832	Oberlin College, OH, becomes the first co-educational college.		*1196–1206* – Genghis Khan establishes a Mongol empire and begins expansion towards China.	

EUROPE	NORTH AND CENTRAL AMERICA	SOUTH AMERICA		

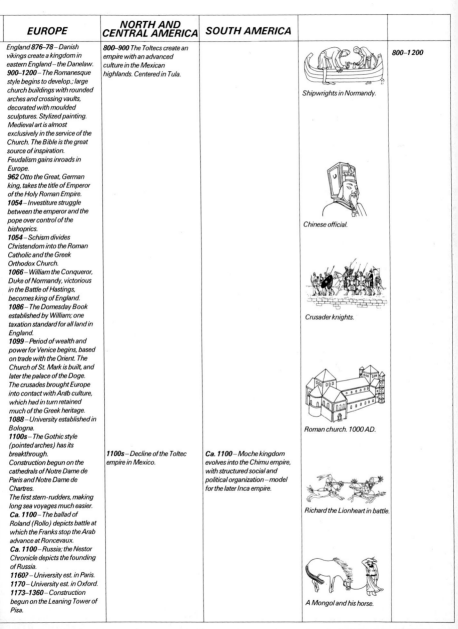

EUROPE

England 876–78 – Danish vikings create a kingdom in eastern England – the Danelaw.

900–1200 – The Romanesque style begins to develop.; large church buildings with rounded arches and crossing vaults, decorated with moulded sculptures. Stylized painting. Medieval art is almost exclusively in the service of the Church. The Bible is the great source of inspiration. Feudalism gains inroads in Europe.

962 Otto the Great, German king, takes the title of Emperor of the Holy Roman Empire.

1054 – Investiture struggle between the emperor and the pope over control of the bishoprics.

1054 – Schism divides Christendom into the Roman Catholic and the Greek Orthodox Church.

1066 – William the Conqueror, Duke of Normandy, victorious in the Battle of Hastings, becomes king of England.

1086 – The Domesday Book established by William; one taxation standard for all land in England.

1099 – Period of wealth and power for Venice begins, based on trade with the Orient. The Church of St. Mark is built, and later the palace of the Doge. The crusades brought Europe into contact with Arab culture, which had in turn retained much of the Greek heritage.

1088 – University established in Bologna.

1100s – The Gothic style (pointed arches) has its breakthrough. Construction begun on the cathedrals of Notre Dame de Paris and Notre Dame de Chartres. The first stern-rudders, making long sea voyages much easier.

Ca. 1100 – The ballad of Roland (Rollo) depicts battle at which the Franks stop the Arab advance at Roncevaux.

Ca. 1100 – Russia; the Nestor Chronicle depicts the founding of Russia.

1160? – University est. in Paris.

1170 – University est. in Oxford.

1173–1360 – Construction begun on the Leaning Tower of Pisa.

NORTH AND CENTRAL AMERICA

800–900 The Toltecs create an empire with an advanced culture in the Mexican highlands. Centered in Tula.

1100s – Decline of the Toltec empire in Mexico.

SOUTH AMERICA

Ca. 1100 – Moche kingdom evolves into the Chimu empire, with structured social and political organization – model for the later Inca empire.

800–1200

Shipwrights in Normandy.

Chinese official.

Crusader knights.

Roman church. 1000 AD.

Richard the Lionheart in battle.

A Mongol and his horse.

	UNITED STATES	AFRICA	ASIA	AUSTRALIA
		The Mandingo people found the Muslim kingdom of Mali, with Timbuktu as the leading centre of trade.	Japan – **1200s** The ritual No drama is born. India ink drawing is developed.	
1836	Texans at the Alamo in San Antonio are besieged by Mexicans under the command of Santa Anna; Texas declares its independence from Mexico; the first white women cross the plains.		China – **1200s** The classical Chinese drama develops.	
1838	The US government forces Cherokees to leave their homes in the Southeast and march 1,200 miles on what was called the "Trail of Tears."			
1844	Samuel F.B. Morse sends the first telegraph message.			
1846	War with Mexico ignites over disputed Texas land.			
1848	The Mexican War ends with the US gaining vast tracts of land in the West; gold is discovered in California; Lucretia Mott and Elizabeth Cady Stanton conduct the first women's rights convention in Seneca Falls, NY.			
1850	Senator Henry Clay's Compromise admits California to the Union as a non-slave state.			
1854	The Republican Party is formed in Ripon, WI; Henry David Thoreau publishes Walden; in the Dred Scott decision, the US Supreme Court upholds slavery and denies citizenship to Blacks.			
1858	Presidential candidates Abraham Lincoln and Fredrick Douglas debate in Illinois.		**1271** – Venetian trader Marco Polo goes to China. In 1295 he returns to Venice.	
1859	Abolitionist John Brown raids a US arsenal at Harper's Ferry, WV; Brown is hanged for treason.		Japan – **1274 & 1281** Mongols under Kublai Khan make failed attempts to conquer Japan.	
1860	Abraham Lincoln is elected the 16th president; the Pony Express begins service between Sacramento, CA and St. Joseph, MO.		**1279** – Genghis Khan's grandson, Kublai Khan, conquers all of China and begins the Mongol dynasty.	
1861	Seven pro-slavery Southern states cede from the Union and, under the leadership of Jefferson Davis, set up the Confederate States of America; Civil War breaks out at Fort Sumter, SC.	In the **1320s** The Muslim king of Mali, Mansa-Musa, undertakes a pilgrimage to Mecca, and upon his return begins construction of the Great Mosque in Timbuktu.		
1862	The Homestead Act promotes settlement of the Midwest by granting land to farmers.			
1863	Harriet Tubman's "Underground Railroad" ushers hundreds of slaves to freedom in the North; Lincoln issues the Emancipation Proclamation, freeing the slaves, and delivers the Gettysburg Address.			

EUROPE	NORTH AND CENTRAL AMERICA	SOUTH AMERICA		
1200s – A time of blossoming for the cities. The universities become centres of learning and culture. The writings of Aristotle are studied intensively. Romantic chivalric poetry popular among the upper classes. The many cloisters are centres of teaching, medical care, and the development of agricultural methods. Italy *1210 – Francis of Assisi founds the Franciscan order – beggar monks.* England *1215 – Magna Carta; protection against arbitrary judgments by the crown in legal and taxation matters.* Spain *1216 – Dominican order founded.* France *1235 – Leoninus, the first known composer, dies. Choral music evolves.* England *1245 – Construction begun on Westminster Abbey, which becomes the site of all future coronations.* England *ca. 1259 – The English parliament begins to take form.* England *1300s – Wool trade flourishes.* *1300s – The plague (Black Death) strikes Europe and Asia. Ca. 75 million people thought to have died. Lack of manpower and changes in climate likely causes of decline in agricultural production. Transition to money-based economy, with inflated prices and devaluations. Social unrest leads to many rebellions. Secular music begins to take its place alongside church music.* Italy *1303–05 – Giotto completes his frescos in Padua. He can be said to have prefigured the Renaissance through a more humanistic approach to religious motifs. Dante writes (ca. 1310–20) his Divine Comedy, in which the journey through Hell, Purgatory and Paradise reflect the Medieval world-view. In Italy the great writers, Dante, Petrarch and Boccaccio, shape the modern Italian language.* *1337–1453 The Hundred Years' War between England and France.* France *1309–1377 – Popes forced to reside in Avignon. The popes' «Babylonian Captivity».*		*1300s – The Incas begin building their empire on South America's west coast.*	Man wheeling his wife home. Wine grapes are trampled. Mongol horseman. Ploughing with a harrow. Mistreated prisoners. Plague doctor wearing protective mask.	*1200* *1340*

	UNITED STATES	AFRICA	ASIA	AUSTRALIA
1864	Awaiting a surrender agreement, hundreds of Cheyenne and Arapahoes are massacred by US cavalrymen at Sand Creek, CO.		China – **1300s** The Mongol empire is overthrown and the Ming dynasty commences. Chinese renaissance. The Great Wall reaches its present dimensions. Working in porcelain (Ming porcelain) flourishes. Ming porcelain is the forerunner of the so-called East-Indian porcelain which is later exported to Europe.	
1865	The Civil War ends with General Robert E. Lee surrendering at Appomattox Courthouse, VA; Lincoln is assassinated; the 13th Amendment, abolishing slavery is passed.			
1866	The Ku Klux Klan is formed secretly in Pulaski, TN, to terrorize Black voters.		Persia – Hafiz (1325–1390), Persian lyric poetry's great master, writes his collection of verse – Divan.	
1867	The US buys Alaska from Russia for $7.2 million.		**1399** Mongol emperor Timur Link conquers India, Persia and Asia Minor. With his death in **1450**, the empire falls apart.	
1869	Central Pacific and Union Pacific railroad tracks are joined at Promontory, UT uniting the East and West coasts.			
1870	Victoria Claflin Woodhull is the first woman to run for president.			
1872	Congress establishes Yellowstone as the first national park; Women's suffrage leader Susan B. Anthony is arrested for voting.			
1875	Congress passes the Civil Rights Act, giving Blacks equal access to public places and jury duty privileges. (The US Supreme Court invalidates it in 1883.)			
1876	Members of the Sioux, Northern Cheyenne and Arapahoe Nations, in part led by medicine man Sitting Bull, defeat General George Custer in the "last stand," Battle of the Little Big Horn, Montana; Custer, 264 7th Cavalry soldiers and an estimated 30 Native Americans are killed.			
1877	The US violates a land treaty with the Dakota Sioux by seizing the Black Hills in South Dakota; eleven leaders of the Molly Maguires, a society of Irish miners in Scranton, PA, are hanged for killing mining officials, and policemen.	Portugal **1432** Prince Henry («The Seafarer») organizes voyages of exploration along the west coast of Africa. The Portuguese begin construction of fortified trading stations along the west coast. The birth of a colonial empire.		
1879	Thomas Edison invents the electric light bulb; F.W. Woolworth opens his first five-and-ten cents store in Utica, NY.	**1442** – The Portuguese begin exploiting Africa's northwest coast, and find gold at Rio de Oro.		
1881	James A. Garfield, the 20th president, is assassinated soon after taking office; Chester A. Arthur becomes the 21st president; Black educator Booker T. Washington founds the Tuskegee Institute, Alabama, for Black students.	Trade along the Atlantic coast in competition with the caravan trade across the Sahara.	Turkey – **1453** Mohammed II occupies Constantinople – the Byzantine empire ceases to exist.	
1885	The Statue of Liberty is dedicated in New York Harbor.		Russia **1453** After the fall of Constantinople, the patriarch of Moscow takes over the leadership of the Greek Orthodox Church.	

EUROPE	NORTH AND CENTRAL AMERICA	SOUTH AMERICA		

France **1358** – Peasant rebellions.

Germany **1370** – The Hansa – confederation of northern German cities – dominates trade in Northern Europe.

England **1381** – Peasant rebellions.

Poland and Lithuania enter into union in **1386**.

England **1387** – Geoffrey Chaucer, «father of the English language,» publishes his Canterbury Tales.

Northern Europe **1397** – Denmark, Norway, Sweden and Finland enter into a union that exists formally until 1521.

In Northern Italy the Renaissance develops – a rebirth of Antiquity – «mankind's Golden Age». Finds expression in painting in Masaccio (1401–1428), who creates an intensively human mood in his paintings. In architecture Brunelleschi defines the style – cathedral cupola in Florence.

The search for gold and silver (to pay for the costly imports from Asia) driving force behind European explorations.

Bill of exchange becomes common form of payment. Italian system of dual-entry bookkeeping used.

1432 – Jan van Eyck completes the alter at Gent. A realistic Northern European style blossoms. With the help of a flexible new material – oil paint – it is possible to give paintings greater nuance.

France **1439** – Joan of Arc, a peasant girl from Lorraine, takes part in the Hundred Years' War to drive out the English. Taken prisoner, judged a witch and burned at the stake. Becomes a saint and national symbol.

Germany **1450** – Johann Gutenberg invents printing press with moveable type.

English wagon from the 14th century.

1300
1450

Arab slaves.

Timur Lenk on his throne.

Threshing grain.

Sailing ship in the 15th century.

English archer from 1415.

	UNITED STATES	AFRICA	ASIA	AUSTRALIA
		1464–92 Under the reign of Sonni Ali the Songhai empire reaches its largest extension in West Africa.		
1886	Seven policemen and four workers are killed during a bitter labor battle in Chicago's Haymarket Square; the American Federation of Labor is founded; Apache Chief Geronimo surrenders to Arizona Territory leaders.			
1890	Sitting Bull is killed by police officials at Standing Rock Reservation in South Dakota; an estimated 200 Sioux are massacred by US troops at Wounded Knee, SD; the Sherman Antitrust Act begins a government effort to curb monopolies; Ellis Island in New York Harbor opens as an immigration depot.			
1896	The US Supreme Court approves racial segregation in Plessy vs Ferguson.			
1898	The US blockades Cuban ports, declares war on Spain and invades Puerto Rico; Spain cedes the Philippines, Puerto Rico and Guam, and approves Cuban independence.			
1899	Seeking an end to US intervention, Filipino insurgents begin guerilla warfare in the Philippines; through the Open Door Policy, the US trades with China.			
1900	The International Ladies Garment Workers Union is founded; prohibitionist Carry Nation begins raiding Kansas saloons.			
1901	The US captures Emilio Aguinaldo, the leader of the Filipino insurrection, ending the movement; President McKinley is assassinated; Theodore Roosevelt becomes the 26th president; J.P. Morgan founds the US Steel Corporation.		China – *1498* The modern toothbrush is described in a Chinese reference work.	
1902	US gains control of the Panama Canal.	*1505* – Portuguese establish trading stations on the Zambezi river on Africa's east coast; present-day Mozambique.		
1903	Orville and Wilbur Wright complete the first air flight near Kitty Hawk, NC; Henry Ford establishes the Ford Motor Company.			
1905	Bill Haywood, Mother Mary Harris Jones, Eugene Debs, and others found the IWW– the Industrial Workers of the World union.			
1906	US troops occupy Cuba; San Francisco is destroyed by an earthquake.			
1908	Roosevelt stops Japanese immigration into the US; demanding labor improvements, women demonstrate in New York City.			
			India *1525* Empire of the Great Moguls is established.	*1519–21* – The Spanish sponsor Portuguese mariner Magellan's circumnavigation of the globe. Magellan dies during the voyage.

EUROPE	NORTH AND CENTRAL AMERICA	SOUTH AMERICA		
Russia **1480** – Ivan III frees Moscow from the Mongol empire («Golden Horde») and joins with other princes in a Russian kingdom. Spain **1492** – The Moors (Arabs) are driven out of Spain. All Jews expelled. **1492** – Columbus discovers America, but believes he has found India. Germany **1492** – Martin Behaim constructs the first globe map. Most intellectuals now agree that the world is round – not flat. **1493** – The Spanish begin conquest of portions of North Africa. **1493** – The first Spanish settlement in the New World at Hispaniola. Italy **1495–97** – Leonardo da Vinci paints the Last Supper. **1497** – The Italian Cabot discovers Newfoundland. **1497–98** – Vasco da Gama finds the sea route to India. **1498** – Columbus discovers the South American continent. **1499** – Switzerland frees herself from the German empire. **1500s** – Beginning of the modern age. Europeans have contact by sea with Africa, Asia and the Americas. National states form. Renaissance culture has breakthrough in Europe. Church unity is broken. The printed word makes an impact in secular and religious struggles. **1516** – Erasmus of Rotterdam translates the New Testament from Greek. The Reformation Bible. Germany **1517** – Martin Luther puts forth his theses on man's way to salvation. With the printing press his ideas are spread far too quickly to suit the Church. Germany **1519** – Charles V becomes Holy Roman Emperor and inherits present-day Germany, Austria, The Netherlands, Spain, and vast areas of South America. France **1520s** – First textile factories for weaving silk. Switzerland **1525** – Zwingli's reformation in Zurich. Austria **1529** – The Turks' advance into Europe reaches its peak, and Vienna is threatened.	**1492** – Columbus discovers America. Mexico **1519–21** – Cortéz conquers Mexico and lays waste to the Aztec kingdom, the youngest of advanced cultures in the Americas. The capital of Tenochtitlàn, built on the waters of Lake Tetzcoco, is destroyed. The king, Motecuzoma, is killed. The city was at the time one of the world's largest, with some 400 000 inhabitants.	**1498** – Columbus discovers the South American continent. **1493–ca. 1527** – Huayana Capac expands the Incan empire across Ecuador to Chile.	 Europeans being carried by East Indians. Goa in India ca. 1500. Aztecs being interrogated by Cortez. Spaniard beating an Indian. Aztec woman at her loom. Holy Roman Emperor Charles V.	**1475** **1530**

	UNITED STATES	AFRICA	ASIA	AUSTRALIA
1909	Admiral Robert E. Perry reaches the North Pole; Walter White helps found the National Association for the Advancement of Colored People (NAACP); "Free Speech Movement" springs up in cities in Washington, Montana, and California: thousands of people are arrested for speaking on street corners.			
1911	At the Triangle Shirt Waist Company in New York City, an estimated 146 textile workers, most of them women and children, die in a fire.			
1913	Income tax collection is ratified under the 13th Amendment.		Japan – *1542* The Portuguese land in Japan and begin preaching Christianity, which is forbidden.	
1915	More than 100 Americans aboard the British cruise ship Lusitana die when it is sunk by a German submarine; 25,000 women march in New York City demanding the right to vote.		*1557* – The Portuguese conquer Macao on the coast of China – remains a Portuguese possession to this day.	
1916	Due to the persistent work of Margaret Sanger, public birth control clinics open in Brooklyn, NY; the National Park Service is formed; Jeanette Rankin, Montana, becomes the first US Congresswoman.			
1917	The US declares war on Germany after German submarines wage "unrestricted" warfare; Puerto Rico becomes a US territory.			
1918	When the war ends in November, more than one million American troops are in Europe. Fifty thousand American soldiers died there.			
1919	The US Supreme Court holds that free speech doesn't apply to draft resistance (Later decisions overturn this ruling.); general strike of 100,000 shuts down Seattle, WA for five days.			
1920	Women get the right to vote under the 19th Amendment; during the "Red Scare," nearly 4,000 people are arrested and deported as alleged communist spies.			
1922	Rebecca L. Felton, Georgia, becomes the first woman US senator.			
1924	Congress recognizes Native Americans' citizenship.			
1925	John T. Scopes is fined $100 for teaching evolution in a Dayton, TN high school.			
1927	Charles Lindbergh completes the first solo flight across the Atlantic.			

EUROPE	NORTH AND CENTRAL AMERICA	SOUTH AMERICA		

England **1534** – Henry VIII breaks with the pope and founds the Church of England. Manages to outlive six wives. Henry's daughter, Mary, attempts to reintroduce Catholicism and marries Philip II of Spain. Her brutal methods gave her the nickname «Bloody Mary», perhaps best remembered in the cocktail «Bloody Mary», made from vodka and tomato juice.
Germany **1530s** – The financial house of Fugger at the height of its power.
Spain **1540** – The Jesuit order founded – to counter the Reformation.
Switzerland **1541** – Calvin's reformation in Geneva.
1543 – Copernicus presents his view of the world, where the Sun is the centre of the universe, and Earth only a small part of the whole.
Germany **1556** – Emperor Charles V abdicates. The Habsburg empire is divided.
1558–1603 – Elizabeth I reigns – the Elizabethan era - a shining epoch in the history of England.
1558 – Russian czar Ivan the Terrible advances to the Baltic.
1571 – The Spanish defeat the Turkish fleet at Lepanto. Turkish hegemony over the eastern Mediterranean ended. One of the combatants is Cervantes, who later writes Don Quixote.
1570s – Palestrina and Orlando di Lasso develop and perfect Gregorian church music.
Venice **1570** – Andrea Palladio publishes «Four Books on Architecture», which has great influence on the art of building construction.
France **1572** – Religious wars (Huguenot wars) and wars of succession. Peace when Henry of Navarre made king after converting to Catholicism. «Paris is well worth a mass.»
1587 – Mary Stuart, queen of Scotland, executed for slandering Elizabeth I and making claims to the English throne.
1588 – Philip II of Spain sends the «Great Armada» against England. The English fleet, incl. circumnavigator Sir Francis Drake, victorious.

1585 – English found the colony of Virginia on the east coast of North America.

1531–1533 – Spaniard Pizarro's conquest of the Inca empire in Peru.

Areas conquered by the Spanish organized into viceroyalties: New Spain (Mexico), the vice-royalty of Peru, and New Granada (Colombia).

The Europeans in South America gained knowledge of a number of cultivated plants and vegetables: potatoes, tomatoes, maize, and tobacco.

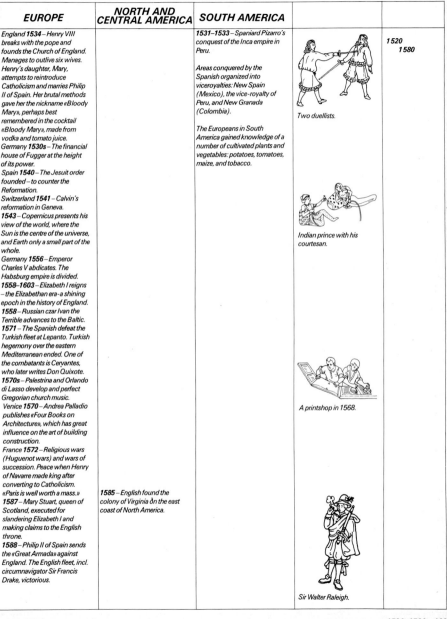

Two duellists.

Indian prince with his courtesan.

A printshop in 1568.

Sir Walter Raleigh.

1520
1580

	UNITED STATES	AFRICA	ASIA	AUSTRALIA
1929	Stock prices plummet, the market crashes and the Great Depression begins; much of the Midwest suffers under a drought.			
1931	The Empire State Building opens.			
1932	Charles Lindbergh's baby son is kidnapped and found dead.			
1933	Franklin Delano Roosevelt becomes the 32nd president; US Secretary of Labor Frances Perkins becomes the first woman cabinet member.		Japan – **1603** The Tokugawa period commences. After a short time of openness and expansion, Japan again closes herself to the world. A strictly controlled and hierarchical society is imposed. Continues until 1868.	
1935	Under the Wagner Labor Relations Act, workers are permitted to organize unions; Roosevelt signs the Social Security Act.			
1936	Roosevelt is re-elected; at the Olympic Games in Berlin, Black US athlete, Jesse Owens wins four gold medals, challenging Hitler's notion of Aryan racial superiority.		India – **1605** Akbar the Great dies. During his reign the empire of the Great Mogul is expanded, achieving a stabile military and political organization.	
1937	Aviator Amelia Earhart and co-pilot Fred Nooman disappear during a cross-Pacific flight.			**1606** – The Dutchman Willem Jansz sails through the Torres Strait between Australia and New Guinea and goes ashore at the eastern part of the Bight of Carpentaria.
1938	The national minimum wage is enacted.			
1940	Roosevelt takes the presidential oath for a third time.			
1941	After Japanese fighter pilots bomb Pearl Harbor, the US declares war on Japan; war is declared on Germany and Italy.			
1942	Japanese-Americans are forced into detention camps for the duration of the war. Their homes, property, and businesses are confiscated.			**1642** – Dutch seafarer Tasman sails around Australia and discovers New Zealand and Tasmania.
1944	Roosevelt is elected for a fourth time; US and other allied forces stage the D-Day invasion of Normandy.			
1945	Roosevelt dies, and Harry S. Truman becomes the 33rd president; Germany surrenders; US drops the first atomic bombs on Hiroshima and Nagasaki, and Japan surrenders.		India **1631** Construction of the queen's mausoleum Taj Mahal in Agra is begun. China – **1644** The Manchurian Qing clan, China's last imperial dynasty, takes power and a new period of greatness begins.	
1946	US Navy tests the atom bomb in the Bikini Islands.			
1947	Congress passes the Taft-Hartley Act to curb labor union strikes; under the Marshall Plan, the US gives war-torn European countries aid; the Central Intelligence Agency (CIA) is established; Jackie Robinson becomes the first Black major league baseball player.	**1652** – Dutch found the Cape Colony on the southern point of Africa.	– **1645** The Russians reach the Pacific Ocean.	

EUROPE	NORTH AND CENTRAL AMERICA	SOUTH AMERICA		
1600s – are marked by religious conflict and wars. North America is colonized. Birth of modern science. Emergence of the Baroque. Hansa trade monopoly is broken. England, The Netherlands and France become the new trading nations, as seen in their establishing of the East India companies. Baroque painting reflects in colour, light and movement, people's feelings during an era of unrest. The 17th century's turmoil and struggle for power reflected in Baroque architecture. Monumental and full of life. The Baroque is spread over all of Europe and Latin America. Through the work of Galileo, Kepler and Newton, a new world-view is formed, based on mathematical formulae. **1600**, Shakespeare's great tragedies appear, among others, Hamlet. England **1617** – William Harvey discovers the circulatory system. **1618** – Thirty Years' War begins. Conflict over religious and political power in Europe. **1622** – First potatoes grown in Germany. France **1625** – Peter Paul Rubens paints 18 panels in the Palais de Luxembourg in Paris. Baroque art is established. Sweden **1628** – The royal ship the Vasa sinks on its maiden voyage, and isn't recovered until 1956. Holland **1632** – Rembrandt paints «Doctor Tulp's Anatomy Lecture». **1635** – Acadimie Française founded. **1648** – Thirty Years' War ends. Germany remains religiously and politically divided. France and Sweden great-powers. France – In the **1650s** Louis XIV begins construction of the palace of Versailles, where his court became the model for European royalty. Establishment of absolute monarchy. «The state is me,» as Louis is supposed to have said. His Allonge wig. Symbol of power and strength, modelled on the lion's mane. Italian Monteverdi (1567–1643) and Englishman Purcell develop opera as art form. **1662** – Royal Society founded in London.	**1607** – Henry Hudson sails to Greenland, and up the Hudson River. **1608** – The French found Quebec in Canada. **1620** – The Pilgrim Fathers, radical protestants, land the «Mayflower» in Massachusetts, where they found the city of Boston in 1630. **1626** – The Dutch found New Amsterdam (later New York). The French push further inland along the St. Lawrence. Interested mostly in trading (furs), not in farming. **1640s and 50s** – English royalists colonize the southern parts of the North American east coast. Plantation farming with imported black slaves.		 Transport by sleigh ca. 1600. Soldier with musket ca. 1600. Combat during the Thirty Years' War. Peace is proclaimed in 1648. The Tower of London in 1641. Prince James playing tennis.	**1 600** **1 650**

	UNITED STATES	AFRICA	ASIA	AUSTRALIA
1950	Truman sends US troops to South Korea to stop invasion from North Korea.			
1951	Presidents are limited to two terms in office.			
1952	Jonas Salk develops a polio vaccine; the first hydrogen bomb is exploded over the Pacific Ocean.			
1953	The Korean War ends; Julius and Ethel Rosenberg are executed for espionage.			
1954	Senator Joseph McCarthy (R-Wis.) is reprimanded for "witch hunting" during the House Unamerican Activities Committee hearings; in Brown vs the Board of Education, the US Supreme Court rules racial segregation in schools unconstitutional.			
1955	Rosa Parks refuses to give her bus seat to a white man in Montgomery, AL, touching off the "Great Montgomery Bus Boycott"; America's two largest labor unions merge to form the AFL-CIO.	**1700s** The export of slaves from Africa is estimated at 15 million.	India – **1700** The Mogul Empire is weakened, giving the English an opportunity to control the India trade. They begin exporting Indian opium to China.	
1958	Explorer 1 becomes the first earth-orbiting satellite; the National Aeronautics and Space Administration (NASA) is established.		China – **1715** The English granted permission to establish trade mission in Canton.	
1959	Alaska and Hawaii become the 49th and 50th states.			
1960	Black College students begin staging "sit-ins" after four Black students are denied service at a Woolworth's lunch counter in Greensboro, NC.			
1961	John F. Kennedy becomes the 35th president; Alan B. Shepard, Jr. completes the first manned space flight aboard a Mercury capsule.			
1962	John Glenn orbits the earth in the space capsule Friendship 1; in spite of campus rioting, James Meredith becomes the first Black student to enroll at the University of Mississippi.			
1963	President Kennedy is assassinated in Dallas, TX; Lyndon B. Johnson becomes the 36th president; the US Supreme Court bans prayer in public schools and rules that states must provide free legal counsel for indigents; Civil Rights leader Martin Luther King, Jr. delivers his "I have A Dream Speech".		**1756–1763** – The colonial war between England and France strengthens British influence in India.	

EUROPE	NORTH AND CENTRAL AMERICA	SOUTH AMERICA		
France **1670s** – Paris becomes cultural capital of Europe. England: Declaration of Rights **1689** defines the power of the parliament and rights of individual citizens. **1690** – John Locke publishes «On Human Understanding». Due to his ideas on human rights and freedoms, he becomes the father of enlightenment and liberalism. **1694** – Bank of England established. Peter the Great begins modernizing his empire according to Western model, and expands into the Baltic. **1700** – Peter introduces a tax on facial hair, and forcibly clips the beards of noblemen. Germany **1710** – Saxons duplicate art of porcelainmaking, which has been a Chinese secret. Meissen factory founded. Germany **1710** – Leibniz formulates the problem of 'theodicy': how to reconcile the concept of a good and omnipotent God, with all the misery that afflicts the world. In Great Britain two novels published which are important to the Enlightenment: Defoe's «Robinson Crusoe» (1719) and Swift's «Gulliver's Travels» (1726). Germany Baroque music flourishes; J.S. Bach: Matteus-passion (1729) and G.F. Händel: The Messiah (1742). France **1748** – Montesquieu's On the Spirit of the Laws – source of inspiration for – among other things – the U.S. constitution, with its separation of powers. France **1759** – Voltaire's novel «Candide» published as piece of social criticism. Great Britain **1760** – Macpherson publishes «The Works of Ossian», gives impulse to Pre-Romanticism. Russia **1762** – Catherine II (the Great) regent. Her love-life presumably the most costly in history: equivalent to $1, 600, 000, 000 (U.S.) **1762** – Rousseau: The Social Contract. Attack on private ownership as the root of all evil. England **1776** – Adam Smith: «On the Wealth of Nations» – basis of classical liberal economy.	**1755–1763** – Colonial war between England and France gives the English all land east of the Mississippi and all of Canada. **1767** – Mason-Dixon Line drawn across the eastern colonies. Separates slave-holding colonies from those which do not accept slavery.	**1713** – Importation of slaves from Africa to the Spanish colonies. The English slave trade reaches its peak.	Harvesting in 1675. English pillory. 1700s. Apartment buildings in Paris. 1700 s. French execution in 1757. Basic steps in the Minuet.	**1690** **1770**

	UNITED STATES	AFRICA	ASIA	AUSTRALIA
1965	Anti-war protests escalate due to US military intervention in Vietnam; on the third try, Martin Luther King, Jr. leads civil right marchers from Selma to Montgomery, AL. This attempt is successful because of federal mobilization of National Guard Units to protect the marchers.	Egypt – **1798–1799** Napoleon's expedition to Egypt makes the country a sought-after area for archaeological research. Among other things, the so-called Rosetta Stone is found, which leads to an interpretation of the hieroglyphs (1822).		1770 – James Cook lands in Australia and claims the land for the British crown.
1966	The National Organization for Women (NOW) is founded.	The British fleet under Nelson defeats the French at Abukir.		
1967	66 die in Newark, NJ, and Detroit, MI race riots; Thurgood Marshall is sworn in as the first Black US Supreme Court justice.	West Africa – **1805** The Fulani people occupy the Hussa kingdom and establish a Muslim empire with Sokoto as its capital. The beginnings of present-day Nigeria.		1788 – Botany Bay becomes a penal colony.
1968	Martin Luther King, Jr. is assassinated in Memphis, TN; Senator Robert F. Kennedy is assassinated in Los Angeles; Representative Shirley Chisholm, New York, is the first Black woman elected to Congress; a coalition of women's groups disrupt the Miss America Pageant in the first mass demonstration of the modern day women's movement.	Egypt – **1811** Mohammed Ali occupies the country, which during his reign becomes more independent of the Turks. Southeast Africa – **1816** Shaka the Great founds a Zulu empire, which continues until 1887.		1793 – The first voluntary immigrants come ashore. 1797 – Lieutenant John MacArthur introduces the Spanish Merino sheep, laying the cornerstone for future sheep raising.
1969	Richard M. Nixon becomes the 37th president; Neil Armstrong, becomes the first man to walk on the moon; the modern day gay rights movement starts with the Stonewall rebellion in a New York City bar.	West Africa – **1822** Liberated black slaves found the state of Liberia. North Africa – **1830** The French begin the conquest of Algeria, which later comes under French administration.	India – **1818** The British East India Company now controls the entire country. The Malacca peninsula **1819** sir Stamford Raffles founds an English colony on the southern tip of the peninsula – Singapore.	1802–03 – Matthew Flinders sails around the entire continent and charts the coastline. He proposes to name it Australia.
1970	National Guardsmen kill students at Kent State University, OH, and Jackson State, MS during anti-war demonstrations; members of the "Chicago 7" are acquitted of conspiring to incite a riot during the 1968 Democratic National Convention.	Southern Africa **1836** The Cape Colony's original colonizers, the Dutch-known as the Boers-, dissatisfied with British rule, migrate northward (The Great Trek) and found Transvaal, the Orange Free State.	Due to its location and free trade, the city quickly becomes an important trading centre. China – **1839–42** China halts the import of opium, leading to war with England – the Opium War. The British take Hong Kong.	
1971	The 26th Amendment gives 18-year-olds the right to vote; Lieutenant William L. Calley, Jr. is convicted of killing Vietnamese civilians, many of them women and children, in the 1968 My Lai massacre.	1840 – The Boers defeat the Zulus in the Battle of Blood River.	1850 The Taiping Rebellion – history's most destructive and bloody civil war; ca. 17 million dead. India – **1853** The country gets its first railways and telegraph lines.	1840 – The deportation of prisoners to Australia is halted. 1850 – Australia's first university founded in Sidney.
1973	In Roe vs Wade, the US Supreme Court, in part, bans state anti-abortion laws; Nixon refuses to release tapes relevant to the Watergate break-in; two of the Watergate "burglars" are convicted; in the "Saturday Night Massacre," Attorney General Elliot Richardson resigns and Nixon fires special prosecutor Archibald Cox and William Ruckelshaus when they try to secure a court order forcing him to release Watergate tapes.	1853 – The Scottish missionary Livingstone begins his explorations of Africa.	Japan – **1853** An American naval squadron under commodore Perry forces Japan to open itself to the West, leading to the demise of the shogunate and the fedual system. The rapid industrialization of Japan begins.	1851 – Gold-rush to Bathurs and Ballarat. 1854 – Gold miners and the military clash in Eureka – the only armed conflict on Australian soil.
1974	Under public pressure over the "Watergate Scandal," President Nixon resigns; Vice President Gerald Ford becomes the 38th president, pardoning Nixon for all federal crimes he "committed or may have committed."		India – **1857** Sepoy Rebellion breaks out, led by the native soldiers of the Company's army – the Sepoys. The East India Company loses its control of India, which is placed under the British crown.	

EUROPE	NORTH AND CENTRAL AMERICA	SOUTH AMERICA		
Germany **1781** – Immanuel Kant publishes «Critique of Pure Reason,» where he discusses the limits of human knowledge. One of Romanticism's philosophical starting points.	**1773** – Boston Tea Party. Colonists disguised as indians dump a ship's cargo of tea overboard. Bitterness due to tax on tea.		Neo-classicism in Munich.	**1770** **1860**
France **1783** – Flight of the first manned balloon, constructed by the brothers Montgolfier. England **1780s** – The Industrial Revolution is in full swing. Seen in the textile industry in inventions such as mechanical spinning wheels and looms (1785); in the iron industry, the Puddel process, by which malleable iron could be produced through the addition of carbon (steel). James Watt's steam engine (1769) is improved and becomes the new power source. Austria **1780s and 90s** – Mozart's great works produced. France **14 July 1789** – The storming of the Bastille. The French Revolution begins. Feudalism disappears.	**1776** – The American colonies declare their independence. «We hold these truths to be selfevident, that all men are created equal, endowed by their creator with certain inalienable rights, among which life, liberty and the pursuit of happiness.»		Russian village ca. 1800.	
1792 – France becomes a republic. **1799** – Napoleon seizes power. Poland **1795** – The 3rd division of Poland. In effect, Poland ceases to exist. Austria **1800–1810** – Beethoven creates his best known works.	**1783** – Peace. England recognizes the USA. **1789** – The American Constitution completed. George Washington becomes the country's first president.			
1812 – Napoleon attacks Russia and occupies Moscow. The French withdrawal in the bitter cold is a catastrophe for the French army. **1815** – Napoleon defeated by Wellington at Waterloo and sent into exile on St. Helena. France **1830** – The July Revolution inspires revolutionaries in Italy and Germany. England **1830s** – Charles Dickens, writes The Pickwick Papers and Oliver Twist. Ireland **1845** – The Great Potato Famine. Mass immigration to the USA. France **1848** – The February Revolution. France becomes a republic. Marx and Engels writes the «Communist Manifesto». **1852** – Napoleon III takes power. **1853–56** – Crimean War. Horrific conditions for the wounded inspires Florence Nightingale's epochmaking work. In 1860 she starts a school of nursing at St. Thomas hospital in London.	**1803** – France sells Louisiana west of the Mississippi to the U.S. **1804–1806** – Lewis and Clark explore the American Northwest and reach the Pacific. **1818** – The 49th parallel becomes boundary between U.S. and Canada. **1823** – Monroe Doctrine declared to prevent European intervention in American (esp. S. American) affairs. **1830** – First railroads in the U.S. **1844** – Dentist Horace Wells begins using aesthetics on his patients. **1848** – Gold discovered in California. Goldrush to the west coast – «He was a miner, forty-niner...» **1852** – Henry Wells starts the Wells Fargo delivery service to the West.	**1810–1826** – The Spanish and Portuguese colonies become independent nations. **1822** – Brazil becomes empire – lasting until 1889. The poorly defined borders in the South American interior lead to numerous border-clashes in the 1840s and 50s.	Napoleon returns home from Russia in 1812. Indian locomotive ca. 1850. Florence Nightingale in the Crimea.	

	UNITED STATES	**AFRICA**	**ASIA**	**AUSTRALIA**
		Egypt– 1869 The Suez Canal completed. Built by Ferdinand de Lesseps and financed by France. Verdi was inspired to write his opera Aida, set in ancient Egypt.		*1860 – Burke and Wells cross the continent from south to north, but starve to death on the return trip.*
1975	*US troops leave Vietnam.*			
1976	*July 4th, marks the country's 200th anniversary; Viking I and II land on Mars; 29 people attending a Philadelphia, PA convention die from "legionnaires' disease."*	*1871– During his search for the source of the Nile, Livingstone disappears and is later found by the American journalist Stanley.*		
1978	*President Carter facilitates peace treaty between Eygpt and Israel.*	*1875– To secure British access to India, prime minister Disraeli buys majority shares in the Suez Canal.*		
1979	*Emergency crews prevent a total melt down at the Three Mile Island nuclear reactor near Middletown, PA.*	*Congo – 1885 Leopold II of Belgium gains control of the area and enforces merciless*	*1877 – Queen Victoria is proclaimed empress of India.*	*1880 – Highwayman Ned Kelly is taken prisoner and hanged.*
1980	*Carter places a grain embargo against the Soviet Union for its invasion of Afghanistan; to further protest the invasion, the US Olympic Committee decides to boycott the Moscow games; Washington State's Mount St. Helens volcano erupts, killing at least 60 people.*	*policies of forced labour and physical torture. This inspires Joseph Conrad to write his masterpiece, Heart of Darkness. 1886 – Gold found in Transvaal, leading to a gold-rush. 1890 – Cecil Rhodes, who amassed a fortune from*	*1900 China – The Boxer Rebellion; Europeans are persecuted, and the embassies in Peking are under seige. 1904–1905 – The Russo-Japanese War. Due to Japan's rapid industrial and technological advancement, her*	*1901 – The first parliament assembles in Melbourne. The six colonies form the Commonwealth of Australia.*
1981	*Sandra Day O'Connor is appointed the first woman US Supreme Court justice.*	*diamond mines, founds Rhodesia.*	*fleet was able to quickly crush the Russians. The first time in history that an Asian nation had*	
1982	*Unemployment hits 10.8 percent, the highest rate since 1940; the Equal Rights Amendment is defeated; Barney B. Clark receives the first artificial heart.*	*1899 – Boer War between England and the Boers, who are defeated. The Boer states are incorporated in the British empire.*	*defeated a European foe. China 1911–12 – Revolution – the emperor is overthrown, a republic established. Yuan*	
1983	*AIDS, a mysterious and deadly new virus is first diagnosed in homosexual males; US Marines invade Grenada; Space Shuttle Challenger crew member Sally Ride becomes the first American woman in space.*	*1910 – The South African Union is formed. Member of the British Commonwealth. 1911 – Italy conquers Libya. 1922 – Following a nationalist rebellion, Egypt is liberated from British and French influence.*	*Shih-kai China's first president. 1917 – The Balfour Declaration promises the Jews a new homeland in Palestine.*	*1917 – Railway spanning the continent completed. 1051 miles long. 1927 – Canberra becomes seat of the Parliament.*
1984	*CIA officials acknowledge they helped mine Nicaraguan harbors; Geraldine Ferraro is first female vice presidential candidate; Ronald Reagan is re-elected for a second term; Dr. Katheryn D. Sullivan is first female astronaut to walk in space.*	*1934 – Italy, led by the fascist dictator Benito Mussolini, attacks Ethiopia, Africa's oldest independent nation. UN sanctions have no effect. Ethiopia falls.*	*1919 – Gandhi introduces passive resistance to British rule. 1932 – The kingdom of Saudi Arabia is formed.*	
1986	*First official observance of Martin Luther King, Jr.'s Birthday; the Space Shuttle Challenger explodes, killing all seven crew members, including teacher Christa McAuliffe; spacecraft Voyager II at 2,000 million miles from earth sends pictures of Uranus.*		*1931–1932 Japan's expansion on the mainland continues with the conquest of Manchuria and attacks on China proper (1937).*	
1987	*Lt. Col. Oliver North and other key Reagan officials are questioned about their involvement in the Iran-Contra affair, in which weapons were traded for US hostages; Reagan and Russian Premier Gorbachev sign an agreement to dismantle intermediate range missiles; after a record high on Wall Street, the Dow drops 508 points in one day.*			

EUROPE	NORTH AND CENTRAL AMERICA	SOUTH AMERICA		
Between the years 1845–1895 many of the things now part of everyday life are invented: the sewing machine, the refrigerator, the telephone, film, the automobile and the gramophone. Sweden **1867** – Alfred Nobel invents dynamite, his wills grants annual prizes for literature, medicine, physics chemistry and peace. **1870s** – Rapid industrialization of the U.S. initiated. The Netherlands, England and Russia. **1871** – In connection with the Franco-German War, the new, united German Empire is proclaimed at Versailles. Scandinavia **1880s** – Dramatists Ibsen and Strindberg produce their epoch-making dramas. France **1894** – Captain Alfred Dreyfus is deported to Devil Island, sentenced for treason. **1861** – Italy united. **1861** – Serfdom abolished in Russia. France **1863** – Edouard Manet, pioneer of French Impressionism, creates scandal when he exhibits his «Luncheon on the Grass». Emile Zola, writes his naturalistic novel, first great work, «Thérèse Raquin» 1867. **1911** – The Norwegian explorer Roald Amundsen reaches the South Pole. **1914** – The gunshot in Sarajevo – the Austrian heir apparent is murdered by a student, Gavrilo Pricip. The murder triggers the First World War. Russia **1917** – Revolution. The czar abdicates. The communists under Lenin take power. The first socialist state. **1918** – First World War ends. **1919** – The Peace of Versailles: Germany forced to pay reparations and greatly reduce its armed forces. New, independent states formed: Estonia, Latvia, Lithuania, Hungary, Poland, Czechoslovakia and Yugoslavia. Germany **1925** – Inflation runs wild. DM becomes worthless. Germany **1933** – Hitler comes to power.	**1860** – The Southern States secede from the union and civil war breaks out. Abraham Lincoln elected president. **1865** – The Southern States defeated. Slavery is forbidden. Lincoln is assassinated. **1869** – The Pacific Railroad completed. **1870s** – Rapid industrialization of the U.S. initiated. **1876** – Battle of the Little Big Horn. Sioux indians, led by Sitting Bull, defeat general Custer's cavalry. One of the last attempts by natives to stop the white man's exploitation of the Wild West. **1898** – War with Spain. The U.S. annexes Puerto Rico and the Philippines. At the turn of the century, jazz is born in New Orleans and entertainment district of Storyville is closed. During WW1 jazz is spread across the U.S., esp. to Chicago and New York. USA **1903** – The Wright brothers make the first motorized flight. **1909** – Henry Ford begins mass-production of the Model-T Ford. USA **1912** – Hollywood becomes centre of the film industry. **1927** – The first films 'The Jazz Singer' with sound – «talkies». **1927** – Charles Lindbergh makes the first trans-Atlantic flight. **1928** – October. The great stock market crash on Wall Street. The Great Depression begins. USA **1931** – Empire State Building. 449 meters, 102 stories high. USA **1935** – Hitchcock has breakthrough with «The Thirty-nine Steps». USA **1936** – Chaplain creates his parody of modern industrial society – «Modern Times».	 **1930** – Military coup in Brazil. **1932** – War between Bolivia and Paraguay over possession of the Gran Chaco region.	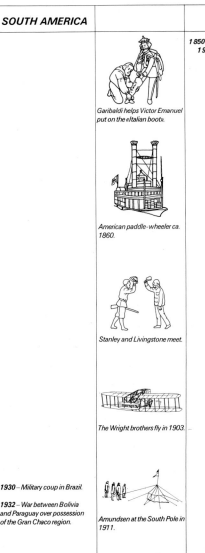 Garibaldi helps Victor Emanuel put on the «Italian boot». American paddle-wheeler ca. 1860. Stanley and Livingstone meet. The Wright brothers fly in 1903. Amundsen at the South Pole in 1911. British tank 1914–18.	*1850* *1940*

	UNITED STATES	AFRICA	ASIA	AUSTRALIA
1988	Nearly four million acres of forest land are destroyed by fire during the worst drought in 50 years.	*1941* – German-Italian force under Field Marshal Rommel attacks Egypt.	*1945* – The U.S. drops atomic bombs on Hiroshima and Nagasaki – Japan capitulates.	*1973* – The Opera House in Sidney completed. Drawn by Danish architect Jørn Utzon. Roofed with a million Swedish manufactured ceramic tiles.
1989	George Bush becomes the 41st president; Former President Reagan and Bush are subpoenaed during early Iran-Contra trials; he US Supreme Court's "Webster" ruling permits states to regulate abortions again; Lt. Col. Oliver North is convicted of destroying National Security Council documents in the Iran-Contra affair; San Francisco is rocked by a large earthquake, collapsing the Oakland-San Francisco Bay bridge.	*1943* – The war in North Africa ends. General Montgomery drives Rommel's army out.	*1947* – British India is divided into two independent states – Islamic Pakistan and Hindu India.	*1974* – Prime Minister Gough Whitlam removes restrictions on non-white immigrants.
1990	In response to the invasion of Kuwait, President Bush deploys the largest number of troops since the Vietnam War to the Persian Gulf.	*1949* – South Africa introduces Apartheid. Kenya *1952* – The secret organization Mau Mau begins a nationalist rebellion. *1956* – Egypt's dictator Nasser nationalizes the Suez Canal. The British, French and Israeli attack. The UN intervenes. *1960s* – Twenty independent African nations are formed. *1961* – South Africa leaves the Commonwealth. *1960* – The Sharpeville massacre in South Africa. *1965* – Rhodesia declares independence. *1967* – South African doctor Christiaan Barnard performs the first successful heart transplant.	*1949* – Mao Tse-Tung's communist armies drive the nationalists to Taiwan. *1947–1955* The «French» part of the Vietnam war. *1955–1976* The «American» part of the Vietnam war. China *1966* – Mao leads the Cultural Revolution against bourgeois tendencies. *1971* – The war between India and Pakistan results in East Pakistan separating and becoming the state of Bangladesh. *1973* – The oil-producing Arab nations cut back production and quadruple oil prices, resulting in poor economic times throughout the world. *1979* – The Shah of Iran is overthrown and Iran becomes an Islamic republic, led by the fundamentalist Shiite ayatollah Khomeini. *1979* – Sovjet troops invade Afghanistan. *1980* – The bloody Iran-Iraq war begins. Peace 1988. *1982* – Israel invades Lebanon. The PLO is expelled from Beirut. *1984* – The Bhopal catastrophe in India: 2500 people die, as poisonous gas is leaked from a Union Carbide factory. *1988* – The Sovjet Union leaves Afghanistan. *1990* – Iraq invades Kuwait. *1991* – War starts between Iraq and UN-allied troops from U.S., Saudi Arabia, Great Britain, France and others.	*1979* – Plans begun for a new parliament building in Canberra. *1988* – Bicentennial of the arrival of the first immigrants. Queen Elizabeth dedicated the new parliament building.
		1985 South Africa – Racial unrest is growing and spreading, leading to a declaration of matrial law. *1990* – Nelson Mandela, leader of the African liberation organization ANC, is freed after decades of imprisonment.		

EUROPE	NORTH AND CENTRAL AMERICA	SOUTH AMERICA		
1939 – Hitler's invasion of Poland begins the Second World War.	*1941* – Japan's attack on the American fleet at Pearl Harbor in Hawaii leads to U.S. entering the Second World War.	*1939* – Australia becomes a base for the war in the Pacific.	American aircraft carrier.	*1939* *1990*
1945 – Second World war ends. Germany defeated, Hitler has committed suicide, 40 million people (of which 6 million Jews) have died, 34 million are wounded.	*USA 1944* – The first computer is built, but doesn't have its breakthrough until after 1971 when the microchip is developed.			
1949 – North Atlantic Treaty signed (NATO).	*1945* – The United Nations (UN) is formed and head-quartered in New York.	*Argentina 1946* – Juan Perón comes to power.		
1953 – Joseph Stalin dies.				
1955 – The Warsaw Pact formed. The Cold War develops. Hungary *1956* – Popular uprising against the communist regime. Soviet troops called in to quell the revolt.	*1954* – Hemingway receives the Nobel Prize for literature as leader of the «hard-boiled school».	*1959* – Fidel Castro leads the revolution in Cuba. He introduces communism and allies the country with the Soviet Union.	UN's insignia from 1945.	
1961 – The Berlin Wall is erected. The USSR sends up the first manned spacecraft with Jurij Gagarin aboard. England *1962–1971* – The Beatles' melodious music takes the world by storm. The Soviet Union *1964* – Khrushchev toppled when his economic policies fail. He had promised the people of the USSR a higher standard of living than in the U.S. by the year 1980.	*UN 1960* – Khrushchev pounds his shoe on the podium when displeased with General Secretary Hammarskjöld. *USA 1962* – Film star and sex-symbol Marilyn Monroe dies of an overdose. *1963* – President Kennedy murdered in Dallas.	*1962* – Cuban Missile Crisis; the Soviet Union attempts to station long-range missiles in Cuba. Solution negotiated over the «Hot Line».	Stalin lying in state.	
Czechoslovakia *1968* – Attempt made to liberalize the communist system – known as the «Prague Spring,» it was put down by Soviet troops.	*1964* – Laws passed against racial discrimination. *1968* – Black civil rights activist Martin Luther King is murdered.			
1974 – Portugal becomes democracy. *1975* – Spanish dictator, general Franco, dies. Juan Carlos becomes king, and the development of democracy begins.	*1971* – President Nixon and Secretary of State Kissinger initiate detente with China and the Soviet Union. *1974* – President Nixon forced to resign over the Watergate Scandal.	*1970* – Salvador Allende is the first democratically elected Marxist leader in Chile. *1973* – Allende toppled in military coup led by general Pinochet, who becomes country's dictator.	The Soviet Vostok from 1962.	
Poland *1980* – the trade union Solidarity is formed and begins the struggle for democracy. *1983* – Two Soviet cosmonauts spend 150 days in space. *1985* – Gorbachev comes to power in the Soviet Union.	*1979* – Civil war in Nicaragua. Sandanistas come to power. *1980* – Ronald Reagan elected president in U.S.	*1980* – First free elections in 17 years held in Peru. *1982* – Argentina invades the Falklands Islands, but gives up following a British counter-attack.	American bomber over Vietnam.	
1986 – Melt-down at the nuclear reactor in Chernobyl. Radioactivity spread over vast areas. *1989* – Democratic elections in Poland. Gorbachev launches «perestrojka». Romanian dictator Ceausescu flees, but is captured and executed. Dismantling of the Berlin Wall begins. A wave of liberation and democratization sweeps over Eastern Europe.	*1986* – Spacecraft Voyager II sends back pictures of the planet Uranus from a distance of 2 billion miles. *1987* – Reagan and Gorbachev reach agreement in Washington on banning land-based medium range ballistic missiles. *1988* – George Bush president in U.S.	*1985* – Democracy reintroduced in Brazil and Uruguay.		
1990 – The reunification of East and West Germany is begun. Single currency introduced.	*1990* – Free elections in Nicaragua. Sandanistas lose power.		Line of jobless people.	

PICTURE CREDITS

In addition to the artwork collected from J.W. Cappelen's archives, the following picture sources are used:

AAA photo, Paris, p. 35 (above).
Biblioteca Angelica, Roma, p. 49 (below).
Biblioteca Riccardiana, Firenze, p. 49 (above).
Bibliothèque National, Paris, p. 41, 56 (below).
Bridgeman Art Library, London, p. 52 (to the right), 61 (below), 66, 67, 74 (below to the left), 76 (below), 81, 90 (above), 92 (below), 98 (both), 99, 104, 105 (both), 107, 110.
British Museum, London. p. 60.
Camera Press, London, p. 119 (below), 122 (all three to the right), 123 (above to the left), 126 (to the right).
Cinevision, Stockholm, p. 20.
Douglas Dickens, London, p. 39 (below).
C.M. Dixon (Photoresources), Kingston, Kent, p. 7, 9 (above), 13, 17, 19 (above), 22, 23, 25 (below), 43, 72, (above).
E.N.I.T., Rome, p. 27 (above).
The Eremitage Museum, Leningrad, p. 89 (above).
The Frederiksborg Museum, Hillerød, p. 69 (above).
Galleria Villa Borghese, Rome, p. 26.

Mats Halling, Stockholm, p. 31 (below).
Robert Harding Picture Library, London, p. 11 (above to the right and below), 14 (above), 21 (in the middle), 33 (below), 62 (above), 64 (above), 68, 71, 73 (below), 74 (above), 75 (above), 77 (all three), 85 (above), 90 (below), 96 (below).
Herakleion Museum, Athens, p. 8 (to the left).
Michael Holford, London, p. 12 (above), 15, 18 (above and below to the left), 21 (above), 25 (above), 27 (below), 28, 31 (above), 35 (below), 63 (below), 65, 89 (below and to the right), 91.
Hulton Picture Library, London, p. 54 (in the middle), 106 (below), 126 (to the left).
Robert Hunt Library, London, p. 102, 111 (above).
Imperial War Museum, London, p. 112 (below).
Iraqi Museum, Baghdad, p. 11 (above to the right).
Heikki Kirkinen, Joensuu, p. 51.
Library of Congress, Washington D.C., p. 94 (below), 109 (in the middle to the left).
Louvre, Paris, p. 19 (below), 29 (above), 73 (above).
Mansell Collection, London, p. 54 (above), 64 (below), 83 (above), 101, 106 (above).

Musée Carnavalet, Paris, p. 78 (above).
Musée Guimet, Paris, p. 39 (above).
Museo Curco, Como, p. 61 (above).
Museo del Risorgimento, Milan, p. 87 (above to the right).
Museo Nacional, Lima, p. 94 (to the left).
Museo Nacional de Antropologia, Mexico City, p. 62 (below).
National Army Museum, London, p. 97 (above).
National Gallery, p. 88 (above).
Heikki Partanen, Helsinki, p. 10, 14 (below).
Politikens Forlag, Copenhagen, p. 12 (below), 16, 18 (below to the right), 20 (above), 21 (below), 29 (below), 36 (below), 38 (below), 47 (below), 55, 61, (in the middle), 63 (above), 74 (below), 83 (below), 87 (above to the left and below), 92 (above), 103, 105 (to the left), 120 (to the right).
Politikens Pressefoto, Copenhagen, p. 108, 118 (to the right), 120 (to the left), 121, 122 (farthest left), 123 (above to the right), 127, 128, (below to the left and the two above to the right).
Popperphoto, London, p. 124 (above).
Prähistorisches Museum, Hallstatt, p. 8 (to the right).
Rex Features Ltd., London, p. 115

(below to the right), 118 (to the left), 123 (below).
Scan-Foto, Frankfurt p. 128 (below to the right).
Schloss Charlottenhof, Sans-souci, Berlin, p. 95.
Staatsarchiv, Hamburg, p. 56 (above).
Stadtbibliothek, Nuremberg, p. 58 (below).
Sundahl Foto, Stockholm, p. 69 (below).
Toledo Museum of Art, Ohio, p. 58 (above).
Universitätsbibliothek, Geneva, p. 59 (in the middle).
The Vatican Museum, Rome, p. 50 (below).
Zefa, London, p. 38 (above).

Illustrations:
Sv. Aa. Voigt Andersen, Copenhagen, p. 20 (below).
Arne Gaarn Bak, Copenhagen, p. 116.
Lars Tangedal, Copenhagen, p. 9 (below).

Whilst every effort has been made to trace copyright holders, the publisher will be pleased to make the necessary arrangements at the first opportunity if they have overlooked any.

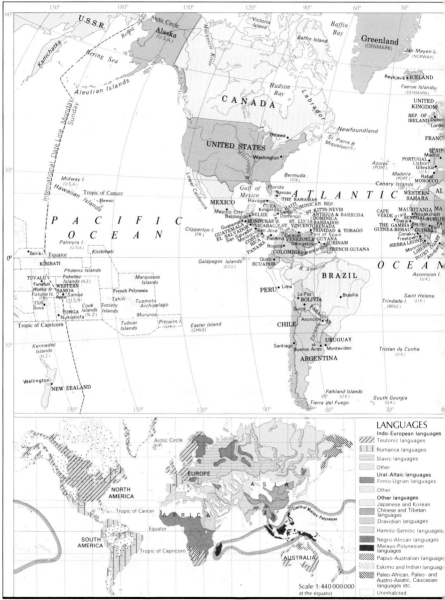